AN ILLUSTRATED DICTIONARY OF JEWELLERY

An Illustrated Dictionary of

JEWELLERY

Anita Mason

Illustrated by Diane Packer

Osprey Publishing Limited

First published in 1973 by
Osprey Publishing Ltd, P.O. Box 25
707 Oxford Road, Reading, Berkshire

ISBN 0 85045 109 4

Filmset and printed by BAS Printers Limited,
Wallop, Hampshire

Preface

This book is intended as a reference book both for those involved in the jewellery trade and for those with a less specialized interest in jewellery. Although a number of excellent publications are already available dealing with gemstones and their identification, with the techniques of jewellery-manufacture, with the history of jewellery, and with subjects of interest to the retail jeweller such as hallmarking, there is no book in which all these related subjects are covered in a form which allows of easy reference. We hope that the present volume will help to fill this gap. For the benefit of the layman technical language has been avoided where possible, and such technical terms as have been used are explained under the appropriate headings.

The attempt to cover a fairly wide field has necessitated some compression, and the book does not pretend to provide more than an outline of jewellers' techniques, which are fully treated in other publications.

We should like to express our appreciation to the many retail and manufacturing jewellers who have provided us with information and advice, to Miss Hare and other officials of Goldsmiths' Hall, London for their co-operation and help, and to Messrs Tiffany & Co. and Georg Jensen for permission to illustrate some of their pieces.

A.M.
D.P.

ABBREVIATIONS

H. = Hardness
S.G. = Specific gravity
R.I. = Refractive index

These terms are explained under the appropriate headings in the text.

A

Abalone. A salt-water univalve (the *Haliotis*) fished both for its pearls and shell. The pearls are small and sometimes hollow inside, are often baroque in shape, and are of unusual colours – green, yellow and sometimes blue. The shell is also very colourful and is used for a variety of mother-of-pearl ornaments. The abalone is also known as the ear-shell since it is thought to resemble the human ear in shape.

The abalone is found along the Great Barrier Reef off the eastern coast of Queensland, in the waters of New Zealand, where it is known as Paua, and off the coasts of California and Florida. The smaller ormer shells (*Haliotis tuberculata*), found in great numbers in the shallow waters off the Channel Islands, produce a rather inferior pearl which is seldom good enough to use in ornamentation. (See also *Pearls* and *Shell*.)

Abrasives. Materials used in jewellery work to abrade and polish metal and to cut, facet and polish stones. They are marketed in the form of powders, grits, grease compositions, papers and cloths charged with grit and powder, and powdered synthetic or natural stones. Their hardness is measured on Mohs's scale (q.v.). The hardest stones are cut and polished with powdered crystals of a harder mineral, usually diamond or corundum. Diamonds can be cut only with diamond powder. Other abrasive materials used by the jewellery trade include: powdered garnet, quartz, emery, pumice, oilstone, Arkansas stone, Water of Ayr stone, tripoli, crocus, rottenstone, diatomite, rouge, green rouge, carborundum (silicon carbide), boron carbide, putty powder (tin oxide), synthetic aluminium oxide ('Aloxite', etc.) (qq.v.). (See also *Diamond-cutting*, *Gem-cutting* and *Polishing metals*)

Abraxas stone. A stone engraved with the cabbalistic word *abraxas* or *abrasax*, originating among the Gnostics and used as a talisman in North Africa and Asia Minor in the first centuries of the Christian era, and later in Europe during the Middle Ages. The stone bore a variety of engraved symbols, of which the commonest was a creature with a human body, the head of a cock and serpentine legs. This has been taken in the past to be a representation of a god called Abraxas, but it is now established that *abraxas* was not primarily a name but a symbolic word. The numerical value of its letters in Greek is 365, which was the number of orders of spirits believed by the Gnostics to emanate from the supreme God; both the word and the figure thus symbolised this idea. Abraxas stones later lost their specific symbolism and were used for a variety of magical purposes. (See also *Talisman*.)

Absorption spectra. Dark bands or lines which appear on the spectrum when a coloured stone is examined through a spectroscope (q.v.). They correspond to the wavelengths of light absorbed by the stone. Since many gemstones have characteristic absorption spectra this furnishes a means of identifying stones and sometimes of distinguishing natural stones from synthetic ones.

Accidental pearl. Term for a natural pearl.

Acetone. A colourless organic liquid which softens cellulosic plastics and can therefore be used to identify them. It is also used by jewellers for removing cellulose varnish.

Acetylene tetrabromide (Tetrabromoethane). A liquid used in the measurement of specific gravity and refractive index (qq.v.). (S.G.2.96, R.I. 1.638.) It is less widely used than bromoform as it does not form such a clear and stable solution, but it may be preferred for some purposes on account of its higher specific gravity.

Achroite. Colourless tourmaline.

Acicular. Having a needle-like form, such as the crystals of rutile in rutilated quartz.

Acid testing of metals. See *Touchstone testing*.

Adamant. An old synonym for diamond. The word has a complicated history, and early usages of it can be very misleading. It is derived from the Greek *adamas*, 'unconquerable', which was used by the Greeks as a name for the hardest known metal, steel. In Roman times it was used as a poetic word for anything very hard or indestructible, and Pliny used it as a name for a gem-stone which was probably white sapphire. In this sense the word was finally transferred to the even harder diamond. At the same time 'adamant' developed the secondary meaning of 'loadstone' or 'magnet', following the mistaken assumption of medieval Latin writers that the word was derived from *ad-amare*, 'to have an attraction for'. The two senses became confused in the Middle Ages and as a result the diamond was often believed to have magnetic powers. The confusion persisted until the seventeenth century, after which 'adamant' was used only as a synonym for diamond. It is now obsolete in this literal sense and is used only poetically or metaphorically. The word 'diamond' derives from the medieval 'diamant', which arose as a variant form of 'adamant' or 'adimant'.

Adamantine. The type of lustre (q.v.) shown by a diamond. (See *Adamant*.)

'Adamite'. An artificially-produced corundum powder used as an abrasive.

Adhesives. These are used in very cheap jewellery for securing stones in their mounts. In the case of a difficult setting an adhesive may also be used to keep the stone in place while the setting is completed. Epoxy-resin adhesives are generally used.

Adularescence. Name given to the whitish or bluish sheen seen in the moonstone. The sheen is due to the reflection of light from alternating layers of mineral in the stone. The word is taken from *adularia,* the type of feldspar (q.v.) of which moonstone is the gem variety.

'African emerald'. Misnomer for the green fluorspar found in South West Africa. Not to be confused with the real emerald which comes from South Africa.

'African jade'. Misnomer for massive green grossular garnet.

Agate geode with typical banding

Agate. (See *Chalcedony*.) A common gem variety of chalcedony. It is usually banded, showing layers of clear quartz alternating with opaline layers. In *eye agate* the bands form concentric circles or ovals, and in *fortification agate* they form an angular pattern which suggests the outline of a fortress. Most banded agate on the market is artificially coloured (see *Dyeing of stones*) – a process to which it lends itself because of its porosity. Some agate is not banded but contains mineral inclusions – black, red or green in colour which give a moss-like or tree-like (dendritic) effect. These stones are known as *moss agate* or *Mocha stone*. (In England and America the names are synonymous, but in Europe generally only the black and red type are known as Mocha stone.)

Agate is an extremely attractive stone and is extensively used in rings, pendants and brooches as well as for larger ornamental objects such as ashtrays. It also has a number of commercial applications, for instance in burnishers (q.v.), pivots for laboratory scales, mortars for crushing stones, etc. The centre of the agate industry is at Idar Oberstein (q.v.).

Agate occurs in the amygdaloid cavities of decomposed lava and is usually found in the form of nodules or geodes with a dark outer skin, varying in size from small stones a few centimetres across to small boulders. The most important source of agates is now South America (mainly Brazil and Uruguay). Deposits are also found in India, particularly of green moss agate. Less important deposits are found world-wide.

Agate was much used in the ancient world. The Egyptians collected it from the desert areas around Jebel Abu Diyeiba over 3000 years ago, and quantities of Sumerian agate beads have been found. Agates which probably came from India were being traded by Arab merchants in the fifth century B.C. Agate was first mentioned by name by Theophrastus, (372–287 B.C.), who attributed its name to the river Achates (now the Drillo) in Sicily where it was believed to have been first found. It was popularly believed to protect the wearer against dangers. In ancient Rome the possession of an agate cup or bowl was a mark of social status. The stone continued to be worn as a talisman during the Middle Ages. (For supposed magical properties of stones see *Magical jewellery*.)

Agate jasper. See *Jasp-agate*.

Agatized coral. Fossilized coral in which the original substance has been replaced by chalcedony (q.v.). There is a considerable deposit of this at Tampa Bay, Florida. It is cut and polished in cabochons, and is often dyed pink or blue.

Agatized wood (Petrified wood). Fossilized wood in which the original substance has been replaced by chalcedony in the form of agate (q.v.). Much of what is called agatized wood is really jasperized wood (q.v.). (See also *Opalized wood*.)

Sixteenth-century Italian aglet. Victoria and Albert Museum

Aglets. Decorated metal loops, tags or spangles worn as an ornament on the dress during the Renaissance (see illustration). They were moved from one garment to another, like brooches, and were often worn in the cap. Aglets of enamelled gold in such shapes as small animals, cherubs' heads, rosettes, fruit, etc., are regularly mentioned in sixteenth-century inventories, and Elizabeth I had several pairs set with pearls and precious stones. Few examples have survived.

Ahrens prism. A modification of the Nicol prism, q.v.

Aigrette. A jewelled ornament in the shape of a feather (see illustration), or supporting a feather, or occasionally having no connection with a feather at all, worn in the hair or cap from the end of the sixteenth century onwards. They were very popular in the middle of the eighteenth century (see *Eighteenth-century*

Nineteenth-century design for a diamond aigrette

jewellery). The word is adopted from the French word for heron (*aigrette* – hence the English word 'egret') which was transferred to apply to the heron's crest and thence to helmet-plumes and head-dresses in general.

'A jour'. A setting which leaves the pavilion facets of a stone open to the light; the same as an open setting.

Akabar (Accarbaar). A black coral (q.v.) found off the Cameroon coast and in the Mediterranean. The material from the Mediterranean is called *giojetto*. Specimens have been carved and mounted in jewellery.

Akbar Shah diamond. An Indian diamond weighing 120 carats in the rough and 74 carats when cut, which was once the property of the Great Mogul Akbar. It was engraved in Arabic on two faces by the order of his successor Jahan. The inscriptions read, in translation, 'Shah Akbar, Shah of the World, 1028' (A.D. 1618), and 'To the Lord of Two Worlds, Shah Jahan, 1039' (A.D. 1629).

The diamond disappeared for a time, but turned up again in Constantinople under the name 'Shepherd's Stone'. It still retained its inscriptions and was thereby recognized. In 1866 it was bought by an English merchant who unfortunately had it re-cut, reducing the weight to

71 carats and destroying the inscriptions. It was subsequently sold to the Gaekwar of Baroda, reputedly for about £26,000.

Alalite. See *Diopside.*

'Alaska diamond'. Misnomer for rock crystal.

Alasmodon pearls. Freshwater pearls from the *Alasmodon margaretifera*. (See also *Pearls.*)

Albert chain. A slender gold watch-chain worn during the nineteenth century, sometimes by women as well as men. It survived until the advent of the wrist-watch in the early part of this century. 'Albert' was, of course, the Prince Consort.

Alcohol. A liquid useful in the measurement of refractive index (q.v.) (R.I. 1.36) and for diluting heavy liquids in the measurement of specific gravity (q.v.).

Aldur. American name for an amino plastic. (See *Plastics.*)

Alexandria shell (Egyptian shell). Decorative shell from the pearl-oyster *Pinctada margaretifera* fished in the Red Sea. It was formerly marketed at Alexandria. (See also *Shell.*)

Alexandrite (Beryllium-aluminium oxide. S.G.3.64–3.74; R.I.1.75–1.76; H. $8\frac{1}{2}$). A variety of chrysoberyl (q.v.), characterized by its change of colour from grass-green in daylight to red in artificial light. The stone, which owes its green colour to chromium oxide, strongly absorbs light in the blue and yellow parts of the spectrum so that the light which emerges from it consists largely of green and red rays. In light which is rich in green rays (daylight) it therefore looks green, and in light rich in red rays (artificial light) it looks red.

Alexandrite was first found in 1830 on the banks of the Takovaya river in the Urals, on the day when Tsar Alexander II came of age, and was named after him. It now comes also from Brazil, Burma, Ceylon and Rhodesia. Ceylonese alexandrites are much larger than the Russian variety but less prized. They are greener by daylight and show a brownish-red by artificial light instead of the violet-red of the Russian stones. Alexandrite is comparatively rare and good specimens are valuable.

The stone is frequently imitated by synthetic corundums and spinels which are manufactured to give the colour-change effect. True alexandrite may be distinguished by its refractive index, specific gravity and absorption spectra (qq.v.). (See also *Synthetic gemstones*.)

The Alfred Jewel. Ashmolean Museum, Oxford

Alfred Jewel. A rich jewel believed to have belonged to, or at least been made for, the Saxon king Alfred the Great (831–99). (See illustration.) It is pear-shaped, 5.2 cm. in length and 3.1 cm. at its greatest width. The obverse shows a design in cloisonné enamel of a man carrying two sceptres on his shoulders; this is soldered to a gold plate and covered with a sheet of rock crystal. The back of the jewel shows an elaborate tree pattern traced on a gold plate. The front and back are joined by a wide band of gold filigree and openwork lettering which reads AELFRED MEC HEHT GEWYRCAN – 'Alfred ordered me to be made'. At the narrow end of the jewel the frame terminates in the head of an animal, probably a boar, made of sheet gold and holding a socket in its mouth.

There is no mention of the jewel in Anglo-Saxon records and its purpose remains a mystery. It looks suitable for a pendant, but if worn round the neck it would hang upside-down, and in any case pendants are not usually fitted with sockets. The socket suggests that it was attached to a wooden or ivory rod, and in this case it may possibly have been the head of a sceptre, the central jewel in a crown, or the head of a valuable pointer used with religious texts. None of these suggestions seems particularly likely. The identity of the figure on the obverse is also doubtful: Christ, Alfred, the Pope, and a selection of saints have been variously suggested.

The jewel was found in 1693 during drainage excavations at a site 4 miles north of Athelney in Somerset, a place traditionally associated with King Alfred. It was bequeathed to the University of Oxford in 1717 and is now in the Ashmolean Museum, Oxford.

For further information on jewellery of the period see *Anglo-Saxon jewellery*.

Allochromatic minerals. Minerals which when chemically pure are colourless. Most gemstones are allochromatic. The colouring is given by impurities in the stone, generally a metallic oxide or inclusions of some coloured mineral. (See also *Idiochromatic minerals*.)

Alloy. A mixture of two or more metals. (This is the usual current meaning of the word, but its meaning has changed rather confusingly over the centuries. It originally meant the fineness of gold or silver, as in the phrase 'silver of the sterling alloy'. Later it was used to mean the base metal which was mixed with the gold or silver; it still retains something of this

Alloy

meaning. It has been suggested that the derivation of the word is from the French '*à la loi*' (according to the law), meaning the amount of base metal which may legally be added to gold or silver, but the Oxford Dictionary gives the derivation as *aloi*, a mixture.)

Alloys have been used by man since metalworking began, sometimes intentionally, as in the case of bronze (an alloy of copper and tin), sometimes because the metal occurred in a naturally alloyed form and either it was not possible to refine it or the metal was good enough as it was (an example being electrum, a natural alloy of gold and silver often used in ancient work). There are numerous reasons for combining metals – utilitarian (to produce a metal which is harder or more durable or has better working qualities), economic (a common reason for alloying precious metals), and decorative (the colour of a metal may be altered by mixing it with another one). To some extent all three motives have always been operative, but the extensive use of alloys to simulate precious metal did not really begin until the eighteenth century (the best-known example is probably pinchbeck, q.v.), and the use of alloying metals to vary the colour of gold did not become common practice until the nineteenth century.

All gold and silver has to be alloyed before use because in their pure state these metals are too soft to be satisfactorily worked. The proportion of pure gold or silver in the metal is regulated by law. The standards vary from country to country; in Britain they are 92.5% silver (sterling) and 95.84% silver (Britannia), and 91.66%, 75%, 58.5% and 37.5% gold (22-carat, 18-carat, 14-carat and 9-carat respectively). The remaining proportion in the silver alloys is made up with copper. Gold can be alloyed with a number of metals, including copper, silver, palladium and nickel, each of which will produce an alloy of different hardness, colour (see *Gold*) and melting-point.

From its beginnings as a somewhat hit-or-miss affair, the production of alloys has in this century become an exact science. As certain manufacturing processes require metals with particular characteristics, alloys to meet these requirements have been developed by the refiners. Some of these special requirements are alloys for enamelling (which requires constituent metals of a very high degree of purity), deep spinning (a process used for making trophies, cups, etc., which calls for a soft alloy), chain-making (in which the metal has to withstand severe bending, flattening and elongation), engine-turning (the metal is treated to make it a suitable surface for very fine lines), and casting (some alloys cast 'cleaner' than others). A current refiner's catalogue for jewellers and silversmiths lists 14 different alloys for 9-carat gold, 7 for 14-carat, 8 for 18-carat and 2 for 22-carat; they have different melting-points and slightly different working characteristics, and are in a range of colours which includes yellow, white, green and red. This is by no means a complete list; many more are available, including gold and silver alloys made to foreign standards. The solders used in jewellery, which have to contain the same proportion of precious metal as the rest of the work in order to conform to the hallmarking laws, are of course also alloys and are produced in a wide range to provide a series of different melting-points; these are discussed under *Solder*.

Platinum also has to be alloyed with other metals to give satisfactory working qualities. The usual alloying metals are copper, palladium and iridium. A standard for platinum is not yet legally enforced in Britain, but the proportion of 95% platinum is generally accepted.

Alloys consisting solely of base metal are used in cheaper jewellery and plated with gold or silver. Examples are gilding-metal (an alloy of copper and zinc – the proportions vary), nickel silver (an alloy of copper, nickel and zinc) and bronze (sometimes used as a basis for rolled gold). Two base-metal alloys which appear in jewellery undisguised are pewter (tin, copper and antimony) and stainless steel (iron, chromium and nickel).

Alluvial deposits. Deposits of minerals which have been washed out of their original matrix and are found concentrated in the beds of past or present streams and rivers, from which they are recovered by mining or panning. Alluvial deposits yield a large proportion of the world's gemstones.

Alma trace chain. A chain with broad-ribbed oval links. (See *Chain.*)

Almandine (Almandite). (Iron-aluminium silicate. S.G. 3.85–4.20; R.I. 1.77–1.82; H. 7½.) A variety of garnet which has a deep red colour, often with a blackish or purplish tinge. Almandine often contains inclusions of smaller crystals or of 'needles' of a foreign substance, and the latter if distributed thickly enough may produce a weak four-pointed star of light (asterism) when the stone is cut *en cabochon*.

Almandines can be cut in many ways. They are often cut *en cabochon* and hollowed out at the back to lighten the colour. Cabochon-cut garnets are known as carbuncles. In Anglo-Saxon times almandine was the most popular stone and was extensively used for inlay work on brooches, buckles, etc. About the middle of the nineteenth century it again enjoyed a vogue in jewellery.

Almandine tends to exhibit anomalous double refraction (q.v.). Its most striking optical property is the presence of strong absorption bands (see *Absorption spectra*), one in the yellow and two in the green parts of the spectrum, which serve to distinguish it from any other red stone.

India supplies good quality almandine including most of the star-stones. Other sources are Ceylon, Central and South America and the U.S.A. (See also *Garnet.*)

'Almandine spinel'. Name given to precious spinel of a reddish-purple colour resembling that of almandine. (See *Spinel.*)

Almandite. A synonym for almandine; also a misnomer for synthetic spinel.

'Aloxite'. (Trade name.) A hard abrasive made of artificially produced aluminium oxide.

Alpine diamond. A misnomer for pyrites.

Aluminium. A lightweight, silvery metal discovered in the nineteenth century and at first quite highly valued. Since the introduction of anodising (q.v.), which gives aluminium a coloured finish, it has been much used in costume jewellery. Its lightness makes it suitable for wear with very lightweight fabrics, but the same quality makes it rather an unsatisfactory metal for the jeweller, and it is also difficult to solder well. The melting-point is 660.2°C.

Aluminium has been known to be alloyed with gold in order to simulate platinum (the heaviness of the gold masks the lightness of the aluminium). Since, like platinum, aluminium does not react to nitric acid, the imitation has a good chance of passing undetected.

Aluminium bronzes. Alloys of copper, aluminium and small amounts of other non-ferrous metals. Since these alloys have high tensile strength and cast well, and are acid- and oxide-resistant, they may be used in jewellery.

'Alundum'. (Trade name.) A hard abrasive made of artificially-produced aluminium oxide.

Amalgamation. The mixing of mercury with another metal; the process was employed until very recent times in the gilding and silvering of metals. It is more commonly known as mercury-gilding (q.v.).

'Amaryl'. (Trade name.) A light green synthetic corundum. (See *Synthetic gemstones.*)

Amatrice (Amatrix). An ornamental stone consisting of a concretion of variscite (q.v.) in quartz or chalcedony. The material is found in America and the name is a contraction of 'American matrix'.

· 7

Amazonstone (Amazonite). Potassium-aluminium silicate. S.G. 2.56–2.58; R.I. 1.52–1.53; H. 6½.) An opaque verdigris – green to bluish-green variety of microcline feldspar (see *Feldspar*). Only richly-coloured material has any value as a gemstone. The stone has a mottled texture and the polished surface has a shimmering appearance caused by small incipient cleavage cracks. The tendency to cleave easily has to be borne in mind when fashioning the material, which is usually cut *en cabochon* or as beads.

Sources of good material include Kashmir and other localities in India, Colorado, U.S.A., Brazil, the Urals, Madagascar and South Africa. In spite of its name, none appears to come from the region of the Amazon river.

'Amazon jade'. A name for amazonstone; it has little resemblance to jade in fact.

Amber. (S.G. 1.05–1.10; R.I. 1.53–1.54; H. 2½.) Translucent or transparent fossil resin, usually yellow or brown in colour, originating from coniferous forests of the Oligocene period. Most commercial amber comes from the Baltic Sea area, near what is now Kaliningrad. This variety is called *succinite* (the Latin word for amber was *succinum*, from *succus*, meaning juice) and the acid it contains is called succinic acid. It is recovered as sea amber – washed up on the shore, and pit amber – mined from the Oligocene deposits of glauconite. Sea amber is found washed up along the shores of Baltic countries and also the coasts of eastern England and the Netherlands. A Burmese variety (*burmite*) is redder and harder than succinite and is mined from clayey soil in the Hukong valley; most of this material goes to China. There is also Sicilian amber (*simetite*) which is reddish-brown and is found along the banks of the river Simeto, and Romanian amber (*roumanite*), which is highly fluorescent and may be of a blackish, bluish or greenish colour as well as the usual yellow and brown. Amber has also been found in various parts of North America and in small quantities elsewhere.

Amber is light in weight and warm to the touch. It will float in pure water and sink in brine. It possesses a number of unusual qualities. It occasionally contains insects, small animals, pieces of vegetation or inorganic matter which were caught up in the resin before it hardened; such specimens are of great scientific interest. When rubbed it produces a negative electric charge and will pick up light objects. (From the Greek word for amber, *elektron*, our word electricity is derived.) The word 'amber' is derived ultimately from the Arabic *anbar*, meaning ambergris; there is no connection between the two substances beyond the fact that they are both washed up on beaches, but a confusion between them existed for many centuries. Ambar has been known and used for ornament, mainly as beads, at least since the Bronze Age. In Greece and Rome it was valued as a luxury, and was an important item of trade between the Baltic and Mediterranean in the centuries before Christ. Yellow amber was used by the Greeks as a varnish, and powdered amber was much prized in Germany in the early Middle Ages as an aromatic incense. The sweet smell of heated amber is one of its most distinctive properties.

The main use for amber now is in necklace beads (there was a vogue for amber necklaces in the late Victorian period), mouthpieces for pipes, cigarette holders, umbrella handles and small ornamental objects. Its softness and toughness make it very suitable for carving. Amber must be fairly clear to have value; when it contains many bubbles which give it a cloudy appearance it is known as bastard amber. It may also have a bony or chalky appearance. Amber which is not of good quality is used for the production of succinic acid, amber oil and colophony (used in varnish). Small pieces of good-quality amber can be pressed together under gentle heat to make larger pieces. This reconstructed amber is known as *pressed amber* or *ambroid*, and can be distinguished from true amber by its flow structure and the elongation of the air bubbles.

Amber can be imitated by a variety of substances. Copal or kauri gum, a recent fossil resin, resembles it in density and optical properties but melts much more easily. Synthetic resins such as bakelite, celluloid, casein and perspex can be distinguished from amber by their different densities and refractive indices (see *Plastics*) and – as a quick test – by the fact that they can be cut cleanly with a knife whereas amber will splinter. Glass has a higher specific gravity, feels colder, and is harder than amber. The distinctive aromatic odour given off by amber when a small piece is heated on a knife-blade is also a good means of identification.

'Amberine'. A name given to yellowish-green moss agate. (See *Agate*.)

Ambroid. Reconstructed ambers. (See *Amber*.)

American brilliant cut. A modification of the brilliant cut in which the width of the table is reduced to approximately one-third the width of the stone, and the height of the crown is approximately two-thirds that of the pavilion. This enables eight additional bezels to be ground on the stone, thereby increasing its sparkle. (See also *Brilliant cut* and *Diamond-cutting*.)

'American jade'. Misnomer for californite (see *Idocrase*).

'American ruby'. Misnomer for pyrope garnet.

Amethyst. (See *Quartz, crystalline*.) Transparent violet or purple quartz. The colour varies considerably and is often irregularly distributed in the same specimen. When heated to between 400° and 500°C amethyst changes colour, usually to a brownish-yellow or red, although material from some localities changes to green (see *Heat-treatment*). Most yellow quartz on the market is heat-treated amethyst. Amethyst sometimes behaves unpredictably on heating and should not be exposed to excessive heat. Untreated amethyst is distinctly dichroic (see *Dichroism*), the colours being bluish-violet and reddish-violet.

The stone has been popular since ancient times, when it was often fashioned into necklace beads. It was used as an amulet, and was believed to protect the wearer against harm in battle, act as an antidote against poison and sharpen the wits. Its name is probably derived from the most famous of its supposed properties, that of preventing drunkenness (Greek *amethystos* = not drunk), although Pliny suggested that it was so named because its colour approaches but does not quite attain the colour of wine. Because of its supposed powers it was sometimes made into drinking-goblets.

Amethyst is one of the stones traditionally used in ecclesiastical jewellery and has often been set in the finger-rings of bishops. Two fine amethysts are mounted in the British Regalia. The value of the stone has declined considerably since extensive deposits of large crystals were found in Brazil and Uruguay in the nineteenth century. Most of the amethyst used in jewellery now comes from this area. Other sources are Russia, U.S.A., Ceylon, India, Madagascar and South Africa.

Amethyst is popular both as a cabochon stone and faceted. It can be imitated by glass (which is softer) and synthetic corundum (see *Synthetic gemstones*).

Amethystine quartz. Quartz with patches of violet or purple colouring. It is sometimes used for small carvings.

Amino plastics. See *Plastics*.

Ammonium sulphide. A compound in lump form used for oxidizing copper, silver and carat golds to give a soft or antique appearance or to give recessed parts greater depth. The surface of the metal is brushed with a solution of ammonium sulphide and water and the colour develops from a pale golden straw through deep crimson to purple and bluish-black. When the required tint is reached the metal is quickly washed clean. (See also *Colouring of metals*.)

Amorphous. Without crystalline form or structure. (See *Crystal*.)

Ampullar pearl. A pearl from the epidermis of the oyster.

Amulet. A protective charm usually worn on the person, often hung round the neck. It can be of any material. In primitive times it might be an object of unusual shape or colour, since to the primitive mind anything mysterious has magical possibilities, or perhaps part of an animal (wolf's teeth, the claws of a bear, etc.), believed to endue the wearer with the animal's strength, courage or speed. In the ancient civilizations of the East amulets were almost universally worn and their form was dictated by religion. Primitive materials were replaced by clay modelled into magical figures, and by gemstones, which because of their colours, rarity and hardness were thought to have magical properties. In ancient Egypt amulets were an essential part of everyday life and there were over a hundred different types, of which the most important was the *scarab* (q.v.). Other important types were the *udjat*, in the form of an eye carved in stone, the *tet*, a representation of a man's backbone, and the *aakhu*, representing the rising sun. They were buried with the dead and worn as jewellery by the living (see *Egyptian jewellery*).

The early Christian Church condemned magic and the wearing of certain types of amulets, but in the East they continued to be worn by Christians and in the West also there was soon a revival of the practice, although Christian rather than pagan symbols were used. Amulets of a completely non-religious character were also worn as a protection against sickness and other dangers; in many cases the Church turned a blind eye to these. During the Middle Ages and until the end of the seventeenth century amulets were worn as jewellery by all classes of society in Europe. By this time, however, the various magical traditions had become so interwoven that it is impossible to distinguish amulets from other types of magical jewellery, and amulets of the Middle Ages and Renaissance are therefore dealt with under *Magical jewellery*

(q.v.). (See also *Talisman*.)

Amygdaloid. Literally, almond-shaped (Greek *amygdale* = almond). The word refers to rounded or almond-shaped cavities in volcanic rocks which later become filled with mineral matter, often chalcedony.

Amyl-acetate. A liquid which softens cellulosic plastics and can therefore be of use in identifying them. It can be used on its own or mixed with acetone.

Anatase (Octahedrite). (Titanium oxide. S.G. 3.82–3.95; R.I. 2.493–2.554; H. $5\frac{1}{2}$–6.) A brown, blue or black almost transparent stone occasionally used in jewellery. It has an adamantine lustre. The alternative name 'octahedrite' refers to its habit of crystallizing in a bipyramidal form. Sources include France, Russia, Switzerland, Brazil and part of the U.S.A.

'Ancona ruby'. A misnomer for rose quartz.

Andalusite. (Aluminium silicate. S.G. 3.1–3.2; R.I. 1.633–1.644; H. $7\frac{1}{2}$.) A clear olive-green to brown stone which comes mainly from Minas Gerais, Brazil. Other localities are Andalusia in Spain (where it was first found), Ceylon and Madagascar. Andalusite is strongly dichroic (see *Dichroism*): a green stone will display a strong red tint when viewed in the direction parallel to the prism edge. This has to be borne in mind when cutting the stone.

An unusual variety of andalusite, *chiastolite*, contains impurities which give a cruciform pattern to the crystals when cut in sections. These pieces are sometimes cut and polished as religious amulets. Chiastolite occurs in Siberia, Brittany, Southern Australia and the U.S.A.

Andradite. (Calcium-iron silicate. S.G. 3.80–3.90; R.I. 1.82–1.89; H. $6\frac{1}{2}$.) The 'common garnet'. Two varieties are used in jewellery: *melanite*, an opaque black stone which has been used for mourning jewellery, and *demantoid*, a very attractive transparent green stone (colour varying from emerald to olive) which is the most valuable of the garnets.

Melanite comes from France and Italy, among other localities. It can be distinguished from black tourmaline, black-dyed chalcedony and black glass, which have also been used for mourning jewellery, by its high specific gravity.

Demantoid is so called because it has certain properties in common with diamond: an adamantine lustre and large colour dispersion. In fact this stone has greater fire (q.v.) than the diamond, but because it is coloured the effect cannot be so clearly seen. The disadvantage of demantoid as a gemstone is its comparative softness, which limits it to settings where it will not be subject to much wear. Demantoid characteristically shows fine inclusions of asbestos fibres in a radiating pattern and this feature, together with its high refractive index (1.888–1.889) and high colour-dispersion, make it easily distinguishable from other green gemstones. It was first found in Russia in 1868, and the Urals are still the major source.

A yellow andradite is found in the Ala Valley, Piedmont, and Zermatt, but the crystals found so far are too small for use as gems. (See also *Garnet*.)

Anglo-Saxon jewellery. The Germanic tribes loosely referred to as Anglo-Saxons began to settle in Britain from the middle of the fifth century A.D., bringing with them their own art-forms and technical skills. Jewellery was for them, as for other barbarian and nomadic peoples, virtually the only visual art, and over and above its practical and decorative functions it had an extremely important social role. It was the outward sign of rank and authority, and also – since looted jewels were traditionally given by the victorious chieftain to his warriors – the sign of a man's prowess. The jewellery was therefore of a formal and fairly rigid nature, resistant to innovation, using traditional forms developed over many centuries – interlacing patterns, geometric designs, and animal and bird forms so

highly stylized that today they are only recognizable to the expert. The jewellery of kings and chieftains is magnificent both in its use of precious materials and in its workmanship. It has been estimated that it would have taken one man between four and five months simply to cut the stones in one of the more ornate disc-brooches.

The important metals in Anglo-Saxon jewellery were gold, silver and bronze. The gold and silver were probably all imported from the Continent and most of the bronze came from melted-down Roman pieces. The standard of metalwork was very high: the techniques included elaborate filigree in twisted, coiled and plaited wire, granulation, chasing and engraving. The metalwork was often enriched with niello, and bronze and sometimes silver were gilded. Occasional use was also made of iron and pewter. Extensive use was made of cloisonné inlay, an art learnt from the Goths, and a wide variety of shapes was used for the inlays of garnet, enamel and glass. Garnet inlay is a characteristic of Anglo-Saxon jewellery. The stone was polished and cut in slices to fit the cell, and mounted on a filling of cement.

The best-known and most attractive pieces of Anglo-Saxon jewellery are the *brooches*, which were universally worn. There are various types, of which the finest is the jewelled disc-brooch which

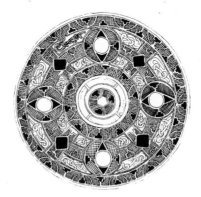

The Kingston brooch. Gold inlaid with garnets and lapis lazuli. Liverpool Public Museum

11

Anglo-Saxon jewellery

was worn in the Kentish region. Some of
these are cast in silver or bronze, with a
nielloed border and garnets in isolated
settings. The more splendid ones, known
as composite brooches since they are
made of two plates bound together with
strip metal, are in silver or gold and
elaborately inlaid with almandine garnets,
red and blue glass, shell, a white material
resembling meerschaum, and sometimes
lapis-lazuli. The metal surfaces are decorated with intricate patterns in filigree.
The Kingston brooch (see illustration) is
the most famous example of this type. A
complete contrast is the cruciform brooch,
a heavy cast ornament of gilded bronze,
which was never gem-set. The shape is
basically that of an arched bow with a
long 'foot', at the back of which is the
catch for the pin; at the top of the brooch
is a rectangular head-plate covering the
spring, and this is fitted with three
terminal knobs. The shape is therefore
roughly that of a cross (see illustration),
but it has no religious significance, having
been adopted from a Scandinavian type
some centuries before the conversion of
the Anglo-Saxons to Christianity. Similar
to the cruciform brooch is the square-
headed brooch, which ends in 3 rounded
terminals at the foot while the head-plate
characteristically has a serrated or decorated edge. The ornament on the cruciform
and square-headed brooches is usually of
highly stylized animal forms, typical of
early Germanic art.

The so-called saucer brooches, which
were often worn in pairs, are concave and
decorated with geometric and animal
patterns. Some are made in two pieces; a
thin gilded bronze plate with a pattern in
repoussé is cemented on to a heavier disc
of beaten bronze. The ring and penannular
brooches (see *Brooches*), with a hinged or
movable pin lying across the centre, are
adopted from old Celtic types; they are
comparatively rare, but one of the
surviving examples is strikingly beautiful.
This is the Sarre brooch in the British
Museum; it is of silver, chased with a
formalized animal pattern in two concentric bands, and further decorated with

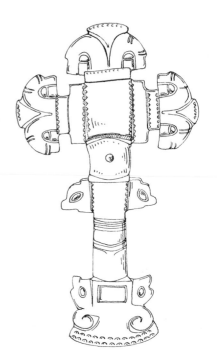

*Cruciform brooch of cast bronze. University
Museum of Archaeology and Ethnology,
Cambridge*

two birds cast in the round below the
point of the pin. The style of the decoration is more Celtic than Saxon. Other
types of brooch are the simple disc-
brooch, usually of chased or engraved
bronze, the small button-brooch, only
about $\frac{3}{4}''$ in diameter, cast with the design
of a human face, and the rare equal-armed
brooch, shaped like an H on its side,
decorated with animal and scroll patterns
adopted from Roman art.

Buckles were as universally worn and
often as ornate as brooches. They reached
a particularly high level of development
in Kent, where the typical form was a
triangular buckle-plate with 3 bosses in
relief and an ornamented plate at the base
of the tongue. These buckles are frequently inlaid with garnet, and are richly
decorated with interlacing animal designs
in filigree. The most magnificent Anglo-
Saxon buckle known is the solid gold one

found in the Sutton Hoo ship burial; it is over 5 inches long and is decorated with chasing and niello in an intricate interlacing pattern of animal forms and birds' heads (see *Buckles* for illustration). Interlocking *clasps* were sometimes used instead of buckles and decorated in a similar manner. The pair of gold clasps from the Sutton Hoo ship burial are unique in Anglo-Saxon jewellery and it is not known on what part of the body they were worn. They are curved, nearly 5 inches in length, and inlaid with a central mosaic of garnets and blue and white glass in a border decorated with an interlacing zoomorphic pattern. A rounded panel at the end of the clasp has a design of bears set with garnet and glass against a bird-pattern in filigree.

Queen Ethelswith's ring. British Museum

Rings were fairly common ornaments, and it was with gold rings that the pagan chieftain traditionally rewarded his warriors. Women wore fairly simple rings of silver or bronze; mostly they were of wire, with a flattened coil of wire or a bead forming the bezel, or of strip metal coiled in a snake pattern. On gold rings niello was often used with great skill; an example is the heavy gold ring of Queen Ethelswith, sister of King Alfred, which is chased and nielloed with two small animals on the shoulders and the Lamb of God on the bezel (see illustration). There is a ring of similar workmanship which belonged to King Ethelwulf of Wessex.

Other types of jewellery are less elaborate. *Earrings* were frequently worn but are mostly a simple ring of silver wire carrying a glass bead. Beads were also very popular in necklaces and bracelets; occasionally they were made of gold or other precious materials, but the commonest materials are amber, amethyst and glass. The glass beads display to the full the Anglo-Saxon love of colour; they are blue, green, red and yellow, and sometimes of mixed colours – blue spotted with white, yellow streaked with red, etc. Objects such as shells and the teeth of animals were worn as amulets, and there is little doubt that magical properties were also ascribed to the very popular stones amethyst and amber.

One of the most interesting products of the Anglo-Saxon jeweller is the Alfred jewel (q.v.), made in the ninth century. In its fine enamelling and elaborate goldwork it combines elements of barbaric and civilized art, which were to reach a gradual synthesis in the course of the Middle Ages. (See *Medieval jewellery*.)

Aniline. A chemical used in the measurement of refractive index (q.v.); R.I. 1.58.

Anisotropic. Exhibiting double refraction (q.v.).

Annealing. The process of heating metal to red-heat and then cooling it to render it more pliable for working. As metals are subjected to stresses such as hammering, rolling, twisting, etc., the grains are stretched and distorted and the metal becomes brittle; when it is raised to red heat the grains recrystallize in an undistorted form and the metal is again soft and easy to work. Silver is annealed at a maximum temperature of 650°C. This is also the temperature for annealing yellow, red and green gold; most white gold alloys require a temperature of 700°C. It is important that the entire piece is evenly heated; the heating can be done with a blow-torch for small work but large pieces have to be annealed in a furnace. The length of time for which the metal is kept at the required heat varies from a few seconds to a few minutes depending on the thickness of the metal. Silver and

Anodising

some gold alloys are quenched immediately in water or pickle, but certain golds have to be cooled in air, or cooled to black heat before quenching, or they will become stressed. Details of appropriate procedures are provided by the suppliers of precious metals.

Anodising. The process of giving aluminium (used in cheap jewellery) a protective finish which can then be dyed in a range of colours. This is done by electro-chemical action. The article to be treated is made the anode in the circuit and oxygen is liberated at the anode face, causing an oxide film integral with the metal to be built up. If the anodised article is immediately washed in cold water and placed in a hot dye solution it will take dye readily. (Dyestuffs for aluminium are available in a range of pastel and bright colours.) The dye is usually sealed by immersing the article in boiling water for half an hour.

Anomalous double refraction. An apparent double refraction seen in singly-refractive material, such as garnet or glass, when viewed between crossed polarizers (see *Double refraction*). It is usually caused by internal strain in the material. In most cases anomalous double refraction can be distinguished from true double refraction by the fact that the extinction of light occurs patchily instead of at intervals of 90°. Some garnets are an exception and show a pattern of light and dark which is difficult to distinguish from that of true double refraction. Synthetic spinel may be identified by its characteristic anomalous double refraction pattern of alternate light and dark stripes (the 'tabby' effect); the effect in this stone is caused by the excess of alumina which strains the crystal lattice. Paste gemstones may exhibit anomalous double refraction when the glass has been cooled quickly.

Anorthite. See *Feldspar*.

Antigorite. A jade-like variety of green serpentine, q.v.

Antilles pearls (Oil pearls). Pearls cut from suitable pieces of the shell of the sea snail, occasionally used in jewellery. They have a pearly top surface and a yellowish non-nacreous (see *Nacre*) underside. (See also *Shell*.)

Antique green. (See *Colouring of metals*.)

Antique jewellery. For ancient jewellery see *Egyptian jewellery, Greek j., Roman j., Etruscan j., Byzantine j., Celtic j., Anglo-Saxon j.* For later periods see *Medieval j., Renaissance j., Seventeenth-century j., Eighteenth-century j., Nineteenth-century j., Art Nouveau j., Modern j.*, See also items of jewellery, e.g. *Bracelets*, classes of jewellery, e.g. *Mourning j., Magical j.*, and jewellers, e.g. *Cellini*. Historical material is also included under e.g. *Enamel, Cameos, Gold*, etc.

Antwerp rose cut. A version of the rose cut in which the stone has 12 facets. (See *Diamond-cutting*.)

Anvil. See *Beck-iron*.

Anyolite. Green Tanzanian zoisite (q.v.) fashioned complete with the ruby crystals for which it is the matrix. It is used as an ornamental stone for small objects. The name is taken from the Masai word for green, *anyoli*.

'Apache tears'. A name given to the pebble-like cores of natural glass found in the south-west of the U.S.A. (see *Obsidian*). The transparent ones when cut are greyish in colour and may give a silky cat's eye effect owing to the presence of fine striations in the glass.

Apatite. (Calcium phosphate. S.G. 3.15–3.22; R.I. 1.63–1.64 to 1.64–1.65; H. 5.) A clear stone with a resinous lustre which occurs in a wide variety of colours – green, yellow, blue, violet and purple. A yellowish-green variety first found in south-east Spain is called Asparagus stone. Some blue stones from Ceylon and Burma are fibrous and show a cat's eye effect. Apatite is very attractive but its brittleness and softness make it rather unsuitable for use in jewellery, so it is not often encountered. Its name comes from the Greek word *apate*, deceit, because in the past it was often confused with other minerals.

Fine quality apatite comes from Ceylon, Burma, India, Mexico, Germany, the Urals and the U.S.A.

Aphrizite. Black tourmaline.

'Apricotine'. (Trade name.) Apricot-coloured garnet.

Apyrite. Tourmaline of a peach colour.

Aqua Fortis. Trade term for a mixture of one part nitric acid to five parts dilute sulphuric acid, used to produce a bright surface on base metals. (See *Bright-dip* and *Pickle*.)

'Aquagem'. (Trade name.) A light blue synthetic spinel.

Aqua Regia. Trade term for a mixture of one part nitric acid to two parts hydro-chloric acid. It is used in the testing and refining of gold and platinum, and takes its name ('royal water') from the fact that it was the only liquid known which could dissolve gold.

Aquamarine. (Beryllium – aluminium silicate. S.G. 2.65–2.85; R.I. 1.560–1.565; H. $7\frac{1}{2}$–8.) A transparent blue, bluish-green or yellowish-green variety of beryl, identical in chemical composition and crystal form to emerald, but of much lower value, partly because it often occurs in large unflawed crystals. The most acceptable colour for aquamarines is sky-blue, but this colour rarely occurs naturally and most blue aquamarines have been heat-treated to produce the desired colour, which is then permanent. Aquamarine is dichroic (q.v.), giving a blue and a colourless image. The stones are usually faceted in the step cut or brilliant cut (qq.v.).

Aquamarines occur in the cavities of granite rocks. Good quality material comes from Brazil, Madagascar, the Urals, Burma, U.S.A. and Southern Africa.

Aquamarine can be simulated by glass, synthetic spinel and garnet-topped doublets (See *Doublet*), all of which may be distinguished from true aquamarine by their physical properties (specific gravity, etc.) (See also *Synthetic gemstones*.)

Arabesque. A form of surface decoration characterized by flowing lines and scrollwork and intertwined leaves, branches, floral forms and fanciful motifs such as griffins, dolphins, etc. The arrangement is basically symmetrical. Arabesques of this type were introduced into western Europe in the sixteenth century and were exceedingly popular in all branches of the applied arts including jewellery. The term 'arabesque' implies that these designs were taken from Islamic art, but in fact the Renaissance arabesques were based on Graeco-Roman work and included representations of living creatures, which in Islamic art are forbidden. The Islamic type of arabesque is usually known as Moresque and is purely abstract.

'Arabian diamond'. A misnomer for rock crystal.

Aragonite. A translucent banded yellow stone from South-West Africa; it is a variety of calcite (q.v.).

Arbour. The threaded adaptor fitted on a motor spindle to take polishing mops (q.v.).

Archimedes. A name in the trade for a bow-drill (q.v.).

'Arizona ruby'. Misnomer for pyrope garnet from the Arizona district.

'Arizona spinel'. Misnomer for garnet.

'Arkansas diamond'. Misnomer for rock crystal.

Arkansas stone. A natural abrasive used by jewellers for smoothing off the surface of metal and for sharpening tools.

Armada jewel. See *Heneage jewel*.

Armenian stone. A name for lapis-lazuli.

Peacock pendant by Gautriat, about 1900.
Gold with enamel, diamonds, moonstones and a drop pearl. Victoria and Albert Museum

Art Nouveau jewellery. The Art Nouveau style became fashionable in jewellery in the early 1890s and lasted until about 1910. It was partly a reaction against what was worst in mid-Victorian jewellery: the unimaginative copying of ancient styles, the flamboyant display of jewels as wealth, and the ugliness and vulgarity of much mass-produced jewellery. Art Nouveau was a development from the earlier Pre-Raphaelite movement which had been an attempt to re-establish aesthetic principles in art and design. Some rather poorly executed jewellery had been produced by the Pre-Raphaelites, which was the precursor of Art Nouveau jewellery.

Art Nouveau was a relatively free, and at first simple, Romantic style, influenced considerably by Japanese art, which was enjoying a vogue in Europe at the time, and also by elements of Renaissance, Gothic, Baroque and Celtic art. The characteristic forms of Art Nouveau are curved and flowing, often asymmetrical, and based on natural forms. Recurrent motifs are intertwining creepers, leaves and flowers (particularly convolvulus, cornflowers and nasturtiums), insects (especially butterflies and dragonflies), wraith-like forms and dreaming faces.

In materials, Art Nouveau jewellery broke away from convention in using precious, semi-precious and worthless materials side by side. Greater importance was attached to the beauty of a stone than

The Sylvia pendant made by Paul and Henri Véver, about 1900. Enamelled gold, chalcedony (the head and hands), diamonds and rubies. Musée des Arts Décoratifs, Paris

to its intrinsic value. Stones were generally cut *en cabochon* rather than faceted, as a rounded, flowing effect was desired; and milky, soft-looking stones such as opals, moonstones and pearls were much favoured. Enamel was extensively used, often in preference to gemstones, and very delicate effects were sometimes achieved with it.

The most popular types of jewellery in this period were necklaces and pendants and fantastically-decorated hair-combs and pins, which were made in great numbers. Rings were also elaborate; a

17

Pendant by Lalique, about 1900. Gold, blue enamel, white carved stone (the face) and a baroque pearl. Musée des Arts Décoratifs, Paris

Mermaid comb in tortoiseshell and gold with coral and enamel, by the Danish jeweller Slött-Muller

favourite design was of two serpents or two dragonflies holding a stone such as an opal. Bracelets were not particularly fashionable.

The Art Nouveau movement began with individual artists and craftsmen, not with big established firms, and in essence this tradition continued. Although some designers employed a large number of craftsmen and produced jewellery on a large scale, a lot of jewellery was also made by private individuals who had no previous training in the trade and worked mainly for their own pleasure. The most gifted and influential of the Art Nouveau jewellers was René Lalique (q.v.), whose

jewellery was a triumphant success at the Paris Exhibition of 1900 and was worn at the courts of Europe. Lalique was the most original of the Art Nouveau jewellers, using a wide variety of materials including horn, ivory, tortoiseshell, copper and steel. He experimented with new processes of enamelling and his enamels are the finest in the style. He was responsible for introducing many of the motifs which became so popular in Art Nouveau work, particularly the nude or semi-nude female figure. Lalique's work was widely imitated, often badly, and his influence lasted for some twenty years.

Among other important French designers of the time were Véver (q.v.), Georges Fouquet (q.v.) and Marcel Bing. Jules Desbois produced delicately-worked buttons and brooches in chased gold and other materials depicting a female head or form in languorous attitudes, often against a background of flowing hair. Philippe Wolfers (q.v.) produced fine jewellery in Art Nouveau style in Belgium. In England the pioneer was C. R. Ashbee (q.v.). In other European countries the influence of the style was less profound. In America, Art Nouveau jewellery was produced by Tiffany and Co. (q.v.). Fabergé (q.v.), the most renowned jeweller of the period, was not much interested in the Art Nouveau style and is not considered here.

Art Nouveau jewellery ultimately declined as a result of its own extravagances and because, being dependent on individual talent, it could not be mass-produced. It gradually gave way, around 1910, to a more sober and geometric type of design. (See also *Modern jewellery*.)

Artificial resins. A general term for the plastics used in the manufacture of imitation stones. (See *Plastics*.)

Ashbee, C. R. (1863–1942). The pioneer of Art Nouveau jewellery (q.v.) in England. He was not by training a jeweller, but in the 1880s he became involved in the Arts and Crafts movement which was trying to educate the public to appreciate Pre-Raphaelite styles in design and understand the importance of craftsmanship, and as a result he became interested in designing jewellery. His designs were carried out by the Guild and School of Handicraft in London, and at Campden in Gloucestershire. Ashbee detested commercially-produced jewellery and believed that the monetary value of a jewel should not be thought important. For his own designs he frequently used materials of little value such as amethyst, amber and blister pearls. He liked silver, but with a dull polish which gave it a rich, aged appearance. Amethyst with silver was one of his favourite combinations. Many of his designs were either abstract

Peacock brooch in gold, pearls and diamonds. Designed by Ashbee, made by the Guild of Handicraft

or taken from flowers, especially the rose, carnation and heartsease.

Ashbee's early work had considerable influence in England, and other artists and craftsmen were encouraged by his example to produce their own designs in the Art Nouveau style.

Asparagus stone. See *Apatite*.

Asprey & Co. Ltd. High-class manufacturing and retail jewellers, also specializing in fine gold, silver and leatherwork. The business was established at Mitcham in 1781 by William Asprey, a skilled metalworker and descendant of a distinguished family of Huguenot craftsmen. In the 1830s William Asprey's son Charles opened a shop at 49 New Bond Street and in 1848 moved to larger premises at 166, where the firm has been ever since (having subsequently expanded

Assaying

into 165–169 New Bond Street). The tradition of individual craftsmanship is carefully preserved – Asprey's design and make their own merchandise in workshops above the showrooms – and the business is still handed on from father to son. The firm has been granted a royal appointment by every reigning British sovereign since Queen Victoria, and has lately executed some important jewellery commissions in the Middle East.

Assaying. The process of determining what proportion of precious metal is contained in a piece of gold or silverwork. Articles made of gold or silver must be of a minimum standard of fineness. In Britain the minimum standards for gold are 22-carat (22 parts out of 24 pure gold, or 91.66%), 18-carat (18 parts out of 24, 75%), 14-carat (14 parts, 58.5%) and 9-carat (9 parts, 37.5%). The standards for silver are 95.84% pure silver (the Britannia standard, rarely used) and 92.5% (sterling). The gold and silver solders used in the work must also be of the required standard.

Legislation concerning the compulsory assaying of gold and silver has been in force in European countries since the Middle Ages (though not always very effectively). The first English legislation is a statute of Edward 1 in 1300, which fixed the minimum standards at sterling for silver and at 19½ carats for gold, and laid the responsibility for assaying on the 'guardians' of the goldsmiths' craft in London, who were supposed to assay not only the wares of the London goldsmiths but those of provincial goldsmiths as well. Provincial assay offices were subsequently set up (see *Assay offices*), but many later closed. Assaying is now carried out at four assay offices in Britain, and if the articles assayed are of the required standard they are then hallmarked. Certain articles are exempt from assaying and hallmarking: they include gold rings (except wedding rings), gold watch-chains, articles of gold or silver which consist entirely of filigree work or are so small, or so heavily engraved or set with

stones, that they cannot be marked without damage, the actual settings of stones, and most silver articles weighing under 5 dwt. (0.25 oz. Troy.).

Before sending his work to be assayed the jeweller or silversmith must stamp it with his mark, which consists of his initials, and it must be sent to the assay office at which his mark is registered. With it he sends a form stating the weight of the piece and the standard of the metal. A fee is payable for the assay.

Methods. The oldest method of assaying was to rub the metal on a touchstone and compare the resulting streak with the streak left by metal of a known quality. This method is much more accurate than it sounds and is still used by retail jewellers and in many Continental assay offices (see *Touchstone testing*), but in British assay offices more scientific techniques are used for testing gold and silver. Even some of these techniques, however, are many centuries old; they were probably in use in the fourteenth century, and the basic principles were being applied (but for refining, not testing) in the ancient world.

All gold and silver wares which arrive at the assay office are first weighed. Tiny scrapings of metal are then taken from the various parts of the work so that a representative sample is obtained; the amount which may be removed in this way is fixed by law at 8 grains to the pound Troy. The removal of these scrapings without damaging the work is of course a highly skilled operation. The scrapings are carefully weighed, and the assay proceeds as follows.

Gold. To the gold scrapings is added a proportion of fine silver. The gold and silver are then wrapped in small sheets of lead and placed in a cupel (a porous crucible) which is put in a furnace. At 1100°C the base metals oxidize and are absorbed by the cupel, leaving an alloy of gold and silver in the form of a small pellet in the bottom of the cupel. When it is cool this pellet is hammered and rolled into a thin strip and placed in nitric acid which is then brought to the boil. The nitric acid dissolves the silver and when it is poured off pure gold is left behind. The gold is brought to red heat, quenched, and weighed. From the weight of the gold in proportion to the weight of the original scrapings, the percentage of pure gold in the sample (i.e. the fineness of the gold) can be calculated.

Silver. Silver can be assayed in the same way as gold (the scrapings are weighed, wrapped in lead, heated in a cupel until pure silver remains, the weight of the silver being compared with the weight of the scrapings), but in practice a titration method (volumetric analysis) is used.

There are some differences in the way the technique is applied at the various assay offices, but the basic principle is the same. The procedure used at the London assay office is briefly as follows. Scrapings are taken and an accurately weighed portion of the sample is dissolved in nitric acid; the silver content is determined by titration with sodium chloride solution. An exact volume of sodium chloride is added as a concentrated solution sufficient to precipitate all but one or two parts per thousand of the silver as silver chloride. The silver still remaining in solution is then determined either by potentiometric titration with dilute sodium chloride solution, or by the addition of dilute chloride solution and measurement of the density of the 'cloud' which is formed. This method allows the exact proportion of fine silver in the scrapings to be determined.

Platinum. There is no legal requirement for platinum to be assayed in Britain. A method of spectrographic analysis has been formulated in case assaying is made obligatory at some future date.

If a piece fails the assay the first time it is assayed again, and a third time if necessary. If the third assay still shows it to be below the legal standard it is cut through and returned to the maker. If the assayer suspects that base metal is contained inside the piece he is authorized to cut it, and if he finds base metal the entire piece is confiscated; if he does not, compensation is paid. If however the assay shows the piece to be of the required standard, it is then stamped with the appropriate hallmark (see *Hallmarking*) and returned to the maker. It is usual for jewellers and silversmiths to send their work to be assayed before it is quite finished. Pieces of jewellery which are to be gem-set are sent for assay before the stones are put in.

Assay offices. There are statutory offices for the assaying and hallmarking (qq.v.) of gold and silver in *London* (at Goldsmiths' Hall), *Birmingham*, *Sheffield*, *Edinburgh* and *Dublin*. The London office is the oldest-established, since a statute of 1300 gave the 'guardians of the craft' of London goldsmiths the duty of assaying every piece of gold and silver work made in the city before it left the workshop. The wares of provincial goldsmiths were also supposed to be assayed at London, but in view of the travelling conditions of the time this was clearly not a practical proposition, and in 1423 provisions for assay offices at York, Newcastle-on-Tyne, Lincoln, Norwich, Bristol, Salisbury and Coventry were made. There is no evidence that offices were ever actually set up in Bristol, Salisbury, Coventry or Lincoln. Of the other offices, Norwich does not appear to have assayed anything after 1700, York closed in 1858 under something of a cloud (plate had been hallmarked without being properly assayed), and Newcastle closed in 1884 when there was no longer sufficient work to justify an assay office.

Meanwhile an assay office had been thriving at Chester since the Middle Ages without, apparently, official royal sanction until the seventeenth century. The probable explanation for this is that the assay was regulated by the Earl of Chester, under whose authority, and not that of the crown, the city and county of Chester had been since early Norman times. The Chester office survived for many centuries but was finally closed in 1962. Exeter, although not mentioned in the statute of

1423, had also been assaying gold and silver for several centuries before the office was officially established in 1701; there was clearly a need for an assay office in the west of England since Bristol and Salisbury had not taken advantage of their privilege. The Exeter office seems to have done good business until the middle of the nineteenth century, when the number of goldsmiths in the west declined sharply and the revenue was insufficient to cover expenses. It was closed in 1883.

When the manufacture of jewellery and plate began to develop into a major industry at Birmingham and Sheffield in the eighteenth century the manufacturers had to send their wares to Chester or London to be assayed. This resulted in delays and sometimes damage to the goods, and in 1772 the manufacturers petitioned Parliament to set up assay offices in Sheffield and Birmingham. The petition was strongly opposed by the officials of Goldsmiths' Hall, who were jealous of their privileges, had always had a low opinion of provincial assay offices, and of course stood to lose revenue if work from the Midlands was assayed elsewhere. The grounds of the opposition were that the Birmingham and Sheffield manufacturers were dishonest and had passed off silver plate as solid silver and marked it as such. In counter-attack the Sheffield silver-smiths alleged corruption at Goldsmiths' Hall and said that the favour of the assayers and scrapers could be bought with drink. A Parliamentary Committee was set up to investigate these and other allegations about the administration of assay offices. They found that most were administered honestly and efficiently, and some were not. The Assay Master at Exeter, for example, was not a trained goldsmith and had never been instructed how to make an assay; he had experimented with the weights used by his predecessor until he arrived at an idea of what he was supposed to do. The oath by which he had been sworn in was not the statutory oath, but he said he was sure that it would do just as well. The main finding of the Commission, however, was that there was a real need for assay offices at Birmingham and Sheffield, and these were therefore established in 1773 under the jurisdiction of the Guardians of Wrought Plate of those cities. One of the reasons for the Commission's decision was that the patterns used by the Birmingham jewellers were being adopted by London goldsmiths and the Birmingham jewellers were getting no credit for the designs. At first only silver was allowed to be assayed at the new offices and the area assigned to each office was restricted to a radius of 20 miles, but in 1824 this was extended to 50 miles and Birmingham was author-ized to assay gold. Gold does not seem to have been officially assayed at Sheffield until 1904. Birmingham (q.v.), now a major centre of the jewellery trade, is proud of the reputation of its assay office, which each year sends to the Mint a sample of the scrapings it has assayed (known as the 'diet'); the sample has never been found unsatisfactory.

The Scottish goldsmiths have never been subject to the authority of Gold-smiths' Hall, as were the provincial gold-smiths of England. A Scottish statute of 1457 (by which time the craft was well established) restricted the amount of alloy which might be added to gold and silver and made the marking of wares by a 'deacon of the craft' in Edinburgh compulsory; in 1586 the deacons were officially authorized to 'search' for substandard work and to assay. The Wardens of the Incorporation of Gold-smiths of the City of Edinburgh had jurisdiction over goldsmiths throughout Scotland except those in Glasgow, where there was a very old-established guild of goldsmiths. The Glasgow assay office was not officially established, however, until 1819; it was closed in 1964.

The Dublin goldsmiths appear to have managed without assaying until the beginning of the seventeenth century, when it was resolved that all silver plate should be marked and should be of the same standard as the silver coinage. The assaying was controlled by the City

Corporation, a state of affairs which the goldsmiths must have found highly unsatisfactory because they petitioned Charles I to incorporate them by royal charter so that they could run their own affairs and establish a 'proper standard' for gold and silver. They had, they said, been granted a charter before, but it had unfortunately been burnt. (The records of it have also apparently perished.) Charles granted them a charter in 1637. Imported gold and silver wares made in the Republic of Ireland are deemed to be 'foreign' and have to be assayed and marked in Britain before being offered for sale; similar conditions apply to British goods imported into the Republic.

Each assay office has its own mark, which it stamps on all the work it assays. It also has its own cycle of date-letters; these are described under *Hallmarking*.

For assay office procedure and techniques see *Assaying*. (See also *Goldsmiths' Hall* and *Worshipful Company of Goldsmiths*.)

Asteria. A stone which exhibits a 4, 6 or 12-rayed star of light when cut *en cabochon* in the appropriate crystallographic direction. (See also *Asterism*.) The finest star-stones are rubies and sapphires, which show 6 or 12 rays. Rose quartz (usually 6 rays) also shows a good star effect, and a weak effect may be seen in spinel and garnet. Star rubies and sapphires are made synthetically. (See *Synthetic gemstones*.)

Asterism. The 'star' effect seen in some gem-stones when they are cut *en cabochon* with the base of the stone parallel with the basal plane of the crystal. The effect is produced by the reflection of light from small cavities or fibrous inclusions in the stone. (See also *Epiasterism* and *Diasterism*.)

Atlas pearl. Misnomer for a bead of satin spar (q.v.).

Auckland shell. Mother-of-pearl from the pearl-oyster, *Pinctada margaritifera*, fished off the islands of the South Pacific,

and exported from Auckland. It has a green nacre (q.v.). (See also *Shell*.)

Augelite. (Hydrated aluminium phosphate. S.G. 2.7; R.I. 1.547–1.588; H. 5.) A mineral which has on occasion been cut into colourless gemstones for collectors. The stones have a vitreous lustre. Localities: U.S.A. and Bolivia.

'Australian ruby'. A misnomer for garnet.

Aventurine feldspar ('Sunstone'). (Oligoclase feldspar. S.G. 2.62–2.65; R.I. 1.54–1.55; H. 6.) A stone which has a spangled metallic appearance owing to the inclusion of small flakes of haematite or goethite. The colour is bronze or reddish-brown. The best source is the south coast of Norway. Other localities are Canada, Russia, India and the U.S.A.

It is used in much the same way as aventurine quartz (q.v.), which it closely resembles but which has the advantage of being harder.

Aventurine glass ('Goldstone'). (S.G. 2.50–2.80; R.I. 1.53; H. 5½.) Glass containing small flakes of copper which give a spangled bronze effect. It is an imitation of aventurine quartz, but is easily distinguishable from it in appearance and on account of its comparative softness. It is also made in blue.

Aventurine quartz. (See *Quartz*. S.G. 2.64–2.69; R.I. 1.544–1.553; H. 7.) A variety of quartzite which has a spangled appearance owing to the inclusion of mica or iron. The colour may be reddish-brown, green, yellow or grey. The green variety is most often used in jewellery, cut with a flat or slightly rounded surface and used in rings and brooches, or made into beads. Sources include India, Russia and Tanzania. (See also *Aventurine feldspar* and *Aventurine glass*.)

Awabi pearls. Japanese name for abalone (q.v.) pearls.

Axe stone. Name given to the variety of nephrite (q.v.) found in New Zealand. It is mostly dark green in colour.

Axinite. (Boro-silicate of aluminium and calcium. S.G. 3.27–3.29; R.I. 1.67–1.68; H. 7.) An unusual translucent to transparent stone with a high lustre. The colours are clove-brown, yellow, and occasionally blue, grey and green; some violet stones are found in Tasmania. Axinite is strongly dichroic (q.v.). It takes its name from the shape of the crystals, which are very thin and sharp-edged. Sources are Isère in France, Tasmania, Norway, Cornwall, Canada, and various localities in the U.S.A.

Axis of symmetry. The axis about which a crystal can be rotated so as to occupy the same position in space more than once in 360°. (See *Crystal systems.*)

Azurite ('Chessylite'). (Copper carbonate. S.G. 3.77–3.89; R.I. 1.73–1.84; H. 3½–4.) An opaque azure-blue copper carbonate which makes an attractive stone in jewellery, although it wears badly because of its softness. It is frequently found in association with malachite (q.v.), with which it has a common origin, and pieces of azurite and malachite concentrically banded together (*Azur-malachite*) are also used in jewellery.

Localities include Chessy in France (hence the name 'Chessylite'), Romania, south-west Africa and Arizona.

Azur-malachite. See *Azurite.*

B

Bacalite. Amber (q.v.) from Lower California.

'Baffa diamond'. Misnomer for rock crystal.

Baguette. A gemstone cut in the shape of a narrow rectangle. (See also *Baton*.)

Bakelite. See *Plastics*.

Baikalite. Diopside from Baikal in Russia.

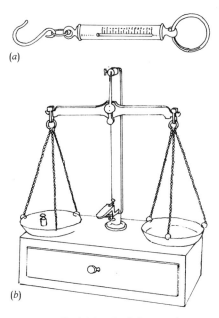

(a)

(b)

Jewellers' (a) spring balance and (b) scale-pan balance

Balances. In several processes involved in the manufacture of jewellery the precise weight of the materials, particularly the precious metals, is of great importance. A variety of precision balances are available for this purpose; previously they measured in Troy weight but they are now metric. They may be of the spring-balance type or the scale-pan type (see illustration). Precision balances are also used in the measurement of the specific gravity (q.v.) of gemstones. Some are specially made for this purpose. Two of these, the Westphal balance and the Jolly's spring balance, are described under *Specific gravity*.

'Balas ruby'. The old name for red spinel, originating at a time when stones were classified largely according to their colour. The derivation of the word 'Balas' is obscure, but it probably comes from Balascia, the old capital of Badakhshan in Afghanistan, whence the stones were exported to Europe in the Middle Ages.

Ballas. A rare multicrystalline form of diamond which, having no cleavage, is much in demand for industrial purposes because of its toughness. It comes from Brazil and certain of the South African mines. (See also *Diamond*.)

Ball catch

Ball catch. A safety-catch much used on brooches. The outer part forms an incomplete circle with a central groove, the inner part is a movable curved tongue to which is soldered a tab which rides along the groove. When the tab is pulled down to the end of the groove the tongue

25

moves round to close the circle and hold the brooch-pin. (See illustration.)

Bamboo pearl. Tabasheer.

Bandeau. A narrow band encircling the forehead. Jewelled bandeaux have been fashionable at various times from the Middle Ages onwards; their last period of popularity was in the early part of the Victorian era, when they might be of plain gold or set with pearls, diamonds, etc. (See also *Diadems* and *Nineteenth-century jewellery*.)

Bandelettes. Decorated ribbons worn in the hair, trimmed with jet, amber, coral or pearls, during the late 1860's.

Bangle. A non-flexible bracelet. (See *Bracelets*.)

Barbor Jewel. A pendant said to have been made to commemorate the deliverance of William Barbor, condemned to be burnt at Smithfield stake for his Protestantism, who was reprieved by the death of Mary Tudor and accession of Queen Elizabeth I. The pendant consists of a small cameo portrait of Elizabeth in an oval enamelled frame, in an outer border set alternately with rubies and table-cut diamonds. Below it hangs a cluster of small pearls. The jewel is now in the Victoria and Albert Museum, London.

Barite (barytes). (Barium sulphate. S.G. 4.47; R.I. 1.636–1.648; H. 3.) A transparent to opaque white, red, blue, green, yellow or brown stone. The variety most used ornamentally is a brown stalagmitic type which shows concentric markings when cut crosswise. The softness of the stone prevents its use in jewellery except as a curiosity. It occurs worldwide.

'Baroda gem'. (Trade name.) Colourless glass with a foiled back. (See *Foil*.)

Baroque. Term for an irregularly-shaped stone.

Baroque jewellery. See *Seventeenth-century jewellery*.

Baroque pearl. A large irregularly-shaped pearl. Such pearls were extensively used in Renaissance jewellery towards the end of the sixteenth century, especially by German craftsmen. They were set generally in pendants in the form of birds, dragons, sea-monsters, etc., the pearl usually forming part of the creature's body (see illustration). In the best examples

Late sixteenth-century enamelled gold pendant using a baroque pearl for the lizard's body. Victoria and Albert Museum

the shape of the pearl has clearly inspired the form of the jewel and the result is an arresting piece of jewellery, but sometimes the pearl was merely fitted into a conventional design, and the effect is rather forced. (See also *Renaissance jewellery* and *Canning jewel*.)

Barrel polishing. See *Tumbling*.

Basanite. A fine-grained black jasper (q.v.) used by jewellers for testing precious metals. The metal is rubbed against the stone leaving a streak, which is then tested with acid (see *Touchstone testing*). The use of basanite goes back to the ancient world, and its name is derived from the Greek word for touchstone.

Base metal. Any metal other than gold and platinum. In the literature on jewellery, silver is usually classed with the precious metals.

Basse-taille. A technique of enamelling in which the metal is worked in relief and overlaid with translucent enamels, so that the shades of colour vary with the depth of the enamel over the high and low parts of the design. (See *Enamel*.)

'**Bastard emerald**'. Misnomer for peridot.

Bastite. See *Enstatite*.

Baton. A gemstone cut in the shape of a long narrow rectangle, larger than a baguette.

Battersea enamels. Brightly-coloured enamels on a copper base produced in Battersea, London, between 1750 and 1775 as a cheap substitute for the fine French enamels then in fashion. The articles produced were mostly small ornamental objects such as snuff boxes and jewel-cases, but enamels for jewellery were also made. These were usually oval and set in gold or gilt frames, and could be mounted in bracelets, clasps or necklaces. They were also popular as buttons. The designs were generally of classical or pastoral scenes, following the taste of the period. (See *Eighteenth-century jewellery;* also *Bilston enamels* and *Enamel*.)

Bayate. Ferruginous jasper (q.v.) from Cuba.

Beading-tool. A tool used for making the beaded wire which is a feature of much ancient goldsmiths' work. As described by the eleventh-century monk Theophilus, it consisted of two blocks of metal (bronze or iron) made to fit one over the other, in which were cut corresponding grooves of varying sizes with small hemispherical depressions. Gold or silver wire was placed in the groove, the blocks were fitted together and hammered while the wire was turned, and the wire took on the impression of the patterned grooves. Modern patterned wire is made in rolling-mills (q.v.), and a graining tool (q.v.) is used to raise beads on metal.

Beads. Beads are among the earliest and most universal forms of jewellery. It is likely that in primitive societies they are worn as much for the sake of their supposed magical properties as for the sake of ornament. This is particularly so in the case of engraved beads, where the

Elaborate bead in filigree and enamel from a sixteenth-century Venetian necklace. Museo Poldi-Pezzoli, Milan

inscription nearly always has some magical purpose. (See *Magical jewellery*.)

The most primitive beads found are often of roughly-chipped stone or hardened clay. A decorative effect is achieved by using clays of different colours. These beads were sometimes worn individually, but usually they were strung together. Other favourite materials, where they could be found, were amber, bone, jet and ivory, all of which are soft enough to be worked by primitive methods.

Ancient civilizations which had learnt the art of glass-making produced some strikingly beautiful glass beads. The Phoenicians were skilled glass-makers and have left a number of necklaces composed entirely of glass beads although many other more precious materials were available to them. Bead necklaces were much in use among the Egyptians, who used highly-coloured glass, faience (q.v.), a variety of gemstones including amethyst, cornelian, garnet, lapis lazuli and turquoise, and also beads of silver and gold. Egyptian beads are frequently cylindrical. Some Egyptian collars consisted entirely of beads. (See *Egyptian jewellery*.)

The bead necklace was a favourite ornament in Roman times. Amber was a popular material and was especially valued if it had an insect embedded in it. Most necklaces dating from the Roman occupation of Britain are of spherical glass beads and show the high standard of skill which Roman glass-making attained. Some of these beads show a beautiful blend of colours and are sometimes decorated with a serpentine pattern fused into the glass.

Many bead necklaces have survived also from the Anglo-Saxon period. Some are of glass, in shapes and colours similar to the Roman. Amethyst, amethystine quartz and amber, probably all brought by trade from the Continent, were also used, either strung together or worn individually. The latter were probably amulets. More valuable materials were used in necklaces for people of higher rank: gold beads, or precious stones in settings of gold filigree.

Necklaces were little worn during the Middle Ages with the exception of rosaries (see *Devotional jewellery*), for which a great variety of beads, some very elaborate, were made. As jewellery became increasingly luxurious with the Renaissance, beads became miniature jewels in their own right (see illustration). Later with the invention of brilliant-cutting for diamonds, beads were relegated to a minor place in jewellery, but they have always regained popularity whenever simplicity is in fashion. (See also *Necklaces*.)

For the way in which stone beads are made see *Gem-cutting*.

Bearing (bearer). A thin collar of metal soldered inside the collet (q.v.), approximately $\frac{1}{16}''$ below the top, to support the stone.

Beccarite. Green zircon.

Beekite. Agatised coral.

Beck-iron. A steel anvil used for hammering jewellery. It has two tapering arms – one round, for working finger-rings or curved metal, the other flat-surfaced for flat metal. (See illustration.)

Beeswax. The natural wax produced by bees, used by jewellers as a lubricant in

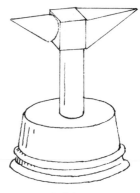

Beck-iron

wire-drawing (see *Drawplate*), as an acid-resist in etching (q.v.), and as an ingredient in the pitch mixture used in repoussé work (q.v.) – it helps to make the pitch more malleable.

Beilby layer. The fused surface layer on a stone caused by the friction of polishing. The surface becomes liquid under the heat and either recrystallizes or remains amorphous according to the mineral. This fusion occurs in all stones except diamond, which has too high a melting-point for it to be produced – the polish on diamond is therefore entirely due to abrasion. The Beilby layer is extremely thin and does not affect refractometer (q.v.) readings. It is named after its discoverer, G. T. Beilby.

Belcher chain. A trace chain made of D-section wire. (See *Chain*.)

Bellows. Foot-bellows are used for increasing the heat of a gas flame for soldering, etc. (See also *Blowpipe*.)

Bell pearl. A drop pearl. (See *Pearls*.)

Belomorite. Moonstone from Russia.

Bench pin. A wedge-shaped piece of wood with a V cut out of the end, fixed to the jeweller's workbench and used to support work while it is being filed or sawn.

Bench skin. An apron of leather or simulated leather fixed to the front of a jeweller's workbench and fitting over his

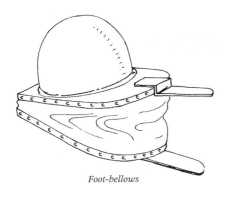

Foot-bellows

lap; it is to catch the precious-metal filings, etc. (See *Lemel*.)

'Bengal amethyst'. Misnomer for purple sapphire.

Benitoite. (Barium-titanium silicate. S.G. 3.65–3.68; R.I. 1.76–1.80; H. $6\frac{1}{2}$.) A rare transparent sapphire-blue stone found only in San Benito Co., California. Benitoite has very strong fire (q.v.), comparable to that of diamond, but the effect is masked by its colour. When first discovered at the beginning of this century it was thought to be sapphire, but was later found to be a hitherto unknown mineral. It may be distinguished from sapphire by its lower specific gravity (q.v.), its more pronounced dichroism, and its fluorescence under ultra-violet light. (See *Luminescence*.)

Benoîton chain. A chain which hung from the bonnet, passed under the chin and lay in a loop on the breast. It could be of gold or silver links or composed of a string of pearls, jet beads, etc. These chains had a brief vogue between 1865 and 1870 and were introduced to replace bonnet-strings which easily became entangled with the very long earrings then in fashion. (See also *Nineteenth-century jewellery*.)

Berghem, Ludwig van (Louis de Berquen). The supposed inventor of diamond-polishing. He is said to have discovered the principle of polishing diamonds with diamond-powder in Bruges in 1476, but as there is evidence that polished diamonds were in circulation in Europe before this date, it seems likely that he did no more than refine and develop existing techniques.

'Berigem'. (Trade name.) Synthetic greenish-yellow spinel.

Berlin iron jewellery. Cast-iron jewellery made in Berlin, or in imitation of the Berlin style, during the first half of the nineteenth century. It is lacquered black and some of the finest pieces are decorated with gold. Much of it has the extreme delicacy of wrought-ironwork in miniature, and is among the most attractive jewellery of the century.

Iron began to be used in jewellery at about the end of the eighteenth century largely because of the scarcity of precious metals. The first factory for the manufacture of iron jewellery (among other ironwork) was opened in Berlin in 1804; in 1806 Napoleon captured Berlin and the casts were taken to France, where presumably they were used, although there is no iron jewellery which is known to be of French manufacture. Meanwhile production was continued in Berlin.

A wide range of jewellery was produced, including buckles, brooches, bracelets, earrings, necklaces and hair ornaments. During the Napoleonic era the designs were predominantly neoclassical. Openwork reliefs of classical scenes were popular, framed by a milled iron rim. Another frequent design was a classical profile in low relief on a polished steel ground framed in whorls of iron wire; these were often used in bracelets arranged alternately with medallions of floral patterns in wire.

Production of iron jewellery reached its peak in the years 1813–15 when Prussia rebelled against the French. The wealthy were asked to donate their jewels for the war funds, and in return were given iron jewellery by the government. Many of these pieces bore inscriptions such as 'Gold gab ich für Eisen, 1813' ('Gold I gave for iron, 1813'). Over 11,000 pieces of jewellery were made in these years, of which nearly half were iron crosses.

Beryl

After the restoration of the Bourbon monarchy the neoclassical designs associated with the Napoleonic era disappeared. Foliate and lattice-work designs and fruit and flower motifs now became predominant in iron jewellery. Classical subjects were occasionally used but they were treated romantically rather than heroically.

other colours which do not have specific names. Dark brown and black beryls showing weak asterism (q.v.) have been found in Brazil and Mozambique respectively. Beryl is colourless when pure (this happens rarely – 'colourless' beryl nearly always has a very pale tint). The colours of the gemstones are due to traces of other minerals: chromium in the case

Emerald crystals

Nineteenth-century Gothic-style iron cross

Towards the middle of the century Gothic motifs were introduced. (A typical Gothic-style cross is illustrated.) By this time, however, iron jewellery was becoming less fashionable, and shortly afterwards it ceased to be made. Comparatively little of it has survived and this accordingly has a value far in excess of its intrinsic worth. The most extensive collection is in the museum at Rouen.

Aquamarine crystals

Beryl. (Beryllium-aluminium silicate. S.G. 2.68–2.90; R.I. 1.57–1.59; H. $7\frac{1}{2}$–8.) A mineral producing in its opaque form the raw material for the beryllium used in industry, and in its transparent form a range of gemstones: *emerald* (grass-green), *aquamarine* (blue-green), *morganite* (pink) *heliodor* (yellow) (qq.v.), and stones of

of emerald, iron in heliodor and (probably) in aquamarine and in other green beryls, and manganese or lithium in morganite.

Beryl crystallizes in hexagonal prisms which terminate, in the case of emerald, in a flat face at right angles to the prism faces, and with other beryls in a number of small inclined faces giving a rounded top to the crystal. It is doubly-refractive and dichroic (qq.v.).

Sources include Columbia, Brazil, Ceylon, Madagascar, India, South Africa and Rhodesia.

Beryl glass. Fused beryl: described under *Glass*.

Beryllonite. (Sodium-beryllium phosphate. S.G. 2.84; R.I. 1.55–1.56; H.5.) A rare transparent mineral, usually colourless but sometimes tinged with yellow. The stone is not particularly attractive and its comparative softness makes it rather unsuitable for use in jewellery, but it has a certain appeal on account of its rarity. Gem-quality material comes from Stoneham, Maine, U.S.A.

Roman gold ring, fourth–fifth century A.D.
British Museum

Betrothal rings. The custom of giving a ring as a token of betrothal appears to date from Roman times. At the betrothal the girl's father or guardian made on her behalf a promise of marriage to the man, who in turn gave her a ring as his pledge. Since the wearing of a gold ring was not permitted, except as a special privilege, in the days of the Republic, the betrothal ring, called the *anulus pronubis*, was at first of iron and contained no gemstone. By the third century A.D. the old ideals of austerity had been abandoned and gold rings were in use. The ring might be decorated with some appropriate inscription or motif: among these were the lovers' knot and the motif of two clasped hands, both of which originated in the Roman period and were adopted in later centuries in the rest of Europe.

The betrothal in Roman times, although a solemn ceremony, was not considered unbreakable. The early Christians, however, who continued to use betrothal rings, regarded the ceremony as increasingly important and finally incorporated the plighting of troth into the marriage ceremony; the betrothal ring therefore became a wedding ring and the giving of it was regarded as the symbol of an unbreakable contract. In time a need was felt for another ring to be given at an earlier stage as the sign of an intention to marry, and this eventually produced the modern engagement ring. However, there is an intervening period of over a thousand years during which it is almost impossible to say for what precise purpose any particular ring was intended – as a betrothal ring, a wedding ring, or simply as a token of love. This is partly because many forms of betrothal were in use in the Middle Ages and different degrees of importance were ascribed to them; some were considered almost tantamount to marriage. In other cases the ring was simply a symbol of a lovers' understanding or a pledge exchanged between parents who had arranged their children's marriage. In the later Middle Ages in particular, the wearing of many rings was fashionable, the giving of rings as a token of regard was almost a social convention, and the ideal of courtly love, even if it was no more than an ideal, made the giving of rings inscribed with amorous mottoes and symbols perfectly acceptable. One has no hope of knowing the meaning behind such gifts.

The surviving medieval rings which could have been betrothal rings are of numerous types. One very large class, the fede ring (q.v.), bears the clasped-hands symbol which originated in Roman times. The hands are often on the bezel, but may be at the back of the hoop, or supporting a heart, etc. The lovers' knot also continued in use from Roman times. These motifs may be combined with an inscription such as 'par grant amour' ('with great love'), 'I am yours, you are mine', etc., or the names of the couple, and such inscriptions also occur on decorative rings which bear no other

Betrothal rings

symbols. Amorous inscriptions also occur on rings and other jewels side-by-side with religious inscriptions and magical symbols (and even, at a slightly later date, with the skull and crossbones – see *Memento mori jewellery*). Finally, of course, many ornamental rings bearing no specific reference to love may well have been given as love-pledges. (During the fifteenth and sixteenth centuries inscribed rings developed as a class on their own – see *Posy rings* – and the composition of suitable mottoes and verses for them became something of a literary pastime. Many posy rings would have been used as betrothal and/or wedding rings; again, it is impossible to cite examples.)

Fourteenth-century ring in form of a lovers' knot

In the Renaissance the gimmel ring made its appearance. Basically it consisted of two or more hoops which fitted together, and it was often surmounted by the clasped hands of the fede ring. (For further description and illustration see *Gimmel ring*.) This type was obviously very appropriate as a wedding ring, but was doubtless used as a betrothal ring as well. Similar in some respects to the gimmel is the puzzle ring (q.v.), which became popular as a form of lovers' ring in the seventeenth century but probably existed much earlier.

The various types of ring mentioned above continued to be worn with comparatively little change for many centuries; they appear to have been much less subject to the changes of fashion than other jewellery. The lovers' ring illustrated, with two hands holding a heart, was made in about 1700, but the design has not changed since the Middle Ages. (Other rings of this period show an

Lovers' ring, made about 1700

increasing elegance of design and emphasis on faceted stones – see *Seventeenth-century* and *Eighteenth-century jewellery*.) There appears to have been no rule as to which finger should be used for betrothal rings, and it was not until the nineteenth century that the custom of having separate rings for engagement and wedding became established in England.

Queen Victoria's engagement ring was in the form of a gold serpent (serpent-rings were very popular at the time) set with emeralds. The diamond-set engagement ring did not become normal for a long time; in the 1850s engagement rings set with pearls were popular, and in 1875 the *Young Ladies' Journal*, an authority on such matters, stated 'any pretty fancy ring may be worn as an engagement-ring', although 'pearls or diamonds are considered the proper gems'. The only stone that should not be worn was opal, since it was associated with sorrow. The greatly increased popularity of diamonds at the end of the nineteenth century made diamond engagement rings particularly fashionable, and in this century diamonds have become the conventional stone for those who can afford precious stones at all. The durability of diamond, and of course its price, make it a very suitable symbol for an engagement ring. Jewellers now stock a very wide range of diamond engagement rings to suit all tastes and all

Modern diamond-set engagement ring

pockets, ranging from those set with diamonds of $\frac{1}{4}$ carat or so, to solitaire rings with large diamonds costing hundreds of pounds. Matching engagement and wedding rings have recently become fashionable, and in America there is now a vogue for pre-engagement or 'promise' rings set with very small diamonds as a promise of better things to come.

In recent years antique rings have become popular as engagement rings. This partly reflects an increased interest in antique jewellery, but is doubtless also connected with the fact that no purchase tax was payable on antique rings. (See also *Wedding rings*.)

Bezel (templet) facet. Four large quadrilateral facets on the crown of a brilliant-cut (q.v.) stone; they are the first to be ground after the table. The four quoin facets which lie between them, and which differ from the bezels only in their orientation to the stone, are usually also termed bezel facets, making a total of eight.

Bezoar stone. A stone believed to be found in the stomach or gall-bladder of an animal and to have miraculous properties, notably against poison. It was worn as an amulet and taken in powdered form as a medicine from the Middle Ages to the early eighteenth century. (See *Magical jewellery*.)

Biaxial crystals. Doubly-refracting crystals which have two optic axes (directions in which they are singly refracting) and

three refractive indices. (For further explanation see *Double refraction*.) Minerals in the biaxial class are those belonging to the monoclinic, triclinic and orthorhombic systems. (See *Crystal systems*.)

Bick-iron. See *Beck-iron*.

Bijouterie. The art of working in gold and enamel, distinguished in earlier centuries from *joaillerie*, the art of mounting precious stones.

Bilston enamels. Enamelled medallions produced in Bilston, Staffordshire, in the late eighteenth century as a cheaper substitute for the fine French enamels then in fashion. They were made in oval form for mounting in clasps, bracelets, etc., and as buttons. The designs were classical – Cupid and Psyche, heads of Greek gods, etc. – in grisaille (q.v.) on a dark background. (See also *Battersea enamels*.)

Binding wire. Annealed iron wire, to which solder will not adhere, used to hold jewellery pieces together for soldering.

Binghamite. Chatoyant quartz with inclusions of goethite.

Bird's eye pearl. A freshwater pearl with dark rings.

Bird's eye quartz. Jasper with circles of colourless material.

Birefringence. The amount of double refraction (q.v.), measured by the arith-

Detail of a bracelet of linked plaques of Bilston enamels, made about 1775.
Victoria and Albert Museum

33

metical difference between the maximum and minimum refractive indices (see *Refractive index*).

Birmingham. The centre of the mass-production jewellery industry in Great Britain; the manufacture of jewellery components, services such as electroplating and casting, and the production of costume jewellery, are all concentrated in this area. The city also has one of the two provincial assay offices in England, the other being at Sheffield.

The Birmingham jewellery industry grew out of the manufacture of such items as sword-hilts, buckles, and small trinkets known as 'toys'. Goldsmiths and silversmiths had worked in Birmingham probably since the Middle Ages (they are first mentioned in records in 1524), but the real founder of the trade is said to have been Charles II, who on his restoration in 1660 brought with him from the Continent the fashion for wearing decorative buckles, buttons, chains, etc. Buckles (q.v.) became a very important item of dress and remained so for over a century, and large numbers were manufactured in Birmingham and exported abroad. The principal materials were cut steel (see *Cut-steel jewellery*) and silver. The manufacture of jewellery was at this stage only a side-line to the buckle and 'toy' trade. By the second half of the eighteenth century Birmingham had acquired a reputation for shoddy work – the word 'Brummagem' originated at this time – and one of the avowed intentions of Matthew Boulton (q.v.) when he set up his factory just outside Birmingham in 1762 was to raise the standard of Birmingham products. Boulton's drive and initiative revitalized the industry, and he was largely responsible for the granting of a much-needed assay office to Birmingham in 1773. (See also *Assay offices.*)

By 1790 buckles were beginning to go out of fashion, and since they were the bread-and-butter of the industry the craftsmen were obliged to turn to other work in order to survive. Jewellery rapidly became a separate and major part of the industry and because of the availability of skilled labour, craftsmen were attracted to the area from other parts of the country. A gas works was built in 1817 and another in 1825, furnishing a more convenient source of power than steam. In the depression following the Napoleonic wars the trade suffered badly, but in the early years of the Victorian era it began to revive and was soon rapidly expanding: prosperity, the Queen's own fondness for jewellery, and the discovery of rich deposits of gold in California and Australia all contributed to this expansion. By the 1860s the jewellery trade was one of the largest industries in the city, employing about 7,500 people. The jewellery was still predominantly hand-made; machine-stamping (q.v.) was used to some extent, but mainly for the cheaper gilt articles and not for gold and silver jewellery of quality. Electroplating (q.v.) had been developed by the Birmingham firm of Elkington in 1840 and was just becoming established as an important commercial process replacing Sheffield plate (q.v.). (Sheffield plate had not by any means been a monopoly of Sheffield: Matthew Boulton had been making it as early as 1764 and a considerable quantity of very good plate had been produced in Birmingham.) Whereas Sheffield plate had little or no application in jewellery, the electroplating process offered a flexible and economical means of gilding or silvering articles of almost any size.

The 1860s were a period of remarkable prosperity in the trade. Women were wearing a lot of jewellery, and the various fashions for antique styles and for novelties that were only in vogue for a few months, but were absolutely essential as long as they were in vogue, ensured that the designers and craftsmen were kept busy. Within ten to fifteen years, however, the trade was sunk in depression, and by 1885 it was on the verge of disaster. The reasons for this were complex, but an important contributory cause was the sudden availability of silver. Silver had not been of much importance in nineteenth-century jewellery up to this time because a variety of cheap substitutes for gold were available, but when large deposits of silver were discovered in the Comstock Lode in Nevada the price began to fall and it became a popular metal. To keep up with the demand the silver branch of the jewellery trade expanded at the expense of other branches, and because of the intrinsic cheapness of the material the workmanship and standard of design were poor. Machinery was relied on more and more, and as the price of silver continued to fall so did the quality of the product. In the mid-70s the export market suffered badly as a result of the Franco-Prussian war and economic trouble in America, and the efforts of the jewellers to stimulate demand gave another turn to the vicious circle of price-cutting, increased reliance on machinery, and further deterioration in quality. Trade was just beginning to revive in 1878 when a series of business failures, headed by the Glasgow Bank crash, plunged it into gloom again. By the 1880s the fashionable world was thoroughly disgusted with silver jewellery, and in 1885 a general depression affected the sale of high-class jewellery in gold. For several years jewellery was just not worn. For many manufacturers this spelt disaster. Bankrupt stock flooded the market, and since at the time there was no system of credit enquiry traders in difficulty resorted to the desperate expedient of buying goods on credit and pawning them to pay creditors. The situation was worsened by the activities of unscrupulous 'factors'. These were middlemen who acted as freelance travelling salesmen for a number of small manufacturers who could not afford to employ their own travellers; they were usually not obliged to sell any of their wares, and some of them promptly turned over the patterns with which they were entrusted to be mass-produced by 'garret-masters' – employers of cheap labour in the city.

In 1887 some Birmingham jewellers petitioned the Princess of Wales for help in reviving public interest in jewellery.

She bought some of their wares and wore them on public occasions, but it was not until 1895 that the trade really began to recover. By the turn of the century prosperity had returned. Meanwhile the Birmingham jewellers had realized that co-operation was the only answer to the peculiar hazards of their trade, and had formed (in 1887) the Birmingham Jewellers' and Silversmiths' Association, the first organized and permanent body of its nature in the trade. (For its subsequent history see *British Jewellery and Giftware Federation.*) Its aims included the promotion of technical education, the removal of restrictions on the trade, the support of measures for the development of trade at home and in foreign and colonial markets, and the prosecution of thieves and receivers. In connection with the latter, the Association set up a Vigilance Committee to apprehend and prosecute thieves, but were assured by the police that police protection was adequate. In 1904, however, when a number of warehouses were burgled and the police were unable to take effective action because of the difficulty of identifying gold and silver, the Association began to press for wider powers for the police. Eventually in 1914 a clause was inserted in the Birmingham Corporation Act which gave the Birmingham courts unique powers under British law; the effect of the clause was that within the city boundaries a man found in possession of precious metals had to account for them to the court's satisfaction: in other words the onus was on him to prove his innocence, not on the police to prove his guilt.

The Association was also largely responsible for the passing of the 1904 Bill which made it compulsory for foreign gold and silver wares entering Britain to be stamped with a set of hallmarks distinctively different from the hallmarks on British wares (see *Hallmarking*). Hitherto foreign goods had only been stamped with an 'F' to distinguish them, and as at the time a number of foreign pieces were appearing on the British market under false descriptions (e.g. '9-

carat' gold that was only 7-carat), and since furthermore British goods were being priced out of foreign markets by tariffs, the Association felt that the competition was more than unfair.

Until the First World War the trade expanded considerably and in 1913 the value of high-class jewellery sold from Birmingham exceeded that of the cheaper jewellery. The larger firms were now dealing direct with retailers and employing their own travellers, which meant extending the range of their products. The war however diverted many skilled craftsmen to the munitions factories, though those that remained were kept busy on patriotic jewellery and identity bracelets. There was a short boom at the end of the war, followed almost immediately by depression. During the early twenties many jewellers had to close down and it was lamented that no young people were entering the trade. The thirties were hardly more encouraging. Apart from the effects of the depression, the Birmingham jewellers also found themselves in competition with a flood of imitation jewellery from Germany and Czechoslovakia which entered Britain between the wars. This jewellery was attractive, was produced in an enormous range of patterns, and was also very cheap: the German jewellery is said to have been subsidized, and the Czechoslovakian jewellery was produced by craftsmen working at home with low wages and low overheads. The Birmingham manufacturers tried to adopt the techniques and styles of their competitors, but were unable to match the inventiveness of design shown in the foreign goods and were quite unable to offer a similar range. They could not afford to supply small orders, whereas the foreign manufacturers, who sent their travellers all over the country and obtained hundreds of small orders from different retailers, manufactured in bulk and split up the orders.

The outbreak of the Second World War disposed of the foreign competition but for a time nearly disposed of the home industry as well. Craftsmen were again diverted to war work, and the Government announced a plan for the 'concentration of industry' with the purpose of emptying and releasing factories for war production. The manufacture and sale of jewellery were severely restricted. The B.J.S.A. fought for and finally obtained concessions by which small firms with people unemployable on war work should be allowed to manufacture. The supply of goods of a gold content of 9-carat or finer was prohibited, but the Board of Trade was persuaded finally to allow the use of 9-carat gold for wedding rings: these were to be of a maximum weight of 2 dwt. and to be sold at £1 1s. The Board of Trade had underestimated the eagerness of the population to marry in wartime: in the following year the quota of wedding rings was insufficient for the demand, and after further representations from jewellers the quota was doubled.

Recovery after the war was of course gradual, but Birmingham has long since consolidated its importance as a centre of the jewellery trade, which continues to be one of the major industries of the city. The sub-division of work which began with the growing prosperity of the 1840s has continued. Firms specialize in one type of article such as chains, studs, etc., or one process such as casting or the mounting of stones, and this assures the firm of a guaranteed market and the customer of a skilled and efficient service.

Birmingham Metal Gauge. See *Metal Gauges.*

Birthstones. The link between gemstones and the months of the year is of very ancient origin and includes elements of pagan, Jewish and Christian tradition. The association is ultimately rooted in the astrological theory that an individual is influenced by the planetary sign under which he is born. This idea, which is at least as old as the Chaldean civilization, was combined with the later neo-Platonic concept of a connection between minerals and the planetary influence under which they were believed to have been formed, the result being a correspondence between a mineral and the individual's natal sign or month of birth.

The choice of gemstone to correspond with the natal month was influenced by various factors. One was the mass of superstitions which surrounded precious stones (see *Magical jewellery*). Another was the fact that very little was known scientifically about the nature of precious stones and they were usually very roughly classified according to colour. The reason why lists of birthstones in various societies do not differ even more than they do is that the pagan beliefs were overlaid by a Judaeo-Christian tradition resting on two lists of precious stones in the Scriptures – the description of the stones in Aaron's breastplate (Exodus 28, xvii–xx), and the list of stones in the foundations of the New Jerusalem (Revelations 21, xix–xx).

Although the tradition was a very old one, the custom of wearing birthstones did not become widespread in Europe until the eighteenth century. Because the association of the stone with the month was made on the basis of the colour of the stone there were naturally many inconsistencies, and in 1937 the National Association of Goldsmiths drew up an 'official' list which it suggested should become the standard. This list is now followed in most English-speaking countries.
It is as follows:

Month	Birthstone	Alternative
January	Garnet	—
February	Amethyst	Onyx
March	Aquamarine	Bloodstone
April	Diamond	Rock crystal
May	Emerald	Chrysoprase
June	Pearl	Moonstone
July	Ruby	Cornelian
August	Peridot	Sardonyx
September	Sapphire	Lapis lazuli
October	Opal	Tourmaline
November	Topaz	Citrine
December	Turquoise	Blue zircon

(*Note*: there are variations in the alternative stones: it is only the first list that has been standardised.)

Bishop's stone. Amethyst (traditionally an ecclesiastical stone).

Biwa pearls. Cultured pearls without a nucleus, produced from the freshwater mussel *Hyriopsis schlegeli* in the Biwa lake in Japan. (For information on cultured pearls see *Pearls*.)

'Black amber'. A misnomer for jet.

'Black diamond'. Misnomer for haematite. Genuine black diamonds occur but are rarely used as gemstones. (See *Diamond*.)

'Black moonstone'. See *Labradorite*.

Black Orloff Diamond. A black cushion-cut diamond weighing 67.50 carats, said to take its name from the Russian princess Nadia Vyegin-Orloff, who owned it in the eighteenth century. It came, according to legend, from a shrine near Pondicherry, India, and is also known as the Eye of Brahma Diamond. It is the possession of Mr. Charles F. Winson, the New York gem dealer.

Black Prince's Ruby, The. A large red spinel, long associated with the British monarchy, now set in the Imperial State Crown of the British Regalia. It measures nearly 2 inches and has been left unfaceted in its original irregular shape. It came into the possession of the Black Prince (son of Edward III) in the fourteenth century, probably as a gift from the King of Castile, and his great-nephew Henry V wore it in his helmet at the battle of Agincourt. In 1649, when the Crown Jewels were broken up by order of Parliament, the stone disappeared, but subsequently reappeared at the Restoration of the monarchy and has been an important part of the regalia ever since.

Blackmorite. Reddish-yellow common opal from Montana, U.S.A.

Blister pearl. An irregularly shaped and sometimes hollow pearl cut from the shell of an oyster. It consists of a nacreous coating (see *Nacre*) deposited over a foreign substance which has penetrated between the mantle and the shell. (See also *Pearls*.)

37

Bloodstone (Heliotrope). (See *Chalcedony*.) A variety of chalcedony consisting of plasma (q.v.) with small red spots of jasper (q.v.). It has been a popular seal-stone (see *Seals*), and in earlier times was worn as an amulet in the belief that it would prevent loss of blood. The best bloodstone comes from the Kathiawar peninsula in India; other sources are Australia, Brazil and the U.S.A.

(*Note*: the German bloodstone (*Blutstein*) is haematite.)

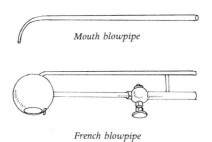

Mouth blowpipe

French blowpipe

Blowpipe. A long pipe used to blow the flame from a gas jet on the jeweller's bench on to the piece being soldered. One type is the mouth-blowpipe which has been in use since Egyptian times, another is the French blowpipe which is fixed to a blowtorch (q.v.) and connected to a foot-operated bellows.

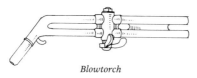

Blowtorch

Blowtorch. A torch used by jewellers for soldering and annealing (q.v.). It may be used with propane gas, oxyacetylene, or a gas and air mixture in conjunction with a foot-bellows or mechanical air-compressor.

'Blue alexandrite'. Misnomer for sapphire exhibiting a change of colour.

Blue chrysoprase. Chalcedony with inclusions of chrysocolla.

Blue gold. An alloy consisting of approximately 25% iron, 75% gold.

Blue-john. A bluish-violet patterned variety of fluorspar (q.v.).

'Blue moonstone'. Misnomer for chalcedony (q.v.) which has been stained blue or is naturally of this colour (the latter comes from S.W. Africa).

'Blue opal'. Misnomer for lazulite.

Blue pearls. Pearls of a lead-grey colour, caused by a layer of conchiolin near the surface or a conchiolin-rich core. (See *Pearls*.)

Blue-point pearl. Pearls from the fresh-water pearl-mussel *Quadrula undulata*, fished in the U.S.A.

Bluestone. Sodalite.

Blue-white. A term used in the colour-grading of diamonds, applied to stones with a very faint bluish tinge. This effect is usually seen in the finest stones. The term is less used than formerly, as the distinction between blue-white and white is difficult to make and open to abuse.

Boakite. Brecchiated green and red jasper.

Board-sweep. See *Lemel*.

Boart (boort, bort, bortz). Diamond which is not of gem quality. It has numerous uses in industry and is used in crushed form for cutting and polishing gem diamonds and other stones. (See also *Diamond*.)

Bobrowka garnet. Demantoid garnet. (See *Andradite*.)

Bodkins. The name given to hairpins in the Renaissance, at which time they were popular and richly jewelled.

Bog-oak. Oak blackened and preserved in peat-bogs. Carved and set with Irish pearls, it was a material much favoured by the Victorians for cheaper jewellery, particularly in the early Victorian period when there was a romantic interest in Ireland and Scotland and when anything unusual was likely to be admired. (See *Nineteenth-century jewellery*.)

'**Bohemia chrysolite**'. Misnomer for moldavite. (See *Tektite*.)

'**Bohemian diamond**'. Misnomer for rock crystal.

'**Bohemian ruby**'. Misnomer for pyrope garnet or rose quartz.

'**Bohemian topaz**'. Misnomer for citrine.

Boke. Japanese term for rose-coloured coral.

Bolt ring

Bolt ring. A hollow or partly hollow connecting ring part of which may be drawn back on an internal spring to open the circle. It is a common fastening for necklaces.

Bombay bunch. A selection of pearls, drilled and ready for making into necklaces, strung on silk and made into bunches for export at Bombay.

Bombay pearl. A fine pearl with a rosée tint, or any pearl marketed through Bombay. (See *Pearls*.)

Bonamite. See *Smithsonite*.

Bone. Bone, being a readily-available material and soft enough to be fashioned with very crude tools, has always been one of the first materials to be used in primitive jewellery. It was much used in prehistoric times for beads and pins (the forerunners of brooches). Not being a particularly decorative substance, it usually fails to compete when more attractive materials become available, but carved bone has been used in the jewellery of civilized societies – in the Minoan civilization, for instance, for seals, and in Europe in the Middle Ages for rosary beads.

Bone appears in modern jewellery as an imitation of ivory. Most people are sufficiently familiar with the appearance of the two substances to be able to distinguish them, and under a microscope the structure of bone can be seen to be completely unlike that of ivory (q.v.). Bone is also slightly heavier than ivory (S.G. about 2.0). The hardness ($2\frac{1}{2}$) is the same. Bone lacks the mellow gloss of ivory, but its appearance is improved by staining.

'**Bone turquoise**'. Odontolite.

Borax. A flux (q.v.) commonly used in soldering jewellery. It consists of crystallized sodium tetraborate, and although it occurs in a natural form it is also manufactured in quantity. There is a lump borax specially made for jewellers which is readily soluble in water, melts more easily than ordinary borax and expands less, and is therefore less likely to displace the solder when heated. (See also *Soldering*.)

'**Bornholm diamond**'. Misnomer for rock crystal.

Bornite. (Sulphide of copper and iron. S.G. 4.9–5.4; H. 3.) A copper mineral sometimes cut as a curiosity. The colour is usually a coppery-red, but as the surface tarnishes, iridescent colours are produced, and on this account the mineral is sometimes known as 'peacock ore'.

Boron carbide. A very hard (H. $9\frac{1}{2}$) artificially-produced abrasive used in gem-cutting.

Bossing-up. Beating out metal into a rough design from the back. (See *Chasing* and *Repoussé work*.)

'**Bottle-stone**'. Moldavite. (See *Tektite*.)

Botryoidal. Having a surface covered with spherical protuberances, caused by a radial arrangement of fibrous crystals. Chalcedony is often of this form.

Boulton, Matthew (1728–1809). Brought up in the Birmingham jewellery trade, Matthew Boulton was one of the most important manufacturers of cut-steel jewellery (q.v.) in England in the late eighteenth century. In partnership with

Bourguignon pearls

John Fothergill he set up a factory for this purpose at Soho near Birmingham in 1762; other factories were later established in Birmingham, Sheffield and Wolverhampton. The business was a great success, thanks partly to Boulton's farsighted idea of bringing together under one management craftsmen specializing in different types of work, and controlling the marketing himself.

Boulton entered into a partnership with James Watt, and gave Watt's improved version of the steam engine its first practical application by introducing it into his own factory. His other commercial interests included the manufacture of Sheffield plate and articles in ormolu, and he was largely responsible for the establishing of assay offices in Birmingham and Sheffield in 1773.

He also, in 1797, undertook the production of a new copper coinage, the press for which was in use until 1882.

Bourguignon pearls. Imitation pearls filled with wax. (For imitation pearls, see *Pearls*.)

Bow-drill. A tool used in the ancient world for engraving and drilling stone, and still used with little modification for

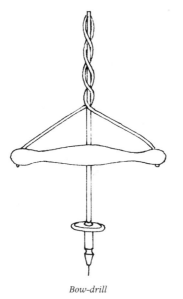

Bow-drill

drilling stones and metal today. The string of the bow is looped around the shaft, and movement of the bowstring makes the shaft rotate to drive the cutting tip. The bow-drill is preferred by craftsmen doing fine work, as greater control is possible than with a mechanical drill. (See also section on drilling of stones, under *Gem-cutting*.)

Bowenite. See *Serpentine*.

Box dust. Boxwood sawdust, used warm for drying jewellery after it has been cleaned.

Box setting. A setting in which the stone is enclosed in a rectangular frame of metal, the top edges of which are pressed down to hold the stone in place.

Brabant rose-cut. See *Antwerp rose-cut*.

Bracelets. The bracelet is one of the earliest personal ornaments worn by man. In primitive societies its use as a decoration by both sexes seems to be almost universal, and although in the West it is now worn only by women, in the East it has always formed part of male dress and is frequently a sign of rank.

Egyptian paintings and sculptures show that four bracelets were normally worn – two on each arm, one on the wrist and one above the elbow. Various types of Egyptian bracelets have been found (see *Egyptian jewellery*). Some are composed of beads of gold and glass, some are plain gold bands, sometimes decorated with chain-work or inlay, some are of twisted gold wire. Serpent bracelets were worn in the Ptolemaic and Roman periods in Egypt.

The bracelet was an important item of Greek and Roman jewellery (qq.v.). The illustration shows a superb Greek bracelet of the fourth century B.C. decorated with sphinxes. In Roman times one bracelet was usually worn on the right wrist, and another on the upper arm. The earliest Roman bracelets were of pure gold, but later they were set with precious stones, engraved gems and – towards the end of the Roman empire – coins. A large number of bracelets from the Roman period have

Greek bracelet in gold with sphinx finials.
Hermitage Museum, Leningrad

been found in Britain. They are mostly of a simple type – the commonest is just a ring to be slipped over the wrist. Others are penannular or are closed with a hook and eye. Glass armlets have also been found.

Bracelets lost their prominent position in European jewellery with the decline of the Roman Empire and have never regained it. They were little worn during the Middle Ages because of the long-sleeved garments which were normal wear. In the fifteenth century wide, loose sleeves became fashionable and bracelets began to be worn again: enamelled designs set with precious stones were popular.

The early Renaissance fashion was for long sleeves falling over the hand, which still did not encourage the wearing of bracelets. They seem to have been worn sometimes over the sleeve, and sometimes the sleeve was slashed at the wrist to show the bracelet underneath. Bracelets set with cameos were popular, reflecting the general enthusiasm for classical engraved gems (see *Cameos*). The bracelets of the wealthy followed the same elaborate form as other articles of jewellery: an inventory of Henry VIII's jewellery in 1530 shows that he had seventeen, some of them very richly jewelled. Pomander bracelets were

worn, composed of filigree beads containing perfumes. The serpent form was still popular: one of Mary Stuart's bracelets was of this type.

During the seventeenth century bracelets were worn infrequently in any part of Europe. They came back into favour in the eighteenth century when there was a fashion for cameos of classical subjects; these were linked together or set into the clasp of the bracelet. For those who could not afford genuine cameos, cheaper substitutes were produced in considerable quantities in the form of Battersea and Bilston enamels (qq.v.) and plaques of Wedgwood ware (q.v.). Fine enamel and grisaille work (qq.v.) also were worn in this way.

The nineteenth century saw a new vogue for bracelets. As many as four were sometimes worn on each arm, and they continued to be popular when other forms of jewellery were temporarily out of fashion. Many were of gold chain with an enamel or precious stone set in the clasp. At times a simple velvet band with an ornamental clasp was fashionable. In the early Victorian period there was a vogue for bracelets with pendants. Bangles were in favour throughout the period; they were often in serpent form or decorated with the motifs fashionable at the time – naturalistic forms in the Romantic period, Greek, Assyrian and

Late nineteenth-century gold bracelet with filigree decoration in the Etruscan style.
Victoria and Albert Museum

41

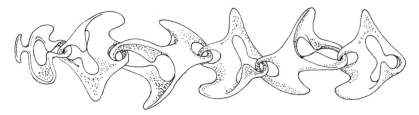

Silver bracelet by Georg Jensen

Egyptian in the middle of the century (see illustration) – but the most popular bracelet of the 1870s was a plain gold bangle. The serpent bracelet developed more and more loops as the century wore on. Cameos retained their popularity for a long time, and many bracelets consisted of linked cameos or other medallions. Bracelets composed of several rows of pearls were worn throughout the Victorian period and were particularly popular in mid-century. Other favourite materials which appear in nineteenth-century jewellery are coral, garnet, ivory, jet, amber, amethyst, topaz, and, of course, diamonds. The cult of sentimental and mourning jewellery produced the bracelet containing, or sometimes entirely woven of, the hair of a departed loved one. (See *Hair jewellery*.)

In the course of the present century bracelets have lapsed into relative obscurity once again. They re-emerge from time to time when there is brief fashion for charm-bracelets or for wearing a chain on the wrist, etc., but with these exceptions the wearing of bracelets is mostly confined to formal occasions when they can be seen to their best effect on a bare wrist. Bracelets of good modern design are nevertheless produced (see illustration).

Bracteates. Thin circular medallions, generally of gold, worn as pendants by the Germanic peoples after the fall of the Roman Empire. They were introduced into Anglo-Saxon England from Scandinavia. They were embossed with human and animal designs and were a very remote and formalized imitation of the gold coins and medallions of the late Roman period. They were die-stamped with a beaded edging, and had a loop at the top. Their normal use in Anglo-Saxon jewellery (q.v.) seems to have been as part of a woman's necklace. They may have been regarded as amulets.

Swedish bracteate

Braganza Diamond. A Brazilian stone, said to be the size of a goose egg and to weigh 1680 carats, which was brought back to Portugal in the eighteenth century. It is now generally believed to be a colourless topaz, but this cannot be verified as no one is allowed to see the stone: indeed, the Portuguese government deny that it is in their possession.

Brass. An alloy of copper and zinc. The proportions are variable. Some brasses are used in jewellery but are known as gilding-metal (q.v.).

Brazilian chain. Alternative name for snake chain. (See *Chain*.)

'**Brazilian emerald**'. Misnomer for green tourmaline.

'**Brazilian peridot**'. Misnomer for yellowish-green tourmaline.

'**Brazilian ruby**'. Misnomer for red Brazilian topaz.

'**Brazilian sapphire**'. Misnomer for blue tourmaline.

Brazilianite. (Hydrous sodium-aluminium phosphate. S.G. 2.98–3.0; R.I. 1.598–1.617; H. 5½.) A yellowish-green translucent to transparent stone first discovered in 1944 in Minas Gerais, Brazil. Crystals have since been found in New Hampshire, U.S.A. Brazilianite occurs in quite large crystals.

Break facet. Another name for the cross facets (q.v.) on a brilliant-cut stone. (See *Diamond-cutting*).

Brecchia. A conglomerate of angular pieces of stone cemented together in a matrix. Cut and polished, such material is often attractive enough for ornamental use. Examples are brecchiated agate and brecchiated jasper.

Crown from eighteenth-century Swedish bridal parure, set with rock crystals. Nordiska Museum, Stockholm

Bridal jewellery. A suite of jewellery loaned to a bride to be worn on her wedding-day. The custom developed from the late medieval fashion of wearing a bridal crown (itself a development of the unmarried girl's chaplet), and has con-tinued in Scandinavia until the present day. The jewellery is generally owned by churches or local authorities. Bridal parures are usually extremely pretty but of low intrinsic value; the crown illustrated is part of an eighteenth-century Swedish parure of rock-crystals set in silver. The suite also includes a Sévigné brooch, girandole earrings and a chaplet.

Bright-dip. A solution in which articles of brass, nickel-silver, copper and copper alloys are immersed to give a bright surface. (See *Aqua fortis*.)

Bright-line spectra. Bright lines which appear superimposed at certain wavelengths on the spectrum of light transmitted by a substance when it is subjected to intense heat. The lines are the wavelengths of radiations emitted by chemical elements in a state of disturbance. The observation of these spectra in gemstones can help in identification, since the spectrum given by the stone can be checked against the known spectra of elements and the stone's composition be thus established. The substance may be volatilized in a flame or by electrical means, and the spectra are observed with the aid of a spectrograph or spectrometer (qq.v.). The bright-line spectra of gemstones correspond to the absorption-spectra (q.v.) – the wavelengths of light absorbed by the stone.

Brilliant. A synonym for brilliant-cut diamond. (See *Diamond-cutting*.)

Brilliant cut. The style of cutting most often used for diamonds, and sometimes for other gemstones as well. It has 58 facets. For description and diagram, see *Diamond-cutting*.

Briolette. A drop-shaped stone faceted all over with triangular (occasionally rectangular) facets, and often pierced at the top so that it can be worn as a pendant. (See *Diamond-cutting* for illustration.)

'**Bristols**' or '**Bristows**'. Colourless quartz (rock crystal) found in Bristol limestone, at Harrogate and in the iron mines of

· 43

Cornwall, worn as a substitute for diamonds in Elizabethan times. The term is also applied to paste (q.v.), since glass was made at Bristol.

'Bristol diamond'. Misnomer for rock crystal. (See above.)

Britannia metal. The modern equivalent of pewter. (See *Pewter*.)

Britannia silver. Silver which is 95.84% fine (11 oz. 10 dwt. to the pound Troy). This higher standard for silver (sterling is 92.5% fine) was introduced in March 1697 as the compulsory standard for wrought plate in an attempt to stop the widespread practice of melting down the coin of the realm to provide silver plate. It was found too soft to be serviceable and the Act of 1697 was repealed in 1719, but Britannia remained one of the two legal standards for silver in Britain and silver of this quality is still produced. Being so soft, its use is almost entirely restricted to the faking-up of silverware of the 1697–1719 period. It is stamped with a hallmark depicting the figure of Britannia. (See also *Hallmarking* and *Silver*.)

British Jewellers' Association. See *British Jewellery and Giftware Federation Ltd.*

British Jewellery and Giftware Federation Ltd. A federation of associations representing the interests of manufacturing, wholesale and retail jewellers, stone dealers, silversmiths and allied trades. Member Trade Associations include the British Jewellers' Association, British Wholesale Jewellers' Association, Metal Finishing Association, and Art Metalware Manufacturers' Association.

The Federation was founded in 1887 as the Birmingham Jewellers' and Silversmiths' Association. (For the circumstances in which it was founded, see *Birmingham*.) Over the years as similar associations were founded in various parts of the country it became clear that some form of national amalgamation or federation was desirable. In 1945 the Birmingham association was reorganized on national lines, and after an amalgamation with the Scottish Wholesale Jewellers' Association a section was set up in Glasgow. In 1946 the Association's title was changed to the British Joint Association of Goldsmiths, Silversmiths, Horological and Kindred Trades, and shortly afterwards practically all the other trade associations covering the industries represented in the new title were incorporated in its membership.

Membership of a member trade association automatically confers membership of the Federation, and membership is not confined to one trade association. The Federation offers special insurance services, etc., to members, and organizes trade fairs in Britain and participation by members in overseas trade fairs. Two trade journals are published, the *British Jeweller and Watch Buyer* (monthly) and the quarterly export journal *Britannia*. (See also *National Association of Goldsmiths*.)

Brittleness. The tendency of a material to fracture easily. Hardness (q.v.) does not imply that a stone is not brittle.

Broach. A 3-sided tapered tool of hardened steel with sharp edges, used for boring out holes or tubes to enlarge them.

Brogden, John. A nineteenth-century London jeweller who specialized in high-quality work in the antique style (see *Nineteenth-century jewellery* for the styles in vogue). He was particularly influenced by Castellani (q.v.). A partner in the firm Watherston and Brogden in the 1840s, he quickly gained public recognition and began to work on his own. Brogden's most celebrated piece of jewellery is his bracelet, modelled on an Assyrian relief, depicting king Assurbanipal sacrificing on his return from a lion hunt (see illustration). He also made a number of jewels in the Egyptian style, as well as the normal jeweller's stock-in-trade. He continued to produce jewellery until some time in the 1880s.

Bracelet by Brogden depicting the return of Assurbanipal from the hunt. Victoria and Albert Museum

Bromoform. A colourless liquid of formula $CHBr_3$ used in testing the specific gravity (q.v.) or refractive index (q.v.) of a stone. It has a specific gravity of 2.90 at 15°C and a refractive index of 1.598 at 19°C. It darkens when exposed to the light, and should be kept in a dark cupboard.

Bronze. An alloy of approximately 8 parts copper to 1 part tin, sometimes also containing small amounts of lead and zinc. The earliest use of bronze seems to have been in the 3rd millennium B.C. in Mesopotamia and Egypt, whence it spread to Mediterranean countries. The search for copper and tin led to the opening up of the early trade routes. Bronze was used predominantly for tools and weapons and ornamental work of some size, for instance on chariot-fittings, although some early personal ornaments of bronze have been found. Later in the Bronze Age, brooches and pins of bronze were common items of functional jewellery (see *Brooches*). The Bronze Age came to an end some time after 1000 B.C. (the date varies in different regions according to the availability and use of iron), but bronze long continued to be used in jewellery as a substitute for precious metals. It was, for instance, much used by the Anglo-Saxons in brooches and buckles (see *Anglo-Saxon jewellery*). Most bronze jewellery was probably gilded.

Since the merging of barbarian and classical styles of jewellery at the beginning of the Middle Ages bronze has had very little place in jewellery. A variety of base metals, cheaper and sometimes more attractive than bronze, are now available for cheap jewellery, and bronze has become preeminently a sculptor's material. (See also *Phosphor bronzes*.)

Bronzing. See *Colouring of metals*.

Bronzite. See *Enstatite*.

Brooches. The brooch is as old as man's use of clothing, for in its earliest form it was simply a sharp object, perhaps a thorn or a splinter of flint, used to keep clothes together. It gradually evolved in a number of well-defined forms. There are basically four types of brooch, all originating from the simple pin.

1. The safety-pin type. The pin, having been passed through the fabric, was bent up and caught behind the head. Later it was twisted in a circle at the point of bending to make it more secure, thus providing a spring, and later still this loop was elaborated into a series of coils and the brooch was now made in two pieces, hinged at the coils. The bow or top of the brooch, and the catch-plate in which the pin was held, gradually became more important in the design and were eventually very richly ornamented. Most early brooches are of this type (see illustration). (Ancient brooches are often referred to by the archaeological name of *fibula*.)

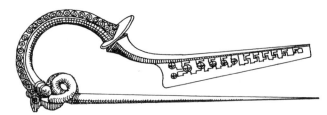

Roman safety-pin brooch of Celtic type.
British Museum

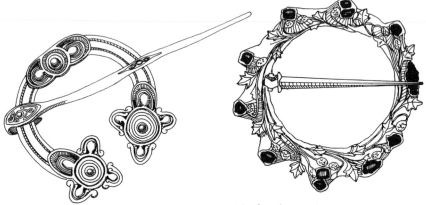

Late Celtic silver penannular brooch

Ring brooch set with rubies and sapphires,
made about 1300. Victoria and Albert Museum

2. The circular brooch. This is a flat disc with a hinged pin. It appears to have developed from a pin decorated with a flat disc of spiral wire: the disc gradually grew larger and became the major part of the brooch. This type of brooch is familiar in modern jewellery.

3. The penannular brooch. This consists of a circle with a small break in it, fitted with a long movable pin (see illustration). The pin is pushed through the fabric at two points, and the end of the ring is then pushed under the exposed end of the pin and turned, so that the pull of the fabric holds the pin against the ring. This type is characteristic of Celtic jewellery, and presumably originated from a pin with a circle of wire bent through the head.

4. The ring brooch. This is the characteristic brooch of the Middle Ages. It is a ring fitted with a pin as long as its diameter, which crosses the ring and rests on the opposite side. The fabric is pulled up inside the ring and the pin is inserted

through it, then the fabric is drawn back and its pull keeps the pin in place. This type presumably had a similar origin to the penannular brooch, but it seems to have developed independently.

Early Greek, Etruscan and Roman brooches were mostly of the safety-pin type. Brooches in precious metal do not appear to have been much worn in Greece, although a number of fairly ornate silver fibulae, originating in Asia Minor, have been found there. A few circular brooches from the Hellenistic period also have been found. The safety-pin brooch reached its highest point of development in Etruscan jewellery; as well as numerous everyday bronze fibulae, many were made in gold and silver with extremely elaborate designs. (See *Etruscan jewellery* for illustration.) One fibula of the seventh century B.C. (in the British Museum) is of gold richly covered in granulation and decorated along the bow with a row of little lions and other animals modelled in gold. The Etruscan fibula died out in about the fourth century B.C. with the assimilation of Etruria by Rome.

Roman brooches are of several types. The safety-pin brooch, which the Romans adopted not from the Etruscans but from the Celts, underwent various modifications, the commonest of which was the crossbow brooch, which had a high arched bow and a horizontal extension on either side of the hinge. This type developed in the second and third centuries A.D. Circular brooches were also worn, often consisting of gold coins or medallions. Very often, however, they were of bronze richly decorated with champlevé enamel. This type has been found mostly in the Roman provinces. Enamel was also used on brooches of the safety-pin type, and on brooches in the form of animals and birds which are probably of Celtic origin.

The bronze safety-pin brooch was used by the Celts for many centuries, in the course of which the design underwent various changes, although the brooch's essentially functional nature was never quite forgotten; there is nothing, for instance, corresponding to the extravagance of the Etruscan fibula referred to above. The safety-pin brooch is a characteristic of early Celtic jewellery; it was gradually replaced as the commonest type by the penannular brooch, which originated in Iron Age Britain, survived through the Roman conquest and was brought to a high pitch of artistry in Celtic lands in the eighth century. It continued to be worn in parts of the Highlands for another thousand years. These brooches are discussed in more detail under *Celtic jewellery*.

Most Anglo-Saxon brooches are circular or cruciform. The cruciform brooch, a heavy and rather primitive affair, was always made of plain metal and never set with stones. It was a development of the Scandinavian fibula and had no connection with the Christian cross. The circular brooches are flat or saucer-shaped. The flat disc brooches provide some of the most magnificent examples of Anglo-Saxon jewellery, and are often richly decorated with niello or relief work and inlaid stones and glass. The concave saucer-shaped brooches, which are in bronze, are less often jewelled, but are elaborately decorated with interlacing animal or geometric designs. A fourth type is the annular or ring brooch, with a movable or hinged pin lying across its centre; this type is rare, and is the forerunner of the medieval ring-brooch. A beautiful example is the Sarre brooch now in the British Museum (see *Anglo-Saxon jewellery*).

Continental brooches showing the same richness as Anglo-Saxon work continued to be produced into the eleventh century. Magnificent and traditional in design, and showing Byzantine influence in their use of enamel, they represent the last elements of barbaric art in Europe before a more civilized and flexible style was attained.

Little jewellery was worn in the early Middle Ages, but the ring-brooch, used for fastening the dress at the neck, was universal among the wealthier classes. The early brooches were small and with narrow rings, decorated with simple designs. They were of gold or silver. In the thirteenth and fourteenth centuries they were usually inscribed, very often with amatory inscriptions in French, sometimes with a devotional inscription such as 'JHESUS NAZARENUS REX JUDAEORUM'. The devotional inscriptions were generally of the type regarded as having a magical power (see *Magical jewellery*) and were sometimes cabbalistic.

During the fourteenth century inscribed brooches began to be worn in base metal by the poorer classes. At the same time the brooch began to develop away from its utilitarian design; the circle is sometimes twisted like a wreath, or made into an octagon, or expanded into projecting lobes which are set with jewels. The pin, instead of passing through the fabric to be held on the opposite rim, began to be held in a catch at the back, as in the modern brooch. Once this had happened there was no longer any point in restricting the brooch to a ring-shape, and the centre therefore began to be filled in. This was first done by putting ribs across the central space, like the spokes in a wheel; this type is known as the wheel-brooch. Finally the centre was completely filled, and the brooch became readily adaptable to the ensuing changes in fashion. A very fashionable type during the fourteenth century was the cluster brooch. Gradually the central stone or motif became more prominent until the type was superseded by a design consisting of a central plaque of enamelled gold in a fairly unimportant jewelled rim. The designs on these brooches were often of traditional themes such as a pair of lovers, a lady in a garden, a huntsman, etc., and many were of animals and birds – dogs, squirrels, roe deer, stags, eagles, goldfinches, etc. These continued to be very popular among the nobility into the fifteenth century. (See also *Medieval jewellery*.)

Brooches were not always worn at the neck. Those with a heraldic or personal significance, such as the eagle brooches often worn by the royalty and nobility on state occasions, were apt to be worn on the breast and could therefore be larger and more imposing than the neck-brooch. They are known as pectorals and were worn more in a purely ornamental capacity than for fastening clothes. Other types of brooch were *morses* used for fastening the copes of the clergy, and hat brooches, which in various forms were fashionable until the late sixteenth century. (See *Renaissance jewellery*.)

With the Renaissance came a change in styles of dress, and the neck-brooch of the Middle Ages ceased to be necessary. Brooches were still worn, and those of the nobility were often very extravagant, but with the exception of the hat-brooch they were not an important feature of dress. From this time onwards the wearing of brooches was purely a matter of fashion, and they followed fashion in their design and the materials of which they were made; thus in the eighteenth century, when diamonds were the most popular stone, most brooches were diamond-set. (See *Eighteenth-century jewellery*.) In the mid-seventeenth century there was a vogue for knot-brooches, usually worn on the shoulder. In the nineteenth century brooches were to some extent interchangeable with pendants, and some were fitted with a ring or hook so that they could be worn on a chain. Sometimes pendants of pearls, gemstones or tassels hung from them. Victorian brooches followed all the vagaries of fashion of the Victorian era – medieval themes, brooches of Scottish pebbles (mid-nineteenth century), Egyptian and Etruscan styles (the 1860s), animals, insects, and such unlikely subjects as ships, violins and wheels (1880s onwards). Hair brooches were very much in vogue, particularly in the 1840s and '50s, as part of the cult of mourning and sentimental jewellery (see *Hair jewellery*). In 1890, some thousands of years after the emergence of the Bronze Age fibula, a safety-pin brooch with a twisted spring instead of a hinge was patented as a new invention.

Brown pearl. Conchiolin-rich pearls of low value. (See *Pearls*.)

Browne and Sharpe Gauge. See *Metal Gauges*.

Bruting. The process of roughly fashioning diamonds before the facets are ground. Until recently this was done by hand: two diamonds were cemented into wooden holders and worked one against the other. The process is now carried out mechanically, one diamond being held in a chuck on a special lathe, while the other, mounted on a rod, is held against it by the bruter. (See also *Diamond-cutting*.)

Buckles. Basically a simple attachment for securing a belt or strap, the buckle has at various periods in its history become an important item of jewellery. In Anglo-Saxon England buckles were worn by both sexes and all social classes and some of them were extremely elaborate. The main focus of ornament was the buckle-plate, a sheet of metal hinged to

Gold buckle richly decorated with niello from the Sutton Hoo ship burial. British Museum

the buckle or made in one piece with it, and riveted to the end of the belt, originally to strengthen it at the point of greatest strain. The other end of the belt which was passed through the buckle was also often strengthened with a metal tip, known as the mordant, and this too was frequently decorated. Anglo-Saxon buckle-plates are of gold, silver or bronze, sometimes set with garnets. Some have a single large stone in a chased setting. The most elaborate type are those in the shape of a long isosceles triangle; these are usually ornamented with three bosses in relief, while the rest of the plate may be decorated with filigree work and garnet inlay. The design is often of highly stylized animal or bird forms. Perhaps the finest example is the solid gold buckle over 5 inches long found in the Sutton Hoo ship burial, decorated with chasing and niello in an intricate interlacing pattern with formalized animals' and birds' heads (see illustration). Continental buckles of the same period were sometimes equally magnificent and used such materials as onyx and rock crystal. Frankish buckles were of iron, often inlaid with silver and gold. They must have been something of a burden to wear: some of the largest ones are in the region of 8 inches long and 4 inches wide.

The tradition of elaborate buckles was carried on after a lapse of several centuries by the goldsmiths of the later Middle Ages. The buckles were sometimes chased with figures so exquisitely modelled that they are miniature sculptures. (See *Medieval jewellery*.) Towards the end of the Middle Ages the designs were dominated by Gothic tracery and the mordant and buckle-plate were often treated as two parts of a single design. These highly ornate buckles survived into the sixteenth century.

The wearing of ornamental buckles declined in the sixteenth and seventeenth centuries, but was vigorously revived with the Restoration. During the eighteenth century all types of buckles were worn, but the most important were shoe-buckles. They were worn by everyone, in diamonds, paste, cut steel or gilt according to one's means and social position. Many buckles were made of the new cheap materials invented in the course of the century, such as pinchbeck (q.v.) and 'Tutania' – base metal covered in silver leaf, painted, varnished and stoved. The use of cheap materials did not necessarily make for an inferior product: some very attractive buckles were made of steel, and paste was worn in the highest society alongside precious stones.

With various fluctuations in size and materials, shoe-buckles retained their importance throughout the eighteenth century. Buckles for other parts of dress went in and out of fashion. In the later eighteenth century small buckles, diamond-set for the wealthy, were worn to fasten a velvet bracelet or throatlet. In

49

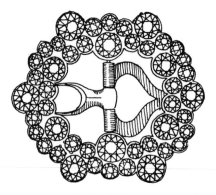

Spanish shoe-buckle of about 1770, set with blue and white pastes

1783 diamond buckles to fasten the gloves were in fashion, and in 1784 the fashionable gown known as the 'Robinson vest' was fastened at the front of the bodice with a series of small buckles set with diamonds or pearls.

Towards the end of the eighteenth century shoe-buckles began to be replaced by shoestrings, and by the end of the century they had virtually disappeared. Buckles of other kinds also declined in popularity, and although they were worn as part of women's dress in the nineteenth century they were not important. Victorian buckles were sometimes worn *en suite* with a matching brooch, and their designs reflect the changing fashions in Victorian jewellery —lizards, serpents, butterflies, leaves and scrolls, etc. In the 1890s there was a fashion for very large buckles – some of a high rectangular type, others set with paste and often worn at the back of the dress. The buckle is still rescued from time to time by fashions of this nature, but whatever importance it now has is as a part of dress: the age of the buckle as a piece of jewellery appears to be over.

Buddstone. (See *Chalcedony*.) A bright green chalcedony, sometimes veined with white, found in Southern Africa. It is usually tumble-polished. (See *Tumbling*.)

Buff. A polisher. The word usually applies to discs of felt or leather dressed with abrasive material and turned on a spindle or lathe. (See also *Polishing mops* and *Buff stick*.)

Buff stick. A tool for hand-polishing metal. It is basically a flat piece of wood to which is glued some type of fabric – felt or chamois which can be charged with abrasive powder and grease, or sheepskin, which is used with rouge (q.v.) for final polishing.

Buffing. Polishing (q.v.). Generally used of the final light polishing of metal or stones with lambswool or a soft cloth.

Bulla. A hollow receptacle for an amulet, worn in the ancient world. Etruscan bullae were usually made of two concave gold plates, and were worn by both men and women in necklaces and bracelets. In Roman times they were of various shapes – square, cylindrical, vase-shaped or circular – and were worn as part of a woman's necklace or individually by children. They ceased to be worn after the first century A.D. For illustration, see *Etruscan jewellery*.

Burin. See *Graver*.

Burmese shell. Pearl-shell from the waters around the Mergui archipelago.

Burmite. Burmese amber. (See *Amber*.)

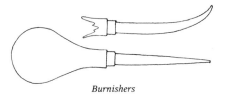

Burnishers

Burnishers. Handled tools with variously-shaped tips for polishing metal (see *Burnishing*). The tips may be of hardened steel, agate, bloodstone or haematite.

Burnishing. Polishing metal by compression (as distinct from abrasion). It is done with burnishers (q.v.), and used on fine work in which it is important to preserve the definition. (See also *Polishing*.)

Burr. The sharp raised edge of an incision made in metal by a chisel or cutting tool, often used to hold inlay work.

Buttons. Buttons are seldom elaborate enough to be considered as articles of jewellery. Some examples of gold or gilt buttons and button-tops have been found dating from the classical period, but they do not appear to have been common. Buttons did not become a focus for decoration until the end of the Middle Ages, when dress became increasingly luxurious and tight-fitting coats and bodices, necessitating long rows of buttons, were worn. In the Renaissance (see *Renaissance jewellery*) buttons replaced the medieval brooch as the usual way of fastening garments, and were also used on sleeves and to close the decorative slashings in the clothes. They were often richly jewelled and enamelled. Rows of buttons were also worn for purely ornamental purposes; the design of many of them is so delicate and irregular that they could not have had any practical value. In the second half of the sixteenth century jewellery became more specifically a part of female dress and the men wore fewer jewels than before, but buttons retained their extravagance and were sometimes the richest part of a man's costume. In 1591 the King of France had no fewer than 143 sets of them.

Buttons next came into prominence in the late seventeenth and eighteenth centuries. At first diamond buttons and buttons enamelled with a floral design were most popular. Later, a very wide range of materials was used. The wealthy had buttons set with diamonds or precious stones, and also paste, while cheaper materials included lapis 'lazuli, agates, tortoise shell and marcasite. In the second half of the eighteenth century cut-steel jewellery was very popular and many buttons were made of this. Some of the openwork steel buttons of this period are of a very high standard. Sometimes the whole button was made of steel; alternatively, the steel was used as a setting for the Wedgwood cameos or Battersea and Bilston enamels (q.v.) then in fashion as an inexpensive substitute for genuine cameos and French enamels (see *Eighteenth-century jewellery*).

Jewelled buttons were not a feature of nineteenth-century jewellery, except for a period in the 1840s when they were worn very large. Enamel surrounded by marcasite, and garnet surrounded by pearls, were popular, and marcasite, cut steel, amethyst and turquoise were worn in fancy buttons which were often flower-shaped. In the present century ornamental buttons have never had more than a passing vogue, and it seems likely that their role will remain keyed to very transient fashions such as the one at the end of the 1960s for wearing old-fashioned military uniform, where rows of decorative metal buttons were an essential part of the effect.

Button pearls (Bouton pearls). Pearls with a rounded top and flat base. (See *Pearls.*)

'Buxton diamond'. Misnomer for rock crystal.

Byewater. A term used in the colour-grading of diamonds, applied to stones with a faint yellowish tinge. (See also *Diamond.*)

Byzantine jewellery. Byzantine jewellery, like all Byzantine arts, was a mixture of the classical traditions of Greece and Rome and elements of Oriental art. The latter influenced Byzantine style by its highly formalized animal designs, delight in intricate geometric patterns, and an expressionism which was in direct contrast to the detached classical style. All these elements were welded together under the dominating influence of a Christian culture. Byzantine jewellery, however, is not only interesting in itself but of considerable importance to the medieval jewellery of the West, for from the eleventh century onwards trade and cultural contacts between the East and West were stimulated by the Crusades and Byzantine styles and techniques were imitated in Europe.

The techniques most characteristic of Byzantine jewellery are rich metalwork and enamelling. Metalwork was an important industry; indeed, Constantinople was the first place where a method of silver-marking was used which makes it possible to date the pieces. The most usual forms of goldwork seem to have been filigree – a classical technique passed on to Western goldsmiths – and openwork. The openwork was of a type developed by the Romans, and consisted of piercing designs in sheet-metal with a chisel. The lacy effect which this produces is characteristic of Byzantine jewellery. Repoussé work also often appears, sometimes in combination with engraving, and niello was used with great delicacy. Granulation – a technique perfected by the Etruscans – was also employed, often in geometric designs.

Byzantine enamelling reached a high degree of perfection and established a tradition which was carried on almost until the present day in Russia, as well as influencing the techniques of enamelling in the West (see *Enamel*). Whereas Western enamelling in the Middle Ages was confined to the champlevé process (q.v.), the Byzantines had developed the cloisonné technique, in which the enamel was run into compartments made of thin gold strips which had been soldered to the metal ground. This method permitted much more flexibility and subtlety of design than champlevé, and, in combination with the pure, bright colours which began to be used in the tenth century, produced enamels of superb quality.

A third characteristic of Byzantine jewellery is its lavish use of precious stones. These were available in great quantity through trade and conquest in the East, and were not used only in jewellery but were also worn, sewn on to their garments by members of the Imperial family.

Unfortunately, comparatively few pieces of Byzantine jewellery now survive. Many were probably destroyed in the iconoclast period (726–834) when figural representations were forbidden, and later pieces were looted and melted down for their intrinsic value in the sack of Byzantium by the Fourth Crusade (1204). Byzantium being a Christian state, personal jewellery was not placed in the tombs of the dead, a practice which has preserved much pagan jewellery for later ages. Our knowledge of the jewellery is therefore partly dependent on paintings and mosaics of the time.

From these and from the jewellery that survives it appears that earrings and necklaces were important ornaments and possessed a highly individual style. The *earrings* are basically of two types. One, an early style, is a development of a Roman type and consists basically of a rectangular bar from which hang pendants of pearls or precious stones. The second type, which is of later development and is specifically Byzantine, is crescent-shaped and is usually in openwork or enamel,

Typical Byzantine earring in gold openwork with peacock design

Byzantine earring of the bar-pendant type. Victoria and Albert Museum

very often showing a bird-design. (See illustrations.)

Necklaces generally were composed of rows of precious and semi-precious stones and pearls interspersed with plaited gold chains or gold beads and medallions.

Medallion pendants were popular, decorated with openwork, filigree or enamel and often set with stones or pearls. The most frequently-worn pendant after about the fifth century was the cross, which was often decorated with pendant gemstones on the arms. Many of these crosses were reliquaries, such as the Beresford Hope cross in the Victoria and Albert Museum, London.

Rings have survived in greater numbers than other types of Byzantine jewellery. They are of gold, silver, copper and bronze and the metal is very often engraved with inscriptions showing that the ring was a gift: ring-giving was a

Byzantine gold bracelet with enamels. Archaeological Museum, Salonika

custom in early Christian times. Other rings are set with engraved gems.

Bracelets often seem to have consisted of funnel-shaped bands of gold, enamelled in square segments marked off by filigree (see illustration). A gold bracelet in the Franks Bequest is in open-work and has a design of swans and peacocks in scrolls; on the clasp is a repoussé bust of the Virgin.

Brooches seem to have been mainly of circular type; from them hung three chains set with jewels. (The pendant chain of jewels was a characteristic of Byzantine jewellery.) Coins were frequently mounted as brooches – a continuation of an old Roman practice.

The richness of Byzantine jewellery is evident from the examples we possess, but how universally it was worn is largely a matter of conjecture. To judge from the paintings and mosaics, it seems that in spite of the availability of precious materials jewellery was less a part of everyday wear in Byzantium than it was in Europe, at least towards the end of the Middle Ages. Certainly the commoner articles of jewellery – pendant crosses, reliquaries, rings – are of a more pronounced religious nature than the commoner types of jewellery in the West.

(For the classical precursors of Byzantine jewellery see *Etruscan, Greek*, and *Roman jewellery*.)

C

Cabochon. A stone with a smooth curved surface. This is the oldest style of stone-cutting and was the only style (excepting inlay) until faceting was introduced in the late Middle Ages (see *Medieval jewellery*). Opaque and badly flawed stones, and those exhibiting special optical effects such as star stones, are still cut in this way, and the cut is also used when a soft effect is desired (as in Art Nouveau jewellery, q.v.) and in imitations of antique work. (See *Gem-cutting* for further description and illustration.)

Cabra stone. Fluorspar.

Cacholong. See *Opal*.

Cairngorm. (See *Quartz, crystalline*.) Clear brown quartz taking its name from the Cairngorm mountains of the Scottish highlands, where it was mined to be worn with the traditional Highland dress. This supply is now virtually exhausted and much of the cairngorm used in Scottish jewellery is heat-treated Brazilian amethyst. Brown quartz also comes from the Swiss Alps and the U.S.A.

Cairo star cut. A complicated cut for diamonds introduced in this century; its main characteristics are a six-fold arrangement of facets, a small table and a large cutlet. (See *Diamond-cutting* for description.)

Calaite (Kalaite). Turquoise.

Calbenite. See *Myrickite*.

Calcite. (Calcium carbonate. S.G. 2.71; R.I. 1.486–1.658; H. 3.) Transparent and colourless in its pure form but sometimes showing tints of pink, yellow, blue, etc., this mineral has little use as a gemstone but is valuable for its optical properties; it exhibits very pronounced double refraction (q.v.) and when of suitable quality is used in nicol prisms and dichroscopes (qq.v.) for polarising light and producing a double image. Marble (q.v.) is a massive form of calcite sometimes used in jewellery as an ornamental stone, and the so-called 'onyx marble' (q.v.), which often shows very beautiful patterns, is a stalagmitic variety. Calcite satin spar is a fibrous form of the massive material.

Calibre-cut. Trade term for stones, usually small, cut in special shapes to fit commonly-used designs. They are generally rectangular and faceted in the step cut. (See *Gem-cutting*.)

California cat's eye. A fibrous serpentine (q.v.), exhibiting faint and occasionally pronounced chatoyancy (q.v.).

'California hyacinth'. Misnomer for hessonite. (See *Grossular garnet*.)

'California iris'. Misnomer for kunzite.

'California jade'. Californite. (See *Idocrase*.)

'California lapis'. Misnomer for blue dumortierite quartz.

'California moonstone'. Chalcedony.

'California onyx'. Banded stalagmitic calcite. (See *Onyx marble*.)

'California ruby'. Misnomer for garnet.

California tiger's eye. Chatoyant bastite. (See *Enstatite*.) Also used synonymously with '*California cat's eye*'.

'California turquoise'. Misnomer for variscite.

Californite. See *Idocrase*.

Calipers. Instruments for measuring the size of an object. The commonest type are spring calipers in which the jaws are placed in contact with the object and the distance between them is then measured on a rule. One type is made for measuring outside surfaces and another for inside surfaces. The latter can be compressed in order to withdraw them when the measurement has been made and will afterwards spring back to the same distance. Sliding caliper gauges marked in millimetres and small fractions of an inch are used for fine measurements. (See also *Micrometer*.)

Cambay stone. Indian cornelian.

Cameos. A true cameo is a hard stone on which a design is cut in relief. The stone is usually a banded chalcedony and the design is cut in the pale layer leaving the darker layer underneath as the background. Modern cameos are cut on a power-driven grinding wheel to which the stone, attached to a dop-stick (q.v.) is applied. In the ancient world where cameo-cutting originated the stone was often held rigid and carved with a hand-operated bow-drill (q.v.). The abrasives used were quartz and corundum. Modern engravers work with a magnifying lens but there is no direct evidence that ancient engravers did so; they may have used some form of magnifying device, perhaps of crystal, but if so it is surprising that the fact is not mentioned by Pliny, who in his *Natural History* has much to say about gems and engraved stones in Roman society.

The art of engraving stone first developed in Mesopotamia and for thousands of years was used almost solely for cutting in intaglio (i.e. with the design incised into the stone, as opposed to standing in relief), since the purpose of the engraving was to produce a seal-stone which would leave an impression in relief on a softer material (see *Intaglios* and *Seals*). The cutting of cameos did not begin until the Hellenistic period in Greece, and was presumably the result of a new attitude to engraved gems which

regarded them as ornamental rather than purely functional: a cameo has an immediate appeal, whereas an intaglio has to be carefully looked at before it can be appreciated. The Greek cameos of this period were made for setting in a finger-ring or pendant, and are of banded agate or sardonyx, with the design cut in the pale layer. Occasionally a range of colours was achieved by cutting as many as four layers in relief, some of them thinly so as to be translucent. Hellenistic cameos are miniature sculptures of a very high order, for gem-engraving in the ancient world was regarded as one of the major arts and attracted the skills of the best artists.

In the first century B.C. many of these Greek engravers took their skills to Rome, where cameos rapidly became an enthusiasm among the wealthy and large collections were acquired by connoisseurs.

Roman cameo of Victory in her chariot, cut in sardonyx with two layers of relief

Most Roman cameos are small, of finger-nail size, but some are very much larger. The subjects are mostly portraits, often idealized representations of generals, statesmen or patrons, and themes from mythology – Dionysus, Eros, Leda and the Swan, etc. Some are signed, and in the case of others the artist can be guessed at. Some of the names of engravers which have come down to us are Gnaios, Aulos, Dioskorides and his son Hyllos, Tryphon, Solon and Sostratos.

Cameos

Towards the end of the Roman Empire the interest in gem-engraving declined, and such cameos as were produced show much cruder workmanship. Through the Dark Ages the techniques and some of the stones themselves somehow survived, and during the Middle Ages a few cameos were cut showing portrait heads and religious themes. The ancient cameos that were still in circulation were very highly valued and were used in crowns, reliquaries, and to adorn the shrines of saints. Their pagan subjects were interpreted in Christian terms; thus the triple mask of Bacchus, worn in Roman times as an amulet, was revered as a symbol of the Trinity. Knowing virtually nothing of the history of classical times, the people of the early Middle Ages did not understand the nature of antique cameos and various beliefs as to their origins were current. One was that they had been made by the tribes of Israel during their sojourn in the wilderness; cameos were for this reason known as 'pierres d'Israel'. The designs carved on them were thought to indicate specific magical powers in the stones. With this belief in their magical properties, they were naturally in demand for personal wear as well as for the use of the Church.

In fourteenth-century Italy engraved stones began to be cut in greater numbers, but still in a predominantly Gothic style, showing Christian motifs and personal insignia. With the rediscovery of ancient art from the fifteenth century onwards, however, gem-cutting was revived, and antique cameos were much sought after by collectors and assiduously copied by artists. They were worn in a variety of ways – as hat-brooches, medallions, in pendants, rings and brooches – and were also inlaid in plate and other ornamental pieces. Renaissance cameos were only rarely direct copies of the ancient ones; more often they were a free rendering of a classical subject and followed contemporary styles in art and sculpture (see *Renaissance jewellery*). There is little danger, on the whole, of confusing a Renaissance cameo with the classical original which inspired it. As in the ancient world, the craft of gem-engraving was highly regarded, and many of the foremost sculptors and artists tried their skill at it, encouraged by the patronage of noble families such as the Medici. Many of the cameos produced were portraits of these ruling princes. In the sixteenth century a variation of the normal type appeared; only the head and part of the body were in chalcedony, the rest of the design being in enamelled gold. Sometimes this arrangement was reversed; the figure was in enamelled gold, and the background of stone. The most famous of these pieces is a medallion bearing the arms of Francis I, showing Leda and the Swan. It was previously wrongly attributed to Cellini. The origin of these unusual cameos is not known, but may be French.

Cameo of Lodovico Sforza, about 1500. Bibliothèque Nationale, Paris

By the seventeenth century enthusiasm for cameos had waned, and gem-cutters were soon employing their skill in the newly-invented art of brilliant-cutting diamonds. The cameo was revived again during the eighteenth century and copies of ancient cameos were now made in great numbers. Books of engravings were published, making a range of designs widely available, and cameo-collecting again became fashionable. The wealthy collected what they believed to be genuine antique stones, and the less wealthy made do with the moulded paste imitations produced in considerable quantity by James Tassie (q.v.). Many of the stone cameos produced at this time were

56

close copies of the antique but were not actually intended as forgeries; they are often signed with the engraver's real name, although in Greek letters. On the other hand, deliberate forgeries were certainly made, and were subjected to artificial roughening to give them an aged appearance. (This artificial treatment can usually be detected by the expert, and the copyists were also apt to give themselves away by such errors as anachronisms in hairstyle on portraits, misunderstanding of ancient conventions, misspelling of Greek signatures, and the introduction of unnecessary details, which classical artists always avoided. The use of modern tools is also detectable.)

The enthusiasm for cameos reached its height at the end of the eighteenth century. They were particularly popular in French jewellery, influenced by the neo-classicism of the Napoleonic empire. In England imitation cameos were made of Wedgwood pottery and worn in bracelets, clasps and pendants (see *Wedgwood*). Shell cameos (q.v.) were also very popular.

The boom in classical stones as collectors' pieces ended quite suddenly in the early nineteenth century. The reason was partly that a new kind of Greek sculpture, typified by the Elgin marbles, was reaching Europe and showing scholars and artists that there was more to classical art than the Hellenistic and Roman styles they were familiar with. Collectors of antique gems became much more critical, and scholarly interest gradually turned to the archaic and true classical periods of Greek history. However, cameos and their imitations continued to be worn in jewellery throughout the nineteenth century, partly no doubt owing to Queen Victoria's fondness for them. In the mid-Victorian period when there was delight in clever craftsmanship, cameos *habillés* were made; the head carved in the stone was shown wearing a necklace and earrings which were set with tiny diamonds. The art of hard-stone cameo-cutting is now practised only by a handful of dedicated engravers, although the cutting of shell cameos continues to be a healthy industry in Italy.

Distinction between a hard-stone cameo and paste is not difficult, the paste being softer and having a glassy appearance. (See also *Intaglios*.)

Canada moonstone. Peristerite (q.v.) feldspar.

Canary beryl. Greenish-yellow beryl.

Canary diamond. A yellow diamond.

Canary stone. Yellow cornelian.

Cancrinite. (S.G. 2.42–2.50; R.I. about 1.51; H. 5–6.) A complex mineral occasionally cut *en cabochon* or as beads. The material used for gem purposes is massive, fibrous and of a yellow colour, and comes from Canada. Cancrinite which is not of gem quality is found in many parts of Europe and the U.S.A.; the mineral was first discovered in Russia and named after Count Cancrin, the Minister of Finance.

Candite. Blue spinel.

Candling. American term for a quick process of identifying thin-skinned cultured pearls which are strung in a necklace. Each pearl is held in a beam of strong light and rotated; if light and dark stripes are seen this indicates that the pearl has a straight-layered nucleus and is therefore cultured. The method may not work with cultured pearls which have a thick nacreous coating, so the absence of stripes does not mean that the pearl is natural. The principle is a simplified version of that employed in the lucido-scope (q.v.). (See also *Pearls*.)

'Candy spinel'. Misnomer for almandine garnet.

Cannetille. A rather coarse type of gold (or imitation gold) filigree used in nineteenth-century jewellery, particularly in the early part of the century. Pyramids, rosettes and beads of coiled wire figured prominently in this style of decoration.

Canning jewel. A magnificent late-sixteenth-century jewel, probably Italian, brought back from India in the nineteenth

The Canning jewel

century by Lord Canning and now in the Victoria and Albert museum. It is a pendant in the form of a triton or merman. The upper part of the body is a single baroque pearl, the head and arms are of white-enamelled gold, and the tail, which is enamelled bright green, is set with a row of diamonds and a large carved ruby. In his right hand the triton wields a scimitar, and with his left he holds a shield in the form of a mask of Medusa, enamelled blue and green and set with a ruby to indicate the gaping mouth. Three pendant pearls complete the design. The ruby medallion above the largest pendant pearl, and the carved ruby set in the flank, were probably added when the jewel was in India.

Cap-cut. Term for stones which are irregularly or haphazardly faceted.

Cape. A classification used in the sorting of diamonds: Cape stones have a faint yellowish tinge. (See also *Diamond.*)

'Cape chrysolite'. Misnomer for prehnite from South Africa.

'Cape emerald'. Misnomer for prehnite from South Africa.

'Cape ruby'. Misnomer for pyrope garnet.

Caradosso (*c.* 1445–1527). A renowned goldsmith, medallist, gem-engraver and sculptor of the Renaissance. He has the distinction of being almost the only goldsmith regarded by Benvenuto Cellini (q.v.) as a serious rival; Cellini praised in particular his hat-badges in gold repoussé-work. Caradosso (his real name was Ambrogio Foppa) was born in Como and for some years was goldsmith to Lodovico il Moro at Milan. In 1499 he went to Rome and was thenceforth employed at the papal court making, among other things, medals, gold and silver plate and dies for coins, and engraving gemstones. It is recorded that he engraved a diamond in 1500 (a remarkable feat for that time) and offered it to Pope Julius II. His contemporaries rated him very highly as a gem-engraver – he has been compared with the Greek master Dioskorides – but as he never signed his gems it is impossible now to identify and assess his work.

Carat. (1). The unit of weight used for precious stones and pearls (although the weight of pearls is actually *expressed* in grains [see *Pearls*]). It has been standardized in this century as one-fifth (0.200) of a gram (the metric carat). The origin of the carat weight was probably the seed of the carob or locust tree (*Ceratonia siliqua*), used as a weight by Eastern pearl-traders. These seeds are remarkably uniform in weight – about 0.197 grams. When the unit was adopted in Europe its weight varied considerably from one country to another and at different times; in the middle of the nineteenth century the carat weighed 0.205 g. in Berlin and London, 0.206 g. in Vienna, and 0.197 g. in Florence. An attempt was made by Paris gem dealers in 1871 to standardize the carat at 0.205 g., but the standard failed to obtain international recognition. In 1907 a second attempt was made, this time by the Comité International des Poids et

Mesures, who proposed a standard weight of 0.200 g. (the metric carat). Over the next few years this weight was adopted by most countries concerned with the precious stone trade, although somewhat surprisingly South Africa, the major diamond-producing country, did not legalize the metric carat until 1923.

Although legalized, the metric carat was not made compulsory. The old carat, however, more or less ceased to be used because of the confusion that would have resulted. (See also *Weights for gemstones*.)

Carat. (2). A measure of the fineness of gold. The standard is divided into 24 parts and pure gold is therefore 24-carat. 18-carat gold contains 18 parts of gold to 6 parts base metal, etc. Pure gold is too soft to be a useful metal and has to be alloyed with at least 2 parts in 24 of base metal to give it the necessary hardness. Different legal standards for gold are in force in various countries; in Britain they are 22-carat, 18-carat, 14-carat and 9-carat.

The spelling 'karat' is used in many countries, including America, to avoid confusion between this meaning of the word and the carat weight for precious stones (See *Carat* [1].)

See also *Gold* and *Alloy*. For the standards for gold which have been legally in force at various times in Britain. (See *Hallmarking*.)

Carat gold. A gold alloy conforming to one of the legal standards for the fineness of gold: in Britain, 9-carat, 14-carat, 18-carat and 22-carat. (See *Carat* [2].)

Carat punches. Punches used to mark the quality of the metal on precious-metal articles – '9ct', '18ct', 'Sterling silver', 'Plat', etc. They are made angled as well as straight so that pieces can be marked in inconspicuous but inaccessible places.

Carbonado ('Carbons'). A rare black form of diamond which has no cleavage and is highly valued in industry because of its toughness. It comes from Bahia in Brazil.

Carborundum. Silicon carbide; a very hard substance (H. $9\frac{1}{2}$) used as an abrasive,

produced by heating coke and sand in a furnace.

Carbuncle. A red garnet cut *en cabochon*. In earlier times any red cabochon stone was likely to be called a carbuncle.

Carcanet. A short necklace or jewelled collar, of the type fashionable in the sixteenth century. (See *Renaissance jewellery*.)

Carnelian. See *Cornelian*.

'Carneol' (Trade name). Pink-dyed chalcedony.

Cartier Ltd. Court jewellers with an international reputation for fine craftsmanship. The firm was founded in 1849 by Louis Francois Cartier who started a small workshop in Paris. His work soon attracted the attention of the Empress Eugénie, and 1859 Cartier opened a shop on the Boulevard des Italiens. In 1874 he was joined by his son Alfred. The firm prospered and the premises were transferred to the Rue de la Paix in 1898. Cartier's patrons now included the Prince of Wales, who suggested that it would be convenient to have a branch in London. A branch was opened in Old Burlington Street in 1903, and was transferred to the present premises at 175 New Bond Street six years later. This branch was under the management of Jacques Cartier, a grandson of the founder, who, having a great flair for design, decided to open his own workshop in London instead of importing jewels from Paris. The workshop, registered as the English Art Works, was started in 1921 in two small rooms over a shop in Oxford Street, but it grew rapidly and was later transferred to the upper floors of the Bond Street premises. Most Cartier jewels are still made there today.

Under Jacques Cartier the business consolidated its reputation, and built up a distinguished foreign clientèle which included the ruling Indian princes. The past thirty years have seen the disappearance of many of these clients, but the firm has adapted itself to the changing times without sacrificing its high standards, and produces jewellery to suit the informal style of modern life as well as jewellery of the traditional kind. The present Chairman and Managing Director is Jacques Cartier's son, Jean-Jacques.

Carving. Metal is carved with chisels (q.v.) and hammer, and with a graver (q.v.). For carved openwork, much of the metal can also be cut away with a piercing-saw (q.v.). A fairly complicated design in bas-relief is usually modelled in wax first. The piece to be carved may be held in a vice or engraver's block or on a bowl of pitch (qq.v.), depending on the size and shape. When the carving is finished the background is usually smoothed with a riffle (q.v.) to remove the tool marks. Metal-carving is practised particularly in the East.

Gemstones are carved or engraved with a bow-drill (q.v.) or on a wheel charged with abrasive; the softer stones can be worked with a steel file. (For engraved stones see *Cameos*, *Intaglios* and *Seals*.)

Casein. See *Plastics*.

Cassiterite (Tinstone). (S.G. 6.95; R.I. 2.01–2.1; H. 6½.) Cassiterite is the principal ore of tin; normally black or opaque, it is occasionally found in yellowish-brown or colourless crystals transparent enough to be used as gemstones. They can be distinguished from other stones of similar appearance such as sphene by their very high specific gravity. Sources include Australia, Bolivia, the Malay peninsula, Mexico, Saxony, and Cornwall.

Castelbolognese, Bernardi Giovanni (1495–1555). A famous gem-engraver and medallist of the Renaissance, who worked for the Duke of Ferrara, Pope Clement VII, and Cardinal Alexander Farnese. His work included figures of the apostles cut in rock crystal (for the Pope), an engraving in crystal for the Duke of Ferrara of the attack on the fort of Bastia, in which the duke was wounded, numerous medals, and engraved gems of which the finest include the Fall of Phaeton, Bacchus and his attendants, the Abduction of Ganymede, and scenes from the life of Christ.

Castellani, Fortunato Pio (1793–1865). One of the most influential and gifted jewellers of the nineteenth century. It was Castellani who was responsible for the revival of Greek and Etruscan styles in jewellery (see *Nineteenth-century jewellery*); unfortunately his many imitators usually lacked his skill and taste.

Castellani opened a shop in Rome in 1814 for the sale of jewellery which was mostly in the prevailing French and English styles. Becoming dissatisfied with this, he looked for fresh ideas and became interested in the chemical aspects of metallurgy – the colouring of gold and the possibilities of electro-gilding. He found these techniques unsympathetic, however, because he had no interest in mass-production. He then saw some recently-excavated Etruscan jewellery and, struck by the spirit of the work and by its extraordinarily delicate craftsmanship, decided to try to reproduce the jewellery of the ancient world with as much fidelity as possible as a corrective to what he considered to be the increasingly bad taste of his own times. Roman jewellery proved not difficult to copy, but in attempting to reproduce the jewellery of the Etruscans and Greeks Castellani encountered enormous difficulties because modern techniques proved quite incapable of achieving the same results. The granulation (q.v.) practised with such virtuosity by the Etruscans (see *Etruscan jewellery*) was particularly difficult to imitate; no satisfactory method could be found of attaching the grains (see *Gold*). Searching for craftsmen who might still possess this apparently forgotten knowledge, Castellani found in a remote part of the Umbrian marches peasant communities where some of the ancient traditions were still handed on. He brought these craftsmen to Rome and set them to work in his workshop, and after much patient experiment techniques were evolved by which very good imitations of the ancient work could be produced. Beautifully made though these pieces are, however, Castellani and his sons, who followed him into the business, did not succeed in rediscovering the technique used by the Etruscans for attaching their grains of gold to the surface. Castellani's son observed that although by using arseniates instead of borax and by powdering the solder to a fine dust they had obtained satisfactory results, they were nevertheless convinced that the ancients had 'some special chemical process' for affixing the grains, of which modern craftsmen were ignorant. He was almost certainly right; it is now assumed that the process used for granulation in the ancient world was colloid hard-soldering (q.v.), which was rediscovered in the 1930s by H. P. Littledale.

Castellani sold his reproduction Etruscan pieces under the name 'Italian archaeological jewellery', and the style, spreading to France and England, rapidly became fashionable. Other jewellers attempted to do the same thing; the Neapolitan jeweller Giuliano (q.v.) was probably the most talented of those influenced by Castellani. As the style became more popular, however, the imitations became cheaper and cheaper until towards the end of the century 'Etruscan' meant a piece of sheet-metal stamped with little raised bosses.

As well as the Greek, Roman and Etruscan jewellery, Castellani imitated early Christian, Byzantine and Renaissance jewellery. He was particularly interested in traditional Italian peasant jewellery; the Castellani family made many pieces in this style and Alessandro Castellani amassed a fine collection of peasant jewellery which is now in the British Museum, with which in later life he was associated. Castellani left the business to his sons Augusto and Alessandro in 1851 and for many years they continued to make jewellery of fine quality, improving the techniques developed by their father. The technical knowledge of the Castellani probably died with them, but there is still a tradition of fine filigree and granulated goldwork in Rome.

Casting. Casting is the process of forming an object by pouring molten metal (or some other substance in a liquid state) into a mould so that when it solidifies it has taken on the shape of the impression in the mould. The mould may be made of a variety of materials, and the original impression in the mould may be made by simply hollowing the mould out or by first making a solid pattern, forming the mould around this and then removing the pattern. Casting is a very old technique – it was used in Egypt, and later by the Greeks, by the goldworkers of Mexico and Peru before the Spanish conquest, and by other ancient civilizations. The process used was generally lost-wax casting (see below). A less sophisticated process, casting into a hollowed-out stone mould, was used for making weapons and axe-heads in the Bronze Age.

The casting processes most used by jewellers now are cuttlefish casting and lost-wax casting with a centrifuge (a mass-production method). Sand casting is occasionally used.

Cuttlefish casting. This is used when only one or two casts are required. The mould is the soft inner bone of the cuttlefish. Two pieces are needed; a large cuttlefish may be cut down the edges into two halves or two small cuttlefish may be used, one surface of each being rubbed perfectly flat with emery paper. The top end of the cuttlefish is cut off. A solid pattern of the article to be cast is made by hand, usually in lead; it must not have any undercuts which would pull away the mould when the pattern was removed. Three small register pegs are inserted in one face of the mould, leaving enough space between them for the pattern, and the two halves of the mould are pressed together so that the pegs make corresponding holes in the other face. The mould is then separated, the pattern is placed in position in the mould, and the two halves are pressed tightly together, located by the pegs. The mould is opened again and the pattern removed. It should have left a sharp impression in the cuttlebone. A funnel-shaped channel is cut in both faces of the

Casting

mould leading from the impression to the edge, and a few small channels are made to allow air to escape. (See illustration.) The two parts of the mould are tightly bound together with binding-wire, and the molten gold or silver is poured into the funnel-shaped channel. When the metal has cooled the mould is separated and the metal 'pour' is cut away from the casting, which has to be finished off with a file.

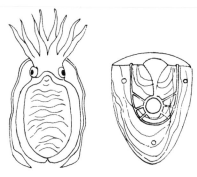

Cuttlefish and cuttlefish mould

Lost-wax casting. This method allows objects with undercuts to be cast. As the method has been practised for upwards of 4000 years there have been many variations of it, but the principle is as follows. A pattern of the article to be cast is made in wax. This is encased in a mould of some fire-resistant material (in ancient times often a mixture of clay, charcoal and water, now usually a proprietary brand of plaster), and an opening is left in the mould leading from the pattern. When the mould has hardened it is heated and the wax melts and runs out; molten metal is then poured in through the same opening. When the metal has cooled the mould is broken away. In recent times the lost-wax process has been used in conjunction with a method of forcing the metal into the mould under pressure; this produces castings of much higher quality. Compressed air and steam pressure have in the past been used (the latter particularly by dentists), but the method now generally used in the jewellery trade is centrifugal casting.

Centrifugal or investment casting. By this method quite complex patterns can be produced in quantity. A model is first made by hand in metal. Thin sheets of rubber are packed around this model and the rubber is put into a vulcanizing press where it is heated, flows around the model and becomes hard. The rubber mould is cut cleanly in half, the model is removed and the two halves of the mould are bound together. A channel has previously been made in the mould and the opening is placed over the nozzle of a wax injector – a can containing molten wax – and wax is spurted into the mould under pressure. When the wax has hardened the mould is separated and it is removed. A number of wax models are made in this way from the same rubber, and the models are then mounted on a cone-shaped frame and placed in a metal flask, and plaster (or a substance having similar properties) is poured over them. This plaster investment is placed in an oven and under the heat the wax runs out through a hole in the bottom, leaving a plaster casing containing numerous moulds. This is mounted on a centrifuge, a machine with two arms rotating (usually) on a horizontal plane. One arm holds counterweights, and on the other arm is placed the plaster mould with, immediately behind it, a crucible of molten metal. The arms are released and, driven by a spring or electric motor, rotate at high speed, so that molten metal is flung by centrifugal force from the crucible into the mould. The plaster mould is subsequently broken away and the castings separated from the cone.

Sand casting. This process, which seems to have been invented in the fourteenth or fifteenth century, was used for jewellery until recently, when it was replaced by centrifugal casting. It is now mainly used in iron foundries, etc. The process requires two casting flasks (iron boxes without a top or bottom, and with register-marks on the edge of one which fit into holes on the other), and casting sand, which is a special type of sand with good binding qualities. The sand is mixed with water so that it just holds together when squeezed in the hand. One of the boxes is placed with its register-marks upwards and filled with the sand, which is tightly packed in. The surface is dusted with French chalk or some other substance which prevents the parts of the mould from sticking to each other or to the pattern, and the model of the object to be cast, also dusted with French chalk, is pressed halfway into the sand. The other box is placed in position on top and filled tightly with sand. The boxes are then reversed, and the first one to be filled is lifted off and the sand knocked out (because the impression is probably imperfect); it is then replaced on the other and filled again with sand, firmly packed. The flasks are then separated, the pattern is removed and a pour for the metal and a number of air-vents are made. The flasks are bound together and when the mould is completely dry the molten metal is poured in.

Cast-iron jewellery. See *Berlin iron jewellery.*

'Catalin'. (Trade name). A phenol plastic. (See *Plastics.*)

Catalinite. Jasper from Cataline Island, California.

Cateye. Name sometimes used for operculum (q.v.), and sometimes for a chatoyant ('cat's-eye') stone.

Cat's eye. Any stone exhibiting chatoyancy (q.v.) when cut *en cabochon* in the appropriate direction.

Cat's eye (chrysoberyl). (S.G. 3.71–3.72; R.I. 1.75–1.76; H. 8½.) A silky yellowish-brown to honey-coloured variety of chrysoberyl, which when cut *en cabochon* exhibits a moving streak of light over the surface of the stone. The effect is caused by the reflection of light from a series of fine canals penetrating the stone.

A similar effect is given by certain other gemstones, notably quartz and tourmaline, and these are also known as cat's eyes. To avoid confusion they are usually referred to as 'quartz cat's eye', etc., while the term 'cat's eye' is restricted to the chrysoberyl type. The quartz cat's eye is similar in colour to the chrysoberyl but has a lower specific gravity and hardness. Chrysoberyl cat's eye possesses a characteristic opalescence which is not seen in other chatoyant gemstones. The most important source for the stone is the gem gravels of Ceylon.

Cat's eye effect. See *Chatoyancy.*

Cat's eye opal. Harlequin opal showing a streak of light. (See *Opal.*)

C-clamp. A c-shaped clamp, adjustable by means of a wing-nut at the bottom, fixed to the edge of a workbench and used to hold down metal for sawing, drilling, etc.

Cedarite. Amber from Manitoba, Canada.

Celebes pearl. Pearl from the Celebes archipelago.

Celestial stone. A name for turquoise.

Celestine (Celestite). (Strontium sulphate. S.G. 4.0; R.I. 1.62–1.63; H. 3½.) A colourless or bluish mineral sometimes cut as a gemstone. The stone is not really interesting enough to compensate for its softness. It occurs in various parts of the U.S.A. and Europe, but most of the cut stones probably come from S.W. Africa.

Cellini, Benvenuto (1500–1571). Cellini was among the foremost Renaissance goldsmiths, a virtuoso in metalwork, jewel-setting and enamelling. Nevertheless, although he records that he made numerous pieces of jewellery, ranging from simple rings to elaborate pendants, none of these pieces seems to have survived, and we know very little about his work as a jeweller except from descriptions. His reputation is such that fine pieces of sixteenth-century jewellery have frequently been attributed to him in the past, but it is now agreed by art-historians that there is no known piece of jewellery that can confidently be said to be his. His skill can, however, be judged from a magnificent salt-cellar in enamelled gold, surmounted with a male and female figure in the round, which he made for Francis I and which is now in the Kunsthistorisches Museum, Vienna.

The main source of information about Cellini's life and works is his *Autobiography*, written between 1558 and 1566. He was born in Florence, the son of a musician, and became apprenticed to a goldsmith at an early age in spite of his father's wish that he too should become a musician. He showed considerable talent for goldsmith's work but an equal aptitude (which accompanied him through life) for getting into trouble, and was banished from Florence for fighting. He worked in Siena and Bologna and went finally to Rome, where he set up his own workshop and remained, except for brief intervals, until 1540. Here he met some of the greatest of Renaissance artists, including Raphael and Michelangelo, who influenced his style for many years. (The figures on the Vienna salt-cellar, for instance, are strongly reminiscent of Michelangelo.) During this period Cellini worked for numerous patrons and notably for Pope Clement VII, for whom he made medals, a chalice (unfinished), and a large cope-morse set with a diamond, showing a figure of God the Father. Some eighteenth-century watercolour studies of this survive. He also made dies for the papal mint. His other activities at the time included playing a heroic part (by his own account) in the defence of Rome in 1527, and the murder of a jeweller named Pompeo, for which he had to flee Rome but was later pardoned. Some years later he incurred the enmity of Pope Paul III's son and was thrown into prison on the charge of having stolen some of the papal jewels during the sack of Rome. He was finally released on the intervention of the Cardinal of Ferrara, acting on behalf of King Francis I, who wanted Cellini to work at his court.

Cellini worked for Francis I at Paris and Fontainebleau from 1540 to 1545. His interest now lay in sculpture rather than goldsmith's work and in France he was one of a group of artists working in the mannerist style, a sophisticated and to some tastes decadent reaction against Renaissance classicism. Cellini's major work of this period is the *Nymph of Fontainebleau* – a decorative and not particularly impressive piece of sculpture. In 1545 he returned to Florence and there remained for the rest of his life, working for Duke Cosimo de'Medici. He made a few small pieces of jewellery but concentrated on sculpture, in which he returned to a more classical and powerful style. His finest work is the bronze *Perseus*, now in the Loggia dei Lanzi, Florence.

Cellini wished to be remembered as a sculptor rather than a goldsmith, and even in his early work such as the coins and medals made in Rome his fascination and talent for sculpture are evident. The salt-cellar is pure miniature sculpture. Ironically, his fame rests neither on his sculpture nor his goldsmithing but on his Autobiography, an extraordinarily vivid document written without a shred of modesty. It casts much light on the social background against which the sixteenth-century jeweller worked. Even more valuable is Cellini's treatise on goldsmithing and sculpture written towards the end of his life, which is our main source of information on the methods used in Renaissance jewellery and the state of technical knowledge at the time.

Cellon. (Trade name). A celluloid (cellulose acetate) plastic used as an imitation of amber. (See *Plastics*.)

Celluloid. See *Plastics*.

Cellulose acetate. 'Safety celluloid' – it is less inflammable than ordinary celluloid. (See *Plastics*.)

Celtic jewellery. *Pagan period*. In the course of the first millennium B.C. Celtic tribes migrated through many parts of Europe, bringing with them the knowledge of the use of iron and spreading techniques of metalwork learnt from the classical cultures of the Mediterranean. They were themselves highly skilled metalworkers with a genius for the elaboration of abstract and geometrical ornament. These qualities are well displayed in their jewellery, the forms and decoration of which show an unmistakably Celtic stamp in whatever countries they settled.

The pre-Christian Celtic culture is divided by archaeologists into the pre-historic or Hallstatt culture, and the 'La Tène' culture which originated in the Rhine area in the fifth century B.C. and includes elements of Greek and Eastern art. The 'La Tène' culture was brought to Britain by Celtic settlers in about 250 B.C., but the Celts of the earlier culture had already been living in the country for several centuries.

Among the earliest Celtic jewellery found in the British Isles are bead necklaces of amber, jet and glass, and the crescent-shaped gold plates, known as lunulae, found in Ireland. There is some doubt as to whether these were worn as headdresses or collars. They are decorated with fine lines in a zig-zag pattern around the edges and horns of the crescent. Characteristic of later Celtic jewellery are the magnificent collars known as *torcs*; these are tubular in section and penannular (broken circle) in shape, with ornamented terminals. They are often of bronze but sometimes of gold or electrum. One of the most splendid examples, found at Snettisham in Norfolk, is made of eight twisted strands of electrum, each strand itself consisting of eight fine twisted wires; the terminals are decorated with an abstract pattern in relief. (For the development of the torc, see *Necklaces*.) Other neck-

ornaments were strung with gold beads or thick beads of bronze.

The commonest *bracelets* and armlets are also penannular, and of a similar style to the torcs. They are chiefly of highly-ornamented bronze.

The typical early Celtic ornament is the *safety-pin brooch*. This was of very ancient origin. It originated from a pin, which, having been pushed through the clothing, was bent up and caught behind the head to keep it in place. Later a coil was added to provide a spring, and the catch plate at the other end was elaborated (see *Brooches*). Various features of the brooch developed along different lines in different countries. The earlier 'La Tène' brooch had a roughly triangular catch-plate; later this became an open loop which resembled a serpentine head bending back to touch the curved bow of the brooch. By the time of the Roman occupation of Britain this loop had been filled in and the catch-plate was now in the form of an elongated triangle, and the bow was curved in a shape reminiscent of a harp (see illustration). Another type of brooch was the ring-headed pin with a bent shoulder; early examples are made out of twisted wire, but later the pin is cast and the head is decorated, sometimes with inlay.

Although the richest pieces of Celtic jewellery are made of precious metal, bronze was much more commonly used and was quite highly prized by the Celts in Britain, since it was less easily available than on the Continent. It was sometimes

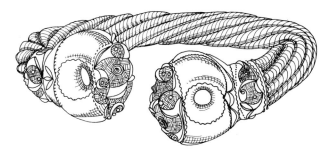

The Snettisham torc. First century B.C., British Museum

65

Celtic jewellery

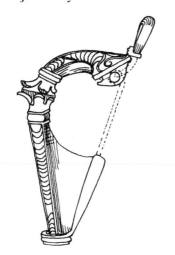

*Silver-gilt Celtic brooch, second century A.D.,
British Museum*

cast, sometimes wrought and nearly
always superbly decorated. On the cast
pieces the basic decoration was part of the
moulding, and the surface was sometimes
afterwards chased and engraved. The
wrought bronze was usually decorated
with repoussé work. Separate pieces were
riveted together, as the Celts did not use
solder. The ornament was almost entirely
in the metalwork itself; virtually the only
ornamental stone used with any frequency
was amber, and that was comparatively
rare. The Celts were, however, skilled at
enamelling, and champlevé enamel in
bright colours was applied to many
armlets, brooches and pins. It is not
known where the Celts learnt this art or
whether they invented it themselves;
certainly it was well established before
the Roman invasion of Britain.

The decorative forms used on Celtic
jewellery are highly distinctive. The
earliest forms were based on the chevron
or zig-zag and the spiral, and on ancient
Bronze Age symbols such as the swastika.
With the rise of the 'La Tène' culture a
new style entered Celtic art, characterized
by curved, flowing lines, trumpet-shapes
and scrolls. Many of the shapes are
probably ultimately derived from foliage,

since the undulating curves branch out at
intervals from a central 'stem', but the
design is so formalized that the natural
motif on which it is based is barely
recognizable. The same process occurred
in all the motifs used in Celtic art: human,
animal and bird forms, although used
rarely in early Celtic work, all became
formalized into an abstract or geometrical
pattern, and are subsequently elaborated
with further spirals, circles and zig-zags
until the original idea is completely
submerged in the complexity of the
design.

Christian period. The Roman occupation
to some extent broke the continuity of
Celtic art, and characteristic types of
jewellery such as the torc and safety-pin
brooch died out. After the withdrawal of
the Romans, the invasion of the Teutonic
tribes drove the Celts westwards. In
Ireland and western Scotland Celtic
culture continued and developed under
the influence of Christianity while the rest
of Europe was still predominantly pagan.
The importance of Christianity for Celtic
art of this period cannot be overestimated;
it introduced elements of Italo-Byzantine
art from the Christian East, it facilitated the
combination of designs and their elaboration and transmission through the
medium of illuminated manuscripts, and
it provided a new patron for the craftsman
in the form of the Church. The result of
this influence is that there is a marked
difference between Christian and pagan
Celtic art, although the development can
still be clearly traced.

The most characteristic pattern in
Christian Celtic decoration, seen in stone-
work, metalwork and manuscripts, is
interlaced work. This was derived from
classical art and its earliest form is a simple
over-and-under plait. At some stage the
continuous lines began to be broken,
producing the effect of knots, and this
knotwork developed into a variety of
highly complex types in which it is almost
impossible to follow the interwoven lines.
Sometimes the lines terminate in the heads
of serpents or animals; it is difficult to
decide whether this is another example of

the Celtic habit of formalizing natural shapes, or whether the artist simply decided to add a serpent's head to what was obviously a serpentine shape. More recognizable zoomorphic shapes sometimes occur, probably derived from Eastern art. The Greek key-pattern appears, but its effect is completely transformed by slanting it at an angle of 45°, in which form it combines harmoniously with other Celtic motifs. The old Celtic forms, particularly the spiral, also continue to be used. All these motifs appear in combination, nearly always arranged in balanced panels. The traditional skill of the Celtic metalworker reached a high degree of perfection in Ireland around the eighth century. The techniques used included enamelling, niello, plating and gilding, chasing, engraving, chainwork, and a skilful use of filigree and occasionally granulation. As in the pagan period, inlay was sparingly applied and pieces were still riveted rather than soldered.

By far the commonest surviving examples of Christian Celtic jewellery are the *penannular brooches*. This form appears to have been independently invented by the Iron Age Celts in Britain, and was fully developed in the Christian period. It consists basically of a broken ring along which moves a pin considerably longer than the ring's diameter. The pin is pushed through the fabric, and one end of the ring is then pushed under the exposed end of the pin and turned, so that the weight of the fabric holds the pin against the ring. The brooch was worn with the pin pointing diagonally upwards. Penannular brooches were at first simple in design, but increasingly elaborate decoration was applied to them, particularly to the finials, which were often in the form of birds' heads and were widened on the inside of the ring so that only the outside rim of the brooch was circular. A stage was reached at which the decoration was more important than the practical function of the brooch, and at this point the break between the finials began to be closed, at first with bars, so that the brooch was in effect a disc-brooch with a long pin. In the final stage the brooch is completely closed but the finials are still represented in the decoration as separate panels. The most beautiful of Celtic brooches, the Tara brooch, is of this type (see illustration). It is made of gilded bronze, divided into panels bounded by gold filigree, and decorated with nearly all the processes known to the Celtic jeweller – niello, cloisonné enamel, inlaid stones, and chasing and engraving. The reverse is decorated with a pattern of birds' heads and the old Celtic trumpet motif. A fine gold chain was originally attached to each

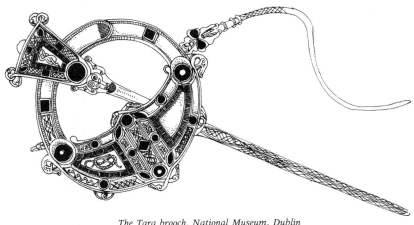

The Tara brooch. National Museum, Dublin

side of the brooch; only one now remains. Probably few brooches were as magnificent as this, but the Hunterston brooch, found in Scotland, is similar in type.

Apart from the penannular brooches, few examples of Christian Celtic jewellery survive. There were some brooches of the simple pin variety, and a type of which the so-called Clonmacnois pin is a fine example. This is of silver and is in the form of a long pin, attached to the head of which by a short bar is a kite-shaped pendant beautifully decorated with gold filigree, enamel, niello and inlay. Like the Tara brooch it is fitted with a finely-plaited chain.

Towards the tenth century Celtic art began to decline. By this time it had had considerable influence on Anglo-Saxon art, but this in turn was cut short by the Norman conquest. In Europe generally, Celtic forms were either forgotten or were absorbed, leaving little trace, into the stream of medieval art. The penannular brooch itself died out in the early Middle Ages and was replaced by the independently-evolved ring-brooch, except in a few remote Celtic districts such as the Western Highlands of Scotland.

Centre punch. A steel tool with a sharp pointed end, used to make an impression in metal at a point which is to be drilled. The hand punch is used in conjunction with a hammer, and it may also be used to texture the surface of metal. An automatic type is available which dispenses with the hammer; downward pressure on the barrel releases a spring which forces the point outwards.

Centrifugal casting. A casting process used for mass-production in which molten metal is flung by centrifugal force into a mould. The moulds are made by the lost-wax (q.v.) process. (See *Casting*.)

Ceragate. Waxy yellowish chalcedony.

Cerium oxide. A polishing agent for gemstones. (Cerium is a rare metallic element.)

Cerulene. Calcite coloured green and blue by malachite and azurite.

Ceylon cat's eye. Chrysoberyl cat's eye. (See *Cat's eye*.)

'Ceylon chrysolite'. Misnomer for greenish-yellow tourmaline.

'Ceylon diamond'. Misnomer for colourless zircon.

'Ceylonese peridot'. Misnomer for yellowish-green tourmaline.

Ceylonite (Pleonaste). An iron-rich variety of spinel (q.v.), dark green and almost opaque. It is occasionally used in jewellery. It is appreciably heavier (S.G. about 3.80) than the normal gem spinel.

'Ceylon opal'. Misnomer for moonstone.

'Ceylon peridot'. Misnomer for greenish-yellow tourmaline.

Ceylon ruby. A ruby from Ceylon or an almandine garnet.

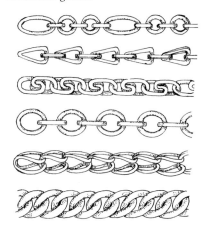

Various types of chain: from top downwards – fetter and five, barleycorn, S-curb, trace, loop-in-loop, curb

Chain. Nearly all chain is a series of linked loops of metal wire. Some time seems to have elapsed in the ancient world between the discovery of methods of making wire (q.v.) and the use of wire to make chain, but once chain was invented it was used in a variety of forms in jewellery and with considerable decorative effect (particularly in Greek jewellery, q.v.). One of the oldest types of chain is the loop-in-loop.

To make this, the individual links are first prepared and are pressed into an oval shape and then bent upwards so that they form about three quarters of a circle. Each link is then slipped through the looped ends of the one below it, and the last link is soldered to complete the chain. A more compact chain is produced by passing each link through the looped ends of the two preceding ones, and the chain can be broadened by cross-linking it so that it can be used as a belt, etc. Extremely complex loop-in-loop chains were built up in this way and it is often almost impossible to see how such a chain is constructed without taking it apart. The more complex chains of this type are also known as Trichinopoly chain or plaited chain.

During the Renaissance chains became a regular part of costume and were used not only as jewellery but as a form of currency. It was common practice to give gold chains as gifts or in payment for services. The usual type of chain at this time was made of broad flat links, but more decorative types were also produced. The wearing of one of these heavy chains did not preclude the wearing of a jewelled collar or pendant as well. Chains lost their popularity in the seventeenth century but returned to favour in the eighteenth, when they were used in chatelaines (q.v.) and much trouble was taken to make the links interesting and decorative. About 1830 the plain gold chain made a re-appearance when the Albert chain (q.v.) became fashionable; this survived well into the present century.

In modern times a bewildering variety of chains are produced and their manufacture is largely carried out by firms who specialize in chain-making. There are basically three types of chain – trace, curb and fancy, but there are numerous varieties of each type and the names given to them vary. Many do not have a name, merely a manufacturer's catalogue number. *Trace* chain is a chain of equal-sized oval links which when stretched out does not lie flat because the links are set alternately in a horizontal and a vertical plane. The wire may be round in section or flattened; when flattened it is known as *diamond trace*. In *curb* chain the links are twisted so the chain lies flat. Fancy chains are often developments or combinations of these. *Belcher* chain, for instance, is a trace chain made from D-section wire. In *rope* or *double-trace* chain two or more trace links are caught up in the next link. *S-curb* is a variety in which each link is internally coiled into an 'S'. The type known as '*barleycorn*' has its links arranged as in trace but the links are long and wider at one end than the other. *Fetter* chain is a chain of long links, but these are usually combined with smaller trace or curb links in groups; a chain in which there are five small links between each two fetter links is known as 'fetter and five', etc. Some chains are used predominantly for one purpose; examples are *snake* chain or *Brazilian* chain, made of a series of linked cups that fit into one another, extensively used for key-rings, and *Milanese* chain, a mesh of interwoven rows of links, which can be made in broad bands and is used for bracelets and watch-straps. There are many more, and different varieties are made on the Continent. A lot of chain is made in Germany.

Chain is produced in a range of precious metal alloys, in rolled gold and in base metal. Much of it now is machine-made, but some is still made by hand. Since every link has to be individually formed, set in the next one and soldered, this is naturally a very time-consuming process.

Chalcedony. (Silica. S.G. about 2.60; R.I. 1.53–1.54; H. $6\frac{1}{2}$–7.) Cryptocrystalline or microcrystalline quartz, a mixture of quartz in crystal form and opal. *Agate*, *cornelian*, and *chrysoprase* are the most important gem varieties of chalcedony and *jasper* may be regarded as a highly impure sub-variety. The terms 'chalcedony' and 'agate' are to a certain extent interchangeable, but 'chalcedony' usually refers to the common whitish or brownish material, which is sometimes carved, while 'agate' refers to the strongly-banded material suitable for use in jewellery (see *Agate*). All chalcedony is porous and can be stained, and this is regularly done with agate.

Chalcedony occurs world-wide, in the cavities of volcanic rocks, as nodules in sedimentary rocks, and sometimes as stalactites. Only the material from Brazil and Uruguay and from India and Madagascar is of commercial importance. Chalcedony often acts as a fossilizing agent on materials such as wood, shell or bone, and the resulting stone can be used for ornamental purposes.

Chalchihuitl (or similar names). Mexican name for jade, turquoise, and a variety of greenish compact stones; sometimes even applied to any stone that can be carved whether it is green or not.

Chalcomalachite. A mixture of calcite and malachite.

Chalcopyrite (Copper pyrites). (Sulphide of copper and iron; S.G. about 4.2; H. $3\frac{1}{2}$–4.) A mineral sometimes used as a gem material, but of greater importance as an ore of copper. It is brassy yellow in colour, like iron pyrites (see *Marcasite*), but is softer and of deeper colour. It occurs world-wide.

Chameleonite. A rare variety of tourmaline (q.v.) which is olive-green in daylight and brownish-red in artificial light.

Champlevé. A technique of enamelling in which the enamels are placed in recesses cut or stamped out of the metal. (See *Enamel*.)

Chank pearl. A pink, non-nacreous (see *Nacre*) pearl from the *Turbinella scolymus*.

Chaplet. A circlet for the head, often decorated with gold flowers or precious stones. Chaplets were worn by unmarried girls in the later Middle Ages. (See also *Diadems*.)

Charcoal. A substance which has been indispensable to the jeweller for thousands of years; its capacity for retaining an even red heat for a long period of time makes a charcoal fire ideal for metalworking processes such as annealing and soldering (qq.v.). Powdered charcoal can also be used in the material for casting moulds, as a polishing agent (mixed with oil), and for producing grains of gold for granulation (see *Gold*). Although the heat required in jewellery-making is now usually supplied by some form of gas jet or (for enamelling) electrically-heated kiln, a charcoal fire is still often used where a wide area of heat is required or where it is desirable that the work should be evenly heated from below rather than above.

Charcoal is most often seen in a modern workshop, however, in the form of a block on which work is rested during soldering or annealing. During annealing the charcoal helps to ensure an even spread of heat, and it has the advantage that depressions can be cut in it to hold objects or for other purposes such as making spherical beads of metal.

Charm bracelets. Gold or silver chain bracelets hung with a variety of small trinkets such as figures of animals or holiday souvenirs (models of Bath Abbey, Cornish pixies, etc.). These 'charms' (their connection with magic seems slight) originated in the novelty jewellery of the Victorian era (see *Nineteenth-century jewellery*), and in the early part of this century they were often quite expensive ornaments. A jeweller's catalogue of 1905 has a page of cast gold charms in such forms as rabbits, owls, pigs, guardsmen and motor cars, set with diamonds and emeralds and with prices ranging up to £11. The modern type are on the whole very much cheaper (allowing for the difference in the value of money) and are often stamped instead of cast. In 1961 self-illuminating charms fitted with miniature batteries were introduced.

Chasing. The working of sheet metal from the front with hammer and punches. A piece of repoussé work (q.v.) is nearly always chased when the process of beating up the relief from the back is finished; the purpose of the chasing is to give further definition to the relief,

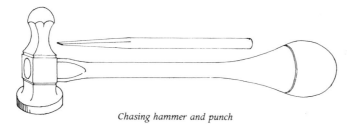

Chasing hammer and punch

increase the light-and-shadow contrast and give additional texture to the background. Pieces may also be chased as the only means of achieving relief (in this case the background is beaten down, and the metal pushed into ridges, etc., by holding the punch at an angle), and castings are also often finished off by chasing. The work may be laid on a bed of pitch as for repoussé, but for most chasing a less yielding surface is required and a block of hardwood or steel is generally used. For chasing continuous outlines, the punch is held at a slight angle at the beginning of the line to be chased, and is given a series of continuous rapid blows with the chasing hammer. Some punches with specially-shaped ends are hammered only once to give a single impression.

For much chasing and repoussé work the tools can be used on either side of the metal. (See *Chasing tools, Repoussé tools* and *Chasing hammer*.)

Chasing hammer. A lightweight hammer (4–6 oz.) specially designed for use with chasing and repoussé tools (qq.v.). It has a wide flat face and a springy wooden handle with a bulbous end which fits into the palm of the hand for maximum control.

Chasing tools. Steel punches of square or rectangular section, used in conjunction with a chasing hammer (q.v.) to give definition, texturing and relief to sheet metal from the front (see *Chasing*). Many of these tools are also used for repoussé work (q.v.).

There are several classes of chasing tools, and various types and sizes are available within each class. *Tracers* are used to create lines; they are shaped like a blunted chisel and are driven along the metal with a series of light blows from the hammer. Various widths are available. *Modelling tools* have flat or convex tips and are used to flatten and shape the metal around relief which has already been raised. *Matting tools* have patterned tips and are used to give texture to the surface with a single impression, and a variety of other punches with specially-shaped tips are used to impress with one blow the shape of the tool. Punches of this type with concave circular tips are also known as *ring tools*.

A large range of chasing tools is available from retailers, but craftsmen who specialize in this kind of work and usually have a hundred or so such tools, each for a particular purpose, often prefer to make their own from steel blanks. The end of the blank is shaped first with a coarse file, then with a finer one, finished off with abrasive, polished and finally tempered. (See also *Repoussé tools*.)

Chatelaines. The chatelaine originated in the seventeenth century as a device for suspending seals, which were beginning to take the place of signet rings, from the belt or girdle. It soon also came to be used to hold the watch, which previously had just hung from the belt by a chain or had been kept in the pocket, and by the middle of the eighteenth century it had developed into a major item of jewellery to which a variety of small objects could be attached. The basic form of the chatelaine was a metal shield or hook-plate fitted at the bottom with hooks from which hung a number of short chains. Sometimes the objects were attached directly to these chains, sometimes the

Early nineteenth-century German chatelaine

chains were united by a second shield, which in turn held another series of chains. The first article to join the watch was the *étui* – a small case, roughly cylindrical in shape, containing an assortment of objects such as scissors, thimble and pencil, used in needlework or drawing. The *étui* made its appearance in the 1720s. Later other useful objects such as keys were added, and also a variety of purely ornamental trinkets. Chatelaines of this type were of course only worn by women and served roughly the same purpose as a handbag, but the masculine equivalent was often equally heavily equipped with watch, watch-key and bunches of seals.

The chatelaine was a characteristic feature of eighteenth-century dress and the finest workmanship was lavished upon it. While all other items of jewellery were dominated by precious stones, chatelaines were almost exclusively of metal-work, sometimes set with enamels. The finest examples in the first half of the century are in chased and repoussé gold, beautifully worked. For those of modest means, a great number were made in imitations of gold, particularly pinchbeck. These were made up from cast sections and the designs therefore tend to be standardized. In the 1760s solid gold became unfashionable, and there was a trend towards lighter designs. Many gilt chatelaines incorporated contrasting metals such as silver and steel, and those in gold were sometimes decorated with *taille d'épargne* enamel or had delicate goldwork on a ground of agate. In the last quarter of the century there was a vogue for gold chatelaines and watches with painted enamels; the subjects were usually of classical or sentimental nature.

A hookless chatelaine known as the Macaroni came into fashion in the early 1770s; it was worn looped over the belt with both ends hanging down. The watch hung at one end, and the other held usually a seal or tassel or a sham watch (*fausse-montre*) balancing the real one. These chatelaines normally consisted of enamelled gold chains linked by plaques, also of enamelled gold, and were sometimes set with diamonds or pearls. Both sides were equally ornamental. The backs of the watches were enamelled and jewelled to match.

The chatelaine declined in popularity at the end of the eighteenth century but was revived as an 'antique' in the 1830s. Steel chatelaines were fashionable from 1849 to 1855, and in 1851 one was shown at the Great Exhibition. They went out of fashion again in the 1860s, but from 1870 onwards were moderately popular in such materials as steel, sometimes combined with jet, and electroplated silver.

Chatelaines with a silver watch and silver-bound prayer-book were worn from 1875 to 1885. In 1893 Ashbee, one of the leading exponents of Art Nouveau jewellery (q.v.) produced a chatelaine in silver openwork; but by this time the chatelaine had ceased to be a common item of jewellery, and before long it was entirely forgotten.

Chatham emerald. An American synthetic emerald. (See *Synthetic gemstones*.)

Chaton. Term for the central ornament of a finger ring; also a name for mirror-foiled stones. (See *Foil*.)

Chatoyancy. (*Cat's-eye effect*.) The characteristic displayed by certain stones of exhibiting a streak of light across the surface, which moves as the stone is moved. The effect is due to the reflection of light from numerous parallel cavities or fibres within the stone. The chrysoberyl cat's eye is the best-known chatoyant stone, but other minerals which produce 'cats' eyes' include quartz, tourmaline, apatite, beryl and scapolite. Chatoyant stones are cut *en cabochon* or in flat plates to display the effect fully, and it is important that the fibres should be running parallel to the base of the stone or the streak of light will not be 'centred'.

Chatoyant. Exhibiting chatoyancy (q.v.).

Chatter-marks. See *Fire-marks*.

Cheapside hoard. A hoard of early seventeenth-century English jewellery

Amethyst hair-jewel from the Cheapside hoard

found in Cheapside, London, in 1912 when a house was being demolished. It is presumed to have been the stock of a jeweller. The hoard included bracelets, necklaces, earrings, hair-ornaments and several carved stones, including an amethyst and emeralds carved in the form of bunches of grapes, and a number of cameos. The jewellery shows a predominance of pendant briolette stones in light enamelled settings. There are some very attractive enamelled chains in floral designs set with precious stones, including one of white and gold Tudor roses linked with enamelled green leaves. One bracelet is made of faceted rings of amethyst, joined with enamelled links. The jewellery is interesting in showing the progress that had been made in gem-engraving and gem-cutting, and the increased emphasis on faceted stones that was to become a characteristic of seventeenth-century jewellery. It also illustrates very clearly a decline of the imaginativeness and grand conception of form which had gone to produce the best of Renaissance jewellery, and the emergence of a more delicate and dainty style. (See *Renaissance jewellery* and *Seventeenth-century jewellery*.)

73

The hoard is now in the London Museum and the Victoria and Albert Museum.

Chelsea colour filter. A small instrument resembling a hand lens fitted with a piece of coloured glass or gelatine which allows only two colours of the spectrum to be transmitted through it – red and yellowish -green. It was designed primarily to distinguish between emeralds and their imitations. Emerald, although a green stone, absorbs a considerable amount of light in the yellow-green part of the spectrum, and transmits red light strongly. When seen through the filter, therefore, an emerald will appear a good red colour, whereas most of the green stones used to imitate emerald, including glass, appear green. Synthetic emeralds show a much stronger red than the natural stones.

The filter may also be used in the identification of certain other gemstones. It is particularly useful in distinguishing between blue synthetic spinel, which appears red or orange through the filter, and aquamarine and blue zircon, both of which appear green and are often simulated by the synthetic spinel.

'Chemin de fer' jewellery. Massive and ugly jewellery made of chains, bolts, screws, etc., presumably intended to be an expression of an industrial age, briefly fashionable when it was produced by the French jeweller Duval in 1861. (See *Nineteenth-century jewellery* for other jewellery of this period.)

Chenier. A short length of metal tube of the sort used for hinges. (See *Tube*.)

Cherry opal. Red common opal from Mexico.

Chessylite. See *Azurite*.

Chiastolite. See *Andalusite*.

Chicken-bone jade. Yellowish jade discoloured by burning or having been buried. (See *Tomb jade*.)

Chicot pearl. Alternative name for a blister pearl.

'Chinese cat's eye'. Operculum.

Chinese jade. Jadeite. (See *Jade*.)

'Chinese turquoise' A misnomer for a mixture of calcite, quartz and blue-dyed soapstone.

Chisels. Small chisels with blades of tempered steel are used by jewellers and silversmiths for carving metal (see *Carving*) and for pierced work (q.v.). Although in the West pierced work is mostly done with a saw, in parts of the East chisels are used exclusively and complex decoration is produced in this way.

Large chisels may be used in conjunction with a heavy hammer to cut sheet metal which is too thick to be cut with shears, but this type of work is not normally done by jewellers.

Ch'iung Yü. Red jadeite: valuable. (See *Jade*.)

Chlorastrolite. (Calcium-aluminium silicate. S.G. 3.1–3.5; R.I. about 1.70; H. 5–6.) An unusual chatoyant stone with green and white markings. It occurs in small aggregates of green fibre found as pebbles along the shores of Lake Superior. It is usually cut *en cabochon* to bring out the unique markings, to which its name ('green star') refers.

Chloromelanite. Jadeite (see *Jade*) of a dark green to black colour.

Chloropal. (1) Green common opal. (2) An opal-like hydrous silicate of iron.

Chlorophane. Fluorspar which fluoresces on heating.

Chlorospinel. Green spinel.

Chlor-utahlite. Variscite.

Choker. A short necklace, usually about 15 inches long.

Chromepidote. Chrome-rich epidote from Burma, also known as tawmawite.

Chromium. A hard white metal, resistant to corrosion and with a high melting point (1765°C). It is the constituent which makes stainless steel (q.v.) resistant to rust.

Chromium plating is now extensively used on costume jewellery, to which it gives a hard, bright finish often relieved by touches of enamel. Coloured chromium plate was introduced some years ago but did not prove popular. Chromium plate has a bad reputation for peeling and pitting, but this only occurs when the coating is thin or the plating is carelessly done. Good chromium plate is a quite satisfactory material and has on occasion been used in good quality modern jewellery.

In minute quantities chromium is responsible for many of the richest colours displayed by gemstones, notably emerald and ruby.

Chromium oxide. A polishing agent. (See *Green rouge*.)

Chromium plate. See *Chromium*.

Chrysanthemum stone. An aggregate of xenotime and zircon with radial markings. It comes from Japan.

Chryselephantine. Made of gold and ivory.

Chrysoberyl. (Beryllium aluminium oxide. S.G. 3.71–3.72; R.I. 1.75–1.76. H. 8½.) Most gem-quality chrysoberyl is a transparent greenish-yellow. It was popular in Victorian and Edwardian jewellery and was sometimes referred to as chrysolite (a name properly reserved for a variety of olivine). The major sources are Brazil and Ceylon. This type of chrysoberyl is now much less in demand than the two rarer varieties *alexandrite* and *cat's eye* (qq.v.).

Chrysocarmen. Red-to-brown copper-bearing ornamental stone from Mexico with green or blue spots.

Chrysocolla. (Hydrated copper silicate. S.G. 2.0–2.5; H. 2–4.) An opaque blue or bluish-green mineral which makes an attractive ornamental stone. Its composition is rather variable and it is found in the upper veins of copper mines in many parts of the world, notably U.S.A., Russia, the Congo and Chile. It is usually polished as cabochons. Some chrysocolla is found embedded in rock crystal and cut and polished in the matrix.

Chrysolite. A name misleadingly used for a variety of stones. In the Victorian and Edwardian periods it referred to greenish-yellow chrysoberyl; it is sometimes used now, particularly in America, to refer to peridot. In earlier centuries it could refer to any yellowish stone.

Chrysopal. Green common opal.

Chrysoprase. (See *Chalcedony*.) A variety of chalcedony stained green by nickel; the best chrysoprase is a translucent apple-green. It is used for cabochons and beads and for carving intaglios and cameos. A stone called 'chrysoprasus', which may or may not have been true chrysoprase, was highly esteemed in the ancient world and is listed as one of the stones in the foundations of the New Jerusalem (Revelations 21, xx). The source of this material is unknown.

Chrysoprase was popular in Victorian times and was often cut in flattened cabochons with a rim of facets round the edge. At that time it was mined in Silesia and in Tulare County, California, but these mines are no longer productive and chrysoprase now comes from Goias, Brazil and Queensland, Australia. An imitation of chrysoprase is produced by stained agate. Where the staining is done by chromium salts the imitation can be detected with the Chelsea colour filter (q.v.), through which the chromium-stained agate shows red instead of green. Nickel staining is more difficult to detect. The glass imitations of chrysoprase can usually be distinguished by the bubbles they contain.

Chrysoquartz. Green aventurine quartz.

Cinnabar matrix. Minerals with inclusions of cinnabar (a red mineral of no importance as a gemstone). The term has been applied particularly to a Mexican jasper.

Cinnamon-stone. A name for golden-yellow hessonite. (See *Grossular garnet*.)

Cire-perdue. Alternative name for the lost-wax process of casting. (See *Lost-wax casting* and *Casting*.)

Ciro pearl. (Trade name). Imitation pearl.

Citrine. (See *Quartz, crystalline*.) Transparent yellow quartz, the colour varying from pale lemon to a golden or reddish shade. Natural citrine is rather rare, and much of the citrine used in jewellery is actually heat-treated amethyst (amethyst, being purple quartz, is identical with citrine except for the colour).

The best citrine comes from Brazil.

Clam pearls. Pearls from clams, for instance the quahog (see *Quahog pearl*) and the giant clam. They are of comparatively little value. The word 'clam' is sometimes incorrectly applied to fresh-water mussels, particularly those from the Mississippi basin.

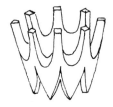

Claw setting

Claw setting. A setting in which the stone is gripped just above the girdle (q.v.) by projecting claws. Claw settings may be of various shapes, and they are often made out of strips of gallery (q.v.).

The claw setting allows considerable light to enter the stone and is therefore used mainly for transparent faceted stones. It first became popular in its modern form in the nineteenth century. (See also *Setting*.)

'Clean'. Trade term for stones free from noticeable flaws.

Cleavage. The tendency of a crystallized mineral to split or break along certain planes producing a more or less smooth surface. The cleavage planes are always parallel to a possible crystal face in the mineral ('possible' because minerals rarely crystallize with the full symmetry of which they are capable – see *Crystal systems*). Diamond cleaves easily parallel to the octahedral faces of the crystal, and this fact is exploited in the preliminary stage of diamond-cutting when rough crystals of awkward shape or containing

a flaw in one part are split along a cleavage plane (see *Diamond-cutting*). In most other respects, however, easy cleavage is a nuisance, as tiny cleavage cracks in a stone may be developed under the stresses involved in faceting and polishing it, and if it survives these it is likely to break along a cleavage plane if dropped on a hard surface. Few gemstones, however, cleave as easily as this: the ones worth noting are topaz, euclase, and kunzite. Some other minerals, including garnet and quartz, do not cleave at all readily.

In very rare cases the type of cleavage can help in identifying a stone. This situation occurs when a stone purporting to be of a certain species shows under the microscope cleavage cracks which could not occur in the crystal system to which that species belongs.

Cleiophane. Zinc blende.

Clerici solution. A poisonous liquid consisting of a hydrated solution of thallium salts, used in the determination of specific gravity (q.v.). Its specific gravity is 4.15; it is diluted with water for use.

Clinozoisite. See *Epidote*.

Cloison. A cell made of strip metal to enclose enamel (see *Cloisonné*) or a suitably-cut stone.

Cloisonné. A technique of enamelling in which the enamels are contained in cells of strip or filigree metal, usually soldered to the base. (See *Enamel*.)

Cloud agate. Agate with dark cloud-like markings.

Coated stone. Term for a stone painted with coloured lacquer (see *Tinting*). Diamond crystals with a coloured natural coating are also called coated stones.

Coconut pearl. Pearl from the clam of Singapore, similar in appearance to the white flesh of a coconut.

'Coconut pearl'. Misnomer for pearl-like concretions found in coconuts: they are of no value at all.

Collaert, Hans (c. 1540–1628). Engraver and designer of jewels who in 1581 published one of the most important collections of designs of the period, the *Monilium bullarum in aurumque icones*. His engraved designs for pendants seem, from existing pieces, to have been widely used. Some of them are very similar to Erasmus Hornick's designs for pendants in the form of sea-horses, etc. (see *Hornick*), but they have a rather more abstract quality. Many of Collaert's designs have a somewhat geometrical feeling.

Collaert visited Italy, but apart from this seems to have spent most of his life in Antwerp.

Collars. See *Necklaces* and *Dog-collars*, also *Renaissance jewellery*.

Collet. A round band of metal which encircles a gemstone and holds it in place.

Colloid hard-soldering. A process patented in 1933 by H. P. Littledale which makes it possible to effect a join in gold or silver without using a prepared solder. It is assumed that this process, or one very similar to it, was used in antiquity to solder the grains in granulated work (see *Granulation*) and on certain other ancient pieces in which no soldered joints are visible.

The process depends on the fact that the melting-point of gold (or silver) and copper when they are in contact is lower than the melting-point of either metal separately. The pieces to be joined are glued together with a mixture of glue and ground-up copper salt. They are then heated (in ancient times this would be done in a crucible on a charcoal fire). At 100°C the copper salt changes to copper oxide. At 600°C the glue changes into carbon. At about 850°C the carbon absorbs the oxygen from the copper oxide and vapourizes as carbon dioxide, leaving a thin layer of copper between the parts to be joined. At 890°C the copper and the gold melt and the joint is made. The melting-point of pure gold is 1063°C, so there is little danger of overheating the metal to the point where the gold itself melts. A clean joint is made which will stand subsequent re-heating, and the higher the temperature reached the less visible the joint.

Colorado aquamarine. Aquamarine from Mt. Antero, Colorado. Usually pale and with a green tinge.

'Colorado diamond'. Misnomer for transparent smoky quartz.

Colorado goldstone. Aventurine quartz.

'Colorado jade'. Misnomer for green microcline feldspar (amazonstone, q.v.).

'Colorado ruby'. Misnomer for pyrope garnet.

'Colorado topaz'. Misnomer for yellow quartz (citrine).

Colour dispersion. The splitting up of white light into colours of the spectrum when it passes through a transparent medium such as a gemstone. The light is split up because each of the colours composing it is refracted (see *Refraction*) to a different extent according to its wavelength; on emerging from the stone the colours are again refracted and separated still further. The resulting flash of colour is known as 'fire'. The ability to disperse light in this way is very strong in some stones (diamond, zircon, demantoid garnet, sphene) and negligible in others. For most practical purposes, the dispersive power of a stone is measured by the difference between the refractive index (q.v.) for red light (6870Å) and the refractive index for blue light (4308Å) (this is known as the B–G interval). This measurement is carried out with a table spectrometer (see *Refractive index*) using the minimum deviation method, or less accurately with a refractometer (q.v.) using red and blue lights or filters.

Colour filter. A device usually consisting of a piece of coloured glass or gelatine used to filter out certain parts of the spectrum and aid in the identification of some gemstones, particularly emerald. The type most commonly used in England is the Chelsea colour filter (q.v.).

Colour in gemstones. The appearance of colour is caused by the absorption of certain wavelenths of light. Light from the sun or from an ordinary incandescent light-bulb is known as 'white light' and contains the entire visible spectrum of colours, each of which corresponds to a wavelength of visible light. Certain elements absorb selected wavelengths of light, and therefore when one of these elements is present in a substance the substance can only transmit those wavelengths which have not been absorbed: these make up the resulting colour of the substance. Each element has its own absorption-spectrum, and where these spectra are known they can be of great assistance in identifying gemstones (see below).

The colouring agents in gemstones are metallic elements. In some cases the colouring mineral is an essential constituent of the gemstone (as in turquoise, a copper-aluminium phosphate, owing its colour to the copper); gemstones of this type are called idiochromatic. Most gemstones, however, would be colourless if they were chemically pure; the colouring agents are impurities which happened to be present when the mineral crystallized, or they may be sub-microscopic particles of another coloured mineral. Gemstones of this type are called allochromatic, and they may assume a very wide range of colours. Corundum, quartz, spinel and beryl are examples.

The principal colouring elements in gemstones are: *copper*, giving characteristic green, blue and greenish-blue hues to idiochromatic minerals such as malachite and turquoise, but of no importance in the colouring of allochromatic stones; *chromium*, to which the finest colours in gemstones are due – the rich crimson-red of ruby, the green of emerald, and many others; *iron*, which is present in many gemstones and responsible for the bluish-green of aquamarine, the purplish-red of almandine garnet, the green of tourmaline and nephrite, etc., but which on the whole produces rather subdued and even drab colours because it absorbs light over a very broad spectrum; *nickel*, responsible for the apple-green of chrysoprase but not a common element in gemstones; *cobalt*, which is used to produce a blue colour in synthetic stones and glass although it does not colour any natural gemstone blue; *manganese*, which gives a pink or orange colour to rhodonite, rhodochrosite and spessartite garnet; *vanadium*, the colouring role of which in natural stones has not yet been established, but which is used in the synthetic corundum imitation of alexandrite (coloured naturally by chromium); and *titanium*, which is partly responsible for the blue in natural and synthetic sapphire.

In idiochromatic gemstones the colour is usually so characteristic that they can be immediately identified. Many allochromatic gemstones also display characteristic shades of colour; emeralds, for instance, are not difficult to recognize, and experienced jewellers and gem-dealers rarely have difficulty with the more commonly-encountered stones. The time has gone, however, when jewellers believed that the colour of a stone was a sure guide to its identity; with such a wide range of gemstone materials now available, and the commercial production of synthetic gemstones (q.v.) in colours which simulate those of other natural stones, colour can be more misleading than helpful. An examination of the stone's absorption-spectrum, however, can often give a conclusive identification, since the typical absorption-spectra of the major gemstones are known. The examination is carried out with a small instrument called a spectroscope (q.v.). A simpler but more limited text is to examine the stone through a Chelsea colour filter (q.v.), which was devised as an aid to distinguishing emerald from its imitations but is of use with some other stones as well.

Some doubly-refracting stones (see *Double refraction*) show two or sometimes three colours according to the direction in which the stone is viewed. (This is explained under *Dichroism*.) In many cases this effect cannot be seen by the naked eye, but in a few stones, such as green tourmaline (q.v.), the effect is very noticeable. Dichroism is detected by the dichroscope (q.v.), and since it is only manifested in doubly-refracting stones it is another aid to identification.

The colour of a cut gemstone is very important to its value; a sapphire of poor colour, for example, is likely to be of less value than a very fine sherry-coloured topaz, although topaz is generally thought of as a 'semi-precious' stone. This is why poorly-coloured stones are often sold under names which imply that they are stones of a different species (see 'Oriental emerald', etc.). Generally speaking, coloured stones should have as rich or 'saturated' a colour as possible, while colourless stones should be water-white with no tinge of yellow (this applies particularly to diamonds). When stones are of an unsatisfactory colour, the colour may in some cases be altered by heating. This is often carried out with quartz, topaz and zircon (see *Heat-treatment*). Diamonds change colour on exposure to radium and bombardment with atomic particles (see *Irradiation of diamonds*). In most cases the resulting colour is permanent.

For other methods of changing the colour of stones, see *Colouring of stones (artificial)*.

Colouring of metals. Metals may be given a coloured finish in several ways – by enamelling (see *Enamel*) by the application of a thin coat of varnish or lacquer (see *Lacquer*), by plating with a coloured metal or alloy (see *Electroplating*), and by chemical processes in which the surface of the metal undergoes a chemical change. Chemical colouring is a final process carried out after all soldering, etc., is finished and after the metal has been polished. The type of polish on the surface before colouring affects the appearance of the metal after colouring: if it is highly polished in the first place the coloured surface will be glossy. The temperature at which the colouring is

done, the duration of the process and the composition of the metal also affect the result. It is essential that the metal surfaces should be completely free of grease, dirt, oxide, etc. before being coloured. The principle of most chemical colouring is that oxides or sulphides are created on the metal surface by immersion in the appropriate solution. When an article cannot be immersed the solution can be painted on. Silver in reaction with a sulphur compound develops a layer of silver sulphide; copper develops cuprous oxides or sulphides, and gold, which in its pure state does not react to most chemical agents, depends for its colouring on the base metal with which it is alloyed.

Gold alloys can be coloured black by immersion in a hot solution of half a cube of potassium sulphide (liver of sulphur) in 2 pints of water. The gold is heated before immersion. A surface layer of pure gold can be produced on a low-carat gold alloy in several ways. One recipe is to combine in a heated crucible 2 parts potassium nitrate, 1 part common salt and 1 part alum – this becomes fluid when heated. The gold article is first dipped into a solution of 1 part nitric acid to 10 parts water, then rinsed in boiling water, then agitated for a few minutes in the crucible solution. It is rinsed again in boiling water and dipped in the crucible, and this process is repeated until the colour of pure gold appears on the surface.

Silver can be coloured black by the potassium sulphide solution described above. Dark grey is obtained by taking the article out of the solution before the colour becomes too deep and rinsing immediately in water. This solution is used mainly to give silver jewellery an 'antique' appearance. A golden colour can be obtained by immersing in a cold solution of ammonium sulphide (1 gram to 7 fl. oz. of water). By repeated immersions, or by heating the solution, various shades from crimson to purple and brown may be achieved; the article must be withdrawn immediately the required colour appears. Silver may be coloured blue by placing it in a closed steel box with a small quantity of pure sulphur, which must not actually touch the silver, and heating the box.

Copper and its alloys can be given an attractive range of colours. 'Antique green' is produced by prolonged immersion in a solution of 1 oz. copper nitrate, 1 oz. calcium carbonate and 1 oz. ammonium chloride to 4 pints of water. The article and the solution are both warmed first. Various other greens can be obtained: sage green by a hot solution of 1.5 gram copper nitrate to 6 oz. water, olive green by 1 part ammonium chloride or iron perchloride to 2 parts water, and dark green by equal parts of copper sulphate and zinc chloride. Blue-black is obtained with a hot concentrated solution of barium sulphide or ammonium sulphide. A bronze colour is produced by a hot solution of 1 part copper sulphate to 2 parts water. Copper-zinc alloys can be given a range of colour from yellow to bright red by immersion in a solution of 2 parts copper carbonate and 1 part caustic soda to 10 parts water.

Polished *steel* can be turned black with a solution of $\frac{3}{4}$ oz. nitric acid, $1\frac{1}{2}$ oz. copper sulphate and 1 oz. selenious acid to 1 gallon of water. However, steel is normally coloured by heat (see below).

Colouring by heat alone.

Steel. This must first be brightly polished. Heated with an even source of heat, e.g. a charcoal fire, it goes through a range of colours; light yellow at 410°F, bronze at 510°F, light blue at 560°F, dark blue at 610°F. (The precise colour depends on the composition of the alloy.) When the required colour is reached it is quenched immediately in water or oil.

Copper. On heating, this passes through pale yellow and red to violet and finally black as the layer of cuprous oxide builds up. The colour is not always permanent, but is more likely to be so if the heat is fairly slow. The oxide may flake off if the metal is suddenly quenched.

Gold. The copper in a low-carat gold alloy oxidizes on heating and becomes red and then black; the lower layers remain red and can be partially revealed by polishing. This varicoloured effect is quite often used on castings.

Colouring of stones (artificial). There are various ways of altering or improving the colour of stones. One of the commonest, although it can only be done with porous material, is dyeing or staining (see *Dyeing of stones*). This is done with the rough material before it is cut. Transparent coloured stones which have been cut may be foiled or tinted (see *Foil* and *Tinting*). Some gemstones change colour on heating and retain this colour permanently. Quartz, topaz and zircon are often treated in this way (see *Heat-treatment*). Diamonds assume a green colour on exposure to radiation (see *Irradiated diamonds*). In composite stones (see *Doublet*) pale or colourless material may be given a colour by the use of a coloured cement layer.

In synthetic stones colour is given by the addition of metallic oxides. These may be used to produce colours which do not occur in the natural stones. (See *Synthetic gemstones.*)

Combs. These have appeared as items of jewellery at various times. In the fifteenth century when head-dresses were elaborate (see *Medieval jewellery*) crown-shaped combs of gold were worn, usually set with precious stones. The great age of the comb, however, was the nineteenth century (see *Nineteenth-century jewellery*), when for a time combs were the chief head-ornament. In the early part of the century they were very often set with cameos, partly owing to the Empress Josephine's fondness for engraved gems. Throughout the century they were made in a great variety of materials (a Victorian glass comb is illustrated under *Nineteenth-century jewellery*). Tortoiseshell first became fashionable in the 1850s and remained popular for a long time. In the 1860s combs were the most popular head ornament and could be worn either on the chignon at the back of the head or on the forehead as a diadem. The latter type were hinged so that the teeth folded backwards and the tops were wide and often elaborate. Gold (or gilt)-topped combs were at first fashionable, set with pearls, stones, cameos, or enamelled (usually with Greek patterns), but in about 1868 tortoiseshell replaced metal in popularity. Soon afterwards there was a vogue for high Spanish combs in tortoiseshell, worn with a mantilla. These were still popular in the 1880s, by which time combs were becoming more vertical and were worn in a high top-knot. Most combs were now of tortoiseshell with gold or jewelled tops.

Combs continued to be a favourite with Art Nouveau designers, particularly the less talented ones. They were nearly always enamelled. A fairly typical example in this style is illustrated under *Art Nouveau jewellery*. Since the early part of this century the decorated comb has relapsed into obscurity, from which it can only be rescued by a revolution in hairstyles.

Commemorative rings. In the seventeenth century a practice began of wearing rings which commemorated a specific event, and in the seventeenth, eighteenth and nineteenth centuries many such rings were worn. The events were usually of political importance, and although they included royal marriages and military victories there is a preponderance of rings commemorating defeats, disasters and deaths. Most commemorative rings are therefore also a type of memorial jewellery (q.v.).

Commemorative ring with portrait of Charles I. Victoria and Albert Museum

A large class of English commemorative rings relates to the execution of Charles I, the Restoration, and later the Jacobite rebellions. These were worn by supporters of the Stuarts and were generally enamelled with a portrait head or bust on the bezel. The Jacobite rings sometimes have a portrait of the reigning monarch on the lid of the bezel, which lifts up to reveal a portrait of the Pretender inside. A series of rings were made in commemoration of the deaths of Lords Balmerino, Kilmarnock, Lovat, Derwentwater and others, executed in 1746–7 for their part in the 1745 rebellion. Two of these are in the British Museum.

Also in the British Museum are a number of Polish rings. One is inscribed 'In memory of the partition of Poland 1772', and another is enamelled with a crown of thorns, palm branch and cross and with the dates 25–27 February and 8 August 1861; on these dates Polish peasants were shot in the Warsaw uprisings.

The siege of Paris in the Franco-Prussian War is commemorated by a ring decorated in relief with the arms of Paris flanked by olive branches and inscribed *'Tous aux dangers tous à l'honneur. 1870–1871.'* The turbulent history of France in the late eighteenth and early nineteenth centuries provided many subjects for commemoration. A ring in the Victoria and Albert Museum bears the portraits of Jean Paul Marat (murdered 13 July 1793) and Louis Michel Lepelletier de Saint Fargeau (murdered 20 January 1793), and a ring in the British Museum

Ring said to have been made to commemorate Napoleon's escape from Elba (see text). British Museum

commemorates Napoleon's escape from Elba. It has a hinged locket bezel enamelled on the outside with three flowers in a wreath, and inside is a head of Napoleon in relief in gold. It is said to be one of six rings which were made for the conspirators involved in the escape.

81

Composite stones. See *Doublet.*

Comptonite. An opaque variety of thomsonite found in the Lake Superior region and also in Italy.

Conchiolin (Conchine). A brown organic substance secreted by pearl-producing molluscs, and one of the constituents of pearl. (See *Pearls.*)

Conchoidal fracture. See *Fracture.*

Conch pearls/shell. The giant or Queen conch (*Strombus gigas*), found in the waters of the West Indies and off the Florida coast, produces pink or white pearls which are non-nacreous (see *Nacre*) and have a porcelain-like appearance. The shell is used for cameo-carving; the colour is white on a rose-pink background, or vice versa. (See also *Pearls* and *Shell.*)

'Congo emerald'. Misnomer for dioptase.

Connemara marble. A green serpentine marble from County Galway, Eire. (See *Marble.*)

Contact liquid. A liquid of high refractive index, used to bring the stone being tested into optical contact with the dense glass of a refractometer by excluding air. (See *Refractive index* and *Refractometer.*)

Copal. A recent fossil resin sometimes used to imitate amber, q.v.

Copper. A malleable, rich-coloured metal which has been used by man for some 10,000 years. It oxidizes readily, but this tendency can be controlled by combining it with other metals, and as a constituent of bronze (q.v.) copper was of great importance in the ancient world.

Unalloyed, copper is now a popular metal in cheap hand-made jewellery. It is often enamelled, since its rich colour sets off the enamels well and they fuse to it readily (see *Enamel*). It can be bought in sheet, strip and wire. Since the invention of pinchbeck (q.v.) copper has been used in alloys which simulate gold. It is now a constituent of gilding metal (q.v.) (a type of brass), which is extensively used, electroplated, in cheaper jewellery. It is also used in nickel silver (q.v.) and Britannia metal (the modern equivalent of pewter, q.v.) and as an alloying metal for silver and gold (qq.v.). It has in addition numerous industrial applications, particularly in the electrical industry.

The melting-point of copper is 1083°C.

'Copper emerald'. Misnomer for dioptase.

'Copper lapis'. Misnomer for azurite.

'Coque de perle'. A section cut from the central whorl of the shell of the Indian nautilus. It looks somewhat similar to a blister pearl, but is thinner and is usually given a backing of cement. (See also *Shell.*)

Coral. (S.G. 2.6–2.7; H. about 3½.) The axial skeleton of the coral polyp. Of the many varieties of coral only the red and rose-red 'noble coral' (*Corallium nobile* or *Corallium rubrum*) is used in jewellery. This coral was a valued ornament in the ancient world and was worn as an amulet. There was a vogue for it, particularly in carved form, in the Victorian era (see *Nineteenth-century jewellery*), and it was again popular in the 1920s.

Noble coral is found, not in the atolls of the Pacific, but in the Mediterranean and Japanese waters. The most important sources are off the coasts of Tunisia and Algeria, Sicily, Corsica, Naples and the Calabrian coast of Italy. The coral is usually dredged from the sea bed and most of it is then taken to Torre del Grecco near Naples, where it is fashioned into beads, cameos and small carved objects. Some pieces are left in their natural tree-like form and are simply polished and bored through the centre so that they can be strung on a necklace. Much coral is exported to the Far East, where it is more highly valued as an ornamental stone than in western countries.

The commonest imitations of coral are made in glass, plastic or porcelain. Coral should be easily distinguishable by its density and hardness. Also, being largely composed of calcium carbonate, it will effervesce if touched with a drop of acid.

Coral agate. See *Agatised coral.*

Coralline. (Trade name). Chalcedony dyed red.

Corbeille. A gift of jewellery made by the bridegroom to the bride on their wedding.

Cordelière. A long beaded girdle knotted in front with the ends hanging down, fashionable from about 1837 to 1840. It was part of the cult of the Middle Ages. Cordelières were made of various materials – silver beads were fashionable in 1837 – and might have chatelaines (q.v.) attached. (For jewellery of the period, see *Nineteenth-century jewellery.*)

Cordierite. See *Iolite.*

Cornelian (Carnelian). (See *Chalcedony.*) A translucent reddish or yellowish-red variety of chalcedony. The fleshy colour was responsible for the introduction of the alternative name, carnelian (from Latin *carnis*, 'flesh') in the fifteenth century.

The main sources of cornelian in earlier times were the Arabian and Egyptian deserts, where the stones were often found as loose pebbles on the surface. Brazil, Uruguay and India are now the major commercial sources.

'Cornish diamond'. Misnomer for rock crystal.

Corn tongs. See *Stone tongs.*

Coronet setting. A circular claw-setting.

Coro pearl. (Trade name). Imitation pearl.

Corozo nut. See *Ivory,* under '*Vegetable ivory*'.

Corundolite. (Trade name). Synthetic white spinel.

Corundum. (Aluminium oxide. S.G. 3.96–4.01; R.I. 1.759–1.767; H. 9.) The mineral which provides the gemstones ruby and sapphire (qq.v.). Pure corundum is colourless (white sapphire) and very uncommon; the colour of the gems is provided by various metallic oxides – chromic oxide in ruby, titanium in blue sapphire, ferric oxide in yellow sapphire,

etc. Most corundum, however, is impure and opaque. Since corundum is harder than all other natural substances except diamond, the impure material is extensively used as an abrasive, while small crystals of transparent corundum are used in industry where a substance with high resistance to friction is required. Much of the corundum used industrially is now synthetic (see *Synthetic gemstones*).

Large deposits of corundum are found in Burma, Thailand, Ceyon, Kashmir, Australia, Tanzania and the U.S.A. Transparent corundum has unusual internal features which may on occasion help to establish where a stone has come from (this affects its price). Burmese stones, especially rubies, show internal patterns of rutile needles intersecting at angles of 60° and 120°, and these produce a sheen in the stone which is known as 'silk'. Corundum from Thailand contains curving systems of canals known as 'feathers'. Ceylon stones exhibit rutile needles and feathering, often include small crystals of zircon, and frequently have bands of colour. Kashmir sapphires have a rather hazy appearance owing to the presence of fine lines intersecting at 120°. The most striking internal feature of corundum is its ability to produce fine star-stones (see *Asterism*). Corundum crystallizes in the trigonal system (see *Crystal systems*) and is therefore doubly refractive (q.v.).

The name of the mineral comes from the Tamil word for ruby, 'kurundam'. The first stones brought to Europe came from India.

'Cosse de pois'. A style of ornament which became popular in jewellery, particularly for aigrettes and the surrounds and engraved backs of miniature cases, etc., in the early part of the seventeenth century. It consisted of carving elongated leaf-shapes, rather like pea-pods (hence the name). The style probably originated in France just before 1600; it is most clearly seen in work of about 1620, and thereafter developed in the direction of more naturalistic flower-

Costume jewellery

Cosse de pois ornament on the frame of a cameo, about 1610. Bibliothèque Nationale, Paris

and-leaf patterns. (See also *Seventeenth-century jewellery*.)

Costume jewellery. Mass-produced jewellery which is made of non-precious materials and is not designed to last. Much of it is designed to be thrown away within a very short time, since it is made for a prevailing fashion.

'Costume jewellery' is a rather vague term which is sometimes applied to all cheap jewellery and sometimes only to the fashion-oriented jewellery just mentioned. The latter is really a product of this century, although novelty jewellery which was only destined for a very short life made its first appearance in the Victorian era (see *Nineteenth-century jewellery*). Such jewellery was not, however, particularly cheap; it was usually of gold set with diamonds, emeralds, etc. Jewellery made of non-precious materials first began to be extensively worn in the eighteenth century, when paste and cut steel were substitutes for diamonds, pinchbeck for gold, and Wedgwood for hardstone cameos (see *Eighteenth-century jewellery*). This type of jewellery, however, was cheap only in its materials: it was well designed and well made, and was intended to last.

Modern mass-production of jewellery utilizes the many technical advances that have been made in, for instance, casting, stamping, plating and finishing processes, and the development of synthetic materials and new alloys. By these means costs are kept to a minimum. Imitation jewellery, i.e. jewellery which follows the designs and styles of precious jewellery, is usually of silver or a plated base metal, set with pastes, marcasite, etc., which are generally cemented in and not hand-set. (Hand-made jewellery in materials of low intrinsic value does not really fall into the category of costume jewellery.) The cheap 'fashion jewellery' which does not follow the designs of precious jewellery makes considerable use of plastics, chromium plate and anodized aluminium (qq.v.).

Cotter pins. Small pegs or clips of iron wire used to hold work together for soldering. (See also *Binding wire*.)

'Crackled'. Term applied to stones which have been heated and then suddenly cooled in water, producing numerous small fissures. The stones are frequently cooled in dyed water so that the dye is absorbed and dries out in the cracks, colouring the stone.

Crafts Centre of Great Britain. An organization which for many years has promoted work by craftsmen: the range of work displayed and sold at the Centre includes silver, jewellery, enamels, ceramics, glass, woodwork, embroidery, bookbinding, etc. Craftsmen pay a small fee for membership and an additional fee for exhibiting work, which if accepted by the selection committee is handled by the Centre on a sale-or-return basis. The centre provides a London showplace for the best quality work, and concentrates on work for which there is not a mass market. It can be of great help in launching young craftsmen straight from Art School, who normally find the first few years very difficult.

The Centre is a registered charity and receives a government grant. It has recently been merged with the Craft Council and will in future be known as the British Crafts Centre, with showrooms at 43, Earlham St., W.C.2, and 12, Waterloo Place, Lower Regent St., S.W.1.

Cramp rings. See *Magical jewellery.*

Cramp setting. A variation of the rub-over setting (q.v.). Instead of the projecting rim of the setting being simply pressed down to hold the stone, parts of it are cut away with a saw leaving a serrated edge. Each projecting tooth or 'cramp' is then pressed down on to the stone.

'Created emeralds'. American trade name for synthetic emeralds. (See *Synthetic gemstones.*)

Creole earring. An earring in the shape of a hoop broader at the bottom than at the top. They were extremely popular in the 1850s.

Creolin. Brecciated jasper.

Creolite. Red and white banded jasper from California.

Crispite. Quartz or agate with green hair-like needles. (See *Sagenitic quartz.*)

Crocidolite. A fibrous mineral which when decomposed into quartz produces the gemstones tiger's eye and hawk's eye (qq.v.). These gemstones are sometimes wrongly called crocidolite.

Crocus. A polishing powder, usually in block form, produced from iron oxide.

Crop pearl. Baroque pearl.

Cross cut. A modification of the step cut in which the table is surrounded by triangular facets. (See *Gem-cutting* for illustration.)

Cross facet. The small triangular facets above and below the girdle of a brilliant-cut stone (see *Diamond-cutting*). There are altogether 32 of these triangular facets and some of them have the alternative names of skew, skill or break facets, or halves. It is now usual for all of them to be classed together under the same name, since they are of identical shape and differ only in

their orientation, which dictates the direction in which they are ground and the order in which they are placed on the stone.

Cross rose cut. A modification of the rose cut in which 18 of the facets are quadrilateral. (See *Diamond-cutting.*)

'Cross stones'. Stones which exhibit a cruciform pattern and are used as religious amulets. (See *Andalusite* (chiastolite) and *Staurolite.*)

Crown. The upper part of a cut gemstone, lying above the girdle (q.v.).

Crowns. Although the words 'crown' and 'diadem' may be used interchangeably, 'crown' usually refers to a metal circlet from the upper edge of which rise pinnacles, crosses or foliate shapes, and which may be crossed at the top with one or more arches. This type developed in post-classical Europe and is not found in the ancient world, although certain Greek diadems of the Mycenaean period, consisting of gold circlets with leaves and rosettes attached to the upper edge, are clearly forerunners of the European type. (See *Diadems.*)

A variety of imperial headdresses were worn by the Roman emperors, from a simple wreath to a 12-rayed crown of Eastern origin which was held to be a symbol of divinity. Neither type survived in Europe. It is difficult to know what sort of crowns were worn in Dark Age Europe because the main sources of information are the portrait-heads on coins, and these were often copied directly from Roman coins. Illuminations in Anglo-Saxon manuscripts show kings wearing open crowns with foliated pinnacles, and also a square crown, which must have been somewhat uncomfortable. It is probable, however, that the type of crown actually used during this period was more in the nature of a helmet than an open crown. The helmet type was probably used until the tenth century; at the coronation of King Edgar (A.D. 973) an open crown was used, and from then on was the standard crown for coronations.

Edgar's crown is shown in manuscripts as having three trefoils along the upper edge. The trefoil was adopted by Western rulers from the Roman Empire, having first been used as a royal emblem by Constantine. In the course of the Middle Ages it became formalized into the fleur-de-lys, and as such has appeared on all English crowns ever since.

The regular use of arches on English crowns dates from the late Middle Ages, when Henry V introduced an arched crown as the crown of state. The origin of the arched crown is not clear – it was introduced into the West by Charlemagne and his successors, who may have adopted it from a Byzantine model or from the helmet-crown. Whatever its origin, it was worn by various European rulers during the Middle Ages, including apparently William the Conqueror, but no particular importance was attached to the arches. By the end of the Middle Ages, however, the arches had come to be seen as symbolizing independent sovereignty, and it is likely that Henry V established an arched crown of state to signify his independence of the Holy Roman Emperor.

In the reign of Henry VI the crown was made more ornate and the intersection of the arches was surmounted by a small orb and cross. This idea was taken from the personal crowns worn by the Holy Roman Emperors; it became a permanent feature of the English crown and was soon almost universally adopted by the rest of Europe. In the following centuries the shape of the arches underwent various transformations. At first they rose almost to a point; later they became more and more flattened at the top, and, instead of receding inwards from the circlet, began to project beyond it. Meanwhile the type of crown with pointed arches was not discarded but came to be recognized throughout Europe as an imperial crown, the type with flattened arches being the crown of royalty. The flattening of the arches continued until the nineteenth century, when they were bent almost at right angles and were further depressed at the point where the orb and cross rested.

Arched crowns are generally lined with a velvet cap, turned up at the bottom with miniver. The cap is a survival of the Cap of Maintenance or Cap of Estate, an ancient symbol of rank or official status formerly worn on its own or carried in procession on public occasions.

The type of crown described above is characteristic of Western Europe (the Russian imperial crown is of quite a different shape, resembling a priest's mitre), and although the elements of which it is composed can be traced back to the Middle Ages or earlier, it is modern rather than ancient in style. The crowns in the English regalia are all of this type since the oldest of them dates only from the seventeenth century, the earlier crown jewels having been broken up by order of Parliament after the Civil War. Other European countries, however, possess much older crowns, around which many legends and religious beliefs have accumulated over the centuries. One of the most famous of these is the Iron Crown of Lombardy, a circlet of hinged gold plaques in Byzantine style, around the inside of which runs an iron band said to have been made from the nails of the Cross. It is extremely old, having been given by Pope Gregory to Queen Theodolinda in the seventh century, and both Charlemagne and the emperor Charles V are said to have been crowned with it. Another ancient crown with religious associations is the Crown of St. Stephen, also known as the Holy Crown of Hungary, which since the Second World War has been in American custody. This was made in Byzantium, probably in the eleventh century, and also consists of a circlet of hinged plaques. These are richly decorated with enamels and set with large cabochon jewels, and the crown is surmounted by arches bearing a central cross. The crown was given to the first Duke of Hungary in 1072 by the Emperor of Byzantium, after which it had a fairly chequered history. There is a delightful story that on one occasion Queen Elizabeth of Hungary, fleeing from her enemies, concealed the crown by inverting it (it is lined with a gold cap) and feeding the baby out of it.

The lower edge of St. Stephen's crown is hung with three pendant chains set with rubies. These pendant chains, known as *cataseistae*, denoted supreme power in Byzantium and were worn only by the Emperor himself. During the Middle Ages, however, they appeared briefly on the crowns of Western kings, who did not appreciate their lofty significance and used them as chin-straps.

Crown glass. Glass which does not contain lead oxide; it is used for some imitation gemstones. (See *Glass*.)

Crown setting. See *Coronet setting*.

Crucible. A cup-shaped vessel of fireclay or some other fireproof material used primarily for melting metals, although it is also useful for such purposes as containing acids. The name is said to derive from the fact that crucibles were formerly stamped with the sign of the Cross.

Crucible furnace. A furnace for melting large quantities of metal. Most types are fired by gas. (See also *Muffle kiln*.)

Crusite. Chiastolite.

Crypto-crystalline. Occurring in closely-packed crystals of sub-microscopic size. (See *Crystal*.)

Crystal. (1). Occasionally used to mean rock crystal, q.v.

Crystal. (2). A solid with a definite and orderly atomic structure which results in a symmetrical external appearance. Minerals are classified into seven crystal systems (q.v.) according to the type of symmetry they display.

The most valuable gemstones are those cut from fairly large transparent crystals. When a mineral occurs in very small closely-packed crystals it is said to be crypto-crystalline, and will yield a translucent or opaque gemstone, as in chalcedony and its varieties. Minerals composed of crystals of microscopic size are said to be massive (an example is lapis lazuli). Amorphous minerals are those which have no crystalline structure; there

are no important gemstones of this type except opal. Glass is amorphous.

Common forms assumed by crystals are described under *Crystal habit*.

Crystal habit. The crystal form characteristically assumed by a mineral. Gemstone minerals may assume several different forms all showing the same basic type of symmetry (see *Crystal systems*), and the forms are apt to vary with location and with the colouring agent present in the mineral. For instance, emerald, aquamarine and morganite, which are all varieties of beryl, typically assume three different crystal forms.

The commoner crystal habits are: *prismatic* (an elongated shape with parallel sides, as in emerald and tourmaline), *tabular* (flattened and short, as in morganite), *octahedral* (eight faces, as in diamond), *dodecahedral* (twelve faces, as in garnet), *acicular* (needle-shaped, as in the rutile in rutilated quartz), *platy* (in very thin plates, as in some haematite – this is an extreme of the tabular habit). Several forms may be combined in one crystal.

Crystal systems. Crystals are classified into 7 'systems' according to the symmetry they exhibit. The system to which a gem crystal belongs determines many of its most important characteristics, notably its optical properties. Three kinds of symmetry are involved. (For the purpose of classification crystals are regarded as being perfectly formed; in fact crystals are frequently distorted owing to unfavourable conditions of growth and other factors, but the angles of inclination of corresponding faces in crystals of the same system are always the same). A *plane of symmetry* is an imaginary plane dividing a crystal into two equal parts, each of which is a mirror-image of the other. An *axis of symmetry* is an axis about which a crystal may be rotated so as to occupy a precisely similar position in space more than once in 360°. It may occupy a similar position twice (i.e. every 180°), in which case it is said to have a digonal axis, three times (every 120°, a trigonal axis), four times (every 90°, a tetragonal axis) or six times (every 60°, a hexagonal axis.) A *centre of symmetry* is said to be present when there are similar faces parallel to each other on opposite sides of the crystal. Crystals are described by reference to their *crystallographic axes*; these are imaginary lines running through the crystal in definite directions and intersecting at its centre, and are usually parallel to the axes of symmetry or perpendicular to the planes of symmetry. The distance and inclination of the faces of the crystal are measured by reference to the crystallographic axes.

The seven crystal systems are as follows. (Within each system are minerals showing greater and lesser degrees of the full symmetry.)

1. Cubic system. 3 crystallographic axes of equal length at right angles to one another. 9 planes of symmetry, 13 axes of symmetry (3 tetragonal, 4 trigonal, 6 digonal), and a centre of symmetry. Examples: cube and octahedron. Important gemstones crystallizing in this system include diamond, garnet, spinel. Minerals in this system are singly-refractive.

2. Tetragonal system. 3 crystallographic axes at right angles to each other, the two horizontal axes being equal and the vertical axis either longer or shorter than these. 5 planes of symmetry, 5 axes of symmetry (4 digonal, 1 tetragonal), and a centre of symmetry. Example: a 4-sided prism terminating in 4 triangular faces. Gemstones include zircon, rutile, idocrase.

3. Hexagonal system. 4 crystallographic axes, the three horizontal axes being of equal length and intersecting each other at 60°, and the vertical axis being longer or shorter than these and perpendicular to them. 7 planes of symmetry, 7 axes of symmetry (1 hexagonal, 6 digonal), and a centre of symmetry. Example: a 6-sided prism terminating in a single face. Gemstones include emerald and aquamarine, and apatite.

4. Trigonal system. Similar crystallographic axes to the hexagonal system, but 3 planes of symmetry, 4 axes of symmetry (1 trigonal, 3 digonal), and a

centre of symmetry. Example: a rhombohedron. Gemstones include tourmaline, sapphire and ruby, and the quartz stones.

5. Orthorhombic system. 3 crystallographic axes of different lengths at right angles to each other. 3 planes of symmetry, 3 digonal axes of symmetry, and a centre of symmetry. Gemstones include chrysoberyl, topaz and peridot.

6. Monoclinic system. 3 crystallographic axes of different lengths, two at right angles to each other and the third inclined at an angle to them. 1 plane of symmetry, 1 digonal axis of symmetry, and a centre of symmetry. This is a very large crystal group. Gemstones include sphene, moonstone (orthoclase feldspar), kunzite, diopside, brazilianite, malachite and jade (both jadeite and nephrite).

7. Triclinic system. 3 crystallographic axes of different lengths, all inclined to each other. A centre of symmetry but no planes or axes. This, the least symmetrical of the crystal systems, contains no gemstone of importance except turquoise. Labradorite, amazonstone, axinite and rhodonite also belong to this group.

The trigonal and hexagonal systems are sometimes grouped together, making only six systems in all.

The above groups refer only to the types of symmetry the crystals exhibit; within these groups minerals may crystallize in a great variety of different *forms*. These are discussed under *Crystal habit*.

Crystolon. Trade name for a silicon carbide abrasive.

Cufflinks. Cufflinks first appeared in the nineteenth century when white shirts with long sleeves and starched cuffs were worn. They were usually fairly simple, made of gold, silver or ivory, sometimes set with diamonds. The basically simple design of cufflinks made them an obvious subject for mass-production, and links quickly became one of the staple commodities of the Birmingham industry. The designs at this time were hardly imaginative. A Birmingham manufacturer's catalogue of 1905 has two pages devoted to gold cufflinks which are almost identical except for one pair which is decorated with a fox's head and hunting horn and another which has turquoise set in hammered gold. By and large, cufflinks remained the same for the next fifty years – round, oval or square, set with mother-of-pearl or onyx, or perhaps enamelled with regimental colours, or simply made of engine-turned gold. In the past ten years or so, however, with the gradual erosion of the idea that men's dress should be sober and men's jewellery invisible, there has been a minor revolution in cufflinks. They are now likely to be made of any material and to be of any shape, provided it will go through a shirt buttonhole. Cufflinks of traditional type are still produced in considerable quantities, but hand-made cufflinks in modern and often arresting styles are increasingly popular.

There are several types of connection for cufflinks. The simplest is the ordinary chain. Expanding links, which allow the shirt-cuffs to be pushed up, have a length of chain coiled up inside the link-head which uncoils to allow the distance between the links to be widened by an inch or more. Another connection is a fixed metal bar to which one of the link-heads is soldered while the other is fixed on a swivel, so that it can be bent back to go through the buttonhole. Finally, some links fit together with press-studs.

Culet. The small facet ground on the base of a brilliant-cut stone to prevent splintering. It is not used much in modern stones. (See *Diamond-cutting*.)

Cullinan diamond. The largest diamond ever discovered. Found in 1905 at the Premier Mine in South Africa, it weighed the extraordinary amount of 3106 carats (about $1\frac{1}{3}$ lb.) and was of perfect quality. One face of the crystal appeared to be a cleavage face, suggesting that it was only part of a much larger crystal which had been split by natural processes.

The stone was named after the chairman of the mining company. The Transvaal government purchased it for £150,000 and presented it in 1907 to King Edward VII

on his birthday. The somewhat alarming task of cutting this enormous stone was entrusted to the Amsterdam firm of J. J. Asscher. The initial cleaving of the crystal into smaller pieces suitable for fabrication was attended with great anxiety, since it was suspected that the stone was heavily strained and might shatter under the blow. It did not, but Mr. Asscher, having successfully cleaved it at the second attempt, fainted and had to be revived with brandy.

The crystal was cut into nine major stones. The largest, Cullinan I, is a pendeloque brilliant with 74 facets weighing 530 carats; it is the largest cut diamond in the world. It is known as the Star of Africa, and is set in the head of the royal sceptre in the British regalia. Cullinan II is a cushion-shaped brilliant weighing 317 carats, and is set in the Imperial State Crown. Cullinan III is a 94-carat pendeloque brilliant, and Cullinan IV is a 63-carat square brilliant; both these were set in Queen Mary's coronation crown in 1911. Cullinans II, III and IV are known as the Lesser Stars of Africa. The five remaining major stones are considerably smaller; the largest weighs nearly 19 carats and the smallest just over 4 carats. 96 very small brilliants were cut from the remaining pieces.

Cultured pearls. See *Pearls*.

Cupel. A block of refractory material containing a cup-shaped depression in which metal is placed for purifying. (See *Cupellation*.)

Cupellation. The process of refining gold or silver by heating it in a porous crucible or cupel together with base metals, which oxidize and are absorbed by the cupel leaving the precious metal in a pure state. This method of refining was practised in the ancient world (see *Gold*, under *History*), and is the basis of modern assaying methods (see *Assaying*).

'Cupid's darts'. Rutilated quartz.

Curb chain. Chain with twisted links. (See *Chain*.)

Cushion-cut (cushion-shaped). A term for stones with a squarish outline and rounded corners. The facets usually follow the standard arrangement of the brilliant cut. (See *Diamond-cutting*.)

Cushion tool. See *Repoussé tools*.

Cut-down setting. A setting in which metal is worked up round the edge of the stone and reinforced with vertical metal ridges. It was much used in the eighteenth century. (See also *Settings*.)

Cuts of stones. See *Gem-cutting* and *Diamond-cutting*.

Cut-steel jewellery. Jewellery set with studs of faceted steel instead of gemstones probably first began to be made in the early eighteenth century, and well before the end of the century had become exceedingly fashionable. It was not a new invention, for ornamental sword-hilts and other articles had been made of steel in the seventeenth century and probably earlier, but the use of steel in jewellery was encouraged by the financial difficulties which were common to many parts of Europe in the mid-eighteenth century.

The first centres of production were Woodstock in Oxfordshire, and Birmingham. The work from Woodstock was said to be the finer, and was certainly made with great care – one of its features was that it could be dismantled for cleaning. It is not clear how long Woodstock continued to produce jewellery, but it is unlikely that when cut steel became really popular, from about the 1770s onwards, a small business could cope with the demand or compete with the enormous output of Birmingham (q.v.), which had been engaged in the light steel trade for a century. The most important manufacturer of cut-steel work in the later part of the century was Matthew Boulton (q.v.), who in partnership with a James Fothergill set up a factory near Birmingham in 1764, and owed much of his success to the fact that he brought all the processes of production under one roof.

The purpose of cut-steel jewellery was to imitate the brilliance of diamonds. This was achieved by the use of large numbers of densely-packed steel studs, faceted to reflect the light. (The candlelight of the eighteenth century would have created a much more sparkling effect than modern artificial lighting.) The greater the number of facets the more brilliant the effect, and the more expensive the piece of jewellery. In the eighteenth century there were sometimes as many as 15 facets on a large stud, but in the nineteenth-century work when standards began to decline the average number dropped to 5. The studs were individually faceted and then riveted to the base-plate, which might be of steel or some other base metal such as silver alloy or tin. In a complicated design several interlocking base-plates would be used, and in the earlier jewellery the base-plate was often reinforced by a solid backing.

Virtually every item of jewellery was made. Chatelaines, buckles and buttons were particularly popular in the later eighteenth century. Chatelaines ranged from the very modest, with a simple polished steel hook-plate and chains of faceted steel beads, to the very elaborate with a delicate openwork hook-plate and chains set with steel 'gems'. Buckles of all types and sizes were produced in great quantity until towards the end of the eighteenth century, when they went out of fashion. The demand for cut-steel buttons, which were worn ornamentally much more than for their practical function, was enormous, and they were exported to many parts of Europe as well as produced in great numbers for the home market.

Necklaces and bracelets show much of the finest work done in cut-steel. The most usual pattern for necklaces is a series of linked rosettes or stars, sometimes graded in size. The finest are those that have pendants. Bracelets also often consist of linked rosettes; the most elaborate have one large central rosette, often with a movable centre, closely set with steel studs, while the more modest ones are made of a series of linked sections of uniform width in a conventional pattern – interlinked circles, the Greek key design, etc. The bangles are less interesting and often consist simply of three rows of studs on a solid backing, with a flange clasp. Others have a central feature in the form of a rosette, buckle, star, or similar conventional shape.

Some of the surviving brooches are quite elaborate and have cascades of steel drops hanging from a large rosette. Most of them, however, seem to date from the mid-nineteenth century and conform to the contemporary fashion for bees, butterflies, lizards, and other representational themes.

Hair-ornaments were very fashionable in the nineteenth century and the cut-steel tiaras and combs are often very impressive. The combs in particular show fine workmanship with richly-studded formalized patterns on the crown. The comb itself was usually of tortoiseshell.

Apart from this combination with tortoiseshell in combs, cut-steel was frequently used in conjunction with other materials. The commonest was blue-and-white Wedgwood (q.v.) ware, made into plaques for setting in jewellery. Matthew Boulton was at one time working in association with Josiah Wedgwood in the production of this type of jewellery. Other materials set in cut steel included Bilston enamels (q.v.) and miniature Italian mosaics.

The trade in cut-steel jewellery was given an added impetus by the hardships caused by the French Revolutionary wars, but unfortunately for the British manufacturers the wars also cut off their export markets in Europe. By the time peace was restored the manufacture of cut-steel jewellery was firmly established in France. A Yorkshireman by the name of Sykes had set up a shop dealing in cut steel in France in about 1780, and his example was soon followed by the French jewellers, the first of whom was Dauffe. In the early nineteenth century the jewellers Frichot, Henriet and Schey were said to be making more money out of cut steel than the court jeweller was making out of diamonds. Napoleon, unable to afford precious stones, bought a splendid parure of cut steel for his second wife, Marie Louise of Austria.

During the nineteenth century the standards of workmanship in cut-steel jewellery declined sadly, the turning-point coming when it began to be made from stamped-out strips of metal instead of with individually faceted and riveted studs. Genuine cut steel continued to be made for some time, but it had lost its appeal and was virtually a dead craft by the end of the nineteenth century.

Cutting punches. Hardened steel punches with concave circular tips, used for cutting out circular sections of sheet metal. They are manufactured in a range of sizes.

Cuttlefish casting. Casting in a mould made from cuttlefish. The pattern is pressed into the soft bone, which takes a perfect impression, and molten metal is poured into this. (See *Casting* for more detailed account.)

Cyanite. See *Kyanite*.

Cymophane. Chrysoberyl cat's eye.

Cyprine. See *Idocrase*.

Cyst pearl. A natural pearl formed within the tissue of the oyster: the most perfect type of pearl. (See *Pearls*.)

D

Damascening. The art of inlaying metal with gold and silver, (see *Inlaying*). (This is the modern meaning of the word. It originally referred specifically to the ancient art, practised in India and the Near East, of producing a watered pattern in steel.)

'Damburite'. (Trade name.) A synthetic light corundum.

Danburite. (Calcium boro-silicate. S.G. 3.0; R.I. 1.63–1.64; H. 7.) A transparent colourless or yellow stone, closely similar to topaz in its crystal formation and often in appearance, although its colour is inferior to that of topaz. Its specific gravity (q.v.) is lower than that of topaz and higher than that of yellow quartz, which is useful in distinguishing it. Danburite is so called because it was first found at Danbury, Connecticut, but most of the gem material comes from the Mogok Stone Tract in Upper Burma.

Dark-field illumination. The illumination of specimens under a microscope by oblique instead of direct rays of light. This method is often valuable in the examination of gemstones, since the inclusions in the stone reflect the light and appear as bright areas on a dark ground; by direct illumination such inclusions are often much less clearly seen. The method is particularly favoured in America and Continental countries. Some gemmological microscopes incorporate special devices for producing oblique illumination, but the effect can be simply produced by placing a dark patch centrally below the substage condenser to cut the central rays of light from the microscope mirror.

The Darnley jewel

Darnley (Lennox) Jewel. This sixteenth-century jewel is typical of later Renaissance jewellery (q.v.) both in its richness and in its use of emblems possessing a secret meaning for the wearer; in this case the meaning has been lost. The jewel, which was made for Lady Margaret Douglas, mother of Lord Darnley, in memory of her husband the Earl of Lennox (died 1571) and as a gift for her grandson, later James I of England, is a heart-shaped gold pendant about $2\frac{1}{2}$ inches long. The front has a large heart-shaped cabochon sapphire between a pair of wings, under a crown set with rubies and an emerald. At the corners are four enamelled figures: Victory holding an olive branch, Truth holding a mirror,

Hope with an anchor, and Faith with a cross and a lamb. Both the crown and the sapphire open to show various mottoes and ciphers. Round the rim of the pendant runs the inscription: 'QVHA HOPIS STIL CONSTANLY VITH PATIENCE SAL OBTEIN VICTORIE IN YAIR PRETENCE'.

The reverse of the pendant is enamelled with a further series of emblems: the sun in glory and the crescent moon, a crowned salamander in flames, a pelican in her piety, a phoenix in flames, and the reclining figure of a man with a sunflower growing from a crown on one side and a laurel bush with birds on the other. The inscription round the edge reads: 'MY STAIT TO YIR I MAY COMPAER FOR ZOU QHA IS OF BONTES RAIR'. The locket opens to display a miniature, which is now missing but was presumably that of Lennox. The inside of the locket is enamelled with a number of emblems of even greater obscurity: a stake surrounded by flames with crosses in them; a crowned lady in a royal chair; a two-faced figure holding an hourglass and pulling a female figure (Truth) out of a well; Hell with demons; and two warriors, one standing victorious over his foe and the other, who is crowned, holding a female figure by the hair with his sword drawn to slay. Although the precise meaning of all these figures can only be guessed at, it is clear that they refer to the political intrigues of Lady Margaret Douglas and her relations with Mary Queen of Scots and Queen Elizabeth.

The jewel was once in the possession of Horace Walpole, from whom it was purchased to be given later to Queen Victoria. It is now in the collection of H.M. the Queen.

Dary-i-noor. A rose-cut diamond said to weigh 186 carats which was among the loot taken from Delhi in 1739 by Nadir Shah. Its name means 'River of light'. It has been identified with the Great Mogul (q.v.), which in turn might be the same stone as the Orloff or Koh-i-noor (qq.v.). However, it is said to have been seen among the Persian crown jewels in 1827, in which case it could not be identical with either of these stones. Another suggestion is that it was re-cut from the Great Table diamond (q.v.).

Datolite. (Calcium boro-silicate. S.G. 2.9–3.0; R.I. 1.63–1.67; H. 5.) A stone rarely used in jewellery: it may be either transparent and colourless (or palely tinted with green or yellow), or granular and varying in colour from cream to brown. The transparent variety is cut for collectors; the granular variety is sometimes cut en cabochon for ornamental wear.

The best gem-quality material comes from Habachtal, near Salzburg, Austria. Other sources include the U.S.A. and Cornwall.

Davidsonite. A yellowish-green beryl.

Dear pearl. A pearl which lacks lustre.

De Beers Consolidated Mines Ltd. The foremost diamond-producing concern in the world, with a controlling interest in the mines of South Africa and South-West Africa, an extensive network of associations with diamond-producers in other parts of the world, and investments in many other industrial concerns apart from diamonds.

The company was the creation of Cecil Rhodes, who first arrived in South Africa in 1870 at the age of 17 and in 1880 founded the De Beers Mining Company, in which were amalgamated the De Beers mine (discovered in 1871) and several others. After a bitter financial struggle with his rival Barney Barnato, Rhodes, who had obtained the backing of the Rothschilds, bought control of Barnato's company in 1888 and formed a new company under the name of De Beers Consolidated Mines Ltd. By a series of amalgamations the company subsequently acquired control of all the other important South African mines.

Following this consolidation, a syndicate of diamond merchants in South Africa and London attempted to establish a marketing policy which would keep the price of diamonds stable. The attempt was largely successful as long as South Africa continued to be the world's leading source of diamonds, but in the early years of this century extensive deposits of alluvial diamonds began to be discovered in other parts of Africa and in 1928 the yield from alluvial deposits was greater than that from deep mining. It was increasingly difficult to finance the sale of these large quantities of diamonds and to ensure that output from the new mines was limited, and when the world recession came the diamond industry was on the verge of disaster. At this point the late Sir Ernest Oppenheimer, who had recently been appointed chairman of De Beers, formed the Diamond Corporation as a sales channel. In 1934 negotiations between the Corporation and the diamond-producers in South and South-West Africa resulted in the formation of the Diamond Producers' Association, the members of which agreed to market their diamonds through the Corporation on a quota basis. The Diamond Trading Company was formed to deal with the actual selling of the diamonds. Subsequently another company, Industrial Distributors (Sales) Ltd., was formed to market the industrial diamonds, and the Corporation was thus left free to act as a link between the De Beers group of companies and producers outside the group.

This policy of seeking co-operation from other diamond-producers has proved very fruitful, and over 85% of the world's diamonds are now sorted and marketed through the Central Selling Organization of which the companies mentioned above are the nucleus. The organization contracts periodically to purchase the output of diamond-producing countries irrespective of the current demand for diamonds, thus safeguarding the producers against temporary recessions (which of course would be particularly damaging to the developing countries where diamond-mining is a major source of revenue). The diamonds are released on to the market at a rate which enables price stability to be maintained, and, to ensure that the public do not lose interest in the commodity around which this enormous organization is built, the C.S.O. mounts large-scale international advertising campaigns to publicize diamond jewellery, and by means of international competitions seeks to stimulate new ideas in jewellery design.

The C.S.O. has offices in South Africa and London, and it is to the London offices in Charterhouse Street that the diamonds are sent to be sorted, valued and sold. (See *Diamond*.)

Engraved design for a pendant by Etienne Delaune

Delaune, Etienne (1518–1583?). One of the most gifted designers of goldsmiths' work and jewellery in the Renaissance period (see *Renaissance jewellery*). Delaune was born at Orléans and was principal medallist to Henri II of France, but being a Huguenot was forced to flee to Strasbourg in 1572 to escape religious persecution. Several years later he became associated with, or perhaps actually established, a workshop at Augsburg, where he published a widely-circulated series of engraved designs for goldsmiths. His designs for jewels, which involve an elaborate use of the masks, strapwork and other motifs of the Mannerist style, reveal a fine sense of harmony coupled with a firm grasp of the practical side of the jeweller's work; it has been assumed from this that he was himself a working goldsmith, but this has never been established.

'De la Mar pearls'. (Trade name.) Imitation pearls. (For imitation pearls, see *Pearls*.)

Delawarite. Aventurine feldspar from Delaware Co., Pennsylvania.

'Delta pearls'. (Trade name.) Imitation pearls. (For imitation pearls, see *Pearls*.)

Demantoid. See *Andradite*.

Demi-parure. A small matching set of jewellery (literally 'half a parure'). It might consist of a brooch with matching earrings, a necklace with bracelet, etc. (See *Parure*.)

Dendritic. Resembling a tree or fern. The word is used to describe minerals which assume this form, the commonest examples being the inclusions which appear in moss agate. (See *Agate*.)

Density (of stones). See *Specific gravity*.

Dentelle. A term sometimes used for the lower 18 facets of a rose-cut stone. (See *Diamond-cutting*.)

Desert glass. Natural glass. (See *Obsidian* and *Tektite*.)

Devotional jewellery. The earliest form of jewellery which bore specifically Christian symbols or inscriptions was the signet ring of the early Christians. While rings were worn in abundance in the pagan Roman Empire, the early Church exhorted its followers to wear only one ring, a signet, which at that time was essential for the sealing of documents. Since pagan or other undesirable elements were apt to creep into the devices on signet rings, St. Clement of Alexandria advised Christians to use one of the accepted Christian symbols: the palm branch (signifying peace), a ship in full sail (symbol of the Church), an anchor (symbol of hope), a dove, a fish (symbol of Christ), etc. Many rings survive bearing these devices and other symbols such as the Cross and the Chi Rho monogram. The rings are often

of bronze or iron, but were also made in precious metal.

The signet ring with a religious device became commonplace in Byzantium, but as the wealth of the empire increased jewellery became more luxurious. Much of Byzantine jewellery is of a religious nature, but is executed with a richness of materials and workmanship which is completely foreign to the asceticism of the early Christians (see *Byzantine jewellery*). A good example is the Beresford-Hope cross in the Victoria and Albert museum; this dates from about the eighth century and consists of two hinged cruciform plates of gold which formerly contained a sacred relic. It is decorated with translucent enamels, one side showing Christ on the cross with the Virgin and St. John, the other side showing a full-length picture of the Virgin surrounded by the heads of four saints. Of about the same date was the pendant reliquary worn by Charlemagne, containing parts of the Crown of Thorns and the Cross under a large sapphire set in gold and surrounded by precious stones. It is said to have been given to Charlemagne by Haroun-al-Raschid. These two jewels are among the earliest pendant reliquaries known, and they illustrate quite clearly the shift from the ideal of simplicity and the use of religious symbols purely as symbols and nothing more, to the veneration of sacred objects *per se* and the idea that only the finest workmanship and the best possible materials should be used in the treatment of religious subjects. This attitude developed further during the Middle Ages and was responsible for the many superb and elaborate reliquaries produced in Western Europe.

During the thirteenth century a new element entered western Christianity and was spread by the mendicant orders: it was an emotional piety which emphasised the bond between God and man and concentrated on the suffering figure of Christ. It culminated in the mystical movements of the fourteenth century. From the fourteenth and fifteenth cen-

95

Devotional jewellery

turies date many beautifully delicate
devotional pendants. Among the pendant
reliquaries of this period is a small jewel,
now in the British Museum, said to have
been given by St. Louis to an Aragonese
king: the outer case consists of two large
cabochon amethysts enclosing an inner
case which once contained a relic from the
Crown of Thorns. The inner lids are
decorated with small translucent enamels
depicting the Crucifixion and other
scenes from the life and Passion of Christ.
Many reliquaries were in the form of
hinged tablets which opened out into a
diptych or triptych enamelled with
religious scenes. A fine example made at
about the end of the fourteenth century
opens into a triptych of which the
central panel is enamelled with a half-
length figure of the suffering Christ
between two angels holding the Crown of
Thorns. Below this is a small compartment
which once held a piece of Christ's
mantle.

Reliquaries such as these were worn on
a chain round the neck or suspended from
the girdle. Richly-enamelled gold reliquaries containing such important relics
as part of the Crown of Thorns could of
course only be afforded by the nobility,
but as the poorer classes could buy relics
of extremely dubious authenticity from
the travelling preachers, pendant reliquaries of much lower intrinsic value
were also produced by the goldsmiths.
Towards the end of the Middle Ages a
considerable number of silver and silver-
gilt reliquary pendants were produced in
Germany. An extremely popular pendant
of the reliquary type was the Agnus Dei:
this consisted of a small circular box,
usually of silver-gilt, containing a wax
medallion which had been made from the
Paschal candle at Rome, stamped with the
impression of the Lamb of God and blessed
by the Pope for distribution to the
faithful. The box itself was decorated with
the figure of the Lamb in niello or
repoussé. Other substitutes for relics were
pieces of vellum on which were written
verses from the Bible or the names of
Christ, the Virgin Mary, or the saints.

*German pendant with figure of St. Sebastian,
about 1500. Österr. Museum für angewandte
Kunst, Vienna*

The cult of the saints resulted in the
production of large numbers of medallion
pendants bearing the figures of saints,
and pendants in which the figures were
wrought in high relief. Among the silver
and silver-gilt devotional ornaments produced by German craftsmen in the
fifteenth century is a large pendant in the
shape of a Gothic tabernacle with four
niches each containing the figure of a
saint; surmounting the whole are the
figures of the Virgin and Child. A simpler
pendant in the same sculptural style is
illustrated.

The saints also appeared on rings. There
is a large class of devotional rings which
have the figure of a saint or some other
sacred personage engraved on the bezel;
they are usually enamelled and have
wreathed hoops, and appear to have been
common only in England. The favourite
subjects included the Virgin and Child,
the Trinity, St. John the Baptist, and the
saints Barbara, Catharine, Christopher,
George and Margaret. Wearing an object
which bore the figure of a saint was not

merely an act of piety; it was thought to protect the wearer, as were the sacred relics. These inconographic rings were often engraved with non-religious mottoes such as 'mon coeur avez', 'en bon an', suggesting that they were used as betrothal rings and New Year gifts.

Rings also contained relics; many are mentioned in medieval records and inventories. Gregory the Great presented to certain princes rings containing filings from St. Peter's chains; a piece of the Cross was set in an iron ring for the sister of St. Gregory of Nyssa; and in 1427 Elizabeth, Lady Fitz-Hugh bequeathed to her son 'a ring with a relic of St. Peter's finger'.

An interesting class of devotional rings are the decade rings which date mostly from the sixteenth century or later. These have a series of knobs, usually ten, set around the hoop, and an engraving of the cross, sometimes combined with other religious symbols, on the bezel. These rings were used in the same way as rosary beads for the recitation of Aves; the ring was placed on one of the fingers and turned with the thumb, an Ave being repeated for each knob, and when the cross on the bezel was reached the Paternoster was said. It has been suggested that the rings, being much less conspicuous than a rosary, were used by Roman Catholics during times of religious persecution.

Rosaries themselves became increasingly elaborate during the later Middle Ages and at various times it was fashionable to wear them as necklaces and bracelets. Some were made of beads which opened to show carved or enamelled religious scenes inside. The craftsmanship in these miniature works is superb. One which is now in the Louvre is made of agate beads containing enamelled scenes in relief from the life of Christ. Another is enamelled with scenes from the life of the Virgin. A small rosary which belonged to Henry VIII is in boxwood; the Ave beads are carved with the articles of the Creed, Apostles and Old Testament figures, and the Paternoster bead bears the King's name and arms and opens to reveal carvings of the Mass of St. Gregory and the Virgin and Child. The rosary, which is only of one decade, hangs from a finger-ring. Few rosaries would be as elaborate as these, but many were made of valuable materials: gold (sometimes engraved and nielloed), carved coral, amber, crystal, chalcedony, lapis lazuli and silver gilt. For children's rosaries there were beads of white bone. Ornaments or trinkets, called gaudees, were attached to the rosary, and there was also of course a pendant cross or crucifix. (Crosses were also worn as pendants on their own; they were often very ornate and decorated with a flower or foliage design.) The manufacture of rosary-beads was a thriving business by the end of the Middle Ages, as the names of the little streets around St. Paul's Cathedral, Paternoster Row and Ave Maria Lane – where the bead-turners had their shops – testify.

An extremely popular devotional jewel in the late Middle Ages was the pilgrim's badge. These were simple cast medallions, usually of lead or pewter (perhaps gilded), issued by the many centres of pilgrimage and showing the effigy or symbol of the actual place of pilgrimage; they are possibly the earliest example of souvenir jewellery. Their popularity may be judged from the fact that in 1466 one monastery alone (Einsiedeln) issued 130,000 of them. The fourteenth-century poet Langland describes a much-travelled pilgrim as wearing 'an hundred' of such badges, which was probably an exaggeration but certainly not an impossibility. Even the nobility wore these badges – though not, of course, in base metal. They were worn on the hat, and were probably the forerunners of the splendid hat-badges of the sixteenth century (see *Renaissance jewellery*).

Devotional jewellery is not a tidy category to which a piece either does or does not belong. Devotional and secular elements are frequently combined in medieval jewels, a notable example being the fashion for pendants with a religious scene and perhaps a space for a

Devotional jewellery

relic on one side, and a vanity-mirror on the other. Often jewels combined a religious picture with a love-motto (the iconographic rings mentioned above are an example of this), and even the Paternoster beads of rosaries were sometimes decorated with secular motifs. Conversely, an otherwise secular piece of jewellery might have a religious inscription engraved on it. Certain inscriptions occur very frequently on medieval jewellery: the names of the Three Kings, the last saying of Christ, the *titulus* of the Cross (Iesus Nazarenus Rex Iudaeorum), the Ave Maria, and verse 30 of St. Luke iv. The popularity of these texts is explained by the fact that they were believed to exert a protective power on behalf of the wearer. In other words, they were thought to be magical.

It is impossible to draw a dividing line between magical and religious elements in medieval jewellery because no such distinction existed in the minds of the people who made and wore it. It is only a short step from using a relic as an aid to spiritual contemplation or invoking a saint as an intercessor or protector, to incorporating the relic, the saint's image or a written invocation in a jewel which is then regarded as possessing certain supernatural properties in its own right. The step was taken at a very early stage, and by the end of the Middle Ages not only were religious images and texts being used in a magical way but they were being used side by side with symbols and inscriptions derived from pagan magical traditions. There are innumerable examples of this incongruous combination (see also *Magical jewellery*). A fifteenth-century gold ring found at Coventry, for instance, is engraved with a typical series of pious images (see illustration): Christ standing in the tomb, the Cross and the instruments of the Passion, and the Five Wounds and their descriptions ('the well of pitty, the well of merci, the well of confort, the well of gracy (grace), the well of everlastingh lyffe'). Inside the hoop is a further series of inscriptions: Vulnera quinque dei sunt medicina mei,

98

The Coventry ring. British Museum

pia crux et passio xpi sunt medicina michi, jaspar melchior baltasar ananyzapta tetragrammaton. The first two lines of this are a common pious inscription, but the names of the Three Kings were a protective charm against epilepsy, as also was 'ananyzapta', a magical word of unknown origin, while 'Tetragrammaton' is one of the Ten Names of God and was frequently used as a word of power. Certain devotional symbols were also thought to be particularly powerful; the Cross is an obvious example, and the Tau cross was also thought to be a powerful amulet. This symbol, which is in the shape of the Greek letter T, became the emblem of St. Anthony because it was thought to resemble the stick which he would have carried as a swineherd, but from an early date mystical associations gathered round it because of its resemblance to the Cross, and it was thought to be the mark which was set on the foreheads of the elect in the vision of Ezekiel (Ez. chap. 9).

Medieval theologians were aware of the delicate line between religion and magic. St. Thomas Aquinas when questioned about the use of inscriptions replied that they were only permissible 'if no evil spirits were therein invoked, no incomprehensible words used, no deceit or belief in any other power than the power of God, no character used other than the sign of the Cross, and no faith placed in the manner of the inscription'. It is unlikely that many of the inscribed devotional jewels of the time fulfilled all these conditions.

With the Reformation the more crudely superstitious elements of religion were discarded, although of course superstition persisted among the uneducated. Reliquary pendants or rings were not worn by Protestants. A type of devotional jewel which can have offended few sensibilities and was fashionable throughout the

IHS pendant made about 1600; diamonds set in enamelled gold. Victoria and Albert Museum

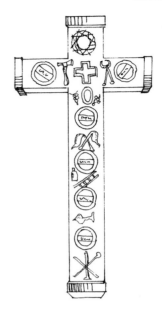

Spanish devotional pendant of about 1580; rock crystal with compartments for relics, and the instruments of the Passion in enamelled gold. Metropolitan Museum of Art, New York

sixteenth century and for some time afterwards was a pendant in the form of the IHS monogram (see illustration). In Spain, the stronghold of Catholicism, the traditional types of devotional jewellery of course continued to be worn. The Spanish devotional jewels of the Renaissance period are of extremely fine workmanship and are sometimes executed in the difficult and delicate technique of verre églomisé (q.v.). The pendant cross bearing the emblems of Christ's Passion (see illustration) seems to have been a fairly popular type in Spain. Devotional jewellery has continued to be worn in Catholic countries until the present time, although it now forms a class of popular, as distinct from precious, jewellery. In non-Catholic countries, however, it is difficult to think of any religious emblem which is now acceptable as jewellery apart from the simple pendant cross. (One can hardly count St. Christopher, particularly since his demotion.)

Diadems. The wearing of a diadem as a mark of nobility or royalty is an extremely ancient custom, and the forms which diadems have assumed are so diverse that it is very difficult to generalize about them or to trace a continuous line of development. The diadems of some of the Eastern Kings in ancient times were extremely ornate and heavy, while in classical times supreme power was often denoted in the simplest way – by a band of cloth worn round the head and tied in a knot behind. When Gibbon says of Diocletian that he 'ventured to assume the diadem', the diadem in question was only a fillet of white cloth set with pearls. Yet much richer head-dresses had been worn at an earlier date, notably by the Egyptians.

Some of the diadems of the Egyptian princesses are amazingly delicate. One which belonged to the Princess Khnemt is made of delicate flowers in gold wire, inlaid with stones, and has all the fragility of a wreath made of real wild flowers. Another consists of fine rings of gold strung from a gold head-band and falling over the temples. Although the basic form of the diadem of the pharaohs – a gold band meeting in a stylized knot at the back of the head – was simple enough, the inlaying of coloured stones became more lavish in time, and the figures of the vulture and the sacred cobra, fixed to the front of the diadem as the protectors of royalty, are often superbly modelled and inlaid. Long metal streamers hanging down at the back completed this imposing head-dress. The finest example is the diadem of Tutankhamun, described under *Egyptian jewellery*. As a complete contrast, the diadem of one of the wives of Tuthmosis III is decorated at the front with the beautifully-modelled heads of two gazelles in solid gold. Gazelles were the insignia of the royal concubines.

The earliest diadems found in the Greek world are made of gold or silver sheet decorated with simple patterns of dots embossed from the back. As in Egypt, some diadems were made purely for funerary use, and it is not always easy to tell whether a surviving piece was made for the living or for burial. By the Mycenean period the upper edge of the diadem was sometimes decorated with attached gold leaves or rosettes – the forerunner of the pinnacled crown (see *Crowns*). Dot-repoussé had now been replaced by embossed circles and other patterns, and on Cyprian diadems of the same period the designs – rosettes, palmettes, spirals and animal-forms – were embossed with a stamp. A new type of diadem appears in the Greek islands in the seventh century B.C. – a band of leather or some other material to which were attached elaborate gold rosettes. These rosettes are beautifully decorated with filigree and granulation, embossed work, and attached figures of animals' heads, birds, insects, etc.

In classical times the diadem of sheet gold decorated with embossed patterns was joined by the wreath. Extremely naturalistic imitations of wreaths of real leaves were made in gold, silver, and materials plated with gold, and were worn on ceremonial occasions such as processions, given as prizes, and also buried with the dead. These continued to be made in the Hellenistic period, by which time a very elaborate type of diadem had been developed. This had a centrepiece in the form of a Heracles-knot (i.e. a reef-knot) – a popular amuletic symbol – inlaid with garnets and set in a decorated framework, the rest of the diadem consisting of chains or bands of gold from which hung complicated pendants.

Wreaths were awarded by the Romans for valour, and in the days of the Republic they were of real leaves. The highest honour was a wreath of grass; it was given to the commander who delivered a besieged army. A wreath of bay leaves was worn by a victorious general at his triumph, a wreath of oak leaves was awarded for saving the life of a fellow-soldier. There were several other kinds, and usually only certain ranks were eligible for them. Under the Empire, however, the system gradually lost its meaning; a gold crown was introduced in

Greek silver wreath of fifth or fourth century B.C. British Museum

place of the oak wreath, awards were given without merit, and many decorations could only be awarded to the Imperial family. The laurel wreath of the victorious general was worn by Roman Emperors regardless of their martial prowess, and thus became a symbol of supreme power. In time the luxurious habits of the East infiltrated Roman society, and the Emperors adopted first the radiated crown which had originated in the sun-worship of the East, and then a diadem of gold and precious stones. In the Byzantine Empire, which inherited both Roman culture and the traditions of the East, this tendency was naturally strengthened, and a mosaic of the Empress Theodora shows her wearing an extremely elaborate head-dress set with pearls and jewels and having long pendant strings of jewels hanging down to below the shoulders.

In Western Europe during the early Middle Ages the pinnacled crown began to develop towards its present form and was worn as the symbol of kingship (see *Crowns*), but plainer head-ornaments based on the simple band or wreath were worn by those not of royal birth, generally by women. They consisted either of narrow bands of metal, sometimes decorated with pearls and precious stones, or an embroidered band on to which were sewn gold flowers (the latter are described in inventories as 'chaplets'). During the fourteenth century circlets were often made of hinged plaques of embossed metal, and at about the same time the fleur-de-lys began to appear on the upper edge. Diadems such as these were not confined to the nobility – many of them were of quite cheap workmanship and materials – but the wearing of them gradually crystallized into a system of privilege and in this sense they are the forerunners of the modern coronets of the peerage (though in form these are a modest version of the modern royal crown).

In the following centuries jewelled head-dresses might be worn at Court but were not a regular part of jewellery; in

Mid-nineteenth century diadem in antique style; gold set with carbuncles

Tiara made by Giuliano about 1890, set with four large topazes

the nineteenth century, however, they returned to fashion with the pomp of the Napoleonic empire, and owing to the Empress Josephine's fondness for engraved gems, were very often set with cameos. The diadem, which by now was often confined to a semicircle with the ornament concentrated in the front, was worn as part of a parure. Diadems became widely popular in the 1850s and followed the current enthusiasms for ancient jewellery; there were 'Gothic' diadems of remarkable ugliness surmounted by architectural pinnacles, and simpler varieties set with cabochon gems. Floral designs were also popular. Diamond tiaras were worn during this period, but their greatest popularity was reserved for the last decade of the century when a new source of diamonds had been discovered in South Africa; the forms of these late-

101

Victorian tiaras range from conservative coronets to delicate designs in the Art Nouveau style. Necklaces were often made in such a way that the central portion could be worn as a tiara. This was the heyday of the jewelled head-ornament: with the increasing informality of social life the market for diadems and tiaras has sadly declined, and those that are worn are not likely to be of modern design.

'Diakon'. One of the trade names for acrylic plastic. (See *Plastics*.)

Diamanté. Colourless paste, or imitation jewellery set with it.

Diamantine. (Trade name.) An abrasive consisting of aluminium oxide.

Diamond. (Carbon; S.G. 3.52; R.I. 2.417; H. 10.) A transparent, usually colourless precious stone, the hardest of all natural substances, popularly thought to be the most valuable stone although in fact its price may be lower than that of a fine emerald. Diamond is not an uncommon stone: its high price is due partly to the fact that both the production from the major sources and the release of diamonds on to the market are controlled, and partly to the considerable amount of skilled work involved in fashioning the stone, which requires different treatment from other gemstones because of its hardness and unique optical properties.

The important optical characteristics of diamond (a singly-refractive stone) are pronounced colour dispersion and a high refractive index (qq.v.). Light entering the stone is broken up into the colours of the spectrum, producing the 'fire' which is the outstanding feature of diamonds. The high refractive index means that a high proportion of the light which strikes the stone undergoes total internal reflection (q.v.) within it, being thrown from one facet to another so that the stone appears to be filled with light. The combination of these qualities together with the characteristic adamantine lustre account for the diamond's peculiar beauty, but they are only fully displayed when the stone is cut in the brilliant style (see *Diamond-cutting*), and it is only since this cut was invented that diamonds have been so highly esteemed.

The extraordinary hardness of diamond (see *Hardness*) results from its very closely-packed atomic structure. It belongs to the cubic system (see *Crystal systems*) and crystallizes usually in octahedral or dodecahedral form. However, many variations, some extremely distorted, occur, and since in addition the more rounded type of crystals are frequently covered with a skin of other material it is not surprising that on several occasions when new sources of diamonds were discovered the stones were not immediately recognized. The origin of diamonds is not understood. They are found either in alluvial deposits, which give no clue to their source, or in vertical pipes of igneous rock which are believed to have been forced up from great depths in the earth. The crystals are obviously formed under enormous heat and pressure, and since their composition is pure carbon it should not be difficult to synthesize them, but so far this has proved impossible except for very small crystals which do not approach gem quality. (See *Synthetic gemstones*.)

The preferred colour for gem diamonds is water-white, but many other colours occur: brown, yellow, pink, red, blue and green. These are called 'fancy stones' and their value is rather unpredictable; fine specimens may command high prices but it is rare for the colour to be evenly distributed through the stone. The colour is thought to be due to defects in the crystal lattice and not to traces of other minerals, as is the case with most gemstones. 'Colourless' diamonds have very faint tinges of colour, usually only recognizable to the expert eye, and are classified in a graded system of which the main classes are blue-whites, whites, Capes, browns, and yellows. 'Blue-white' diamonds, which are often of the finest quality, have a faint bluish tinge which may be an effect of fluorescence; this classification is less used than in the past because it has often been abused. A perfectly clear and flawless stone is said to be 'of the first water'. Diamonds are colour-graded by hand and eye, and the system for grading them is far from uniform in different parts of the world. An instrument called a colorimeter, on which stones can be matched against standardized depths of colour, is now used in some countries.

It is unlikely that diamonds have been known for much more than two thousand years. The stone in Aaron's breastplate (Exodus 28, xviii) which is called a diamond could not have been one, for it could not have been engraved at that time. (The word 'adamant' [q.v.], from which 'diamond' is derived, was applied in antiquity to the hardest known substance, and therefore could not be used of diamond until diamonds were in circulation.) Diamonds make their first appearance, uncut, in late Roman jewellery, and appear sporadically in the jewellery of the Middle Ages. The pointed natural octahedron of diamond is itself an attractive stone with a certain sparkle

Renaissance ring set with a pointed crystal of diamond

(such crystals, set in rings, were popular into the seventeenth century – see illustration), but comparatively few crystals are of perfect form and many of the diamonds worn in the Middle Ages were rough and unattractive. The main virtue of the diamond lay in its hardness, and since gemstones were at the time credited with supernatural powers (see *Magical jewellery*) the diamond was believed to bestow on its wearer invincibility in battle and numerous other blessings. (It was also believed for many centuries that, being so hard, a diamond would

resist the blow of a hammer. This is not so; diamond is brittle and cleaves readily along certain planes, and many stones must have been destroyed in this test.)

Being harder than all other substances, diamond can only be abraded by its own powder. The art of diamond-cutting seems to have been invented some time during the fourteenth century, and the earliest cut was the table cut in which the tip of the octahedron was ground away leaving a flat rectangular surface. This remained the basic style until the sixteenth century, when the rose cut, in which the stone was covered with small triangular facets, was introduced. This greatly increased the sparkle of the stone and during the seventeenth century diamonds rose high in popularity. Then at the end of the seventeenth century the brilliant cut was invented by a Venetian, Vincento Perruzzi; this revealed for the first time the amazing fire of the diamond. Twenty-five years later a new source of diamonds was discovered in Brazil – hitherto the only source of European diamonds had been India, which had provided the very earliest stones. The combination of these discoveries made the eighteenth century the era of the diamond (see *Eighteenth-century jewellery*). Since then many other sources have been discovered, and the diamond has not only retained its pre-eminent position as a gemstone but has come to play a vital role in industry. (See *Diamond-cutting* for a description of the various cuts and their history.)

The diamonds used by industry are those which are not of gem quality because they are too small, of a bad colour, or of unsuitable structure. There are several types. Carbonado is a black variety which has no cleavage and is therefore extremely tough; it was used in rock drills until it became very scarce. It is extremely valuable. Ballas is a multi-crystalline form which also has no cleavage and again is very scarce. 'Boart' is a collective term covering all other industrial-grade diamonds. There are innumerable uses for boart in industry, both as an abrasive, and in tools and machinery where a high

Diamond

resistance to abrasion and chemical action are needed.

Sources of diamond. India, the oldest source, is now unimportant. There are three main deposits, of which the most important in early times was the area on the eastern slopes of the Deccan near the river Kristna, where the famous Golconda (q.v.) mines are situated. The Koh-i-Noor is reputed to have come from this area, as are many other historic Indian stones. The only mines which are productive now are those near Panna in Central India, where good octahedral crystals of a light green colour are found in alluvial terraces, in conglomerate, and in a volcanic pipe similar to those in the South African diamond fields.

Diamonds were discovered in the early eighteenth century in *Brazil* by gold-prospectors who did not realize what they were and were using them as chips in their card games when the stones were recognized by a Portuguese diamond-dealer. For a time they had to be marketed as Indian stones because the Dutch diamond-merchants feared that news of the discovery would upset the market. The original find was in the area now known as Diamantina in Minas Gerais. This has continued to be a productive region, and there are now numerous less important sources as well as a rich deposit at Bahia. Brazil produces carbonado and ballas (see above), as well as good gem-quality stones, the most notable example being the 'President Vargas' diamond weighing 726 carats. The stones occur chiefly in river deposits, in a gravel known as 'cascalho', from which they are recovered by mostly primitive methods.

South Africa is now by far the most important source of gem diamonds. The first diamond was found in 1866 on the banks of the Orange river; the children of a farmer brought it home as a pretty pebble. It was finally identified as a diamond of 21 carats and named the 'Eureka' (q.v.) diamond. When three years later a crystal weighing over 83 carats was found (the 'Star of South

Africa'), the trickle of prospectors to the area became a flood. There were no dramatic finds along the Vaal or Orange rivers until 1870, when rich alluvial deposits were found at Klipdrift, now Barkly West. These deposits, known as 'river diggings', have continued to produce gem diamonds of very high quality. The real wealth, however, lay in the arid country south-east of the river: in 1870 and 1871 diamonds were found at a number of farms in this area – Jagersfontein, Dutoitspan, Bultfontein, Vooruitzigt (later De Beers mine) and Colesberg Kopje (later renamed Kimberley). After a lapse of some years there were further discoveries at Wesselton (1890) and at a site some 20 miles east of Pretoria. This last was the Premier mine, discovered in 1902, the richest in South Africa.

The early miners on the 'dry diggings' found the diamonds in a loose surface deposit which they assumed was the only gem-bearing layer. Having struck a yellowish bedrock underneath this most of them abandoned their claims. However, the diamonds were found to continue into the yellow rock, and then into the harder blue rock which lay 50 to 60 feet below it. The surface of each mine, which was roughly elliptical in shape, was in fact the mouth of a vertical 'pipe' of iron-rich igneous rock (kimberlite) which had oxidized at its upper level to a yellowish colour and weathered to a gravelly layer at the surface. The diamonds were found only in these volcanic pipes, never in the surrounding rock which they penetrated. The claims therefore had to be worked vertically downwards, and soon the narrow roadways between them, and the surrounding rock itself, began to collapse. By the late 1880s open-pit mining had been more or less abandoned and it was clear that the only future lay in under-ground mining by shaft, for which financial backing and co-operation were essential. An epic struggle for financial control of the mines between Cecil Rhodes and Barney Barnato resulted in 1888 in the purchase of Barnato's company, the Kimberley Central, by Rhodes, who formed a new company under the name of De Beers Consolidated Mines. This company subsequently acquired the other pipe mines, and now exerts a controlling influence in the world's diamond markets (see *De Beers*).

The diamond-bearing pipes extend downwards to an unknown depth and the supply of diamonds therefore seems to be, for all practical purposes, inexhaustible. Mining is highly mechanized. A main shaft is sunk through the rock surrounding the pipe, and horizontal shafts are driven from it into the pipe at intervals, connecting with the level above. The 'blue ground' containing the diamonds is removed in stages, working backwards along the shaft, and is brought to the surface and crushed. The crushed ore is then passed over greased shaking-tables, and the diamonds adhere to the grease while the other materials are washed away. (Some diamonds do not stick to grease and other methods have to be used for the separation.) The diamonds are sent to be graded and sold by the Central Selling Organization in London, which handles the bulk of the world's diamond production (see 'Sorting and marketing', below).

Other African sources of diamond include South-West Africa, the Congo, Ghana, Sierra Leone and Tanzania. Rich marine deposits are found along the coastal belt of South-West Africa, and are mainly worked by a branch of the De Beers group. The Congo produces more diamonds, by weight, than any other country, but about 95 per cent are of industrial grade only. Most of the material from Ghana is also of industrial quality. Sierra Leone, where diamonds were found in 1930, produces a quantity of well-crystallized diamonds of good quality. All the above sources are alluvial deposits, but in Tanzania diamonds are mined from a kimberlite pipe which is the largest in Africa. This is the Williamson mine, which has produced a number of large diamonds including one of 240 carats.

Diamonds occur in various other countries including the U.S.A., but the deposits are not of much commercial importance. They have been found since very early times in Borneo and Indonesia, but are usually not more than one carat in weight. These diamonds are unusually hard and are marketed in the East. Russia also produces diamonds, but the extent of production is not known.

Sorting and marketing. Over 85% of the world's rough diamonds, of both gem and industrial quality, are sent to London to be sorted, valued and marketed through the Central Selling Organization (see *De Beers*). The industrial diamonds, which amount to about 75% of the total in terms of weight, are sold by Industrial Distributors (Sales) Ltd., while gem diamonds are handled by the Diamond Trading Company, both being subsidiary companies of the CSO. The gem diamonds are sorted into five main categories: (1) *Stones,* diamonds of a regular shape weighing over 1 carat; (2) *Cleavages,* pieces of diamond which have broken along the cleavage plane; (3) *Macles,* triangular-shaped twinned diamonds, and *Flats,* flattish irregular crystals; (4) *Mélée,* diamonds weighing less than 1 carat but of a good shape; (5) *Chips,* small cleavages. Within these main categories the diamonds are sorted into many other classes, including colour and clarity. There are altogether more than 2000 classifications. (It takes seven years to train a diamond-sorter.) The diamonds are sold at 'sights' held ten times a year at the London offices of the Diamond Trading Company. Shortly before each 'sight' some two hundred regular customers from the main diamond-cutting centres are invited to submit a list of their requirements, and parcels of suitable rough diamonds are made up for their inspection. The buyers inspect their parcels in private rooms facing a north light, and are under no obligation to buy. (The large stocks held in reserve by the CSO protect diamond merchants from fluctuations in supply and demand which could prove disastrous in a luxury market.)

Identification and valuation. The commonest diamond simulant is the heat-treated white zircon, which has considerable fire. Zircon, however, is doubly refractive, and shows an apparent doubling of the back facet-edges if looked at from the front under a magnifying glass. (The stone must be rotated because there is one direction in which this doubling is not seen.) The facet-edges of a diamond will appear as single sharp lines. Two synthetic stones used as diamond simulants, strontium titanate ('Fabulite') and synthetic rutile ('Titania'), betray themselves to the experienced eye by having too much fire; strontium titanate has about 4 times and synthetic rutile 6 times as much fire as diamond. Also strontium titanate is much heavier than diamond, and synthetic rutile has a yellowish tinge and exhibits strong double refraction. Synthetic white sapphire and synthetic white spinel have considerably less fire than diamond, although the spinel is more convincing owing to its high lustre. Rock crystal, often dignified by such names as 'Cornish diamond', almost completely lacks fire, while paste can be identified by scratches and other signs of wear on its surface. All the stones mentioned are of course softer than diamond, some considerably so, and one of the quickest ways of testing an unmounted stone which purports to be a diamond is to try to scratch a piece of corundum with it. The only gemstone which will scratch corundum is diamond. Unfortunately one of the most convincing fakes is a stone which is partly made of diamond. This is the diamond doublet, in which a diamond crown is cemented on to a base of some other colourless material. If looked at obliquely these stones are seen to contain a shadow, which is the shadow of the edge of the table facet projected on to the thin layer of cement.

The value of a diamond depends very largely on how free it is from flaws; few diamonds are completely free of small imperfections or inclusions, but a stone is said to be 'clean' if no flaws are visible under a lens which magnifies ten times.

Colour is important – a yellowish tinge, for instance, detracts from the value of a 'colourless' stone – and the value is also proportionate to the weight. The price per carat (q.v.) rises for stones above about 4 carats. This may not apply to exceptionally large diamonds, the price of which is dependent on a very small market. (Large diamond crystals are nowadays usually cut into several stones. Most large stones which appear on the market are those with historical associations.) Finally, an otherwise good stone may lose appreciably in value if it is badly cut.

Many diamonds have become famous through legend, historical associations or merely because of their size. Among the most famous are the Akbar Shah, Braganza, Cullinan, Eureka, Excelsior, Great Mogul, Hope blue, Idol's Eye, Jonker, Jubilee, Koh-i-Noor, Niarchos, Nizam, Orloff, Pitt, Savoy, Star of South Africa, and Star of the South (qq.v.).

Diamond Corporation. See *De Beers*.

Diamond-cutting.
History.
It is not known when or where the art of diamond-cutting originated. Being the hardest natural substance, diamond cannot be cut or polished by any material other than its own powder, and even if the possibility of doing this had occurred to the ancient lapidaries it is unlikely that they would have been willing to sacrifice one diamond to polish another since diamonds were until comparatively recent times exceedingly rare. Also it is only when diamond is cut in a very sophisticated way (the brilliant cut, see below) that the point of cutting it becomes evident; a roughly-fashioned diamond has very little life or sparkle at all. The first diamonds worn in jewellery were therefore uncut and were valued primarily as amulets (see *Diamond*). Then during the fourteenth century cut diamonds began to appear in European jewellery and a diamond-cutting industry grew up in the Low Countries. The diamonds were fashioned in what is known as the *table*

cut (see illustration), a simple form which was probably achieved by grinding off the tip of a natural octahedron, this being one of the forms in which diamond crystals occur. (The octahedron was worn in jewellery in its natural state, simply cut in half and polished, for many centuries.) The table cut may have originated in India and reached Western Europe by way of Venice; it was a cut extensively used by the ancient Indian lapidaries, who had been faceting diamonds for generations when Tavernier visited them in the seventeenth century. Another cut employed by medieval lapidaries was the lozenge; this is obtained by grinding away one of the corners on the girdle (widest part) of the octahedron until what is commonly known as a 'diamond-shape' is achieved. The result is attractive but wastes a lot of material, and the cut was therefore not very often used. Both the table cut and the lozenge cut are comparatively easy to achieve, since the hardness of a diamond varies slightly in different directions and the table and lozenge faces are ground along two of the softer planes.

The next advance in diamond-cutting was the rose cut, which appeared in the sixteenth century. While the table and lozenge cuts exploited the shape of the octahedral crystal, the rose cut made use of the dodecahedron form in which diamonds very frequently occur. Basically the rose cut consists of a series of small symmetrically-placed triangular facets rising in a dome over a flat base. This cut was particularly useful for small stones, and its introduction led to an increase in the popularity of diamonds during the seventeenth century. At the end of the seventeenth century a Venetian cutter named Peruzzi invented the brilliant cut in which 58 facets were placed in a regular geometric relationship. This cut, which was again based on the octahedron, revealed for the first time the fire of the diamond. (Fire is the dispersion of light into the colours of the spectrum. It is intensified by increasing the length of the path the light travels within the stone,

and in a brilliant-cut diamond the facets are so arranged that light is internally reflected from one to another and travels through as long a path as possible before finally emerging from the stone. This phenomenon is explained under *Total internal reflection*.) The introduction of the brilliant cut set the seal on the diamond's popularity, and many old table-cut and rose-cut diamonds were re-fashioned in the new style although this involved sacrificing a considerable proportion of the stone. It is not known how much geometry Peruzzi used when he designed the brilliant cut, but the earliest brilliants were cut deeper than modern stones and had less fire. With the development of optical science the brilliant has been improved and numerous modifications have been introduced to cope with crystals of different shapes and with very large stones, and also to provide compromises which lack the fire of the true brilliant but are much cheaper to produce. *Modern styles of cutting.*

1. The rose cut. This is still extensively used for small diamonds because it is economical; small fragments of crystals can be cut in this way. It is also sometimes used for large diamonds when a special effect is desired (Fabergé used rose-cut diamonds almost exclusively because he did not want the diamonds to distract the eye from the rest of the piece). In the standard rose cut, sometimes known as the Dutch rose or crowned rose, there are 24 triangular facets arranged in multiples of six (see diagram) over a flat base. The height of the stone is usually equal to half its diameter. In the *Antwerp rose* the stone is flatter and has only 12 facets (see diagram). The *cross rose* has 24 facets but 16 of them are quadrilateral and the remaining 8 triangular (see diagram).

2. Double rose and briolette. The double rose is simply a fully-rounded form of the standard rose cut in which the bottom half of the stone is the same as the top. It is used for pendant stones. The briolette may be described as a double rose with an extremely elongated top half (see diagram). The facets on a briolette need not be triangular, however; they are sometimes rectangular.

3. *The brilliant cut*. The standard brilliant cut has 58 facets, of which there are 33 on the top part of the stone (the crown) and 25 on the base (the pavilion). (See diagrams.) The large central facet at the top (the table) is octagonal and is surrounded by 8 triangular star facets. Between these are 8 larger quadrilateral bezel facets which meet the girdle of the stone (the point of greatest diameter). Surrounding the bezels and meeting the girdle are 16 small triangular facets known as cross or skill facets ('skill' because they are difficult to place correctly). Below the girdle are another 16 corresponding cross or skill facets, below which are 8 long pavilion facets which meet at the bottom. At the point where they meet a small facet known as the culet is ground to prevent splintering. The culet is often omitted in modern stones, since the base of the stone is usually adequately protected by its setting and the presence of a culet can give the impression of a black spot at the bottom of the stone. Without the culet the number of facets is 57. To secure the greatest fire from the diamond the angle between the bezel facets and the plane of the girdle should be about 35° and the angle between the pavilion facets and the plane of the girdle about 41°. The outline of most modern brilliants is circular, but older stones were often cushion-shaped – squarish with rounded corners.

4. *Modifications of the brilliant cut.* Some stones differ markedly in outline from the standard brilliant but have a similar arrangement of facets. The commonest examples are the *marquise* or *navette*, a boat-shaped stone, and the pear-shaped *pendeloque* (see diagrams). There are numerous simplified versions of the brilliant which are often used for small stones. The *eight cut* (see diagram) has 8 facets surrounding the table and 8 facets on the pavilion. The *English brilliant cut* has 17 facets on the crown including the table, and 12 on the pavilion, plus the culet if there is one (see diagram). The *Swiss cut* has a crown

similar to the English brilliant cut but has 8 pavilion facets instead of only 4. On large diamonds more facets may be added to the original 58 to increase the stone's brilliance or to reduce the amount of weight lost in cutting. In some of these elaborate cuts small facets are put on the girdle. In the *American brilliant cut* the proportions of the original brilliant are considerably altered; the table facet is only about one-third instead of half the width of the girdle, and the crown is appreciably deeper in proportion to the pavilion (see diagram). This enables 8 additional bezel facets to be ground on the crown. The *king cut* has a 12-sided table surrounded by 48 facets on the crown (see diagram), and 36 facets, not counting the culet, on the pavilion. The *magna cut* is even more elaborate, having a 10-sided facet surrounded by 60 facets on the crown, and 41 facets on the pavilion including the culet. These last two cuts closely resemble the standard brilliant in symmetry, but cuts designed earlier in this century were devised less to display the stone's fire than to retain its weight. In the *Cairo star cut*, for instance, the table is only one quarter the width of girdle and the culet is much larger than usual (see diagram). The table is hexagonal and surrounded by 6 star facets, 6 bezel facets and 12 cross facets. The pavilion is cut with a complicated system of 49 facets of widely different shapes and sizes. The Cairo star is unusual in that the facets are based on a six-fold instead of an eight-fold symmetry. In the *jubilee cut*, invented at the beginning of this century, there is no table facet (see diagram). Instead there are 8 star facets meeting in a point, surrounded by 8 bezel facets, below which are 16 skill facets and 16 cross facets above the girdle. On the base of the stone an extra 16 facets are added and there is no culet. The stone has less fire than the brilliant but has considerable glitter because of the large number of facets.

5. *The profile cut*. This was invented in 1961 by Mr Arpad Nagy, founder of the Diamond Polishing Works in London. It

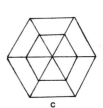

(a) Table cut

(b) Rose cut, side view and crown

(c) Antwerp rose, side view and crown

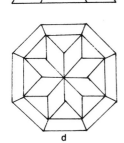

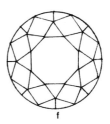

(d) Cross rose, side view and crown

(e) Briolette

(f) Brilliant cut, crown

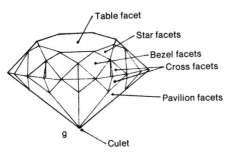

Table facet
Star facets
Bezel facets
Cross facets
Pavilion facets
Culet

(g) Brilliant cut, side view, with names of facets

(h) Marquise

(i) Pendeloque

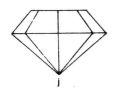

(j) Eight cut

(k) English brilliant cut

(l) American brilliant cut, side view and crown

Diamond-cutting

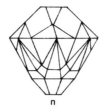

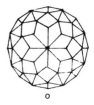

(m) King cut　　　　　　　*(n) Cairo star cut*　　　　　　　*(o) Jubilee cut*

was formerly known as the princess cut. It is a completely new way of fashioning diamond and is extremely economical in its use of material. The crystal is sawn on a gang-saw into parallel plates approximately 1.5mm. thick. Each plate is cut to the desired outline and the top surface polished, and the bottom is cut with a series of narrow paralleled V-grooves which create the necessary total internal reflection. This technique provides a large surface area of diamond at comparatively low cost, and the stones can be produced in a variety of shapes in standardized sizes.

Methods. Apart from the fact that the machinery involved is now electrically-powered instead of being driven by horses, steam or the diamond-cutter's daughter, the way in which diamonds are fashioned has not changed very much in 500 years. The first step is to eliminate any flawed part of the crystal and to separate it into pieces of a workable size. This is done by cleaving or sawing. Diamond cleaves readily along a plane parallel to the octahedral face. The diamond is set in a holder and a groove is made in it with the point of another diamond. A heavy blunt steel blade is placed in the groove and tapped with a mallet, and the stone splits cleanly in the required direction. Sawing is used to separate well-formed octahedral crystals; the stone is cut along its greatest width to give two equal halves, each of which can then be fashioned as a brilliant. The sawing is done on a phosphor-bronze disc revolving at about 6000 r.p.m., the cutting edge of which is impregnated with a mixture of olive oil and diamond powder. (Each diamond-cutting workshop has its own recipe for the abrasive mixture, and in many the mixture is still prepared by pounding diamonds by hand in an iron mortar.) The sawing has to be done across the grain, i.e. against the direction of cleavage. It can take up to eight hours to saw through a one-carat crystal; in earlier centuries, when sawing was carried out by using brass or iron wires charged with diamond powder, it could take as many months. In modern workshops one man usually looks after a battery of saws, replenishing them with abrasive as needed.

The stones are then roughly fashioned or 'bruted' to remove corners and obtain a rough approximation of the facet positions. This used to be done most laboriously by hand, the bruter working two diamonds set in holders against each other. It is now done mechanically; one diamond is mounted on the headstock of a special lathe and another is set in a long holder held under the bruter's arm and ground against it. When the process is completed both diamonds are the same shape: a double cone with one end slightly flattened (this will be the table facet).

The diamond is now ready to be faceted by the polisher. This is done on a horizontal cast-iron wheel, known as a scaife, charged with oil and diamond powder and revolving at about 2500 r.p.m. The diamond is mounted in a cup-shaped holder called the 'dop'; in the older form of dop the diamond was embedded in solder, and although mechanical dops with clamping screws are now exten-

110

sively used, the older solder dops are still better for certain cuts and many polishers prefer them. The dop is set on a flexible copper stalk which is held in a clamp (the 'tang'), and the inclination of the diamond faces to the wheel can be altered by moving the stalk. Lead weights are placed on the arm of the tang to give added pressure during the grinding. Before any facets are ground the stone is very carefully inspected to ascertain the direction of the grain: grinding can only be carried out against the grain. The first facets to be ground are the table, four bezel facets (the first four bezel facets to be ground are also known as templets), four pavilion facets corresponding to these, and the culet. This arrangement is called the cross. Next the remaining bezel and pavilion facets are put on, and then the small facets. The latter are done in groups. On the crown of the stone one star facet and the two cross facets below it are worked together, and on the pavilion each pair of cross facets is worked together. It is essential that the facets should be placed with geometrical precision, and although the diamond-cutter has gauges and protractors to help him, in the main he relies on his eye. When the finishing touches have been given to the stone it is cleaned in an acid solution and is then ready to be mounted in jewellery; unlike other gemstones, diamonds require no final polishing – the polish is given by the grinding on of the facets. When the cutting process has been completed, the stone has lost 50–60 per cent of its original weight.

The major diamond-cutting centres of the world today are Amsterdam, Antwerp, Bombay, London, New York and Tel Aviv. (See *Diamond* for information on the sorting, marketing, etc. of diamonds.)

Diamond gauges. Instruments for assessing the weight of diamonds which are set and therefore cannot be weighed. They are basically of two types, the stencil gauge and the caliper gauge. Stencil gauges consist of thin sheets of metal or plastic containing holes of different diameters; the holes are tried over the diamond until one is found which just fits the girdle of the stone, and the carat weight corresponding to this size will be found marked beside the hole. Caliper gauges are much more accurate. They consist of a pair of spring calipers fitted with a pointer which moves over a scale. The diameter of the stone across the girdle and the depth from table to culet are measured, and the measurements recorded on the scale are looked up in a set of tables supplied with the instrument which give the corresponding weight. Some gauges allow the weights of fancy-cut diamonds as well as brilliants to be assessed.

Diamond-milling. A modern mechanical process used to give an interesting textured surface to mass-produced jewellery. A pattern of sharp bright cuts is made in the metal by a machine which has its cutting blade set with a diamond. The diamond not only cuts the pattern but also gives it a bright finish. The pattern depends on the way the machine is set up and also on the size and shape of the diamond. Diamond-milling is extensively used on modern wedding rings.

Diamond powder. Crushed or powdered boart (q.v.) and waste diamond material from cleaving, bruting, etc., used as an abrasive in diamond-cutting and the fashioning of other hard stones, and also in industry. It is sorted into grades, the finest of which is 1 micron (0.001 mm.). (See also *Diamond* and *Diamond-cutting*.)

Diamond Producers' Association. See *De Beers*.

Diamondscope. An American instrument incorporating a binocular microscope used for observing internal features in stones. Its use is not restricted to diamonds – coloured stones, pastes and synthetics may also be examined.

Diamond Trading Company. See *De Beers*.

Diasterism. A 'star' effect (see *Asterism*) which is best seen in transmitted light, i.e. by looking at a source of light through the stone, as distinct from a star seen by reflected light (epiasterism).

Diatomite. A polishing powder produced from the silicified cell-walls of microscopic fossilized plants (diatoms).

Dichroic. Exhibiting dichroism, q.v.

Dichroism. The property in doubly-refracting coloured stones of exhibiting two or more different colours according to the direction in which they are viewed. (In biaxial [q.v.] stones there are three colours and the property is properly termed trichroism or pleochroism, but 'dichroism' is the term commonly used.)

The appearance of colour in gemstones is caused by selective absorption of parts of the visible light spectrum. Doubly-refracting stones split up light into two rays (see *Double refraction*), and in each of these rays a different part of the spectrum is absorbed and thus a different colour transmitted. The range of colour depends on the basic body-colour of the stone, which is determined by its chemical composition, and the precise tint exhibited depends on the direction in which the light rays travel. In uniaxial (q.v.) stones there is one direction (the optic axis) in which light is not doubly-refracted but travels as a single ray (the 'ordinary ray'); when viewed in any other direction than along its optic axis the stone shows a colour which is a mixture of the ordinary and extraordinary rays, and at right-angles to the optic axis the colours are equally mixed.

In some gemstones such as the green tourmaline the dichroism is perceptible to the naked eye. In others it can only be detected by the dichroscope (q.v.), which analyses the colours by polarizing the light. The presence of dichroism may help to identify a stone, since only those stones which are doubly-refracting exhibit it. On the other hand not all doubly-refracting stones are dichroic, so the absence of perceptible dichroism does not mean that a stone is singly-refractive.

The dichroic properties of a stone are extremely important to the gem-cutter, since in a strongly dichroic stone the predominant colour of the cut gem will depend on the angle at which he cuts it. Green tourmaline, for instance, appears almost black if viewed along the optic axis, which is parallel to the prism edge of the crystal, but light green if viewed across it; to capture the lighter colour, therefore, the stone must be cut with its table facet parallel to the optic axis so that the observer looking down on the stone is looking across the optic axis. Rubies display their best colour along the optic axis, and are therefore cut across it.

Dichroite. See *Iolite.*

Dichroscope. An instrument for examining dichroism (q.v.) in gemstones. It consists basically of a hollow metal tube with a lens at one end and a small aperture at the other, containing a rhomb of transparent calcite. When a gemstone is viewed through this the calcite, being strongly doubly-refractive, produces a double image of the stone and also polarizes the light emanating from it, so that the colours of the two rays can be seen side by side. When the stone is rotated in front of the aperture, there are four positions at intervals of 90° where the two images are identical in colour; between these points the colours gradually diverge until at 45° they reach a maximum difference, after which the difference decreases until they are again identical. In the case of ruby, for example, the two colours at their maximum difference are pale yellowish-red and deep red; at 45° from this position they are the same red colour, and at a further 45° they are again at maximum difference, but this time the first image is deep red and the second pale yellowish-red.

In biaxial (q.v.) stones there are not two but three principal colours, but since only two of them can be seen at any one time they may be said for practical purposes to be dichroic.

Stones show no double refraction, and hence no dichroism, when viewed along an optic axis (q.v.), and it is therefore important that the stone should be examined from more than one angle.

Die-casting. Casting into a cut-steel die; a method which has been used in the past for mass-producing jewellery but has now been replaced by centrifugal casting. (See *Casting*.)

Die-stamping. See *Machine-stamping*.

Diffraction (of light). The breaking up of light into the spectral colours when it passes through a narrow aperture; it is caused by interference of the rays by deflection. Some spectrometers (q.v.) use a diffraction grating (a sheet of glass covered with a series of finely-ruled lines) instead of a prism to disperse light.

Diffusion column. A tube containing two heavy liquids of different density which diffuse to form a liquid of varying density along the tube. Used in the measurement of specific gravity (q.v.).

Diopside (Alalite). (Calcium-magnesium silicate. S.G. 3.27–3.31; R.I. 1.67–1.70; H. 5–6.) Most gemstones cut from this mineral are a transparent bottle-green, although some are a brighter green owing to the presence of chromium (the dark green is caused by iron, and stones containing a lot of iron are almost black). Diopside is dichroic (q.v.), but the effect is only distinct in dark stones, which are sometimes mistaken for tourmaline. Chrome diopside from Burma is fibrous and is cut into attractive cat's eye cabochons. A very dark green star diopside (see *Asterism*) has been found in India. Other sources of gem-quality material include the diamond-mines of South Africa, the Ala valley in Piedmont (hence the alternative name alalite), the Tyrol, Brazil, Ceylon and the U.S.A.

Diopside is sometimes known as malacolite, and the material from Baikal in Russia has been called baikalite. A dark violet-blue variety is known as violane or violan (q.v.).

Dioptase. (Copper silicate. S.G. 3.3; R.I. 1.64–1.70; H.5.) A translucent emerald-green stone which, although very attractive, is not really suitable for use as a gemstone because of its softness and strong cleavage, and is therefore not often cut. Dioptase has a higher colour-dispersion and therefore more fire than many gemstones, but the rich colour of the stone masks this. Good crystals are found in the Kirghiz Steppes in Russia, and in the Congo, Chile, Argentina and the U.S.A.

'Dirigem'. (Trade name.) A synthetic green spinel. (See *Synthetic gemstones*.)

Dispersion. See *Colour dispersion*.

Disthene. See *Kyanite*.

Ditroite. Sodalite.

Dog-collars. Jewelled dog-collars were sometimes worn during the sixteenth century, but were never an important feature of dress until the late Victorian period, when they became indispensable for fashionable women. In 1885 they consisted of broad bands of velvet – worn plain or decorated with beads for those of modest means, covered with precious stones for the wealthy. In the following year these collars were replaced by rows of pearls held in position by jewelled strips of gold or silver. The pearl dog-collar remained extremely popular for many years. By the turn of the century it sometimes contained as many as eleven rows. Collars of coral and jet were also worn. It was not unusual for a necklace to be worn as well.

(For further information on the period, see *Nineteenth-century jewellery*.)

Doming block. A metal cube, usually of brass or steel, with hemispherical depressions of various sizes on each surface, used in conjunction with doming punches (q.v.) for doming up thin pieces of sheet metal.

Doming punches. Punches with globular heads which fit the hollows on a doming block (q.v.). (See illustration.)

Dop. The holder in which a diamond is held while it is being fashioned (see *Diamond-cutting*). The old dops were cup-shaped and filled with a tin and lead

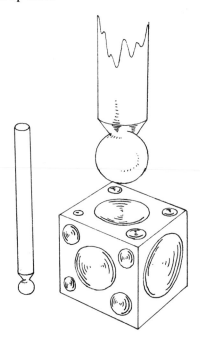

Doming block and punches

solder in which the diamond was embedded; modern dops are mechanical and hold the stone by screw clamps, but the old type are still in use. 'Dop' is an old Dutch word meaning 'shell', referring to the shape of the holder. (See also *Dop-stick*.)

Dop-stick. A stick, usually of wood, to the end of which the lapidary attaches a stone which is to be cut or polished (see *Gem-cutting*). Resin or a similar substance is melted on to the end of the stick and the stone is embedded in this and is held securely when it cools. (See also *Gem-stick*.)

Doublet. A composite imitation stone consisting of two or three separate layers cemented or fused together. (A stone consisting of three layers is properly called a triplet, but 'doublet' is now the common term for all such composite stones in Europe, although 'triplet' continues to be used in America.) A doublet may be made of two pieces of the same

mineral in order to produce a larger stone but the usual intention is to produce an imitation of a valuable stone using either inferior material of the same kind or a different mineral altogether. The advantage of the doublet over a glass imitation is that the crown of the stone is made of a hard mineral and thus will not be scratched if tested for hardness (q.v.) with a steel file. Doublets are not necessarily produced with fraudulent intention, and several types are marketed under recognisable trade names, but obviously they lend themselves to fraudulent use.

The commonest type of doublet is the *garnet-topped* doublet. This consists of a thin layer of almandine garnet (q.v.) fused to a base of coloured or colourless glass; the stone is faceted after the two layers have been joined. The layer of garnet is too thin to have much effect on the colour of the resulting stone, which is determined by the colour of the glass. The doublets are made in pink, red, aquamarine-blue, blue, green and other colours. Unset stones other than the red and pink ones usually show a red ring round the girdle if they are placed table-facet downwards on a piece of white paper. The composite nature of the stone can also be detected by bubbles along the plane of fusion and by the discrepancy in refractive index which can be observed if the stone is immersed in a highly-refractive liquid. (See *Refractive index – immersion methods*.)

The doublet imitation of emerald, known as *soudé emerald*, originally consisted of two pieces of colourless quartz cemented together and given an emerald colour (when viewed through the top) by a thin layer of green gelatine. This stone, like the true emerald, showed red through a colour filter (q.v.). This type is now less common since the gelatine was found to yellow with time, but there is another type, also using quartz, in which a different colouring matter – probably containing copper – is used. These stones have a slightly higher specific gravity (q.v.) than emerald; the first type have the specific gravity and refractive index of

114

quartz (q.v.). A more recent type of soudé emerald uses synthetic white spinel (see *Synthetic gemstones*) for the crown and base. The refractive index is 1.73 and the specific gravity 3.36–3.69. Doublets using synthetic spinel have been made in other colours as well. White sapphire may also be used (in which case the specific gravity and refractive index approximate to those of sapphire, q.v.), and a doublet marketed under the trade name of 'Smaryll' in the 1960s was made of two pieces of beryl cemented together with a green duroplastic cement. All soudé emeralds may easily be recognised if they are unset by immersing them in a suitable liquid (methylene iodide for the spinel type, otherwise water) and looking at them from the side; the coloured layer and the pale or colourless crown and base can be clearly seen.

A number of doublets consist of a crown of colourless quartz cemented to a colourless glass base. The specific gravity of such stones is usually between 2.55 and 2.61 and the refractive index near 1.51. Triplets are much less common than twolayer stones; they usually consist of a top and base of quartz with a layer of coloured glass between.

The potentially most deceptive doublets are those consisting of a crown of the species of stone simulated, cemented on to a base of another or inferior material. These, however, are not common, although diamonds are simulated in this way. Diamond doublets can usually be quickly identified by inspecting them obliquely in a good light, when the edge of the table facet will be seen reflected as a shadow on the layer of cement. 'True doublets', consisting of two pieces of the same mineral cemented together along the plane of the girdle to produce a larger stone, are even rarer; a microscope will generally reveal the cement layer in such stones and also the lack of continuity of internal features such as inclusions.

Other specific imitations. Opal doublets are quite common. The usual type is a thin layer of precious opal cemented on to opal matrix or black glass. The 'Triplex

opal' is a doublet of this kind with a layer of colourless quartz cemented over the top. A doublet consisting of a thin layer of mother-of-pearl used as backing for a glass or quartz cabochon is a recent imitation of opal. *Star sapphires* are imitated by a composite stone containing star rose quartz. A cabochon of this quartz is cemented on top of a layer of blue glass, which in turn is backed with a mirror. The mirror is necessary because the star in sapphire is shown by reflected light (epiasterism), whereas the star in rose quartz is shown only by transmitted light (diasterism). If this stone is examined under an electric light the image of the light bulb will be seen at the centre of the star; this effect is not seen in natural starsapphire. *Cameos* and *intaglios* are often imitated by doublets; the top of the stone is usually glass and the base chalcedony, but sometimes both sections are glass and the colour is given by the cement.

Modern materials have increased the possibilities of the doublet, but the idea is not new. Cellini in his *Treatises,* written in the middle of the sixteenth century, mentions that stones consisting of a thin layer of ruby or some other precious stone cemented on to a glass base were being sold as genuine by Milanese jewellers. One of the unsuspecting customers was Henry VIII.

Double refraction. The splitting-up of a ray of light into two rays as it is refracted into a different medium (see *Refraction*). This phenomenon can sometimes be seen with the naked eye; for instance an object viewed through a thick piece of transparent calcite will appear to be doubled. In cut gemstones it can often be seen without difficulty through a handlens; the back facets of the stone will appear doubled if looked at through the top of the stone.

Of the seven systems of crystal formation into which gemstones are divided (see *Crystal systems*), all except the cubic exhibit double refraction. Determining whether a stone is doubly or singly refracting will help to identify it – it will, for instance, distinguish between a ruby and a garnet. The usual method of testing for double refraction relies on the fact that light travelling through a doubly-refractive stone is polarized: that is to say, the ray vibrates in one direction only instead of in many directions, as in ordinary light. The two rays into which the original ray is split up vibrate in directions at right-angles to each other. The stone to be tested is examined between two pieces of Iceland spar (calcite), known as nicol prisms or nicols, which are usually mounted in a microscope, one above and one below the stage. The calcite has been cut and re-cemented in such a way that it only transmits one of the light-rays passing through it; the other is totally reflected and is absorbed by the casing. (Polaroid, a plastic material which transmits only one polarized ray, may be used instead of nicol prisms.) The prisms are set in a 'crossed' position to each other so that the ray emerging from the lower prism (the polarizer) is vibrating at right-angles to the vibration-direction of the upper prism (the analyser). This ray cannot travel through the analyser but is also absorbed. Through 'crossed nicols', therefore, the field of view is completely dark. If a singly-refracting stone is placed between the prisms the field of view will remain dark because the stone cannot affect the vibration-directions of light. If however a doubly-refracting stone is placed between the prisms and turned in a complete circle, there will be four positions at 90° to each other where the field is dark (this is when the vibration-directions of the stone are parallel to those of the prisms), and four positions at 45° to these where the field is light (the light from the polarizer having been resolved by the stone in such a way that it can be transmitted by the analyser). This test is a reliable way of determining whether a stone is doubly-refractive, but it is necessary to examine a stone which appears to be singly-refractive in more than one direction in case it has been viewed along an optic axis (q.v.), in which

case the double refraction will not be seen. Singly-refracting stones are apt to exhibit anomalous double refraction (q.v.) when they are in a state of strain; this can usually be distinguished from true double refraction without difficulty.

The twin rays in doubly-refracting stones have different refractive indices (see *Refractive index*). In uniaxial (q.v.) crystals one ray has a constant refractive index (denoted by the sign ω) and is known as the ordinary ray. The other, known as the extraordinary ray, has a variable refractive index (denoted by ε) which is related to the direction of travel. In biaxial (q.v.) crystals there are still only two rays but there are three refractive indices; these correspond to the three mutually perpendicular directions of light-vibration, which are again related to the direction of travel. The refractive indices in biaxial stones are denoted by the signs α for the lowest refractive index, γ for the highest, and β for the intermediate.

Double rose. A form of the rose cut in which the bottom half of the stone is the same as the top. For the rose cut, see *Diamond-cutting*.

Dravite. Brown tourmaline.

Draw-bench. A low bench with a winch at one end, used for drawing wire when the quantity to be drawn or the thickness of the wire make it difficult to draw by hand. At the far end of the bench from the winch are a pair of stops which hold the draw-plate (q.v.); the wire is fed through the draw-plate and gripped by the draw-tongs (q.v.), the hooked handles of which are held in a triangular iron ring at the end of a strap which is attached to the winch. When the winch is turned the iron ring pulls back the tongs and the wire is drawn through the draw-plate.

Draw-plate. A sheet of hardened steel pierced with holes of graduated sizes, used in drawing wire. The holes are slightly wider at the back of the plate than at the front. The draw-plate is held in a vice and the wire is fed in through

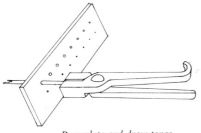

Drawplate and draw-tongs

the back of the hole and pulled through with a pair of draw-tongs (q.v.); by pulling the wire through a series of holes of decreasing sizes its diameter can be considerably reduced. A lubricant such as beeswax is used, and after a while the wire has to be annealed (see *Annealing*) to restore its ductility.

The draw-plate was introduced some time before the Middle Ages – possibly in Roman times. Before this, wire was made by rolling thin strips of metal between stones or plates of harder metal, or by twisting strips in a tight spiral. The draw-plate is no longer as essential as it used to be, since wire in a variety of gauges can be obtained ready for use from the refiners.

(See also *Draw-bench* and *Rolling mills*.)

Draw-tongs. Heavy square-nosed pliers with a hooked handle designed for drawing wire through a draw-plate (q.v.). (See illustration.)

Dresden White, Green and Yellow diamonds. Six very fine Indian diamonds which were formerly in the Green Vaults at Dresden; they are said to have passed into Russian possession after the Second World War. The Dresden White, a square diamond weighing nearly 50 carats, was set in a shoulder knot. The Dresden Green, a flawless apple-green stone of 41 carats, was set in a hat ornament. Both these were purchased by Augustus the Strong in the eighteenth century. There are four yellow diamonds cut as brilliants; the largest weighs in the region of 38 carats.

Drill. For fine work a bow-drill (q.v.) is used by jewellers; ordinary hand drills fitted with a fine bit are also used for drilling holes in metal, and power-operated flexible-drive-shaft drills are used for drilling and, when fitted with the appropriate heads, for grinding and polishing.

Drilling. For drilling of stones see *Gem-cutting*, for drilling of pearls see *Pearls*. Metal is drilled for two purposes: to allow the insertion of a saw blade in pierced work (q.v.), and to provide the holes in which stones are sunk in a pavé setting (q.v.). (See also *Drill*.)

Drop-pearl. A pear-shaped pearl.

Drop stone. A pear-shaped stone, usually worn as a pendant.

Ducerceau, Jacques Androuet (*c.* 1510–1585 ?). Engraver and architect who published numerous designs for jewels in the Mannerist style (see *Renaissance jewellery*), including pendants with rather heavy strapwork frames. His designs were widely used. He was born in Paris but except for a visit to Italy lived for most of his life in Orléans, where he is said to have studied under Etienne Delaune (q.v.). He died in Geneva.

Dumortierite. (Aluminium boro-silicate. S.G. 3.26–3.41; R.I. about 1.68; H.7.) A rare violet or blue stone sometimes used in jewellery. It occurs usually in massive fibrous or columnar form rather than in distinct crystals. The stone is strongly dichroic (see *Dichroism*). It occurs in California, Nevada and Arizona, Madagascar, Norway, and near Lyons in France.

Dunstan, St. Patron saint of goldsmiths, jewellers and locksmiths. The most famous of Anglo-Saxon saints, Dunstan was largely responsible for the revival of English monastic life and played a part in the reunification of England under King Edgar. Owing to his outspokenness he had a somewhat stormy political career.

Dunstan was born about 910 near Glastonbury of a noble family. He was given a scholarly education and sent

Dürer, Albrecht

while still a youth to the court of King Athelstan. Here he incurred the displeasure of certain people who accused him of practising magical incantations; he was expelled from court and apparently thrown into a cesspool on his departure. Shortly after this he took holy orders at the hands of his uncle St. Alphege the Bald and went to live the life of a monk at Glastonbury, studying, illuminating manuscripts, and making bells and sacred vessels for the church.

Athelstan's successor Edmund, however, recalled Dunstan to court and in 943 made him Abbot of Glastonbury. Edmund was murdered after a reign of 6½ years and succeeded by his brother Edred, who made Dunstan one of his chief advisers. Dunstan initiated many moral and ecclesiastical reforms, and advocated the unification of the country by placating the Danes who had settled in the eastern parts; this earned him powerful political enemies, and when on the accession of Edred's nephew Edwy in 955 Dunstan dared to rebuke the young king for unseemly behaviour on his coronation day he was exiled in disgrace and had his property confiscated. He found refuge in Flanders, but was soon recalled to England again by Edgar, who had been installed as king as a result of a rebellion against Edwy. The country was united under Edgar in 959 and Dunstan was made Archbishop of Canterbury. He was appointed Papal legate by Pope John XII and, armed with this authority, set himself with renewed vigour to combat the laxity in the Church and restore the monasteries destroyed by the Danish invasions. For many years he was chief adviser to Edgar and his successor Edward, but on the accession of Ethelred the Unready in 970 he expressed grave forebodings about the future of the realm and retired from political life to Canterbury, where he taught until his death in 988. He was canonized soon afterwards. His love of discipline must have been tempered with great kindness, because the young scholars are said to have remembered him with longing when they

suffered under the harsh discipline of his successors.

St. Dunstan's status as the patron saint of goldsmiths and jewellers rests on a somewhat insecure foundation, since the first references to him as a goldsmith are after the Norman conquest. During the Middle Ages, however, the figure of the metalworker-saint with an uncompromising tongue captured popular imagination, and Dunstan became one of the best-loved saints in the calendar. From the Middle Ages dates the legend that he once seized the Devil's nose with a pair of blacksmith's pincers when the Devil was trying to tempt him.

Design for a belt-end by Dürer, engraved by Wenceslas Hollar (q.v.)

Dürer, Albrecht (1471–1528). The son of a Nuremberg goldsmith, Dürer was, like many other great artists of the period, taught the goldsmith's craft in his youth, and later in life produced a number of designs for jewels. These were probably intended to be carried out by his brother Endres. The surviving designs include belt-buckles, brooches, clasps, pendants and pendant whistles. They are full of the fantastic and mythological creatures – dragons, dolphins, mermaids – which towards the end of the sixteenth century became almost commonplace in jewellery, but in Dürer's designs these appear with startling power and freshness. There can be no doubt that Dürer's genius exercised considerable influence on German decorative art and contributed to the importance of Augsburg and Nuremberg as centres of the goldsmith's craft.

Durosol. Abrasive powder consisting of aluminium oxide.

Dust pearls. Trade term for very small seed-pearls.

Dutch rose cut. The standard form of rose cut. (See *Diamond-cutting*.)

Dwt. Abbreviation for pennyweight (=24 grains). (See *Weights for precious metals*.)

Dyeing of stones. The colour of a porous stone may be altered or improved by dyeing, and although a comparatively small range of stones are treated in this way, one type in particular, the banded chalcedony (agate) is almost invariably found dyed. The treatment is carried out on a large commercial scale at Idar-Oberstein (q.v.) in Germany. Banded agate is dyed in a range of bright colours – blue, red, green, etc. – and the dye is absorbed by the more porous layers, the harder opaque bands remaining white. The effect is extremely attractive. Onyx, which is simply agate with straight bands, is dyed black, and a reddish dye produces sardonyx. (Black onyx and red sardonyx do occur naturally but are uncommon; all the onyx, and most of the sardonyx, used in jewellery are artificially dyed.) Dyeing is used to intensify the colour of pale stones as well as to give colour to almost colourless stones.

The material may be stained by soaking in an aniline dye, but the resulting colours tend to fade and most dyeing is done by depositing a coloured chemical precipitate in the pores of the stone. The black onyx is achieved by soaking the material in a hot sugar solution for several days (honey may be used instead), and then washing it and soaking it in sulphuric acid. The acid converts the sugar into a fine deposit of carbon. Blue is obtained by soaking the material first in potassium ferrocyanide and then in a solution of ferrous sulphate. (Jasper dyed in this way is marketed as an imitation of lapis lazuli under the names 'German lapis' and 'Swiss lapis'; the colour is not particularly convincing.) Red is obtained by soaking in iron nitrate and then raising to red heat; the heat turns the iron compound into a deposit of ferric oxide. Much of the cornelian used in jewellery is chalcedony stained in this way. Soaking in a solution of chromic acid or nickel salts, and then heating, produces a green colour, and such material is often marketed as chrysoprase (which, strictly speaking, it is not, since chrysoprase is an apple-green chalcedony naturally stained by nickel.) Finally, yellow is obtained by soaking the material in hydrochloric acid in gentle heat. All these colours are virtually permanent.

Other stones are sometimes dyed, either to improve their natural appearance or to produce an imitation of a different stone. An artificial rainbow quartz is produced by heating quartz and cooling it quickly in water which contains dye; cracks are produced by the temperature-change and the dye dries out in them. Coral may be dyed to improve its colour. Turquoise of poor colour may be stained with Prussian blue, but a more usual treatment is to soak the stone in paraffin wax. Jade is dyed to improve its colour and is imitated by other dyed stones. Examples of the latter are a Mexican calcite which has in the past been dyed green and called 'Mexican jade', and a bowenite type of serpentine which is dyed to the colour of Imperial jade (a rich apple-green to emerald-green.) Jadeite which is of an uninteresting greyish colour may be dyed an Imperial jade colour by a combination of yellow and blue organic dyes. This fades within a period of months. The artificial colour tends to concentrate in the cracks of the material, but otherwise the appearance is very convincing.

For other methods of changing the colour of stones, see *Colouring of stones (artificial)*.

E

Earrings. Earrings are more a feature of Eastern than of Western jewellery, although in their most primitive form – a hoop of wire pushed through a perforation in the ear-lobe – they are common to nearly all races. They were an important part of the jewellery of the ancient world, and reached a very high standard of design and workmanship in ancient Greece.

There were numerous types of Greek earring. One of the commonest, a spiral of metal wire pushed through the lobe, was eventually elaborated into a type with ornamented ends and a rosette, decorated with filigree, at the top of the central loop. The boat-shaped earring – basically a hoop with a thick, boat-like lower half – was of very ancient origin; it was in use in Mesopotamia in 2500 B.C. In classical Greece it developed into a very elaborate form; the 'boat', suspended from an enamelled rosette, sometimes held a figure such as a siren, while from it hung short chains terminating in bird-shapes or cockleshells. The whole earring, which was of gold, was decorated with intricate filigree work. An earring of this type is illustrated under *Greek jewellery*. Equally popular were disc-earrings in silver or gold, sometimes enamelled; most of these covered the ear-lobe instead of hanging from it and were in the form of studs, the back of which was simply pushed through a hole in the lobe. In the Hellenistic period these types were replaced in popularity by the tapered hoop, usually of coiled gold wire, terminating at one end with an animal's, or sometimes human, head. This type of earring has been found in many parts of the classical world and its origin is not known. Heads of lions or horned

lions, goats, gazelles and bulls were most popular. Later the hoops were threaded with coloured stones or glass. Pendant earrings, worn for many centuries, also became extremely popular; the hook of the earring was usually masked by a rosette, while the pendant took a variety of forms of which the most striking are small figures of Eros and of the winged Victory.

Earring of twisted gold wire with lion's head finial, Hellenistic. British Museum

Etruscan earrings are in many respects similar to Greek, with the exception of the *baule* earring (so called because it looks rather like a bag), which was an Etruscan invention. It consisted of a strip of gold bent into a near-cylinder, closed at the ends with a disc, and decorated with fine filigree-work and sometimes enamel. It was fitted with a hook for insertion into the ear. Disc-earrings, lavishly decorated with goldwork and inlay, were also frequently worn and were sometimes as much as 6 cm. in diameter. (See also *Etruscan jewellery*.)

Hoop-shaped earrings of the Roman period sometimes have a very long hook for insertion into the ear, giving the whole earring an S-shape. This type is often threaded with small beads. Characteristically Roman types are the ball earring, consisting basically of a hemisphere of gold with an S-shaped hook, and the bar-pendant. The latter consists of a horizontal bar hanging from a mounted stone, with two or three drop-pendants suspended from it. This type persisted for some centuries and became one of the two main types of Byzantine earring, the other type being crescent-shaped with, usually, bird-figures depicted in open-work or enamel (see *Roman jewellery* and *Byzantine jewellery* for illustrations).

For a thousand years after the fall of Rome earrings were virtually not worn in the West because the long hair-styles of the women left no scope for them. Even when the hair was worn high on the head at the end of the fourteenth century earrings were still uncommon. They were not widely worn until the second half of the sixteenth century, and they were then more popular in Spain than in the rest of Europe. The Spanish taste was for long pendant earrings, featuring the use of enamel and faceted stones, particularly emerald. In England pendant pearl earrings, of the type seen often on portraits of Elizabeth I, seem to have been the most popular for women, but there was a greater vogue for earrings among men, who usually wore only one. This fashion, which was probably of Spanish origin, lasted until the time of the Civil War in the next century; Charles I wore a large pearl in his left ear and parted with it only on the scaffold. Spanish influence continued into the seventeenth century and most of the existing earrings from the early part of the century are of Spanish or Portuguese origin (see illustration). In the later part of the century the *girandole* earring made its appearance. This was a pendant earring with three pear-shaped stones or pearl drops hanging from a bow-shaped ornament or large stone at the top (see *Eighteenth-century jewellery* for illustration). The girandole became extremely fashionable in the eighteenth century as it provided an ideal way of displaying diamonds, the full splendour of which had only been realized at the end of the seventeenth century when the brilliant cut (q.v.) was invented. The free movement of the pendant stones increased

Seventeenth-century Spanish earring in pearls, enamel and gold. Museo Poldi-Pezzoli, Milan

their glitter in candlelight, and this fact was further exploited by a design in which a large diamond was freely suspended in the centre of a diamond-set oval hoop, which in turn hung from another large diamond at the top. To increase their reflectivity diamonds were at this time usually set in silver.

Worn consistently throughout the eighteenth century, earrings went in and out of fashion in the nineteenth according to how the hair was worn. In the late 1830s long elaborate jewelled earrings, including some of girandole type, were worn for evening wear, but in the 1840s the hair was worn over the ears and earrings were hardly worn at all. They came back in the following decade, and a popular type at this time was the Creole earring – a tapered hoop thicker at the bottom than at the top. Gothic motifs were also fashionable. During the 1860s earrings grew gradually longer (see illustration) until by 1870 they sometimes

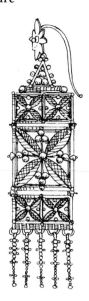

*Gold earring by Giuliano, about 1870.
Victoria and Albert Museum*

reached the shoulders. Drop earrings were a popular form, and, following the contemporary enthusiasm for antique styles, many were made in imitation of Etruscan, Greek and Egyptian designs. The smaller earrings of the 1860s and '70s reflect the worst of Victorian taste, which was not confined to England; earrings in the shape of monkeys, bird-cages, spurs, epaulettes and shovels were worn as happily in Paris as in London. The enthusiasm for earrings waned in the 1880s and the few that were worn were very small. In 1890 the stud earring with a screw fitting was introduced, but interest in earrings did not begin to revive until the end of the century. Earrings were then again popular until the outbreak of war and during the 1920s, when the creole earring was all the rage for a time. However, the present century, with its increasing accent on casual dress and casual hairstyles, has not encouraged the wearing of earrings except on formal occasions, for which traditional styles with diamonds and pearls are the most suitable. On the whole, earrings of truly modern design are not often seen.

Earthenware. Baked clay of variable composition, sometimes used to produce opaque imitation gemstones. It is moulded and glazed in appropriate colours. It can usually be detected immediately by its lightness; the specific gravity is about 2.30, which is appreciably lower than that of almost any stone it is likely to resemble.

Ebonite. Vulcanized rubber; occasionally used, for example, in mourning jewellery.

Ecclesiastical rings. The early Christian church disapproved of the wearing of any rings other than the practical signet ring, but in the course of the centuries it became customary for high ecclesiastical dignitaries to be invested with a ring and to wear it as a sign of office.

The investiture ring of the Pope is known as the Fisherman's ring or *anulus piscatoris*. Traditionally this is the ring with which the Pope seals documents, but in practice a stamping die is used for the purpose. The bezel of the ring is engraved with a representation of St. Peter letting down a net into the sea from a boat, and with the Pope's name. When the Fisherman's ring first began to be worn by Pontiffs is not known; the first mention of the ring is in a letter from Clement IV in 1265, at which time it was used to seal the Pope's private correspondence. The ring does not descend from one Pope to another; after the death of a Pope his ring, together with other Papal seals, is given into the keeping of the Cardinal Chamberlain and publicly broken at the next meeting of Cardinals. A new ring is then prepared with a space left blank for the name, and when the new Pope is elected the Chamberlain places this ring on his finger and asks him what name he will take. The Pope replies, and returns the ring for the name to be engraved on it. This custom seems to have originated in the sixteenth century and to have continued unbroken ever since, except on the death of Pope Pius VI in 1799, when the ring was not destroyed but simply re-engraved with the name of the new Pope, Pius VII. This practical expedient was in vain; ten years later the ring was forcibly taken from the Pope by a French general and was damaged in the process, and although subsequently returned it had to be engraved again. In the Victoria and Albert museum is a Fisherman's ring set with a bloodstone intaglio of St. Peter which has a blank space for the Pope's name; presumably it was made for the investiture of a new Pope and for some reason never used.

The so-called Papal rings (q.v.) are not discussed here since it is unlikely that they had any ecclesiastical use.

The Cardinal's ring is the ring given by the Pope to a new cardinal on his election. These rings are first mentioned at about the end of the thirteenth century, but in most of the records there is very little indication of their appearance. They seem to have been usually but not invariably set with a sapphire, a stone which from ancient times had been associated with purity and spirituality. The sapphire is still the traditional stone for cardinals' rings, and the underside of the bezel is decorated with the arms of the Pope.

As far as can be established, the oldest ecclesiastical ring is that worn by bishops. Episcopal rings are first referred to in writings of the late sixth or early seventh centuries, and were probably in use some time before that. In the seventh century the Synod of Milan decreed that the consecration rings of bishops should be of pure gold and set with a gem that was not engraved. They were to be worn on the third finger of the right hand. The gem would probably be sapphire (though ruby and amethyst were also used), but even so the description is so unspecific that it is almost impossible to identify any surviving ring with certainty as a bishop's consecration ring. Other rings were, however, worn by bishops; they have been found in tombs and are often represented in Renaissance paintings. These are known as pontifical rings and were worn during the celebration of High Mass. They were generally worn over gloves and are therefore large and impressive. The pontifical ring bequeathed by William of Wykeham to his successor was set with a sapphire surrounded by balas rubies (spinels). Two 'pontificals' described in an inventory of Charles V were set respectively with a cameo, twelve pearls, two sapphires and two emeralds, and with a large sapphire surrounded by turquoises and garnets. On the death of a bishop his rings were supposed to be handed over to the royal treasury, but as many rings have been found in bishops' coffins this rule cannot have been very strictly enforced. Owing to the great variety of stones with which they were set and the absence of any prescribed form, pontifical rings are not much easier to identify than the consecration rings; large rings were not uncommon in the late Middle Ages and Renaissance because rings were frequently worn on the thumb. It is therefore only those rings which were actually found on a bishop's fingers that can safely be assumed to be episcopal rings.

During the early Middle Ages abbots began to wear a ring as a sign of office, an innovation which was apparently deeply resented by the bishops. Like episcopal rings, abbots' rings were worn on the third finger of the right hand and presumably also had to be surrendered to the treasury on the abbot's death, since several of them are mentioned in royal inventories. A gold ring set with a single stone – amethyst, sapphire, topaz, etc. – seems to have been the usual form; some abbots' rings are simply described as 'gold'. Towards the end of the Middle Ages abbesses also took to wearing a ring, but Gregory XIII put a stop to this in 1572. The abbesses had to be content with the simple nun's ring symbolizing their marriage to Christ.

Certain other ecclesiastical dignitaries are permitted or have at some time been permitted to wear a ring. Protonotaries apostolic, for example, may wear a ring except during the celebration of Mass, for which they may wear a 'pontifical' ring instead. It is doubtful whether the rules against the wearing of rings by the clergy except as a privilege were much regarded until comparatively recent times. Although the ordinary priesthood were supposed never to wear rings there are references to priests' rings in many old records, and in the Victoria and Albert Museum is a sixteenth-century silver ring inscribed with the name of one 'Egidius the priest'.

Edema collarettes. A form of dog-collar (q.v.) for daytime wear briefly fashionable at the beginning of this century. They consisted of a soft material such as velvet or lace threaded through a series of jewelled bars.

Egeran. Idocrase (q.v.) from Eger in Hungary.

Egg pearls. Oval or egg-shaped natural pearls.

Egyptian jasper. A variegated yellow and brown jasper.

Egyptian jewellery. With the exception of enamelling on metal, the jewellers of Ancient Egypt were acquainted with all the basic processes used in modern jewellery. There has been some debate as to whether they used solder, but although many pieces of jewellery were joined by the colloid hard-soldering process (q.v.) for which no solder is required, ordinary hard-soldering of the modern type was certainly also employed. The materials most commonly used were gold and silver, cornelian, lapis lazuli, jasper, amethyst (in certain periods), green feldspar, turquoise, glass, faience (q.v.) and steatite. All of these were obtainable in Egypt, with the exception of lapis lazuli, which was imported from Afghanistan. Most if not all Egyptian jewellery had a magical or religious significance in addition to its ornamental value.

Most of the jewellery that has survived was made for burial with the dead person and was intended to protect and help him on his journey through the underworld. Signs of wear on some tomb-jewellery, however, indicate that it was worn during life, and sculptures and wall-paintings depict the living as wearing very similar types of jewellery to the dead. It is there-

fore impossible to draw a distinction between the two types, except in the case of very flimsy pieces which were obviously not designed to be worn in life, and a few emblems such as the *akh*-bird symbolizing the soul of the deceased, which never appear on jewellery worn by the living.

Since the jewellery reflects a religious and magical system, it has a limited number of formalized motifs which occur repeatedly. There are many of these, but among the most important are the scarab, a beetle-form symbolizing rebirth (see *Scarabs*); the sacred cobra (*uraeus*), emblem of supreme power and protector of the king; the falcon, symbol of the god Horus and also of the king; the *udjat*, the eye of Horus; and the various hieroglyphic signs, which were used both for their literal meaning and as having amuletic power in their own right. Of the numerous amuletic symbols perhaps the most important is the *ankh*-sign, in the shape of a T surmounted by a loop, which was of very ancient origin and was the symbol of life. Floral designs are common, particularly the papyrus and lotus, and these also are usually symbolic; the lotus, for instance, is a symbol of resurrection. In addition to these there are the specific emblems of the gods, such as the sun's disc, and a variety of naturalistic forms which were also regarded as amulets. An example is the fly, which somewhat surprisingly was an honorific decoration.

Egyptian history is usually divided into three major periods; the Old Kingdom (*c.* 2686–2181 B.C.), the Middle Kingdom (*c.* 1991–1786 B.C.) and the New Kingdom (*c.* 1567–1085 B.C.) (the gaps are accounted for by periods of anarchy). Throughout this time and for centuries before and after it the main characteristics of Egyptian jewellery remained essentially the same.

One of the most important items was the *collar*, which had amuletic powers in itself. It was worn in all periods and by both sexes. The commonest type was that known as the *usekh*; it consisted of numerous rows of beads held together by connecting spacer bars and covered the shoulders and chest. The beads were of various materials – steatite or glazed faience, lapis lazuli, turquoise, sometimes glass. In the Middle Kingdom beads were often replaced by small amulets, sometimes inlaid with coloured stones and glass. In the same period terminals in the shape of falcon-heads were added to the collar. At the back of the neck hung a counterpoise to the collar and this was sometimes decorated to match. Other types of collar were the *menat*, which had religious significance and consisted of numerous strings of beads gathered together and threaded through several circular spacer-beads, and the *shebiu*-collar, an honorific decoration consisting of up to four rows of thick biconical beads closely strung. Some rich *shebiu*-collars found in Tutankhamun's tomb were strung with beads of red and yellow gold, and had inlaid terminals in the shape of lotus buds.

The *pectoral* or breast-ornament originated before the Old Kingdom as an apron of beads hanging from the collar; during the Old Kingdom a pictorial design was incorporated above the beads, and in the Middle Kingdom the picture alone remained. It developed into the most distinctive form of Egyptian jewellery, displaying fine craftsmanship and a highly sophisticated grasp of design. The usual form of pectoral was a fairly large openwork ornament representing the activities of the Kings or conveying some symbolic meaning. It was usually contained in a rectangular frame representing a shrine, and was lavishly inlaid with lapis lazuli, turquoise, cornelian and other materials. The design was repeated in repoussé on the back, and the details brought out by chasing. One of the finest examples is the pectoral of the princess Sit-Hathor-Int, daughter of Sesostris II (see illustration); this is rather unusual for the Middle Kingdom period in that it is not contained in a shrine. The design shows two falcons (symbol of royalty) each resting one foot against palm-branches held up by a god. Above the palm branches is the royal cartouche of Sesostris II, held by two sacred cobras from whose necks hang *ankh*-signs. All parts of the design are covered with cloisonné inlays of lapis lazuli, cornelian and turquoise, and the falcons' eyes are picked out with chips of garnet. Pectorals do not seem to have been worn by men until the New Kingdom.

Diadems were basically simple – a band of metal encircling the forehead and meeting at the back in a stylized knot – but in the Middle and New Kingdoms they were often inlaid with coloured stones

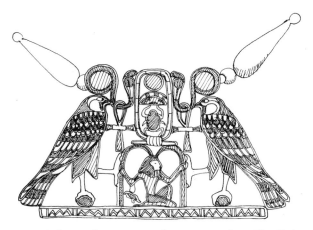

Pectoral of Sit-Hathor-Int. Metropolitan Museum of Art, New York

125

and decorated with streamers of precious metal hanging down at the back. The diadems of the kings were surmounted by the protective figures of the cobra or vulture, and Tutankhamun's diadem (described below) is a superb example. Some of the floral headdresses of the princesses are of amazing delicacy and lightness, and a diadem belonging to one of the wives of Tuthmosis III (1504–1450 B.C.) is decorated at the front with two beautifully-modelled gazelle-heads cast in gold.

Bracelets were worn in all periods by both sexes, but apparently more by women. The number varied. The earliest types are narrow bangles and rows of beads joined by spacer-bars. Queen Hetepheres, the mother of Cheops, had 20 bracelets of sheet silver inlaid with turquoise, green jasper, lapis lazuli and cornelian in butterfly designs. These types continued in use and became more elaborate; in the Middle Kingdom the clasp of the bracelet was inlaid, and amulets in the shape of small gold lions were made exclusively to be worn on bracelets; they were set facing each other.

Anklets were usually similar to bracelets and can only be distinguished by the position in which they were found. From the Middle Kingdom onwards they were worn by both sexes.

Earrings were a very minor part of Egyptian jewellery and were not regularly worn until the XVIIIth dynasty (c. 1567–1320 B.C.). The designs included hoops decorated with a feather pattern or a cornflower pendant, discs with pendant strings of beads, and inlaid discs decorated with rosette patterns. Tutankhamun had several elaborate pairs, including one pair in inlaid gold in the shape of falcons, their outstretched wings forming a circle round the head, which was of blue glass.

The *ring* was important from the Middle Kingdom onwards, since it was the usual setting for the scarab in its role as a signet (see *Scarabs*). The name or device of the owner was cut in intaglio on the base of the scarab, which was mounted as a swivelling bezel with the carved back normally facing outwards. Scarabs were the most usual feature of rings, but some rings were simply decorated with granulation, and others have beads of turquoise, amethyst or quartz. At the beginning of the New Kingdom the solid signet-ring with an engraved oblong bezel made its appearance and gradually replaced the scarab-ring. There was also a type with a rectangular plaque bezel which swivelled like the scarab.

Egyptian jewellery reached its peak of splendour in the treasure of Tutankhamun (1361–1352 B.C.). The extravagant jewellery buried with the young king is not only much richer than anything that precedes or follows it, but is often in a freer and more imaginative style. It notably lacks the restraint of earlier work. There were, for instance, twenty-six pectorals in the tomb, some in the traditional style described above, but others in a new baroque style that is almost three-dimensional. The scarabs are large and fully modelled and almost look as though they are crawling; the flowers have a fleshy appearance and are sometimes completely in the round. A similar style is found in the bracelets, of which the most impressive is completely covered along its top surface with a large free-standing scarab beetle carved in lapis lazuli and mounted on gold legs. Numerous collars were found on the mummy, some of them of engraved sheet gold in the shape of falcons or vultures with outstretched wings. The diadem (see illustration), which is thought to have been Tutankhamun's diadem in life and not merely a funeral ornament, is an inlaid gold circlet attached to the front of which is the head of a vulture in the round, superbly modelled in gold. Next to the vulture is the head of the sacred cobra, the body of which winds snakily over the top of the head to the back of the circlet, where it is joined by long gold streamers inlaid with glass and stones. After the XVIIIth dynasty, to which Tutankhamun belonged, artistic standards in Egypt gradually declined as the country lost its foreign possessions and

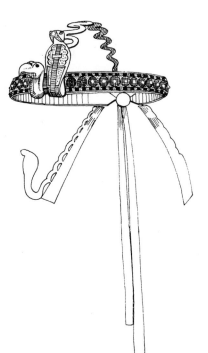

Tutankhamun's diadem. Cairo Museum

which showed best by candlelight were usually too ostentatious for daytime wear, two distinct types of jewellery – precious stones for evening, semi-precious for day – now developed.

Evening jewellery was totally dominated by the diamond. The principal reason for this was the invention just before 1700 of the brilliant cut (q.v.); this revealed for the first time the superb fire of the stone, which would be particularly dazzling by candlelight. (Diamonds were also plentiful; the Golconda mines were at the height of their production and after 1725 there was a rich source in Brazil.) To increase their brilliance the diamonds were nearly always set in silver (gold has less reflectivity and gives the stones a yellow tinge), and the settings were open at the bottom to allow light into the stones from below.

The characteristic designs were based on stars and crosses and on the flowers,

began to disintegrate politically. There was an artistic revival under the XXVIth dynasty (c. 664–525 B.C.) but nothing important was produced in the way of jewellery. In 525 B.C. Egypt was conquered by the Persians and in 332, after Alexander the Great's conquest of Persia, it came under the rule of the Ptolemies, from which time it progressively adopted Hellenistic styles from the Greek craftsmen who settled there.

Egyptian shell. See *Alexandria shell.*

Eight cut. A very simplified form of the brilliant cut used for small diamonds. It has a total of 18 facets including the culet. See *Diamond-cutting* for description.

Eighteenth-century jewellery. Eighteenth-century jewellery reflects a new phenomenon in European social life which had begun just before the turn of the century; the importance of social gatherings in the evening. As jewels

Portuguese brooch in asymmetrical design, about 1760. Victoria and Albert Museum

127

Girandole earring and brooch from a mid-eighteenth century demi parure. Spanish. Victoria and Albert Museum

leaves, and ribbons that had been popular in the seventeenth century, but the style was on the whole lighter and more flowing. Asymmetrical designs became fashionable in the 1730s (see illustration) and remained so until mid-century. The parure or matching set of jewellery was now indispensable for ladies of fashion; its basic constituents were girandole earrings, a Sévigné brooch worn below the décolletage, an aigrette or a jewelled hairpin, and perhaps a necklace, bracelet or stomacher.

Girandole earrings had been fashionable since the later seventeenth century. The characteristic form was a bow, star, or ribbon shape from which hung three pendant stones (see illustration). Large drop-shaped pendants were also fashionable, sometimes featuring a briolette stone which would swing freely to enhance its glitter.

Sévigné brooches were often in the girandole form. Others were based on delicate floral sprays or bunches. The brooch might be replaced by a long triangular *stomacher* (q.v.) which covered the front of the bodice and would also be based on a floral or ribbon design. Some of these jewels were made in detachable sections so that their size could be altered according to whether a modest or a grand effect was desired.

Aigrettes were very fashionable during this century; the traditional form was a plume of feathers, but there were also stars, butterflies and other forms. Small rose-cut diamonds, pavé-set in glittering masses, were used alongside brilliants.

Necklaces and *bracelets* were of less importance, although some of the diamond necklaces were magnificent. A band of silk or velvet worn round the throat was fashionable, and similar bands were worn as bracelets, often with an enamelled miniature set in the clasp. Other bracelets often consisted of several strands of pearls. Coloured stones were not merely less popular than diamonds for evening wear during the greater part of the century; they were actually unfashionable. Colour was not thought desirable, which is one reason for the complete disappearance of enamelled settings (except in Spain, where the taste for colour was never quite lost). In the 1760s, however, coloured stones – topazes, emeralds, sapphires – began to appear again, possibly encouraged by an increasing naturalism in flower designs. Precious stones of all kinds were imitated in paste (q.v.), for by now the paste industry was well established. George Ravenscroft had invented a good flint glass in 1676, and in the early eighteenth century Georges Stras produced a lead glass which when suitably cut gave a very passable imitation of diamond. These pastes were extremely popular, as was rock-crystal as another substitute for diamonds. Paste and crystal jewellery was not merely the bourgeoisie's answer to the diamond parures of the Court; it was made by some of the most distinguished jewellers, and worn by the queens and empresses of Europe – though not, of course, in the evening. Besides its attractiveness, there was a further sound reason for the use of imitation jewellery by the rich. In an age when travelling was fashionable but hazardous, it made the toll exacted by the highwayman less costly.

Daytime jewellery might be of paste or a wide variety of inexpensive and ornamental stones. There were parures of agate, amethyst, cornelian, smoky quartz, turquoise (very popular), river pearls, amber, and many other stones. Enamels were fashionable, usually thinly cut and backed with a foil to increase their brilliance. The fashions for daytime jewellery – whether, for instance, earrings should be worn – tended to change much more frequently than fashions for evening wear. Besides paste and the cheaper

gemstones, the middle classes could choose from a considerable range of less expensive materials. Cut steel (q.v.), long manufactured in Birmingham and Woodstock, became extremely popular in the latter half of the century, and marcasite (iron pyrites) was also widely used. The glittering faceted metal studs were the poor man's diamonds. The poor man's gold was pinchbeck (q.v.) or one of the other recently-invented alloys. The eighteenth century saw a revived enthusiasm for cameos, and those who could not afford the genuine hardstone variety could choose from shell cameos, from the moulded pastes produced in great number by James Tassie (q.v.), or from the pottery cameos, often set in rims of cut steel, made by Wedgwood (q.v.) towards the end of the century. Finally, as substitutes for the French painted enamels fashionable among the wealthy, there were the Battersea and Bilston enamels (qq.v.) which were produced in the form of small plaques suitable for setting in bracelets, etc., as well as in the form of snuffboxes and other ornamental objects. It will be noticed that all these substitute materials were of British origin; they fulfilled an increasing demand for inexpensive jewellery from the middle classes in an era of industrial prosperity, but they were also very successfully exported to the rest of Europe, including – ironically – the fashion-centre of Paris.

The items of jewellery in which these cheaper materials were most likely to be used were buckles and chatelaines, both essential for fashionable daytime wear. The *chatelaine* (q.v.), basically an attachment worn at the belt for suspending a watch, took on an all-purpose function in the course of the century and might have numerous small objects suspended from it including an *étui* (a cylindrical case) containing such useful things as scissors, pencil, tweezers, etc. The chatelaine and its accompaniments offered almost the only opportunity in eighteenth-century jewellery for high-class metalwork, and in the early part of the century superb examples were made in chased

129

gold. Later painted enamels were incorporated. The cheaper variety were made in cast pinchbeck or some other gold-substitute, and later cut steel was very popular, often in combination with Wedgwood cameos. (See *Wedgwood*.)

Apart from jewelled buttons (q.v.), *buckles* were the main focus of jewellery for men. They were universally worn – set with diamonds for those at Court, with paste or cut steel for the middle class. They were worn, according to fashion, on various parts of the attire, but almost until the end of the century it was essential to have them on the shoes. Small jewelled buckles were also fashionable for women. (See also *Buckles*.)

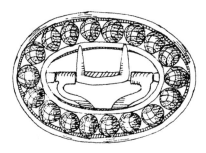

Late eighteenth-century cut-steel buckle

Men also wore *rings*, but they were less popular than in previous centuries and were much lighter in form. Fashionable types were the *giardinetti* ring (one of these is shown under *Rings*), in the shape of a floral spray set with delicately-coloured stones, and the marquise ring, which became popular in the second half of the century and had an oval or shuttle-shaped bezel set usually with a coloured stone surrounded by small diamonds. The commemorative and mourning jewellery of the seventeenth century continued into the eighteenth with rings commemorating political events and mourning rings in which the bezel is in the shape of a miniature urn. The latter were particularly popular in England, where the wearing of mourning and sentimental jewellery was almost a national trait. (See *Memorial jewellery*.)

The ordered society of the eighteenth century was brought to an abrupt end by the French Revolution (1789), which shattered the class structure that had regulated, among other things, the wearing of jewellery. The effect was felt to some degree throughout Europe, not only indirectly through political influences, but directly in that France had been the acknowledged leader of European fashion. In the years immediately following the Revolution French jewellery sank to its nadir: the designs were trivial, the motifs patriotic, the materials of little intrinsic value. The Paris company of goldsmiths was abolished in 1791, and many of the Crown Jewels were sold off to raise money.

This enforced egalitarianism, however, was short-lived. In 1799 Napoleon declared himself First Consul of the Republic, and it was not long before France again had a court to provide patronage for the jewellers and standards of fashion for the rest of Europe. (See *Nineteenth-century jewellery*.)

Eilat stone (Elath stone). An opaque, variegated blue or green stone found near Eilat on the Gulf of Aqaba and usually cut as cabochons or tumbled. It is a mixture of copper minerals including turquoise, chrysocolla and pseudomalachite (qq.v.), and is said to come from the copper mines of King Solomon.

Elbaite. Pink tourmaline from Elba.

Elco pearls. Imitation pearls.

El Doradoite. Local name for a blue quartz from El Dorado Co., California.

Electric jewels. A form of novelty jewellery introduced in the late 1860s. They consisted of moving hair-jewels which were kept in motion by an electrical battery worn under the clothing.

Electro-gilding. See *Electroplating*.

Electroplating. The process of depositing a layer of metal (e.g. gold, silver) on an object by means of an electric current. The object to be plated is connected to the negative terminal (the cathode), and a sheet or bar of the plating metal is connected to the positive terminal (the anode). Both are immersed in a plating bath containing acid and a solution of the plating metal, and when a low-voltage direct current is passed through, ions of the plating metal are attracted to the negative terminal and are deposited on the article to be plated. The thickness of the coating depends on the amount of current and on how long the process continues. The use of electroplating in jewellery is mainly confined to plating with gold, silver and the platinum metals. Rhodium is often electroplated on to silver to protect it from tarnishing. Other metals which can be used for plating are copper, brass, nickel, chromium and cadmium. Non-metallic substances such as plastic can be electro-plated, but have to be treated first to make them electrically conductive.

The first experiments in electroplating were made at the end of the eighteenth century. By the 1830s it was possible to electroplate silver with copper or gold, and lead with silver. However, it was not until 1840 that satisfactory results in silver and gold-plating were achieved. The process, using cyanide of silver and cyanide of gold, was patented by the Birmingham firm of Elkington Bros., who attempted to exploit it commercially but met with such strong opposition from shopkeepers and manufacturers of Sheffield plate (q.v.) that they made no profit on their invention for seven years. In the 1860s, however, the electroplating industry expanded rapidly, and by about 1866 the manufacture of Sheffield plate had virtually ceased and the workers had joined the new plating factories in the Midlands and London.

Electrotype. A facsimile made by electro-typing (q.v.).

Electrotyping. The process of producing an exact replica of an object by electrolytic deposition of copper in a mould. The process was used by jewellery manufacturers in the last century (see below) but has now been replaced by centrifugal casting (q.v.). It is still used in the printing trade for making blocks, etc. Electrotype replicas of medallions and other objects for use in jewellery are made in the following way. An impression is taken of the original in a suitable medium (a modern recipe is 2 parts gutta percha to 1 part lard, with a little linseed oil), and the surface of the impression is rendered electrically conductive by coating with plumbago. The mould is immersed in a plating bath and coated with a layer of copper by ordinary electro-plating (q.v.) methods. The layer of copper is subsequently separated from the mould and the surface which was in contact with it is a replica of the original. (The method obviously cannot be used for reproducing a three-dimensional object in the round; for this two surfaces have to be made and soldered together. Alternatively the article itself may be coated with plumbago – assuming it is non-conductive – and the copper deposited on top, but this is electroplating and not electrotyping.)

The principles of electrotyping seem to have been discovered in the late 1830s by several people independently. In 1839 a Mr. Spencer of Liverpool announced that he had discovered a method of producing facsimiles of copper coins using a Daniell's cell. The idea created immediate interest and the copying of medals, coins and seals soon became a fashionable amusement. The method involved either taking a mould of the original in metal, or else plating on to the original, removing the coating, which then became the mould, and then depositing copper on to that to produce a replica of the original. It was quickly discovered, however, that a mould made in almost any material could be coated with metal if its surface was rendered conductive with a thin layer of graphite. This extended the possibilities of the process and by the 1850s it was being used commercially to make reproductions of the ancient jewellery so dear to the Victorians.

Electrotype facsimiles of Celtic brooches were shown by a Dublin firm at the 1851

Exhibition, and within a short time other manufacturers were producing similar reproductions in other styles. Since several copies could be produced at once, electrotyping was a mass-production process, but the quantity of jewellery produced by this method in the nineteenth century was considerably less than that produced by machine-stamping. (See *Machine-stamping* and *Nineteenth-century jewellery*.)

Electrum. A natural alloy of gold and silver used in the ancient world from Egyptian times onwards. One of the sources was probably the gold-bearing river Pactolus in Asia Minor. The proportion of silver varied; Pliny gives it as one part in five. An alloy of gold and silver is nowadays known as 'white gold' (q.v.).

Eligius, St. (St. Eloi). Patron saint of jewellers and metalworkers. St. Eligius was born near Limoges about 588, the son of an artisan, and, showing considerable manual skill at an early age, was apprenticed to a goldsmith who was master of the mint at Limoges. After completing his apprenticeship he went to Paris where he attracted the notice of the treasurer of King Clotaire II. According to tradition, the King commissioned him to make a throne in gold and precious stones and Eligius, out of the materials provided, made two. Impressed by his honesty as much as by his technical skill, the king made him master of the mint and he retained this post through the next three succeeding reigns. His biographer records that he made a number of fine jewelled cups and ecclesiastical vessels, and numerous reliquary shrines are attributed to him, including those of St. Martin at Tours and St. Dionysius at St. Denis.

A pious and philanthropic man, he was made bishop of Noyon and Tournai in 641 and founded a monastery at Solignac in Limousin, the monks of which were well known for their work in the arts. Eligius continued to practise the goldsmith's art all his life (he died in 660), and a guild of French jewellers and goldsmiths was founded in his name in the thirteenth century. Paintings and sculpture usually represent him holding a hammer, beating metal on a goldsmith's anvil, or presenting a jewelled shrine to the king. (See also *Dunstan, St.*)

Elite pearls. Imitation pearls.

Email en résille sur verre. A delicate form of enamelwork, basically a type of champlevé (q.v.), in which the design is cut in glass or rock crystal, and the recesses lined with gold foil and then filled with translucent enamels. (See *Enamel*.)

'Email en ronde bosse'. See *Encrusted enamel*.

Embossing. See *Repoussé work*.

Emerald. (Beryl. S.G. 2.68–2.77; R.I. 1.57–1.58; H. $7\frac{1}{2}$–8.) A transparent grass-green stone, the most valuable variety of beryl (q.v.). The characteristic colour is due to chromium: the green beryl which is coloured by vanadium or iron is of a different shade and is not classed as true emerald, and is therefore much less valuable. The extreme rarity with which emerald of the correct colour is found comparatively free from flaws makes it one of the most precious, if not the most precious, of gemstones. Even when unflawed the crystals are rarely quite clear and usually contain characteristic inclusions. These give the stone its depth and character.

Emerald is doubly refractive and dichroic (qq.v.), the two colours being blue-green and yellowish-green. Which of these predominates depends on the direction in which the table facet is cut. Good emeralds are nearly always faceted in the step-cut style (see *Gem-cutting*) with the corners mitred – a cut which displays the depth of colour to best advantage and is now generally known as the emerald cut. Poorer quality stones are cut *en cabochon* or made into beads (particularly in Indian jewellery). Badly flawed emerald with a good colour may be carved.

Many superstitions have gathered around the emerald. In the ancient world it had associations with the sight. It was thought to be beneficial to the eyesight and even to heal diseases of the eye, and was supposed to have the power of blinding serpents. It is recorded that Nero used an emerald crystal to help him watch gladiator fights, but exactly how he used it is not clear. Emeralds were said to change colour to reveal the inconstancy of a lover: this presumably has something to do with the fact, remarked on by Pliny, that emeralds are unusual among green stones in retaining their colour in any light. The emerald is the birthstone for May, its colour being reminiscent of spring green.

The name 'emerald' is derived from a Persian word rendered into Greek as 'smaragdos', and the term was applied somewhat indiscriminately in the ancient world to cover a variety of green stones. It is most unlikely that the 'emerald' in Aaron's breast-plate really was an emerald. The earliest known source of emeralds were the so-called Cleopatra's mines in Egypt at Jebel Zubara and Jebel Sikait. These mines were being worked at least by 1650 B.C. and may have provided all the emeralds of the ancient world. Knowledge of their whereabouts was lost during the Middle Ages and they were not rediscovered until 1818. Various attempts have since been made to work them, but the emeralds they produce are cloudy and light-coloured, and much inferior to the best South American stones.

South American emeralds first reached Europe after the conquest of Peru by Pizarro, who seized the hoarded emeralds of the Incas and sent them back to Spain. The Spaniards later discovered the source of the stones in the eastern range of the Andes, in what is now Columbia. There are three principal mines – at Muzo, Cosquez and El Chivor. The Indian name for El Chivor was *Somondoco* – 'god of the green stones'. This was the first mine to be worked by the Spaniards, and it is said that its position was betrayed to them by an Indian. In the following century it was abandoned, was rapidly obliterated by the tropical vegetation, and was not rediscovered until 1896, since when it has been sporadically worked.

The mine at Muzo is said to produce the finest emeralds in the world – they have a velvety appearance which is highly prized. They occur in calcite veins in a bituminous limestone and are mined by digging the soil in terraces and washing away the debris. (Emerald is always mined from the parent rock: it is never found in alluvial soil.) A common internal peculiarity of Muzo stones is the 'three-phase inclusion', which consists of a flat cavity containing a bubble of gas and a crystal which is probably common salt. The Columbian emerald mines are operated by the government and the emeralds recovered are released for sale according to demand: when the stock exceeds market requirements the mines are temporarily shut down.

Brazil was long thought to be a potential source of emeralds and the quest for them played an important part in the opening up of the country to Europeans in the sixteenth century. In fact, however, Brazil produces few emeralds and none of high quality. They are pale in colour and unusually free from inclusions, which would suggest that they are not true emerald were it not that they have been found to contain chromium.

Emeralds were found in Russia in 1830, when a peasant noticed some green stones at the foot of an uprooted tree. The mine, which has been worked intermittently, produces large crystals of somewhat poor quality but also small crystals of a very good colour. Russian emeralds have characteristic inclusions of mica and actinolite.

Emerald has been used in Indian jewellery for over a thousand years, but the material was probably all imported. As far as is known, true emerald was not found in India until 1943. The stones are of variable quality. A characteristic of Indian emerald is that the inclusions (liquid-filled cavities and biotite) run usually at right-angles to each other.

Other sources of emerald include Austria, Australia, South Africa, Rhodesia, Norway.

The colour of true emerald is so characteristic that the experienced eye can usually distinguish it from other green stones without difficulty. Where there is a superficial resemblance, emerald can be distinguished by its dichroism, its low specific gravity (qq.v.) or its comparative softness. Very good imitations of emerald can be produced using glass, which is often made with realistic-looking flaws and inclusions, but glass is not dichroic and is softer than emerald. Finally, a decisive test can usually be made by means of a colour filter (q.v.) through which emerald shows a red tint while most other green stones appear greenish. Unfortunately some emeralds, particularly those from India and South Africa, do not show red through the filter. Emerald is most often imitated by composite stones, particularly 'soudé emeralds' which consist of two pieces of colourless quartz or synthetic colourless spinel cemented together with a layer of some green substance, usually a copper compound (see also *Doublet*). If these stones are dropped in water and looked at from the side the three layers can be clearly seen. Real emeralds of poor colour may be painted on the back to improve the colour and then put in a closed setting, which makes the 'improvement' difficult to detect. Synthetic emeralds are now manufactured and marketed for use in jewellery: for their characteristics, see *Synthetic gemstones*.

Emerald glass. Fused emerald (see *Glass*). Also used to mean any green glass, or a colour filter (q.v.) used for identifying emeralds.

'Emeraldine'. A misnomer for chalcedony which has been stained green by chromic oxide. The colour is not unlike that of emerald and the material shows red through a colour filter. (See *Emerald*.)

'Emeraldite'. A misnomer for pale green tourmaline.

Emerald jade. Jade of the finest emerald-green colour, also known as imperial jade.

'Emerald matrix'. A misnomer for green fluorspar. Also used to mean the mother rock in which emerald occurs.

'Emerita'. See '*Symerald*'.

Emery. A coarse form of corundum (q.v.) containing a proportion of haematite and magnetite. It is used in the grinding and polishing of gemstones, and is available in many grades for various types of work.

Emery cloth. A cloth coated with emery powder. (See *Emery* and *Emery stick*.)

Emery stick. A stick to which emery cloth (q.v.) is stuck, used for abrading flat metal surfaces.

Empress Eugénie Diamond. A 51-carat Indian diamond which was first heard of as belonging to Catherine the Great, who presented it to one of her favourites, Potemkin, as a reward for his military services. It was later purchased by Napoleon III as a wedding present for the Empress Eugénie, and set in a diamond necklace. After the collapse of the Second Empire it was bought by the Gaekwar of Baroda.

Enamel. Enamelling is the process of fusing coloured glass in powdered form to a surface. The surface is usually metal, but other materials may be used if they can withstand red heat. The glass is a flint glass containing 25–40 per cent lead oxide, and the colours are obtained by adding small quantities of metallic salts. Gold chloride gives a dark red, oxide of cobalt gives blue, iron oxide gives green, uranate of soda yellow, permanganate of potash purple, etc. These are mixed with the powdered glass, and tin oxide is added if an opaque enamel is desired. After being washed, the powdered enamel is mixed with water and applied to the surface, and the piece is fired in a furnace. Many coats of enamel may be required and the piece has to be fired again each time. After the last firing it is ground smooth and polished with pumice.

In jewellery the surface to be enamelled is usually gold, silver or copper. The best results are obtained with fine gold, which is ductile, has a high melting point and imparts a soft glow to translucent enamel. For obvious reasons solid gold is not often used, but a similar effect can be obtained by enamelling a piece of copper, coating the enamel with gold leaf and firing it, and then applying translucent enamels over the gold leaf. Copper itself is a quite satisfactory base for enamel although it gives a more subdued effect than gold. The cold appearance of silver lends itself well to blue and green enamels and is less satisfactory with warm colours. Other metals which have been enamelled for jewellery are bronze and iron (for which the enamels have to be opaque).

The principal types of enamelling are as follows.

In *cloisonné* enamelling the different-coloured enamels are placed in cells consisting of narrow strips of metal wire which have been soldered to the base. The back of the cell may be roughened to allow the enamel to grip well. The metal strips may be glued to the base instead of soldered, in which case the glue melts during the firing and the strips are held in place by the enamel when it hardens. Cloisonné is one of the oldest methods of enamelling and can be very beautiful; the effect is similar to that of a stained-glass window. An extension of this method is *plique-à-jour* enamelling, in which the enamels have no metal backing and are open to the light. There are various ways of achieving this: the enamel may be mixed to a consistency which will hold together in an open setting without coming out, or it may be placed on a thin metal backing which is scraped away after the firing. If it is placed on a copper base this can later be dissolved away with acid. Another way is to set the enamels over a base to which they will not adhere, and which will separate easily from them when cool. Cellini used clay for this purpose. Plique-à-jour is a technique rarely practised because of its difficulty, and few examples of earlier work have survived, owing to their fragility.

In *champlevé* enamelling the enamels are placed in recesses which have been cut out of the base metal. Work done in this style tends to be coarser than cloisonné and is most effective on a fairly large scale, although some very delicate champlevé work was produced in the seventeenth century on such articles as watch-cases. A development of champlevé is the difficult technique known as *émail en résille sur verre*. The design is cut into glass or rock crystal and the hollows are lined with very thin gold foil and then filled with translucent enamel. The glass, if glass is used, must of course have a higher melting-point than the enamels. This technique was introduced in the early seventeenth century and as far as is known was practised only for a very short period.

Basse-taille is similar to champlevé in that the enamels are placed in recesses in the metal, but the base is previously chased with a design in relief so that the surface is of uneven depth. The enamels are arranged over this to give a flat surface, and the resulting variations in thickness of the enamel produce subtle gradations of colour and shadowing. Another type of enamelling in relief is *encrusted enamel*, also known as *émail en ronde bosse*. Here the enamel is applied to figures or modelling in high relief. (To make enamel stick to a vertical surface a little gum tragacanth is mixed with it before application.) Encrusted enamel was popular during the Renaissance and used widely on the splendid pendants worn at the time.

The other major technique is *painted enamel*, also known as *Limoges enamel* after the centre where it was developed. For this technique it is usual to use a slightly convex copper plate as the base and coat it with a layer of white enamel. When this has been fired, the design is drawn on the white enamel and the colours are applied with a fine brush or a palette-knife in the same way as paint. There are no dividing walls between the

135

colours, but they do not run together when fired if carefully applied. Many layers of enamel may be applied to obtain the desired depth of colour, the piece being fired again after each new application.

Grisaille is painted enamel using dark and neutral colours which give a monochromatic effect. For this the surface is first coated with black enamel and fired, then with opaque white enamel and fired again, leaving a grey surface on which tone-contrasts are gradually built up with successive coats of enamel. Blacks, greys, browns and purples are the colours most commonly used. Grisaille is very suitable for the reproduction of engravings and similar fine work. It was popular in the eighteenth century for enamelled medallions set in jewellery.

History. Enamelling is an ancient art, but appears to have developed considerably later than most of the other techniques used in jewellery. As far as is known, although the ancient Egyptians practised the inlaying of stones and glass with great skill they did not use enamel until Roman times. The earliest examples of enamel yet found are a primitive type of champlevé used to decorate certain Mycenaean gold ornaments of the late fifteenth and fourteenth centuries B.C. Some rings of the twelfth century B.C. found in Cyprus contain a primitive cloisonné enamel, as does a gold sceptre of the same date. Some Syrian ornaments of about the tenth century B.C. are decorated in the same way. No further examples have been found until the sixth century B.C., when cloisonné enamel appears again, set in filigree instead of metal strips, in Greek jewellery (q.v.). From this time onwards enamel, generally set in filigree, was regularly used in Greek jewellery but was never an important technique. In the third and second centuries B.C. earring-pendants were decorated with 'dipped enamel' – a heated metal core was dipped into molten glass, which adhered to it and was shaped by ordinary glassworking methods.

The Romans used enamel even less than the Greeks, except in the provinces where Celtic influence was strong. The Celts appear to have developed enamel independently, and were using it extensively in metalwork well before the Roman invasion of Britain. The enamels were all of the champlevé type, in bright reds, yellows and blues, laid in hollows scooped out of the metal in the characteristic Celtic curvilinear designs (see *Celtic jewellery*). The metal was usually bronze. Celtic work of the Christian period includes cloisonné enamel. By this time Celtic art had been influenced by the Byzantine art which dominated the Christian East, and the cloisonné is probably a reflection of Byzantine influence.

Enamelling was brought to the status of a fine art in Byzantium. It seems to have been first practised there in the sixth century A.D., probably as an independent development, and reached its highest level in the tenth century. The usual form was cloisonné enamel on gold or electrum (a gold-silver alloy), and in the work of the best period the flexibility of cloisonné is combined with a skilful use of bright pure colours. After the tenth century the colours deteriorate, notably the flesh-tints, which become dead white instead of the earlier delicate pink. Champlevé and enamelling on relief were also practised, though more rarely. Most of the Byzantine enamels were destined for ecclesiastical use, but there are some splendid surviving examples in jewellery (see *Byzantine jewellery*). Byzantine influence percolated westwards during the Dark Ages and was instrumental in the revival of culture in the eighth century and subsequently. Cloisonné enamels in a style reminiscent of the Byzantine were produced in France, Germany and Italy, and the ninth-century Alfred jewel (q.v.) is a notable English example. Byzantine influence was particularly strong in Germany in the tenth and eleventh centuries, but then declined, and cloisonné began to be replaced by champlevé. Translucent enamel on gold gave way to opaque enamel on large vessels and ornaments of copper and bronze, made for the Church. Limoges became an important centre for this work. During the fourteenth century important developments occurred in enamelling. More varied effects were sought for, and translucent enamels on silver became popular. The basse taille technique was developed, probably in Italy, and some fine work in this style was done in France. Towards the end of the century the difficult technique of encrusted enamel was invented and very quickly perfected. Superb examples of it are seen on some early fifteenth-century brooches (see *Medieval jewellery*). Enamel was at this time fairly lavishly used on brooches, pendant reliquaries and other items of personal jewellery, as well as in ecclesiastical work. Encrusted enamel was initially only popular for a short period, but was subsequently revived in the later sixteenth century.

Towards the end of the fifteenth century it was discovered that dividing walls between different-coloured enamels were not necessary to keep the colours from mingling, and that a piece could be re-fired many times to allow colours to be built up without damage to the enamel. At the same time counter-enamelling was invented. This was the process of coating the back of the piece with a layer of enamel before firing. As glass has a different rate of contraction and expansion from metal, a thin sheet of enamelled metal will curl on cooling and push the enamel off unless it is strengthened with cloisons. A counter-enamel holds the metal rigid and forces it to set slightly stretched. The combination of these discoveries resulted in the production of painted enamels on thin sheets of copper. It is doubtful whether the technique originated at Limoges but it was certainly quickly taken up there, and most of the painted enamels now surviving are products of the Limoges school. The early examples are in vivid colours, notably cobalt blue, with a lavish use of gold 'enamel' (fine gold dust, laid on with gum arabic) for the highlights. The subjects were frequently religious and

many of the enamels were for ecclesiastical use. The art of enamelling at Limoges was transmitted from father to son, but the talent was often very unequally distributed within families. The two most famous enamellists of the sixteenth century were Nardon Pénicaud (died mid-sixteenth century) and Léonard Limousin (died 1577). Pénicaud's work shows a mixture of Renaissance and medieval styles; Limousin's after 1535 is purely Renaissance. Among Limousin's work are a number of striking portraits. It was mainly in the form of portrait medallions that painted enamel was used in jewellery at this time.

Enamel was used lavishly in Renaissance jewellery but mostly in the form of encrusted enamel. Its most striking application was in the large figured pendants popular from the later sixteenth century onwards (see *Renaissance jewellery*). Particularly effective use was made of opaque white on a gold surface. Enamel was by no means confined to fairly large areas, but was regularly used on the settings of stones in any form of jewellery. During the seventeenth century the use of enamel on settings declined (see *Seventeenth-century jewellery*) but it was still used with extreme delicacy, usually in the form of translucent champlevé, on miniature cases and watches, and the backs of jewels were also enamelled in engraved designs. In the following century enamel retreated altogether before the advance of the diamond, which required a practically invisible setting to be seen in its full splendour. Painted enamels, on the other hand, became ever more popular, though their use in jewellery was of course limited. Miniature enamel-painting had developed in the early seventeenth century and was taken up in several centres including Paris, Geneva and Dresden. The best work is that of Jean Petitot (born 1607). Probably the most delicate enamels ever produced are to be seen in the French snuff-boxes and similar pieces of the later eighteenth century, generally depicting pastoral and romantic scenes. Similar

137

enamels in the form of small plaques and medallions became popular in jewellery, and since few people could afford the finer work, cheaper substitutes were produced in England – the Battersea and Bilston enamels (qq.v.). These ranged from pieces in a grisaille colouring or printed in black or sepia from copper plates to copies in bright, almost garish colours of well-known paintings. Etuis for chatelaines (q.v.) decorated in this way were particularly popular. Enamel was revived again, in a somewhat self-consciously artistic way, in the jewellery of the nineteenth century. Carlo Giuliano (q.v.) was a master of the technique of encrusted enamel which had been favoured in the Renaissance. Towards the end of the century enamel was enthusiastically adopted and often very delicately used in Art Nouveau jewellery (q.v.). The jeweller of this period most famed for his use of enamel is, of course, Carl Fabergé (q.v.), who employed a wider range of colours than any enamellist had achieved before. He used special techniques to obtain new effects, such as applying transparent enamels over an engine-turned metal surface so that the enamel appears to shimmer. He specialized in 'en plein' enamelling – the covering of large surfaces with a perfectly smooth layer of enamel. He also revived the ancient techniques of champlevé and cloisonné; in fact his work was, although absolutely contemporary, a continuation of the old Russian school of enamelling derived from the Byzantine tradition.

Since Art Nouveau there has not been a period when enamel was consistently popular. In commercial jewellery, in fact, it has been unfashionable for many years. However, it is increasingly attracting the interest of jewellers who design individual pieces and do not cater for the mass market, and as a hobby it is becoming very popular indeed.

Enamelling kiln. See *Muffle kiln*.

En cabochon. Cut in the shape of a cabochon (q.v.).

Encrusted enamel. A type of enamelwork consisting of the covering of figures in high relief with a layer of enamel. (See *Enamel*.)

Endoscope. An instrument invented in 1926 for distinguishing between genuine and cultured pearls. Only pearls which have been drilled can be examined. The instrument consists basically of a source of light and a system of condensing lenses, a low-powered microscope, and a fine hollow needle at the end of which are two mirrors placed at 45° in opposite directions. There is a small aperture in the top of the needle just before the first mirror. Light is directed through the needle and is thrown up through the aperture by the first mirror, and when a pearl is threaded on to the needle and over the aperture the light is reflected up into the pearl. Natural pearls have a concentric structure, and light entering them is internally reflected in a semicircle along one of the layers. If the aperture is not immediately under the centre of the pearl this light is reflected out again on the wall of the drill-hole and lost, but if the aperture is under the centre of the pearl the light is immediately reflected back on to the second mirror and reflected again as a brilliant flash to the microscope eyepiece. The pearl is usually moved backwards and forwards along the needle, and the appearance of a flash of light proves the pearl to be genuine. Cultured pearls have a nucleus of mother-of-pearl in which the layers are not concentric but run straight. The light therefore does not return to the drill-hole but is reflected up to the surface of the pearl, where it appears as a streak which moves as the pearl is moved along the needle. A special lens enables this surface streak to be observed; all that is seen through the microscope eyepiece is an unchanging dull grey colour. (See also *Pearls*.)

En esclavage. Term for a necklace of several strands in which the strands separate at a certain distance from the catch and are evenly spaced.

Engagement rings. See *Betrothal rings*.

Engine-turning. A method of decorating metal surfaces which was invented in the nineteenth century and began to be widely used in jewellery in the 1940s. The object to be decorated is fixed to the carriage of the machine and moved against the cutting-blade. By controlling the direction of movement, straight lines, zigzags, and wavy and circular patterns can be produced, and with modern machinery several lines can be cut at the same time. (See also *Diamond-milling*.)

English brilliant cut. A simplified form of the brilliant cut, having a total of 30 facets including the culet. (See *Diamond-cutting* for description.)

English Dresden diamond. A diamond weighing 119½ carats in the rough, found at the Bagagem mines in Minas Gerais, Brazil, in 1853. It was bought by a London merchant named Dresden and cut into a pendeloque brilliant of 76½ carats. It was later bought by the Gaekwar of Baroda.

Engraver's block. The pivoting block on which work is held while it is being

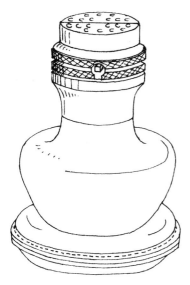

Engraver's block

engraved. The top part has jaws which open like a vice to grip the outside edges of the piece, and the lower part consists of a heavy metal ball which is cushioned on a pad of felt or leather and can be easily rotated with slight pressure. The top part of the block has numerous holes in which a variety of attachments can be fitted to hold work of odd shapes.

Engraving. The production of a linear pattern on metal or some other surface by cutting away the surface with a sharp tool. Sheet-gold was being engraved by the third millennium B.C., the earliest tools being made of flint, copper, bronze and later iron. Modern engraving tools (see *Graver*) are made of steel. The engraver first transfers his design to the surface of the metal using ink, pencil, carbon paper, etc., then fixes the piece to some surface which enables it to be turned easily (see *Engraver's block*). With one hand he steadies and turns the piece, and with the other directs the graver. Much engraving is now done by machine, particularly for work on awkwardly-shaped surfaces and hard metals. A specially-treated silver is available from refiners on which lines can be engraved more cleanly than on ordinary silver.

The engraving of stones has as long a history as the engraving of metal, and in classical times and during the Renaissance it reached a high level of perfection. For information on gem-engraving, see *Cameos*, *Intaglios* and *Seals*.

Enseignes. Hat-badges worn by men during the sixteenth century. (See *Renaissance jewellery*.)

Enstatite. (Magnesium-iron silicate. S.G. 3.26–3.28; R.I. 1.663–1.673; H. 5½.) A generally green or brownish-green transparent stone sometimes faceted for jewellery. This material comes from the South African diamond mines and the Mogok Stone Tract in Burma. Some chatoyant grey enstatite from Ceylon is cut *en cabochon*, and a 6-rayed star enstatite has been found (see *Asterism*). As the proportion of iron increases enstatite becomes *bronzite* (S.G. 3.2), so called because of its bronzy lustre, and *hypersthene* (S.G. 3.4), an almost opaque stone which may be cut *en cabochon* to display the spangled effect caused by small included flakes of other minerals. A transparent brown stone intermediate between enstatite and hypersthene, found in India, is faceted.

Bastite (S.G. about 2.6; H. $3\frac{1}{2}$–4) is an altered enstatite, leek-green in colour, sometimes cut *en cabochon*. Gem-quality material comes from Burma.

Epiasterism. A 'star' effect (see *Asterism*) produced by reflected as distinct from transmitted light.

Epidote (Pistacite). (Calcium-aluminium silicate with iron. S.G. about 3.4; R.I. 1.74–1.77; H. $6\frac{1}{2}$.) A translucent to opaque yellowish-green stone; the colour (pistachio) gives the mineral its alternative name. The greater the percentage of iron, the darker the stone. Epidote is strongly pleochroic (see *Dichroism*), the colours being green, brown and yellow.

Clinozoisite is an epidote containing a smaller percentage of iron and is usually a much lighter green. The specific gravity is similar to that of epidote but the refractive indices are slightly lower. Epidote is found in many parts of the Alps and in North America; clinozoisite in many parts of Europe, Lower California and in Mexico. A deep green epidote coloured by chromium is found at Tawmaw in Upper Burma and is known as *tawmawite*.

Epidote and clinozoisite crystallize in the monoclinic system (see *Crystal systems*), and are closely related to *zoisite* (q.v.) which is of similar composition but crystallizes in the ortho-rhombic system. The name 'epidote' is applied by mineralogists to the whole group.

Episcopal rings. See *Ecclesiastical rings*.

Erinide. (American trade name.) Yellowish-green synthetic spinel.

Erinoid. A casein plastic. (See *Plastics*.)

Essence d'Orient. A fish-scale essence used to produce the 'pearly' effect in imitation pearls. It consists of a silvery substance (guanine) extracted from the scales of certain fish and suspended in a suitable substance such as isinglass. (See *Pearls*.)

Etching. The removal of part of a metal surface by acids to achieve a decorative effect. (Other substances such as glass may also be etched, but these materials have little importance in jewellery.) The areas of the surface which are to remain intact are covered with an acid-resistant substance (there are many recipes for these, the main constituents being wax, gum and asphaltum), and the entire piece is then immersed in the appropriate acid solution until the exposed areas have been etched away to the required depth.

If fine lines are required the entire piece is coated with resist and the lines are engraved in the coating to expose the metal. The acid solutions normally used for etching in jewellery-work are diluted aqua regia (q.v.) for gold and diluted nitric acid for silver and copper.

Etching has many possible applications in jewellery. It may be used to texture areas of metal, to produce a surface pattern, to create the depressions or grooves for champlevé enamels or other inlays, or to model the surface for basse-taille enamelling (see *Enamel*). Although an old technique, it has been encouraged by technical advances in chemistry, and now permits the metalworker to accomplish more quickly what was previously done with the graver or hammer and punches (qq.v.).

Eternity rings. A modern class of ring consisting of a simple band, usually set with a continuous line of stones. The circle is a traditional symbol of eternity.

Ethylene dibromide. A liquid used in the measurement of specific gravity (S.G. 2.19). As it has a much lower surface tension than water it is useful in hydro-static weighing. (See *Specific gravity*.)

Etruscan jewellery. The Etruscans settled in the part of central Italy known as Tuscany towards the end of the eighth century B.C., and were for some centuries a thriving civilization until defeated and absorbed by Rome. Their finest jewellery, which displays the greatest technical skill seen in ancient metalwork, was produced in the seventh and sixth centuries B.C., and was later the inspiration for much of the jewellery produced in the 'antique revival' of the nineteenth century.

The most distinctive feature of early Etruscan jewellery, and the one which most challenged the ingenuity of nineteenth-century imitators, was granulation (q.v.). This is a technique in which minute grains of gold are soldered to a background to form a pattern. (Silver can also be used, but the Etruscans worked mostly in gold.) It is a difficult technique and the difficulty increases with the smallness of the grains: in the finest Etruscan work the grains are often only 0.25mm. in diameter, and sometimes as little as 0.14mm. The main difficulty lies in attaching the grains; if an ordinary soldering process is used the solder floods and displaces the grains before they are fixed. Since the art of granulation died out around A.D. 1000 the method used by the Etruscans is not known, but it is presumed that they used the colloid hard-soldering process (q.v.) recently rediscovered in this century, which does not require solder.

Etruscan jewellery falls into two quite distinct classes: that made between the seventh and fifth centuries B.C., and that made from 400 to 250 B.C., which shows a decline in skill and inventiveness.

Bracelets, earrings, necklaces and brooches are predominant in the first period.

Bracelets were often in the form of a large rectangular strip of gold decorated with embossed figures outlined with granulation. Other types were made of openwork filigree – a technique which again required considerable skill, being much more difficult than filigree applied to a background. This technique was used in spiral bracelets, and also for bracelets in the form of a band in which strips of openwork filigree were placed side by side; this variety was frequently decorated with small human heads in relief.

Etruscan baule earring, sixth century B.C. British Museum

The characteristic Etruscan *earring* was the *baule* type, consisting of a strip of gold bent round until it was almost a cylinder, and decorated with filigree and small rosettes, berries, etc., applied in panels (see illustration). The ends of the cylinder were closed with decorated discs, and the wire which fastened the earring in the ear was often masked by another decorated metal plate. An equally ornate type was the disc-earring, decorated with granulation, filigree and sometimes inlaid stones. These fitted into the ear by a projection in the centre of the back of the earring, and were sometimes very large. An attractive type of eastern origin which does not seem to have survived very long is a chiselled openwork disc with a crescent-shaped nick at the top, decorated with a central inlay.

Necklaces were of many types. Bead-necklaces were popular in the seventh century and the beads were usually of granulated gold; multi-coloured glass beads, thought to be of Phoenician origin, were also worn and many necklaces included both types. A common type of necklace in the earlier seventh century had a circular pendant with a central boss which sometimes was inlaid with amber. Another pendant was in the form of a scarab or scaraboid, introduced by the Phoenicians from Egypt, and usually made of gold, amber or faience. Unlike the Egyptian scarabs it was not usually

Etruscan jewellery

engraved with a seal (see *Scarabs*). The pendant which became a characteristic of Etruscan jewellery did not become widely worn until rather later; this was the *bulla*, a hollow and originally globular pendant, usually of gold, made to contain an amulet. Bullae were worn individually or strung together in a necklace, and some are very elaborately decorated with filigree, granulation and embossing. Other pendants of the sixth and fifth centuries are in the shape of satyrs' heads, sirens, flowers, rosettes and acorns.

The safety-pin type of brooch (see *Brooches*) was adopted by the Etruscans from a type already existing in Italy, and in their hands became a luxurious item of jewellery rather than simply a means of fastening the clothes. The supreme example is the large gold fibula in the British Museum, which is not only richly granulated but is literally covered with small figures in the round – lions, horses' heads and sphinxes. A similarly elaborate example (in the Louvre) is decorated with geometric patterns and the owner's name. There were of course simpler types (see illustration) in which the decoration was more austere.

similar to a Greek design of a slightly later period. (See *Earrings* for illustration.) Hoop-earrings with pendants are fairly common, the pendants being often in the form of a jar, or sometimes a human head. These also show Greek influence. Another type, which appears from wall-paintings to have been very popular, is a development of an earlier Etruscan earring consisting of a hoop with globular pendants; in the later variety the hoop is decorated with an embossed gold plate in the shape of an inverted horseshoe, which becomes larger in the course of time until the pendants form the terminals of the horseshoe and the whole earring is made out of one sheet of embossed metal.

Rings, little worn in the earlier period and then usually only in the form of an Egyptian-type hoop with an oblong engraved bezel, became more popular in the late period. One variety, also of Egyptian origin, was a scarab-ring with a swivelling bezel. Another type which was peculiar to the Etruscans had a large convex bezel with a stone set in the centre, surrounded by embossed goldwork.

Wreaths were also a feature of the later period. They mostly consisted of a stylized arrangement of leaves flimsy in construction and not particularly impressive. Scenes from Greek mythology were often embossed on the terminals.

Etruscan gold fibula with ram's head, decorated with granulation. Sixth century B.C. British Museum

Embossed gold bulla from an Etruscan necklace. Fourth century B.C. British Museum

There are few examples of Etruscan jewellery from 500 to 400 B.C., and when it becomes plentiful again the style has changed considerably. Granulation and filigree are very seldom used, and the decoration consists mainly of fairly simple embossed designs. Bracelets are now rare, and the baule earring has been replaced by types demanding less technical skill. One of these is a hoop with one end terminating in a human or animal head –

The bulla was now very widely worn and was richly decorated with embossed work, also showing subjects from Greek mythology (see illustration). By 250 B.C., when Etruria was finally absorbed by Rome, the jewellery of the Roman republic had for centuries been Etruscan in style if not in manufacture, and the bulla was one of the Etruscan ornaments most widely accepted by the Romans. It was highly regarded as an amulet, and was hung round the necks of children and worn by victorious generals at their triumphs, to avert the power of the evil eye.

(For other jewellery of the ancient world see *Egyptian jewellery, Greek jewellery, Roman jewellery*.)

Etui. A small case, usually in the shape of an elliptical cylinder, which was suspended from a chatelaine and contained various useful items such as scissors, pencils, etc. The étui was made to match the chatelaine and many are of exquisite workmanship. (See *Chatelaines*.)

Euclase. (Beryllium silicate. S.G. 3.10; R.I. 1.65–1.67; H. $7\frac{1}{2}$.) A transparent blue-green stone, very similar in appearance to aquamarine (q.v.) but rarely used in jewellery because its easy cleavage makes the crystals difficult to cut and the stones liable to fracture. The attractive smooth prismatic crystals are sought after for mineral collections. Euclase is, like aquamarine, distinctly dichroic (q.v.), but it may be distinguished from aquamarine by its higher specific gravity and refractive indices. The principal source is Brazil.

Eureka diamond. The first diamond to be found in South Africa (1866). It weighed 21 carats in the rough, and was found by the children of a Boer farmer. The farmer's wife, thinking it to be simply an unusual pebble, gave it to a neighbour, van Niekerk, who offered it to a trader; the trader was for a long time unable to interest anybody in the 'pebble', but he eventually showed it to the Civil Commissioner for Cape Town, who sent it to a mineralogist, Guybon Atherston. Atherston found it to be a diamond and it was bought for £500 by Sir Philip Wodehouse, Governor of the Cape. It was exhibited at the Paris Exhibition and subsequently cut into a 10-carat stone and set in a ring. The finding of a solitary diamond in South Africa did not attract much interest in Europe; it was not until 1869, when a much larger diamond was found on the banks of the Orange River, that the prospectors began to arrive. (See *Diamond*.)

'Evening emerald'. A poetical but misleading name for peridot; it appears greener by artificial light.

Excelsior diamond. A fine bluish-white diamond found at the Jagersfontein mine, South Africa, in 1893, weighing 995 carats in the rough. Until the Cullinan (q.v.) was found in 1905 it was the largest diamond ever discovered. The African who found it was rewarded with £500, some pistols and a horse. It was cut by the Amsterdam firm of Asscher to produce 21 brilliants, the largest of which weighed just under 70 carats. The stones were sold separately and it is possible that some of them are in the English Crown Jewels.

Eye agate. See *Agate*.

Eyestone. Thomsonite.

F

Fabergé, Peter Carl (1846–1920). Fabergé has been called the last of the great goldsmiths. Critical opinions of his work differ widely, but its ingenuity and craftsmanship cannot be doubted. He was not primarily a jeweller; the reputation of his firm is based mainly on his 'fantasy' pieces such as the delicate imitation flowers and the famous series of Easter eggs made for the Russian Imperial family.

Carl Fabergé was born in St. Petersburg, the son of a successful jeweller of Huguenot descent, and after serving an apprenticeship in Germany and travelling through Europe he took over the family business at the age of 24. The business at this time was based on the manufacture of conventional articles of jewellery. At some stage this policy was changed and Fabergé began to concentrate on purely decorative objects, beautifully designed and made but of lower intrinsic value. Encouraged by his success at the Moscow exhibition of 1882 he continued with this policy, and the first of the Imperial Easter eggs was made in 1884 or 1885. Shortly after this the Tsar granted the firm his Royal Warrant. International recognition came in 1900 when Fabergé exhibited at the Paris Exhibition and was awarded the Legion of Honour. His work was now as fashionable in Western Europe as in Russia, and among other commissions he made a piece each year for Edward VII to present to Queen Alexandra on her birthday; he was also commissioned to make stone-carvings of the domestic animals at Sandringham. In 1903 he opened a shop in London. The firm now employed in the region of 500 people and had four branches in addition to the main establishment at St. Petersburg. The out-break of the First World War, however, sounded the knell for Fabergé; his particular blend of luxury and fantasy became an anachronism, and even the Imperial Easter eggs had to be created around a military theme – with disastrous results. The workshops were largely given over to the manufacture of armaments, and following the Revolution the whole business was taken over by the Bolsheviks. Fabergé left Russia and died in Lausanne in 1920.

Although Fabergé must have made jewellery and other objects himself, at least during his apprenticeship, none of these are known. In his position as head of the firm he was manager of the enterprise and the principal source of ideas. He was of course a designer, but the man principally responsible for the designs was Francois Birbaum, a Swiss, and numerous other talented designers were at various times employed by the firm, notably Agathon, his young brother, and later his sons. The various types of articles made by the firm were produced in different workshops under work-masters personally responsible for them: thus the Easter eggs were made in the workshop of Michael Perchin and after Perchin's death Henrik Wigström; the jewellery in the workshops of August Holmström and Alfred Thielemann. Other craftsmen specialized in stone-carving, silverware, small enamel objects, and so on. The chief enameller was Alexander Petrov.

As has been remarked, the type of work which gained Fabergé his reputation, and at which his firm excelled, was the production of what have been called 'objects of fantasy'. The Easter eggs epitomize this kind of work; one, carved out of rock-crystal, contains an enamelled mechanical peacock which when placed on the table struts about and spreads its tail; another is covered in rose enamel and decorated with lilies of the valley in pearls and diamonds, and contains miniatures of Nicholas II and the royal children which pop out of the egg when a button is turned. A particularly beautiful one is composed of a pattern of clover leaves in plique-à-jour enamel. Equally delicate are the imitation flowers, with slender gold stalks, leaves of carved nephrite, and petals of enamelled gold or carved gemstone. In addition to these and to the often superb animal-carvings, Fabergé produced an enormous variety of 'functional' objects such as enamelled cigarette-cases, small boxes, clocks, desk ornaments, carved bowls, and so on.

The jewellery was, artistically speaking, a subsidiary, in that although a considerable quantity was made this was mainly the ordinary stock-in-trade of a fashionable jeweller, produced for the wealthy middle classes and showing little originality or invention. Fabergé did however make some fine jewellery, including replicas of antique pieces, and also designed some of the Crown Jewels. The Easter eggs reappear in a modest form as small enamelled, jewelled or stone eggs worn as pendants on a gold chain. Fine Fabergé jewellery is now rare, as much of it had to be sold by refugees after the Revolution.

The characteristics of Fabergé's work are impeccable craftsmanship and a very careful selection of materials. The craftsmanship can be seen in the smallest details – settings, rivets, hinges and fastenings are very often almost invisible. The materials were chosen with an eye to their harmonious combination, not their value. The diamonds were nearly always rose-cut so that they would blend with the design instead of distracting from it, as brilliants would do. Sapphires, rubies and emeralds were usually cut *en-cabochon* and were used sparingly; less valuable but highly ornamental stones

such as moonstones, jade and stained agate were preferred. The stones were cut and stained in Fabergé's own workshops. Different coloured golds were carefully combined. Fabergé is famous for the perfect finish and delicate colouring of his enamels. He specialized in translucent enamelling on an engraved surface, but also produced champlevé and cloisonné enamels in traditional styles. (See *Enamel*.)

'Fabulite'. (Trade name.) A simulant of diamond consisting of strontium titanate. For distinction from diamond, see *Diamond* under *identification*.

Facet. A flat face ground on a gemstone. For the names and arrangement of facets see *Diamond-cutting* and *Gem-cutting*.

Faceting of gemstones. See *Gem-cutting* and *Diamond-cutting*.

Faience. A general term for glazed earthenware and porcelain. It has been used at various times in jewellery, particularly for beads, and was commonly used in ancient Egypt for scarab amulets which were coated with a bluish glaze. The name is thought to be derived from Faenza in Italy where much ceramic ware was made.

Fairburnite. Name for fortification agate (see *Agate*) from South Dakota.

Falcon's eye. See *Tiger's eye*.

Falize, Alexis and Lucien. Parisian court jewellers and goldsmiths. The firm was founded by Alexis (1811–1898) and expanded by his brother Lucien, whose sons continued the business after their father's death. Alexis and Lucien specialized in the imitations of antique jewellery popular in the early and middle part of the nineteenth century (see *Nineteenth-century jewellery*), and produced work of high quality and greater originality than most of the jewellery inspired by antique styles (see illustration).

'False amethyst'. Misnomer for purple fluorspar.

'False emerald'. Misnomer for green fluorspar.

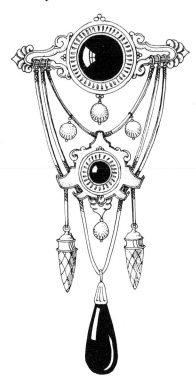

Sketch for a brooch by Alexis Falize

Typical fede ring

'False lapis'. Misnomer for lazulite, or jasper dyed blue to imitate lapis lazuli.

'False topaz'. Misnomer for yellow fluorspar or citrine.

'Falun brilliants'. (Trade name.) Imitation diamonds made of lead glass.

Fancy pearls. Trade term for natural coloured pearls. (See *Pearls*.)

'Fancy shapes'. A name used for cut stones of unusual shapes, e.g. lunette (half-moon), triangle, kite.

Fancy stones. A trade term for coloured diamonds. (See *Diamond*.)

Fausse montre. A sham watch worn on a hookless chatelaine to balance the real watch at the other end of the chain. (See *Chatelaines*.)

'Feathers'. See *Inclusions in gemstones*.

Fede rings. Rings bearing the motif of two clasped hands (see illustration). Generally the hands are moulded to form the bezel of the ring, but they are frequently combined with other motifs, and in a number of fifteenth-century Italian fede rings the clasped hands are at the back of the hoop and the bezel is in the form of a circular plaque bearing a picture of a woman's head. Some fede rings also have religious or magical inscriptions along the hoop. The motif of clasped hands is first found on Roman rings and continued in use until the nineteenth century. Such rings were used as love-rings, betrothal and wedding-rings, and also probably as pledges of friendship or trust. ('Fede' is the Italian word for good faith, belief, etc.).

At some time during the Middle Ages the fede was elaborated into the gimmel ring (q.v.), in which the hands are set on separate linked hoops and actually lock together.

Fei ts'ui. Originally kingfisher-blue jade; now used for almost any jade.

Feldspar. (Silicate of aluminium with potassium or sodium and calcium.) A geologically important group of minerals which however produces no gemstone of importance except moonstone. There are two groups of feldspars: orthoclase and microcline, which have the same chemical composition (potassium-aluminium silicate) but crystallize in different systems, and plagioclase (these constitute a series between sodium-aluminium silicate [albite] and calcium-aluminium silicate [anorthite]). Orthoclase and microcline produce respectively the gemstones *moonstone* and *amazonstone* (qq.v.), and the plagioclase group produce *aventurine feldspar* (sunstone), *labradorite, peris-*

terite ('pigeon stone') (qq.v.) and several other varieties which have little or no use in jewellery.

Orthoclase feldspar crystallizes in the monoclinic system, and microcline and plagioclase in the triclinic (see *Crystal systems*).

Feldspar occurs abundantly in igneous and metamorphic rocks, but the amount of material that can be used for ornamental purposes is very small.

'Ferrer's emerald' ('Ferros emerald'). (Trade name.) A glass imitation of emerald.

Ferronnière. A narrow chain or band encircling the forehead with a small jewel in the centre. This head-ornament was popular for a time at the very beginning of the sixteenth century, and when Renaissance styles became fashionable in the nineteenth century (see *Nineteenth-century jewellery*), the ferronnière was revived (about 1840). The fashion was taken from a portrait ('La Belle Ferronnière') attributed to Leonardo da Vinci in which such a jewel is worn. In their enthusiasm the Victorians failed to realize that the word 'ferronnière' referred not to the jewel but to the blacksmith's wife who wore it and was the subject of the painting.

Fetter chain (Fetter trace chain). A chain with long links. (See *Chain*.)

Fibrolite (Sillimanite). (Aluminium silicate. S.G. 3.25; R.I. 1.66–1.68; H. $7\frac{1}{2}$.) A mineral of fibrous appearance from which transparent sapphire-blue and chatoyant greyish-green stones are sometimes cut. The stones are strongly dichroic (q.v.), and to give the best effect a blue stone must be cut with the table facet at right angles to the length of the crystal. Transparent gem-quality material is found in association with ruby in the Mogok Stone Tract in Burma, and the chatoyant green stones are found in Ceylon. Brazil is another source.

The commoner form of fibrolite is densely compact, brownish or greenish in colour, and resembles jade. Its specific gravity is 3.14–3.18. Pebbles of this massive fibrous material are found in the valley of the Clearwater river, Idaho, and are tumbled to produce baroque stones.

Fibula. Archaeological term for a brooch.

Files. Steel files are used by jewellers to remove rough edges and irregular surfaces from metal. There are numerous types, designed for a wide variety of filing jobs. Those most often used by jewellers are needle files (slender files with the handle and filing blade made in one piece). They are made in various sections, e.g. round, half-round, square, three-square (triangular), knife-edged (triangular with one narrow and two wide sides), fish-belly (convex both sides). Broader files of different sections may also be used. Files of circular section which taper sharply are known as rat-tail files. A riffle or riffler (q.v.) is a special type of file with two curved ends.

Filigree. Decoration with fine gold or silver wire twisted into patterns. The wire may be soldered to a sheet of metal, or several strands may be twisted together without a background. The latter technique, which is difficult and not often practised, is known as openwork.

Filigree was being used on jewellery by the middle of the third millennium B.C. The earliest examples are rather clumsy and the wire is thick, but by Classical

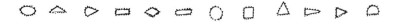

Needle file and variety of shapes available

Filigree enamel

*Greek filigree earring of the early Christian
period. Benaki Museum, Athens*

times the technique was highly developed,
and the filigree work which is one of the
main features of Greek and Etruscan
jewellery (qq.v.) is extraordinarily light
and delicate (see illustration). The use of
filigree spread from Mediterranean countries to the more northern parts of Europe
during the Dark Ages, and the so-called
'barbaric' jewellery of this period uses the
technique with great skill. Filigree continued to be an important feature of
jewellery until the fifteenth century (see
Medieval jewellery), when with the
development of gem-cutting interest
gradually shifted from the goldwork to
the stones. The Renaissance produced
goldsmiths' work of virtuoso standard,
but the accent was now on stones and
enamel and on sculptural forms, and
filigree became a more or less neglected
art. It made a brief appearance in the
mid-seventeenth century when watch-
cases of delicate filigree were worn, but
it was not systematically revived until the
nineteenth century when a whole class of
filigree jewellery was produced, largely
as a result of the interest in ancient and
medieval styles. (See *Nineteenth-century
jewellery*.)

Filigree cannot be said to be a popular

technique in modern jewellery, which
prefers bold and sculptured forms. It is
however still used, and the modern
jeweller has the advantage of being able
to purchase almost any gauge of wire
he requires from the refiners instead of
hammering it and rolling it or pulling it
through a drawplate (q.v.). Metals of as
high a degree of purity as possible should
be used, since the more base metal they
contain the less malleable they are. (See
also *Gold*.)

Filigree enamel. Enamelwork similar to
cloisonné (q.v.), but with the cells made
of round instead of flat wire, and with
opaque enamels. Filigree enamel was
developed comparatively early in Greece
(see *Enamel*) but was very sparingly used.
It does not seem to have been used
subsequently in Europe except in Hungarian work of the sixteenth century and
Hispano-Moresque work.

Findings. Mass-produced jewellery components which can be bought from the
refiners ready to make up into jewellery.
They include stone-settings, gallery strip
(q.v.), fittings for earrings, catches,
shoulder pieces for rings, and eternity
rings with the holes drilled ready to take
the stones.

'Fine' (of precious metals). Pure. Fine
gold and silver are gold and silver which
contain no alloying metals. They are too
soft to be used in jewellery and are
alloyed in certain proportions which are
fixed by law (see *Alloy*). The fineness of a
precious-metal alloy is the proportion of
precious metal it contains; thus 18-carat
gold is said to be 18 carats fine (see
Carat), etc.

Fire. The flashes of prismatic colour displayed by some gemstones, notably
diamond. (See *Colour dispersion*.)

Fire-free silver. Silver which has been
annealed (see *Annealing*) in an oxygen-free
atmosphere at the refinery to prevent the
formation of firestain (q.v.).

Fire-gilding. See *Mercury-gilding*.

Fire marble. See *Lumachella*.

Fire-marks (Chatter-marks). Small cracks seen near the facet-edges of corundum, both natural and synthetic. They are caused by local overheating during cutting and polishing.

Fire opal. See *Opal*.

Firestain. The black film of copper oxide which forms on the surface of a silver-copper alloy when it is heated in air during annealing, soldering, etc. (As all silver used by the trade is alloyed with a small proportion of copper, it is all susceptible to firestain.) The stain can be removed by rubbing with an abrasive stone or pickling (q.v.) in acid, but when the silver is heated numerous times the stain begins to penetrate the metal and becomes difficult to remove without removing an excessive amount of metal. In the past silver articles often had to be electro-plated to cover the stain, but techniques have now been developed which enable silver to be annealed at the refineries without the formation of copper oxide (see *Fire-free silver*); this means that the jeweller buys his silver free from firestain and the stain it subsequently acquires in working can usually be removed without much difficulty.

Firestones. An imitation of rainbow quartz (q.v.) produced by heating rock crystal to crack it and then cooling it in water which contains a dye. The dye dries out in the cracks and an iridescent effect is produced.

Firing (enamel). The process of subjecting enamels to red heat to fuse and 'mature' them. This is nowadays done in electric kilns. (See *Muffle kiln*.)

First water. A term of unknown origin used to describe diamonds which are perfectly clear and free from flaws.

Flange. A reinforcing rim set inside a bezel which acts as a bearing (q.v.) for the stone.

Flats. Term used in diamond-sorting for flattish irregular crystals.

Flaws in gemstones. These may take the form of small cracks or cleavages in the stone, or inclusions, which are normally particles of other minerals or liquid-filled cavities (see *Inclusions in gemstones*). The extent to which flaws detract from the value of a stone varies, since in some cases features which are technically flaws enhance the stone's appearance. Examples of this are the dendritic inclusions in moss agate (see *Agate*), the cavities or inclusions which produce a 'star' in rubies and sapphires (see *Asterism*), and the peculiar structure of opal (q.v.) which gives the stone its beautiful play of colours. Emerald (q.v.) is very rarely found free from minute inclusions, and unless these are so numerous as to make the stone cloudy they are regarded as giving it character and are not counted a fault. As a general rule, however, any transparent stone which contains a visible flaw loses considerably in value. An otherwise clear diamond of good colour, containing a small inclusion visible to the naked eye, might be valued at only one-fifth of the price it would have fetched had it been free of flaws. For this reason flawed portions of gem crystals are usually cut away before the stone is shaped, even though this means sacrificing a considerable amount of material.

In some stones, particularly diamond, a tinge of colour or of the wrong colour is an imperfection which detracts from the value. Nearly all diamonds have a very faint tinge of colour but this is often detectable only by the expert eye. The colour of a stone is best seen by inspecting it in the morning in a north light. Most diamonds also contain minute inclusions – usually specks of carbon – or tiny hair-cracks. A diamond is said to be 'clean' if it shows no flaws under a lens which magnifies ten times. Flaws in transparent stones are more easily detected by examining them when they are immersed in a colourless liquid of high refractive index (q.v.).

Another defect which detracts from a stone's value is bad cutting. There may be tiny chips, especially on the girdle, or small unpolished surfaces, or there may be a lack of symmetry in the placing of the facets (a common fault in stones cut in the East). Chips may be masked by the way the stone is set, as may many other flaws, and a stone of poor colour may be 'improved' by placing a coloured foil behind it or painting the back facets. (See *Foil*.)

Flèches d'amour. Name for the needle – like crystals of rutile in rutilated quartz (q.v.), and thus for the whole stone.

Flint glass. A rather soft glass containing lead oxide, used in paste jewellery. (See *Glass* and *Paste*.)

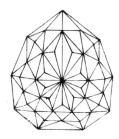

The Florentine diamond, crown

Florentine diamond (Austrian Yellow, Tuscany). A yellow briolette diamond weighing 137.27 carats. Its early history is uncertain. It is said to have belonged to a sixteenth-century Indian prince who was conquered by the Portuguese; another story is that it belonged to Charles the Bold and was lost in battle. At the beginning of the seventeenth century it was bought by Ferdinand, Duke of Tuscany, and was seen by Tavernier among the Duke's treasures. A Venetian lapidary cut it into its present shape and it subsequently passed into the possession of the Austrian royal house. It was appropriated by the Germans when Austria was taken over, but was restored after the war by the American government.

Florentine mosaic. See *Mosaic*.

Flower agate. Chalcedony with inclusions resembling flowers, similar to moss agate. (See *Chalcedony* and *Agate*.)

Flowering obsidian. See *Obsidian*.

Fluorspar (Fluorite, Fluor). (Calcium fluoride. S.G. about 3.18; R.I. 1.43; H. 4.) A stone rarely used in jewellery because of its softness, low refractivity and easy cleavage, but which nevertheless provides a very attractive range of colours – translucent to transparent pink, violet, blue, green, yellow, and brown. Colourless stones are also sometimes seen. The fluorspar most used in the past for ornamental work was blue-john, a massive variety attractively patterned in curved bands of violet or purple on a usually reddish or colourless ground. It came from only one locality: Treak Cliff in the Kinderscout district of Derbyshire, which source is now said to be exhausted. The material had been worked since Roman times.

Other types of massive fluorspar may be used for ornamental work and there is a massive green variety which resembles massive green beryl and is often carved. Fluorspar crystallizes in the cubic system (see *Crystal systems*). Apart from its ornamental qualities it has important industrial uses, notably as a flux in the manufacture of steel.

Some of the best fluorspar comes from England – Derbyshire, Durham, Cumberland and Cornwall. There are also sources in Switzerland, Germany, Poland, Czechoslovakia, Italy, Norway and North America.

Flux. A substance used in soldering to encourage the flow of solder and to exclude air from the surface of the heated metal, thus preventing the formation of a film of oxide which would make satisfactory soldering impossible (see *Soldering*). The flux is spread over the surfaces to be joined before the solder is applied. In the ancient world natron and the burnt sediment of wine were probably used as fluxes. In modern work borax (q.v.) is commonly used, but as it is not entirely satisfactory for all purposes a range of proprietary fluxes has been developed. These are normally available in the form of a fine powder, which has to be mixed to a paste with water before use. For soft-soldering – not often used in jewellery – zinc chloride or Baker's fluid may be used as a flux.

Flux fusion. A method of growing crystals artificially from solutions, used in the production of synthetic emeralds and some rubies. (See *Synthetic gemstones*.)

Typical eighteenth-century fob set with a swivelling seal-stone

Fob. A trinket hung on the watch-chain or chatelaine (q.v.) from the eighteenth century. The word was originally used to denote the pocket in which the watch was kept; later when watches were suspended on chains or chatelaines it was transferred to the chain ('fob-chain'), and finally it came to mean a decorative object worn on the chain. Numerous objects were so worn (see *Chatelaines*), but the trinkets usually known as fobs were small elaborate pendants with an engraved seal-stone set in the base (see illustration). Unengraved stones were also set in this way. Elaborate fobs were the height of fashion in the 1770s and 80s, but ceased to be regularly worn when men's dress became sober and unadorned at the end of the eighteenth century.

Foil. A thin leaf of metal placed under a mounted gemstone to improve its colour or brilliance. The foiling of precious stones was common practice in the Renaissance, and the preparation of a foil suitable to the stone was something of an art in itself. Cellini in his *Treatises* gives recipes for yellow, blue, red and green foils for ruby, sapphire and emerald; the constituents are gold, silver and copper in varying proportions. Diamonds were not foiled

but tinted – the base of the stone was painted with a dark liquid which increased the stone's brilliance.

The development of more sophisticated styles of gem-cutting in the sixteenth and seventeenth centuries (see *Gem-cutting* and *Diamond-cutting*) made the artificial improvement of stones by foiling less of a necessity, but the practice was still continued, particularly with paste, which in the eighteenth century was commonly backed with a foil when in a pavé or rub-over setting. Almandine garnets were also foiled – they were thinly cut and set over a pink foil in an imitation of rubies. In the nineteenth century also coloured stones were often foiled; this was particularly so with amethyst and topaz.

Foiling is still practised today, and although it is no longer a matter of course it is something for which the jeweller buying mounted stones has to keep his eyes open, since a foil can give a mis-leading impression of the value of a stone and even suggest that it is another stone altogether. Thus a green foil placed behind a pale emerald makes it appear of deeper colour and therefore of greater value, and a green foil placed behind a stone which is not an emerald may make it look like one and may even transmit red through a colour filter (q.v.), which is one of the distinguishing characteristics of emerald. Paste is still quite often foiled to give it more brilliance. A technique which has been used since the 1840s is known as mirror-foiling and consists of backing the pavilion facets of the stone with a mercury amalgam in the same way as a mirror. This differs from the old method in that the foil is actually in contact with the stone. Almandine garnets are also still foiled to lighten their colour, which otherwise is very dark. They are generally cut as hollow cabochons (see *Gem-cutting*) and the foil is placed in the hollow as a lining.

'Fool's gold'. Iron pyrites, which in its natural state often resembles a gold vein.

Fossilized wood. See *Agatized wood*, *Jasperized wood*, *Opalized wood*.

Fossil ivory

Corsage ornament in enamelled gold, designed by Mucha and made by Fouquet

Fossil ivory. The tusk of the woolly mammoth. (See *Ivory*.)

Fossil marble. See *Marble*.

'Fossil turquoise'. Misnomer for odontolite.

Fouquet, Georges. (1862–1929). A distinguished French jeweller, son of Alphonse Fouquet, who worked in the Art Nouveau (q.v.) style but produced jewellery of striking originality with a greater use of geometric and synthetic forms than was usual at the time. Like other Art Nouveau jewellers he employed a wide range of coloured stones, pearls and enamels. He was described by an English critic in 1902 as being 'generally complicated, somewhat Byzantine, and thoroughly modern'. Fouquet exhibited widely and won international recognition, and among many distinctions was awarded the Legion of Honour. Between 1898 and 1905 Alphonse Mucha designed jewellery for Fouquet's shop in the Rue Royale; one of these pieces is illustrated.

Fortification agate. See *Agate*.

Fossil tripoli. See *Diatomite*.

Fracture. The term for the type of surface a stone shows when broken or chipped. There are various types of fracture but only two are really distinctive. Conchoidal fracture, so called because the surface is concentrically ridged like a shell, is characteristic of glass and other amorphous substances. Splintery or hackly fracture, where the broken surface shows long jagged splinters, is produced by fibrous minerals such as nephrite. Fracture may in rare cases be of use in identifying an uncut stone, and a conchoidal fracture in the interior of a stone will suggest that it is glass, although quartz can also show this type of fracture.

French chalk. A soft powder derived from steatite. Its main use in the jewellery trade is to prevent patterns from sticking to the mould in casting (q.v.).

Freshwater pearls. Pearls found in river mussels. (See *Pearls*.)

Friction gilding. An old method of gilding. Linen rags are soaked in a

152

solution of gold chloride and are dried and then burnt. The ashes are preserved, and are rubbed over the surface of the article to be gilded with a piece of damp leather. When the article has taken on the colour of gold it is washed and well burnished. (See *Burnishing*.)

Friedelite. (Manganese silicate. S.G. about 3.07; R.I. 1.63–1.66; H. 4–5.) An unusual rose-red to orange-red stone. The mineral mostly occurs in massive form. It is found in France, Sweden and the U.S.A.

Frit. A term for clear enamel before metallic oxides are added to colour it.

Froment-Meurice, F. G. (1802–1855). A Parisian jeweller noted for his work in the medieval and Renaissance styles. He is said to have been responsible for the introduction of Gothic themes into jewellery. His pieces make lavish use of angels (see illustration), knights, architectural and heraldic motifs, and other themes which the nineteenth century considered to be representative of medieval art. A bracelet of his depicting scenes from the life of St. Louis in an elaborate Gothic architectural framework was particularly admired at the Exhibition of 1851. Although his work in this style is of a higher standard than that of most of his contemporaries it is still unmistakably stamped with nineteenth-century sentimentality and could not possibly be confused with genuine medieval or Renaissance jewellery (qq.v.). Froment-Meurice's work was not however confined to antique styles; he produced a

Brooch in enamelled silver showing an angel playing a violin. Made by Froment-Meurice. Victoria and Albert Museum

wide range of high-class jewellery, including jewels in the naturalistic style popular in the first half of the century, and also executed commissions for the Church. (See also *Nineteenth-century jewellery*.)

Frost agate. Agate with white markings.

Furnace. See *Muffle kiln* and *Crucible furnace*.

G

Gahnite. (Zinc-spinel. S.G. 4.40; R.I. 1.805; H. 7½–8.) A stone usually occurring in very dark green crystals; lighter-coloured material is sometimes cut as a gemstone. It is found in zinc deposits in many localities. Although belonging to the spinel group it is regarded as a separate mineral. A synthetic gahnite has been produced which has a slightly higher refractive index than the natural stone and a specific gravity of 4.6. (See also *Spinel*.)

Gahnospinel. A name sometimes used for blue spinel containing a high proportion of zinc. These spinels are rare and have a considerably higher specific gravity and refractive index than ordinary spinel, from which they cannot be distinguished by eye. (See *Spinel*.)

'Galalith'. A casein plastic (see *Plastics*).

Gallery strip

Gallery. A perforated metal border, supplied in strips by refiners in both a 'closed' and 'open' form (see illustration); the open type is used by jewellers as a ready-made claw setting for stones.

Garnet. A general name for a group of minerals having the same crystal habit and a similar chemical composition. The six varieties of gem-quality garnet are

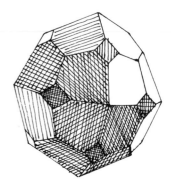

Typical crystal of garnet

as follows: *pyrope* (blood red; magnesium-aluminium silicate); *almandine* (purplish-red; iron-aluminium silicate); *spessartite* (yellowish or brownish-red; manganese-aluminium silicate); *grossular* (mainly hessonite, an orange or brownish gem-stone; calcium-aluminium silicate); *andradite* (*melanite*, an opaque black gemstone, and *demantoid*, transparent green; calcium-iron silicate); *uvarovite* (green crystals too small for use as gemstones; calcium-chromium silicate). (For further description of the stones see under separate varieties.) The chemical composition of stones within the six classes varies considerably and there is much overlapping. For instance, the pyrope and almandine groups are actually continuous, and it may be difficult to decide to which group a stone belongs.

Gem quality garnets occur mainly in schists, metamorphic limestone and alluvial deposits. Being composed of some of the principal elements of the earth's crust, garnet is a fairly common mineral. Partly because of this and partly owing

154

to the extensive use of rather unattractive Bohemian garnets in Victorian jewellery, garnets are not now very popular as gemstones. In earlier times they were more highly regarded. They were much used for ornamental work, particularly in combination with gold, both in the ancient world and in the Middle Ages, and the Crusaders used them as talismans. The present low opinion of garnet is not merited, as very fine examples are seen and it may, for instance, be difficult to tell a good almandine from a ruby.

Formerly garnets were cut *en cabochon* but they are now mostly faceted. Garnet crystallizes in the cubic system (see *Crystal systems*), and is therefore singly refractive (q.v.) and not dichroic, which serves to distinguish it from many other stones of similar appearance.

Material which is not of gem quality is sometimes used in industry as an abrasive.

Garnet is the birthstone for January.

'Garnet jade'. Misnomer for massive green grossular garnet.

Garrard & Co. The crown jewellers. The company was started by the silversmith George Wickes, who opened a shop in the Haymarket, London for the sale of 'all sorts of jewells and curious works in gold and silver' in 1720. It quickly gained a high reputation; Wickes was appointed goldsmith, jeweller and silversmith to the Prince of Wales in 1735, and executed many commissions for royalty and the nobility. In 1792 the firm passed into the hands of Robert Garrard, whose family had long held a distinguished position in the city, and royal patronage continued. Among the important commissions executed by the firm in Victorian times were the pendant designed by the Prince Consort which Queen Victoria presented to Florence Nightingale in 1885, a suite of diamonds and pearls given by the City of London as a wedding present to Queen Alexandra, and a similar suite given to Queen Mary on her marriage to the future George V. Several pieces of the British regalia were re-made by Garrards for Queen Victoria, and the firm also made crown jewels for foreign powers.

In 1952 Garrards were amalgamated with another famous firm, the Goldsmiths and Silversmiths Company, which had been established in the 1880s by William Gibson, and all business was transferred to the present premises at 112 Regent Street under the name of Garrard and Co. Here the firm continues to supply high-class jewellery and gold and silverware made by its own craftsmen, and quality clocks and watches. Much work is done for the export market, and the company are proud of the fact that many of their modern pieces have been officially classed as works of art, which exempted them from purchase tax.

Gedanite. A variety of amber found near Danzig; it is softer and rather lighter than most amber (S.G. about 1.02, H. $1\frac{1}{2}$–2). (See *Amber*.)

Gem-cutting. (For diamonds see *Diamond-cutting*). Relatively soft gemstones such as cornelian and lapis lazuli were being cut to shape, sliced and polished in ancient Egypt, using copper blades and an abrasive which was probably quartz sand mixed with water. Harder stones which could not be cut with quartz were left in their natural state. Later, powdered corundum, which can abrade any stone other than diamond, was used in the treatment of the harder stones. For several thousand years, the only style of cutting for gemstones (apart from beads, and stones intended for inlay or engraving) was the dome-shaped cabochon (see below). During the Middle Ages however gems began to be faceted in simple shapes, and over the centuries a variety of cuts evolved as techniques and tools became more sophisticated.

Methods. The rough material, still in its natural state, is first sawn to the required size. This operation is known as slitting and is done with a vertically-rotating metal disc, charged with diamond powder for cutting the harder stones such as sapphire, or emery or corundum powder for softer minerals. The material is held against the cutting edge by hand. The facets are then ground on the stone, using a horizontal grinding wheel of copper, gunmetal or iron (the lap) charged with abrasive and lubricant. The stone is cemented to a holder held in the gem-cutter's hand and lowered on to the flat surface of the grinding wheel. It is held vertically until the central table facet has been ground on. To enable the side facets to be ground at the correct angle, the upper end of the holder is inserted into a vertical piece of wood pierced with a series of holes; the point at which the holder is inserted determines the degree of inclination of the stone to the wheel. The cutter guides the stone and controls the depth of cutting by hand. When the top or crown of the stone has been faceted it is taken off the holder and reversed, and the bottom facets are ground on. The stone is then cleaned to remove any abrasive, and polished. The facets are polished individually in the same way as they were cut, but the lap is normally of wood or pewter and polishing powder is used instead of hard abrasive. There are numerous polishing powders and their use varies according to local preference. The most commonly used ones are rouge, green rouge, putty powder, tripoli, rotten-stone and pumice (qq.v.). After polishing the stone is again cleaned and is then ready to be set by the jeweller.

The grinding of facets can be done mechanically, but as mechanical cutting wastes material (it is unnecessarily accurate), usually only cheap or synthetic stones are treated in this way. Polishing wheels are generally mechanically driven, but for grinding a hand-driven wheel is often preferred for delicate work.

The preparation of unfaceted stones is of course simpler. Cabochon stones and beads are roughly shaped on a carborundum wheel which may be grooved to facilitate the rounding of the stone, and then further ground and polished on vertical wheels or laps. Flat-cut stones are simply held against the grinding wheel until a level surface is achieved. The softer stones such as agate, lapis lazuli, malachite and turquoise are often polished on beech-wood rollers covered with soft leather.

Drilling of beads and other stones is carried out as follows. The pieces to be drilled are cemented in rows on a board or slab and placed under the drilling frame. The drill is an iron or steel shaft set with pieces of black diamond (carbonado), and pivots on a long wooden arm, the free end of which is held under the driller's left armpit. The drill is hand-operated by a bowstring wound once round the drill-shaft and held in the driller's right hand. A to-and-fro working of the bowstring drives the drill, which is controlled by the pressure of the driller's left arm on the wooden arm holding the drill. This method, by which stones have been drilled for thousands of years, is still preferred to mechanical methods, although electrically-powered drills are used for making large holes or drilling thick pieces of material.

There are gem-cutting workshops in major cities all over the world, but the most important centre is Idar-Oberstein (q.v.) in Germany. Stones which are found in quantity in the East, such as garnet, alexandrite, ruby and sapphire, are often native-cut, but when sent to Europe they usually have to be re-cut in European workshops because the aim of the native cutters is to retain as much of the stone as possible and the stones are therefore, to European eyes, badly proportioned and not faceted symmetrically. Nevertheless the skill of the native cutters, using primitive machinery and traditional methods, is considerable.

Styles of cutting. The principal cuts for stones other than diamonds are as follows.

1. The cabochon. This, the earliest form of cutting, is still used for opaque and translucent stones, which do not benefit from faceting, and for stones which exhibit special optical effects that are best brought out by cabochon-cutting. These are star-stones (see *Asterism*), cat's eye stones (see *Chatoyancy*), and stones which have a particular sheen or play of colour, such as opal, moonstone and

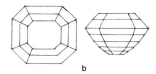

(a) Cabochon, hollow cabochon and tallow-topped cabochon

(b) Step cut (emerald cut). Crown and side view

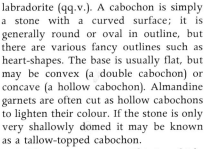

(c) Scissors or cross cut, crown

(d) Zircon cut, side view

labradorite (qq.v.). A cabochon is simply a stone with a curved surface; it is generally round or oval in outline, but there are various fancy outlines such as heart-shapes. The base is usually flat, but may be convex (a double cabochon) or concave (a hollow cabochon). Almandine garnets are often cut as hollow cabochons to lighten their colour. If the stone is only very shallowly domed it may be known as a tallow-topped cabochon.

2. The step or trap cut. This is a fairly popular cut for transparent coloured stones. The shape of the stone is usually square, oblong, octagonal or hexagonal, although there are other possible variations. The *table* (the large central facet) is surrounded by a series of rectangular facets which slope down to the *girdle* (the point of greatest circumference), while similarly-arranged rectangular facets slope from the girdle into the facet at the base (see illustration). The *emerald cut*, so called because it is nearly always used for emeralds, is the rectangular variety of step cut with the corners mitred, producing an octagonal stone. Large diamonds are sometimes cut in this way. The *scissors cut* or *cross cut* is a modification of the step cut in which four triangular facets fill each of the rectangular spaces between the table facet and the girdle (see illustration). The purpose of the step cut is to display the stone's colour; however, it allows quite a lot of

light to escape and does not bring out the stone's brilliance.

3. The mixed cut. This is designed to display the stone's brilliance to better advantage than the step cut, and is very popular for transparent coloured stones. The crown or upper part of the stone is faceted in the brilliant cut (see *Diamond-cutting*), and the pavilion or lower part in the step cut. The number of facets may be varied, as long as there is a balance between the two halves of the stone.

4. The brilliant cut. This was originally developed to exploit the special properties of diamonds, but modifications of it are now used for colourless stones and on occasion for coloured stones as well. The varieties of the brilliant cut are described under *Diamond-cutting.*

5. The zircon cut. This is similar to the brilliant cut (see *Diamond-cutting*) but has a second set of facets between the pavilion facets and the culet (see illustration). It is frequently used for zircon, which has a similar brilliance to diamond.

6. The rose cut. This is also basically a cut for diamonds but has been used for other stones, notably the garnets so popular in Victorian jewellery. It is described under *Diamond-cutting.*

The barrel-polishing of minerals to produce baroque stones has recently become very popular among amateur lapidaries. The process is described under *Tumbling.*

157

Gem of the Jungle. A magnificent sapphire weighing 958 carats in the rough, found in 1929 in the Mogok Stone Tract (q.v.) just below the surface. It was bought by Mr. Albert Ramsay and cut into nine stones, the largest of which weighed 66.5 carats.

Gemmological Association of Great Britain. An association for the further-ance of the study of gemmology. It was founded in 1908 as the educational committee of the National Association of Goldsmiths (q.v.), reconstituted as the Gemmological Association in 1931 and incorporated under its present title in 1947. The educational work of the Association includes the holding of examinations and the awarding of diplomas and certificates, and the main-taining of libraries and collections of gem materials. A correspondence course is organized and is studied by students all over the world. Through the Association, members may have gemstones and pearls tested at the laboratories of the London Chamber of Commerce. Other services of the Association include an inquiry bureau covering all kinds of gemmological inquiry, the loaning of mineral specimens and slides, library facilities and the supply of books and gem-testing instruments. The Association maintains links with gemmological associations in other coun-tries, and its quarterly journal, the *Journal of Gemmology*, has a worldwide circulation.

Gemolite. An American binocular micro-scope designed purely for the study of gemstones; it incorporates a zoom lens and provision for dark-field illumination (q.v.).

Gem-stick. A stick shaped like a pen-holder with a metal cup at the end, into which a gemstone is cemented to be held against a grinding or polishing wheel. (See *Gem-cutting*.)

'Geneva rubies'. Reconstructed rubies (made by the fusion of many small fragments of ruby) which appeared on the market in the 1880s and caused some trouble at the time since they were sold as genuine. They were said to have been made by a priest in a village near Geneva.

Geode. A hollow cavity in rock lined with crystals. Many gemstones, particularly those of the quartz group, occur in this form. The crystals are deposited by mineral-rich water which has percolated into the cavity.

'German lapis'. See '*Swiss lapis*'.

'German mocoas'. (Trade name.) A German-made imitation moss agate.

German silver. Nickel silver (q.v.).

Giardinetti rings. Rings in which the central ornament is in the shape of a spray or garland of flowers set with a variety of coloured stones. They are often enamelled, and the general effect is very delicate and colourful. Such rings began to be worn at the end of the seventeenth century and were extremely popular in the eighteenth century; quite a number of them have survived. For illustration, see *Rings*.

Gibsonite. Pink thomsonite.

Gidgee opal. (See *Opal*.) (S.G. 2.65–3.00.) Stone cut from iron-rich opal which has impregnated the roots of the gidgee tree (a variety of acacia). The density is considerably higher than that of true opal.

Gilding. The process of covering silver, base metal or some other substance (e.g. wood) with a thin layer of gold, which may be either pure or a gold alloy. Gilding has been practised since remote antiquity (see *Gold*). An early method was to cover the object with gold leaf, attached with an adhesive. A later method in use from Roman times and still sometimes employed is mercury-gilding (q.v.). Various other methods have been devel-oped by craftsmen over the centuries, such as contact gilding and friction gilding (qq.v.), but the method now commonly employed is electroplating (q.v.), which was developed in the 1840s and can be used to deposit various thicknesses of gold, from a very thin coating (known as a 'flash') which is little more than a surface colouring, to a layer of appreciable thickness which may fairly be described as a plating. (See also *Rolled gold* and *Hard gold plating*.)

Gilding-metal. A base-metal alloy composed mainly of copper and zinc (80–90% copper, 20–10% zinc) widely used in cheap jewellery. It is nearly always gilded. Various alloys of this type are available to meet different requirements; a higher proportion of zinc makes the metal more malleable, while the addition of lead and tin instead of some of the zinc produces an alloy more suitable for casting.

Gilt. This term properly refers to any article of base metal or some other material covered with a layer of gold (pure or alloyed). However, it is now generally used to describe cheap articles on which the gold coating is very thin. (See also *Gilding*.)

Gimmel ring

Gimmel (gemmel) ring. This is basically a ring formed of two or more linked hoops which fit together (see illustration). The loops were often surmounted by hands, which would clasp when the ring was put together, and if the ring was in three parts the middle loop might be surmounted by a heart in such a way that the hands would clasp over it. Gimmel rings were used both as betrothal and wedding rings, and in some cases they were so made that they could be taken apart at the betrothal and worn separately by the couple, and then symbolically joined together at the wedding. There was frequently an inscription running along the facing halves of the hoops, which would only be visible when the hoops were separated. 'QUOD DEUS CONIUNXIT HOMO NON SEPARET' – 'What God hath joined, let no man put asunder' – was, not surprisingly, one of the more frequent of these inscriptions. Most surviving gimmel rings were made in Italy by Renaissance craftsmen (although some are English or German), and are of silver, often decorated with niello.

Gipsy ring. A wide gold ring with a stone or stones deeply set in it (see *Gipsy setting*). Gipsy rings set with pearls and diamonds became popular in the nineteenth century.

Gipsy setting. A setting in which the stone is deeply sunk into the surrounding metal so that the top or table facet is almost on a level with the metal surface. The metal around the stone is sometimes engraved with radiating lines to represent a star.

Girandole. A type of earring or brooch in which three pear-shaped stones or pearls hang from a large stone or decorative motif (often a bow). The design originated in the seventeenth century and was the characteristic form for earrings in the eighteenth century. (See *Eighteenth-century jewellery* for illustration; see also *Earrings*.)

Girasol. A word literally meaning 'to turn to the sun'; it is applied to various stones which exhibit a flash of fire or some other striking optical effect, particularly fire opal and water opal (for which see *Opal*). A *girasol sapphire* is a chatoyant sapphire.

Girasol pearl. A type of imitation pearl. (See *Pearls*.)

Girdle. The widest part of a cut gemstone, dividing the crown or upper part from the pavilion or base. Stones are normally set with the girdle plane with the metal surface (an exception being the gipsy setting), and the girdle is accordingly also known as the setting edge. Some crystals, e.g. the octahedral crystals of diamond, are sometimes described as having a girdle, this referring to the widest part of the crystal.

Giuliano

Enamelled pendant by Giuliano. Victoria and Albert Museum

Giuliano, Carlo (d. about 1912). A Neapolitan jeweller who migrated to England, opened a business in Piccadilly in the late 1860s and achieved a lasting reputation, notably for his very fine work in the Renaissance style. He did not make slavish copies of antique pieces, but used the cabochon and table-cut gems, and the scrolls and arabesques of late Renaissance jewellery, to create pieces which are distinctively his own. He used encrusted enamel (q.v.) frequently and with great skill. Giuliano's work is marked by a high standard of design and a delicacy of treatment which are not characteristic of nineteenth-century jewellery and certainly owe nothing to the jewellery produced in England at the time; he was influenced most strongly by his fellow-Italian Castellani (q.v.). His best work was not confined to the Renaissance style; he produced at the beginning of his career some very skilled imitations of Greek and Etruscan work, several of his later pieces show Oriental influence, and the tiara illustrated under *Diadems* (q.v.) is in the Art Nouveau style. In the 1880s Giuliano's sons Federico and Fernando opened a jeweller's shop in Howland Street and produced work in the same style as their father. (For further informa-

tion on the period, see *Nineteenth-century jewellery*.)

Glass. A non-crystalline substance produced by a fusion of oxides (or one acidic oxide) at a high temperature. Numerous materials may be used in making glass, but a major constituent of nearly all glasses is silica. To this are added other substances which thin out the glass, lower its melting point, and give it other properties required for particular purposes. Colouring agents may be added and these are usually metallic oxides. Among the many possible colouring agents are copper oxide (red and pale blue), cobalt oxide (blue), chromium oxide (green), silver salts (yellow), manganese oxide (purple or brown depending on the composition of the glass), tin oxide (an opacifying agent).

Glass has been used to imitate gemstones since Egyptian times. It was common in the first two centuries of the Roman Empire (the Romans were skilled glass-makers), was again highly developed in Italy in the fifteenth and sixteenth centuries, and became very popular as a substitute for diamonds in the eighteenth century. The eighteenth-century pastes owed their brilliance to lead oxide, which is one of the constituents of the better-quality pastes made now. Two types of glass are used in modern imitation stones. One, which is generally known as crown glass, consists of silica, lime, soda, potassium oxide and appropriate colouring agents. This is the glass used for cheap moulded imitation gems. The molten glass is poured into iron moulds, and after cooling the stones may be polished on a lap; sometimes only the crown is polished. Glass of this type is generally used only in costume jewellery.

The second type, which can produce pastes of high quality, consists of silica, lead oxide, potash or soda, and sometimes compounds of thallium. These pastes are carefully faceted to simulate gemstones. The effect of the lead is to increase the colour-dispersion and brilliance but to make the glass softer, and although lead pastes are, if well cut, very attractive when new, they quickly lose their polish and can even be scratched by window glass. They also tend to discolour, as the lead is attacked by sulphur in the air.

Few glass imitation stones are likely to deceive an experienced jeweller or gem dealer; in the first place, the colour is rarely quite right. Glass also feels warm to the touch (the way to test this is with the tip of the tongue, avoiding holding the stone in one's fingers) whereas a stone feels cold, and it is much softer (hardness usually less than 6) than most of the stones it is used to imitate. Characteristic bubbles are likely to be present, particularly in the cheaper type of glass. If these tests do not detect the imitation, measurement of the refractive index (q.v.) usually will. The refractive index of the glasses used in jewellery lies between about 1.44 and 1.70. Glass, being an amorphous substance, is singly-refracting, and there are no singly-refracting gemstones of any importance in this range except opal (R.I. 1.44–1.46), and the glass imitations of opal so far produced have either been completely unconvincing in appearance or have not in fact approached opal in their physical characteristics. The fact that glass is not dichroic (q.v.) is also useful. The specific gravity of glass, ranging from about 2.00 to 4.20, is not however particularly helpful in identification. Translucent and almost opaque pastes are made to imitate such stones as the chalcedonies, jade, turquoise and lapis lazuli. There is a tendency in the translucent pastes for the colour to appear in swathes, and in both translucent and semi-opaque pastes there are often a lot of bubbles. When it is not possible to see these in the body of the stone there may be evidence of them in the form of tiny pits on the surface – these are bubbles which have been cut through in polishing.

The colouring of pastes is not confined to the addition of oxides to the glass melt; colourless pastes may be sprayed on their pavilion facets with an adhesive coloured pigment and then backed with silver or aluminium (see also *Foil*).

Composite stones consisting wholly or partly of glass are often coloured by the cement layer; these are described under *Doublet*.

The source of a great many glass imitation stones is Czechoslovakia; Germany and France also produce a considerable quantity.

A glass which has the same composition as a natural gemstone is beryl glass, which was originally produced by the fusion of real but poor-quality emeralds in an attempt to produce a 'reconstructed' emerald (see *Reconstructed stones*). Beryl glass has been made in a variety of colours (the colouring agents are those used in ordinary glass) and faceted. The stones may be distinguished from natural beryl by their lower specific gravity and refractive index (about 2.42 and 1.52 respectively), their slightly lower hardness (7), the inclusion of gas bubbles, and the fact that, like glass, they are singly refractive and therefore show no dichroism. Natural glasses also occur and are sometimes used in jewellery; see *Silica glass, Obsidian* and *Tektite*. For historical information on glass in jewellery see *Paste*.

'Glass agate'. Misnomer for obsidian.

Glass meteorite. Moldavite. (See *Tektite*.)

Glass opal. Hyalite. (See *Opal*.)

Glass paper. A fine emery paper; the final abrasive used on metal before polishing.

Glyptic. The art of carving and engraving gems (or other materials), or pertaining to that art.

Golconda. The area in southern India which is reputed to be the world's oldest source of diamonds, and to have supplied many of the more famous and historic Indian stones. The diamonds were found in the valley of the river Kistna or Krishna and the deposits were worked from very early times. When Tavernier visited the mines in the seventeenth century he found 30,000 men employed there. All stones over 2 carats in weight were the property of the local ruler. The city of Golconda itself, which is now in ruins and lies about 5 miles west of Hyderabad, was the trading centre not only for local stones but for diamonds found over a very wide area extending from the Godivari river in the north to the Pennar river in the south. From 1518 to 1687 this city – a large fortress standing on a granite hill – was the capital of a powerful kingdom, one of five sultanates set up after the disintegration of the Bahmani Kingdom of the Deccan. Its rulers were overthrown by Aurang Zeb in 1687 and Golconda was incorporated in the Mogul empire. The mines were at the time highly productive, but within 40 years India lost its ancient monopoly when diamonds were discovered in Brazil, and although the Golconda deposits continued to be worked for some time they declined in importance and are now virtually abandoned. Among the famous stones said to come from the region are the Hope diamond and the Koh-i-Noor (qq.v.), both reputed to have been found in the Kollur mine. (See also *Diamond*.)

Gold is in many ways the ideal metal for jewellery, and its advantages have been recognized since very early times. Its natural colour is rich and appealing, it is sufficiently rare to be highly valued, it does not tarnish or rust – gold ornaments are dug up after thousands of years looking as bright as the day they were made – and it is a remarkably easy metal to work, even with primitive tools. It can be beaten out into sheet so thin it is almost transparent, and drawn into extremely fine wire (50 miles of wire can be drawn from one ounce of gold). Its weight (it is very much heavier than lead) gives a satisfying heaviness to articles made from it, and also makes it fairly easy to separate from other minerals with which it is associated by panning in water: the gold sinks to the bottom and the unwanted minerals are floated off. A further advantage of gold for the craftsman is the range of colours it can be made to assume by alloying it with different metals (see

Green gold, Red gold, etc.); the combination of golds of different shades can be very effective.

Gold occurs mostly in quartz veins associated with granite masses. Until a century ago most gold was obtained from alluvial or 'placer' deposits. The gold had been washed out of its matrix and settled, because of its weight, along the beds of rivers, sometimes collecting in masses which had become compressed into solid lumps or nuggets. The enormous South African deposits discovered at the end of the last century, however, consist of reefs of a pebbly conglomerate in which the grains of gold are often too small to be seen by the naked eye. The nature of these reefs – whether they are a fossil placer deposit which has been covered by deposits of other rock and tilted – is still disputed. They now supply almost half of the world's gold. Most of the remainder is supplied by quartz-vein mining, and the output of alluvial gold is now comparatively small.

Gold is to be found in all parts of the world, but only in certain areas does it occur in sufficient quantity to make its extraction commercially worthwhile. Most of the ancient sources of gold are no longer productive. Modern sources of gold other than South Africa include Russia, Australia (Victoria), Alaska (the Yukon), U.S.A., Canada, central and western Africa, and parts of Europe. Some gold has been obtained in Britain but the deposits are no longer worth working; a Welsh mine near Dolgellau traditionally provides the gold for the ring at royal weddings, but on the last occasion when this was required it had to be re-opened specially for the purpose.

Various ways of extracting and refining gold have been used in the past (see *History* below). In modern times the cyanide process has been found the most efficient means of recovering gold. The gold-bearing ore is crushed and ground very fine, and then subjected to cyanide of potassium, which dissolves the gold. The gold-bearing solution is filtered off and the gold precipitated by the addition of zinc dust, after which the zinc is removed in sulphuric acid and the gold is smelted to produce ingots. These are then sent to a refinery where the gold is purified of the other metals, including silver, which it still contains. The refining process entails passing chlorine gas through the gold to turn the other metals into chlorides, which are then removed, boiling in aqua regia (q.v.) to separate the gold from any remaining trace of silver chloride, and finally precipitating the gold by means of an agent such as iron chloride. When all traces of the precipitating agent have been removed with acid, the gold is virtually pure.

Pure gold is too soft to be usable, and has to be alloyed. Various metals such as copper, silver, palladium, nickel and iron are alloyed with gold, and the hardness and colour of the resulting alloy depend on the metal used and its quantity. The purity of gold alloys is measured by the carat (q.v.), pure gold being of 24 carats. 18-carat gold therefore contains 18 parts of gold to 6 parts of another metal, 14-carat gold contains 14 parts of gold, etc. The four legal standards for gold in Britain are 22 carat, 18 carat, 14 carat and 9 carat. (These are *minimum* proportions: a piece of jewellery may be made of 11-carat gold, but it will be hallmarked in this country as 9-carat.) Other standards such as 20-carat, 15-carat, 12-carat and 10-carat are used in other parts of the world. (The ways in which the fineness of gold is tested are described under *Assaying*.)

For different standards of gold which have at various times been in force, see *Hallmarking*.

The refiners produce gold of various carats and colours in a variety of forms: sheet, wire, tube and solder (to pass the assaying tests, gold articles must be soldered with a solder containing a stipulated proportion of gold). In these forms the gold is bought by the manufacturing jeweller. The refiners also supply findings (q.v.) – ready-made jewellery components which the jeweller then assembles.

Gold has in the past been imitated by alloys of copper and zinc, such as pinchbeck (q.v.). Modern imitations of solid gold are usually produced by covering base metal with a thin layer of gold. (See *Gilding, Electroplating, Rolled gold, Hard gold plating* and *Lacquer*.)

History. The history of the use of gold in jewellery begins in ancient Egypt and Mesopotamia, where gold was being worked with proficiency by the fourth millennium B.C. The earliest gold ornaments were made from gold sheet, since this could be quite simply obtained by hammering flat a pellet or nugget of gold. After it has been hammered for a time gold becomes brittle and has to be annealed (raised to red heat and quenched in water) to make it malleable again. During the fourth millennium this became possible with the invention of the blowpipe to control the heat of a charcoal fire, but before this time gold had to be hammered 'cold'. The gold sheet was decorated in relief with hammer and punches (see chasing) and engraved with a sharp tool – flint or copper in the Bronze Age, iron after this had been introduced. By hammering the metal over a shaped core of wood, or hammering it into a mould, three-dimensional pieces could be made. One of the most superb pieces of ancient jewellery, a gold helmet from the royal graves at Ur, is decorated entirely with these simple techniques of repoussé work and engraving; it is beaten from a single sheet of gold and chased and engraved in the form of an elaborate wig encircled by a diadem. Sheet-metal could also be decorated by stamping; punches were made with ends shaped, usually in cameo, in a particular pattern, so that the design could be exactly reproduced as often as required.

During the third millennium B.C. a technique of hard-soldering gold and silver was discovered (see *Soldering*). The flux used was probably natron or the burnt sediment of wine. There are other ways of joining pieces of jewellery together apart from soldering – riveting (the method used by the Celts), the use of hinges, folding pieces together and burnishing them, or binding them with wire – but soldering is a more reliable and less clumsy method and its invention made possible the more ambitious projects of the goldsmith.

By the middle of the third millennium B.C. gold wire was being used for filigree work and for making chains, finger-rings, etc. There are various ways of making gold wire; the earliest method was to cut a thin strip of sheet metal and roll it between stones or plates of a harder metal until it was cylindrical. Wire could also be made by twisting a strip into a tight spiral. A later method was to draw the strip through a drawplate (q.v.) punched with holes of varying diameter; the date of the introduction of the drawplate is uncertain, but it was unknown before the Roman period. (The use of a drawplate can be detected by striations along the wire, and also by its uniform thickness.) Beaded wire was produced with the aid of a beading-tool (q.v.).

The use of gold wire was one of the most important features of ancient jewellery. It was soldered in patterns on to sheet gold and sometimes worked in open designs with no backing. Greek and Etruscan jewellery (qq.v.) shows a particularly skilled use of filigree of this type. Very fine loop-in-loop chains (see *Chain*) were also made for suspending pendants. A development of filigree is *granulation*: the decoration of a surface with tiny gold granules.

A crude type of granulation is found on ornaments from the royal graves at Ur (about 2500 B.C.); the technique was improved during the following centuries and reached Greece in about the middle of the second millennium, and was practised with extraordinary skill by the Etruscans some thousand years later (see *Etruscan jewellery*). The granules were probably made by placing small pieces or filings of gold in a clay crucible in alternating layers with powdered charcoal, and bringing the crucible to red heat so that the gold melted into spheres. After cooling, the charcoal would be washed away and the gold grains sorted into sizes over a mesh. The art of granulation died out in about A.D. 1000, and the problem which until fairly recently perplexed jewellers and historians was how the grains were attached to the surface. Attempts to copy pieces of ancient granulation using a normal hard-soldering process were unsuccessful, because the solder flooded and the flux boiled up and displaced the grains from their position. In 1933, however, a process known as colloid hard-soldering was discovered by which pieces of gold could be joined without using a prepared solder; the pieces are stuck together with a mixture of copper salt, glue and water, and heated to a temperature of 890°C, at which temperature a clean joint is made. (See *Colloid hard-soldering* for detailed explanation.) The process would have been well within the capacity of gold-smiths of this period, and was almost certainly the technique employed for granulation and often for other work as well.

The jewellery of Mesopotamia and the Greek world was almost entirely a gold jewellery (and perhaps silver, but owing to the more perishable nature of silver little survives). Stones and enamel were rarely used. In Egypt however, the *inlaying* of stones in gold was a major feature of jewellery and was practised with great skill. Inlay was later adopted by the Goths and spread to western Europe.

Casting of precious metal was not much practised in the ancient world, because to obtain an ornament in the round it was sufficient to beat two pieces of sheet-gold into hemispherical moulds and solder them together, if necessary with a filling of sand or some other material. Alternatively a sheet of gold could be beaten right over a core, probably of wood, in which case of course the core could not then be removed. Ornaments were, however, sometimes cast solid, and for this the lost-wax process was used. A model of the article was made in wax and covered with clay, and heated. The wax melted and ran out through a funnel previously made in the clay, and molten metal was poured in through the funnel to take the shape of the mould. When the metal cooled the clay was removed and the metal cast finished off with the appropriate tools. It is not known at what stage lost-wax casting was introduced, but it was in use in ancient Egypt.

Finally, objects could be *gilded*. Gold leaf – sheet beaten extremely thin – could be stuck over another metal with an adhesive. A more sophisticated method, used from Roman times onwards, was to mix powdered gold with an equal weight of mercury, spread the mixture over the metal to be gilded and heat it. The mercury vapourized and a thin coating of gold remained. This process is known as amalgamation.

The gold of the ancient world came from numerous sources, of which the richest was probably Egypt. There were rich deposits along the Red Sea and in Nubia, and probably a considerable amount of alluvial gold in the Nile. Mesopotamia had no native gold sources. The gold was probably Egyptian or Arabian. There were deposits in Asia Minor (home of the legendary Midas), in Arabia, in Thrace and Macedonia (supplying some of the gold for Hellenistic jewellery), and some islands of the Cyclades. Rome in the republican period had access to Italian deposits, and later gained control of the rich gold sources in Spain.

Organized mining probably started in Egypt in the fourth millennium B.C. Diodorus, a writer of the first century B.C., describes techniques which had probably not changed much in the intervening three thousand years. The gold-bearing rock was hewn out with a pickaxe if it was soft enough, otherwise split by fire. The stone was crushed and ground by hand and the gold recovered by washing off the other materials in water. Criminals and captives provided the work-force. The Roman mining techniques were, as would be expected, highly organized, involving a great deal of undermining of alluvial terraces and diversion of water-sources to wash out the gold. According

to Strabo, a writer of the early Roman Empire, a tribe in the Caucasus known as the Lice-eaters placed layers of fleeces in the gold-bearing water and the gold, sinking to the bottom, was trapped by the grease in the wool. It has been suggested that this is the origin of the legend of the Golden Fleece. Another ancient method of extracting gold was to place the crushed gold-bearing rock in a mortar with mercury, to which the gold adhered. The combined gold and mercury were heated and the mercury was vapourized, leaving the gold. This method and the washing of gold in a pan or bowl of water – panning – were both used until the last century; indeed a modification of the mercury-amalgamation process is still used, alongside cyanide recovery, at some mines.

Gold *refining* was understood in the third millennium B.C. but was not much practised until classical times. Mostly the craftsman used gold in the state in which it was found, i.e. usually alloyed to some extent with silver and copper. The metal known in antiquity as electrum was a natural alloy of gold and silver in which the silver constituted about one-fifth; nowadays it would be called white gold. When refining was carried out it was by the process known as cupellation. Diodorus, describing the Egyptian method of refining, says that the gold-bearing material was ground and put into earthenware pots with a piece of lead, lumps of salt, a small quantity of tin and some barley. The pots were sealed and baked in a kiln for five days and nights, after which the impurities had been absorbed by the pot and pure gold remained. This would then be melted down and cast into ingots.

A popular way of testing the purity of gold was to rub it on a touchstone – a piece of black Lydian jasper – and compare the colour of the resulting streak with that of gold of a known purity. This test came into use in a comparatively late period in antiquity.

The techniques for the extraction and working of gold changed very little over thousands of years. A few improvements were made in tools and in the construction of furnaces, etc., but it was not until the industrial revolution of the eighteenth century brought about the mechanization of mining and the mass-production of jewellery that radically new techniques were introduced. Even so, although the craftsman now buys his gold in strip, wire and sheet from the refiners instead of beating it out himself, the tools and methods he uses to fashion it are basically the same as those used in the earliest civilizations.

The discovery of new sources of gold however has, to a great extent, determined the course of history. Gold, being virtually imperishable and also (unlike precious stones) easily divisible, has always formed the basis of a nation's economic stability: this role has only begun to change in very recent years. By the end of the classical period the gold of the Mediterranean and the East was in the hands of Rome, but as Roman power weakened much of it was used to buy off the encroaching barbarians, thus of course accelerating Rome's decline, and when Rome fell the barbarians had enough gold to start their own gold currencies. As Christianity spread, gold was increasingly used for Church ornaments, and as the Church was under the protection of the kings this was both an act of piety and a useful way of accumulating a reserve. Organized mining had come to a halt with the collapse of Rome, however, and soon a shortage of gold began to be felt in the West, since increasing quantities were being attracted to the one powerful and stable civilization of the time – Byzantium. Byzantine gold, obtained from central Asia, the Caucasus and north-east Africa, furnished a pure gold currency which was the foundation of the empire's stability for many centuries. Increasing extravagance and costly wars, however, undermined this stability and more and more gold fell into the hands of the rising Arab nations, who, extending their power by conquest and trade, established a gold coinage of their own and also obtained gold from new sources in West Africa. During the thirteenth century the effects of this

revived circulation of gold were felt in Europe and gold coinages were again minted, particularly by the Italian states. Mining was also revived; Hungary was an important source of gold. During the thirteenth century the goldsmiths' guilds of Paris were regulated, and in 1327 a royal charter was granted to the goldsmiths of London. By the close of the Middle Ages the Portuguese had reached the rich deposits of the Gold Coast and were in the process of setting up a trading monopoly.

This was the beginning of the great period of exploration which resulted in the discovery of the riches of the New World. Columbus sailed for the Indies in 1492, and in the early years of the following century Mexico was discovered. The Indians of Mexico were skilled goldworkers, practising all the techniques known in Europe with the exception of enamelling. Cortes found a fortune in gold ornaments, which were melted down and sent back to Spain. Spanish exploration spread from Central to South America and rich sources of alluvial gold were found in Colombia, Venezuela, Guiana and Ecuador. The Andes were a source of many minerals including gold. In 1531 Pizarro conquered Peru. Gold was plentiful in this area too, and goldworking had been practised for some two thousand years. The Incas beat their gold into thin masks, vessels and other ornaments for religious and ceremonial use. Pizarro demanded, as ransom for the Inca king Atahuallpa, enough gold to fill a small room, and obtained it. A strictly organized system was set up for transporting these huge quantities of gold to Spain in treasure-ships. Some of them fell prey to English privateers, but most of them reached their goal, and for a century Spain was the richest country in the world. In the long term, however, the people who benefited from this influx of wealth were not the Spaniards but the merchant bankers of Europe, to whom the control of gold supplies was gradually being transferred after millennia in which gold had lain in the power of kings.

The next rich source of gold to be discovered was in Portuguese Brazil; the resources of Minas Gerais were developed in the course of the seventeenth century and reached their peak of productivity in the mid-eighteenth. Much of this gold found its way to England, which had always suffered from a shortage of gold but which now became an important gold market. In 1717 the mint price of gold was fixed at £4 4s. 11½d. per Troy ounce and remained at this level until 1914. However, despite the Brazilian sources and later the production of gold in Russia, the world output of gold was becoming insufficient to match increased industrial output towards the middle of the nineteenth century. Then gold was discovered in California.

In 1848 a man building a mill-race on the Sacramento river near Sutter's Fort noticed specks of gold in the water. At the end of the year when this and other similar finds were officially announced, an international gold-rush started. The Californian find was unlike all previous ones in that it was not controlled by a government or monopoly – the gold belonged to whoever could find it, although mining licences had to be bought and the state was able to buy the gold if it wished. The deposits were rich; there was alluvial gold in the streams, and reef-gold in the foot-hills of the Sierras. Soon gold was found in other parts of America – in Colorado, Nevada, Montana and South Dakota. Some of the mines were productive for many years; others were quickly worked out and the settlements became ghost towns.

In 1851 an Australian prospector called Hargreaves who had been in California found gold in a tributary of the Macquarie river in New South Wales. Other areas were prospected and rich sources of gold were found at Ballarat in Victoria, at Kalgoorlie in Western Australia, and in Queensland. The Australian gold-rush rivalled the Californian, and Australian output at its peak surpassed that of California. It declined sharply in this century.

Gold had been found intermittently in South Africa for some time but had not excited much interest. In 1886, however, a prospector crushed and panned some rock from an outcrop on the Witwatersrand slopes and found a rich deposit of gold. As the reef was traced from farm to farm an army of miners moved in, but it soon became obvious that this was not the sort of find that could be exploited by the lone prospector. The gold was contained in a pebbly conglomerate which had to be extracted in large quantities from shafts; organization and considerable capital were required. Numerous mining companies were formed and the mining camp of Johannesburg began to expand into a city. The gold-bearing reef turned out to be by far the largest ever discovered – it stretched in an arc 300 miles long from the eastern Transvaal to the Orange Free State, and extended in places to a great depth below the surface (mining at present is carried out to a depth of 10,000 ft.). Because of the complexity and expense of the mining (the richness of the reefs varies considerably and smaller reefs branch off from the main ones), the initial proliferation of mining companies was succeeded by a period of increasing centralization, and there are now fewer than 50 mines (as against 450 in 1889) owned by seven major groups which pool their experience and pursue a common policy. The gold is refined at a central refinery and bought by the South African treasury, which then sells it; much of it is shipped to London, where it is sold on the London gold market.

The last great gold-rush was to the Yukon valley in Canada, where gold was found in 1896 in the Klondike river. It was a wild and barren region and much of the gold lay in frozen ground, but the prospectors poured in, and in two years the little settlement of Dawson (pop. 500) had become Dawson City, with over 30,000 inhabitants. Fortunes were made, and often lost, very quickly, and the deposits were worked out within a few years. Dawson City became another of the ghost towns littering the exhausted goldfields of North America and Australia. However, the area has recently turned out to contain wealth of another kind: oil has been found there, and is now being extracted on quite a large scale.

Gold opal. Fire opal. (See *Opal*.)

Gold plating. The covering of silver or base metal with a coating of gold. This is done electrolytically (see *Electroplating*), and various shades of colour can be obtained by plating with a coloured gold alloy (see *Alloy*). A recent development is hard gold plating (q.v.), which provides a more durable coating than was formerly possible. (See also *Gilding*.)

Gold quartz. Quartz containing small particles of gold, sometimes used in jewellery. The name may also be used for quartz of a golden yellow colour.

Goldsmiths' Hall. An imposing nineteenth-century building close to St. Paul's Cathedral which is the headquarters of the Worshipful Company of Goldsmiths (q.v.), housing the Company's collection of historic plate, a reference library, and the London Assay Office.

The hall is the fourth to be built on the site. The first hall, of which little is known, was purchased in 1339 by the London guild of goldsmiths, who had been incorporated by royal charter in 1327. A second hall of larger proportions was begun early in the following century and contained, in addition to an assembly hall, a chapel, an armoury, a granary and an assay office. Although the hall appears to have been very impressive in Tudor times the accommodation was obviously felt to be insufficient, because when a new hall was built between 1634 and 1636 the sites of ten adjacent houses were added to the area. Inigo Jones acted as consultant to the building. The new hall was extensively damaged in the Great Fire of 1666, and the Company were at the time so impoverished after the recent political upheavals that they were obliged to sell much of their plate in order

to restore it. When rebuilt it was a large and dignified building in red brick surrounding a small paved courtyard, and contained a dancing gallery and card room in addition to its more sober amenities. In the later eighteenth and early nineteenth centuries, however, the Company's finances were again at a low ebb, and the hall fell into a dilapidated and eventually dangerous condition. A serious fire in the Assay office in 1830 was the deciding factor, and plans for a new building were commissioned from Philip Hardwick, R.A.

The new hall, built of Portland stone in the Italian style and with a frontage of 150 feet, was opened with ceremony in July 1835. The interior was described at the time as having 'an air of palatial grandeur', and this was before the marble staircase, built of marble from six different countries, was added in 1871. The hall then remained virtually unchanged until the Second World War, when it suffered minor damage from incendiary bombs and severe damage to the south-west wing, which was directly hit by a high-explosive bomb. The company carried on their work in what remained of the building and restoration was started in 1947. The former Court Dining Room was replaced by an Exhibition room housing a permanent display of the Company's plate, extra room was added at the top of the building to provide space for a laboratory, photographic studio and a smaller exhibition room, and what had formerly been the Committee Room was converted into a reference library, opened in 1951 for use by students. The ceremonial rooms in the hall now comprise, in addition to those mentioned, the Livery Hall, Binding Room, Court Room, Drawing Room, North and South Ante Rooms and a Luncheon Room. All the business of the Assay office has been carried on inside Goldsmiths' Hall since the war, when the premises on the other side of Gutter Lane hitherto used for this purpose were destroyed by bombing. In the Assay office are a copper plate stamped with the marks of London gold and silversmiths from 1675, and a set of Troy weights dating from 1588. Among the many interesting objects in the rest of the building are a Roman stone altar to Diana, found during the excavations on the site in 1830 and now kept in the Court Room, and a seventeenth-century gilded wooden statue of St. Dunstan (q.v.) which was formerly a figurehead on one of the Company's barges: it now stands on the main staircase. (For history of the London goldsmiths' guild see *Worshipful Company of Goldsmiths*.)

Goldstone. See *Aventurine glass*.

'Gold topaz'. Misnomer for golden-yellow quartz.

Goshenite. A name formerly used for colourless or white beryl (q.v.).

Gothic jewellery. For jewellery of the Gothic period, see *Medieval jewellery*. For revival of Gothic styles, see *Nineteenth-century jewellery*. The jewellery of the Goths is not considered.

Grain (1). A unit of weight. The grain Troy is equal to the grain Avoirdupois, and there are 480 grains to the Troy ounce. As a unit of weight for diamonds and pearls, the grain is 0.25 carat. (See *Weights for precious metals* and *Weights for gemstones*.)

Grain (2). Name for a small spherical bead of metal.

Graining tool. A hand tool with a cup-shaped depression at the tip, used to round over any small projecting piece of metal into a grain or boss.

Granulation. The process of decorating a metal surface with tiny spherical grains of metal. It was practised from the third millennium B.C. to about A.D. 1000. The surviving pieces are in gold; the technique could also have been used with silver, but owing to the perishable nature of silver few silver ornaments have survived from antiquity and it is not known whether silver granulation was in fact practised.

Granulation was used most regularly, and with the highest degree of skill, in Etruscan jewellery (q.v.). Various styles of granulation have been distinguished: *massed*, in which the grains cover the entire surface or a large part of it; simple *linear* granulation; *outline* granulation following the contours of embossed decoration; *silhouette*, in which the grains are used to block in figures; and *reserved silhouette*, where the background is blocked in with grains.

The method used in antiquity for attaching the grains was the subject of some speculation in the past, since ordinary hard-soldering did not seem to produce satisfactory results. It is now assumed that the process used was colloid hard-soldering (q.v.). For further details of this process, see *Gold*.

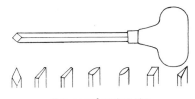

Graver and various tips

Graining tool

Graver (Burin). A tool with a sharp steel edge like a chisel, and a round wooden handle which is held in the palm of the hand, used for engraving metal.

Great Mogul. A large Indian diamond found in the Kollur mines near Golconda (q.v.) in the seventeenth century. It was

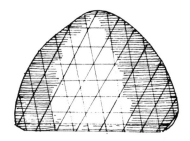

The Great Mogul diamond, from Tavernier's original drawing

shown in 1655 to Tavernier, who made several drawings of it, by the Great Mogul Aurang Zeb, and at the time apparently weighed something in the region of 790 carats. It was subsequently very badly cut and the weight was drastically reduced – some sources say to 280 carats, others to 188. The unfortunate Venetian cutter to whom the stone had been entrusted was deprived of all his possessions by the wrathful owner. It is not known what became of the diamond after this: it may have been among the booty taken by the Persian conqueror Nadir Shah, who sacked Delhi in 1739. It has been suggested that the stone is identical with one of the other famous Indian diamonds, perhaps the Orloff or the Koh-i-noor (qq.v.)

Great Southern Cross. A series of nine pearls naturally adhering together in the form of a cross, discovered in a pearl-oyster fished in 1886 off the coast of Western Australia. (It is thought that there were originally only eight, and another was added to make the cross symmetrical.) Pearls are sometimes found naturally united, but a discovery of this nature is quite exceptional.

Great Table diamond. A large tabular diamond seen by Tavernier in 1642 at Golconda; it weighed 242 French carats (see *Carat*). Its later history is unknown, but it has been suggested that it was re-cut to produce the Dary-i-noor (q.v.), the present whereabouts of which are also unknown. It is unlikely that a large stone of such uninteresting form as the Great

Table would survive long without re-cutting.

Great White diamond. See *Imperial diamond*.

Greek jewellery. The jewellery of the Greek world begins just after the middle of the third millennium B.C., when some of the styles and techniques of Babylonian jewellery reached the Aegean. By the seventeenth century B.C. the art had developed considerably and some very fine jewellery was produced by the Minoan civilization in Crete. The techniques now used included filigree and granulation (qq.v.), the inlaying of coloured stones, and a means of mass-producing embossed pieces from the same pattern. Minoan jewellery includes diadems, earrings in the shape of a tapered hoop, bracelets and necklaces of beads, gold rings, some inlaid with lapis lazuli, and – most striking of all – large pendants of embossed gold. One of these depicts a nature-god standing among lotus-flowers and holding a bird in each hand. The style shows Egyptian influence.

The Minoan techniques were continued on the Greek mainland by the Mycenaean culture, which flourished from the sixteenth to the twelfth centuries and was an offshoot of the Minoan. Mycenaean jewellery reflects an increased and skilful use of granulation, and also provides the first known examples of the use of enamel (q.v.). Its more notable features are gold signet rings (q.v.) with pictorial devices, and hollow gold beads decorated in shallow relief with stylized representations of plants and marine life. These beads were made in two halves: the decorated half was stamped out of sheet-gold, and a flat piece of gold was soldered to the back, with a filling in the centre. There are many different patterns, and the best examples are further decorated with fine granulation and small dots of enamel placed in hollows on the surface.

About 1100 B.C. the Mycenaean culture collapsed, probably under the Dorian invasions, and was followed by three centuries of poverty in which the only jewellery produced was of a very primitive kind. Contacts with the East were then gradually re-established, and the jewellery of the next two centuries shows a combination of Oriental influences and forms and motifs from Mycenaean jewellery, which were presumably re-introduced by the Phoenicians. Some very fine jewellery was produced in this period of revival, notably in Athens and Corinth and the Greek islands. The mainland jewellery includes some finely-granulated gold *earrings*, some in the shape of a crescent hung with gold chains, others in the form of a disc with a central inlay. The safety-pin type of brooch was widely worn in Greece at this time and had a large square plate, which was often engraved, covering the catch for the pin; most examples are in bronze, but some have been found in gold, delicately engraved with pictures of animals, birds and other subjects. Among the more interesting jewellery from the Greek islands are sets of rectangular gold plaques with embossed figures which were worn in a row along the top of the dress as *pectoral ornaments*. These were made in Rhodes. The subjects include sphinxes, centaurs, the winged goddess Artemis, and a bee-goddess of Hittite origin. (See illustration.) The basic decoration was carried out by stamping or by beating the metal into a mould, and further decoration in the form of filigree, granulation, applied rosettes, etc., was then added. These pectorals were also made in silver and electrum (q.v.). Other rich jewellery of this period comes from Crete, where some very elaborate *pendants* have been found. One of these is particularly unusual in that its central feature is a large half-moon of rock crystal set in gold. It has three subsidiary pendants set with amber, and is hung on gold chains with terminals in the shape of snakes' heads. This pendant suggests Phoenician influence, while the Rhodian pectorals are reminiscent of Egyptian art.

By the sixth century B.C. foreign influences had been assimilated and Greek jewellery had a style of its own. The main

Rhodian gold pectoral embossed with figure of Artemis with lions (The Mistress of Beasts). The plaque is one of five worn on a string. Seventh century B.C. British Museum

features of seventh-century work continued, but as Greek sculpture became more naturalistic so did the style of jewellery. The naturalistic trend continued during the Classical period (475–330), the era of the greatest achievements in Greek culture. Jewellery from the sixth century onwards shows an increasing use of filigree as opposed to granulation, which is now rarely used, and the appearance of enamel in a new form – set in areas on the surface bounded by filigree. The use of inlaid stones is rare; the standard of the metalwork is all-important. The finest work is found on the whole in earrings, necklaces and bracelets.

Earrings (q.v.) were commonly worn and there were numerous types. The type based on a spiral of wire pushed through the ear had been worn for some centuries and now developed in a variety of ways, usually in the direction of more and more elaborate terminals. A number from Cyprus are decorated with lions' or griffins' heads. In another very popular variant of the spiral the middle loop has become elongated and flattened so that the earring resembles a letter W, and a

171

Greek jewellery

Greek earring of fifth century B.C., decorated with filigree, granulation and enamel. British Museum

central rosette is attached to the apex of the loop; these earrings could no longer be pushed through the ear and were worn suspended from a wire. Another common type is the boat-shape, basically a hoop with a thick boat-like lower half. These were frequently hung with pendants in the form of buds, and in some cases a figure such as a siren sits on the 'boat', which by this time is no longer the lower part of a hoop but a pendant in itself, hung from an enamelled rosette (see illustration). Other very popular types of earring were the disc variety, sometimes enamelled, and earrings with pendants in the shape of an inverted cone of gold decorated with filigree and granulation. Some very fine *necklaces* date from the fifth and fourth centuries. They are usually strung with gold beads and pendants in such forms as melons, pomegranates, acorns, buds and bulls' and lions' heads (see *Necklaces* for illustration). One very elaborate one from Tarentum has pendants in the shape of human heads, a popular motif during the fourth century.

Bracelets were mostly penannular (i.e. an incomplete circle) made out of tubular metal with animals' heads on the terminals. The finest known examples are a pair

which terminate in sphinxes (illustrated under *Bracelets*); other bracelets have rams' or horses' heads or the figures of lions.

Up to this time rings had been predominantly functional, carrying the owner's seal engraved in metal or on a stone scarab (q.v.). In the Classical period the decorative element became more important and some purely decorative rings ornamented with filigree are found. Towards the end of the Classical period there are rings decorated with animals in relief, and also a number of spiral snake-rings. Scarab seal-rings of the Egyptian type, with a swivelling seal, had been in use since the sixth century and were usually of cornelian, and the beginning of the fourth century saw the appearance of the simple intaglio stone, without the scarab top, set in the fixed bezel of a ring. This type was to endure for many centuries in the classical world and to be revived in Renaissance and eighteenth-century Europe. (See *Intaglios*.)

Head-ornaments in the form of wreaths and diadems were a characteristic feature of Greek jewellery in this period. Wreaths were worn on ceremonial occasions and were also buried with the dead. They were extremely naturalistic and delicate imitations of leaves and branches (laurel, myrtle, ivy etc.), in precious metal, gilded bronze or wood covered in gold leaf (see *Diadems* for illustration). Diadems had been buried with the dead for many centuries and were also worn by the living. The simplest are a circlet of metal decorated with embossed or attached rosettes; more elaborate types depicted scenes, and a remarkable example found in southern Russia has a griffin-head attachment at the front.

Brooches were not normally used in Greece at this time; the clothing was fastened with a pin. Some of these are very elaborate, the heads being decorated with such motifs as rampant lions, sphinxes, and plant-forms. In the Hellenistic period the pin began to be replaced by the circular brooch.

Greek culture was radically changed by

the conquests of Alexander the Great, which, beginning in the latter part of the fourth century, brought vast areas of the East under Greek control and thus exposed Greece itself to Eastern culture. An incidental result of the conquest was that for the first time since the Bronze Age there was no shortage of gold in Greece. The jewellery of the Hellenistic period (about 330 B.C. onwards) is therefore plentiful and different in style from earlier Greek jewellery, although the new forms took about a century to establish themselves. The most important innovation is the widespread use of coloured stones and glass, previously very rare in Greek jewellery. The most favoured stone was red garnet; other stones used were amethyst, cornelian, chalcedony, pearls, and occasionally emerald. A new type of enamelling was introduced: dipped enamel, mostly used for earring-pendants, in which a metal core was dipped into molten glass and the glass shaped to the required form by ordinary glass-working techniques. Among the new motifs of the Hellenistic period are the 'Heracles knot' (a reef-knot), imported from Egypt where it had an amuletic significance, and the figure of Eros, which was very commonly used. The Heracles knot, inlaid with garnets, appears as the centrepiece in some very elaborate *diadems* of the third and second centuries. They are decorated with gold figures and enamelling and have pendants which are also inlaid with garnet. Another type of diadem rises to a point over the forehead and is decorated in a pictorial style in low relief and filigree.

Wreaths are mostly, like those of the preceding period, naturalistic imitations of real leaves in precious metal or gold foil. Some more elaborate ones have been found decorated with figures in the round, with filigree, and even with beads of stone and glass representing berries.

Earrings continued to be important, but the most popular types were now the pendant-earring and the tapering hoop with an animal-head, or sometimes human-head, finial. This second type

Earring with amphora pendant set with garnets. Second–first century B.C. British Museum

(which is illustrated under *Earrings*) first appeared in Greece in the late fourth century and survived for several hundred years with certain modifications. The hoop was generally formed of twisted gold wires and the most popular decorations until the second century were the head of a lion, bull, goat, gazelle, and sometimes the head of a woman. During the second century beads of coloured stone or glass began to be threaded on to the hoop, and the head of a dolphin became the commonest motif. Of the pendant earrings, the variety with a conical pendant continued from the Classical period; from the second century the cone or pyramid was of coloured stone or glass, set in gold. Other popular earring-pendants sometimes combined with the cone were the winged Victory, Eros (extremely common and often cast in solid gold), jars (see illustration), sirens, and birds in dipped enamel.

Necklaces were frequently in the form of a strap of fine gold chain hung with small pendants, usually in the shape of jars or spear-heads. They are decorated with small enamelled rosettes which mask

Green garnet

Hellenistic serpent-ring. British Museum

the joins in the chain. Necklaces with animal-head terminals were also widely worn; the body of the necklace might be of chain or beads of various materials. Necklaces of linked cabochon stones mounted in gold made their appearance in this period and lasted into Roman times.

The tubular bracelets terminating in animal heads continued to be very popular, as did spiral snake-bracelets, which had also originated in the Classical period. Spiral snake-rings were equally popular (see illustration). A new type of ring which is typical of Hellenistic jewellery has an oval bezel set with an engraved or cabochon stone. Some of these stones are cameos (q.v.), cameo-cutting being another innovation of the Hellenistic period.

In the course of the second century B.C. Greece fell more and more under Roman domination and was finally reduced to the status of a Roman province. This political change, however, had little immediate effect on the Greek arts, since many elements of Greek culture had by this time been adopted by the Romans and had also been spread by Greek settlers to other parts of the East. Hellenistic jewellery therefore does not stop short at the Roman conquest but survives for several centuries in the jewellery of the Roman Empire. (See *Roman jewellery;* also *Etruscan* and *Egyptian jewellery.*)

Green garnet. Demantoid garnet (see *Andradite*). The name has in the past been incorrectly used for enstatite (q.v.).

Green gold. A gold alloy containing a high proportion of silver – 30–40%. (Cadmium may be used instead of silver.)

Green onyx. Chalcedony stained green. (See *Chalcedony* and *Dyeing of stones.*)

'Green quartz.' Misnomer for fluorspar.

Green rouge. Chromium oxide, used in the polishing of gemstones.

Green star-stone. Chlorastrolite.

Greenstone. Nephrite (see *Jade*). Chlorastrolite (q.v.) is also sometimes known as greenstone.

Grelots. Small elongated pendant beads.

Grey gold. An alloy consisting of 15–20% iron, 85–80% gold.

Griqualandite. Tiger's eye (it comes from Griqualand in South Africa).

Grisaille. A type of painted enamel (q.v.), making exclusive use of dark and very pale colours to give a monochromatic effect. (See also *Enamel.*)

Grossular garnet. (Calcium-aluminium silicate. S.G. 3.55–3.67; R.I. 1.74–1.75; H. $6\frac{1}{2}$–7.) The variety of grossular garnet most used in jewellery is *hessonite* (*essonite*), a transparent brownish, honey-yellow or orange stone. Yellow hessonite (and sometimes all hessonite) is also known as cinnamon-stone, and the brownish and orange stones are sometimes called hyacinth or jacinth. The stone is said to have more fire in artificial light than in daylight. Internally, hessonite has a peculiar granular structure which can often be seen with a hand lens: it is caused by the inclusion of many small transparent crystals, probably of zircon or diopside. The interior of the stone may also show oily-looking streaks which are known as 'treacle'. Most gem-quality hessonite comes from Ceylon; other localities are U.S.A., Canada and Brazil. Some fine crystals of brownish-green grossular garnet are found in Siberia but it is doubtful whether they are cut as gemstones.

'*Transvaal jade*', which is found about 40 miles west of Pretoria and is fairly similar to some jade in appearance, is a variety of massive grossular garnet. The best material is bright green, but greyish, bluish, and pink stone is also found. The green stone has been marketed as jade, but its higher refractive index (1.72–1.73) distinguishes it from both jadeite and nephrite (see *Jade*), as does the fact that it is strongly luminescent under X-rays (q.v.).

A third type of grossular garnet consists of crystals of pink grossular garnet in a matrix of white marble. This attractive ornamental stone is variously known as landerite, rosolite, and xalostocite (after its locality, Xalostoc in Mexico). (See also *Garnet*.)

Guard chain (Guard). A long chain of silver or gold, usually gold, from which keys, a watch and other useful objects were hung; later extended to mean any long gold chain. Silver guard chains were introduced into general wear in about 1806, and gold ones about 1830. They survived, with fluctuations in popularity, until the 1920s, when the wristwatch was almost universally adopted and they became redundant.

Guard ring. A ring worn above a more valuable ring on the same finger to guard against its loss. (See also *Keeper ring*.)

Gunmetal. An alloy of 9 parts copper to 1 part tin which may be used in jewellery.

Gypsum. (Hydrous calcium sulphate. S.G. 2.20–2.40; H. about 2.) A mineral best known in the form of its massive variety, alabaster, which is used ornamentally but not in jewellery. A fibrous form of gypsum known as *satin spar* is, however, sometimes made into cabochons or beads; it is generally white and has a silky appearance. It is attractive but much too soft to make a serviceable gemstone. (A fibrous variety of calcite, q.v., is also known as satin spar.) There are numerous sources in Europe and the U.S.A.

H

Habit. See *Crystal habit.*

Hackle-back pearl. Pearl from the freshwater mussel *Symphynota complanata* found in the Mississippi valley.

Haematite (Hematite). (Iron oxide; S.G. 4.95–5.16; H. 6½.) A blue-black opaque stone with a brilliant lustre. Its most common use in jewellery is as an intaglio seal stone, but it is also used for beads (sometimes to imitate black pearl) and as brilliant-cut and trap-cut stones.

Haematite was used in ancient jewellery, and derives its name from the fact that in powdered form it is red and when rubbed on stone it leaves a red streak, both reminiscent of blood. It occurs in nodular kidney-shaped masses and is accordingly sometimes known as 'kidney ore'. Beautiful crystals of haematite occur on the Island of Elba. Most of the haematite used in jewellery, however, comes from Cumberland in England and is cut and polished at Idar Oberstein (q.v.) in Germany.

Hair amethyst. Amethyst containing needle-like crystals of rutile. See also *Rutilated quartz.*

Hair jewellery. Jewellery partly composed of hair seems to have made its first appearance in the seventeenth century, when medallions in the form of initials in gold wire on a background of woven hair, set under crystal, were worn as a type of memorial jewellery (q.v.). When the taste for memorial jewellery revived towards the end of the eighteenth century hair jewellery was again produced, and it remained extremely popular until the 1860s in England, Germany and Scandinavia, and also – somewhat surprisingly – in France.

The hair was worked in various ways. It might be woven and used as a background, as in the seventeenth-century examples, made into a picture or incorporated as part of a picture, or it might be plaited into a bracelet, the clasp of which would probably also consist of a medallion containing hair-work. A small lock of hair might be set under crystal or glass in the bezel of a ring or woven to form a rim round the bezel. Hair was frequently worn as a remembrance of a loved one: in memorial jewellery the hair of the deceased was often formed into appropriately funereal designs of which weeping willows over tombs and weeping widows by broken columns were among the most popular. Hair jewellery was by no means always of a memorial nature, however; the hair might be that of a friend, relative or sweetheart, and worn as a token of sentiment. In that case a variety of designs might be used, the most popular being flower and leaf patterns and the Prince of Wales' feathers (see illustration).

The hair could be taken to a professional to be made up into the required pattern and set in a frame – gold frames set with seed-pearls were very popular – but the work was often done by amateurs. A book entitled *The Lock of Hair,* published in 1871, gives detailed instructions for making designs in hair, including the tomb and weeping-willow scene. Young ladies wishing to preserve a memento of a dear friend in this way were advised that it was much better to undertake the work themselves, since 'unscrupulous tradesmen' were likely to substitute the hair of a stranger for the hair they were given on finding that there was not enough of it

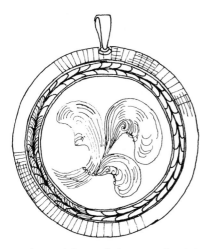

*Pendant medallion with the Prince of Wales'
feathers in hair-work*

for the pattern required. The author of
the book, obviously a professional
jeweller, supplied sets of tools for hair-
work, and gold brooches and lockets
specially made for mounting it.

The book was published at a time when
hair jewellery had passed the peak of its
popularity (the 40s and 50s), but was
still acceptable. Two decades later it was
thought quite hideous. Long after hair
ceased to be made into patterns and
woven into chains and bracelets, however,
it was still worn in a small compartment
at the back of a locket or brooch. (See also
Nineteenth-century jewellery.)

Hairstone. Rutilated quartz.

'Half cornelian'. Yellow cornelian.

Half facets. Alternative name for cross
facets. (See *Diamond-cutting*.)

Half tin-cut. Term applied to cheap glass
imitation stones which have been partly
polished on a tin lap. (See *Glass*.)

Hallmarking.
Modern hallmarks. Hallmarks are marks
stamped by assay offices (q.v.) on gold
and silver wares after they have been
assayed (see *Assaying*) and have been
found to contain the proportions of

precious metal required by law. The
hallmark is a guarantee of the quality of
the metal. There are four legal standards
for gold in Britain: 22-carat (22 parts gold
in 24, or 91.66%), 18-carat (75%),
14-carat (58.5%) and 9-carat (37.5%), and
two for silver: sterling (92.5% silver) and
Britannia (95.84%) (rarely used). Each
has its own hallmark. There are also marks
denoting the assay office at which the
piece was marked and the year in which
it was marked. Finally there is the maker's
mark, put on by the manufacturer before
the piece is assayed.

(i) *The maker's mark* (fig. 1). This should
consist of the initials of the Christian
name and surname of the maker. Sometimes retailers require their own initials
to be placed on work intended for them
instead of those of the manufacturer.

(ii) *The standard mark*. Sterling silver
marked in England is marked with the
lion passant, and sterling silver marked in
Scotland with the thistle (figs. 2 and 3).
Britannia silver is marked with the figure
of Britannia (fig. 4). 22-carat gold and
18-carat gold are marked with figures
denoting the number of carats and with a
crown (figs 5 and 6). 14-carat gold and
9-carat gold are marked with figures
denoting the number of carats and with
the proportion of gold given as a decimal
(figs 7 and 8).

(iii) *The Assay Office mark*. The
London marks are the leopard's head
(fig. 9), which is put on gold and sterling
silver, and the lion's head erased (i.e.
torn from the shoulders), which is put on
Britannia silver (fig. 10). The Birmingham
mark is an anchor for both gold and
silver (fig. 11), the Sheffield marks are a
crown for silver (fig. 12) and a York rose
for gold (fig. 13), and the Edinburgh
mark is a castle for both silver and gold
(fig. 14).

(iv) *The date-letter*. This is a letter of the
alphabet enclosed in a shield (fig. 15).
The letter is changed every year. The
letters run in cycles of 20, from A to U or
V, omitting J. When the end of the
alphabet is reached a new one is started in
different lettering, and as there are not

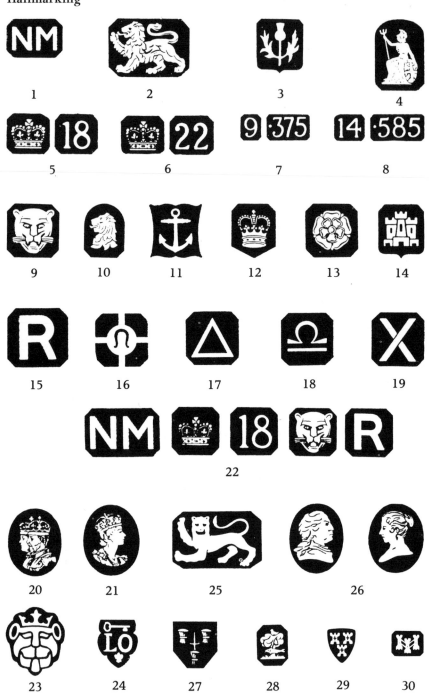

Hallmarks on gold and silver. Reproduced by kind permission of the London Assay Office

many distinctively different styles of lettering the shape of the shield is also varied. No two cycles are exactly the same, therefore, and it is thus possible to tell in which year a piece was hallmarked. First of all, however, it is necessary to find where the piece was marked by looking at the assay office mark. The date-letter is then looked up in the published tables of date-letters issued by each assay office. This is because all the assay offices have different cycles and change the date-letter at different times of the year – London changes in May, Birmingham and Sheffield in July, and Edinburgh in October. The system is somewhat confusing for the uninitiated.

(v) *Marks on foreign wares*. Articles of gold or silver imported into Britain are stamped with marks different from those used on British goods. The marks replace the normal assay office marks. They are: for London, the sign of the constellation Leo (fig. 16); for Birmingham, an equilateral triangle (fig. 17); for Sheffield, the sign of the constellation Libra (fig. 18); for Edinburgh, St. Andrew's cross (fig. 19). The initials of the importer are struck on the piece instead of the initials of the maker.

(vi) *Commemorative marks*. Special marks are sometimes authorized to be struck to commemorate a particular occasion. These are struck voluntarily and do not appear on all goods marked during the period. A mark to commemorate the silver jubilee of King George V and Queen Mary (fig. 20) was authorized to be struck on silver wares made in 1933, 1934 and 1935, and a mark commemorating the coronation of Queen Elizabeth II (fig. 21) was authorized to be struck on gold and silver wares hallmarked in 1952–1953 and 1953–1954.

A set of hallmarks on a piece of jewellery or plate therefore give a great deal of information. They tell one by whom the piece was made, whether it was made inside or outside the United Kingdom, where and when it was hallmarked, and what is the quality of the metal. The set of hallmarks illustrated in fig. 22, for example, show that the piece is of 18-carat gold, was made in Britain by 'N.M.', and was hallmarked in London in the year 1952–1953.

History of hallmarks. Hallmarking was instituted in 1300 by Edward I in an attempt to stop goldsmiths defrauding their customers by pretending that their wares contained a higher proportion of precious metal than they in fact did. This type of fraud was widespread and, judging from the number of statutes enacted in subsequent years to deal with the problem, remained widespread for many centuries. As the legal standards for gold and silver fluctuated over the centuries the use of hallmarks varied, and from time to time new ones were introduced to meet particular needs. The assaying and marking of gold and silver were at first restricted to the officials of Goldsmiths' Hall, London, from which the term 'hallmarking' is derived.

(i) *The leopard's head*. The statute of 1300 laid down minimum standards for gold and silver wares – the 'Touch of Paris' ($19\frac{1}{5}$ carats) for gold, and sterling for silver – and said that these wares were to be marked with a leopard's head by the 'gardiens of the craft' of London goldsmiths. In a subsequent statute the leopard's head is referred to as the King's mark. The leopard at first was a regal-looking animal with a beard and crown (fig. 23) (the crown seems to have appeared some time in the fifteenth century), but during the reign of George II the size of its head diminished, and in 1821 when new punches were engraved it was deprived of both its crown and beard. The reason for this is not known: possibly the official responsible for having the new punches made had consulted a document in which the head was not described as being crowned. Whatever the reason, the modern leopard is decidedly less impressive. (It is not in fact a leopard but a lion, *leopart* being the old French heraldic term for a lion passant guardant [a lion standing sideways with head turned to the front]. As the arms of

England have been three lions passant guardant since the reign of Henry III, it is likely that the 'leopard's head' was taken from the royal arms.) In the sixteenth century a new mark (the lion passant) was adopted as a mark of quality (see below) and the leopard's head came to be used as the town mark of the London assay office. Since 1300 the mark has been in continuous use for silver except for the period 1697–1719, when the only legal standard for silverware was Britannia silver (see below), which was not marked with the leopard's head.

(ii) *The maker's mark*. This is almost as old as the leopard's head; a statute of Edward III in 1363 required every goldsmith to have 'a mark by himself, for which he should answer', to be struck beside the leopard's head. In the days when most of the population was illiterate the goldsmiths' marks were pictorial symbols, probably allusions to the goldsmith's name or reproductions of the pictorial signs hung above goldsmiths' shops. During the seventeenth century letters began to be used, but the signs continued in conjunction with the letters for many years. (Fig. 24 is the mark of Nathaniel Lock, 1705–1706.) The Act of 1697 which made Britannia the compulsory standard for silver also instituted new makers' marks: these were to be the first two letters of the maker's surname. When the Act was repealed in 1719, allowing silversmiths to use either sterling or Britannia silver as they wished, the old maker's marks were also restored, with the result that silversmiths who used both standards of silver used two different makers' marks. This confusing state of affairs continued until 1739, when silversmiths were ordered to destroy their existing marks and use new ones consisting of the initial letters of their Christian names and surnames, which were to be in a different style of lettering from those previously used. This rule has remained in force ever since.

There are continuous records of London makers' marks from 1675 onwards at Goldsmiths' Hall; they are punched into a large copper plate. The identity of some of the goldsmiths before this date is known, but the records are very scanty.

(iii) *The date-letter*. This was introduced during the fifteenth century. The probable reason for its introduction was a statute of 1478 in which the entire guild of goldsmiths was held to be responsible if it were discovered that the Warden had passed inferior metal as being of the required standard. The guild would therefore need to know, in case of future trouble, when a piece had been assayed so that they could identify the Warden responsible. The usefulness of the date-letter to collectors and dealers of a later age was not envisaged at the time. Before 1629–1630 there are no written records referring to date-letters, and the task of reconstructing the early cycles of date-letters therefore depends on the few pieces whose date of manufacture is known.

(iv) *The lion passant*. In the reign of Henry VIII the silver coinage, which in better times had been sterling, was seriously debased; in 1551 there were only 3 ounces of silver in every pound weight of coins. Goldsmiths and silversmiths, however, were still working in silver of the sterling standard, and to indicate the difference in quality between this and the silver coinage a new mark was introduced at Goldsmiths' Hall: this was the lion passant (fig. 25). At first it was a lion passant guardant (the head is turned to the front), but in 1821, at the same time as the leopard's crown was removed, the lion's head was turned in profile and has remained so ever since. Until 1798 both gold and silver were marked with the lion passant. The legal standard for gold had been made 18 carats in 1477 (superseding the 'Touch of Paris') and 22 carats in 1576. From 1576 to 1798 22-carat was the only permitted standard for gold wares. In 1798 a statute was passed permitting the use of 18-carat gold as well, and ordering that this should be stamped with a crown and the figure 18 (the modern hallmark) instead of the lion passant. In 1844 a further statute required

22-carat gold to be stamped with a crown and the figure 22 instead of the lion passant. The lion passant thenceforth was used solely as the standard mark for sterling silver. (In 1854, when for some years British gold-wares had been unable to compete with foreign wares because the compulsorily high standards for gold made them too expensive for the average pocket, the lower standards of 15-carat, 12-carat and 9-carat were legally recognized in Britain and were hallmarked as '15.625' etc. In 1932 15-carat and 12-carat were replaced by 14-carat, marked '14 .585', as now.)

(v) *The lion's head erased and Britannia.* To provide funds for the Civil War in the seventeenth century much silver plate had been melted down. When political stability returned, craftsmen were commissioned to replace this plate, and there was also a great demand for silver tankards for inns. There was not enough silver to meet the demand, and the silversmiths therefore resorted to melting down the silver coinage, which after its debasement in the mid-sixteenth century had been restored to sterling by Elizabeth I. Alarmed by this, the Government passed various statutes designed to stop the melting-down of coins, and finally in 1697 passed an Act which raised the standard for silver plate to 95.84% fine silver. The new plate was to be stamped with the marks of the lion's head erased and Britannia. At the same time a new maker's mark consisting of the first two letters of the surname was introduced. (This Act is the first in which silver wire and very small articles were exempted from hallmarking.) The new standard, which came to be known as Britannia, remained compulsory until 1719, by which time it had been found to be rather soft for domestic use and the Act was repealed. Britannia has remained one of the legal standards for wrought silver, however, and the same marks are still used for it. The Act of 1697 caused considerable hardship to the provincial assay offices because, probably owing to an oversight, they were not empowered

to use the hallmarks for Britannia silver; all wrought silver therefore had to be assayed at London, and until the situation was remedied in 1701, when York, Chester, Norwich, Exeter and Bristol were empowered to assay the new plate, these offices lost nearly all their revenue. The Britannia standard was not operant in Scotland.

(vi) *The duty mark.* The Act of 1719 by which the Britannia standard was made no longer compulsory also introduced the first excise duty on silver plate: it was 6d per ounce and was repealed 38 years later because it was difficult to collect. In 1784, however, the duty was re-imposed and was extended to gold as well: it was 6d per ounce on silver and 8s per ounce on gold (this was later increased from time to time). The duty was collected by the assay office and a special mark was struck on wares to indicate that duty had been paid. This was the sovereign's head in profile (fig. 26). Many people were naturally tempted to forge the duty mark, and this offence carried the death penalty (replaced in 1841 by transportation). On 1st May 1890 the duty was abolished and the duty mark therefore became obsolete, but it should be found on all gold and silver wares, except the very small and delicate articles which were exempted, assayed between 1st December 1784 and 30th April 1890.

(vii) *Assay office or town marks.* At various times from the late Middle Ages onwards provincial guilds of goldsmiths were authorized to assay gold and silver (see *Assay Offices* for details). Each of these guilds had its own town mark. Other towns also hallmarked wares although not expressly permitted to do so. A great variety of town marks can thus be found on old gold and silver wares. Some of these are: Chester, a sword and three wheatsheaves (fig. 27); Glasgow, a tree, bird, bell, fish and ring (the city arms) (fig. 28); Newcastle, three castles (fig. 29); Exeter, at first a letter X, after 1700 a triple-turreted castle (fig. 30). York had a strange-looking mark which was at first half leopard's head and half fleur-de-lys,

181

and was later changed to half a crowned rose and half fleur-de-lys; in 1700 this was changed again to a cross with 5 lions passant. Norwich's mark was at first the city arms (castle and lion), later a crowned rose. Lincoln's mark was a fleur-de-lys, but although some plate is stamped with this mark and although Lincoln was authorized to make assays, oddly enough there is no record that an assay office was ever set up there. The marks for the Dublin assay office are a harp crowned and the figure of Hibernia. (The marks of the other assay offices which are now in operation are described in paragraph 4.)

Faking of hallmarks, etc. There has always been an inducement to fake hallmarks on gold and silver, but whereas previously the intention was to defraud the customer by selling metal of inferior quality, the usual motive now is to pass off a piece of modern work as antique by forging an old hallmark. This can be done in various ways – by cutting punches which will impress the required mark, by taking a casting or electrotype of the marks on an antique piece, or by cutting out genuine hallmarks from a piece which is of the right date but of little value and soldering them into the fake piece. Signs of soldering can often be quite easily detected, and many fakes give themselves away by some discrepancy between the apparent date of the decoration on the piece and the date of the hallmark. Forging and transposing of hallmarks carry a maximum prison sentence of 14 years: a considerable deterrent, although less drastic than the death penalty which was in force from 1758 to 1773.

(*Note:* The above is a simplified account of a complicated subject. The reader wishing to identify an old hallmark is advised to consult the booklets on hallmarks published by the assay offices or a comprehensive book on the subject, such as Jackson's *English Goldsmiths and Their Marks* [reprinted 1964].)

Hambergite. (Beryllium borate. S.G. 2.35; R.I. 1.55–1.63; H. $7\frac{1}{2}$.) A rare colourless stone resembling rock crystal. It is notable for its low specific gravity and strong double refraction (qq.v.). It is of no particular interest except on account of its rarity. Gem-quality material comes only from Madagascar.

Hammered pearl. A pearl showing small indentations like hammer-marks on its surface.

Hammer pearls. Baroque pearls shaped like the head of a hammer.

Hammers. Hammers are used directly on metal in jewellery work for stretching and forming metal and for finishing. Many types of hammers are available for special jobs, but most of them have more application in silversmiths' work than in jewellery proper. *Embossing hammers* have smooth, rounded heads and are driven against the inner surfaces of the work, while it rests on a yielding surface such as a sandbag or bowl of pitch, to raise the relief. *Raising hammers* generally have wide rectangular heads with rounded edges and are used on the outside surface to shape the metal. *Planishing hammers* have two flat faces and are used to smooth out irregularities in the surface and give the metal a finish after other hammers have been used to shape it. A *riveting hammer* has a slightly concave face and is used to round over rivet heads. The *pein hammer* is an all-purpose hammer with one flat face and one rounded (ball pein) or wedge-shaped face. All these hammers have heads of

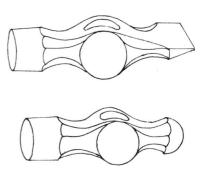

Pein hammer heads

forged and polished steel fixed to wooden handles, and are made in a range of weights.

A special hammer is used in conjunction with punches for chasing and repoussé work (qq.v.). (See *Chasing hammer* and also *Mallets*.)

Handkerchief ring. A fashion in 1870. A small gold ring worn on the little finger was connected by a chain with a larger octagonal gold ring, engraved with the owner's name, in which the handkerchief was held.

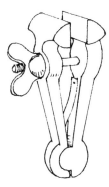

Hand vice

Hand vice. A small vice to be held in one hand. It is used to grip small objects while they are being worked on, and for various other purposes such as twisting wire – one end of the wire is held in the hand vice and the other in a fixed vice. Several types are available; a common type is V-shaped with a spring, and the jaws are tightened with a wing-nut (see illustration). Another is shaped like a pair of pliers, and the jaws are tightened by pulling down a metal hoop over the handles. A special type of vice is made for holding rings. (See *Ring-clamp* and also *Vices*.)

Han jade (Han Yü). Term for jade of the Han dynasty, also for tomb jade (q.v.).

Hard clam pearl. See *Quahog pearl*.

Hard gold/silver plating. A recently-developed technique of electroplating

(q.v.) by which a metal coating considerably harder than that previously obtainable can be achieved. The technique involves the use of special metallic salts and anodes. It is used for watch-cases and to a lesser extent for jewellery, and the plating produced is much more durable than ordinary gilt and also has better wearing qualities than rolled gold (q.v.). (See also *Gilding*.)

Hard mass. Trade term for glass imitation stones. It was originally applied only to unusually hard glass (H. 6 or more), but has now been extended to glass of any hardness and particularly to artificially-flawed glass imitations of emerald. (See also *Glass*.)

Hardness. The power of a substance to resist abrasion. (This definition is not satisfactory for scientific purposes but it is adequate for gemmological work.) There is considerable difference in the hardness of gemstones. Hardness is important, firstly, to the appearance of a stone – the harder it is the better polish it will take and the less easily it will be scratched, not only by contact with hard substances but by particles of grit in the air – and secondly because it furnishes a method of identifying stones. The hardness of gemstones is rated on a scale devised in 1822 by Friedrich Mohs, who selected ten minerals as standards. Mohs's scale is as follows:

1. Talc
2. Gypsum
3. Calcite
4. Fluorspar
5. Apatite
6. Feldspar
7. Quartz
8. Topaz
9. Corundum
10. Diamond

The principle of the scale is that each mineral can scratch the one below it on the scale but not the one above. All other known gemstones have been assigned places on this scale, and some are of intermediate hardness. Thus the hardness of chrysoberyl is $8\frac{1}{2}$. Some gemstones vary slightly in hardness; the most striking example is kyanite (q.v.), which has a hardness of 5 along the length of the crystal and 7 across it. The numbers on Mohs's scale are *not* quantitative, they merely indicate an order. Diamond, for instance, is not ten times as hard as talc but over a hundred times as hard. (The difference between 10 and 9 on the scale is greater than the difference between 9 and 1.)

There are two ways of testing the hardness of a gemstone. One is to attempt to scratch it with another mineral. For obvious reasons this is not a procedure to be recommended with faceted stones unless there is no alternative. A stone may be tested with a steel file (hardness about $6\frac{1}{2}$), a piece of ordinary window glass (about $5\frac{1}{2}$), or with a set of 'hardness points' (q.v.) which are obtainable for this purpose. The mark made should be as small as possible and as near as possible to the girdle of the stone – actually on the girdle if the stone is unmounted. The 'feel' of the point as it is drawn over the stone tells an experienced jeweller whether the stone is harder or softer than the point. If it is harder, some of the testing point may be ground off as powder leaving a mark which looks like a scratch on the stone, so any mark must be rubbed and inspected with a hand lens to make sure of its nature.

The other way is to use the stone itself to try to scratch something else. This is usually only practicable if the stone is unmounted. Small polished pieces of standard minerals such as quartz and sapphire (corundum), on which stones can be tested, can be obtained from lapidaries for this purpose and are not expensive since they need not be of gem quality. (See *Hardness plates*.)

Hardness should not be confused with toughness. Toughness is the quality which makes a substance resistant to blows, etc., and results from an interlocking crystal structure. A gem diamond, in spite of its hardness, will not survive a heavy blow with a hammer (as was once thought). The multicrystalline form of diamond known as carbonado, however, which is composed of an interlocking mass of tiny crystals, is useless as a gem material but extremely valuable industrially because it is not only hard but enormously tough: it has been used in the crowns of rock-drills.

The hardness of metals is rated on a different scale (the Vickers scale). It has no use in identification of metals and does not normally concern the jeweller, beyond the fact that metals used in jewellery need to be comparatively soft.

Hardness plates. Sets of polished minerals of different hardness, used for testing the hardness of gemstones. (See *Hardness*.)

Hardness points (pencils). Sharp conical fragments of standard minerals set in metal, plastic or wooden pencil-type holders for testing the hardness of gemstones. A set usually consists of feldspar, quartz, topaz, sapphire and diamond. (See *Hardness*.)

Harlequin opal. See *Opal*.

Harz cat's eye. Quartz cat's eye from the Harz Mountains; sometimes used to mean any quartz cat's eye.

Hat badges. See *Renaissance jewellery*.

Hatton Garden. A street in the heart of London which has become famous as the centre for diamond, precious-stone and pearl dealers, jewellers and suppliers to the jewellery trade; it also contains the office of Johnson Matthey and Co. (q.v.), refiners of precious metals, who have occupied premises in Hatton Garden for a century and a half. It is really only during the past hundred years that Hatton Garden has become a centre for the jewellery trade and allied businesses. Clerkenwell, just to the north, was previously the centre of the London jewellery trade, and the businesses overflowed into Hatton Garden during the nineteenth century. There are now comparatively few jewellers and clock-makers left in Clerkenwell, but a current revival of interest in the area suggests that it may soon again become a centre for crafts, including jewellery.

Hatton Garden takes its name from the Hatton family, who lived there from the late sixteenth to the eighteenth century. In 1576 Sir Christopher Hatton, Privy Councillor and eventually Lord Chancellor to Elizabeth I, applied to the Queen for a lease on part of Ely Place in Holborn. Ely Place – a palace with orchards, vineyards and gardens – had since the Middle Ages been the residence of the bishops of Ely, but Elizabeth nevertheless granted Hatton a lease on very favourable terms (the annual rent was £10, ten loads of hay and a rose at midsummer) and when the bishop died in 1581 Hatton took over the entire property. The dispossessed bishops spent the next 180 years trying to get it back. In the middle of the seventeenth century the current Lord Hatton, finding himself financially embarrassed as a result of supporting the Royalist cause at a time when the royal fortunes were at a low ebb, began to lease part of the estate for building. The bishop of Ely's protestations that the land was his were ignored, and the first of a series of streets of houses rose along the western part of the estate. Hatton Garden was untouched by the Great Fire of 1666, which occurred almost as soon as the first buildings were finished, and was soon joined by other streets. By 1706 there were 320 houses, occupied mostly by the prosperous merchant class.

The business affairs of the Hatton family were complicated, and when the last Hatton died in 1760 there were a horde of claimants to the estate. The lawyers took seven years to reach a decision, and when they finally did so the bishop of Ely, whom everybody had forgotten, demanded £3,000 as compensation on the strength of an old agreement of 1690 which the lawyers had overlooked. The estate had to be mortgaged to pay him. Over the next few years the whole property was sold off piecemeal. In the early nineteenth century a number of small businesses sprang up in Hatton Garden, among them a platinum-refining business started in 1817 by Percival

Norton Johnson in a stable behind number 79. This was the beginning of the great refining company of Johnson Matthey. By the 1830s a number of jewellers occupied premises in the street and there was also some trade in cut diamonds, but Hatton Garden did not become an acknowledged centre for diamond-dealers until the discovery of the South African diamond fields towards the end of the century (see *Diamond*). Early in the 1880s the Barnato Brothers and Solly Joel opened a business in Hatton Garden, and this provided the nucleus for the centralization of the diamond and precious-stone trade for which the area soon became famous.

Haüynite (Haüyne). (Sodium-aluminium silicate. S.G. 2–4; H. about 6.) A bright blue to greenish-blue translucent or opaque stone better known as a constituent of lapis lazuli (q.v.) but sometimes encountered as an ornamental stone in its own right. It has various sources, particularly Italy and Germany. It was named after Abbé Haüy, one of the pioneers of mineralogy.

'Hawaiian diamond'. Misnomer for rock crystal.

Hawaiite. Peridot from Hawaii.

Hawk's eye. See *Tiger's eye*.

Heat-treatment. The colour of certain stones, notably quartz, topaz and zircon, may be altered by controlled heating. The colour is permanent in many cases but tends to fade in others. It is a commercially-acceptable way of improving the colour of stones and has been practised for many years.

The amethyst (q.v.) variety of quartz when brought to a heat between 400° and 500°C changes colour to (usually) brownish-yellow or red. The preferred colour for heat-treated amethyst is golden-yellow, and such stones are often sold under names implying that they are a variety of topaz. Most stones sold as citrine (q.v.) are in fact amethysts heated to a yellow colour; this appears to be commercially acceptable, since both are varieties of quartz. If heated to above

575°C amethyst becomes colourless and develops a schiller (q.v.); it may then be used to simulate the moonstone (q.v.). Some amethysts from Brazil turn green on heating and have been sold under the name 'Prasiolite'. Amethyst from the Fenn Peaks region of Arizona also turns green. The dichroism (q.v.) of the heat-treated stones is very much fainter than that of the natural ones.

Reddish-brown topaz (q.v.) from Ouro Preto, Brazil, turns rose-pink if carefully heated to about 450°C and allowed to cool slowly; only crystals from this particular area have this property. Natural pink topaz is rare and probably nearly all the pink topaz on the market has been heat-treated. At over 600°C the stone loses its colour altogether.

Zircon (q.v.) is frequently heat-treated, particularly in the case of reddish-brown crystals from Indo-China, which are used to produce colourless, blue and golden-yellow stones. The treatment is carried out locally using crude but effective methods – clay stoves burning charcoal, in which up to a kilogram of rough is heated at a time to temperatures between 900°C and 1000°C. The colour is not always permanent; blue stones may revert to their originally brownish colour or turn brownish- or greenish-blue. They can sometimes be restored to blue by further heating.

Aquamarine (q.v.) which is naturally of a greenish-yellow colour is often heated to 400°C to produce a clear blue stone – most blue aquamarines have probably been treated in this way. Some brownish-yellow beryls can also be turned blue. The colour is permanent.

Other stones which may be heat-treated are dark green tourmaline (q.v.) from South-West Africa (to emerald-green), and tanzanite (q.v.), which occurs in a variety of colours all of which, it is said, can be changed to a very attractive blue on heating to about 380°C.

(See also *Colouring of gemstones* [*artificial*].)

Heaven stone. Benitoite.

Heavy liquids. Liquids denser than water, used in determining the specific gravity of gemstones. (See *Specific gravity*.)

Hedgehog stone. Transparent quartz containing needle-like inclusions of another mineral; the included crystals are larger than in sagenitic quartz (q.v.).

Heliodor. (Beryl. S.G. 2.68–2.71; R.I. 1.57–1.58; H. $7\frac{3}{4}$.) Transparent golden-yellow beryl (q.v.). The name is sometimes used to cover all shades of yellow beryl. Some crystals contain a small amount of uranium and are therefore radioactive. Heliodor occurs in Brazil, Madagascar and South-West Africa, among other localities. The rich golden stones make attractive centrepieces in jewellery and are usually step-cut (see *Gem-cutting*) like other varieties of beryl.

The name heliodor means 'gift of the sun'.

Heliolite. Aventurine feldspar.

Heliotrope. See *Bloodstone*.

Hematine. A metallic composition made to imitate haematite (q.v.) – mostly used for classical-type intaglios. The material is attracted by a magnet, whereas haematite is not.

Hematite. See *Haematite*.

Hemimorphite. (Zinc silicate. S.G. 3.4–3.5; H. 5.) A mineral closely related to smithsonite (q.v.) and often associated with it. Cabochon stones are cut from the massive green, blue or yellow material; the colours are often banded. The doubly-terminated crystals show hemimorphism (different inclination of the faces at each end), hence the name.

Heneage jewel (Armada jewel). A pendant jewel given by Elizabeth I to Sir Thomas Heneage in appreciation of his services at the time of the Spanish Armada, when he was Treasurer at War of the armies levied to resist the invasion. The front of the jewel shows a bust of the Queen taken from an earlier medal. The rim, which stands a little away from the central part of the jewel, is enamelled in white, red and green and set with

The Heneage jewel. Victoria and Albert Museum

transparent emerald-green variety of spodumene (q.v.), also called 'lithia emerald'. A paler yellowish-green variety of spodumene is also sometimes sold as hiddenite, but differs from the rarer true hiddenite in that it does not owe its colour to chromium. Hiddenite, like all spodumene, is markedly dichroic and needs to be cut with the table facet perpendicular to the prism edge for the deepest colour to be seen. Owing to its strong cleavage it is a difficult stone to cut. Hiddenite was first found in about 1880 at Stony Point, Alexander County, North Carolina, and named after the mine superintendent, W. E. Hidden. The deposit is now said to be worked out and the current sources of hiddenite are Brazil and Madagascar, neither of which produces stones of such a deep emerald colour as the original source.

Hilliard, Nicholas (1537–1619). Goldsmith, jeweller, and the first English painter of miniatures. Born in Exeter, he was taught the goldsmiths' trade but showed an early interest in miniature-painting. (It is said that he painted his miniatures on card, chicken-skin and even playing-cards.) He was appointed goldsmith, carver and portrait-painter to Elizabeth I and painted her portrait several times. In 1586 he engraved the great seal of England and was granted the lease of the manor of Poyle in Stanmore, Middlesex, in appreciation of this. In 1617 after the accession of James I he was granted exclusive rights for 12 years to 'make, grave and imprint any picture or pictures' of the king: a highly profitable monopoly which he was unfortunately unable to exploit fully as he died two years later.

Hilliard's paintings were very highly regarded by his contemporaries but his work as a jeweller received less attention. It is difficult to say now which surviving jewels are by him (but see *Heneage jewel*.)

diamonds and rubies. The back of the pendant is enamelled with a picture of an ark on stormy waters, and with the motto 'Saevas Tranquilla Per Undas' ('tranquil through stormy seas'). This lifts up to reveal a miniature of the Queen by Nicholas Hilliard (q.v.), who probably also designed the jewel. The inside of the lid is delicately enamelled with a rose in a wreath of rose leaves and with a further Latin motto.

After several changes of ownership the jewel is now in the Victoria and Albert museum.

'Herkimer diamond'. Misnomer for rock crystal from Herkimer Co., New York.

Herrerite. Blue and green smithsonite from Mexico.

Hessonite (Essonite). See *Grossular garnet*.

Hessonite glass. Orange-coloured glass used for imitation stones (q.v.).

Hiaqua. American Indian word for a necklace of beads or shells.

Hiddenite. (Lithium-aluminium silicate. S.G. 3.17–3.19; R.I. 1.66–1.68; H. 7.) The

Hinge pearl. Elongated baroque pearl with pointed ends, taken from near the hinge of the freshwater mussel.

Holbein, Hans, The Younger

Design by Holbein for a pendant with the initials RE

Holbein, Hans, The Younger (1497?–1543). The most famous of the great Renaissance painters who produced designs for jewels. Born in Augsburg, Holbein went to Basle in 1514 to design woodcuts and paint portraits and murals. Owing to religious dissensions it became difficult to earn a living in Basle by painting, and in 1526 Holbein went to England, having obtained an introduction to Sir Thomas More from his friend Erasmus. It took him some time to make his way at Court, but in 1536 he became established as one of the court painters to Henry VIII. As well as the numerous portraits he painted in this period he made many designs for craftsmen – goldsmiths, jewellers, armourers, bookbinders, etc. His designs for jewels, which were probably meant to be carried out by his friend John of Antwerp, include many pendants in the form of initials: such jewels were very popular in England at the time and Holbein designed one for the king with the initials H and I (J) for Henry and Jane Seymour. The designs are beautifully executed and have a striking harmony and balance. Holbein died at the height of his powers: his death is generally attributed to the plague.

188

Hollar, Wenceslas (1607–1677). A celebrated engraver whose work included a number of etchings of jewels designed by Dürer (q.v.). Born in Prague, he came to England in 1637, and while under the patronage of the Earl of Arundel published a set of 26 engravings showing the dress of English women of all classes. Imprisoned during the Civil War, he was later released and joined his patron in Antwerp, but the Earl died shortly afterwards and Hollar was obliged to work for very little money for the Antwerp printsellers. He returned to England in 1652, but political unrest and, later, the plague and the Great Fire made London an unpromising place for artists, and Hollar died in abject poverty. His prints, which cover a wide selection of subjects, are said to have numbered over 2700, but very few have survived.

Hollow pearl. A wax-filled imitation pearl. (See *Pearls.*)

Hololith ring. A ring cut from a single piece of gem material.

Holstein. Fossilized wood.

'Honan jade'. Misnomer for soapstone.

Hoop. The part of a ring which encircles the finger. Also known as the shank.

Hope chrysoberyl. A flawless yellowish-green chrysoberyl, faceted as a brilliant and weighing 45 carats, which was formerly in the Hope collection (see *Hope diamond*). It is the finest cut specimen known, and is now in the Geological Museum in London.

Hope diamond. A famous sapphire-blue diamond, cut as a brilliant and weighing just over 44 carats. It is believed to have been cut from a drop-shaped blue diamond found at Golconda (q.v.) and purchased by Tavernier on his visit there in 1642. Tavernier sold this stone, which weighed 67 carats, to Louis XIV, but in 1792 it was stolen from the Garde Meuble with the rest of the French regalia and disappeared. In 1830 the stone now known as the Hope diamond appeared on the London market and was bought for

£18,000 by the banker and gem-collector Henry Philip Hope.

The diamond remained in the Hope family until the early years of this century, when it was sold by Lord Hope who – it is said – was in grave financial trouble. The buyer was later drowned at sea. In 1908 Abdul Hamid II, Sultan of Turkey, bought it for (reputedly) $400,000, but sold it again in Paris the following year when revolution threatened. It is said that he shot his wife while she was wearing it. Marie Antoinette, who had once worn the stone, had of course come to an equally sudden end. The diamond by this time had an unenviable reputation; nevertheless it was bought in 1911 by Mr. Edward McLean as a gift for his wife. The stone remained in Mrs. McLean's possession until her death in 1947 and she apparently did not consider it to be unlucky, although by all accounts she had a long series of personal misfortunes herself. After Mrs. McLean's death the stone was bought for $179,920 by Harry Winston, the New York gem dealer; he subsequently presented it to the Smithsonian Institute, where it remains.

There are two other blue diamonds of the same colour in existence; one is the Brunswick blue (just over 13 carats) and the other a very small stone. There is a widely-held theory that these two diamonds, together with the Hope, represent the large blue stone brought back by Tavernier from India. This would allow for very little loss in weight when cutting: a considerable proportion of the material is normally lost when a stone is re-cut. On the other hand, fine blue diamonds are so rare that the theory deserves consideration.

'Hope sapphire'. The name under which the first synthetic 'sapphires' were marketed: presumably it was an allusion to the blue Hope diamond (q.v.). The stones were not in fact synthetic sapphires but synthetic spinels. (See *Synthetic gemstones*.)

'Horatio diamond'. Misnomer for rock crystal from Arkansas.

Horn coral. Black coral. (See *Coral*.)

Engraved design for a pendant by Erasmus Hornick, 1562

Hornick, Erasmus (15??–1583). An influential jewellery designer and goldsmith of the later Renaissance. A native of Antwerp, he fled to Germany in 1555 to escape religious persecution and after a period in Nuremberg settled in Augsburg, where he was granted citizenship and worked until 1582. He then went to work at the court of Rudolph II in Prague, but died shortly afterwards. His engravings for jewellery, published in Nuremberg in 1562 and 1565, are predominantly Flemish in style and strongly individual. Among his more important designs are a series of figured pendants in the form of dragons and sea-horses, and other pendants in which enamelled figures are framed in an architectural setting. The designs are notable for their vitality and imaginative use of the 'grotesques' of the Mannerist style. (See *Renaissance jewellery*.)

'Hot Springs diamond'. Misnomer for rock crystal.

Hsi jade. Clear colourless or clear black jade.

Hsieh jade. Ink-black jade.

Hsiu Yen. Green and white jasper, sometimes sold as jade.

Hungarian cat's eye. Yellowish-green quartz cat's eye (it comes from Bavaria, not Hungary).

189

Hyacinth

Hyacinth (Jacinth). A confusing name applied to orange-red grossular garnet and similarly-coloured zircon (qq.v.). The words 'jacinth' and 'hyacinth' are interchangeable, both being derived from the Greek *hyakinthos*, meaning a gemstone of blue colour, probably sapphire. This is the meaning of the word in the Bible. 'Hyacinth' is also used as a colour designation for reddish-orange stones. (See succeeding entries.)

Hyacinth of Compostella. Reddish iron-rich quartz from Santiago de Compostella in northern Spain.

Hyacinth of Vesuvius. Golden-brown or yellow vesuvianite.

Hyacinth quartz. Reddish-brown citrine.

Hyacinth sapphire. Reddish-orange sapphire.

'Hyacinth topaz'. Misnomer for zircon. (See *Hyacinth*.)

Hyalite. See *Opal*.

Hyalithe. Trade name for opaque glass of various colours.

Hydrophane. See *Opal*.

Hydrostatic weighing. See *Specific gravity*.

Hypersthene. See *Enstatite*.

I

'Iceland agate'. A misnomer for obsidian, which may or may not be from Iceland.

Iceland spar. Transparent colourless calcite (q.v.); flawless material is used in optical instruments because of its very strong double refraction (q.v.).

Idar-Oberstein. A major centre for gem-cutting, dyeing and related industries. Situated on the river Nahe (a tributary of the Rhine) above Bingen, the town of Idar-Oberstein grew from two adjacent villages in which stone-cutting appears to have been practised from very early times. The raw materials – agate, jasper and amethyst – were found in the hills a few miles from the town and were worked in Roman times by Roman craftsmen who settled in the area. When the Romans withdrew the art was forgotten, but was revived again in the fifteenth century, or perhaps earlier, and from this time Idar-Oberstein grew in importance as a centre of lapidary work until it had gained an international reputation. The dyeing of agates (see *Dyeing of stones*) began in the nineteenth century, and gem-engraving and carving of a high standard were practised until engraved gems ceased to be fashionable.

In the early nineteenth century local supplies of stone were almost exhausted and rough material had to be imported. The industry was beginning to decline when a rich source of agate and other quartz minerals was discovered in Brazil in 1825, and this gave such an impetus to the town's industry that by 1860 there were about 140 workshops in the area engaged in stone-cutting. When the demand for agates, citrines and amethysts began to decline, the industry was again saved by the opening-up of the opal fields in Australia. Since that time many new sources of gem material have been discovered, together with a number of new gemstones, and it is unlikely that the town will ever again suffer from a shortage of material. Rough stones are now imported into Idar-Oberstein from five continents, and the finished stones are exported all over the world, particularly to the huge American market. The industry has in any case diversified; it now also undertakes diamond-cutting, the manufacture of synthetic stones, and to a certain extent the manufacture of jewellery.

The Second World War naturally caused the industry a severe setback, not least because many of the skilled crafts-men were Jewish and emigrated to other countries. (The diamond-cutting industries in Amsterdam and Antwerp suffered for a similar reason.) The recovery of the industry after the war was accompanied by a change to electric power, replacing the water power which had been used for centuries. The old workshops were situated in water-mills along the river, and an ingenious system of pulleys and belts from the large water-wheel drove the grinding and polishing wheels in the mill. For grinding, a huge vertically-rotating sandstone wheel was used; the craftsman lay on his stomach on a specially-shaped rest and held the stone with both hands against the face of the wheel, which dipped in water at each rotation to cool it. All but one of these mills have now been abandoned; the one remaining is retained primarily for the benefit of tourists, who can see the old

191

and arduous methods still in use, and buy the products. (See also *Gem-cutting*.)

Identification of gemstones. Once a hit-or-miss affair of classifying a gemstone by its colour and approximate hardness, the identification of gemstones is now a highly developed science. Colour is still a good guide to the experienced eye, but the great variety of available gemstones, the manufacture of synthetic stones and the heat-treatment (q.v.) of stones to alter their colour makes the task increasingly difficult. The testing of hardness (q.v.), although a simple process, always carries the risk of damaging the stone and is often impossible to carry out if the stone is mounted.

The specific gravity (q.v.) or weight of a stone is a reliable guide to its identity, since few stones of similar appearance have similar weight, but this too can only be tested when the stone is unset. Few methods of identification can in fact be satisfactorily carried out with a mounted stone. One which can (usually) is the measurement of refractive index by means of a refractometer (q.v.). The refractive index of a stone (the extent to which it refracts the light falling upon it) is one of its most important properties, and if this can be determined the stone's identity can often be established at once. The various methods used are described under *Refractive index*. It is important to know whether the stone is singly or doubly refracting (see *Single refraction* and *Double refraction*); this will, for example, distinguish between a ruby and a garnet or a diamond and a zircon. The refractometer shows when a stone is doubly-refracting, but the test is usually made between crossed polarizers under a microscope (see *Double refraction*) or with a dichroscope (q.v.), which reveals the twin colours in coloured doubly-refracting stones. Evidence of the stone's chemical composition is given by the examination of the absorption-spectra and bright-line spectra (qq.v.). A less sophisticated analysis of colours is given by the Chelsea colour filter (q.v.).

The microscope is used primarily for observing the internal features in gemstones, which are helpful in identification and occasionally diagnostic (see *Inclusions in gemstones*). Microscopic examination is particularly valuable in detecting the curved structure-lines which are a feature of synthetic ruby and sapphire (see *Synthetic gemstones*) and the bubbles which appear in synthetic stones and glass. In some cases the fluorescence or phosphorence of stones under radiation is diagnostic (see *Luminescence*), and in the last resort there is the modern technique of X-ray crystallography (see *X-rays*), which photographs the atomic symmetry of the stone.

Chemical tests are very little used on gemstones with the exception of ivory, amber, the plastics (qq.v.), and carbonate minerals such as malachite which effervesce when touched with a spot of acid. (See also *Imitation stones*, *Doublets*, and *Colouring of stones* [*artificial*].)

Idiochromatic minerals. Minerals which owe their colour to an essential constituent, e.g. turquoise, malachite. Few minerals are of this class; most of them are coloured by impurities, inclusions, etc., which are incidental to the formation of the crystal. (See *Allochromatic minerals*.) The characteristic colour of idiochromatic minerals is of course a great help in identifying them.

Idocrase (Vesuvianite). (Calcium-aluminium silicate. S.G. 3.3–3.4; R.I. 1.71–1.72; H. $6\frac{1}{2}$.) A stone not often used in jewellery: transparent green or yellowish-brown stones are sometimes faceted, and there is a rare blue variety known as *Cyprine*.

Xanthite is a transparent yellowish-brown variety found at Amity, New York. A compact green variety called *Californite*, which bears some resemblance to jade, is more often used as a gem material.

The alternative name 'Vesuvianite' was given because the mineral was first found on Vesuvius. The green and brown gem material now comes from the Ala Valley in Piedmont, Italy, and from Canada, Switzerland, Siberia and the Tyrol.

Cyprine is found at Telemark in Norway, and Californite, unsurprisingly, in California.

'Igmerald'. Trade name for German synthetic emeralds produced in the 1930s. (See *Synthetic gemstones*.)

Illusion setting. A setting so shaped that it appears to be a continuation of the stone and thus increases its apparent size. The setting was developed in the later nineteenth century by the French jeweller Massin and was used mainly for small diamonds – diamonds were becoming increasingly fashionable at the time. Unobtrusive settings designed to make the stones as eye-catching as possible had earlier been a feature of eighteenth-century diamond jewellery. (See *Eighteenth-century jewellery* and also *Settings*.)

Image stone. Name for a type of steatite.

Imitation gemstones. Imitation stones are those made of an entirely different substance from the stone imitated, the only resemblance usually being in colour (cf. *Synthetic gemstones*). The use of imitation materials in jewellery goes back to Egyptian times: the Egyptians used a form of glazed ware known as faience (q.v.) for their amulets and also made glass to imitate emerald, turquoise, lapis-lazuli and other stones. Both types of material are still used in jewellery and have now been joined by synthetic products. For the physical characteristics of these materials see *Earthenware*, *Glass*, *Doublet* and *Plastics*. See also *Paste*. For imitation pearls, see *Pearls*.

Immersion liquids. Liquids of known refractive index, used in measuring or assessing the refractive index of gemstones. (See *Refractive index*.)

Imperial (Victoria, or Great White) diamond. A rough diamond weighing 469 carats which appeared without explanation on the London market in 1884; it was thought to have come from the Jagersfontein mine and to have been smuggled out of South Africa. It was cut in Amsterdam into an oval brilliant weighing 185 carats and a circular brilliant of 20 carats. The larger stone was sold to the Nizam of Hyderabad for £20,000.

Imperial jade. Jade of the finest emerald-green colour. In America the term 'emerald jade' is more often used.

'Imperial Mexican jade'. Misnomer for green-dyed calcite.

Inanga. Maori term for a grey variety of New Zealand nephrite (see *Jade*) which is highly prized.

Inca emerald. Emerald from Ecuador.

Inca rose. Rhodochrosite.

Inca stone. Iron pyrites (described under *Marcasite*).

Inclusions in gemstones. Crystals very often contain small inclusions of foreign matter in the form of particles of other minerals, or gas or liquid filling a cavity in the stone. If these are visible to the naked eye they usually detract considerably from the value of a cut stone, but in a few cases the inclusions produce an optical effect for which the stone is highly prized, an example being the fine needles of rutile in star-rubies and star-sapphires. (See *Asterism*.) Although from the jeweller's point of view inclusions often 'spoil' a stone, their occurrence is in fact very useful because they furnish one of the best means of identifying stones and in many cases also indicate from where a particular stone has come.

Inclusions may consist of pre-existing matter which was enveloped by the growing crystal, substances formed at the same time as the crystal, such as gas bubbles which became trapped, or inclusions which developed after the crystal had formed: this can occur when a crystal is subjected to chemical alteration, for instance by heat, and parts of it recrystallize. Structural features such as cracks are generally also classed as inclusions.

There are several ways of classifying inclusions; the most meaningful to a non-gemmologist is probably a classification into solid inclusions, gas and liquid inclusions, cracks and fissures, and phenomena directly related to the growth of the crystal. Solid inclusions may be small crystals of the same mineral as the host, having been enveloped by the larger crystal, or they may be of a foreign substance. Examples are numerous: the small specks of carbon often seen in diamond, the slender crystals of rutile in rutilated quartz (q.v.) and in the star-corundums mentioned above, the small crystals of mica which give aventurine quartz (q.v.) its spangled appearance and occur to a lesser extent in other minerals as well, and the dendritic inclusions in moss agate (see *Agate*). The insects and pieces of vegetation sometimes enclosed in amber also of course belong to this category. A type of inclusion which is frequently seen in gemstones from Ceylon is a small zircon crystal surrounded by brownish markings resembling wings; these are known as 'zircon haloes' and the brownish markings are thought to be stress cracks caused by unequal expansion of the two minerals.

Liquid inclusions occur in cavities; the cavities are of a shape which obeys the crystallographic laws of the host crystal (see *Crystal systems*) but they are not necessarily of the same external form as the crystal; they are known as 'negative crystals'. The liquid contained in them may be water, carbonic acid or some other liquid, or it may be the solution from which the crystal formed. In the liquid there may be a bubble of gas (sometimes called a libella), making what is known as a two-phase inclusion. Three-phase inclusions consist of a liquid-filled cavity containing both a gas bubble and an included crystal; they are characteristic of South American emeralds. Air bubbles on their own occur only in amorphous substances such as glass and amber and in synthetic gemstones (q.v.), and as they occur commonly in these substances they are an extremely valuable aid to identification.

Internal cracks and fissures in a crystal often become filled with liquid, gas or a crystalline material which 'heals' the cracks. These microscopic fissures may take very strange forms, and if of a wispy appearance are known as 'feathers'. Feathers are commonly seen in sapphires and their appearance differs slightly according to the locality in which the stone was found.

Internal features related to the growth of the crystal include parallel markings showing where twin crystals have grown (see *Twinning*) and slight differences in colour between one layer and another. These features are important in distinguishing between natural and synthetic corundum, for whereas the lines of growth in natural stones are straight-sided, in the synthetic corundums they are curved because each new layer of the synthetic stone solidifies on the slightly domed top surface of the boule. (See *Synthetic gemstones*.)

'Indestructible pearl'. A type of imitation pearl consisting of an opalescent glass bead covered with layers of *essence d'orient* (q.v.). It is not indestructible. (For imitation pearls, see *Pearls*.)

Index of refraction. See *Refractive index*.

Indian agate. Moss agate. (See *Agate*.)

Indian cat's eye. Chrysoberyl cat's eye. (See *Cat's eye*.)

Indian cut. Term applied to gemstones cut in the East or cut clumsily or without symmetry.

'Indian emerald'. Misnomer for green-dyed crackled quartz.

'Indian jade'. Misnomer for green aventurine quartz.

'Indian topaz'. Misnomer for citrine or for yellow Indian sapphire. A yellow topaz does come from Ceylon.

Indicolite (indigolite). Blue tourmaline.

Indra. A casein plastic (American). (See *Plastics*.)

Inlay. Inlaying is the technique of embedding a decorative material in another substance in such a way that the two surfaces are completely level. In jewellery most inlay takes the form of pieces of gemstone material or glass embedded in gold or silver; occasionally strips of gold or silver are themselves inlaid into another metal but this type of inlay is mainly confined to decorative metalwork. Inlaying is a very old art; the earliest masters of it were probably the Egyptian jewellers who produced superb jewels inlaid with cornelian, lapis lazuli, turquoise, glass and other materials (see *Egyptian jewellery*). At a later date the technique was taken up by the migrating Goths and reached western Europe, where it became a characteristic of Anglo-Saxon jewellery (q.v.).

The type of inlay used by the Egyptians and Anglo-Saxons was *cloisonné* inlay. For this, small strips of metal set on edge are made into cells (cloisons) of various shapes and soldered to a base-plate, and thin slices of gemstone material are cut to fit the cells and cemented in. The entire base-plate is covered with these to present a perfectly smooth surface. The labour involved in cutting the stones to shape was of course considerable. (See *Anglo-Saxon jewellery*.)

Another method is to use two sheets of metal; one is pierced out with a saw in the required pattern, and then soldered to the other, solid, sheet which forms the backing. The decorative material is then inlaid in the recesses cut in the top sheet. Some fairly soft materials such as ivory can be lightly tapped into the recess with a hammer, but thin sections of stones and other fragile material have to be carefully cut and filed so that they fit the recess and are then cemented in.

There are of course other ways of preparing a recess for inlay. It may be cut out of fairly thick metal with a small chisel or graver, or it may be etched out with acid (see *Etching*). A metal inlay may go right through the background and be soldered in. Gold and silver are good materials to use as inlays because they are soft and, when hammered into the recesses, will spread into the undercuts made in the sides of the recesses to hold them.

Inlaying in recesses in solid metal has never been as popular in jewellery as has inlaying in cloisons, but mention should be made of champlevé enamel, which is basically a form of inlaying in recesses although it is not generally thought of in this way. It is described under *Enamel*. (See also *Niello*.)

Intaglios. An intaglio is an engraved stone or piece of metal in which the design is sunk into the material so that when it is impressed on to a softer substance it leaves an impression in relief. This was the purpose of the first intaglios, the cylinder-seals developed during the fourth millennium B.C., and it was not until Roman times that the intaglio stone was valued for its intrinsic beauty as distinct from its function as a seal. (See *Seals*.)

Hard stones were engraved in the ancient world by means of a hand-operated bow-drill (q.v.) or a cutting-wheel, using abrasives made of a powdered hard stone such as quartz. Soft stones such as steatite were hand-cut with metal tools. The art of cutting hard stones was practised in Mesopotamia and Egypt, where the commonest form of seal was the scarab (q.v.), and was introduced into the Greek world in the late Minoan period. It was then forgotten for many centuries, to be reintroduced in the sixth century B.C. by the Phoenicians. The prevailing form of Greek seal at this time was the Egyptian scarab (q.v.): the intaglio design was engraved on the underside of the beetle, and the stone was pierced lengthwise and worn either as a pendant or in a ring, when it was mounted on a swivel with the beetle facing outwards and turned round when the seal was required for use. The scarab soon degenerated into the scaraboid, a domed shape which bore only the vaguest resemblance to a beetle, and by the fourth century B.C. this form of seal was being replaced by a ring in which the intaglio was set uppermost in a fixed bezel, the beetle back having been discarded completely. (In Etruscan work the scarab, introduced by Greek craftsmen, retained its pure form long after it had been discarded in Greece itself.)

The Greek intaglios from the fifth century onwards are often masterpieces of engraving. They were mostly oval (because of the original scarab shape), about the size of a fingernail, and engraved in amethyst, agate, cornelian, sard, garnet, rock crystal, and other stones of a similar hardness as these became available. In the Classical period the subjects were often scenes from daily life, delicate studies of animals, etc., with occasionally the representation of a deity. The best of them are carved with the economy, simplicity and boldness one associates with Classical Greek sculpture. During the Hellenistic period (beginning about 330 B.C.) a wider variety of stones became available and paste intaglios were also made; these were not cast from existing intaglios but cut on a wheel in the same way as stones. The style of engraving was now more expressive and the favourite subjects included Dionysius, Apollo and the Muses, women playing instruments, and portraits.

With the assimilation of Greece by Rome a number of Greek gem-engravers settled in Rome, where gem-engraving had been practised for several centuries under mixed Greek and Etruscan influences. The Greek element was now predominant, and in the course of the first centuries B.C. and A.D. engraved gems, both intaglio and cameo, became extremely popular and were collected by wealthy connoisseurs. Some of the gems are signed with such names as Dioskorides, Gnaios, Sostratos and Tryphon.

The finest surviving intaglios are mostly portraits, usually of the Imperial family or important citizens or soldiers. The wealth and power of Rome made available such rare stones as sapphire and emerald, and nicolo (onyx in which the design is cut in the translucent white layer) became popular, especially for copies of statues. Paste of a high quality, both moulded and cut, was common for a period but died out in the second century A.D., probably because gemstones were so plentiful that there was no demand for it.

The enthusiasm for engraved gems waned in the third century and the standard of craftsmanship declined. In the Byzantine Empire gem-engraving was practised using Christian subjects, but it was not of a high standard and does not seem to have been very popular. In the Christian west, however, there was a brief and splendid revival of the art during the Carolingian era; the finest example is the Crystal of Lothair (ninth century), a large medallion of rock-crystal engraved with the story of Susannah. The art then seems to have been forgotten for several centuries. Greek and Roman engraved gems, however, were still in circulation and were regarded in the early Middle Ages with superstitious awe. They were used in ecclesiastical work – reliquaries, book covers, shrines, etc. – despite their blatantly pagan subjects, which were not understood. Gem engraving began to revive again in the thirteenth century; antique gems were copied and new ones engraved. By the end of the fourteenth century the art was again flourishing and work of a high standard was being produced, chiefly in France and Italy. Portrait heads of rulers were popular. Within a hundred years the rediscovery of Classical art had brought a new understanding of the themes of ancient intaglios, and gem-engraving became one of the most highly-regarded arts of the Renaissance.

Cellini records that antique cameos and intaglios were being unearthed almost daily from excavations in Rome. These were avidly collected, and as enthusiastically copied by contemporary engravers. Very rarely, however, were the copies intended to deceive; the Renaissance gem-engraver, like the Renaissance sculptor, interpreted classical models in the spirit of his own time. In any case there was little need to make forgeries when contemporary work was so much in demand from wealthy collectors. Pope Gregory XIII remitted a murderer's sentence on condition that the man, who was a gem-engraver, should engrave a stone for him with some Classical subject. Among the earliest wealthy patrons were Pope Paul II and Lorenzo de' Medici, but during the sixteenth century the enthusiasm for engraved gems spread from Italy to the rest of Europe, and Italian gem-engravers migrated to the courts of foreign princes such as Francis I. Among the most famous gem-engravers of this period were Giovanni del Corniole, Giovanni di Castelbolognese, Alessandre Cesati, Valerio Belli, and Jacopo da Trezzo. These men were regarded as artists on a par with the great sculptors of the Renaissance.

Changing tastes and widespread political disturbance brought about a decline in gem-engraving in the seventeenth century. Intaglios were still made, particularly in the form of portraits, but the work is conventional and often poorly done. In the eighteenth century, however, interest in the art revived and large collections were again amassed by the wealthy. This time classical gems were copied with precision and the copies were often passed off as genuine. The signatures of ancient Greek artists were forged (often by people with an inadequate knowledge of Greek). The most famous case of fraud was the collection of Prince Poniatowski, which after its auction by Christie's in 1839 was found to consist almost entirely of contemporary intaglios furnished with the forged signatures of real and imaginary artists of the Graeco-Roman period. There is no infallible way of distinguishing between a good eighteenth-century copy and an antique gem, but the copyists were apt to give themselves away by a misunderstanding of the subject, ignorance of conventions and of styles of dress, careless mistakes such as mis-spelling of ancient signatures, and inability to reproduce the boldness and sureness of the ancient artists, who always cut a design so as to fill the available field and never introduced unnecessary details. There is a preciseness and sometimes a prettiness about eighteenth-century work which betrays its modernity, and the expert can also usually detect the use of hard modern tools. By no means all careful copies, however, were intended as forgeries: many are signed in Greek letters with the names of eighteenth-century engravers. (Although these too might be forged: the greatest engraver of this period, Anton Pichler, had his name cut on many more gems than he engraved.) Nor were the engravings restricted to classical copies: contemporary portraits and engravings taken from sculptures were especially popular.

The improved techniques for the manufacture of paste made possible the reproduction of antique designs in great quantity. James Tassie produced a series of moulded paste gems in over 15,000 different varieties (see *Tassie*). These provided a cheap substitute for those who could not afford the engraved hardstone gems, but they were of high quality and were purchased in sets or cabinets by the aristocracy.

The fashion for classical engraved gems reached its height towards the end of the eighteenth century, began to wane in the 1820s and by 1850 had disappeared. The reason was largely the discovery of true classical, i.e. pre-Hellenistic, art, embodied in such sculpture as the Elgin marbles, which were placed in the British Museum in 1816. Public interest turned to this newly-discovered period, and although collectors continued to acquire gems in the Hellenistic style the impetus to gem-engraving had gone.

It has not revived, and although there are still a few engravers working in hard stone, labour costs are now so high that there could never again be patronage on the scale which made the earlier great periods of gem-engraving possible. (See also *Cameos, Signet rings, Seals* and [for metal] *Engraving*.)

Interference of light. The phenomenon responsible for iridescence (q.v.) in gemstones. When a stone contains thin layers or films of material of a different refractive index (q.v.) from the body of the stone some of the light is reflected from their surface and some is refracted in them, internally reflected and refracted out again (see *Refraction* and *Reflection*). When the light which has been thus split up is refocused by the eye the two rays are out of phase because the one which was refracted has travelled an extra distance, and instead of the light being recombined into white light one or more of the spectral colours is seen, depending on the length of the light-wave.

Interpenetrant twins. See *Twinning.*

Invelite (Trade name.) A phenol plastic. (See *Plastics.*)

Inverell sapphire. Sapphire (blue) from New South Wales, marketed from Inverell.

Investment casting. See *Centrifugal casting.*

Iolanthite. Local name for a banded reddish jasper from Crooked River, Oregon.

Iolite (Cordierite, Dichroite). (Magnesium-iron-aluminium silicate. S.G. 2.58–2.60; R.I. 1.54–1.55; H. 7–7$\frac{1}{2}$.) A transparent blue stone characterized by its remarkably pronounced dichroism (q.v.); the contrast between the principal colours, smoky blue and yellowish-white, can be seen by the unaided eye. The best colour, a deep blue, is seen when looking along the length of the crystal, and stones to be faceted are cut at right angles to the prism edge to display this colour. Some iolite from Ceylon contains small platy crystals of haematite or goethite which, if present in sufficient quantity, give the stones a red appearance. Iolite can resemble sapphire but may be distinguished from it and from blue tourmaline by its lower refractive index and specific gravity (qq.v.).

Most of the gem-quality material comes from the gem gravels of Ceylon. Other sources are the Mogok Stone Tract in Burma, Madagascar, Madras, and South-West Africa.

Iona stone. A serpentine marble (see *Marble*) found on the island of Iona.

Iridescence. The play of prismatic colours characteristic of opal, labradorite and some other gemstones. It is caused by the interference of light (q.v.) at thin films of differing refractive index (q.v.) within the stone. In opal these films are a result of the amorphous structure of the material (see *Opal*); in labradorite the iridescence is largely caused by the lamellar structure (very thin scales of material). In other gemstones iridescence is not normal but occurs when the stone contains minute cracks or flaws, which provide fine layers of differing refractivity; rainbow quartz is an example of this.

Iris agate. Agate (q.v.) so closely banded that the bands diffract light and produce a rainbow effect.

'Irish diamond'. Misnomer for rock crystal from Ireland.

Iris quartz. See *Rainbow quartz.*

Iron. A metal of little importance in jewellery. The only period in modern times when it has been used to any extent in this way was the early nineteenth century, when cast iron was used to make surprisingly delicate ornaments. (See *Berlin iron jewellery.*) It is not an easy metal to join in a way that is both delicate and strong – the best joints are made by welding and brazing, which are rather coarse techniques for jewellery.

The systematic use of iron began about 1200 B.C. in the near East and South East Europe. Iron was worked to some extent before this, however, although bronze was generally preferred because copper was easier to smelt. Where iron was scarce it was highly prized. Homer speaks of a ball of iron being awarded to Achilles as a prize, and the Aztecs valued iron above gold. Iron was used to some extent in jewellery in the ancient world, mostly for brooches. The Celts sometimes decorated it with champlevé enamel (see *Celtic jewellery*). (See also *Steel.*)

Iron pyrites. See *Marcasite.*

Irradiated diamonds. Diamonds may be artificially coloured by exposure to radiation, which alters the structure of the crystal lattice. The first experiments in this direction were carried out beginning in 1904 by Sir William Crookes, who found that after prolonged exposure to radium diamonds took on a tourmaline-green colour. The colour was permanent (unless removed by strong heating or by repolishing the stone to remove the surface), and the stones remained radio-active for an indefinite period (that is to say, the stones treated by Crookes are still radioactive now). Radium being so valuable, this hardly furnishes a commercial method of colouring diamonds, but a small number of radium-treated stones are known to be on the market. They can be easily detected by laboratory tests, since if left in a dark box with a photographic film for some hours they cause the film to fog. Other more sophisticated tests also easily detect them. The colour moreover is not the apple-green of a natural green diamond. The radioactivity is not of a dangerous level; it appears to be no greater than that given off by a radium-dial watch.

A more recent technique is the bombardment of diamonds by atomic particles. Bombardment with protons, neutrons or alpha-particles in a cyclotron produces green diamonds which may be subsequently turned golden-brown or yellow by heating to about 800°C. The radioactivity dies out after some hours and the colour appears to be permanent. The diamonds are treated through one side, and show a peculiar pattern of triangular markings when examined under a microscope. The colour of the green stones is unlike that of green diamond. Bombardment with neutrons in an atomic pile produces similar results but there are no distinctive markings. Treatment with high-speed electrons from an accelerator and bombardment with *gamma*-rays can both produce an aquamarine colour in diamonds but these techniques are not often used. Examination of absorption-spectra (q.v.) and tests with ultra-violet light are used to distinguish these stones.

'Isle of Wight diamond'. Misnomer for rock crystal from the Isle of Wight.

Isle Royale greenstone. Chlorastrolite.

Isotropic. A term applied to substances which affect light similarly in whatever direction it travels through them. These substances are therefore singly-refracting. Minerals of the cubic system and amorphous minerals are isotropic. (See *Refraction, Double refraction* and *Crystal systems.* See also *Anisotropic.*)

'Italian chrysolite'. Misnomer for idocrase.

'Italian lapis'. Dyed jasper, similar to 'Swiss lapis'.

Ivory. A material used ornamentally from very early times on account of its mellow appearance, elasticity and the ease with which it can be fashioned and carved. In China and Japan ivory is highly prized and the carving of it is an ancient tradition (if now somewhat commercialized). In the West the thirteenth century was the great age of ivory carving, but more recently ivory was extremely popular in Victorian times. In the middle of the nineteenth century there was a fashion for jewellery, particularly bracelets, made out of ivory carved in the shape of leaves and branches. Small pieces of carved ivory were also set in other materials such as jet. The centre of the carved ivory industry at the time was Dieppe. Germany, France and Belgium are now the chief European centres. There are various types of ivory. Usually a substance simply called 'ivory' will be elephant ivory, the other types being given their full name, 'Walrus ivory', etc.

Elephant ivory. (S.G. 1.70–1.90; R.I. 1.54; H. about $2\frac{1}{2}$.) The tusk (incisor tooth) of the elephant. The tusks weigh on average about 16lb., but in very rare cases may be of 200lb. or more. The African elephant supplies most of the commercial ivory, since both male and female have tusks. It is shipped to European markets of which London is the most important. African ivory is mellow in colour and very resilient, but tends to crack when dry. Ivory from the Indian elephant is whiter and finer, but yellows more easily. *Fossil ivory*, the tusk of the prehistoric woolly mammoth, is not strictly a fossil since it is not mineralized: it is found mostly in Siberia, where it has been preserved in the frozen ground. Its working qualities are not as good as those of recent ivory, as it is brittle and often cracked, and it also tends to yellow quickly. The tusks of the elephant are permeated in a longitudinal direction with fine canals containing a gelatinous substance, and on transverse sections of the tusk these appear as a pattern of intersecting arcs resembling the marks of engine-turning on metal. This pattern, known as the lines of Retzius, is seen only on elephant ivory and serves to identify it. The gelatinous substance contained in the canals is responsible for the beautiful polish taken by ivory. The horizontal graining along the length of the tusk is not confined to elephant ivory.

Hippopotamus ivory. (S.G. 1.80–1.95.) The tusk (incisor and canine teeth) of the hippopotamus. It is whiter and slightly harder than elephant ivory and covered with a thick layer of enamel, which has to be removed before the ivory is worked. The tusks generally weigh from 1 to 6lb.

Walrus ivory. (S.G. 1.90–2.00.) The tusk (canine teeth) of the walrus. It is coarser than elephant or hippopotamus ivory and has a very dense texture. The tusks weigh from 7 to 15 lb.

Other ivories. A rather coarse ivory similar to that of the walrus is also obtained from the cachalot whale, narwhal and warthog. The horn of the narwhal, an Arctic whale, was believed from the Middle Ages to the seventeenth century to be the horn of the unicorn, and was highly prized for its supposed miraculous properties (see *Magical jewellery*). The molar teeth of elephants are also sometimes used for ivory; the material has a banded appearance owing to the alternating layers of dentine, enamel and cement, and tends to crack along the divisions.

Vegetable ivory. Certain palm trees produce nuts with a strong resemblance to ivory. The most important is the Ivory palm (*phytelephas*), a native of South America, which produces seeds about the size of a hen's egg filled with a milky fluid that hardens as the seeds mature. When quite hard the material is finely-grained and perfectly uniform in texture, and resembles ivory closely. The hardness and refractive index are similar to those of true ivory, but the specific gravity is lower, about 1.4. The seeds are imported under the name 'Corozo nuts' and fashioned into small ornamental objects including buttons. The Doum palm (*Hyphaene thebaica*), a native of Africa, produces fruit with hard white seeds which may be carved into beads, etc. The specific gravity and hardness are slightly lower than for Corozo nuts. Vegetable ivory displays a different structure from true ivory when seen under a microscope, but the simplest way of distinguishing the two is to touch the material with a spot of sulphuric acid. True ivory will not react, but vegetable ivory will show a spot of pink after some minutes (this can be washed off in water).

The material most commonly used to imitate ivory is celluloid, which can be given a convincing colour and weight and an artificial grain. Celluloid is softer than ivory (less than 2), is easily sectile, and can be softened with amyl-acetate or acetone. (See *Plastics*.)

Bone (q.v.) is closely related to ivory but is not likely to be confused with it.

'Ivory turquoise'. Misnomer for odontolite.

Iztac chalchihuitl. White or green Mexican onyx marble. (See *Chalchihuitl*.)

J

Jacinth. See *Hyacinth, Jacinth.*

Jacumba hessonite. Hessonite (see *Grossular garnet*) from the region of Jacumba Hot Springs, San Diego Co., California.

Jade. Jade is a general term for two quite distinct minerals, nephrite and jadeite, which are similar in appearance and texture. Both consist of a mass of interlocking crystals which makes them, although not particularly hard, extremely tough. This toughness has long been exploited in the carving of jade and its use by primitive peoples in tools and weapons. Jade is the traditional precious stone of the East, being valued at least as highly as any other gemstone. Indeed, the Chinese and Japanese names for jade mean both 'jade' and 'precious stone'. Jade has been carved into ornaments by the Chinese for upwards of 3000 years. Its use in jewellery is subsidiary to its use as a medium for carvings, but it is used in necklaces, ring-stones, and so on.

The word 'jade' is said to have been derived from the last word in 'piedra de ijada', the Spanish name for jade, meaning colic-stone – presumably because the rounded pebbles of jade which the Spaniards found in their American conquests resembled the kidneys.

Nephrite (Magnesium-calcium silicate; S.G. about 3.00; R.I. about 1.62; H. 6½.) A translucent to opaque stone with a greasy lustre, it is usually white, green or brownish in colour and is the commoner of the jade minerals. A yellowish-grey variety is called mutton-fat jade. Nephrite was the jade used in the time of the ancient Chinese dynasties. It was carved with tools of stone, wood and bamboo charged with sand and water. The material probably came from the region of Khotan in Sinkiang, where it is found *in situ* in a thick layer between hornblende-schist and gneiss, in large alluvial boulders in the river beds. Much of the nephrite used in modern times by the Chinese has come from this region, but it is also said to occur in various other parts of China. Dark green nephrite was discovered in the Lake Baikal district of Siberia in the last century. In the West, nephrite has been found in various states of the U.S.A. including Alaska, in Mexico, which probably provided some of the jade used by the Aztecs, and in Poland at Jordanon and Dzierzoniów, which was presumably the source of the worked jade found at the site of the prehistoric Swiss lake dwellings. Nephrite of a dark green colour is also found in New Zealand and was used by the Maoris for weapons and carved ornaments; it is known variously as axe stone, New Zealand greenstone and Maori stone or Maori jade.

Jadeite (sodium-aluminium silicate; S.G. 3.30–3.36; R.I. about 1.66; H. 7), also known as *Chinese jade* although it is not found in China, is the more precious variety of jade. It occurs in a much wider range of colours than nephrite – pink, orange, violet and blue jadeite are found, as well as white and green. The most valued colour is translucent emerald-green, and the material of this colour is called imperial jade. The only commercially important source is the Myitkyina district of Upper Burma, where the jadeite, found as alluvial boulders, has been obtained for many centuries. Virtually all the material goes to China. Jadeite is also found in various parts of California.

Jade-albite

There are numerous imitations of jade. Many of them, such as 'Transvaal jade' (grossular garnet), 'Amazon jade' (microdine feldspar), 'Indian jade' (aventurine quartz) etc., do not possess the peculiar lustre of true jade and can be distinguished on sight, as well as by their hardness and density. The *bowenite* variety of serpentine (q.v.) which is found in the Far East and exported as carved pieces from China under the name 'New jade' can be a convincing imitation. It is softer than jade, however, and can be scratched by a knife blade. Massive green *prehnite* (q.v.) approaches nephrite in appearance, density, hardness and refractivity, but it can be distinguished by means of a colour filter, through which it shows a reddish colour while jade shows green. The variety of idocrase (q.v.) known as *californite* can successfully simulate jade; its density (3.25–3.35) is similar to that of jadeite, but its refractive index (1.72) is markedly higher. The refractive index of 1.70 also distinguishes greyish-green *saussurite* (q.v.) from jade, which it otherwise resembles. Jade is also imitated by glass and plastic. These imitations are not difficult to detect. Glass, viewed through a hand lens, often shows marks where gas bubbles have been cut through, and the plastic imitations, although convincing in appearance, are very much lighter than jade. (See *Plastics*.)

Jade-albite. A green stone patterned with dark veins and spots. It consists of an albite rock associated with chrome-rich jadeite and is found in Upper Burma. (See *Jade*.)

Jade glass. Translucent green glass imitating jade. (See *Jade* and *Glass*.)

Jadeolite. Green syenite (a rock composed principally of feldspar) which resembles jade and comes from the jadeite mine at Bhamo, Burma. (See also *Pseudojadeite*.)

'Jadine'. (Trade name.) Australian chrysoprase.

Jade matrix. Suggested name for the mixture of tremolite and albite feldspar

marketed under the names '*Wyoming jade*' and '*Snowflake jade*'.

Jamb peg. The holder in which a gem-stick (q.v.) is held in the correct position for facets to be ground on a gemstone. It is basically a vertical rod carrying a pear-shaped block of hard wood pierced with holes; the end of the gem-stick is inserted into the hole which will hold it at the desired angle to the grinding-wheel. (See *Gem-cutting*.)

Japanese coral. Dark pink coral with a white core or flecked with white, from Japanese waters.

Japan (Japanese) pearls. A term used for cultured blister pearls and later for cultured whole pearls, and also for any pearl from Japanese waters whether cultured or genuine.

Jardin. Trade term for mossy inclusions in emerald.

Jargoon. An old name for zircon, now used for the pale yellow and colourless stones produced by heat-treatment. (See *Zircon*.)

Jaseron chain. A very fine gold neck-chain in fashion during the first decade of the nineteenth century and to some extent later. It was worn with crosses and other pendants and sometimes used in necklaces of mosaics. (See *Mosaic* and *Nineteenth-century jewellery*.)

Jasp-agate (Agate jasper). A mixture of jasper and agate used ornamentally. It is found in the gravels of the Pecos River in Texas.

Jasper. (Silica. S.G. 2.58–2.91; R.I. about 1.54; H. about 7.) An opaque crypto-crystalline quartz, usually red, brown, yellow or green in colour. The colours are due to the high proportion of impurities – usually iron – in the stone. Jasper is a popular ornamental stone and is used for carvings and sometimes for inlay as well as jewellery. Orbicular jasper, an unusual variety, has white or coloured spots on a background of different colour.

Jasper occurs widely. Many types come

from the U.S.A., and other localities are Siberia and the Urals, and India and Venezuela.

Jasperine. Banded jasper of any colour.

Jasperized wood (Petrified wood). Fossilized wood in which the original fibres have been gradually replaced by silica in the form of jasper (q.v.). It is cut and polished for ornamental purposes. Petrified wood occurs widely in the Northern Hemisphere and the most famous locality is the Petrified Forest in Arizona. (See also *Agatized wood* and *Opalized wood*.)

'Jasper jade'. Misnomer for green jasper and a variety of other massive green stones imitating jade. (See also *Jade*.)

Jasper opal (Jasp-opal). A variety of opal very close to jasper (q.v.), reddish or brownish in colour.

Jasper ware. A type of porcelain used by Wedgwood for imitation cameos. (See *Wedgwood*.)

Jaspilite. Jasper banded with haematite, from the region of Lake Superior.

Jasponyx. A banded type of jasp-agate (q.v.).

Jensen, Georg. Leading Danish firm of silversmiths, founded in 1904 by Georg Jensen (1866–1935), who began with a small shop in Copenhagen. Jensen was a goldsmith, sculptor and ceramic artist who turned to the design of silverware and jewellery in silver and semi-precious stones, and aimed at producing work of a high technical and artistic standard in designs which respected the qualities of the material. His workshop became the centre for a group of artists with similar ideals, and as the studio's reputation grew Jensen came to be regarded as the leading silversmith of his generation. The firm which grew from his studio has consistently pursued a progressive policy, working in association with distinguished artists, and has been a stimulating influence in jewellery design for many decades. Recently the firm has added brass, copper, cast-iron and other metals for 'everyday use' to the range of their materials. There are branches in most European capitals and in New York, Toronto and Australia.

A typical piece of Georg Jensen jewellery is shown under *Bracelets*.

Jet. (Fossil wood. S.G. 1.30–1.35, H. 3–4.) A black substance which takes a high polish and carves well, and was extensively used in Victorian jewellery. Jet, which is derived from decomposed driftwood subjected to high pressures, occurs in considerable quantity near Whitby on the Yorkshire coast and was mined and worked in prehistoric times. During the Roman occupation the jet was shipped to Rome. Whitby became a thriving industrial town in the nineteenth century (see *Nineteenth-century jewellery*) when jet came into vogue for mourning jewellery; the first mechanized workshop was started in 1808 and in 1873 there were two hundred. The fashion subsequently declined, and jet is now little used on account of its softness in comparison with other black minerals such as melanite, onyx and tourmaline.

Jet is said to become electrified when rubbed, but this is not true of all specimens. It burns like coal, and the quickest way to distinguish it from glass, plastic or vulcanite imitations is to press a heated needle into an inconspicuous part of it, when the spot touched should melt slightly and give off a smell of burning coal.

Sources of jet other than Whitby are Spain (Spanish jet was imported to Whitby and made into beads at the height of the jet industry), France, Germany and Russia. These deposits are not systematically worked and the material is thought to be inferior to Whitby jet, which is harder and more elastic and takes a finer polish. The word 'jet' is ultimately derived from the Greek name 'Gagas', a place on the coast of Asia Minor which was a source of jet in Roman times.

Jet stone. A name sometimes used for black tourmaline.

Jewel. The commonest meaning of this word is now a gem or precious stone. This is a development of the older sense, meaning a valuable ornament or 'piece of jewellery'; the word is not often used now in this way. *'Jouel'* or *'joyau'*, the French word from which 'jewel' is derived, originally referred to the elaborate table-plate of the nobility in the Middle Ages, but at the end of the fourteenth century when jewellery was becoming increasingly luxurious and was beginning to be worn purely for its decorative value and not as a functional part of dress (see *Medieval jewellery*) the meaning of the word was transferred to precious ornaments that are worn.

Jewel jade. American term for imperial jade. (See *Jade*.)

'Jeweller's topaz'. Misnomer (American) for citrine.

Jewish marriage-ring

Jewish marriage-rings. These are massive and elaborate rings which were not intended for normal wear; they were symbolically placed on the bride's middle finger by the bridegroom in the course of the marriage ceremony. The bezel of the ring is generally in the form of a gabled building, which is thought to represent either a synagogue or Solomon's temple. Most of the rings bear the Hebrew inscription *Mazzāl tōb* ('Good luck'), sometimes abbreviated, and some are decorated with scenes from the Old Testament – the Fall, the expulsion from Eden, the seven-branched candlestick, etc. The best surviving examples are in gold, and are decorated with fine filigree work and often with richly-enamelled floral ornament. These rings are generally of the sixteenth century and were probably made in Venice or South Germany. In later centuries they deteriorated; the metal was often gilded bronze or silver and the workmanship very plain.

Marriage-rings began to be used by the Jews in the seventh or eighth century, but no examples earlier than the thirteenth century have been found.

Job's tears. Local name for peridot from New Mexico and Arizona.

Johnite. Vitreous (glassy) or scaly turquoise.

Johnson, Matthey and Co. Ltd. A group of companies best known to the jewellery trade as refiners and suppliers of precious metals, although the group's other activities include the production of chemicals for industry and the manufacture of precision engineering materials, electronic components and glazes and enamels.

Founded in 1817 and appointed Melters, Refiners and Assayers to the Bank of England and the Royal Mint over a hundred years ago, Johnson Matthey are now among the world's leading refiners and fabricators of gold and silver, and are the largest refiners and distributors of platinum in the world. These metals are produced in a wide variety of forms for use by industry and by the craftsman. The range of materials produced by the Jewellery and Allied Trades Division includes ready-made components such as fastenings and stone-settings in precious metal (these are known in the trade as 'findings'), and fluxes for soldering. The firm also undertakes casting from customers' patterns and the recovery and purchase of precious metals from scrap, lemel (q.v.) etc.

Johnson Matthey Bankers Ltd. are one of the five members of the London Gold Market. Gold bars of various weights and qualities to meet the requirements of international trading are produced by the group's companies in Great Britain, Australia, Canada, Belgium and Italy. The bank also trades in coins and offers a variety of domestic and international banking services.

The offices of the Jewellery and Allied Trades Division are at 81 Hatton Garden, E.C.1. (See also *Hatton Garden*.)

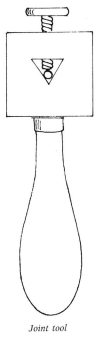

Joint tool

Joint tool. A tool which enables the end of a piece of tube which is to be used for a hinge to be filed quite true. It consists of a flat plate of hardened steel about $\frac{1}{8}''$ thick, pierced with a triangular hole and set in a handle. The tube is inserted into the hole with one end projecting slightly, and clamped into position with a small screw set in the plate. Since the sides of the hole are absolutely perpendicular to the flat surface of the plate the tube is held at a right-angle to the surface, and the end of the tube when filed flat will therefore be square.

Jolly's spring balance. See *Specific gravity*.

Jonker diamond. A flawless blue-white alluvial diamond weighing 726 carats in the rough, found by the prospector Jacobus Jonker on his claim near Pretoria in 1934. A certain amount of romance attaches to it, as having been found by an individual prospector many years after most of the world's diamond fields had come under the control of big companies. Jonker sold the stone to the Diamond Corporation for about £70,000, but it was soon sold again for nearly three times that amount. It was cut into 12 stones, the largest of which, called the Jonker, weighs 125 carats and belongs to the Egyptian government.

'Jourado diamonds'. A name under which colourless synthetic spinels were marketed for a short period when they were first produced. (See *Synthetic gemstones*.)

Juan jade. A mixture of red and white jade.

Jubilee cut. An American modification of the brilliant cut devised at the beginning of this century and named in honour of Queen Victoria's jubilee. It had a total of 88 facets and no table or culet. (See *Diamond-cutting* for description.)

Jubilee diamond. A diamond of fine quality weighing 650 carats in the rough, found in the Jagersfontein mine in South Africa in 1895. It was at first named the Reitz diamond after Mr. F. W. Reitz, then President of the Orange Free State, but in 1897 when it had been cut it was re-named the Jubilee in honour of the 60th anniversary of Queen Victoria's accession. It was cut into a large brilliant weighing 245 carats, and the remaining material was used to produce a pendeloque of 13 carats. The large stone was shown at the Paris Exhibition of 1900; it is now in America.

Jump ring. A connecting ring for necklaces, etc. They can be simply made from wire, but are also among the jewellers' findings (q.v.) manufactured by refiners of precious metal.

Justifier. A tool for truing-up the bearings in which stones are set. It is a type of scorper (q.v.) with the cutting edges ground at a right-angle.

K

'**Kandy spinel**'. Misnomer for the reddish-violet almandine garnet, somewhat resembling spinel, found in Ceylon.

'**Kaolite**'. Trade name for moulded clay medallions in the form of cameos, etc.

Karat. The spelling adopted on the Continent and in America for the English word 'carat' as used to describe the fineness of gold, thus avoiding confusion between this meaning and the use of the word to describe the weight of a gemstone or pearl. (See *Carat* [2].)

Kashgar jade. Nephrite of inferior quality. (See *Jade*.)

Kauri gum. Copal resin, a recent fossil resin often used to imitate amber. (See *Amber*.)

Keeper ring from an early twentieth-century jeweller's catalogue

Nineteenth-century Egyptian ring with double keeper

Keeper ring. Name for heavy gold rings with a chased pattern much worn in the nineteenth century. They were worn on the same finger as wedding rings. The term may also refer to a ring of any kind worn to prevent the loss of a more valuable ring (though these are usually known as guard rings). A curious kind of double-keeper ring, worn in Egypt during the last century, is illustrated: the keepers are of twisted silver wire, held together under the finger by a brace.

'**Kenya gem**'. Trade name for synthetic rutile. (See *Synthetic gemstones*.)

Keweenaw agate. Agate from the region of Lake Superior.

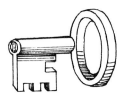

Roman key-ring

Key-rings. In Roman times keys were commonly made in one piece with a ring; in some the key projects vertically from the bezel of the ring, and in others (see illustration) it projects from the side of the hoop. The latter type were worn on the hand, since the key would be along the length of the finger, but the vertically-projecting type must have been kept on a chain since they would have constituted an offensive weapon if worn on the finger. Their function obviously was primarily utilitarian and most of the surviving examples are of bronze, but some decorated examples in precious metal have been found.

In later centuries keys were generally worn on a chain by the mistress of the house. In the 18th century they began to

Modern key-ring in silver by Georg Jensen

be worn on watch chains and chatelaines (q.v.) alongside a variety of objects of greater or lesser utility. In this century the key ring has returned, this time in the form either of an ornamental hoop on which keys are threaded, or a plain ring which holds keys and is provided with a decorative tab.

Keystone. Name for a stone (usually a coloured stone) cut to the outline of the conventional keystone. The arrangement of the facets conforms to the step cut. (See *Gem-cutting*.)

Keystoneite. Chalcedony coloured blue by the copper mineral chrysocolla.

Khiraj-i-Alam ruby. See *Timur ruby*.

Khoton jade. Nephrite of inferior quality (see *Jade*).

'Kidney stone'. A name used for both nephrite (see *Jade*) and haematite.

'Killiecrankie diamond'. Misnomer for Tasmanian colourless topaz.

Kimberley. An industrial city in the centre of South Africa famous for its association with the diamond mines. Diamonds were first found in South Africa, along the Vaal and Orange Rivers, in the 1860s, and in 1870–71 rich finds were made at several farms south-east of the Vaal. One of these farms was Colesberg Kopje, which in 1873 was renamed Kimberley in honour of the Secretary of State for the Colonies, the 1st Earl of Kimberley, at whose instigation the diamond mines had been taken under British protection in 1871. The mining camp which had grown up near the mines was by this time developing into a sizeable town, and this too was named Kimberley. In 1880 the town was incorporated into Cape Colony, and in 1885 a railway was opened between Kimberley and Cape Town. The town was by now a centre for large financial interests, which were finally merged in 1888 when Cecil Rhodes after a protracted and bitter struggle gained control of Barney Barnato's company and consolidated the mines under the name of De Beers (q.v.). After the Boer War, when the town was besieged for 126 days, mining was resumed, and in 1912 Kimberley was amalgamated with the nearby township of Beaconsfield (also a diamond-mining area) and was granted city status. The mines were closed during the First World War and again during the world depression of the early 30s, when the industry was very badly hit, but they were opened again in 1935, and by means of able management and a policy of co-operation with diamond-producers in other countries the industry survived near-disaster.

The head offices of the large organizations which control the marketing of gem diamonds – the Diamond Corporation, the Diamond Producers' Association and the Diamond Trading Company – are situated in Kimberley. (The headquarters of the organization dealing with industrial diamonds is in Johannesburg.) Kimberley is no longer, however, primarily a diamond-oriented city; although the industry is still prominent, the city's importance rests chiefly on its position as the main commercial centre for the northern Cape province, and there is local mining of iron ore, salt, gypsum, asbestos and numerous other minerals less glamorous than the diamonds on which the city's prosperity was founded. (See also *Diamond*.)

Kimberlite. The iron-rich igneous rock which fills the diamond-pipes of South Africa. (See *Diamond*.) It is a variety of

Kingfisher jade

peridotite, and is known as 'blue ground' because of its colour.

Kingfisher jade. Bluish-green jadeite. (See *Jade*.)

King cut. A recent modification of the brilliant cut for large diamonds. There are 86 facets including the culet. (See *Diamond-cutting* for description.)

King's coral. Alternative name for akabar (q.v.).

'King topaz'. Misnomer for deep yellow sapphire from Ceylon.

Kingston brooch. See *Anglo-Saxon jewellery.*

Kinradite. Orbicular jasper. (See *Jasper*.)

'Kismet pearls' (Trade name.) Imitation pearls. (See *Pearls*.)

Kite. Name for a stone (usually a coloured stone) cut to a kite-shaped outline. The arrangement of the facets follows the step cut. (See *Gem-cutting*.)

Kites (Kite facets). Alternative name for the eight bezel facets on the crown of a brilliant-cut stone. (See *Diamond-cutting*.)

Knurling tool. A tool for making a milled or beaded surface; it can be used by jewellers for making plain wire into beaded wire. It consists of a small steel wheel with a concave edge indented with small hollows, set vertically into a handle. When moved along a wire it produces a series of beads on the top surface. It is also known as a mill-graining tool.

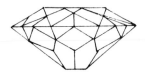

Side view of the Koh-i-noor as re-cut

Koh-i-noor. A famous Indian diamond said to have been discovered in the mines of Golconda (q.v.). The date of its discovery is not known; legend traces its history back nearly five thousand years but its first appearance in recorded history was in 1304, when it fell into the hands of the Mogul emperors. It was clumsily rose-cut to the weight of 186 carats, and according to tradition was set in the great Peacock Throne of Shah Jahan. When Nadir Shah sacked Delhi in 1739 he seized the jewels of the Mogul, and it is said that, finding that the great diamond was not among them and hearing that the Mogul was accustomed to wear it hidden in his turban, he invited the Mogul to a ceremony at which the Mogul was obliged to exchange turbans with him. Whatever the means by which Nadir Shah obtained it, he took the diamond back to Persia with him. After his assassination in 1747 it somehow came into the possession of Ahmad Abdati, who had unsuccessfully attempted to seize the throne and subsequently marched to Kandahar and set up the Kingdom of Afghanistan, taking both the Koh-i-noor and the Timur ruby (q.v.) with him. On his death his successor Timur moved his capital and jewels to Kabul, but when Timur died in 1793 there ensued a long period of disturbance, largely caused by the fact that Timur had had twenty-three sons, and in 1813 the current ruler was so unpopular that he was obliged to

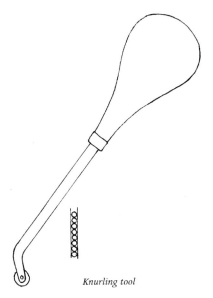

Knurling tool

flee with his jewels to Lahore. The Rajah gave him sanctuary but took the jewels; he did pay, however, for the Koh-i-Noor. After this eventful history the diamond remained quietly in the Toshakhana at Lahore until 1849, but was then annexed by the East India Company as partial indemnity for the Sikh Wars. The Company presented it to Queen Victoria in 1850. The stone was still in its original Indian form, and when it was shown at the Great Exhibition its lack of fire considerably disappointed visitors. Queen Victoria also found it unsatisfactory and took the step, for which historians and gemmologists have never forgiven her, of having it re-cut. The work was done by Amsterdam diamond cutters working in London under the supervision of James Tennant, mineralogist to the Queen. The stone was cut into a shallow brilliant weighing 108 carats, and not only was a great deal of its historical interest thereby lost, but the new shape was still not satisfactory as it did not have the correct proportions of a brilliant, and it accordingly still lacked fire.

Queen Victoria wore the diamond as a brooch but on her death it was transferred to the regalia. A legend has grown up (not surprisingly in view of its history) that the stone brings bad luck to men who wear it, and it is therefore worn only by women. It is at present set in the cross at the front of the crown made for Queen Elizabeth the Queen Mother in 1937.

The name Koh-i-noor means 'Mountain of Light'; this is the cry with which Nadir Shah is said to have greeted it as he unwound the Mogul's turban and the diamond dropped out.

Koranna stone. See *'South African wonderstone'*.

'Korea jade'. A misnomer for bowenite. (See *Serpentine*.)

Kornerupine. (Magnesium-aluminium silicate. S.G. 3.28–3.35; R.I. 1.675–1.678; H. 6½.) A rare greenish stone, generally translucent to transparent, which is occasionally cut for collectors and sometimes turns up in mixed parcels of stones from Ceylon. It was first found in Greenland in the late nineteenth century and was named after the Danish scientist Kornerup, but material of possible gem quality was not discovered until 1912 when sage-green stones were found in Madagascar. The stones from Ceylon are a brownish-green. A star kornerupine is said to have been found in Mogok, Burma, and cat's-eyes are occasionally found. Kornerupine is very strongly dichroic (q.v.); the principal colours, which are distinct enough to be seen by the naked eye, are green and yellow-to-brown. To obtain the best colour the stone is cut with the table facet parallel to the length of the crystal.

Apart from the sources mentioned, kornerupine is also found in Saxony and Quebec, Canada.

Kunzite. (Lithium-aluminium silicate. S.G. 3.17–3.19; R.I. 1.66–1.68; H. 7.) The transparent lilac-pink or violet variety of spodumene (q.v.). Kunzite is strongly dichroic and in order to obtain the deepest colour must be cut with the table facet approximately at right-angles to the length of the crystal. It is a difficult stone to work because of its very easy cleavage.

Kunzite is more popular in the U.S.A. than in Britain, presumably because it is pre-eminently an American gemstone. The first fine-quality kunzite was discovered in San Diego County, California, at the beginning of this century, and much still comes from this area. Other sources are Brazil and Madagascar.

Kyanite (Disthene). (Aluminium silicate. S.G. 3.65–3.69; R.I. 1.72–1.73; H. 5–7.) A transparent blue stone which often resembles sapphire or aquamarine (its specific gravity and refractive index are lower than those of sapphire and higher than those of aquamarine). The colour is frequently confined to the centre of the crystals, which are flat and blade-shaped and have the unique property of being very much harder in one direction than another: the hardness is 5 along the length of the crystal and 7 across it (see

L

Labradorescence. Name for the play of colour seen in labradorite.

Labradorite. (Feldspar. S.G. 2.70: R.I. 1.56–1.57; H. 6–6½.) A gem variety of plagioclase feldspar, basically greyish in colour but displaying a brilliant flash of colour – mostly green, blue or red – when cut and polished along a cleavage surface. The colours are produced by the play of light on lamellar inclusions in the stone.

Labradorite is usually cut with a flat surface to display the flash of colour to greatest effect, but it has also been carved very effectively in spite of its strong cleavage. A dark labradorite with a bluish play of colour has been called 'black moonstone'.

Labradorite was first discovered as large rock-masses along the Labrador coast. It is also found in Newfoundland and various other localities in Canada, in the Ukraine and the Ural mountains, and in the U.S.A.

Labrador moonstone. Labradorite.

Labrador spar. Labradorite.

Labret. A jewel worn in a perforation in or very close to the lip. The wearing of labrets seems to have been customary among primitive peoples all over the world, and is still practised by the few that remain. The labrets are often an indication of rank or of sexual maturity. It appears that the only civilized society in which labrets were worn was that of Mexico, where high rank was denoted by the wearing of a gold crescent in the lip, while lesser officials wore labrets of obsidian.

Lace brooches. Small brooches, usually set with diamonds, worn in the later nineteenth century. (See *Nineteenth-century jewellery*.)

Lacquer. A synthetic resin suspended in a volatile solvent; when painted or sprayed on to an article the solvent evaporates and leaves the resin behind as a thin surface film. Lacquers may be colourless or coloured by pigments, and are used in jewellery for a variety of purposes. Colourless lacquer may be used to give a protective coating to gilt jewellery, and it was earlier used to give an anti-tarnish finish to silver, but has now been superseded in this respect by rhodium-plating (q.v.). Coloured lacquers provide a cheap substitute for enamel, and very cheap costume jewellery is often coated with a gold-coloured lacquer. The lacquer film does not stand up to hard wear or, of course, to abrasion.

A further use of lacquer is in electro-plating (q.v.), when it is applied as a stopping-off material to areas which are not to be plated.

'Lactoid'. (Trade name.) A casein plastic. (See *Plastics*.)

Laguna pearls. Imitation pearls.

'Lake George diamond'. Misnomer for rock crystal from Herkimer Co., N.Y.

Lake Superior agate. May be agate from the region of Lake Superior, or thomsonite from the same area.

Lake Superior greenstone. Chlorastrolite.

Lalique, René (1860–1945). An outstandingly gifted jeweller who became one of the leaders of the Art Nouveau

Lalique, René

Peacock brooch by René Lalique

movement and exercised more influence than any other designer on Art Nouveau jewellery.

Lalique was the son of a merchant, but in view of his talent for drawing, his mother apprenticed him to the jeweller Louis Aucoc when his father died in 1876. He studied at the Ecole des Arts Décoratifs, and from 1878 at an art school in London. Returning to Paris to work as a freelance designer of jewellery, fabrics and other materials, he executed work for several famous Parisian firms including Boucheron and Cartier, and in 1886 was left the Destape workshop. In the early 1890s Sarah Bernhardt commissioned two sets of jewels from him. At this time he also began to study the manufacture of glass. Lalique's work first became widely known in 1895 when he exhibited at the Salon du Champ de Mars and won 3rd prize. In this year he also introduced one of his more famous innovations: the use of the female nude figure in jewellery. In 1897 he was made Chevalier of the Legion of Honour.

At the great Paris Exhibition of 1900 Lalique's jewellery was universally acclaimed and he was henceforth patronized by the royalty and aristocracy of Europe. In 1903 he designed and built his own shop in the Cours Albert I, and two years later opened a larger shop in the Place Vendôme. By this time, however, he was becoming seriously concerned about the widespread imitation of his work by inferior craftsmen (on one occasion he refused to allow the correspondent of an English journal to reproduce or even to see his latest work), and was turning to new materials. He had for many years had an interest in glass and had experimented with the use of it in his jewels, and in 1910 he bought a glass factory at Combes-la-Ville. Not long after this he abandoned jewellery altogether and concentrated on the manufacture of glass, producing some extremely beautiful pieces.

Lalique was an artist of great originality – a quality possessed by comparatively few jewellers of the period. He experimented with new forms (such as the nude), new materials (particularly horn encrusted with silver), and new techniques (for example, he made large models of his pieces and these were reduced to the required size by machine). His work avoids the conventional prettiness into which so much Art Nouveau lapsed, and on occasion is quite startlingly powerful, as in the famous corsage ornament, worn by Sarah Bernhardt, which is in the form of a dragonfly woman whose nude body rises out of the gaping jaws of a lizard with enormous clawed feet. This jewel is one of a spectacular series of jewels commissioned by Calouste Gulbenkian and now in Lisbon.

(See *Art Nouveau jewellery* for illustration of another of Lalique's pieces.)

Lamellar. Composed of thin plates of material. The lamellar structure of some gemstones, e.g. labradorite, is responsible for particular optical effects.

Landerite. See *Grossular garnet*.

Landscape agate. A type of moss agate in which the dendritic inclusions bear some resemblance to a landscape. (See *Agate*.)

Landscape marble. A light grey marble with dark dendritic markings which resemble trees and landscapes. (See *Marble*.)

Lanisher. A machine on which metal can be abraded to a flat surface; it is particularly useful with large pieces of jewellery because it considerably reduces the amount of filing which has to be done. The lanisher consists of an endless belt of emery cloth (various grades are available) running between rollers and over a flat steel face; it is electrically driven. After being smoothed on a lanisher the work is usually ready to be polished. (See *Polishing*.)

Lap. The horizontally-rotating wheel on which gemstones are ground and polished. A lap of iron, gunmetal or copper is generally used for grinding the facets, and a lap of pewter or wood for polishing. (This does not apply to diamonds, which are cut on an iron wheel called a scaife and require no polishing.) The laps are charged with various abrasives according to the type of stone being fashioned. (See *Gem-cutting* and *Diamond-cutting* for further information.)

La Paz pearls. Pearls from the Gulf of California and the Pacific coastal waters of Mexico and Central America; mostly greyish or bronze in colour.

La Pellagrina pearl. A pearl the size of a pigeon's egg, weighing 1,250 grains, found off Santa Margarita in the West Indies in the sixteenth century and presented to Philip II of Spain. The Negro diver who found it was given his freedom in reward. The pearl has remained in the possession of the Spanish royal family.

Lapidaries. Lapidaries were books, written from the time of the Greeks to the seventeenth century, which described the supposed properties of minerals. Most of the minerals were gemstones, although many were not and some were purely imaginary. The properties were magical or medicinal.

The idea that minerals possess hidden powers is of prehistoric origin (see *Magical jewellery*). It was developed into a system by the Babylonians and passed into the culture of the classical civilizations. The earliest surviving lapidaries are Greek and are concerned with the medicinal use of stones; for such ailments as snakebite, skin troubles and eye-diseases they are to be taken in powdered form as a potion, or, if not easily powdered, worn as amulets (these had preventive rather than curative powers). The earliest Greek lapidary is that of Theophrastus, written probably about 315 B.C., and is written as a scientific treatise: it discusses the nature and origin of stones, comments on their different hardnesses and classifies them in various ways. The hidden powers of the stones are mentioned only in passing. This scientific attitude was inherited by the Romans, and Pliny's lapidary, partly based on Theophrastus, is very sceptical in approach.

In Alexandria in the first centuries after Christ, however, lapidaries began to be written incorporating the astrological beliefs derived from the Babylonians and the mystical beliefs of sects such as the Gnostics. These lapidaries are concerned with the magical origins and properties of stones and with how their power can be increased by the inscription of magical symbols on them. Metals as well as stones were thought to have hidden powers according to their correspondence with the planets. The most important lapidary of this school is the Kyranides, a source of many later beliefs including the fable of the unicorn and the medieval belief in a stone of miraculous powers found in the head of a toad.

Two main types of lapidary were thus established: those dealing with minerals, which at first were primarily medicinal in nature, and those dealing with astrological influences, which of course were magical. The Christian Church naturally condemned the magical use of minerals but permitted their medicinal use, and so lapidaries of the medical and scientific type were written by Christians of the West, such as St. Isidore of Seville, and of the East, such as the younger Michael Psellus in Byzantium. The early medieval lapidary by Marbode, the Bishop of Rennes, is an exception; the properties it ascribed to stones are very often magical, and – what is surprising – the stones traditionally revered by Christian writers because of their appearance in the Scriptures are not given any special treatment.

The astrological tradition was continued by the Arabic lapidaries written in Spain. The *Lapidary of Alfonso X*, written in the thirteenth century, is largely concerned with sigils (the occult signs engraved on stones) and their effects in relation to the position of the planets. Another lapidary classifies stones according to the signs of the zodiac and then subdivides them, allotting a stone to each of the 30 'faces' of each sign, and finally ascribing to each stone a star which has power over it and increases its power when the star is in the ascendant. For each stone there is a specific use against some disease or misfortune. This complex astrological system filtered through to Western Europe in the twelfth and thirteenth centuries and was the source of many medieval lapidaries, but it was not always fully understood. Not only was the exact relationship between the sigil and the planet often obscured, so that there was implicit belief in the power of the sigil without any idea *why* it worked, but the system was further confused by the medieval belief that all classical engraved gems – intaglios with portrait heads, mythological scenes, etc. – were of magical and symbolic significance.

An important medieval lapidary is the *De mineralibus* of Albertus Magnus. Part of this deals with engraved talismans and their powers. The book is eminently scientific in its approach, however. This cannot be said of the many popular lapidaries written in the vernacular during the Middle Ages, and based mainly on Marbode and St. Isidore. Much of the material of these was pure fable. The medicinal and amuletic properties of stones were listed, along with quite arbitrary magical powers: sapphire, for instance, 'comforteth a man's heart and limbs' and 'keeps man from poison', but also 'helpeth him out of prison that is imprisoned'. The church, disapproving of the popular and magical lapidaries, produced its own variety – a symbolic treatment of the stones in the Bible (Exodus 28, xvii–xx; Revelations 21, xix–xx).

The lapidaries of the sixteenth and seventeenth centuries are mostly a direct continuation of the medieval ones. A new note is struck by Jerome Cardan (1587), who says that carbuncle strengthens the heart at the expense of harming the brain, and that since diamond makes its wearer 'intrepid' it is better to be without it. In 1636 an important work by Anselmus Boethius de Boot shows the beginning of modern thinking. Stones, he says, are natural products and cannot themselves produce supernatural effects; this can only be achieved by God, using the stone as an instrument. This enabled de Boot to rule out a great many of the traditional powers of stones, such as raising tempests and detecting adultery.

The astrological tradition continued in the sixteenth and seventeenth centuries, though under heavy attack from the new science of astronomy fathered by Copernicus. Two major works of this period are the *Speculum Lapidum* of Camillus Leonardus (1502) and Cornelius Agrippa's *De Occulta Philosophia* (1567). Both of these discuss various types of magical sigils and the way in which they should be engraved.

Lapidaries did not survive the rationalism of the eighteenth century. The complex system of planetary influences which formed the basis of the learned astrological lapidaries was all but destroyed by new astronomical discoveries, which gradually became common knowledge, while the lapidaries of precious stones, which since Boethius de Boot had been purely popular in nature, succumbed to the advance of scientific medicine.

(For further information on the subject see *Magical jewellery*.)

Lapidary. A craftsman who cuts, fashions and polishes gemstones other than diamonds (diamond-workers are known as diamond-cutters or diamond-polishers). The word comes from the Latin 'lapis', meaning a stone. 'Lapidary' is also used to mean the art of fashioning stones, and in this sense it may be used as a noun or an adjective. The process is described under *Gem-cutting*.

(For another meaning of the word, see *Lapidaries*.)

Lapis crucifer. Staurolite.

Lapis-lazuli (Lapis). (Hauynite, sodalite, noselite and other minerals. S.G. 2.7–2.9; R.I. about 1.50; H. $5\frac{1}{2}$–6.) An opaque dark blue stone, usually cut *en cabochon* or flat. The colour may have a greenish or purplish tinge, but the best specimens are a pure intense dark blue. Brassy-looking specks of iron pyrites are often present which detract slightly from the value of the stone but are useful in identifying it. Lapis-lazuli has been highly valued for thousands of years on account of its beautiful colour (see *Egyptian jewellery*), and in earlier times it was used in powdered form to produce ultramarine pigment for painters, which was naturally extremely expensive. (Since 1828 ultramarine has been synthetically produced.)

Lapis-lazuli was known in the ancient world as sapphire. Its present name is a medieval Latin term simply meaning 'Lazulus stone', the 'lazulus' being derived from the Arabic word 'lazward' which meant 'sky' and referred generally to anything blue. 'Lazward' is also the source of the confusingly similar names 'lazurite' and 'lazulite' (lazurite, a combination of hauynite and sodalite (qq.v.), is a constituent of lapis-lazuli, whereas lazulite (q.v.) is a completely different mineral). The word 'azure', which is incorporated in the name of the blue copper carbonate azurite, is also derived from the same Arabic source.

The oldest and most famous source of lapis-lazuli is in the Badakshan district of Afghanistan. These mines, which were visited by Marco Polo, have been worked for some 6,000 years, and were presumably the source of the lapis-lazuli known in the ancient world. The mines are in a remote and almost inaccessible spot in the mountains near Firgamu and are worked by very primitive methods. Another old source of lapis-lazuli is at the southern end of Lake Baikal in Siberia, but it is not known whether the mines are still worked. Chile, Colorado, California and Mogok in Upper Burma are other sources.

Lapis-lazuli is imitated by 'Swiss lapis' (q.v.) (a dyed jasper), and by a sintered synthetic spinel coloured blue by cobalt and sometimes containing gold specks to imitate pyrites. (See *Synthetic gemstones* for means of distinguishing the two.)

Lasque diamonds. Diamonds cut in a flat tabular form by Indian cutters. (See also '*Laxey diamonds*'.)

'La Tausca pearls'. (Trade name.) Imitation pearls.

Lathes. A lathe is a precision instrument for turning metal, wood, etc.: the article is held horizontally between adjustable centres and is rotated against the cutting tools. The lathe is not a normal feature of the jeweller's workshop but it is sometimes used for turning rings, and it has an increasing use in modern jewellery where pure geometric shapes are required.

A special lathe is used for spinning metal (a flat sheet of metal is held in the lathe and is worked, by means of a long steel-headed tool, over a shaped wooden chuck), but this is a silversmithing process and is not likely to be used by a jeweller.

The machine known as a polishing lathe, which is an essential piece of jeweller's equipment, is not, strictly speaking, a lathe. (See *Polishing lathe*.)

Latten. A yellow base-metal alloy, in most cases probably a type of brass, used in the Middle Ages for cheap jewellery, particularly brooches. It was normally gilded.

Lauegram. An X-ray photograph of a gemstone or pearl, used in identification. (See *X-rays* and *Pearls*.)

Laurelite. Idocrase.

Lava jewellery. Jewellery composed of cameos carved from the lava at Pompeii, popular in the nineteenth century as a form of souvenir jewellery. The work was done in Italy and was often very attractive. (See *Nineteenth-century jewellery*.)

'Laxey diamonds'. Trade term for shallow brilliant-cut diamonds; probably derived from the term 'lasque diamonds', q.v.

Lazulite. (Magnesium-iron-aluminium phosphate. S.G. about 3.1; R.I. 1.62; H. $5\frac{1}{2}$.) An opaque blue mineral which is capable of providing very attractive ornamental stones but in practice is rarely used in jewellery. It is found in many localities, including Sweden, Austria, North Carolina, India and Minas Gerais, Brazil.

Lazurapatite. A mixture of lapis-lazuli and apatite; it comes from Siberia.

Lazurfeldspar. Blue orthoclase feldspar from Siberia.

Lazurquartz. Blue chalcedony.

Lead. A soft, malleable and heavy metal with a very low melting-point ($327.35°C$) which has been used for various purposes for many thousands of years. During the Middle Ages it was used, probably gilt, to make cheap brooches and the very popular pilgrims' badges. (See *Devotional jewellery*.)

Its main application in jewellery now is in casting (q.v.) for which it is an excellent material because of the ease with which it can be melted, the density of the castings, and the fact that it can be poured into moulds made of a great variety of materials, including wood, paper, rubber and sand.

Small quantities of lead are used in various alloys, and lead oxide is an important constituent of the glass used in imitation gemstones. (See *Glass* and *Paste*).

Lead glass. Glass containing a high proportion of lead oxide. (See *Glass*.)

Leather sandbag. A leather pad filled with sand, on which an engraver's block (q.v.) is rested; it can also be used to cushion a pitch-bowl (q.v.) during repoussé work, when it allows the bowl to be easily rotated.

Lechosos opal. Opal with deep flashes of colour, particularly green and red.

Engraved design for the back of a pendant by Gilles Légaré

Légaré, Gilles (born *c.* 1610). Court jeweller and enamellist in the reign of Louis XIV, and author of *Livre des ouvrages d'orfevrerie* (1663), one of the most influential books of engraved ornament produced in the seventeenth century. It illustrates very well the transition from lavishly-enamelled jewellery to jewels in which the chief interest lies in the stones; in Légaré's designs the stones are important, but great care is still given to enamelling and engraving. The book contains exquisite examples of floral ornament (see illustration), and the first engravings of the bow-shaped designs which soon became, and remained, extremely popular in the form of the Sévigné brooch and the girandole earring. (See *Seventeenth-century jewellery* for further information on jewellery of the period.)

Legionary rings. Bronze rings with a flattened bezel engraved with Roman numerals. These rings have been found in various parts once occupied by the Romans, and it was once assumed that they were worn by the legionaries and that the numbers were those of the legions. Many of the numbers, however, are too high to be the number of a legion, and it is more likely that they were given out to the soldiers of a centuria (100 men) and worn as a means of identification.

Lemel. Filings and scrap from precious metal, swept up from the jeweller's workbench or caught in the bench skin (q.v.). It is collected and subsequently refined for re-use; refiners offer a recovery service. The word comes from the French 'limaille', meaning filings.

Lennox jewel. See *Darnley jewel*.

Lens. A polished piece of glass with curved surfaces used in magnifying instruments. A convex lens causes light rays to converge at a focus; this type of lens is the more important in microscopes, etc., but concave lenses, which cause the light rays to diverge, are often used in conjunction with convex lenses for the correction of certain optical defects.

For the hand- and eye-lenses used by jewellers, see *Magnifiers*. (See also *Microscopes*.)

Lenticular. Lentil-shaped; doubly convex. A term used often in describing beads.

Leontine chain. A guard chain (q.v.).

Leopard jade. Spotted jade.

Letter punches. Steel punches used for impressing letters of the alphabet on metal. Various sizes and styles are available.

Leucite. (Potassium-aluminium silicate. S.G. 2.45–2.50; R.I. about 1.51; H. $5\frac{1}{2}$–6.) A mineral from which small colourless stones have been cut as curiosities. Most of this material comes from Italy; other sources are Germany and parts of the U.S.A.

Leuco-sapphire. Colourless sapphire.

Liberator (libertador) diamond. A 155-carat diamond found in 1942 in the Gran Sabana region of Venezuela, named in honour of Simon Bolivar, liberator of Venezuela in the 19th century. It was bought by Harry Winston, the New York gem dealer, and cut into three emerald-cut stones (the largest weighing just under 40 carats) and a small marquise stone.

Ligament pearl. Similar to hinge pearl, q.v.

Lime. A polishing powder used instead of crocus (q.v.); it is a calcium-magnesium oxide.

Limoges enamel. See *Painted enamel*.

Limonite. The brown material in which turquoise often occurs; the two are cut together to produce the stone known as turquoise matrix. Limonite is a hydrated iron oxide. (See also *Turquoise*.)

Limousin, Léonard (*c.* 1505–*c.* 1577). A famous enamellist of the Limoges school; he probably studied under Nardon Pénicaud (q.v.). His early work was much influenced by the German style, but after about 1535, when he produced a series of painted enamels from designs by Raphael, he came under the influence of Italian Renaissance art and the school of Fontainebleau. He worked at the court of Francis I, for whom he did a series of enamels of the apostles in colour on a white ground, and also produced a number of striking portraits. His work in grisaille (q.v.) was particularly fine. His predilection, however, seems to have been for very strong colours, and towards the end of his career he placed his figures on a deep blue background. His work is considerably more original than that of most of the Limoges enamel-painters; his copies of Raphael, for example, are very much in his own style. (See also *Enamel*.)

Line spectra. See *Bright-line spectra*.

Lingah pearl. Pearl from the Persian Gulf.

Linisher. See *Lanisher*.

'Linobate'. (Trade name). Colourless or coloured synthetic lithium niobate. (See *Synthetic gemstones,* under 'Other stones'.)

Lintonite. See *Thomsonite*.

'Lithia amethyst'. Misnomer for kunzite.

'Lithia emerald'. Misnomer for hiddenite.

Lithoxyle (lithoxylite). Opalised wood.

Litoslazuli. Confusing name for massive purple fluorspar.

Liver of sulphur. Potassium sulphide, used in solution to colour or 'antique' metals. (See *Colouring of metals*.)

Liver opal. Impure common opal.

Lizardite. A type of serpentine.

Lluvisnando opal. A yellowish water opal with pronounced fire. (See *Opal*.)

Loam. A name for the firmly-bonded sand used in sand-casting. (See *Casting*.)

Loch Buy brooch. An early 16th-century Scottish brooch made out of silver ore from the Loch Buy estate on the Isle of Mull. According to the inscription on the back it was made by a tinker. The maker was fully conversant with jewellers' techniques and the brooch is carefully and richly decorated, but the design is certainly not one which would have occurred to the average jeweller and it has been unkindly remarked that the whole thing looks rather like a jelly-mould.

It is nevertheless a magnificent piece of work. It is dominated by a large central boss of rock crystal, set in a plaque decorated with filigree which rests on a high crenellated platform. Round the edge are ten high turret-like collets set with river pearls; the collets and the spaces between them are also decorated with patterns in filigree.

The brooch is now in the British Museum.

Lockets. The locket as we know it is not much older than the 17th century, but in

The Loch Buy brooch. British Museum

so far as it is basically a jewel which opens on a hinge to disclose something otherwise concealed, its origins can be traced back at least to medieval times. Hinged reliquary pendants, and rings with compartments for relics (and other things – see *Poison rings*) were a very popular form of jewellery during the Middle Ages and the earlier part of the Renaissance period, and the celebrated reliquary pendant of St. Louis, its covers consisting of two large cabochon amethysts and the interior enamelled with scenes from the life of Christ, is not unlike a modern locket in its dimensions. (See *Devotional jewellery* for further information on this class of jewellery.)

During the sixteenth century it became increasingly common for monarchs to present jewels as tokens of favour or appreciation, and these sometimes took the form of a pendant which opened to display the monarch's portrait. Among the finest of these jewels are the Heneage jewel (q.v.), containing a miniature of Elizabeth I, and the Lyte jewel (q.v.), which contains a portrait of James I. Such jewels would not hold any strong personal associations for the wearer; an example of a locket which must have held very powerful meaning for its owner is the late 16th-century Darnley jewel (q.v.) made for Lady Margaret Douglas. This jewel is in fact so rich in personal allusions that it is now impossible to decipher its meaning with any degree of certainty.

During the seventeenth century miniature-cases became important items of jewellery. For many decades, while jewellery of other kinds was progressively invaded by faceted gems, miniature cases continued to be decorated with delicate designs in champlevé enamel and émail en résille sur verre (see *Enamel*); by the 1670s, however, they too were decorated predominantly with gemstones (see *Seventeenth-century jewellery*). Lockets containing miniatures continued to be worn in the 18th century but were no longer a fashionable ornament; they were mostly marriage or betrothal gifts. The miniatures were often set in borders of small pearls or

Victorian locket from a jeweller's catalogue of 1876

faceted stones and enclosed in a case of engraved gold. They were frequently worn on a velvet band round the neck.

The great age of lockets was the nineteenth century. In the sentimental jewellery of the early Victorian period they had a popular role as containers for the locks of hair and little medallions of hair-work which were almost universally worn. Lockets containing a miniature were worn by girls after their engagement, and small lockets were worn on a chain by children. In the 1870s a locket became a fashionable necessity. The lockets of this period are sometimes extremely heavy; these were intended for photographs, the miniature having had its day. Some lockets were jewelled or enamelled, others were of chased gold. Carved jet was also very popular. The shape was generally oval, but a variety of fashionable motifs might be used for decoration – stars, butterflies, flowers, hearts, cupids, etc. Monograms were also favoured. In 1869 a London jeweller produced lockets which could be fitted with removable slides, so that one day the wearer could have a locket decorated with emeralds and opals, the next day a locket decorated with pearl and corals, or a diamond star, or a device in black enamel for mourning, etc. Many of these late-Victorian lockets were mass-produced. (See *Machine-stamping* and *Nineteenth-century jewellery*.)

Lockets containing portraits or some

219

other item of personal significance are still very widely worn, but they are by now a type of sentimental as distinct from fashionable jewellery, and most of those that are worn were probably made many years ago. The trend in good modern jewellery is towards the bold and the unusual, and the locket is essentially something private, unadventurous and rather fiddly.

Lost-wax casting. A time-honoured process which has been used by craftsmen of many different cultures for over 4000 years. In essence the process consists of making a model of the object to be cast in wax, encasing the wax model in some fire-resistant material such as plaster, and heating the mould so that the wax melts and runs out through an opening previously made in the mould. Molten metal is then poured in through the same opening and fills the impression made by the wax model, so that a perfect replica is formed.

The lost-wax principle is now utilized in the mass-production technique of centrifugal or investment casting. (See *Casting.*)

Loupe. A jeweller's or watchmaker's magnifying glass. (See *Magnifiers.*)

Love arrows. Sagenitic quartz.

Love stone. Aventurine quartz.

Lovers' rings. See *Betrothal rings.*

Lozenge. Name for a step-cut stone in the outline of a lozenge (the conventional diamond-shape). (See *Gem-cutting.*)

Lozenge facet. Alternative name for the four quoin facets (q.v.) on the crown of a brilliant-cut diamond (see *Diamond-cutting*). The quoin/lozenge facets are now usually included with the bezel facets (q.v.).

Lucidoscope. An instrument devised for the detection of cultured pearls. It consists basically of a powerful source of light which is directed upwards to illuminate the pearl, and a low-powered microscope, for which a camera can be substituted to record the effect. The pearl rests on a centrally-perforated diaphragm which is placed in a glass receptacle containing liquid of a similar refractive index to that of the pearl.

Light is directed up through the receptacle and the pearl is turned round in the liquid. If it is a cultured pearl with a fairly thin coating of nacre (q.v.), when the layers of the mother-of-pearl core are parallel with the light beam a series of straight light and dark stripes can be seen. This is a conclusive proof that the pearl is cultured, since natural pearls have a concentric structure throughout. If this effect is not seen, however, it does not necessarily mean that the pearl is natural: it may be a cultured pearl with a thick skin of nacre. The lucidoscope is therefore not a completely reliable means of pearl-testing and the instrument now generally used is the endoscope (q.v.). (See *Pearls* for further information.)

Lucinite. Variscite from the vicinity of Lucin, Utah.

'Lucite'. Trade name for an acrylic plastic. (See *Plastics.*)

Silver luckenbooth brooch. National Museum of Antiquities of Scotland

Luckenbooth brooches. Heart-shaped brooches, often surmounted by a crown, worn as popular ornaments in Scotland during the eighteenth and nineteenth centuries and possibly earlier. They were often inscribed with a verse or with the word 'love'. Clearly they were primarily love-tokens or betrothal gifts, but they appear also to have been worn as a protection against witches. During the eighteenth century they were made by silversmiths in country districts, but during the nineteenth century their manufacture was taken over by craftsmen in the cities and these later brooches are often more elaborate and set with stones.

The name 'Luckenbooth' comes from the fact that many were sold in the luckenbooths (street stalls) around St. Giles's church in Edinburgh. Another name for them is 'Queen Mary' brooches, which may perhaps be explained by the resemblance of two hearts placed side by side to the shape of the letter 'M'.

Lulls, Arnold. A Dutch jeweller working at the court of James I. In the early seventeenth century he produced a series of 41 designs in watercolour for jewels for Anne of Denmark. The designs, carefully and delicately drawn, are now in the Victoria and Albert museum and are a valuable source of information about the trends in English jewellery of the time – particularly since a lot of fine jewellery of this period was broken up and sold later in the century to provide funds for the Civil War.

Lulls's drawings reveal the greatly increased importance of gemstones. Although the settings are coloured and linked with graceful scrollwork, it is undoubtedly the gems which are the main feature of the design. This is clearly shown in the drawing of a splendid pendant which has as its focus a large emerald surrounded by table-cut rubies, linked with enamelled scrolls and hung with three pendant pearls (see illustration). There are several designs for aigrettes, in all of which the stones are prominent features, and one of which contains a large square ruby and numerous diamonds. Many of the drawings show rose-cut stones as well as table-cut, and three designs for earrings have pear-

Design for a pendant by Arnold Lulls, about 1610

shaped cabochon emerald pendants.

(See *Seventeenth-century jewellery* for further information on the period.)

Lumachella (Fire marble). An uncommon and attractive dark brown marble containing small whitish fossil shells which exhibit a play of colour rather like that of opal. The name means 'little snail'. The material comes from Bleiburg in Austria and Astrakhan in Russia. (See also *Marble.*)

Luminescence. Under certain types of radiation, including ultra-violet light and X-rays, gemstones, in common with other substances, can be made to emit light. The radiation converts the atoms of the substance from a stable state (the ground state) to an excited state, from which they

221

can only return by emitting the energy they have absorbed. The radiation emitted is always of a longer wavelength than the exciting radiation, and since X-rays and ultra-violet light are of shorter wavelength than visible light, substances irradiated by these emit a radiation which is often within the range of the visible spectrum and is seen as a coloured glow (fluorescence). (An afterglow, seen after the exciting radiation has ceased, is known as phosphorescence.) The colour of this glow will in many cases distinguish between a synthetic and a natural gemstone or give important clues to a stone's identity.

One of the most useful applications of the technique is in distinguishing between synthetic and natural emeralds. For this an ultra-long-wave ultra-violet lamp, which transmits light partly in the visible violet range, is the most useful; under it a synthetic emerald emits a strong crimson glow whereas a natural emerald, possibly because it contains a trace of iron which is absent in the synthetics, appears very dark. To give a few other examples: diamond usually shows a blue or violet fluorescence under long-wave ultra-violet, whereas synthetic white sapphires and spinels, and colourless pastes, barely respond to radiation of this wavelength. Under X-rays diamonds show a bright violet or whitish-blue fluorescence, while synthetic white sapphires may show red, and white spinels blue or green. Benitoite (q.v.), a blue stone which closely resembles sapphire, shows a strong blue fluorescence under short-wave ultra-violet light, whereas sapphire hardly responds to this wave-length. Synthetic blue sapphire shows a dull deep green glow under the same conditions. In some cases an examination of the fluorescent glow through a spectroscope (q.v.) shows the emitted light to be in bands, and the position of these bands may help further in identification.

Although the examination of luminescence is mainly a laboratory technique and not one of the commonly-used ways of testing gemstones, it has the great practical advantage that stones can be examined in their mountings and it does not matter if they are of very small size.

Lunate. Shaped like a half-moon. An outline sometimes used for gemstones.

Lustre. The surface brilliance of a stone or metal, determined by the amount and quality of the light reflected from it. In gemstones this depends on the refractive index (q.v.) of the stone and its degree of polish, the latter being related to the stone's hardness.

There are various kinds of lustre. *Metallic* lustre is the kind possessed by polished metal and many sulphides and oxides. Most transparent gemstones have a *vitreous* (i.e. glassy) lustre; diamond and the very few stones with a similarly high refractive index have *adamantine* lustre. The other types of lustre are *resinous*, as in amber; *silky*, as in tiger's eye and other fibrous minerals; *pearly*, as in moonstone; *waxy*, as in turquoise.

Lustre should not be confused with sheen (q.v.).

'Lustron'. Trade name for a polystyrene-type plastic. (See *Plastics*.)

Lute. A mixture of refractory materials – the constituents may be loam and water, fireclay and water, whitening, tripoli, etc. – used to seal the gap between a crucible and its cover before placing in a furnace, and to protect parts of an object from heat while other parts are being soldered.

Luting. The application of a heat-resistant material before firing in a furnace or soldering. (See *Lute*.)

'Lux sapphire'. Misnomer for iolite.

Lydian stone. Basanite.

Lynx-eye. Labradorite with a green flash of colour.

'Lynx-sapphire'. Misnomer for dark blue iolite from Ceylon.

Lyte jewel. A fine early seventeenth-century pendant given by James I to Thomas Lyte of Lyte's Cary in appreciation of a lengthy pedigree which Lyte had

drawn up for the king showing him to be descended from Brutus, the legendary founder of the British race. The pendant is of enamelled gold and contains a miniature by Isaac Oliver of James as a young man. The rim is set with table-cut diamonds. Over the miniature is a pierced cover bearing the monogram IR (=JR) also set with table diamonds. The back is decorated with a design in outline enamel in white, red and blue.

The jewel passed out of the Lyte family at some stage and came into the possession of the Monypeny family, who sold it to the Duke of Hamilton. It was subsequently bought by Baron Ferdinand de Rothschild, and is now in the British Museum.

The Lyte jewel. British Museum

M

Mabe pearl. A complicated form of cultured pearl, actually a cultured blister pearl. A small object is cemented to the inner surface of the oyster's shell and when it is covered with nacre (q.v.) the resulting blister pearl is cut away. The nucleus is removed, the inside of the nacre shell is polished and the recess is filled with a small bead, which is then covered with a dome-shaped backing of mother-of-pearl fixed on with white cement. There are some variations of the procedure. (For cultured pearls, see *Pearls*.)

Macaronis. Hookless chatelaines, popular in the late eighteenth century. (See *Chatelaines*.)

Machine-stamping. The process of forming and shaping sheet metal mechanically in a press. It is extensively used in the mass-production of cheap modern jewellery. The process known as die-stamping is used for forming metal in relief. Two steel dies are cut, one with the pattern in cameo (the male die) and the other with the pattern hollowed out (the female die). The male die is set in the top, movable part of the press, and this is brought down with considerable force on to the sheet metal placed over the female die, forcing it into the hollow where it takes the required form. This type of stamping is used for making regimental badges, medallions, etc. A similar process is used for cutting out shaped blanks of sheet metal: the metal is fed over the hollow female tool and the male is brought down under pressure to cut it. This is the process more usually known as machine-stamping; it is used to mass-produce jewellery components which are then fitted together by hand.

The mechanical stamping of jewellery began in the nineteenth century. Machine-stamped settings were being made as early as the 1850s, but for the first twenty years or so the press and stamp were used sparingly and for the most part on gilt jewellery. In the 1870s, however, various factors including the necessity of producing silver jewellery at a very low price brought about increasing reliance on mechanical processes, and a considerable amount of late Victorian jewellery consisted of stamped-out components assembled by hand. The centre of the industry was Birmingham (q.v.). The techniques have been refined and improved since the nineteenth century but are still essentially the same, and machine-stamping still offers one of the cheapest means of producing jewellery in quantity (the making of the dies is very expensive, but thereafter the process is extremely cheap).

(Another modern mass-production method is centrifugal casting, for which see *Casting*; see also *Stamping*.)

Macles. Flattish triangular twinned crystals of diamond.

'Madiera topaz'. Misnomer for citrine.

Magical jewellery. During the Middle Ages and the sixteenth and seventeenth centuries jewellery was worn not only for its decorative value but because the materials of which it was made were believed to have hidden properties, most of them magical. It is difficult to judge how important this factor was in the case of the more elaborate and beautiful jewels, but in certain very simple pieces of

Ring set with a 'toadstone'. Victoria and Albert Museum

Pendant of wolf's claw set in silver. Victoria and Albert Museum

Silver ring engraved on the bezel with astrological signs and inside with the legend 'Sadayel – raphael – tiriel' (names of angels). Seventeenth century. British Museum

jewellery such as inscribed rings it was obviously the major consideration, and certain stones such as the 'toadstone', elaborately set in precious materials, would never have been used except on account of their supposed powers since their decorative value is nil.

The belief in the magical properties of stones is older than civilisation, and in the earliest civilizations the materials out of which cylinder-seals were carved – quartz, bloodstone, etc. – were thought to have magically protective powers. In the hands of the Babylonians this ancient belief became associated with astrological ideas, and a system was created in which the known gemstones were associated ac-

cording to their colour with certain stars and said to be under the influence of these stars, and were inscribed with signs denoting the correspondence. Metals were also included in the system; thus gold corresponded to the sun, silver to the moon, lead to Saturn, and so on. The civilizations of Greece and Rome inherited some of these beliefs and they spread eventually to north-western Europe. For many centuries, however, these beliefs were divorced from the Babylonian astrological tradition, which was carried on at Alexandria and later taken up by Arab scholars. The tradition passed on by classical writers dealt mainly with the medicinal virtues of gemstones.

Magical jewellery

In the Middle Ages there were two main types of magical jewellery: that in which the stones themselves were thought to have magical or healing powers and that in which the inscription on the stone or metal was of primary importance. The latter type did not appear in Europe until the thirteenth century.

The powers ascribed to the stones themselves were numerous and often inconsistent. Lapidaries (q.v.) setting out their properties had been written from the time of the Greeks, and the accounts varied widely. Most lapidaries agreed that diamond made its wearer invincible in battle, that carbuncle strengthened the heart, jasper stopped bleeding, emerald was good for afflictions of the eyes and amethyst prevented intoxication. The basis of these common traditions is fairly clear: diamond is the hardest stone, both carbuncle and jasper are the colour of blood, emerald is a soothing colour to look at, and amethyst (according to Pliny) is almost but not quite the colour of wine. There are also a few agreed traditions of unknown origin, such as the belief that turquoise protects the wearer from riding accidents. For the most part, however, the attribution of special qualities appears quite random; many stones have the same property in common, and the same stone is credited with quite different powers by different authors. Often the stones were thought to have not only magical powers but an extraordinary origin. From the time of Theophrastus (about 315 B.C.) it had been thought that stones bred like living things, and a description of a stone called selenite in a twelfth-century English lapidary says that it grows with the crescent moon and diminishes with the waning moon – adding 'The stone is found in the kingdom of Persia', which conveniently left little opportunity for disproving it.

The stones credited with these powers were not all gemstones. Some were minerals of no particular distinction, and some did not exist at all. The outstanding example is the toadstone. This was a stone believed to be carried in the head of a mature toad. Lapidaries gave detailed and unpleasant instructions for extracting it. Once removed it had great virtues: it preserved the owner from all manner of evils and particularly from poison. It was much sought after and was often set in rings. It was in fact the palatal tooth of a fossil fish, the *Lepidotus*. Another stone highly valued for its efficacy against poison was the 'serpent's tongue'. Henry VIII wore one of these as a pendant, and they were often carefully mounted in precious metal and set on the tables of the wealthy. They are thought to have been fossils or prehistoric arrowheads. The horn of the unicorn was another favourite; this was in fact the horn of the narwhal. This too was used against poison – the popularity of these objects is a potent comment on the political intrigues of the time. (The manner in which these stones were supposed to function is not always clear; some gave warning by changing colour, moving in their settings or exuding a sweat when in the presence of poison, others had to be taken in powdered form as an antidote.) Other stones of fabulous origin were the eagle-stone, found in the nest of an eagle, the swallow-stone, found in the maw of a young swallow, the snail-stone, found in the body of a large snail in the Indies, and the bezoar stone, found in the stomach or gall-bladder of an animal. The actual nature of most of these can only be conjectured.

The second type of magical jewellery, that depending on an inscription, became common in the fourteenth century. It developed from several sources: the Babylonian astrological tradition, which in a sense was scientific, and the equally ancient custom of inscribing words of power on some lasting material to make a permanent invocation, which was pure magic. Most of the inscriptions on fourteenth and fifteenth century jewellery are non-astrological; they are either of Christian origin or derived from some old and usually unknown Eastern source. A common inscription of which the source is known is AGLA; this represents the initial letters of the Hebrew phrase 'Atha Gebri Leilan Adonai', meaning 'Thou art mighty for ever, O Lord'. More mysterious is the word A N A N I-Z A P T U S which was frequently used as a charm against epilepsy. Some inscriptions are completely baffling and must represent a very corrupted form of the original words: an example is a ring found in 1841 with the inscription GUTTU: GUTTA: M A D R O S: A D R O S. Names and texts from the Scriptures were also commonly inscribed as charms. The names of the three kings were thought to be very powerful and are inscribed on the fifteenth-century Glenlyon brooch, together with the last saying of Christ, C O N S U M A T U M ('It is finished'). Also very popular were IESUS NAZA-RENUS REX IUDAEORUM, and verse 30 of St. Luke iv, which was often used as a charm by travellers facing the risk of highway robbery. Although inscriptions such as these were Christian in origin, the intention in inscribing them on jewels was that they should work in a magical way. In any case, they occur so often side by side with indisputably magical inscriptions that there can be no doubt that they should be classed as magical.

The magical use of religious inscriptions continued unabated in the sixteenth century. By this time the astrological writings from the East and the related alchemical works of the Middle Ages had been assimilated, and the talisman, an object of stone or metal inscribed with an astrological device, began to be more widely used. An example is the xenexicon, a talisman for use against the plague, which was engraved with the figures of the scorpion and the serpent as the sun entered the sign of Scorpio. The manner and time of engraving the inscriptions were very important. Cornelius Agrippa, for instance, in his *De Occulta Philosophia*, gives instructions for making magical rings and states that this should be done when a fortunate star is in the ascendant, and the sign should be engraved in a metal appropriate to the star, in the smoke of a burning substance also of the appro-priate type. (For the background to this type of magical jewellery see *Lapidaries*.)

The astrological type of magical jewellery was never as popular among ordinary people as that depending on magical stones or religious inscriptions – astrology was essentially a secret knowledge and the province of philosophers. The most popular single type of magical jewellery seems to have been a ring set with a toad-stone; these are listed time and time again in inventories from the fifteenth to the seventeenth centuries. Rings were the favourite setting for magical stones. A variety of ring thought to be magical in its own right was the cramp-ring, used against cramp and epilepsy. These rings were made from the money offered to the church by the king on Good Friday, and the king rubbed them between his hands to impart to them the virtue his hands had received at his anointing. Cramp-rings were apparently of various forms, so it is not possible to say whether any have survived. They were at any rate much sought-after; Benvenuto Cellini records that he asked an influential friend to obtain one for him. Another magical object based on the supposed sacred powers of the king was the touching-piece; these were coins which the king gave as amulets to those whom he touched to heal them of the 'King's evil'. From the sixteenth century the king himself hung them round the neck of the sick man.

Pendants were of course another favourite form for magical jewellery. Many were set with specifically magical materials such as unicorn's horn, which was very highly prized and obtainable only by the nobility. The Campion pendant in the Victoria and Albert museum contains a piece of unicorn's horn elaborately mounted, and signs of scraping on the horn indicate that it has actually been used. A famous Scottish magical pendant was that belonging to the Laird of Lee; it consisted of a yellowish stone set in a silver coin of the reign of Edward I, and in the seventeenth century it was borrowed by the city of Newcastle for protection against the plague. The citizens were so impressed by its efficacy that they attempted to buy it.

Many pendants were in the form of reliquaries, containing the relic of a saint or some other sacred object. As with the religious inscriptions, this category is on the borderline between magical and devotional jewellery, but there is no doubt that the relics were believed to exert a miraculous power in their own right and not merely to act as a focus for medieval piety. This was the whole purpose of actually wearing the relic rather than placing it in a shrine. The overlapping of magic and religion in the Middle Ages is illustrated by devotional jewels which also contain purely magical materials; an example is a jewel which belonged to the Duke of Burgundy containing a piece of unicorn's horn on which was engraved the figure of the Virgin Mary holding the Child. The magical element was, however, probably unconscious, and jewels of this type, including reliquaries, are discussed under *Devotional jewellery* (q.v.).

In the course of the eighteenth century magic retreated before the advance of science. For centuries physicians, under the impression that disease was caused by possession by an evil spirit, had been prescribing powdered gemstones for every ailment: the richer the patient, the more expensive the medicine. In 1715 a Dr. Slare examined the ingredients of a popular remedy requiring bezoar stone, coral and crabs' eyes and declared them to be 'medically negative'. A similar scepticism disposed of the powers of amulets, while the new discoveries of astronomers fundamentally undermined the astrological basis of the talisman. Magical beliefs continued, of course, particularly in remote country districts, but they had now been seriously discredited.

The twentieth century still believes in magic. This does not apply only to people who openly profess magical beliefs and wear charms with an explicit faith in their powers. Jewellery still has for many a somewhat mysterious quality. There are many people who will still not wear opals, and there are many more to whom the loss of a favourite piece of jewellery would seem not merely a financial or sentimental loss, but something 'unlucky'. (See also *Amulets* and *Talisman*.)

Magna cut. A recent modification of the brilliant cut for large stones, having 102 facets in all. (See *Diamond-cutting* for description.)

Magnifiers. The pocket folding magnifiers used by jewellers, also known as hand lenses or loupes, are made in a range of magnifications of which the commonest are × 5, × 8 and × 10. The cheapest type have a single lens. The more expensive aplanatic magnifiers, usually used for gemmological work, have a doubly convex lens of crown glass cemented between two lenses of flint glass; these give better definition over the whole field of view. Eye-glasses with a single lens have less powerful magnification and are made with focal lengths of up to 4 inches. (See also *Microscopes*.)

Maiden pearl. A newly-fished pearl.

Malachite. (Copper carbonate. S.G. 3.7– 3.9; R.I. 1.85; H. 4.) An opaque, bright green stone characterized by its circular banding of lighter and darker green. It occurs in botryoidal (q.v.) form. Cut in flattish cabochons, as beads or in flat pieces for inlay, it makes a very attractive stone, and there was a vogue for it in jewellery from 1820 to 1840 when whole parures of malachite were sometimes worn.

Malachite is an important ore of copper and occurs, often in association with azurite and chrysocolla (qq.v.), in copper mines in Australia, Africa, the U.S.A. and the Ural mountains. Until recently Russia was the main source of the malachite used in jewellery.

Once seen, malachite is not easily confused with other minerals. However, opaque green aventurine quartz sometimes looks very like it – the quartz shows red through a colour filter (q.v.) and is very much harder – and there is another but rarer copper mineral which closely resembles it and is known as pseudo-malachite (q.v.).

Malacolite. Diopside.

Malacon. Brown zircon.

Mallets. Mallets are used in the preliminary stages of forming and raising metal where it is important to mark the metal as little as possible, and in the forming of some soft metals, e.g. pewter, they are sometimes used exclusively. They are made in a variety of shapes (flat-faced, rounded, tapered wedge, etc.) and materials (plastic, rubber, wood, rawhide, etc.). (See also *Hammers.*)

Mammillary. Having a hummocky surface caused by a radial arrangement of fibrous crystals. The word is usually used synonymously with 'botryoidal' (q.v.), but may indicate that the spherical protuberances are larger than in botryoidal minerals.

Mammoth ivory. See *Ivory.*

'Manchurian jade'. Misnomer for soapstone. (See *Steatite.*)

Mandrel. A rod, usually of circular section, tapered and made of metal. There are several types of mandrel for different purposes and they are usually better known by other names. The *triblet* (q.v.) is of steel and is used primarily for forming rings and collets. A mandrel of similar shape but not necessarily of metal is used for measuring the size of rings (see *Ring sizers*). For polishing the insides of rings a leather-covered rod known as a ring stick (q.v.) is used. Metal rods which are not tapered are used for drawing tube and coiling wire.

Manganese spar. Rhodochrosite.

Man yü. Blood-red jade.

Maori stone (Maori jade). Nephrite from New Zealand. (See *Jade.*)

Marble. (Calcite. S.G. 2.71; H. 3.) A massive form of crystalline limestone, occurring in very many different colours and types of patterning owing to the impurities and secondary minerals it contains. It is primarily used for building, sculpture and small ornamental objects, but particularly attractive pieces are sometimes mounted in jewellery.

Marble is found in many parts of the world. Among the most famous varieties are the white Pentelikon marble quarried near Athens and the white Parian marble from the Cyclades, Cipollino (banded white and green) from Euboea, and Travertine (straw-coloured) from Italy.

Among the most decorative marbles are the brecchiated type, in which the marble has been broken up by stress and subsequently recemented by infiltrating minerals. In some marbles magnesia and silica have combined to form magnesium silicate and this has later been chemically altered to a green serpentine marble; examples of this are Connemara marble from County Galway, Eire, and Iona stone from Iona in the Hebrides. Some marble contains crystals of another mineral, an example being the ornamental marble xalostocite. (See *Grossular garnet.*)

The so-called fossil marbles are sedimentary limestones formed from a multitude of organic fragments. When cut and polished these are often extremely attractive. They are of three types – those containing shells, those containing corals, and those containing the remains of crinoids or sea-lilies (these are known as encrinital marbles). Purbeck marble, containing the fossil shells of freshwater snails, is the best known of the shelly marbles, and fire marble or lumachella (q.v.) probably the most beautiful.

Another type of marble shows dark markings in patterns which resemble trees, landscapes or ruined buildings. These result from the infiltration of other minerals. An example is ruin marble (q.v.).

The stalagmitic calcite known as onyx marble (q.v.) is described separately. (See also *Calcite.*)

Marcasite (Iron pyrites). (Iron sulphide. S.G. 5.10; H. $6\frac{1}{2}$.) True marcasite is hardly ever used in jewellery. The mineral sold as marcasite is actually iron pyrites, which is identical in composition to marcasite but crystallizes in the cubic instead of the orthorhombic system (see *Crystal systems*). Pyrites has a brassy yellow colour and a high metallic lustre, on account of which it has been nicknamed 'Fool's gold'.

Iron pyrites was used in jewellery by the ancient Greeks, and has been found in the tombs of the Incas. It became very popular in the middle of the eighteenth century, when it was usually pavé-set in the frames of lockets, cameos, etc., or set in narrow bands to form knot-brooches. Then, as now, it was usually set in silver or some other white metal, as pyrites does not harmonize with gold. The material continued popular throughout the nineteenth century, but by this time was worn not because it was fashionable but because it was cheap, and it was accordingly more cheaply mounted. In cheap modern jewellery marcasite is cemented in place instead of being set in a rub-over setting as in eighteenth-century work. The stone is cut and polished in the form of a low 6-faced pyramid with a flat base. Most of the cut material comes from the Jura Alps in France.

Glass imitations of marcasite can be detected without difficulty. Very often what is called marcasite is simply cut steel or some other metal.

Marekanite. A variety of obsidian (q.v.) from the banks of the Marekanka river in Siberia. It is smoky-brown, grey or black in colour.

'Mari diamond'. Misnomer for rock crystal from India.

'Marmora diamond'. Misnomer for rock crystal.

Marquise. A stone of boat-shaped outline, usually faceted in the brilliant style (see *Diamond-cutting* for illustration). It may however be cut with small strip-like rectangular facets as in the step cut (q.v.).

Marquise ring. A ring with a pointed oval bezel; the term is often also used to refer to rings with a shuttle-shaped bezel. Both shapes became popular for rings in the second half of the eighteenth century.

'Marvella pearls'. (Trade name.) Imitation pearls.

'Mascot emerald'. (Trade name.) A soudé emerald. (See *Doublet*.)

Mass aqua. Trade term for hard glass imitation stones, originally used for imitations of aquamarine. (See also *Hard mass*.)

Massin, Oscar. (b. 1829). One of the most gifted and influential of nineteenth-century French jewellers. His contributions to nineteenth-century jewellery included the popularizing of the naturalistic floral style (his elegant floral sprays are among the finest French jewellery of the mid-century), and the introduction in the 1860s of the illusion setting, which was designed to increase the apparent size of a diamond and helped to return the diamond to favour in the later part of the century. In 1856, although internationally famous, he came to England to study English manufacturing techniques, which at the time were much admired abroad, and stayed in London $1\frac{1}{2}$ years.

Massive. Composed of densely-packed crystals of microscopic size. (See *Crystal*.)

Mass opal. Opal matrix. (See *Opal*.)

'Matara diamond'. Misnomer (Ceylonese) for colourless or faintly smoky zircon.

Matrix. The mother rock in which a mineral occurs. Sometimes stones are cut complete with part of their matrix, examples being opal and turquoise (qq.v.), in which case the stone is known as opal matrix, turquoise matrix, etc.

Matting tool. See *Chasing tools* and *Repoussé tools*.

'Matura diamond'. See *'Matara diamond'*.

Maxixe aquamarine/beryl. A boron-rich aquamarine of deep blue colour from the Maxixe mine, Minas Gerais, Brazil. The colour fades.

Mayaite. White to green diopside jadeite found in Central America.

Mazarine. A name which has in the past been applied to rose-cut diamonds on the strength of a belief that the rose cut (q.v.) was invented by Cardinal Mazarin (1602–1661). Mazarin did not invent the cut, which was in use before his time, but he was a collector of precious stones and doubtless his patronage 'encouraged the cutting of diamonds in this style. (See also *Diamond-cutting*.)

Mecca stone. Cornelian.

Medieval jewellery. *The Dark Ages and Early Middle Ages.* The jewellery worn by the migrating barbarian tribes of Dark Age Europe was basically of a traditional and stylistically rigid type executed mainly in gilded bronze with inlaid stones. Anglo-Saxon jewellery (q.v.) is fairly typical of this so-called 'barbaric' jewellery. Coming into contact with the Classical civilizations, however, the tribes had learnt other techniques such as fine filigree work in gold, and throughout the Dark Ages these two styles co-existed and gradually became fused, with the more civilized element predominating. The Carolingian period (A.D. 751–987) saw a general renaissance of culture in which classical models were imitated and jewels were important as the insignia of kingship. Ancient cameos and intaglios were highly prized, and for a short time the art of gem-cutting was revived; its most famous product was the superb Lothair crystal, made in the 9th century, engraved with scenes from the apocryphal story of Susanna.

Byzantine influence (see *Byzantine jewellery*) spread to western Europe through trade and was particularly marked in the Ottonian period, beginning in the tenth century. Several pieces of Ottonian jewellery survive, but the greater part of the most important find, the treasure of the Empress Gisela, was unfortunately destroyed in the Second World War. It included necklaces, earrings, brooches and finger-rings, many of which were completely Byzantine in character, particularly the pectoral of gold chains set with gemstones, pearls and Roman intaglios. One of the brooches, now also lost, was richly set with three tiers of cabochon gems and pearls set in fine filigree, with a domed centrepiece holding a large blue stone surrounded by enamels; it combined massive form with an impression of surprising lightness, achieved by the use of filigree and pierced settings. A similar combination is seen in the surviving brooch from the treasure, which is in the form of a large eagle in a pierced circle, decorated with cloisonné enamel (see illustration).

Eagle brooch from the end of the tenth century, German. Pierced gold with cloisonné enamel and sapphires. Altertumsmuseum, Mainz

Jewellery until the thirteenth century was almost entirely restricted to court circles, and most of the goldsmith's work was for the Church. Both gold and precious stones were in short supply. Throughout the Middle Ages stones (and to a lesser degree metals) were credited with magical or medicinal powers (see *Magical jewellery*), as were the ancient cameos and intaglios which were still in circulation. The pagan nature of the subjects engraved on them was not understood, and they were re-interpreted in terms of Christian symbolism and used in ecclesiastical ornaments and crowns. The cloisonné enamel which had developed under Byzantine influence died out in the early

231

Medieval jewellery

Middle Ages and was replaced by champ-levé (q.v.), a heavier and less flexible type of enamelling, more suitable for large ornaments than personal jewellery, which remained predominant in the West for several centuries.

One reason for the scarcity of jewellery was that the simple style of dress gave no scope for it. With the exception of cere-monial objects such as crowns, virtually the only type of jewellery worn in this early period seems to have been the brooch. The dominant type until the thirteenth century was the heavy, richly-decorated disc-brooch, which presumably was often used for fastening the cloak.

1200–c. 1400. During the thirteenth and fourteenth centuries various social and economic changes gradually brought about a change in the nature of jewellery. The most important factors were the growth of towns and the rise of a prosperous middle class, who could afford fine jewellery and wore it as a badge of social status. Another new element was the idealization of woman, which, although it may have been more theoretical than practical, did result in jewellery being made and given as love-tokens, and in the inscription of amatory mottoes on rings and brooches.

During this period increasing prosperity brought about increasing luxury, which reached such proportions that laws began to be passed – in 1331 in Paris, in 1363 in England – restricting the use of gems. From the conquests of the Crusades (notably the sack of Constantinople in 1204) more precious materials became available to meet the demand, and con-tact with the East also gave the gold-smiths new models and fresh ideas. There was a movement towards naturalism, culminating in the use of delicate and very realistic plant and leaf forms. Jewellery became more sophisticated. Parallel with this secular trend was a new mood of piety which found expression in the mystical movements of the fourteenth century. Jewellery reflected this also, particularly in the wearing of pendant reliquaries in the later part of the period. (See *Devotional jewellery.*)

Dress until the mid-fourteenth century was still fairly simple; both men and women wore a long-sleeved ankle-length garment with a slit at the neck, and a cloak. Both of these were commonly fastened with a *brooch*. The characteristic brooch of the Middle Ages was the ring-brooch; this consisted of a ring with a pin which crossed the front of the brooch and rested on the opposite side (for illustration of the basic type see *Brooches*). At first the ring-brooch was a fairly small and simple affair, made in precious metal often in-scribed with an amatory or religious motto, and worn by the nobility. Later, inscribed brooches began to be worn in base metal by the poorer people, and simultaneously the ring began to be elaborated into fancy shapes (a heart-shaped brooch is illustrated) and was eventually filled in altogether so that the brooch was now of the disc type with a catch at the back for the pin. (This development is traced in greater detail under *Brooches*). From this time the form of the brooch altered with fashion and became more elaborate as the style of dress

Gold brooch, once enamelled, fourteenth century. Victoria and Albert Museum

The Founder's Jewel bequeathed by William of Wykeham to New College, Oxford. The figures are the Angel of the Annunciation and the Virgin. Late fourteenth century

Brooches became yet more sophisticated in the fifteenth century.

Buckles, an important item of dress in earlier centuries, sometimes attained very elaborate form in the Middle Ages. The example illustrated is typical of the Lotharingian style of the thirteenth century influenced by Gothic sculpture. In the mid-fourteenth century dress, and therefore jewellery, began to be subject to changing fashions, one of which around 1340 was for decorated belts consisting of hinged plaques of gold or enamel. Later, narrow belts with ornate clasps or buckles became fashionable again.

Head-ornaments became increasingly important and in the fourteenth century were an indispensable part of court dress. As they were particularly subject to the caprices of fashion few of them have survived; those that do, consisting of narrow hinged plaques worked in repoussé, give an impression of elegance but rather hasty workmanship. Great ladies wore crowns richly jewelled, and as dress became increasingly luxurious precious stones and pearls were sewn on to hats.

became more luxurious. Cluster brooches richly set with cabochon-cut stones were popular during part of the fourteenth century, and many brooches were in the form of an initial. A beautiful example of the latter type is the Founder's jewel left by William of Wykeham to New College, Oxford (see illustration). This is in the form of a crowned M, set with precious stones and pearls, framing two small figures representing the Annunciation.

Rings were also very popular. Many were worn as talismans (see *Magical jewellery*) and many others which bore no magical inscription were probably regarded as having some special virtue according to the stones they contained. In the early Middle Ages such rings as were worn had mostly been copies of antique models, but during the thirteenth century new styles developed. Claw

Thirteenth-century silver-gilt buckle. Museum of National Antiquities, Stockholm

233

Medieval jewellery

Fourteenth-century ring set with an amethyst, inscribed 'Par grant amour'. Victoria and Albert Museum

settings were still used for stones, but high collets fashioned to the shape of the stone became more usual. Smaller stones were often set on the shoulders of the ring surrounding the central stone or motif. Numerous special types of ring developed, including tradesmen's rings, official rings, and the lovers' rings, often inscribed with a motto or ending in clasped hands or a lovers' knot. The last two motifs were originally Roman, and rings in this form were used in the Middle Ages and for some centuries following for a variety of purposes – as betrothal and/or wedding rings, or as tokens of love or simply friendship. They are discussed under *Betrothal rings*. (See also *Rings*.) The lovers' ring with an inscribed motto was very often a plain circle; it developed further during the later Middle Ages and Renaissance as the posy ring (q.v.).

The Later Middle Ages. The increasing extravagance of the medieval courts reached its height in the fifteenth century, when Burgundy, by now the wealthiest country in Europe, became the centre of fashion. Dress was now very elaborate and was quite different for men and women: the men wore a belted and padded doublet, often with leg-of-mutton sleeves, tight hose and pointed, upward-curling shoes; the women wore high-waisted dresses with tight bodices and low neck-lines, and tall and elaborate head-dresses. The purely decorative element in jewellery now became more important than its functional role in relation to the clothing. A general stylistic change was also taking place as a result of the development of gem-cutting. The Paris lapidaries had formed their own guild by the end of the

thirteenth century, and although their craft was applied mainly to ecclesiastical work – carved vessels for churches, etc. – faceted gems began very gradually to replace cabochon stones in jewellery. Another effect of gem-cutting was that the stones became more important than hitherto; they were no longer merely an accessary to the goldsmith's work. There was a growing enthusiasm for cameos.

Enamelling had developed rapidly in the fourteenth century and at the very end of the century the technique of en-crusted enamel (q.v.) had been perfected. This technique, which consisted in cover-ing figures in high relief with a layer of enamel, was applied in particular to brooches, and those that survive are superb examples of late medieval courtly art. They consist of enamelled figures of lovers, animals, birds, and other popular themes, usually in a gold rim set with pearls or jewels. A particularly delicate one shows a pair of lovers set in a plaited golden wreath; between them are set a triangular diamond and a cabochon ruby, and the wreath is set with five pearls (see illustration). This brooch is of mid-

Fifteenth-century brooch of enamelled gold set with a ruby, triangular diamond, and pearls. Kunsthistorisches Museum, Vienna

fifteenth-century date and belonged to the Duke of Burgundy.

The low-necked dresses which became fashionable in the mid-fifteenth century meant that *necklaces* and *pendants* were universally worn by women. Pendants were also worn by men. They seem often to have been of a heavy, simple design featuring particularly splendid stones; an example is the 'Three Brothers' pendant (q.v.) no longer in existence, which was set with a diamond surrounded by three large rubies and at one time belonged to Henry VIII. Such pieces were also worn in the hat. Reliquary pendants were extremely popular and were often decorated in the painted enamel that replaced encrusted enamel in popularity during the fifteenth century. These pendants generally showed the influence of the large-scale goldsmiths' work done for churches and shrines; many of them are in the form of an opening triptych enamelled with scenes of a religious nature and containing a space for a relic.

Much fifteenth-century jewellery was of a devotional nature. Rosaries were increasingly worn as necklaces and some were very elaborate, with beads which opened to show religious scenes inside. Crosses were worn as pendants and could be elaborately ornamented. The pilgrim's badge, issued by the centres of pilgrimage and bearing the symbol or figure of the respective saint, was worn – in the appropriate metal – by all classes of society. These types of jewellery are described in more detail under *Devotional jewellery*.

Rings were now extremely common – sometimes four or five were worn on each hand. They tended to be heavier and more complicated than in the fourteenth century. The types which had developed earlier in the Middle Ages continued, and some rings contained a small space for a relic (see *Devotional jewellery*). Signet rings (q.v.) abounded.

The wearing of ornamental belts continued, and fashions changed frequently. A number of very fine *buckles* have survived, worked in patterns of late-Gothic foliage. The wide loose sleeves made *bracelets* fashionable for the first time in many centuries; there was a vogue in the early fifteenth century for enamelled ones set with pearls and precious stones. *Pomanders* (q.v.) were very popular, partly because they were believed to give protection against the plague, and devotional jewels often had compartments for ambergris or musk.

There is no clear-cut division between medieval and Renaissance jewellery (q.v.). Gradually the influence of Gothic architecture gave way to that of classical architecture, and the Virgin and saints were replaced by the fauns, satyrs and gods of classical mythology. Some characteristics of Renaissance jewellery, such as the love of superb gems, are already noticeable in the later Middle Ages, while in some parts of Europe medieval forms lingered on well into the sixteenth century.

'Medina emerald'. (Trade name.) Green glass.

Meerschaum. (Hydrated silicate of magnesium. S.G. about 2.0; H. $2–2\frac{1}{2}$.) A soft, whitish, porous material best known for its use in pipe bowls but occasionally encountered in jewellery. It has been used in place of soap, since when first unearthed it has a greasy quality and lathers. When heated it hardens and becomes perfectly white. The most important sources are Turkey, Greece, Spain and Morocco, and the centre of the turning and carving industry, when meerschaum pipe-bowls were popular, was Budapest.

The name means 'sea-foam', an apt description.

Melanite. See *Andradite*.

Mélange. Term for diamonds of mixed sizes weighing more than $\frac{1}{4}$ carat.

Mélée. A classification used in the sorting of diamonds referring to stones weighing less than $\frac{1}{4}$ carat.

Melon. Term for an elongated bead with longitudinal ridges like those of a cantaloupe melon.

Memento mori jewellery

Memento mori jewellery. *Memento mori* means 'remember you must die.' The art of the later Middle Ages and Renaissance was much preoccupied with death, and during the sixteenth century this preoccupation began to manifest itself increasingly in jewellery. Some of the earliest watches were set in pendants shaped as skulls. A pendant surmounted by a skull was among the engravings published by Woeiriot in 1559. Rings enamelled with skulls were worn. One of these, in the Victoria and Albert museum, is a signet ring with a revolving bezel; on one side is a merchant's mark (see *Signet rings*) and on the other an enamelled skull.

The intention behind the wearing of these jewels was mainly religious; they reflected the age of the Counter-Reformation and Calvinism. In the following century the protracted agony of the Thirty Years' War did nothing to diminish the awareness of death, and *memento mori* jewellery assumed elaborate forms. The skull was joined by the coffin, which sometimes contained a corpse or skeleton. A very fine English example of this type is the Torre Abbey jewel, which contains a beautifully-made white-enamelled skeleton (see *Seventeenth-century jewellery*). Another example, rather later, is a coffin-shaped pendant enamelled with skulls, hanging from a chain of cross-bones and with a skull and crossbones hanging below it. The symbol of death sometimes appears in the jewellery of love: an enamelled jewel made in Germany depicts a Cupid with his bow standing over a skull, with a large crown set over the whole (see illustration), while an English wedding ring is tersely inscribed 'Observe wedloke' on one side and 'Memento mori' on the other.

Towards the end of the seventeenth century there was a tendency in England for these reminders of death to be worn as memorials of specific people. In this form they survived into the eighteenth century, but were finally discarded by an age which preferred death to be noble, or at any rate elegant. (See *Memorial jewellery* and *Mourning rings*.)

German pendant of second half of the seventeenth century. Kunstgewerbemuseum, Cologne

Memorial jewellery. The wearing of a particular class of jewellery in mourning is first recorded in the sixteenth century although it probably began earlier. Widows wore death's head jewels in cameo, and an inventory of 1596 mentions a collar for mourning wear enamelled in white and black lovers' knots and set with pearls. An inventory of the early seventeenth century lists a chain of black ambergris beads with nine diamond-set skulls, and a matching pair of skull earrings.

These graphic symbols of death were in fashion during the sixteenth and seventeenth centuries, and although they served for mourning jewellery they were worn primarily as a reminder of one's own mortality (see *Memento mori jewellery*). In the course of the seventeenth century, however, they came increasingly to be worn as specific memorials. This tendency was linked with a fashion for wearing jewellery in commemoration of political events, most of which, in the nature of things, were unhappy. The execution of Charles I is a case in point: slides, pendants and rings enamelled with the portrait of the unfortunate monarch were worn by his supporters, and were the first of a series of Stuart commemorative jewels which later depicted Charles II and the Old and Young Pretenders and commemorated the fate of their followers. Most commemorative jewels were in the form of rings and are further described under *Commemorative rings*. At the same time the giving of memorial rings to mourners at a funeral was becoming something of a fashion and such rings tended to assume a standard form. (See *Mourning rings*.)

Shortly before the end of the seventeenth century a new type of memorial jewellery appeared in which the initials of the deceased in gold thread were set on a background of woven hair under rock crystal. Hair jewellery (q.v.) later became very popular, but skulls and skeletons remained the predominant style for memorial jewellery well into the eighteenth century. They finally disappeared in the 1760s. In the second half of the eighteenth century a prevailing sentimentalism brought the wearing of memorial jewellery into general favour. This phenomenon was more or less restricted to England, although the earlier grim jewellery of skulls and skeletons had been worn also on the Continent. In this new sentimental memorial jewellery the subjects were symbols of romantic grief: weeping willows, urns, tombs, broken columns and compassionate angels. These

appeared on rings, pendants, brooches and clasps, usually in the form of enamelled medallions in which part of the picture (generally the weeping willow) was executed in hair-work. Such medallions were usually oval or shuttle-shaped, and often set in a rim of seed-pearls, amethysts, or perhaps diamonds or paste. Rings became more elaborate: the marquise ring was a popular form, often containing a curl of hair under crystal. This type of memorial jewellery lasted for many decades and was one of the most popular forms of jewellery in the Romantic period (see *Nineteenth-century jewellery*). Hair (see *Hair jewellery*) also enjoyed a remarkable vogue in the Victorian era and was not restricted to memorial wear.

Mourning brooch set with curls of hair under crystal, in a frame of black-enamelled gold. Victorian, mid-nineteenth century

English memorial pendant of about 1785; a miniature with the weeping willow executed in hair-work

As the nineteenth century wore on, memorial jewellery, like other kinds, became heavier and less delicate. This applied particularly to mourning jewellery made of jet. Faceted jet beads had been worn for mourning in the sixteenth century and probably earlier, but in the nineteenth century jet suddenly came into its own. It was the prescribed material for mourning jewellery worn at Court following the death of George IV, and the fashion for wearing it rapidly spread downwards through other classes of society until by the end of the nineteenth century jet was one of the commonest materials seen in jewellery. Its position was assured by the lengthy periods of mourning observed in Victorian society and by the Queen's own uncompromising mourning for Prince Albert; for many years after his death, ladies presented to the Queen were asked to wear no jewellery but jet. The material came from Whitby in Yorkshire (see *Jet*), and was carved into medallions, serpent-bracelets, crosses and many other forms. Whole parures of jet jewellery were worn. Black glass was used to imitate jet, especially in France.

Towards the 1880s the jet jewellery became more and more ponderous and the style of other memorial jewellery more and more funereal. All trace of lightness and elegance disappeared. Rings were largely replaced by heavy pendants, which in the 1880s often took the form of a cross (curiously, religious themes had not been important in memorial jewellery until this time). Flower motifs in white on black had featured in memorial jewellery of the mid-nineteenth century, but by the end of the century these had degenerated into a late-Victorian plainness accentuated by the mass-production methods which were now regularly used in the cheaper kinds of jewellery. When the inevitable reaction against Victorian styles came, these jewels, the acme of gloom, must have been largely responsible for the profound distaste with which the late nineteenth century was regarded.

Memorial rings. See *Mourning rings.*

Menilite. Banded common opal. (See *Opal.*)

Mercury gilding (silvering). The process of gilding or silvering by mixing powdered gold or silver with mercury, applying this liquid amalgam with a brush, and heating the article so that the mercury evaporates leaving an even deposit of precious metal. This method was in use from Roman times until the nineteenth century, when it was replaced as the normal method by electroplating (q.v.). The mercury process gave good results because the gold or silver actually penetrated the surface of the base metal instead of being merely a skin on top, but

it involved the danger of inhaling the highly poisonous mercury vapour.

Metal gauges. Various standards are in use for measuring the thickness of sheet metal and wire. In Britain the Birmingham Metal Gauge is used for measuring sheet gold and silver, copper, brass, etc., and the Imperial Standard Wire Gauge is used for all wire (it is also the standard wire gauge in Canada). In America the standard gauge for non-ferrous sheet metal and wire is the Browne and Sharpe Gauge. The numbers on the Birmingham Metal Gauge are in ascending order of size, and on the Browne and Sharpe Gauge in descending order of size:

B.M.G.	1	= .0085″	=	.216 mm.
	10	= .028″	=	.71 mm.
	20	= .065″	=	1.65 mm.
B. & S.	20	= .0320″	=	.813 mm.
	10	= .1019″	=	2.588 mm.
	1	= .2893″	=	7.346 mm.

The instrument for measuring the thickness of metal on these scales is usually in the form of a metal disc with a series of graduated notches, each notch being marked with the number on the scale and the measurement in thousandths of an inch or millimetres. The correct measurement is that of the smallest notch in which the metal will fit tightly.

A micrometer (q.v.) is also used for measuring the gauge of metals.

Meteoric glass. See *Tektite.*

Methylene iodide. A volatile liquid of formula CH_2I_2 used in the determination of specific gravity and refractive index (qq.v.). It has S.G. 3.32 and R.I. 1.74.

Metric carat. See *Carat (1).*

'Mexican agate'. Misnomer for banded calcite.

'Mexican diamond'. Misnomer for rock crystal.

'Mexican jade'. Misnomer for green-dyed stalagmitic calcite. (See *Onyx marble.*)

Mexican jewellery. *Pre-Hispanic.* Little survives of the jewellery of Central America made before the Spanish conquest, because the Spaniards melted down most of the treasure which fell into their hands. Contemporary accounts give some idea of the richness and the nature of these ornaments. A necklace or collar given to Cortes is described as being of four strands containing 102 red stones, 172 green stones, 26 gold bells, and 10 large stones from which hung altogether 142 gold pendants. Another gift to Cortes was a necklace of hand-wrought gold crabs set with shell. Naturalistic motifs were common: the contemporary descriptions mention metal fish that wiggled, and monkeys with nodding heads. A superb headdress given to Cortes as a gift for his sovereign consisted of long green quetzal feathers sewn into a backing studded with plaques of gold.

These ornaments were Aztec. Of the various Indian peoples who settled in Mexico the Aztecs were among the latest to arrive and the most barbaric. Their barbarism resulted from (or perhaps produced) their religion: although some of their gods were the old gods of the region – such as Quetzalcoatl the plumed serpent-god – their most important deity was their tribal god Huitzilopochtli, who began as a war god and was later identified with the sun. To enable him to overcome the moon and stars every morning and begin his journey across the sky he required nourishment in the form of a constant supply of human blood and human hearts. His followers obtained these by killing prisoners and by ritual sacrifice. It is not surprising that surviving Aztec work shows a preoccupation with death and horror; this goes hand-in-hand, however, with an equal vitality – exemplified in the fish and monkeys mentioned above. Another god revered by the Aztecs was Xipe, the flayed god, who is sometimes represented wearing a mask of skin.

The jewellery and ornamental objects found on Aztec territory are Aztec in spirit (a sacrificial knife found at Tenochtitlan with a chalcedony blade and beautifully-inlaid handle is a good example) but they were probably all made

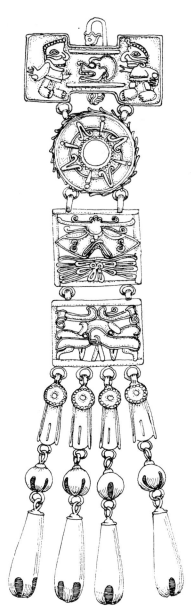

Mixtec gold pendant from the Monte Albán treasure

239

Mexican jewellery

by Mixtec craftsmen or brought from Mixtec territory, to the south of the Aztecs. The Mixtecs were skilled metal workers and stone-carvers. A rich hoard of Mixtec jewellery was discovered in 1931 during excavations at Monte Albán near Oaxaca. (Monte Albán was the sacred mountain of the Zapotecs, but part of it had been re-used not long before the Spanish conquest for a Mixtec burial.) The treasure included many pieces of worked jade, rock crystal, turquoise and obsidian, and gold pendants and masks. There was a gold pectoral ornament (see illustration) in the form of a mask of the god Xipe (whose worship was not confined to the Aztecs), elaborately decorated and made entirely by the lost-wax casting process (q.v.). A gold pendant (see illustration) was found in the form of four linked plaques, one below another, hung with four pendant bells known as *casca-*

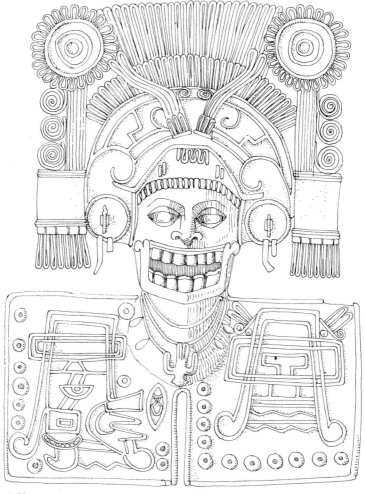

Gold pectoral in the form of a mask of the god Xipe, from the Monte Albán treasure

beles (a characteristic of Mexican jewellery). The top plaque depicted two ball-players with a skull between them (the ball-game was a ritual game with sinister undertones in which the leader of the losing side was apt to be sacrificed); the second plaque showed a solar disc, the third a moon symbol and the fourth an earth-symbol. This also was made by lost-wax casting. The tomb also contained gold rings and nose-ornaments, necklaces of shell, turquoise and pearls, a number of delicately carved jaguar bones, and many examples of the mosaic inlay skilfully practised by the Mixtecs. Turquoise, jade, malachite, quartz, beryl, obsidian, shell and other materials were cut to shape and fitted into complex designs, and were cemented to a base which was usually of wood or stone. In the case of the Monte Albán treasures the wooden backing had disintegrated.

Another famous Mixtec jewel, and the only surviving example of stone mosaic inlay on gold, is a brooch found at the beginning of this century near Yanhuitlán. It consists of a circular shield with four arrows crossing horizontally behind it and pendant *cascabeles* below. The centre of the shield is decorated with a step fret in gold, interlocking with which is a fret in turquoise mosaic. The significance of the design is not known. The Indian who found the brooch took off two of the gold *cascabeles* and prised out the turquoise: the turquoise was subsequently recovered but there are now only 11 instead of 13 *cascabeles*. A replica of the brooch was presented by the Mexican government to Princess Elizabeth as a wedding present.

These jewels and stone-carvings were produced without the use of iron tools and without knowledge of the wheel. The Indian craftsmen worked with hammers and chisels of stone, knives of obsidian or copper, and drills of bone. The chief ways of working gold were by lost-wax casting – an old technique which had spread up the Pacific coast from Peru – and beating in repoussé. Many Mexican gold ornaments look at first glance as if they are decorated with applied filigree, but they are not. They are cast in their entirety, with remarkable skill. The gold for this work was probably mostly obtained from nuggets found in the river beds, although the Indians also mined for metals and apparently knew how to refine gold.

Jade, highly prized by the Indians, was found in ravines in the mountainous regions of Southern Mexico. It was beautifully carved by the Maya, who had no knowledge of metal tools at all. The jade was found as water-worn pebbles and as cores in large boulders; in the latter case it was extracted by sawing the boulder through the centre with strong fibre cords or strips of rawhide charged with powdered rock. The carving was probably done with flakes of flint and with drills made of bird-bones charged with powdered rock. A softer stone, or tree-bark containing silica, would be used for polishing.

Modern. With the Spanish conquest Mexican culture disintegrated. When the Spanish colonists began to arrive they brought with them not only European tastes and European tools, but also European goldsmiths. These obliged the Indian craftsmen to turn out jewels in standard Renaissance styles, and in time the native tradition was lost. Thenceforth the formal jewellery made in Mexico was of European type, with only a slight flavour of the Indian about it. It is only in this century that an attempt has been made to create a new and native style.

The peasant jewellery worn in the villages of Mexico, however, is a different matter. This is not predominantly European in style, although it is largely compounded of European elements. It presents a remarkable hotch-potch of forms and motifs taken from different cultures at different times, and in the various regions of Mexico characteristic types of jewellery are worn which were adopted at some time after the Spanish conquest and have been worn with little or no change ever since. An example is the pendant cross worn in San Juan Yalalag, east of Oaxaca.

Mexican jewellery

This is a cross made of dark silver, from the arms of which hang smaller crosses or coins; these pendants are sometimes larger than the cross itself, and the whole thing may be as much as six inches wide. The cross is made only in this town and has apparently been made there since the sixteenth century. Its origin is not known, but since crosses of a fairly similar nature are worn in some parts of Spain it is probable that the modern crosses are a distant and Mexicanized version of a cross brought over in the sixteenth century by a Dominican missionary. The crescent-shaped earrings which are to be seen everywhere in Mexico were probably also introduced at a very early stage by the Spaniards, and their ultimate origin seems to be Moorish. Many of them are made in filigree and have fringes of small balls or drops. Filigree is widely used in modern Mexican jewellery; it was almost certainly introduced by the Spaniards. Much of it is in silver, but fine gold filigree is a speciality of Chiapas and of Oaxaca. Oaxaca also produces, predictably, replicas of the Monte Albán jewels; they are of very good quality.

The town of Pátzcuaro, the commercial centre of a string of lakeside villages, is

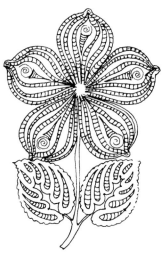

Modern Mexican silver filigree

well known for its fish necklaces. The fish are cast in silver and strung between beads of imitation coral. Some of the fish are stylized, but some are faithful representations of the lake fish on which the prosperity of the villages depends (or did until the tourists started buying the fish necklaces). In Tehuantepec and Juchitán on the isthmus the traditional jewellery is of gold coins. These are treated with great respect; they are often set in pronged bezels, and single pendant coins are usually held in a small carefully-carved gold hand – the coin itself is never pierced.

In the western mountains the Huicholes wear strands of small beads twisted into ropes. The favourite colours are blue and white. There is a great trade in beads, and these come from the unlikeliest places. The blue and white beads of the Huicholes come from France, and in remote parts of the country there are beads from Germany and Czechoslovakia. In San Pedro Quiatoni, a small town south of Oaxaca which until recently was inaccessible by road, Venetian sixteenth-century beads in the form of short glass rods have been worn in necklaces for centuries, handed down from generation to generation. Since the building of a road, however, most of these beads have moved elsewhere. Progress has left its mark in other ways as well; the Tarascan Indians of Michoacán, who used to wear natural branch coral, now wear its equivalent in plastic.

In the 1920s a number of young designers began to produce jewellery which was not traditional in the peasant style and was not slavishly European. Some of them went back to the old pre-Hispanic forms – an interesting experiment but not particularly meaningful in the twentieth century – while others produced work in a modern idiom but using native materials – silver, obsidian and amethyst. The manufacture of this new-style Mexican jewellery has continued and has expanded into an important industry. The centre of the industry is Taxco, a mainly eighteenth-century town which grew from a silver-mining village. In 1927 a highway was built linking it with Mexico City; before the highway there was one jewellery-maker in the town, and there are now several hundred. Various types of jewellery are produced. Some is deliberately primitive, some succeeds in being Mexican without being crude. Some shops practise the old technique of turquoise inlay and of 'metales casados' – a technique of combining silver, silver alloy, brass and copper in designs in such a way that little or no solder is required. Finally, a number of jewellers produce work which is original, individualistic, and completely modern.

'Mexican onyx'. Stalagmitic calcite. (See *Onyx marble*.)

Micatite. (Trade name). A phenol plastic. (See *Plastics*.)

Microcline feldspar. See *Feldspar*.

Micrometer. An instrument used by jewellers for accurate measurement of the thickness of wire or sheet metal. The object to be measured is inserted in a gap in the instrument and the gap is closed by turning a rotating barrel. When the spindle is in contact with the object one measurement is read off from a scale along the sleeve of the micrometer and another from a scale around the barrel, and the two readings added together give the measurement.

Micron. A unit for measuring the thickness of the gold layer in rolled gold. One micron = one-thousandth of a millimetre. The size of the grains in diamond powder is also measured in microns.

Microscopes. Ordinary microscopes consist basically of a system of magnifying lenses fitted in a tube, the raising or lowering of which brings the object examined into focus. The lens at the bottom of the tube, known as the object glass or objective, forms a primary magnified image of the object, and this image is again magnified by the lens at the top, known as the eyepiece or ocular. Both the objective and the ocular are compound lenses. The object examined is placed on a platform called the stage, below which is a movable reflecting mirror; an aperture in the centre of the stage allows light thrown upwards by the mirror to illuminate the object. Between the stage and the mirror is a mounting in which various accessories, such as a condensing lens (substage condenser) to converge light from the mirror on to the object, can be fitted.

For examining gemstones, comparatively low-power microscopes are used and are fitted with various accessories, of which the most important are prisms which permit gemstones to be examined in polarized light. (See *Nicol prisms* and *Double refraction*.) These can be fitted to an ordinary microscope, one slipped into the mounting below the stage, and the other fitted over the eye-piece or screwed into position at the bottom of the tube in place of the objective (which is then screwed in to the bottom of it). Petrological microscopes incorporate these polarizers, together with a rotating stage (an extempore rotating stage can be made for an ordinary microscope), and have crosshairs fitted in the eyepiece to indicate when the polarizers are in the 'crossed' position. (See *Double refraction*.)

Some microscopes, such as the American 'Gemolite', are designed purely for gemmological work. The special features of such microscopes may include gem holders, provision for dark-field illumination (q.v.), a zoom lens, and dichroscope and spectroscope (qq.v.) fittings which can be inserted in place of the eyepiece. Many such microscopes are binocular, which reduces eyestrain, and have an inclined eyepiece so that observations can be made sitting down. Pearl microscopes equipped with an endoscopic stage and pearl illuminator (see *Endoscope* and *Pearls*) are made, and some microscopes incorporate both gem-testing and pearl-testing equipment.

A photographic record may be made of the picture seen through the microscope by fitting a commercial microscope camera over the eyepiece. An ordinary hand camera may also be used, mounted firmly over the eyepiece and with its lens removed, since the optical system of the microscope does duty for that of the camera. Special microscopes incorporating a camera are built for fine photomicrographic work.

Midge stone. Moss agate. (See *Agate*.)

Mignot, Daniel. A French Huguenot

Engraved design for the back of a pendant by Daniel Mignot, 1616

jeweller whose designs for jewellery, published in Augsburg between 1596 and 1616, were widely adopted and are among the earliest to lay emphasis on the display of cut gemstones. The designs are strictly symmetrical, elegant and stylized, and make extensive use of the strapwork and grotesques of later Renaissance work. (See *Renaissance jewellery*.)

Milanese chain. A chain consisting of interwoven rows of small links forming a mesh. (See also *Chain*.)

Milk opal. Translucent milky-white common opal.

Milky quartz (white quartz). (See *Quartz, crystalline*.) Quartz (q.v.) which contains a multitude of small liquid-filled cavities, giving a hazy, milky appearance. It is not much used as a gemstone. Pieces of gold-bearing white quartz are known to have been cut as cabochons.

Millefiori glass. A colourful patterned glass sometimes used in jewellery. The early examples are mostly of the late Roman period and are found in the Gallic provinces and also in Anglo-Saxon work. The glass is now made in Venice. The method is to fuse together a number of thin rods of different-coloured glass and when this has cooled cut it across in slices. The patterned slices can be fashioned into beads or used for inlay work.

Millegrain setting. A setting in which the stone is gripped by a number of small beads or grains of metal. It seems to have been introduced in the nineteenth century. The grains of metal are raised usually by running a milligraining or knurling tool (q.v.) round the edge of the setting. (See also *Settings*.)

Milligraining (mill-graining) tool. See *Knurling tool*.

Mixed cut. A cut widely used for transparent coloured stone; the crown (q.v.) is faceted in the brilliant style and the base of the stone as in the step cut. (See *Gemcutting* for illustration.)

Mixte. Trade term for a composite stone, half real stone and half glass. (See *Doublet*.)

Mizpah rings. Broad gold rings engraved or embossed with the word MIZPAH ('I will watch over thee') – a fashionable gift in the late Victorian period. (See also *Nineteenth-century jewellery*.)

Mocha stone. See *Agate*.

Mock pearl. Imitation pearl. (See *Pearls*.)

Modern jewellery. At the beginning of the twentieth century the development of Art Nouveau had reached its peak and much of the finest jewellery was made in this style (see *Art Nouveau jewellery*). Fine jewellery in precious materials and displaying very high standards of craftsmanship was made in a more traditional style by the great firms such as Cartier and Tiffany, which had grown up in the nineteenth century and had a more conservative clientèle to cater for. This class of jewellery was imitated in cheaper materials by the mass-production methods which had come to be increasingly used towards the end of the nineteenth century.

In the early years of this century the standards of Art Nouveau jewellery began to deteriorate; the inventiveness and originality went out of the designs, which became second-hand and degenerated into a meaningless extravagance, and the best designers, notably Lalique (q.v.), turned their attention to other art forms. Jewellery of the more conservative type, however, was worn in profusion; the years before the First World War saw a great expansion in the trade. This jewellery was mostly heavy and ornate: characteristic items included tiaras, jewelled combs, long earrings, large cameos in heavy gold settings, wide rings with coloured stones in gipsy settings, and watches in richly-chased cases, attached to gold guard chains and worn in the breast pocket or pinned to the dress. Brooches and bracelets were both indispensable. This style of jewellery continued in favour until 1914, but the continuity of fashion was broken by the war and the production of jewellery was greatly curtailed.

When the war ended new fashions and new styles of decoration appeared. Foremost among these was Art Deco, a basically geometric style which introduced smooth polished surfaces and materials such as steel to jewellery. Materials of little intrinsic value were used side-by-side with precious stones; such combinations as coral and diamonds, and emerald and onyx, were popular. The notable designers of this period included Raymond Templier, Georges Fouquet, René Robert and Wiwen Nilsson. Towards the end of the '20s Art Deco gave way to increasingly angular and abstract

Art Deco. Brooch in onyx, coral and brilliant-cut diamonds, set in platinum, by Boucheron, 1925. Musée des Arts Décoratifs, Paris

forms. A jeweller who did not follow prevailing styles but pursued his own ideas was Georg Jensen; he concentrated on silver and devoted himself to producing shapes which were in complete sympathy with the qualities of the metal. His approach to jewellery and standards of craftsmanship gave the firm of Jensen (q.v.) a leading and influential position in the field of design for many decades.

Much jewellery was worn during the '20s and a lot of it was costume jewellery, made of non-precious materials and intended to be thrown away when it ceased to be fashionable. Cheap jewellery and jewellery which relied wholly on its novelty value had been made for decades

Modern jewellery

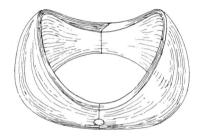

Heavy silver bracelet by Georg Jensen

(see *Nineteenth-century jewellery*) but had always been regarded disparagingly by those with discrimination and wealth; during the '20s, however, boldly designed and purely decorative jewellery in artificial materials was popularized by Chanel and became respectable for daytime wear. One of its most popular manifestations was a choker of large coloured artificial pearls.

Fashions changed fairly quickly during the '20s, but long strings of beads, worn in various ways including wound round the leg, remained in favour for a long time. Bobbed hair brought about a fashion for hair-slides just after the war, but in 1923 the Eton crop arrived, hair-slides disappeared, and long earrings became the rage. Jade, onyx and crystal were popular materials. In the same year Egyptian motifs became very fashionable; Tutankhamun's tomb had just been discovered. Chinese styles were also admired. Gold was now less popular than silver, platinum and even nickel; the use of platinum, a very strong metal, made it possible to set stones in a skeletal framework of metal. There were periodic enthusiasms for the barbaric – Creole earrings, slave bangles, massive African-style armlets in ivory. (In 1919 Georges Barbier had designed a collection of jewellery for Cartier which included linked anklets and bracelets of pearls, pearl breastplates, and a helmet decorated with pearls and pheasant feathers.) Certain items of jewellery which had been worn as a matter of course before the war were no longer to be seen:

they included lockets and cameos, guard rings, and the pocket watch worn on a chain. This had been superseded by the wristwatch, which now often took the place of a bracelet for outdoor wear. Brooches were on the whole much less popular, although in 1925 there was a fashion for pinning them on cloche hats (introduced two years earlier).

In many respects the jewellery of the '30s continued the trends of the '20s: the themes were abstract, white metals were often used in preference to gold, and the same sort of settings, in particular the millegrain setting (q.v.), were used. Artists such as Picasso and Giacometti were taking an interest in jewellery and designed jewels themselves. This movement towards treating jewellery as an art form did not at the time come to much, however; the world depression gave no encouragement to either jewellers or designers. Some small jewellers suffered badly, and at the other end of the scale the entire diamond industry was for a time on the verge of disaster. Some countries did better than others, however; the years between the two wars saw the growth of a major jewellery-manufacturing industry at Pforzheim in Germany, and during the '30s mass-produced cheap (but attractive) jewellery from Germany and from Czechoslovakia, where the production of jewellery was a highly-organized cottage industry, inundated Europe. British manufacturers found it very hard to compete.

The Second World War caused total disruption in the jewellery trade; in Britain virtually the only article of jewellery one could buy in precious materials was a 9-carat gold wedding ring, and there were not even enough of those. When peace was restored it was some years before prosperity returned to the trade as a whole, and for many years the design of jewellery remained more or less static.

It is possible to distinguish four main classes of post-war jewellery, of which two are not new and two are of modern development. The first is what might be called fine jewellery. This is jewellery made with precious materials and impeccable craftsmanship; it is the jewellery of the great firms. The designs are good but are not experimental; they are not intended to do more than display the precious stones to best advantage and to appeal to a discriminating but fairly conservative clientèle. An example of this class of jewellery is the bracelet illustrated, designed by Schlumberger for Tiffany and Co. Its slightly exotic quality is characteristic of modern American design.

Bangle in eighteen-carat gold and light green enamel, by Jean Schlumberger of Tiffany and Co.

The second class of jewellery is that in which the design is based on natural forms but is not actually naturalistic. Jewellery of this type is made usually in silver and with the less valuable stones; it is often highly individualistic, and the materials are subordinated to the design instead of the design being created to show off the materials. The ring illustrated is an example of this type.

Trumpet-shaped ring by J. S. Grigsby

The third class is basically experimental and its existence is made possible by a new attitude which regards jewellery as being an art-form in its own right and approaches the making of jewellery without preconceived ideas. This class of jewellery is much concerned with textures and employs unusual shapes – they may be natural or artificial, but in either case they have an air of being accidental. The brooch by Bjorn Weckström (see illustration), using metal textured as a sculptor would texture it and a baroque pearl, is a good example of this type. Some craftsmen produce this 'accidental' effect by pouring molten metal on to a surface or into water and allowing it to take its own form. Others set their jewellery with natural gemstone crystals.

Sculptural brooch with a blue-grey pearl, by Bjorn Weckström

The fourth type is equally modern but quite different; it is made with geometrical precision in geometrical shapes. Component parts are often turned on a lathe to ensure absolute regularity. This jewellery is smooth, highly-polished, abstract and rather impersonal, but it is also very exciting. The possibilities of geometric shapes are increased by juxtaposing surfaces in such a way that an illusion of movement is created, and in some jewellery of this type there is actually a kinetic element (as in the brooch illustrated overleaf).

In addition to these four main types of jewellery made in precious or at least 'semi-precious' materials, there is of course imitation jewellery, in which paste

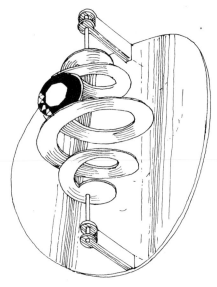

Brooch in white gold with a brown diamond by Friedrich Becker

or crystal provides a substitute for diamonds and gilt a substitute for gold. This type of jewellery follows, with little deviation, the styles of fine jewellery, and is therefore basically conservative. Costume jewellery, on the other hand, follows prevailing fashions in dress and appeals very largely to the taste for novelty. Mass-produced as cheaply as possible, it uses new synthetic materials and modern technical innovations, and thus reflects much more faithfully the age that produces it than the fine jewellery made by craftsmen still using the age-old techniques and tools of the jeweller's craft.

During the past five years or so there has been a great increase in the wearing of jewellery, and the increase has been very largely in the class of jewellery which is hand-made by designer-craftsmen in silver and semi-precious stones. This jewellery is well designed and made, and costs very little compared with fine jewellery. The reason for its popularity is an increasingly widespread appreciation of good design and craftsmanship. In earlier centuries discrimination and wealth normally went hand-in-hand, but this is

no longer the case. There is now a new class of customer with more taste than means, and a new kind of jewellery has accordingly appeared to meet the demand.

Modelling tool. See *Chasing tools* and *Repoussé tools*.

Moe Gauge. A caliper type of diamond gauge. (See *Diamond gauges*.)

'Mogok diamond'. Misnomer for colourless topaz.

Mohs's Scale. A scale used for recording the hardness of minerals, devised in 1822 by Friedrich Mohs. (It is given under *Hardness*.)

'Mojave moonstone'. Misnomer for lilac-coloured chalcedony from the Mojave desert, California.

Moldavite. See *Tektite*.

Molochite. Green jasper.

Momme. A Japanese unit of weight for cultured pearls. (See *Weights for gemstones*.)

Monel metal. A dark grey metal occasionally used in jewellery, particularly for imitations of haematite cameos. The constituents are about 67 per cent nickel and 30 per cent copper, with small quantities of iron, manganese and other substances. The melting-point is about 1300°C. The alloy is strong and has a high resistance to oxidization.

Monobromonaphthalene. An oily liquid of formula $C_{10}H_7Br$ used as a refractometer contact liquid (see *Refractometer*), as an immersion medium in the measurement of refractive index (q.v.), and as a diluent for heavy liquids in the measurement of specific gravity (q.v.). It has refractive index 1.66 and specific gravity 1.49.

'Montana jet'. Misnomer for obsidian.

'Montana ruby'. Misnomer for garnet.

'Mont Blanc ruby'. Misnomer for rose quartz.

Moonstone. (Potassium-aluminium silicate. S.G. 2.57; R.I. 1.52–1.53; H. 6.) The gem variety of orthoclase feldspar (see *Feldspar*), displaying a characteristic shimmering play of whitish or bluish light (adularescence). Moonstone is composed of a combination of orthoclase and albite (see *Feldspar*) arranged in layers, and it is the reflection of light from these layers that produces the sheen. The thinner the layers the bluer the sheen and the more valuable the stone. Moonstones are cut *en cabochon*, and to obtain the best effect the base of the cabochon must lie parallel to the layers.

Most moonstone comes from Ceylon, where it occurs as rough fragments in dykes and also as pebbles in the gem gravels. Other sources are India (which produces stones of unusual colour including brown, plum-blue and green), Burma (fine blue stones), Madagascar, Tanzania and the U.S.A. Some specimens, especially those from Ceylon, have peculiar internal features consisting of straight stress cracks with short branching arms – the effect is rather like an insect.

Moonstone may be imitated by glass (from which it may be distinguished by its double refraction [q.v.]). and by amethyst or synthetic white spinel heat-treated to produce the shimmering effect.

'Mop'. Trade term for pearl shell.

Mordant. The end of the belt or strap which passes through the buckle. In times when ornate buckles were worn the mordant was also frequently decorated. (See *Buckles*.)

Moresque. An Islamic form of surface decoration; an abstract and symmetrical pattern of interlacing curves and straight lines. It was introduced into European art in the sixteenth century and for a time was frequently used on the enamelled backs of watches, pendants and other items of jewellery. Another name for moresque is 'Spanish work'. (See also *Arabesque*.)

Morganite. (Beryllium-aluminium silicate. S.G. 2.70–2.90; R.I. 1.58–1.59; H. $7\frac{3}{4}$.) Transparent pink beryl (q.v.), named after the gem collector and banker

Moresque design for belt-harness by Virgil Solis (q.v.), about 1540

J.P. Morgan. It is found in Brazil, Madagascar and the U.S.A.

Morion. A name given to very dark brown, almost black, crystalline quartz.

Moro coral. Dark red Japanese coral.

Moroxite. A name for blue-green apatite (q.v.) from southern Norway.

Morse. A type of brooch or clasp for fastening the copes of the clergy. This was its ostensible purpose, but although some morses obviously were fixed to one side of the garment and linked to the other side with hooks or a pin, many were quite clearly purely decorative, and have holes or loops by which they could be sewn on.

Little is known about early morses, but the ninth-century Lothair crystal, a large medallion of rock crystal engraved in intaglio with scenes from the story of Susannah, appears to have been used as a morse. In the first centuries of the Middle Ages when the Church was almost the craftsman's only patron, the finest skills of the goldsmith were lavished on cope-morses. Some were decorated with champlevé enamel (q.v.), others set with precious stones and ancient cameos. In 1295 St. Paul's had 28 such morses. The shapes were various, although usually based on the circle, and the size was impressive: the surviving examples range from 5 to 7 inches in diameter.

In the fourteenth century opaque

249

champlevé enamel was largely superseded by translucent basse-taille enamel (q.v.) on silver. The shape was now usually a 4-lobed circle – a form taken from early medieval brooches, which the morse retained for some time after the form of secular brooches had changed. The style of the decoration was influenced by Gothic architecture. This is well illustrated in a fine morse in Aachen Cathedral depicting the Annunciation in an elaborate architectural frame decorated with silver flowers and pearls.

The increasing emphasis attached in the fifteenth century to the sheer beauty of jewels (see *Medieval jewellery*) to some extent affected the jewellery of the Church. A superb morse, said to have belonged to Pope Alexander VI and now in Washington, retains the form of a lobed circle and has as its theme the group of the Trinity, but the treatment is much freer than in earlier morses. The outer rims are of pierced and carved gold set with six large pearls, and out of the centre of the brooch rises the three-dimensional figure of God the Father, holding the Cross with his crucified Son.

During the sixteenth and seventeenth centuries large and splendid morses continued to be worn. Cellini was commissioned to make one for Pope Clement VII set with a large pointed diamond (see *Cellini*). While the forms of secular jewellery changed, and baroque decoration and a lavish display of faceted stones became the fashion, morses kept their traditional sculptural form as long as ecclesiastical jewels of the old and splendid type continued to be made.

Mosaic. A type of decoration which became popular in jewellery towards the middle of the nineteenth century. There were two types: Florentine mosaic, also known as *pietra dura*, and Roman mosaic. Florentine mosaic consisted of small pieces of cut stone (often coral, marble, malachite, turquoise, lapis-lazuli and opal), cemented in a pattern into recesses in, usually, a black marble background. The designs were often floral. In Roman

Part of a bracelet in Florentine mosaic, made about 1870

mosaic the inlays were of coloured glass in a glass background, and the designs were very often pictures of ancient monuments. The mosaics were made as small medallions which were framed generally in gold and made up into necklaces, bracelets, clasps and earrings. They were made in Italy and became popular as souvenirs at a time when travel was becoming easier and there was increasing interest in Italian history. (See *Nineteenth-century jewellery*.)

Roman mosaic is still made in Italy for the tourist trade.

Mosquito amethyst. Amethyst which contains minute platy inclusions of goethite.

'Moss'. Term for the inclusions in emerald which give the stone a cloudy appearance. (See *Emerald*.)

Moss agate. See *Agate*.

Moss opal. Milk opal with black dendritic inclusions.

Mother-of-emerald. Misnomer for either green fluorspar or prase.

Mother-of-pearl. The iridescent nacreous (q.v.) lining of the shell of pearl-producing molluscs. It has been used for inlays in jewellery and ornamental objects since Egyptian times, and is also carved. There is an old-established mother-of-pearl carving industry in Bethlehem. Several species of mollusc produce mother-of-pearl. (See *Shell*.)

'Mountain jet'. Misnomer for obsidian.

'Mountain ruby'. Misnomer for garnet.

Mourning jewellery. See *Memorial jewellery*.

English mourning ring of 1810; gold enamelled in black and white, with the hair of the deceased under glass. Victoria and Albert Museum

Mourning rings. During the seventeenth century it became the custom in England for special rings commemorating the deceased to be distributed to mourners at the funeral. The custom had originated at some time in the Middle Ages when rings belonging to the deceased were bequeathed to friends and relatives as a personal memorial. When the testator wished to leave rings to a large number of people some embarrassment was likely to result from the inevitable difference in value of the rings, and the custom therefore developed of giving instructions in the will for a series of identical rings to be made and distributed. The earliest known instance of this is a will of 1487 in which Sir John Shaw gave instructions for gold rings engraved with the Five Wounds of the Saviour to be made and given to sixteen of his friends. Similar bequests were made in wills of the sixteenth and early seventeenth centuries.

At this time there was no particular form for mourning rings; they followed the taste of the giver. At the same time rings enamelled with skulls were quite commonly worn (see *Memento mori jewellery*) as memorials of specific people. In the 1660s, however, a distinct type of mourning ring came into use. The hoop was engraved inside with the name and date of death of the deceased, and was usually enamelled on the outside with a foliage pattern or with a skeleton on a ground of black. The oval or circular bezel was set with a piece of rock crystal, beneath which was a representation of a skull or else the initials of the deceased in gold thread on a ground of silk or woven hair. The device of setting initials on hair-work under crystal appeared towards the end of the seventeenth century and was the forerunner of the hair jewellery (q.v.) so popular in the Victorian period.

By the second half of the seventeenth century the giving of mourning rings had become a fashionable custom and large numbers were distributed, the recipients often being little more than acquaintances. At Samuel Pepys's funeral 123 were given away. If they were to be distributed in such quantity they obviously could not be very costly, and in a number of wills the sum of one guinea is stipulated: nevertheless quite expensive in those days.

Skulls and skeletons continued to appear on mourning rings until about 1730, and then gradually fell from favour. At the same time there was a trend for the rings to be made without a bezel and for the inscription to be transferred from the inside to the outside of the hoop, where it was enamelled in the style known as *taille d'épargne* (q.v.). Sometimes the hoop was divided into small scrolled compartments each carrying a part of the inscription. There was a convention that married people were commemorated in black enamel and unmarried people in white.

Towards 1770 a new and more sentimental style appeared. This was a plain gold hoop with a large oval bezel which contained a miniature or a lock of hair and was covered with rock crystal. The scene depicted in the miniature was usually a weeping willow over a tomb or some similar symbol of grief. These were popular until the turn of the century (weeping-willow scenes made entirely out of hair-work were made in the Victorian period, but not as rings: see *Hair jewellery*). Another type had a hoop formed of

251

several strands of gold wire spreading towards the bezel, which consisted of a piece of crystal covering some plaited hair and set in a border of seed pearls. Sometimes coloured stones were set in mourning rings, but these were individual rings and not of the kind distributed in quantity at funerals, and in many cases they had probably originated as decorative rings in the late owner's possession and been converted into mourning rings by the addition of an inscription and a touch of black enamel.

In the nineteenth century mourning rings continued to be worn, but at a fairly early stage they lost their uniformity of character and ceased to be distributed wholesale at funerals. For the rest of the century they followed the styles of other memorial jewellery (q.v.).

Mouth blowpipe. See *Blowpipe*.

Muelich, Hans (1515–1572). Designer and goldsmith who worked at the court of Duke Albrecht V of Bavaria. Muelich was a skilled painter of portraits and miniatures, and between 1546 and 1555 recorded in a series of paintings on parchment the entire collection of jewels belonging to Duke Albrecht and his wife; these contribute considerably to our knowledge of the jewellery of the period. Muelich was born and died in Munich.

Muller's glass. See *Opal*.

Multi-facet diamond. American term for a diamond with a polished or faceted girdle (q.v.). It is not standard practice to polish the girdle, which is normally quite thin. (See *Diamond-cutting*.)

Muscle pearl. Small irregularly-shaped pearl found in the muscular tissue of the oyster. (See *Pearls*.)

Mussell-eggs. Regional American name for freshwater pearls.

Mussite. Diopside.

Mutton-fat jade. A greenish- or yellowish-grey variety of nephrite (see *Jade*), mostly used for carvings. It contains more magnesium and less iron than the commoner green nephrite.

'Mutzschen diamond'. Misnomer for rock crystal.

Mya yay. Burmese name for the best-quality translucent green jadeite. (See *Jade*.)

Myrickite (Calbenite). A variety of chalcedony (q.v.), impregnated with the red mineral cinnabar (mercuric sulphide). Most of the material comes from the U.S.A.

N

Nacre. A substance consisting mainly of crystalline carbonate of lime, secreted by certain molluscs. It is the iridescent material of which pearls are composed. (See *Pearls*.)

Nacreous. Composed of or covered with nacre.

Nacrescope. An instrument for the detection of cultured pearls by strong illumination of the body of the pearl. It has been superseded by the more efficient endoscope (q.v.). (See also *Pearls*.)

Narwhal ivory. See *Ivory*.

Nassak diamond. A flawless diamond originally weighing in the region of 90 carats, said to have been the eye in a statue of Shiva in a Hindu temple near Nassak, north-east of Bombay. In the early nineteenth century it fell into the hands of the East India Company and was sent to London, where it was re-cut into a triangular brilliant and sold in 1837 to the Marquis of Westminster, who wore it in the hilt of his dress sword. It remained in the family for almost a century, but was then sold to a Paris jeweller who exhibited it in America. It was subsequently bought by the gem-dealer Harry Winston, for whom it was refashioned as an emerald-cut stone weighing 43 carats. It is now in private ownership in America.

Nassau pearl. Conch pearl.

National Association of Goldsmiths of Great Britain and Ireland. The only national association established exclusively in the interests of retail jewellers. The association was founded in 1894 and is the parent of the Gemmological Association of Great Britain (q.v.). The N. A. G. offers a wide range of services to its members, including a special insurance scheme and an accounts clearing-house scheme, and operates an enquiry bureau which assists members with every kind of trade enquiry. Jewellers who need to identify a hallmark or are uncertain of the period of a piece of old jewellery, etc., can thus obtain expert help from the association. Through the association members can also have pearls and gemstones tested at the laboratories of the London Chamber of Commerce. Library facilities at the association's premises in St. Dunstan's House are available to members. The association runs two diploma courses: the Retail Jewellers' Course, designed for young people entering the trade, and a two-year correspondence course covering all aspects of the jeweller's work including the legal aspect. The official journal of the association is the *Watchmaker, Jeweller and Silversmith* (published monthly), and in association with the journal the N. A. G. sponsors the international watch and jewellery trade fair.

Natural glass. See *Obsidian, Tektite, Silica glass* and *Queenstownite;* also *Glass*.

Nautilus. See *Coque de perle* and *Shell*.

Navette. Another name for the marquise cut (q.v.).

Necklaces. An ancient and universal form of ornament, necklaces in very early times probably had some magical or religious significance in addition to their decorative value. Sculptures and carvings of the Mother Goddess nearly always represent her wearing a necklace, and in one Assyrian wall-sculpture she makes an offering of a necklace before the Tree of Life. In ancient Egypt necklaces and collars were dedicated in the temples, and were bestowed as marks of honour by the pharaoh in public ceremonies on the palace balcony.

Necklaces and collars in Egypt ranged from the comparatively simple to the extremely elaborate. There were several types of collar (these are described in greater detail under *Egyptian jewellery*), including the *usekh*, consisting of numerous rows of beads in a variety of materials, and the *shebiu*, in which the beads were thick and biconical. Splendid and elaborate pectorals were worn by royalty, richly inlaid with cornelian, lapis-lazuli, turquoise and other stones. The single-string necklaces worn by ordinary people were strung with amulets and beads; the beads were of a variety of materials including glass and faience (q.v.). The Egyptians invented a necklace-fastening which was a good deal more sophisticated than the usual method of knotting the strings; it consisted of two metal plaques in the shape of a knot, with a ridge on the lower plaque that locked into a groove on the upper plaque when the two 'knots' were placed one directly above the other.

Phoenician bead necklaces were very often of glass, since the Phoenicians had access to large quantities of raw material in the silica-rich sands along their coast. The glass beads are decorated with a rich variety of colours and patterns. Layers of different-coloured glass were fused together and drawn out in rods, which were then cut and ground to expose the coloured pattern. 'Wrapped' beads were made by drawing molten glass around a metal rod, and many beads were decorated by dragging glass of a contrasting colour across the surface with a wire.

The jewellery of the Greek world was gold jewellery: stones and glass were little used. Early examples of necklaces are the gold plaques embossed with figures of deities and mythical animals which were made in Rhodes; these were worn in a row as pectoral ornaments. (See *Greek jewellery* for illustration.) Later Greek necklaces are among the finest examples of Greek craftsmanship and attention to

Part of a Greek gold necklace with acorn pendants. Fourth century B.C. Ashmolean Museum, Oxford

detail. Often they consisted of small stamped units of sheet metal in the form of rosettes, threaded in a row by means of chenier at the back of the rosettes, and hung with gold pendants. Buds, acorns (see illustration), and pomegranates were popular motifs. The various parts of the necklace were decorated with painstaking care, and joins and spaces were masked with other small rosettes. Another type of Greek necklace consisted of pendants, often in several rows, hung from a very fine mesh strap of gold filigree; the strap looks woven, but it is in fact a complex type of loop-in-loop chain (see *Chain*). The Etruscans also used fine chain for necklace-straps, and hung them with stamped pendants of sirens, gods and centaurs. The bulla (an amulet) was a common Etruscan necklace ornament. (See *Etruscan jewellery*.)

During the Hellenistic period stones began to be used in Greek jewellery and one type of necklace consisted of linked stones in collets. The Romans adopted this type, and an attractive necklace set with sapphires, garnets and rock crystal, with a butterfly-shaped pendant, is illustrated under *Roman jewellery* (q.v.). Elaborate necklaces set with stones and pearls were a feature of Byzantine jewellery (q.v.).

The Celts developed a neck-ornament of a quite different kind: the torc, an incomplete circle of metal which was either large enough or flexible enough to slip over the wearer's head or round his neck. The torc apparently developed out of an Eastern custom of wearing an incomplete circle of thick gold wire round the neck as a convenient way of carrying money. These 'ingot torcs' were succeeded by flat crescent-shaped sheets of metal decorated with engraved patterns; they were of gold, silver and bronze. By the beginning of the Christian era the Celts of Western Europe were wearing heavy and impressive torcs of tubular type, with rounded terminals elaborately ornamented and sometimes decorated with enamel. Some were cast in solid bronze, some were of gold. The most famous example is the Snettisham torc. (See *Celtic jewellery* for illustration.)

Comparatively few necklaces have been found dating from the Dark Ages, but judging from the evidence necklaces of glass beads were much favoured. The beads are often brightly-coloured and patterned. Amber from the Baltic and the North Sea, and amethyst, probably obtained by trade, appear in Anglo-Saxon necklaces; amber was believed to have powers against witchcraft, and amethyst to protect the wearer from the ill effects of drink.

Necklaces were not worn in the first part of the Middle Ages; garments were high-necked and held by a brooch (see *Medieval jewellery*). With a change in fashion in the fifteenth century, accompanied by increasing luxury at Court, necklaces, chains and impressive collars of livery and orders of knighthood began to be worn. Devotional pendants (see *Devotional jewellery*) were popular and often sumptuously decorated. From the early part of the sixteenth century long gold chains were worn by both men and women. They were often heavy and several might be worn at once, or a chain and a jewelled collar might be worn together. A pendant often hung from the chain; the Tau cross (see *Devotional jewellery*) had been a popular pendant in the fifteenth century, and in the sixteenth century there was a vogue for pendants in the form of initials. Towards the end of the century these were superseded by superb enamelled figure pendants. (See *Renaissance jewellery*.)

The seventeenth century saw an increasing emphasis on faceted stones. Mounts and settings were delicately enamelled but the stones were now the main feature (see *Seventeenth-century jewellery*). Floral and ribbon designs were the prevailing style. Very pretty chains were made of enamelled links in flower and leaf patterns, and were worn as necklets and bracelets. (A number of these were found in the Cheapside hoard, q.v.) Strings of pearls were also popular as necklaces, particularly in the earlier part of the century.

By the eighteenth century jewellery was completely dominated by stones and in particular by the diamond (see *Eighteenth-century jewellery*), though coloured stones came into fashion in the 1760s and in some parts of Europe, particularly Spain, were never really out of fashion. The settings for diamond jewellery were usually of silver and were as inconspicuous as possible. Necklaces were a less important item of jewellery than earrings, brooches and aigrettes, but those worn at Court were magnificent. The famous diamond necklace of Marie Antoinette has gone down in history as one of the contributory causes of the French Revolution, in spite of the fact that the unfortunate Queen did not want it and never wore it. The necklace had been ordered some years previously by Louis XV for Mme. du Barry; he died before it was finished and in the succeeding reign Louis XVI and Marie Antoinette declined to buy it on account of the cost. A certain Jeanne Lamotte approached Cardinal Rohan, who was out of favour with the Queen, and told him that the Queen wished to purchase the necklace secretly and that he would be reinstated in her favour if he negotiated the purchase. The Cardinal was given a letter purporting to come from the Queen, and he obtained the necklace from the jewellers and gave it to Mme. Lamotte. She took it to England, had it broken up and sold the diamonds. The Cardinal had of course not paid for the necklace because the jewellers believed him to be acting for the Queen. When they applied to the Queen for payment the fraud was exposed and Mme. Lamotte was sent to prison. However, she paid a lighter price than many others involved in the affair: her husband was imprisoned and flogged, the Cardinal was exiled in disgrace, and the scandal did nothing to alleviate the growing unrest about the extravagance of the Court. The diamonds were never recovered, and Mme. Lamotte herself escaped from prison shortly afterwards and set about securing her husband's release by blackmailing the king.

The necklaces of the nineteenth century were less dramatic, but they were on occasion extremely ostentatious. Engraved gems had been a fashionable interest since the previous century, and the Empress Josephine's fondness for them (she had a necklace of twelve antique sardonyx intaglios, framed in diamonds) encouraged their wear in necklaces and bracelets. Heavy jewellery in neo-Classical style was worn in France at the beginning of the nineteenth century; later the styles became lighter and there was a return to naturalism, but many necklaces of the nineteenth century are still extremely heavy in design, with ornate gold settings which were often machine-made. The heaviness is partly attributable to the fashions for antique and exotic styles of ornament (see *Nineteenth-century jewellery*). At the same time, however, a number of delicate and charming necklaces were made, and the Romantic period of the '30s and '40s saw a vogue for necklaces of seed-pearls, fine gold chains, and ribbons crossed at the throat held with a jewelled button or slide. A great variety of materials were used in the necklaces of the Victorian era; apart from gemstones and pastes (garnets were very popular), there were cameos carved out of lava and jet, Italian mosaics, carved coral, ivory and amber (amber necklaces were briefly but intensely fashionable among aesthetic young ladies from 1878 to 1883). Silver necklaces were popular in the 1870s and Queen Victoria gave one to Jenny Lind. Towards the end of the century diamonds and pearls became fashionable and the dog-collar was a necessity; a jewelled necklace was sometimes worn below it.

In the necklaces of the Art Nouveau period the main focus was usually on the pendant; the best of these pendants are masterpieces (see *Art Nouveau jewellery*), and they normally hung on a fairly simple chain. The idea of an elaborate and often

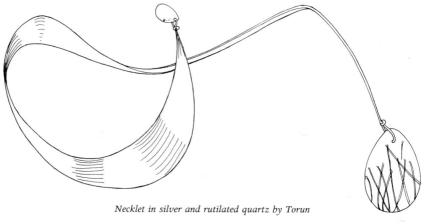

Necklet in silver and rutilated quartz by Torun

enamelled pendant on a simple chain or loop of silver wire has continued into contemporary jewellery, but the necklaces made during the last 20 years show in many cases a completely new concept of what a necklace can be – the forms are sculptural, and the necklace is one unit instead of a series of linked stones or a partnership between a reticent chain and an assertive pendant. Gem-set necklaces in the traditional style, which has not changed much since the eighteenth century, of course continue to be in demand and are an important part of the retail jeweller's stock-in-trade. It is these necklaces, with their matched and graduated stones, on which most of the finest diamonds, emeralds and rubies are lavished, for precious jewellery is of its nature conservative.

Necklet. A short necklace, not more than about 18 inches long. No distinction is usually made between necklaces and necklets. (See *Necklaces*.)

Needle files. See *Files*.

Needle stone. Sagenitic quartz.

Nef. A jewel in the form of a ship. Pendants of this form were very popular during the Renaissance (see *Renaissance jewellery*) among seafaring nations such as England and Spain.

Nepal diamond. A flawless pendeloque diamond of nearly 80 carats thought to have come from the mines of Golconda (q.v.). Until fairly recently it was owned by the Nepalese royalty, but it is now in the collection of the American gem-dealer Harry Winston.

Nephrite. See *Jade*.

'Nevada black diamond'. Misnomer for obsidian.

'Nevada diamond'. Misnomer for artificially decoloured obsidian.

'Nevada topaz'. Misnomer for obsidian.

'Nevada turquoise'. A misnomer for variscite. Nevada does produce turquoise.

Nevada wonderstone (S.G. about 2.53). A stone displaying alternate stripes of red and buff, sometimes with grey patches. It is a weathered volcanic rock, and appears in jewellery in the form of baroque tumbled stones. (See *Tumbling*.)

New Guinea cat's eye. Operculum.

'New jade'. A misnomer for yellowish-green bowenite (see *Serpentine*) exported from China as an imitation of jade.

New rock turquoise. Old Persian term for inferior turquoise or turquoise matrix (see *Turquoise*); also used in parts of the U.S.A. for turquoise which does not retain its colour well. (See also *Old rock turquoise*.)

New Zealand greenstone. Name for the dark green nephrite found in New Zealand. (See *Jade*.)

Niarchos diamond. A flawless diamond weighing 426.50 carats in the rough, found in the Premier mine in South Africa in 1954. It was owned by Sir Ernest Oppenheimer, chairman of De Beers, for a short period, but in 1956 was bought by the New York gem-dealer Harry Winston and cut into a pendeloque brilliant of 130 carats. (Two smaller stones were also obtained from the rough.) The large stone was subsequently bought by the Greek shipping magnate S. Niarchos, reputedly for two million dollars.

Nickel. A hard white metal increasingly used as an alloying metal, particularly for steel (q.v.). It increases the hardness of alloys in which it is used. Among its other qualities are malleability, ductility and high resistance to oxidization. The melting-point is 1445°C. Nickel is best known to the jeweller as a component of nickel silver (q.v.).

Nickel was known in quite early times but was not recognized as an element until the eighteenth century. The modern nickel industry began with the discovery of large deposits in North America in 1866.

Nickel silver (German silver). An alloy consisting of approximately 60 per cent copper, 20 per cent nickel and 20 per cent zinc. (There is no silver content.) The nickel makes the alloy hard and tarnish-resistant. Nickel silver bears some resemblance to silver but has a slightly yellowish-grey tinge; it is used in costume jewellery and may be seen unplated or electroplated with silver.

The alloy was first produced in Europe in the early nineteenth century as a substitute for silver. Many experiments to discover a suitable alloy were carried out in Germany and a copper/nickel/zinc alloy was developed there with similar properties to the modern nickel silver, which is why the name 'German silver' has sometimes been used for this alloy.

Nicolo. The name for a cameo or intaglio (qq.v.) cut in onyx; the design is cut in the white layer which is thin enough to be translucent, and the black base beneath this gives the stone a bluish tinge. The name may also be applied to onyx which has not been engraved.

Nicol prism (Nicol). A piece of Iceland spar (q.v.) cut and re-cemented in such a way that it transmits only one ray of polarized light. Used in the testing of gemstones for double refraction (q.v.).

Niello. A dark grey substance used at least since Roman times, and possibly much earlier, for decorating silver and less commonly gold. It is inlaid into recesses engraved in the metal and fired, in a similar way to champlevé enamel (q.v.). Niello is a mixture of metallic sulphides. Numerous recipes have at various times been published. According to Pliny the niello used in Roman times consisted of 3 parts silver, 2 parts sulphur and 1 part copper. Theophilus in the eleventh century used 2 parts silver, 1 part copper, $\frac{1}{2}$ part lead and a little sulphur. A later recipe from Augsburg gives 1 part silver, 1 part copper, 2 parts lead.

Cellini in his *Treatises* says that when he became a goldsmith's apprentice in 1515 the art of niello work had been almost forgotten and he applied himself to learning it from the masters of the past. Cellini's own instructions are: take 1 part silver, 2 parts copper, 3 parts lead and

half a handful of sulphur. Melt the silver and copper in a crucible, add the lead and stir until it is all well mixed, then empty in the sulphur and shake the ingredients in a flask to mix them. When the mixture is cool, crush it into grains and spread it evenly over the engraved recesses, spread a little powdered borax over it and heat the work gently on a wood fire. A twentieth-century craftsman (H. Wilson, 'Silverwork and Jewellery') commented that this method was 'workable but extremely hard'.

A fairly modern recipe for niello is 3 parts silver, 1 part copper, $\frac{1}{2}$ part lead and 5 parts flowers of sulphur. When the ingredients are thoroughly mixed and are still molten the niello is poured on to a steel slab. Before it cools it is beaten out thin. The required amount is ground up fairly fine and, mixed with a weak solution of borax or sal-ammoniac, placed in the recesses prepared for it. The work is gently heated (usually in a muffle kiln, q.v.) until the niello has melted and filled the recesses. When cool, the work is carefully cleaned with an emery stick, finished with Water of Ayr stone and given a final polish as for silver.

In earlier centuries the niello was usually inlaid into the engraved design, but the modern tendency is to use the niello as a background. The niello may be painted on instead of inlaid into recesses: this of course is a much cheaper process and the decoration is less durable. Niello is now more often seen on eastern than European goods, inlay of all types being a traditional eastern craft.

Niggerhead. A pearl-mussel (*Quadrula ebena*) with dark markings fished in the Mississippi valley, principally for its shell, which is used in buttons. Some pearls are also found. (See also *Pearls* and *Shell*.)

'Night emerald'. Misnomer for peridot. (See also *'Evening emerald'*.)

Nigrine. Black iron-rich rutile.

Nineteenth-century jewellery. The nineteenth century was an age of quickly-changing fashions and enthusiasms, particularly enthusiasms for the past. This is reflected very clearly in the jewellery, in which for the most part the only new elements were the technical processes, such as electroplating and machine-stamping (q.v.), which were employed. A genuinely new style was not seen until the emergence of Art Nouveau in the last decade of the century. Jewellery of high intrinsic value, made for wear at the Court and on state occasions, naturally reflects these changes of taste to a lesser extent than cheaper jewellery, since it is 'made to last', and it is accordingly the cheaper jewellery which is more characteristic of the age.

In the early years of the century Napoleon became Emperor and established a court which consciously imitated the splendour of Imperial Rome. The jewellery worn at Court was designed in the classical style, and such motifs as the laurel wreath, eagles and the Greek key pattern were prominent. Cameos in the classical style were extremely fashionable in the first decade of the century − hardstone antique cameos if possible, otherwise shell. (They remained popular, to a lesser degree, all through the century.) Magnificent parures set with precious stones returned to fashion for formal occasions. The standards were set by the Empress Josephine, who had been given what Napoleon was able to recover of the Crown Jewels and had them re-set for her own use. The 'classical' jewellery of this period is not a great success aesthetically; it is stiff, heavy and rather cold, and completely fails to capture the spirit of ancient work. The same failure is evident in all nineteenth-century revivals of past styles: the features may be carefully reproduced, but the piece 'feels' unmistakably modern.

By 1814, when the Bourbon monarchy was restored, France was impoverished by a succession of wars and it was good taste to wear little jewellery, or at least jewellery of little value. Paste and cut steel (q.v.) were worn, and Berlin iron jewellery (q.v.) was in favour. The diamonds and rubies of the Napoleonic Empire were replaced by amethysts, topazes and aquamarines, in gold settings which were often machine-made. Prosperity had returned, however, by the 1820s and high-class diamond jewellery was again made and worn. The predominant style was now naturalistic: flowers, butterflies and ears of wheat were the dominant motifs, set with rose-cut and brilliant-cut diamonds. Attempts were made at various times to achieve greater naturalism by the use of translucent green enamel for the leaves and coloured stones such as emeralds, rubies and turquoises for flowers and fruit. The jeweller who showed a spray of lilac in diamonds at the Paris Exhibition of 1867 had apparently had a real spray of lilac in front of him all the time he was working at it. This naturalism remained fashionable in precious jewellery until the 1870s. In France, diamond jewellery was also made in imitation of the eighteenth-century style.

Jewellery of lower intrinsic value was much subject to the vagaries of fashion. A fairly long-lasting fashion was the Romantic nostalgia for the Middle Ages, which had reached full strength in both France and England by the end of the '30s. Its manifestations in jewellery took the form of buckles, brooches and bracelets in the style of Gothic architecture, decorated with gargoyles, allegorical figures, angels, knights and their ladies, small figures copied from medieval sculptures, and so on. (See illustration.) Silver was the metal usually employed, and the stones were cabochon-cut. The best examples in this style are by Froment-Meurice (q.v.), who is said to have been the first to use medieval themes in jewellery. Another expression of the Gothic revival was the carving of ivory, tortoiseshell and other materials into twisting branches to form bracelets, and the extensive use of foliage and tracery in designs.

The Renaissance was also fashionable. The *ferronière* (q.v.) (a chain or ribbon worn encircling the forehead with a jewel in the centre) was the height of fashion

Nineteenth-century jewellery

French enamelled silver brooch in 'Gothic' style, about 1840. Musée des Arts Décoratifs, Paris

'Etruscan' gold brooch from a jeweller's catalogue of 1895

between about 1837 and 1844 and was thought suitable for both daytime and evening wear. The arabesques and strap-work of the sixteenth century were revived, jewelled hairnets and chains were worn. The French jeweller Frédéric Philippi produced pendants and decorated pins in the shape of centaurs, using the favourite Renaissance materials of baroque pearls and brightly-coloured enamels. Carlo Giuliano (q.v.), a Neapolitan jeweller who settled in England, was among the foremost interpreters of this style; his necklaces and pendants display a delicate use of antique forms and a mastery of enamels. The high-quality work of such jewellers as Giuliano was imitated in machine-made jewellery.

One of the most influential jewellers of the century was Fortunato Pio Castellani (q.v.), who was responsible for the vogue for jewellery in the Etruscan and Greek styles. He had opened a shop in Rome in 1814 and at first had been content to imitate the styles of contemporary French and English jewellery; on seeing some recently-discovered Etruscan jewels, however, he became interested in the idea of reviving classical jewellery and set about discovering the techniques that had been used by the Etruscans (see *Etruscan jewellery*). His workshops produced some very fine imitations of antique pieces, and after a time these became known abroad and the style was taken up by other jewellers, including Giuliano, the French jeweller Fontenay, and the English jewellers John Brogden and Robert Phillips. By the 1870s Greek, Etruscan and Roman motifs were appearing in cheap jewellery as well as that of the fashionable jewellers. (A mass-produced 'Etruscan' brooch of the '90s is illustrated.)

There were many other fashions for ancient or exotic styles, made topical by archaeological finds or political events. In the 1840s the French wars in Algeria stimulated an interest in Algerian orna-ments, and the knots and tassels of Algerian dress appeared on jewellery. In England, Layard's *Nineveh and its Remains* was published in 1848, and jewellery in Assyrian style was soon pro-duced; the best-known example is probably the gold bracelet made by John Brogden (q.v.) which reproduced an Ass-yrian relief showing the return of King Assurbanipal from the chase. Mariette's excavations in Egypt aroused an interest which resulted in the popularity of jewel-lery in the Egyptian style in the late 1860s, and Queen Victoria's assumption of the title Empress of India in 1876 made Indian-style jewellery all the rage. India returned to fashion ten years later when Indian jewellery was exhibited at South Kensing-ton; this time it was apparently real Indian jewellery that was worn, not European imitations. Discerning Vic-torians were by now beginning to react against the apparently endless succession of secondhand styles.

Two types of jewellery are especially characteristic of nineteenth-century England, and were not as subject to the whims of fashion as other kinds. The first of these is Scottish jewellery. Nineteenth-century romanticism and love of the picturesque would in any case have found Scotland appealing, but its popularity was assured by Queen Victoria's devotion to the country. Jewellery of silver set with cairngorms and 'pebbles' (usually agate) was made by Edinburgh firms and continued to be extremely popular until the 1880s. There was a similar vogue for Irish jewellery: the splendid penannular brooches of later Celtic jewellery were copied, with Victorian heavy-handedness, by the Dublin firm of West.

The second characteristically English type of jewellery (it was also popular in Germany and Scandinavia) was what has been called 'jewellery of sentiment'. This included jewellery worn as a token of love or friendship, and mourning jewellery. The categories often overlap: an example is hair jewellery (q.v.), in which a design was made out of a lock of hair from a friend, relative or sweetheart and mounted in a brooch, bracelet-clasp, etc. This might be worn as a token of sentiment for a distant friend, or as a memorial of the dead. The designs of memorial hair jewellery were often elaborately funereal – weeping willows bending over a tomb were particularly common. Hair jewellery was at its most popular in the Romantic period, during the earlier part of Victoria's reign; by the 1880s the hair was no longer made into patterns but was kept in a small compartment in a brooch, locket or ring. Mourning jewellery proper – the jewellery worn by widows for the prescribed period after their bereavement, and at Court during a period of official mourning – was of jet. The jet came from Whitby, where a thriving industry devoted to the production of carved and polished jet jewellery grew up in the space of a few decades, considerably encouraged by the death of the Prince

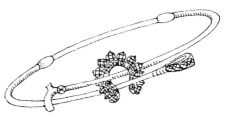

Diamond-set bracelet with horseshoe and crop, from a jeweller's catalogue of 1894

Consort. Miniatures form an important class of sentimental jewellery: they were set in bracelets, brooches, pendants, clasps and, of course, lockets, and towards the end of the century were exchanged by engaged couples, the girl's miniature being worn by the man on his watch-chain. In the second half of the century rings were given as tokens of friendship. The 'regard ring' was set with stones the initial letters of which spelt 'regard': the usual combination was ruby, emerald, garnet, amethyst, ruby, diamond. Names could be spelt in the same way. In the 1880s it was fashionable to give a ring bearing the word MIZPAH, meaning 'I will watch over thee'. Hearts were an extremely popular motif in the same period.

A vogue which began in England and quickly spread to France was for sporting jewellery. Its first manifestation was the horseshoe brooch of the 1860s. In the following decade suites of jewellery were made in the form of harness and riding gear, and in the 1890s golf-clubs in gold with pearl golf-balls, hunting horns and foxes' heads figured prominently in every jeweller's catalogue (see illustration).

Souvenir jewellery became popular as a result of the romantically-inspired desire to visit faraway places and the increasing ease with which this could be done. The country of particular interest at a time when Etruscan art was in fashion and excavations of Roman remains were proceeding was of course Italy. Italian mosaics (see *Mosaic*), delicately inlaid with coloured marble, were worn in necklaces and parures, and Italian shell

Nineteenth-century jewellery

cameos were very popular. Lava from Pompeii was carved at Naples into cameos of classical and medieval heads which, set in gold or silver, were linked to form necklaces and bracelets. Ivory, carved in Switzerland and at Dieppe, was worn in the form of bracelets, earrings and pendants. To a certain extent Scottish jewellery comes into this category, as perhaps do the earrings and brooches set with ammonites (fossils found in the Whitby district) which were worn in the mid-fifties. The latter in particular, and many other types of Victorian jewellery which have been mentioned, illustrate a certain earnestness which was characteristic of the Victorian mind: much as they loved jewellery for the sake of display, the Victorians were always pleased if in addition to being decorative it could be instructive.

The cheaper jewellery made from the 1860s onwards, on the other hand, is increasingly frivolous. Its only virtue was its novelty; it was in fact the beginning of costume jewellery, designed to be worn for a short time and discarded when it ceased to be fashionable. It ceased to be fashionable very quickly, and the motifs employed in this type of jewellery became ever more bizarre as presumably the search for something new became more desperate. The motifs that went in and out of fashion in the last four decades of the century include the following: insects (earwigs and woodlice as well as the prettier kind such as bees and dragonflies – there was even a vogue for house-flies, jewelled or enamelled and set under crystal, about 1867); birds, sometimes in birdcages; peacocks with mechanically-opening tails; goldfish-bowls (for earrings); animals of almost any kind; locomotives; and a range of utilitarian objects in which it is hard to see any aesthetic possibilities at all – watering-cans, lanterns, trowels, coal-scuttles, hammers, ladders and tongs. At the Paris Exhibition of 1867 were jewels for the hair which were kept constantly in motion by a battery worn inside the dress. A brooch made towards the end of the century is in

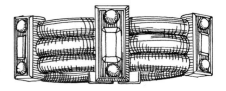

Gold bracelet set with emeralds and pearls. English, made about 1860

the form of a child's blackboard with noughts and crosses written over it, and an issue of the magazine *Queen* for 1880 singles out for mention a gold walnut studded with pearls and a Delft plate with a gold spoon on it.

Since jewellery was by the nineteenth century worn almost exclusively by women (men's dress was very sober and was as a rule only enlivened by a fob on the watch-chain), the changes in fashion reflect to some extent the increasingly active part being played by women in society. This is true particularly of the new boldness which entered jewellery in the 1860s, with flamboyant styles, bright colours and a general effect of massiveness and self-confidence. (The heavy bracelet illustrated is a good example.) At the beginning of the 1880s a reaction against this ostentation was felt in some circles and young ladies of aesthetic sensibilities wore no jewellery but a plain necklace of amber. This degree of restraint was not general, but on the whole much less jewellery was now worn in fashionable society than in the middle of the century, and some jewellers became seriously alarmed for their livelihood.

Among the most characteristic items of nineteenth-century jewellery are *bracelets*. These were worn all through the century and were particularly popular in the Romantic period, when two or three were worn on each arm. Favourite types at this time included the serpent bracelet (the serpent was fashionable for both bracelets and rings more or less throughout the century), link bracelets set with enamels or gems, bracelets made of plaited hair and of carved coral and ivory. In the 1860s the

Early Victorian comb in blue glass and gold

Oriental-style earring from a jeweller's catalogue of 1876

Assyrian, Greek and Egyptian styles came in, and there were bracelets in Algerian style with pendants. Towards the end of the century bangles were very fashionable, made of plain gold or jewelled. *Combs* (see illustration) are another characteristic item. They were often gold-topped and set with cameos or pearls. They were particularly popular between 1860 and 1880, when they might be worn either on the forehead so that the top formed a diadem, or stuck into the chignon at the back of the head. The body of the comb was generally tortoiseshell. Among other jewellery for the head, the *ferronière* was extremely fashionable in the late 30s, and the diamond *tiara* in the last two decades of the century. Towards the end of the century small diamond pins and brooches were also worn in the hair. The wearing of *earrings* fluctuated. Popular in the '30s, they went through a period of neglect in the '40s, came back into favour in the 1850s, and after 1860 were worn consistently for both daytime and evening, becoming longer and longer until by 1870 they sometimes touched the shoulders. Many were in the Egyptian, Etruscan and Assyrian styles (see illustration). Small earrings were also worn in this period, and the designs included novelty-motifs such as flies, horseshoes, croquet-mallets and ladders. By the 1880s small earrings replaced the large ones, and in the last part of the century earrings were hardly worn at all. *Necklaces* were of many types. From the '30s to the '60s there were long fine gold chains, fairly short jewelled or bead necklaces, and – an

English fashion that lasted for many years – ribbons crossed at the throat and held with a brooch. The *croix à la Jeannette* (an antique form consisting of a cross hanging below a heart) was a fashionable pendant. Pendants were particularly common on necklaces from the '60s to the mid-80s; they might be in the popular Greek or Etruscan styles (amphorae, masks, etc.), medallions, or a modest locket. In the last part of the century the dog-collar, set with diamonds or pearls if one could afford it, was the height of fashion, and another necklace might be worn as well. Pearls were much favoured. *Brooches* were often fitted with a ring or hook so that they could be worn as pendants, and quite often had small pendants hung from them. Some brooches with such designs as birds, butterflies and flowers were set on springs so that they vibrated with every slight movement. Brooches were particularly vulnerable to the latest craze, and display the obsession with novelty to its full extent. In the last part of the century the lace-brooch, a small jewelled pin worn in the lace at the neck or used to attach a shoulder-bow, was very popular, and a new type was the bar-brooch, with a fashionable motif set in the centre of a horizontal gold bar. *Rings* were popular in the 1840s and always worn to some extent. They were often enamelled

263

in the earlier part of the century and might be set with lava cameos, mosaics, etc., as well as gemstones. The gipsy ring, in which the stone was set deep in the metal, appeared about 1875. The *parure* was very popular at the beginning of the century; for those unable to afford precious stones there were matching sets in coral, mosaic, seed-pearls, turquoise, etc. In the middle of the century parures were heavy and there was much chiselled and chased gold in evidence. These heavy sets of jewellery were thought extremely vulgar by the mid-80s and large parures ceased to be worn in fashionable society.

Throughout most of the nineteenth century gold was the usual metal for jewellery. In the '70s and '80s there was a fashion for 'coloured' gold: the metal was dipped in an acid solution which removed the base metals from the surface, leaving a thin layer of pure gold covered with minute holes. The effect was a soft bloom on the surface. Various alloys were used as substitutes for gold, but in England the use of low-carat golds (9, 12 and 15-carat) was made legal in 1854 and there was subsequently less demand for imitation metals. Experiments in electroplating (q.v.) were made in the early years of the century, and electroplated gold and silver were commercially developed from the 1840s onwards. Silver completely replaced gold in popularity in the 1880s, and fairly heavy silver necklaces and silver chains and lockets were fashionable for daytime wear. (See *Birmingham* for an account of the disastrous effects of the boom in silver.) By this time machine-stamping (q.v.) was well established as a means of mass-producing cheaper jewellery, and the novelty brooches of this period were mostly made in this way. Silver went out of fashion in the '90s and was thought vulgar. Platinum made its first appearance in this century; it was used in jewellery as early as 1828, and in 1855 Fontenay used it for some of the settings in a diamond diadem, but it only began to be at all widely used in the last years of the century, when its strength and durability were found very useful in

The brooch of the Empress Eugénie, set with diamonds from the Crown jewels. Louvre

the delicate diamond jewellery then in fashion. In the first part of the century both collet and claw settings were fashionable. The pavé setting, which had been in use in the eighteenth century, became very popular towards the middle of the century and at about the same time the illusion setting, which increased the apparent size of the stone, was also much favoured. Enamelled settings were fairly popular at most times, particularly of course in imitations of Renaissance jewellery, but in the mid-70s a trend towards unobtrusive settings began and continued until the end of the century.

The parures worn at Court and on important social occasions were usually of diamonds, emeralds or rubies. Diamond jewellery on the whole declined in popularity during the first half of the nineteenth century, but became fashionable again in the 1850s at the luxurious court of Napoleon III (see illustration). In the second half of the century diamonds became increasingly popular, partly owing to the Empress Eugénie's liking for them and partly owing to the discovery of the vast deposits in South Africa. From the mid-70s jewels began to be set with diamonds only, and fifteen years later rubies, emeralds and sapphires were quite unfashionable. The solitaire ring, set with a single large diamond, became popular in the 1880s and was worn by men as well as women. Modifications of the brilliant cut (q.v.) began to be introduced in an attempt to improve the diamond still further. Pearls, in favour throughout the century, increased in popularity after 1850 and also increased in size; several strings of them were worn round the neck.

For those who could not afford precious stones there was a wide range of other gemstones and ornamental materials. Garnets are always associated with Victorian jewellery; they were extremely popular, particularly the Bohemian pyrope garnets, cut en cabochon or faceted and worn in tiers. The orange hessonite garnets and green demantoids were also quite common. Topazes were very popular between 1810 and 1830, and were worn in rivière necklaces emulating the diamond necklaces of the wealthy. Amethyst, turquoise, aquamarine, malachite, cornelian and agate were other popular coloured stones. There was a great increase in the use of paste ('suitable only for actresses' declared a fashion-paper in 1821). Marcasite became fashionable in the middle of the century and was set pavé or in the frames of medallions; the settings

were now machine-made. Opal was a popular stone, particularly in the latter part of the century, and since large deposits had been discovered in Australia in 1849 it was readily available.

Etiquette prescribed that dress jewels should not be worn during the day. For morning wear such materials as jet, coral, ivory and tortoiseshell were fashionable. (The lava cameos, Italian mosaics and hair jewellery previously mentioned would also be suitable.) Jet was by no means confined to mourning jewellery but enjoyed a general popularity for most of the century, particularly in the mid-Victorian period when large snake-bracelets in carved jet were fashionable. Coral was extremely popular between 1845 and 1865 and was thought particularly suitable for young girls. It was worn both in its natural branching form and carved; the carving was usually done by Italians, but the English jeweller Robert Phillips produced fine jewellery in carved coral. Ivory and tortoiseshell were also carved. Tortoiseshell piqué (see *Tortoiseshell*) was fashionable in the 1860s. Seed-pearls were also popular for morning wear in the first half of the century; they were used in various ways, including the decoration of hair jewellery.

In the 1890s a reaction made itself felt against the ostentation and triviality that had been a feature of so much nineteenth-century decorative art. In its more conservative form this reaction meant the wearing of less jewellery and the appearance of more delicate designs. In its extreme form it produced Art Nouveau, which by the turn of the century was no longer an experimental style favoured by a small group but a commercially-viable style accepted by fashionable society, and affecting the design of both the most valuable and the cheapest pieces of jewellery. (See *Art Nouveau jewellery*.)

Further examples of nineteenth-century jewellery are illustrated under *Berlin iron jewellery, Bracelets, Brogden, Castellani, Diadems, Earrings, Falize, Froment-Meurice, Giuliano, Hair jewellery, Mourning jewellery, Mosaic,* and *Rings*.

O

Obsidian. (Glass. S.G. 2.33–2.42; R.I. about 1.49; H. 5.) A natural glass containing 66–72 per cent silica, formed by the rapid cooling of volcanic lava. Obsidian was extensively used by primitive societies in jewellery and for arrow-heads, etc., and is still sometimes used in modern jewellery. Although mostly of an uninteresting black or grey colour it often has an attractive sheen caused by a parallel arrangement of small bubbles or inclusions. Yellow, brown, red and – rarely – green obsidian is also found. 'Flowering obsidian' is a variety with round inclusions of a white mineral on a black ground, used ornamentally in America.

Most of the obsidian used in jewellery comes from North America: Arizona; California, Colorado, Nevada and New Mexico are all important sources. The obsidian used by the Aztecs for mirrors, masks, ear ornaments and weapons came from vast mines in the state of Hidalgo, Mexico, and that used by the Maya came from quarries at La Joya in Guatemala. Other sources of obsidian include Hawaii, Japan and Iceland.

Obus. Name for a stone cut in such a way that its outline is that of an oblong brought to a point at one end (i.e. five-sided). The arrangement of the facets follows that of the step cut. (See *Gem-cutting*.)

'Occidental'. An almost meaningless word when prefixed to the name of a gemstone; it may mean that the stone was literally found in the Western Hemisphere, or that it is of inferior quality, or that it is not the stone it pretends to be at all. (See also *'Oriental'*.)

Occidental agate. Poor quality agate.

Occidental cat's eye. Quartz cat's eye.

'Occidental diamond'. Misnomer for rock crystal.

'Occidental topaz'. Misnomer for citrine.

'Occidental turquoise'. Misnomer for odontolite.

Ocean-spray. Satin spar (gypsum).

Octahedrite. Alternative name for anatase.

Octahedron. An eight-sided crystal form resembling two pyramids, each formed of four equilateral triangles, placed base to base. It is one of the forms in which minerals crystallize in the cubic system (see *Crystal systems*), and for many centuries diamonds occurring in this form were simply sawn in half across their width and worn without further cutting. (See *Diamond* and *Diamond-cutting*.)

Octavo. A Brazilian unit of weight for gemstones: $17\frac{1}{2}$ carats.

Odontolite (Bone turquoise, Fossil turquoise). (S.G. usually 3.0–3.2; R.I. 1.57–1.63; H. 5.) A blue stone resembling turquoise. It consists of the fossilized bones or teeth of mastodon and other extinct animals, and the blue colour is due to impregnation by the ferrous phosphate mineral vivianite. The original organic material in the odontolite is largely replaced by minerals, mainly apatite, and the specific gravity of different specimens is therefore variable. It is generally higher than that of turquoise (2.60–2.85), however, which may be useful in distinguishing the two. It also shows traces of its

267

organic structure if viewed under a strong lens.

Odontolite is found at Simmore, near Auch, in southern France.

Oeil de boeuf. See *Oxeye.*

'Off-colour'. Trade term for diamonds with a yellowish or brownish tinge.

Oil pearls. See *Antilles pearls.*

Oilstone. A smooth stone used, when moistened with oil, for sharpening jewellers' tools.

Old English cut. American name for the eight cut or single cut (18 facets including table and culet); not to be confused with the English brilliant (30 facets including table and culet). (See *Diamond-cutting.*)

Old mine cut. Term for the old-fashioned brilliant cut in which the stone was cushion-shaped (q.v.) and had a high crown. (See also *Diamond-cutting.*)

Old rock turquoise. Old Persian term for turquoise (q.v.) of fine quality; also used in parts of the U.S.A. for good-quality turquoise which retains its colour. (See also *New rock turquoise.*)

Olive. American trade term for an elongated bead drilled along its length.

Olivine. See *Peridot.*

Onegite. A light amethyst-coloured sagenitic quartz (q.v.) from Lake Onega in Russia.

'Once the weight'. Term used in the calculation of the price of pearls. (See *Pearls.*)

Onyx. (See *Chalcedony.*) Chalcedony with alternating straight black and white bands. It is used for cameos and intaglios, which are carved in such a way that the relief is in one colour and the background in the other. The black onyx used in jewellery has nearly always been stained. (See *Dyeing of gemstones.*)

Onyx alabaster. Onyx marble, q.v.

Onyx marble. Stalagmitic calcite (see *Calcite*) usually showing bands of delicate colour. The name is strictly speaking a misnomer, since onyx is a banded form of chalcedony (q.v.). The onyx marbles generally have a translucent white ground veined with coloured fissures; the colours, which are caused by the infiltration of metallic oxides, include amber, green and orange. The effect is very attractive, and although the material is very rarely encountered in jewellery because of its softness it is extensively used for the manufacture of small ornamental objects such as cigarette-boxes.

Onyx marble occurs very widely but in only a few places are the deposits systematically worked. There are important deposits in Algeria and Mexico. The Mexican stone (white or green, veined with orange and brown) was highly prized by the Aztecs, who used it in the building of their temples, and the name 'Tecali marble' by which the stone is known in America is a corruption of the Aztec word 'teocali', meaning 'temple'. Marble similar to the Mexican type is also found in Argentina and Arizona. The stalagmitic marble veined with brown and amber found in Gibraltar is known as 'Gibraltar stone' and is used mainly for tourist souvenirs. A variety with bright yellow banding from the Karibib district of South-West Africa is known locally as 'aragonite'. Fibrous calcite, which has a pleasant silky lustre when polished, is known as 'satin spar' – a name also used for a type of gypsum (q.v.).

'Onyx obsidian'. Misnomer for obsidian with parallel banding.

Opal. (Amorphous hydrated silica. S.G. 1.98–2.20; R.I. 1.44–1.46; H. $5\frac{1}{2}$–$6\frac{1}{2}$.) A gemstone highly prized for its beautiful play of colours. Opal differs from most gemstones in that it does not have a crystalline form but is basically a hardened jelly. As the jelly cooled, fine films of material formed which, having a different refractive index (q.v.) from the main body of the stone, produce an interference (q.v.) effect when reflecting light, and thus display a flash of prismatic colour.

There are four main varieties of precious opal. *White opal* has a light, milky body colour with the characteristic iridescence. *Black opal*, the most valuable variety, has a black, dark blue or grey body colour showing a vivid flash of colour. *Fire opal* is a translucent or transparent flame-red or yellow stone which may or may not show iridescence. *Water opal*, sometimes called *hyalite* or *Muller's glass*, is a clear colourless stone with a brilliant flash of colour. A fifth type, *harlequin opal*, a variety found in Czechoslovakia, has small points of changing colour.

Unusual types of opal are *hydrophane*, a normally opaque stone which becomes transparent and iridescent when immersed in water, and *cacholong*, a bluish-white variety particularly prized in the East, which has a porcelain lustre and the curious quality of being so porous that it will stick to the tongue. Opal often acts as a fossilizing agent, and opalized shell, wood and bone may be used ornamentally. *Common opal*, which lacks iridescence and is usually of a whitish colour, has little value, but it is sometimes found in attractive colours such as cherry-red (in Mexico) and may then be cut for use in jewellery.

Fire opals may be faceted, but other opals are cabochon-cut to display the movement of colour. Opals are sometimes seen which consist of a thin layer of precious opal on its matrix, which acts as a backing bringing out the colours in the opal. This type of stone, a true opal, may be confused with the opal doublet, in which a thin plate of precious opal is cemented on to a backing of common opal, black onyx or black glass (the black brings out the colours). In doublets the artificial join can be seen with a hand lens. (See also *Doublet*.) The material known as *opal matrix* consists of small patches of precious opal cut complete with its matrix.

Opals require careful handling. Being porous, they must not be immersed in any dirty liquid, and they must not be subjected to heat, as this would dehydrate them. They are liable to shrink slightly in cold weather, which must be borne in mind when the stone is set, and they are easily fractured and fairly easily scratched.

These qualities doubtless help to account for the superstition, prevalent in the nineteenth century, that opal is unlucky. This belief is generally attributed to the influence of Sir Walter Scott's widely-read novel 'Anne of Geierstein' in which an opal brings misfortune to its owner. Queen Victoria was unimpressed by the superstition and gave many opals as presents.

Opal was probably introduced into Europe from India, as the name is derived from the Sanskrit word 'upala', meaning a precious stone. It was greatly admired by the Greeks and Romans, who obtained their opal from the mines near Červenica in Czechoslovakia (formerly the Hungarian Vörösvágás). These mines were worked for many centuries by the local peasants and supplied almost all the world's fine opal until the Australian opal fields were discovered. Although the mines are now in Czechoslovakia the stones produced from them continue to be known as Hungarian opals.

Another ancient source of opal is Mexico, where the deposits were probably known to the Aztecs. However, the mines have been systematically worked for only about a hundred years. Fire opal is the most important product; other types of opal occur but are inferior to those found in Australia.

Australia is now the main source of precious opal. The first discovery was made in 1849 and there are now numerous mines in Queensland and New South Wales. The opal occurs as *boulder opal* (thin veins of opal penetrating boulders of hard rock) or *seam opal* (patches of precious material in seams of common opal between layers of sandstone or basalt.) The famous White Cliffs opal field, discovered in 1889 by a prospector hunting a wounded kangaroo through the bush, produces large quantities of seam opal and it is here that the opalized fossils are found. Black opal was first found in 1903 at Lightning Ridge, and is now also mined at Andamooka. Rich deposits of white opal were discovered at Coober Pedy in 1915. Seam opal is usually mined by sinking a shaft to the layer of 'opal dirt' which lies immediately below a layer of very hard rock known as bandstone, and gouging out the opal from the wall with a knife or spike. It is usually cut and fashioned locally.

Opal agate. Opal occurring in alternate bands with chalcedony (q.v.).

Opalescence. The pearly or milky light seen in some gemstones, including moonstone and some opals, caused by the reflection of light from particles in the stone. The word is sometimes used to refer to iridescence (q.v.), which is a different phenomenon.

Opalescent cat's eye. Confusing name for chrysoberyl cat's eye. (See *Cat's eye*.)

Opal glass. Milky-white glass used for imitation gemstones. Precious opal itself is not much imitated by glass. (See *Glass* for physical characteristics.)

Opalized wood. Fossilized wood in which the organic material has been replaced by opal (normally common opal).

Opalite. Impure common opal. (See *Opal*.)

Opal matrix. See *Opal*.

Open setting

Open setting. A stone-setting in which the pavilion facets of the stone are open to the light; used for transparent stones, particularly diamond.

Openwork. Metalwork which is not 'solid'; it may be filigree (q.v.) which is not fixed to a ground of sheet-metal, or sheet-metal pierced with holes, as in the 'opus interassile' (q.v.) of Roman and Byzantine jewellery. (See also *Pierced work*.)

Operculum ('**Shell cat's eye**'). (Calcareous and organic. S.G. 2.70–2.76; H. about $3\frac{1}{2}$.) The 'door' of the shell of the sea snail *Turbo petholatus*; it closes over the aperture when the snail has retired into its shell and rests on the animal's back behind the shell when it is travelling. The snails occur in great numbers in the waters between northern Australia and Indo-China, and the opercula, which are usually between $\frac{1}{2}$ an inch and 1 inch in diameter and domed on one side, are used locally in jewellery and in some parts as currency. Quantities of them were bought by American servicemen in the Second World War. The operculum is not chatoyant; the term 'cat's eye' refers to its shape and colouring. The centre is generally green, turning to yellow and white at one edge and reddish-brown at the other. The flat undersurface, which is the side attached to the animal, is covered with a brownish skin of conchiolin (q.v.) and shows spiral growth-lines.

Optic axis. The direction of travel in a doubly-refracting stone (see *Double refraction*) in which light is not split up into two rays but behaves as though the mineral were singly-refracting. In crystals of the tetragonal, hexagonal and trigonal systems (see *Crystal systems*) there is one such direction, parallel to the vertical crystallographic axis, and these crystals are accordingly termed uniaxial. In crystals of the monoclinic, triclinic and orthorhombic systems there are two such directions and the optical qualities are much more complex; these crystals are termed biaxial.

'**Opus interassile**'. Latin name for the openwork (q.v.) which became popular in late Roman jewellery and continued in use in Byzantium (see *Roman jewellery* and *Byzantine jewellery*). It consisted of sheet-metal with patterns pierced out of it with a chisel.

Orbicular. Term applied to a mineral containing solid spherical inclusions, usually of contrasting colour to the body of the stone. Mainly jasper (q.v.).

'Oregon jade'. Misnomer for green jasper, also for other massive green stones found in Oregon or California.

Orient. Name given to the characteristic sheen of fine pearls. It is produced by the combination of two optical effects; one is the interference of light (q.v.) at the thin films which make up the nacreous layer of the pearl, and the other is diffraction of light (q.v.) caused by the same films. (See also *Pearls*.)

'Oriental'. As the prefix to the name of a gemstone, this often indicates that the stone is genuine or of fine quality. It is also sometimes used in a misnomer for corundum, prefixed to the name of a stone which is similar in colour – 'Oriental emerald' is thus green sapphire. (See subsequent entries). (See also *'Occidental'*.)

'Oriental alabaster'. Old name for the stalagmitic calcite now generally known as onyx marble (q.v.).

Oriental agate. Agate of good quality.

'Oriental almandine'. Misnomer for purple-red sapphire.

'Oriental amethyst'. Misnomer for sapphire of the colour of amethyst.

'Oriental aquamarine'. Misnomer for blue-green sapphire resembling aquamarine.

Oriental baroque. Trade term for baroque salt-water pearl, as distinct from baroque freshwater pearl.

'Oriental cat's eye'. Misnomer for girasol (q.v.) sapphire. Also used for chrysoberyl cat's eye. (See *Cat's eye*.)

'Oriental chrysoberyl'. Misnomer for yellowish-green sapphire.

'Oriental chrysolite'. Misnomer for greenish-yellow chrysoberyl or sapphire.

'Oriental emerald'. Misnomer for green sapphire.

Oriental jasper. Bloodstone.

'Oriental moonstone'. Misnomer for girasol (q.v.) sapphire, but also used of genuine moonstone.

Oriental pearl. Common trade term for natural pearls produced by the *Pinctada* (i.e. not freshwater pearls, mussel pearls, etc.). Also used for pearls from the Persian Gulf and pearls from the East generally. (See *Pearls*.)

Oriental ruby. Recognized trade term for rubies from Burma.

Oriental sapphire. American trade term for royal-blue sapphire.

'Oriental topaz'. Misnomer for yellow sapphire.

Orleans pastes. Glass imitations of engraved gems made at the beginning of the eighteenth century by Homberg, who copied the collection of the Duke of Orléans, Regent of France. (See also *Cameos*, *Intaglios*, *Paste* and *Tassies*.)

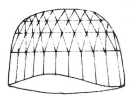

Side view of the Orloff diamond

Orloff diamond. A famous large Indian diamond now in the Diamond Treasury in Moscow. Its early history is largely a matter of legend. According to one theory it was the stone described by Tavernier on his visit to India in 1665 as the Great Mogul (q.v.). In this case it had previously belonged to Shah Jahan and was at the time in the treasury of his son Aurang Zeb; later it was seized by Nadir Shah when he captured Delhi in 1739.

According to an old legend, however, the diamond was originally set as one of the eyes in a statue of Brahma in a temple in Madras, from which it was stolen by a French soldier with the help of a dishonest attendant (later murdered). The soldier sold it to the captain of an English ship for £2,000, and the captain sold it in London for £12,000. It eventually reached

271

Amsterdam and was bought for £90,000 by Prince Gregori Orloff, who was out of favour with the Empress Catherine II of Russia and hoped by this gift to placate her. Apparently he was unsuccessful, but the Empress accepted the gift and the diamond was set in the top of the Russian Imperial sceptre, where it remains. It is a fine bluish-green stone weighing just under 200 carats and still retains its original Indian rose-cut, one of the very few stones to do so.

Ormer. See *Abalone*.

Ornamental stones. Opaque stones of attractive colour which are used for fashioning ornamental objects or for decorating the façade of buildings, etc. (e.g. malachite, serpentine, marble). It is not a precise classification. Opaque or nearly-opaque stones which command a high price, such as jade and lapis-lazuli (qq.v.), are not usually described as ornamental stones. On the other hand the term is sometimes used for translucent stones such as agate (q.v.), which occur fairly commonly and are not usually mounted in gold. (See also *Semi-precious stones*.)

Orthoclase ` feldspar. (S.G. 2.56; R.I. 1.52–1.53; H. 6–6½.) This name is used for the transparent yellow stones found in Madagascar which are in fact only one variety of orthoclase feldspar. The stones are mainly cut for collectors. (See also *Moonstone* and *Feldspar*.)

Ottonian jewellery. See *Medieval jewellery*.

Owl-eye agate. Eye agate (see *Agate*) with a pair of similar 'eyes'.

Ox-blood coral. Coral of a deep red colour – highly valued.

Ox eye. A name for labradorite.

Ox-eye agate. Similar to *owl-eye agate* (q.v.).

Oxidation. See *Oxidization*.

Oxide. A compound of oxygen with another element or elements. Quartz and corundum are oxides. (See also *Oxidization*.)

Oxidization. The process in which an element or compound unites with oxygen to form an oxide (q.v.). The copper with which silver is nearly always alloyed oxidizes on heating, so that silver has to be immersed in an acid solution (see *Pickle*) after heating to remove the copper oxide. Oxidization has to be prevented during soldering or a clean joint cannot be made (see *Soldering*). Firestain (q.v.) develops if silver is annealed (see *Annealing*) too often in air. The terms 'oxidization' and 'oxidation' are commonly used to refer to the process by which silver is coloured chemically. In fact oxidization is not involved because the process depends on the effect on silver of sulphur and its compounds; it is described under *Colouring of metals*.

Pacific cat's eye. A name for operculum.

Padparadscha(h). A name sometimes given to the rare orange-red variety of corundum, or to its synthetic equivalent. The name is a corruption of the Sinhalese word for lotus-flower.

Paillons. Small pellets of solder.

Painted enamel. A type of enamelling in which the enamels are applied to the surface as in painting, with no metal dividing the colours. Also known as Limoges enamel, although by no means all painted enamels were produced at Limoges. (See *Enamel*.)

Palladium. A white precious metal belonging to the platinum (q.v.) group, isolated at the beginning of the nineteenth century but only used to any appreciable extent in jewellery in the past few decades. Like platinum, palladium is untarnishable, quite highly reflective and has good working properties. It weighs little more than half as much as platinum (a great advantage) and is less than half the price. In spite of this, however, it has never become popular in Britain, although in America, where much research into its properties was carried out between the two world wars, it has long been widely used. Palladium is alloyed with a small quantity of ruthenium (another metal of the platinum group) for use in jewellery. There are no legal standards for its quality in Britain. Sources and refining methods are the same as for platinum (q.v.).

Pampilles. Cascades of pendant stones.

Papal rings. Very large rings, mostly dating from the fifteenth and sixteenth centuries, made of base metal and set with stones of little value, bearing the arms of popes, cardinals, etc, and often decorated with other ecclesiastical symbols such as the crossed keys, mitres, and the symbols of the evangelists (see illustration). These rings are traditionally known as 'papal rings' but their precise purpose is something of a mystery. It is exceedingly improbable that the Popes of the Renaissance period, who had a taste for fine jewellery and precious stones, would have worn rings of bronze or copper set with paste, crystal or some other almost worthless stone. Moreover the rings are so massive and cumbersome that one cannot imagine anyone wearing them, even on the thumb, for long. The considerable number of these rings and the fact that some of them are duplicated make it even less likely that they could have been the personal rings of the Popes.

Various theories have been advanced as to the use of the rings, of which the most plausible is that they were souvenirs given by the Pope to pilgrims. This explains their number and their cheapness, but not the symbols found on them (some, for instance, bear the arms of bishops). Another suggestion is that they were carried as credentials by Papal envoys, etc. Rings often were used in this way,

Papal ring

273

and the theory is based on the fact that some papal rings bear the arms both of the Pope and of a king: the second set of arms would be those of the king to whom the messenger was accredited. It is possible that some papal rings were used for this purpose, but a smaller ring would have served just as well and been much more convenient. Yet another theory is that they were rings of investiture conferred on new holders of high Church offices, such as cardinals, but many of them seem to have been made for people who never reached high office, or only did so at a time after the ring was made. And although the Pope did present rings to the cardinals at their consecration these were rings of considerable value usually set with the traditional sapphire.

The Pope's personal ring, known as the Fisherman's ring or *anulus piscatoris*, is described under *Ecclesiastical rings*, as are the rings of cardinals, bishops, etc.

Panama pearls. Black or slate-blue pearls from the Gulf of Mexico.

Paradise jasper. Local name for variegated red jasper from Morgan Hill, California.

Paragon pearls. Unusually large spherical pearls. Also a trade name for some imitation pearls.

'Paris pearls'. Trade name for imitation pearls.

Parting sand (Parting compound). A substance sprinkled over the faces of a two-part mould and the surface of the pattern to prevent the parts of the mould and the pattern from sticking to each other. French chalk (q.v.) and brick-dust are among the substances used. (See *Casting*.)

Parure. A matching set of jewellery, usually consisting of a necklace, earrings, brooch and bracelet. (See also *Demi-parure*.) Much eighteenth-century jewellery (q.v.) was in the form of parures.

Paste. This is the name given to a glass composition used for imitation gemstones, or to imitation stones made of glass. The origin of the term is not known: the derivation usually suggested is from the Italian word 'pasta', but it is rather difficult to see a connection.

The first glass was probably made many thousands of years ago on the shores of the eastern Mediterranean. Here the essential constituent of glass, silica, was readily available in the form of a suitable sand. Sand by itself would not have been a satisfactory material because for fusion it requires a higher and more sustained heat than is obtainable from a wood fire, and the resulting glass is in any case difficult to mould and colour. To lower the melting-point an alkali, probably in the form of soda or potash, would have been added, and since this would have made the glass soft and soluble another constituent, probably lime from seashells, would have been added to make it hard. Traces of iron could be used for colouring.

Because of the shortage of fuel the early glass-makers were probably itinerant, and so the use of glass spread through countries bordering on the Mediterranean. In ancient Egypt glass was used, though not extensively, for jewellery (see *Egyptian jewellery*), and in Myceneaen jewellery it appeared in beads, plaques and inlay work, but during the Roman period glassmaking was developed into a refined art and glass was used for a wide variety of domestic purposes as well as for the production of imitation gems. Roman glass was made in all colours and in degrees of transparency from completely transparent to opaque. It was used in beads, made into individual 'stones' for setting, and moulded into imitation intaglios. It was most popular in the early years of the Empire; after this genuine stones were so readily available that a substitute was not needed. Although undoubtedly cheaper than a real stone, however, glass was not considered an essentially inferior material. The disdain with which paste jewellery is now regarded is a modern attitude.

The basic techniques of glassmaking survived through the Dark Ages and by the 9th century a glassmaking industry was established in Venice. For the next 500 years Venice dominated the production of glass in Europe; it is still an important centre of the industry today. The medieval Venetian glass was still essentially a soda-lime silicate; it had comparatively little lustre and poor optical qualities, and it could not be made in a transparent colourless form because the materials were never pure enough to produce a colourless glass and the Venetians had lost the secret, known to the Romans, of decolouring glass with manganese dioxide. Nevertheless the colours of medieval glass are often superb, and the glassmaker's art was venerated. However, in the case of pastes found in company with precious stones (as in the ornaments found on the body of Edward I), it is difficult to know whether these were recognized as glass or whether they were thought to be genuine stones. The fraudulent use of pastes was certainly not unknown in the Middle Ages; the statute of 1300 which instituted hallmarking (q.v.) in England directed 'that none shall set any stone in gold except it be natural'.

In the fifteenth and sixteenth centuries the manufacture of paste stones was further developed in Milan. The technique for making colourless glass had been rediscovered in the fourteenth century, but there was as yet no demand for colourless imitation stones and the Renaissance pastes were coloured and backed with foil (q.v.) to improve their depth of colour and brilliance. Colourless pastes were not required because diamonds were not sufficiently popular for there to be any need for an imitation; the colourless glasses were in any case uninteresting and lacking in brilliance.

During the seventeenth century, however, the widespread adoption of the rose cut (q.v.) stimulated a growing interest in diamonds and the need for a cheap substitute arose. Rock crystal was widely used, but there was still a market for a glass substitute if a suitably brilliant glass could be produced. A combination of factors led to the development of such glasses in the late seventeenth and early

eighteenth centuries. One of these was economic. In 1615 the English government had prohibited the use of wood as fuel in glasshouse furnaces because a shortage of timber for ships was feared. The glassmakers turned to coal, but this necessitated putting a cover over the glass melt to protect it from the fumes, and the use of a covered container raised the melting-point. To lower the melting-point a flux was added, and the flux used was lead oxide. The introduction of lead oxide into glass, making it heavier and more brilliant, had been suggested at various times since the early Middle Ages, but it had never been consistently tried. The necessity for its use opened up new possibilities which were further explored by George Ravenscroft in the 1670s.

Ravenscroft was attempting to develop a technique of glassmaking which was not dependent on Italian immigrant labour and Italian techniques and materials. In the course of his experiments he substituted English flint for Venetian pebbles and potash for soda, and raised the proportion of lead oxide to over 30 per cent. The resulting glass was heavy, lustrous, highly refractive, had a high colour dispersion (q.v.) and took a brilliant polish. It was manufactured commercially and was soon in great demand.

A few decades later a lead glass with similar optical properties appeared in France and within a short time was being exported all over the Continent. This was 'strass', reputedly invented by Georges Stras of Strasbourg who in 1724 began working as a jeweller in Paris (see *Stras*). (The invention was until recently attributed to one Josef Strasser, but there are no records to indicate that Strasser ever existed.)

The eighteenth century was the great age of paste. No social stigma was attached to the wearing of glass imitation stones; they were admittedly more often to be seen in the jewellery of the middle class than at Court, but paste was nevertheless worn by those who could afford precious stones. There were several reasons for this. One was that many wealthy people preferred to wear jewels of comparatively little intrinsic value when travelling because of the danger of highway robbery. They would not, however, have worn jewellery simply because it was cheap; it also had to be good, and the paste jewellery of the eighteenth century was as well designed and as carefully made as jewellery set with precious stones. The designs of the aigrettes, Sévigné brooches and girandole earrings followed those of precious jewellery (see *Eighteenth-century jewellery*), but paste had an advantage over diamonds in that it could be cut to any outline, and since the aim of eighteenth-century jewellery was to present an almost continuous surface of stones unbroken by gaps which allowed the metal to be seen, this was greatly in its favour. Similar cutting could in theory have been done with diamonds because the techniques of diamond-cutting (q.v.) had been highly developed, but the wastage of costly material and the very high cost of cutting made it impracticable.

Although the pre-eminence of the diamond caused coloured stones to be unfashionable, at least for evening wear, for much of the century, a lot of very attractive coloured paste was made. French jewellery of the period was often set with a beautiful blue paste cut *en cabochon* and foiled. (Foils were normally used with paste and were extremely important to the appearance of the jewellery. The settings [a cut-down setting, q.v., was often used] were finely made and had to be airtight, because air reaching the foil would cause it to deteriorate.) A special type of paste developed in the eighteenth century was opal paste. This was a translucent pink glass which bore little resemblance to opal but was very attractive. It was made by allowing glass of a certain composition to cool in such a way that small particles of it crystallized out, giving the glass a milky appearance. When the particles were of a certain size they gave the glass a pink colour by scattering the blue wavelength of light. This pinkish opalescent glass was cut *en cabochon* and set over rose-coloured foil to deepen its colour. It continued to be produced into the nineteenth century, but the best examples were made before 1820.

In the first half of the nineteenth century the character of paste jewellery changed. In the eighteenth century, although following the prevailing styles of precious jewellery, it had been treated by jewellers as a medium with its own special qualities and had not been purely imitative. By 1850, however, paste was almost wholly confined to a direct imitation of diamond jewellery. Since diamonds were now being set in open claw settings to allow a maximum play of light, paste jewellery followed suit, but open settings were not very suitable for paste, which could not hope to imitate the brilliant lustre and fire of diamonds and had relied heavily in the past on the assistance of a foil. A separate foil could not be used in an open setting, but in 1840 the idea of 'silvering' the back facets of a paste in the same way as a mirror was introduced, and from then onwards colourless pastes were usually treated in this way. This marked a decline in the ancient art of foiling stones. Early in the century, too, pastes ceased to be cut in special shapes and were confined to regulation ovals and circles.

Since the characteristics of paste were no longer exploited it ceased to be an interesting material, and therefore rapidly became a despised material of which nothing was expected except cheapness. Unsuited for use in the antique and exotic styles fashionable at various times during the century (see *Nineteenth-century jewellery*), it was mostly confined to imitating unimaginative diamond jewellery and to the novelty jewellery which became popular in the mid-century. Neither of these roles helped its image, and it has remained the poor relation of gemstones ever since.

(For the physical characteristics of paste, and means of distinguishing it from gemstones, see *Glass*.)

Paternoster beads. See *Rosaries*.

'Patona pearls'. Trade name for imitation pearls.

'Patricia pearls'. Trade name for imitation pearls.

Pavé setting. A style of setting in which small stones are placed close together in holes drilled in the metal, the burr of metal round the hole being pressed over to hold the stone in place. (See also *Settings*.)

Pavilion. The lower part of a cut gemstone, lying below the girdle (q.v.).

Pavilion facet. The name for the eight large 4-sided (5-sided if there is a culet) facets on the lower part of a brilliant-cut diamond (see *Diamond-cutting*). Sometimes four of these facets are called pavilions and the other four quoins; the only difference between them is that they lie at different orientations and therefore have to be ground in different directions.

'Peacock ore'. Bornite.

Peacock stone. Malachite cut to show an eye.

Pea-pod ornament. See *Cosse de pois*.

Pearls. Pearls are among the most precious, and were probably one of the earliest, materials used in jewellery. Their beauty and rarity ensure their high value, and they have the advantage that, unlike nearly all other precious materials, they need no fashioning by man. Both freshwater and saltwater pearls were prized possessions in the East long before the Christian era, and in Rome they were so much a symbol of wealth and prestige that a law was passed restricting the wearing of them to certain classes.

There was much speculation in early times concerning the origin of pearls. One school of thought held that they were formed by drops of rain falling into oyster-shells, and that the oyster secreted a substance that caused the raindrop to harden. This was a not unintelligent guess; pearls are in fact formed by secretion, but the stimulus is a tiny particle of solid matter. This penetrates between the shell of the mollusc and the soft body, which is enclosed in a film of tissue called the mantle. The mantle secretes the material which makes up the three layers of the shell — a dark outer layer consisting of an organic material called conchiolin, a prismatic shelly layer made up of crystalline calcium carbonate, and a smooth inner layer made up of overlapping plates of crystalline calcium carbonate in the form of aragonite. This smooth inner layer is the iridescent mother-of-pearl material and is called *nacre* (q.v.). It is secreted by the entire surface of the mantle, and the mantle continues to produce it throughout the mollusc's life. When an object such as a grain of sand penetrates between the inner layer of the shell and the mantle enclosing the soft body an irritation is set up, and to ease this the mollusc proceeds to coat the foreign object with nacre secreted from the mantle. The object becomes cemented to the inside of the shell and in time a thick coating of nacre is built up over it. The resulting bulge in the lining of the shell is a *blister pearl*, and if large enough may be cut away from the shell and used in jewellery, mounted in such a way that the non-nacreous flattish underside cannot be seen. Blister pearls may be more or less hemispherical or of very irregular shape; they have little value compared with spherical pearls but are nevertheless very attractive. Spherical pearls are formed in another way, when the foreign body which penetrates between the shell and the mantle of the mollusc is not inanimate but a living creature such as a parasite which does not allow itself to be cemented down. To deal with this the mollusc forms a depression in the mantle in which the intruder is trapped; the depression deepens into a narrow-necked pouch and finally the top edges of the mantle close above it, leaving a sac of tissue containing the parasite within the actual body of the mollusc. The inside of this sac is lined with the nacre-secreting cells of the mantle; these cells are still living and in

277

time the parasite – now of course dead – is covered with a fairly even deposit of nacre built up in concentric layers. If the mollusc lives for many years a pearl of large dimensions is produced, bearing no proportion to the size of the minute parasite which caused its production. These pearls formed in the body of the mollusc are termed 'cyst' or 'mantle' pearls. Pearls found very near the mantle are called 'hem pearls' (these are usually of a darkish colour); pearls found near the abductor muscle which closes and opens the two halves of the shell are called 'muscle pearls', and pearls found near the ligament at the hinge are known as 'ligament pearls' (these are dark brown in colour because they contain a high proportion of conchiolin).

Pearls are found in many shapes and colours. The most valuable are those that are perfectly spherical, have a delicate tinge of pink, called rosée, and have a fine 'orient' (q.v.) (the name for the characteristic sheen of pearl). Many pearls have a slightly yellowish tinge; others are classed as silvery or white. Often these tinges of colour are only apparent to the expert. Some pearls however have a very definite colour; these are known as fancy-coloured pearls and they may be green, blue, rose-pink, yellow, bronze, gun-metal-grey or black. The value of these coloured pearls is variable but on the whole does not approach the value of fine rosée pearls. The cause of the different colours is not known. Pearls of unsatisfactory colour are sometimes stained in an attempt to produce the rosée tint, usually without great success. Staining is carried out particularly with dark pearls, which are given a lustrous black appearance by soaking them in a solution of silver nitrate, exposing them to sunlight or ultra-violet rays, and then buffing them up. This treatment is usually difficult to detect. Pearls are often pear-shaped (drop pearls) or have one side slightly flattened (button or bouton pearls). Pearls of very irregular shape are called baroque pearls: they have little appeal now, but were extensively used in Renaissance jewellery (q.v.). Very small pearls are known as seed pearls.

A pearl of some kind can be produced by any shelled mollusc, but only those with a nacreous shell can produce a nacreous pearl. The most valuable pearls are produced by the genus *Pinctada*, commonly known as pearl-oysters, and the most important fisheries for these are in the Persian Gulf, a source which has been known for over 2000 years. The oysters are found on limestone reefs, and are brought up in string bags by skin divers operating from sailing dhows. The divers descend to a depth of from 30 to 90 feet. Since the Second World War the scale of pearl-fishing in the Gulf has declined owing to the growth of the oil-refining industry in Bahrain and on the mainland, which offers more secure employment. The pearl-oyster fished in the Gulf is the *Pinctada vulgaris*, a small oyster (shell about $2\frac{1}{2}$ inches in diameter) which produces small but very beautiful creamy-white pearls. The same oyster is fished in the Gulf of Manaar which separates Ceylon from India. These fisheries, which are as old as those in the Persian Gulf, are now less productive than formerly, as are also the Red Sea fisheries which were a major source of pearls in Roman times but are now unimportant. The pearls from the Persian Gulf are the finest in the world and are known in the trade as oriental pearls; this term is often extended to cover pearls from the Red Sea and the Gulf of Manaar as well. Pearls from all three localities are usually sent to Bombay for drilling (see below).

Other pearl fisheries are off the coast of Bombay, off the Mergui archipelago (here pearls are much less important than the valuable black-lip shell), and right round the northern coast of Australia from Shark Bay to the Coral Sea. Here diving is done mostly in armoured diving suits, and here also pearls are less important than shell (q.v.), although attractive yellowish or golden pearls are obtained from the *Pinctada carcharium* in Shark Bay and large white pearls are found in the *Pinctada maxima*. The *Pinctada maxima* is also fished in the South Pacific, mostly round the Tuamoto archipelago. There are fisheries of varying importance off the coasts of Central and South America. In Venezuelan waters pearls of various colours including translucent white and bronze are obtained from the small *Pinctada radiata*. Off the western coasts of Mexico the greenish-edged *Pinctada margaritifera* is fished. Many of the black and gunmetal-coloured pearls come from the Gulf of California. Yellowish and silvery-grey pearls are obtained from the *Pinctada squamulosa* in the Gulf of Panama.

Other salt-water molluscs which produce pearls are the Abalone (q.v.), the Giant Conch (see *Conch pearls*) and the Giant Clam (see *Clam pearls*). Abalone pearls are brightly-coloured and iridescent, but clam and conch pearls are non-nacreous and less attractive. Several other molluscs sometimes produce pearls but they are of no commercial importance.

Freshwater pearls are produced by several varieties of shellfish, of which the most important is the pearl-mussel *Unio*. The pearls are nacreous and often beautiful, but they do not have the fine orient of oyster pearls. The *Unio* is found in the rivers of Scotland, north Wales and Ireland, in parts of Germany and Austria, and on the American continent. One important source of river-pearls is the Mississippi basin; here pearls are obtained not only from the *Unio* but from the so-called niggerhead clam (*Quadrula ebena*), the warty-back clam (*Quadrula pustulosa*), and many other shellfish. The pearls from the Mississippi basin are often coloured and occur in very irregular shapes such as wings and petals; these baroque pearls have comparatively little value. In Canada freshwater pearls are obtained from the *Alasmodon margaritifera,* and pearls are also found in the Amazon basin.

Sorting and drilling. Pearls are sorted into shapes – spherical, drop, button, etc. – and graded by colour. The drilling, which in the case of oriental pearls is usually done at Bombay, is carried out with a bow-drill (q.v.). Spherical pearls which are to be strung in necklaces are drilled from each side to give a straight hole through the centre. Drop and button pearls, which are used for earrings, pendants, studs, etc., are partly drilled and are cemented on to a metal peg with a special white pearl cement. Some drop and button pearls are 'Chinese drilled': a hole is drilled across the top or bottom of the pearl so that it can be sewn on to material. This type of drilling lowers the value of the pearl. Pearls for necklaces are prepared for marketing at Bombay by stringing them in sizes on silk; a number of strings sufficient to make a necklace are then tied together in a 'Bombay bunch' which is finished off with tassels of silver wire and provided with a label stating the total price of the pearls as calculated by the 'base' system (see below).

Price. To calculate the price of a pearl, the dealer first decides on its 'base' price. This depends on the shape, colour, freedom from flaws and orient of the pearl, and is reckoned from a shilling upwards. The pearl is then weighed; this is done in carats and the weight is converted to pearl grains by multiplying by four. The weight in grains is then squared and multiplied by the base price. Thus the price of a pearl weighing 7 grains at 1s. base price ('once the weight', as it is termed in the trade) would be 49s. (£2.45). At a base price of 3s. a pearl of similar weight would be 147s. (£7.35). To calculate the price of a necklet containing pearls of several sizes, the base value is decided on, the pearls are weighed in groups and the average weight of each group is found, and the price of each group at 'once the weight' is calculated by multiplying the average weight by the total weight of the group (in grains). The prices of the groups are added together and the total is multiplied by the base price previously decided on. This gives the price of the necklet. The base system is not used for seed pearls, which are normally sold by the ounce, or for cultured pearls (see below).

Cultured pearls. A cultured pearl is a pearl formed by the oyster around a nucleus inserted into the shell by man.

Pearls

Attempts to stimulate molluscs into pearl-production have been made for centuries, particularly in China, where small metal figures of Buddha were inserted into the shell of the freshwater mussel to be coated with nacre. Some unsuccessful experiments using a nucleus of limestone were made in the eighteenth century by the Swedish naturalist Linne, but it was in Japan that the first successful cultured pearls were produced. In 1896 Kokichi Mikimoto, a noodle-peddler with an interest in pearls, patented a process for producing a cultured blister pearl by cementing a bead of mother-of-pearl to the inside of an oyster's shell. These pearls were commercially produced, and cultured blister pearls of a similar nature are produced today (see *Mabe pearl*). Usually the original nucleus is removed when the pearl is cut out, a new nucleus is inserted and a backing of mother-of-pearl is cemented over the non-nacreous underside.

Mikimoto is generally credited with the development of the spherical cultured pearl in the early years of this century, but a number of people, mostly Japanese, were experimenting on pearl-culture at the time and it seems probable that Mikimoto was not the first to produce a whole cultured pearl. However, he became, and until his death in 1955 remained, a major figure in the commercial development and marketing of cultured pearls.

The culture of pearls has by now been brought to a fine art in Japan and is a highly organized industry. The oyster used is the small *Pinctada martensi* native to Japanese waters. Some adult oysters which are to be used as hosts are collected from the sea bed by divers, but it is nowadays more usual for oysters to be cultivated for the purpose. Special cages, or straw ropes strung with discarded shells, are suspended from rafts in suitable waters at the beginning of the spawning season and the young oysters, termed 'spat', settle on these. They are transferred to rearing cages at the end of the season, and when they are a year old are sown in shallow water which has a rocky bed to which they can attach themselves. They remain there undisturbed for two years. They are then brought up, cleaned, and prepared for surgery. The shells are induced to open by various means such as placing the oysters in running water, and a wedge of bamboo is inserted to keep them apart. Meanwhile very small squares of graft tissue are prepared, taken from a living oyster. A narrow incision is then made in the body of each oyster, a piece of graft tissue is inserted in the incision at a selected spot, and a spherical bead of mother-of-pearl is placed just above this tissue. (Mother-of-pearl, being a substance not foreign to the oyster, gives better results than nuclei of other materials.) The oyster is then allowed to close. The treated oysters are returned to culture cages in sheltered waters for up to six weeks to convalesce, after which they are transferred to permanent culture rafts. They are left, usually, for $3\frac{1}{2}$ years, at the end of which they are recovered and opened. The pearls are bleached if necessary in a weak solution of hydrogen peroxide, and are graded for size and quality. They are then drilled (a mechanically-operated drill is used), sorted into graduated sizes for necklaces, strung on silk and tied in bunches. They are sold by weight, the unit of weight being the momme (75 pearl grains).

In recent years cultured pearls have been produced in Japan without a bead nucleus. The freshwater mussel *Hyriopsis schlegeli*, found in the Biwa lake, is used. This mollusc grows to 9 inches but on account of its rather complicated internal anatomy solid nuclei cannot easily be inserted in it; small diced pieces of tissue from another mussel are therefore used instead. Twenty such pieces are inserted in the edge of the mantle of each mussel, and the mussels are returned to the lake in baskets for three years. Many mussels produce the full twenty pearls. These Biwa pearls are bright white and usually bun-shaped. In Australian waters non-nucleated cultured pearls are produced using the large pearl-oyster *Pinctada maxima*.

Identification of cultured pearls. Some cultured pearls betray themselves to the expert eye by a greenish tinge and characteristic markings just under the surface. This clearly does not furnish a reliable means of identification, and in the 1920s when cultured pearls first appeared on the market much research was carried out into methods of distinguishing between cultured and natural pearls since if no such method were found the value of real pearls would obviously suffer. Specific gravity (q.v.) was suggested as a test but was not conclusive enough; although the mean density of natural oriental pearl was lower than that of cultured pearls, there was a wide area of overlap. (The ranges of density are 2.68–2.74 for oriental pearls and 2.72–2.78 for Japanese cultured pearls, while the density of natural Australian pearls ranges from 2.70 to 2.79.) Fluorescence under ultra-violet light was suggested but was not conclusive either. It was clear that a conclusive test could be based on the different internal structure of cultured and natural pearls: natural pearls consist wholly of concentric layers of nacre (with the exception of some pearls which have a core of conchiolin), whereas cultured pearls consist of a large core of mother-of-pearl in which the material is arranged in straight parallel layers, covered with a thin coating of concentrically-deposited nacre. It was hoped that X-rays might detect this difference, but with the techniques used at the time they failed to do so.

A number of instruments were therefore devised with the aim of detecting cultured pearls. One was the *lucidoscope* (q.v.), which threw a strong beam of light through the pearl while it was immersed in a highly-refractive liquid; if straight light-and-dark stripes were seen this proved the pearl to be cultured. The test was not completely satisfactory, since if no stripes were seen this did not necessarily mean that the pearl was *not* cultured. An ingenious apparatus called the

pearl compass exploited the fact that a cultured pearl with its straight-layered core will, if placed between the poles of a powerful electro-magnet, turn to align itself with the lines of force of the magnetic field, whereas a natural pearl, being of concentric structure, will remain stationary. However, if the pearl was not perfectly spherical, or was asymmetrically mounted for the test, or had metal in the drill hole, the results were invalidated. The *pearl microscope* (q.v.), a microscope with a strong light source used to inspect the walls of the drill hole by means of a reflecting needle inserted in the hole, was a much more reliable method but was time-consuming to set up. This method is still used, but on the whole the most satisfactory instrument has been found to be the *endoscope* (q.v.). This requires the pearl (only drilled pearls can be tested) to be threaded on to a hollow needle through which is passed a powerful beam of light. The light is sent into the pearl through an aperture in the needle, and from the path the light takes through the pearl the internal structure can be deduced. Up to 200 pearls can be tested in an hour on this instrument.

For testing undrilled or partly-drilled pearls the most conclusive method is to take a lauegram – an X-ray 'photograph' of the internal symmetry of the pearl. (Lauegrams are explained under *X-rays*.) In a natural pearl the crystallites of aragonite (see paragraph 2) are radially arranged; in the nucleus of a cultured pearl they are arranged in more or less straight layers. When a narrow beam of X-rays is passed through a natural pearl in any direction, the rays must travel along the vertical axes of the crystallites because of the manner in which these are arranged. Emerging from the pearl, the rays produce a hexagonal pattern on the X-ray plate. In a cultured pearl, however, the rays will travel along the vertical axes of the crystallites if the pearl is oriented in a particular direction, but at 90° to this orientation the rays will be travelling across the crystallite prisms and will be diffracted in such a way that the pattern they make on the X-ray plate is one of four-fold symmetry – it is in fact the pattern of a Maltese cross. Pearls which on testing show the hexagonal pattern are tested again in another direction, and if this pattern is also hexagonal the pearl is genuine; if however the second pattern is a Maltese cross the pearl is cultured. If the Maltese cross is the first pattern seen there is of course no need to test further.

X-rays are now also used, after the initial failures, to identify cultured pearls by the direct or skiagram method, which utilizes the differing transparency of substances to X-rays (see *X-rays*). The interpretation of the plates is a highly skilled job. The bead nucleus of a cultured pearl is usually rather more opaque to X-rays than the thin coating of nacre, and shows up on the plate as a darker patch, while the organic conchiolin, which in natural pearls sometimes occurs in fine layers near the centre, but in cultured pearls is nearly always deposited over the bead nucleus before nacre is deposited, is transradiant to X-rays and appears as a light circle.

Fluorescence under X-rays is useful in distinguishing the cultured Biwa pearls, which show a strong greenish-yellow glow.

Imitation pearls. Imitation pearls have been made for many centuries. A book written in 1440 gives recipes for making them, and many of the pearls sewn on Elizabeth I's magnificent dresses had never seen an oyster. In the middle of the seventeenth century a French rosary-maker named Jonquin was producing imitation pearls in quantity on the outskirts of Paris. These early imitations were what are known as 'Roman pearls'; they were hollow spheres of glass given a pearly appearance by an inner coating of fish-scale essence, and filled with wax to give solidity.

The iridescent substance on fish-scales, later found to be minute crystals of guanine (an organic chemical compound), is still used for imitation pearls and is known as 'essence d'orient' or pearl

essence. Formerly it was extracted from the scales of the bleak, but since 1919 herrings have been used. The manufacture of the essence was largely a French industry until 1939, but it is now made in many parts including Norway, South Africa, and the herring-fishing area of the Bay of Fundy on the North American coast. The scales are churned to release the guanine crystals, which are strained off, purified, suspended in solvent, and added to a lacquer, usually nitrocellulose, to produce a 'paint'. This is applied by spraying or dipping to the outside of solid glass beads (these have largely superseded the hollow wax-filled type). Usually between five and ten coats are applied. The beads already have a string-hole, since they are formed in a blow-torch flame on a wire which is subsequently dissolved away by acid leaving a central hollow canal.

Imitation pearls are not difficult to detect. Inspection with a hand lens reveals a blotting-paper-like surface quite different from the ridged surface of a nacreous pearl, and usually some wearing-away of the pearl essence at the sides of the string-hole is evident. A traditional test is to pass the pearl over the teeth – imitation pearls feel smooth, real or cultured pearls 'gritty'. Pressure with a pin will mark a coated pearl but not a nacreous pearl. There are numerous other tests, including X-rays (to which the glass beads are opaque) and specific gravity: the coated glass 'pearls' have on the whole a higher density than natural or cultured pearls – it is usually over 3.0. The density of the older hollow glass bead 'pearls' is usually under 1.55.

Care of pearls. Pearls require regular cleaning, since cosmetics seeping into the drill hole cause deterioration. This is if anything more important with cultured than with natural pearls, for there is a discontinuous layer between the nucleus and the nacreous outer layer, and grease and cosmetics penetrating into this show through the pearly coating and make the pearls look 'unhealthy'. The calcium carbonate in pearls is dissolved by weak acids, and pearls which are much worn assume in time a barrel shape as the rounded surface is eroded by acids in the skin. This cannot be prevented, but has a much more serious effect on cultured than on natural pearls since in places the nacreous coating may be completely worn away. Regular restringing by an expert is important, and to prevent the loss of valuable pearls there should be a knot between each pearl and the next one. Pearls should not be kept in too dry an atmosphere, for this will cause the conchiolin in the pearl to dry out, producing cracks.

Pearl compass. See *Pearls.*

Pearl microscope. A device for identifying cultured pearls. Only drilled pearls can be examined. The microscope is used in conjunction with a light source below the stage and an adjustable light to illuminate the pearl from the sides or front. The pearl is set on a special stage called a cardiometer fitted with a fine needle which has a highly polished tip; calibrated adjustments on the cardiometer allow the needle to be raised and lowered by thousandths of a millimetre. The needle is inserted into the drill hole of the pearl and as it is moved up and down the reflection of the walls of the hole in the polished tip of the needle is observed through the microscope. By this means the internal structure of the pearl, which is concentric in natural pearls but straight-layered in the mother-of-pearl nucleus of a cultured pearl, can be seen. (See also *Pearls.*)

Pearlometer. Name for a pearl microscope (q.v.).

Peasant jewellery. Peasant jewellery has virtually disappeared in most parts of Europe; in general it is to be found only in museums. The characteristic of this type of jewellery was not that it was made of cheap materials (admittedly rock crystal and paste were the commonest stones, but there appears to have been no shortage of gold in many parts); it was that both its form and the manner of wearing

Eighteenth-century silver clasp from Heligoland

it were traditional and changed very little over the years. The separate items of jewellery were of much less importance individually than as part of the ensemble in which they were worn. The jewellery was made by local craftsmen in styles which had been in use sometimes for centuries. Industrialization and improved communications dealt the death blow to peasant jewellery in the nineteenth century, when increasing quantities of machine-produced jewellery began to reach hitherto remote country districts and when in many areas the traditional costume was given up.

The most characteristic feature of French peasant jewellery was the pendant cross, usually hung from the neck by a velvet ribbon. The type varied with locality; the best known is the Normandy cross. This was usually of silver, and was in the form of five high bosses each set with a brilliant-cut rock crystal, surrounded with filigree sprays set with smaller crystals. The lower limb of the cross, in which the central crystal was always pear-shaped, was hinged so that it was less likely to get broken in wear. A subject often used in the jewellery of the Rouen area was the Holy Spirit or Dove. This was worn as a breast-ornament or pendant and was set with crystals or coloured pastes. In its beak the Dove carried a branch, spray or bunch of grapes, the latter usually being set with coloured pastes. The Dove was also a popular subject in the jewellery of Puy, but here it was a formalized representation in which pear-shaped bosses set with cabochon stones indicated the wings, body, head and tail of the bird. The jewellery of Auvergne utilized a wider variety of gemstones than was normal in peasant jewellery of other regions, for garnets, opals, zircons and spinels occurred locally in the volcanic rock of the area.

In Belgium also the pendant cross was an important ornament and was worn with matching earrings. The jewellery was largely composed of openwork floral and scroll designs decorated with applied rosettes; gold rosettes were attached to silver ornaments and silver rosettes to gold. A characteristic of Flemish jewellery was that it was set with rose-cut diamonds. Openwork silver pendants in the form of a heart (the *Sacré coeur*) were a common ornament in the region between Antwerp and Malines; in France the heart was often worn immediately above the cross, but in Belgium it was worn as a distinct ornament on its own. The heart was usually crowned, but was sometimes converted into a love-token by the addition of Cupid's arrows, quiver and bow.

Holland retained its peasant jewellery longer than most other European countries; in some parts traditional costume is still worn. Much of the jewellery was worn on the head. In Zeeland the women wore, jutting out at the side of their lace caps, spiral ornaments of gold, silver or gilt on which were hung pendants, sometimes decorated with pearls. In northern Holland similar spiral ornaments were attached to the end of gold or silver bands which encircled the head and were covered with a muslin cap. In Gelderland the women wore complete caps of gold individually shaped to the head. Coral necklaces were worn in Goes and Overyssel, in addition to gold head-ornaments, and men and boys wore gold

and silver buttons. In Overyssel the men wore a pair of large hammered silver discs at the waist.

The commonest material for peasant jewellery in Germany was silver filigree, but the forms were very varied. In some parts large flat hairpins with expanded heads decorated with raised filigree were worn by the women. In the north where amber was readily available amber beads were worn in necklaces. Other necklaces were of hollow beads of silver. Silver filigree was also important in the jewellery of Norway and Sweden. Few stones were used, and those that were were generally coloured paste. The most important item of jewellery was a large circular buckle, from which often hung small concave highly-polished pieces of silver. Some very fine work was also done by casting. Scandinavian brides wore large and elaborate silver-gilt crowns on their wedding day. (See also *Bridal jewellery*.)

Much Italian peasant jewellery of the eighteenth and nineteenth centuries was strongly reminiscent of much older types. (In the nineteenth century Castellani [q.v.] found craftsmen in remote parts of Umbria still making jewellery in a style and by techniques distantly related to those of Etruscan work.) In Lombardy the women wore quantities of hairpins stuck fan-wise into the hair with a long pin passed horizontally through them. Very large but comparatively lightweight earrings, often set with seed pearls, were also worn. The jewellery of the Adriatic shore was of delicate goldwork in the tradition of the old Venetian goldsmiths, decorated with opaque cloisonné enamel (q.v.) and pearls. Elaborate pendants in the shape of fully-rigged ships (a popular Renaissance subject), decorated with painted enamel and hung with clusters of pearls, were worn. Similar work was done in Sicily.

The jewellery of Hungary and Spain in the sixteenth and seventeenth centuries furnishes the only post-classical European examples of filigree enamel (q.v.). Cells of twisted wire were filled with bright opaque colours. In Spain the filigree enamel is seen in work which shows

Moorish influence. Moorish and, apparently, Indian influence is traceable also in Portuguese peasant jewellery; fine gold filigree was much used, crescent-shaped pendants appear in addition to crosses and hearts, and the length of earrings and neckchains (reaching to the shoulders and waist respectively) was of Oriental proportions.

(Types of Mexican peasant jewellery are described under *Mexican jewellery*.)

Pecos diamond. Misnomer for rock crystal from the Pecos river, Texas.

Pectolite. (Calcium-sodium silicate. S.G. about 2.87; R.I. 1.59–1.63; H. 5.) A white or greyish massive stone with a silky lustre which is fashioned into ornaments and cabochons. It is found in the cavities of volcanic rock in Scotland, Italy and parts of the U.S.A.

'Pectolite jade'. Misnomer for pectolite.

Pectoral. An ornament worn on the breast. It may be fastened to the garment like a brooch or worn as a pendant. With the exception of the pectoral cross, pectoral ornaments are not of much importance in Western jewellery, but in Egyptian jewellery (q.v.) they attained great magnificence.

Peg setting. A type of claw setting (q.v.) in which recesses are made in the walls of the claws and the girdle of the stone is set into these. (See also *Settings*.)

Peking jade. Any true jade, but the term usually refers to nephrite. (See *Jade*.)

Pendants. The earliest pendant ornaments worn were probably amulets (q.v.) of shell, stone, the teeth of an animal, etc., pierced or grooved to be carried on a thong round the neck. In many periods of civilization the individual pendant has taken a very subsidiary place to the necklace or collar or has been worn mainly as an adjunct to it. The superb pendant pectorals of Egyptian jewellery (q.v.) for example, developed from, and on the whole remained part of, a symbolic collar. In Greek and Roman jewellery (qq.v.) the formal ornament worn round the neck was a complete and often very intricate necklace. Any object worn alone round the neck was likely to have a magical significance. Branch coral and the Etruscan bulla (see *Etruscan jewellery*) are examples.

In the Middle Ages also, pendants normally had more than a purely decorative role. Some beautiful reliquary pendants survive from the early Middle Ages, together with numerous pendants of devotional nature which were not designed as reliquaries (see *Devotional jewellery*). In the sixteenth century, however, pendants ceased to be primarily symbolic and became ornamental jewels in the grand style. They were large, of sculptural form, lavishly enamelled and set with stones, and were worn not only on a chain round the neck but also pinned to the sleeve. (See *Renaissance jewellery* for further information.)

With a change in fashions in the seventeenth century these magnificent pendants ceased to be worn, and in competition with necklaces, brooches and stomachers in the seventeenth and eighteenth centuries the pendant found little place. There were, however, pendant miniature-cases (see *Seventeenth-century jewellery*) and, towards the end of the eighteenth century, memorial pendants in the form of miniatures (see *Memorial jewellery*).

During the nineteenth century pendants became more popular again and the form they took was often sentimental – small lockets enclosing a lock of hair, jewelled hearts. Pendant crosses were worn more or less throughout the Victorian era and were of many types; the *croix à la Jeannette* and the Maltese cross are examples. (See also *Nineteenth-century jewellery*.)

The Art Nouveau jewellers found the pendant an ideal vehicle for their flowing, asymmetrical designs and areas of enamel, and many of the finest examples of Art Nouveau jewellery (q.v.) are in this form. The pendant has remained fashionable in this century and is now one of the most popular forms of jewellery. It is a very flexible ornament: it can be subdued

285

and discreet and worn in conjunction with other jewels, or it can be big, bold and startling and worn alone. A great point in its favour is that it can be worn with informal clothes, whereas most necklaces cannot.

Pendeloque. A drop-shaped or pear-shaped stone faceted in the brilliant style. (See *Diamond-cutting* for illustration.)

Pénicaud, Nardon (Léonard). One of the great enamellists of the Limoges school. A number of his works, dating from the early sixteenth century and based on engravings of the period, are preserved in France. His method was to lay coloured enamels in juxtaposition on a white-enamelled copper plate, and after firing the piece add highlights in opaque white and touches of opaque red (for blood), finally touching up the picture with gold and decorating it with foiled pastes. The treatment and the architectural elements of the enamels show a mixture of Renaissance and Gothic.

Nardon Pénicaud was one of a distinguished family of Limoges enamellists, the most notable other members being Jean Pénicaud and J. B. Pénicaud. The relationship between them is not clear.

'Pennsylvania diamond'. Misnomer for iron pyrites.

Peridot. (Magnesium-iron silicate. S.G. about 3.34; R.I. 1.65–1.69; H. $6\frac{1}{2}$.) A transparent bottle-green stone with a rather oily lustre. There is often a brownish tinge, and this lowers the value of the stone. True brown peridot is very rare: the stones known as 'brown peridot' before the 1950s have been found to belong to a new mineral species, sinhalite. Peridot is the gem variety of olivine and is sometimes known by that name; it may also be called chrysolite.

The comparative softness of peridot makes it more suitable for use in pendants, brooches and so on than in rings. It may be cut in the trap-cut or mixed-cut style, and sometimes the table facet is slightly domed.

There are various imitations of peridot,

but the oily lustre of true peridot and its strong double refraction are usually sufficient to identify it.

Peridot was the 'topaz' of the ancient world and at that time was found only on the Island of St. John in the Red Sea. This was until recently a major source of peridot, but the mines were closed down in 1914. The sources of peridot now are the Mogok Stone Tract in Burma, Brazil, Australia, Norway and the U.S.A.

'Perigem'. Trade name for a synthetic yellow-green spinel. (See *Synthetic gem-stones.*)

Peristerite ('Pigeon stone'). (S.G. 2.6; R.I. 1.54; H. $6–6\frac{1}{2}$.) A rare variety of albite feldspar, sometimes known as albite moonstone. It is whitish, fawn or brownish-pink with an iridescent flash of blue. Material from Monteagle, Ontario, has been made into cabochon stones and beads, and there are various other sources in Canada.

'Perspex'. (Trade name.) An acrylic plastic. (See *Plastics.*)

Petal pearls. Flat baroque-shaped pearls.

Petosky stone. A fossil limestone from Michigan. (See *Marble.*)

Petrified wood. See *Agatized wood, Jasperized wood, Opalized wood.*

Pewter. A fairly soft alloy of variable constituents. Until the second half of the eighteenth century pewter usually contained a high proportion of lead – sometimes as much as 50 per cent, the other 50 per cent being tin. Other greyish alloys of tin and antimony and tin and copper, the proportion of tin being just over 80 per cent, were also used. Pewter was extensively used for domestic utensils in Roman times and continued to be so used for nearly 2000 years. In Britain, which had a native source of tin in the mines of Cornwall, the craft of the pewterer reached a very high level and British pewter was the model for the fine pewter produced in America in the eighteenth and early nineteenth centuries. The ease with which pewter could be hammered and chased by techniques similar to those of silversmithing, and its low melting-point, which made it an easy material to mend or recast, were the reasons for its popularity as a material for tableware and tankards, but it was also sometimes used in jewellery, either alone or as a setting for paste or other stones of little value.

Pewter lost its position in the eighteenth century when porcelain tableware came into general use; this was cheap, attractive and cleaner than the old pewter, which quickly became dull and greyish. The invention of Sheffield plate (q.v.), which provided a cheap substitute for silver, accelerated its decline in popularity. In the later part of the century, however, a new greyish-white alloy was invented in Sheffield for use in tableware. This consisted of a high proportion of tin, with some antimony and copper. It was stronger than the old pewter, was more silvery, and kept its lustre and polish longer. In spite of these qualities, however, it could not compete with china and Sheffield plate.

This modern substitute for pewter is nevertheless still used for decorative work and sometimes for jewellery. It is now known as Britannia metal and its composition is about 91 per cent tin, 7 per cent antimony and 2 per cent copper. It is a ductile, corrosion-resistant alloy, easily soldered, with a melting-point up to 295°C, which lends itself well to chasing and engraving. This alloy contains no lead; other modern pewter-type metals composed of tin and lead are still sometimes used, but if they are to be employed in utensils for food and drink the lead content is restricted by law to 10 per cent.

Phenakite (Phenacite). (Beryllium silicate. S.G. 2.95–2.97; R.I. 1.65–1.67; H. $7\frac{1}{2}$–8.) A generally colourless, transparent stone not much used in jewellery. In appearance it is very similar to quartz: it was formerly so often mistaken for quartz that its name is derived from the Greek word for 'cheat'. It is harder than quartz and has a higher refraction, but possesses very little fire. Phenakite occurs fairly commonly; sources include Russia, Brazil, France, and various localities in the U.S.A. and Africa.

Phosphor bronze. Bronze (q.v.) to which a small quantity of phosphorus has been added to make the alloy harder and more resistant to oxidization.

Pickle. An acid solution used for removing oxides and hardened flux from metals after soldering, and for cleaning jewellery after all the construction work is finished. In the first case the article when hot is simply dipped in the pickle, in the second it is boiled in it. The acids generally used are nitric and sulphuric, and the proportion of acid to water is varied according to requirements. Half-and-half is an average solution.

Picotite. Black spinel.

Pierced work. Work in which a pattern is cut out of sheet metal. There are several ways of doing this; small chisels (q.v.) may be used to gouge out the metal, the pattern may be stamped out mechanically

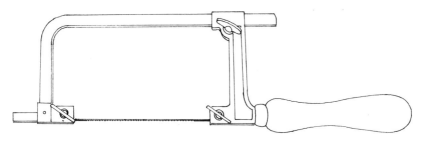

Jeweller's piercing saw

with a stamping die (see *Machine-stamping*) under pressure sufficient to cut through the metal, or the pattern may be pierced out with a piercing saw (q.v.). In the latter case, the pattern is drawn on the metal, a hole is drilled through it and one end of the saw blade (the other end being held in the saw frame) is inserted through the hole and then fixed in the saw frame. The pattern can then be sawn out.

Piercing saw. A frame saw with a thin blade held under tension, used for cutting non-ferrous metals and in particular for pierced work (q.v.). The blades are available in various sizes and the frames are made in several lengths and depths, a depth of 3 inches being the most usual. Some frames are of adjustable length. The blade is inserted with the teeth pointing towards the handle and the cutting stroke is downwards only.

Pietra dura. See *Mosaic.*

Pigeon blood agate. Cornelian or red and white agate from Cisco, Utah.

Piggy-back diamond. A composite stone consisting of a flattish diamond with a large culet (q.v.) set on top of a small diamond; this arrangement gives the appearance of a much larger stone when seen from above.

Pigott diamond. A fine diamond which was once in the possession of Lord Pigott, Governor of Madras, in the 18th century. This is almost the only known fact about the stone; accounts of its weight range from 47 to 85 carats, and its ultimate fate is not known. It is said that Pigott was given the diamond in India in return for protecting the Maharajah's territory, and that the British government, hearing of this and similar occurrences, recalled Pigott to England. He brought the diamond to England with him and according to one version of the story sold it in 1775; according to another version it was inherited by his brothers, who sold it in 1801. In 1818 it was bought for £30,000 by Ali Pasha, Viceroy of Egypt, who on his death-bed ordered one of his followers to destroy the stone. What the follower in fact did with it is a matter of conjecture.

Pilgrims' badges. See *Devotional jewellery.*

Pinchbeck. The most famous of the copper-zinc alloys developed in the eighteenth century to meet the demand for a metal that resembled gold. It was invented by a Fleet Street watchmaker, Christopher Pinchbeck (1670–1732), and was in great demand; after the inventor's death his son continued to trade in the material and in 1733 inserted a long advertisement in the 'Daily Post' warning the public to beware of cheap imitations. The recipe for pinchbeck was never disclosed and various proportions have been suggested: 1 part zinc to 9 parts copper, 1 part zinc to 5 parts copper, 17 parts zinc to 83 parts copper, etc. It has been said that real pinchbeck had much better wearing qualities and a finer colour than other copper-zinc alloys, and that a slight wash of gold might have been applied to the surface to prevent tarnishing.

Pinchbeck or alloys very similar to it continued to be used well into the nineteenth century, but the demand for such alloys diminished when electroplating (q.v.) was introduced. Copper-zinc alloys are still used in jewellery but are now plated; they are nowadays known as gilding-metal (q.v.).

Pin fire opal. Precious opal with pin-point flashes of colour, smaller and more irregular than the points of colour in harlequin opal. (See *Opal.*)

'Pink moonstone'. Misnomer for pink girasol (q.v.) scapolite.

Pin vice (chuck). A type of hand vice (q.v.) with jaws closed usually by a side screw, used for holding very small tools, such as needles, and fine wire. Some are in the form of a chuck, closed by turning the barrel.

Piqué. Tortoiseshell (sometimes ivory) inlaid with a pattern of gold or silver. It was fashionable in jewellery of the mid-Victorian period. (See *Tortoiseshell* for further information.)

'Piqué goods'. Trade term for stones containing small black spots (usually carbon).

Pistacite. See *Epidote*.

Pit amber. Mined amber. See *Amber*.

Pitch. This is used in repoussé work (q.v.); the pitch, held in a bowl or box, provides a firm but yielding surface against which the relief can be punched up, and being sticky it also holds the work in place. The pitch is usually a mixture of burgundy pitch, tallow or beeswax and a little linseed oil. It can be bought ready mixed.

Pitch stone. Obsidian.

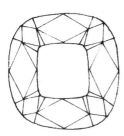

The Pitt or Regent diamond

Pitt (or Regent) diamond. A diamond weighing 410 carats in the rough, found in the Partial mines on the river Kistna in India in 1701. It was purchased by William Pitt, Governor of Fort St. George, Madras, and brought to England for cutting. It was cut into a perfect brilliant weighing 140 metric carats; the cutting is said to have taken two years. Pitt was apparently in constant dread that the diamond would be stolen, and in 1717 he sold it to the Duke of Orleans, Regent of France, for the equivalent of £175,000. It was stolen from the *Garde Meuble* together with the rest of the crown jewels in 1792, but was later recovered (according to one account the thieves returned it, presumably unable to find a way of disposing of it). It was withheld when the rest of the French

Crown jewels were put up for auction in 1886 and, having also managed to elude the Nazis, it is now on exhibition in the Louvre.

Placer. An alluvial or glacial deposit containing minerals. Until recently placer deposits yielded most of the world's gold. (See *Gold*.)

Plaited chain. Very compact loop-in-loop chain (see *Chain*). It looks plaited but in fact is not.

Planishing. The process of smoothing off and finishing silver with a hammer. A flat-faced planishing hammer (see *Hammers*) is used.

Plasma. (See *Chalcedony*). A dark green opaque variety of chalcedony approaching jasper in composition. It often contains small yellow or white spots. Plasma containing spots of red jasper is known as *bloodstone* (q.v.).

Plasma is found in China, India and the U.S.A.

Plaster stone. Gypsum.

Plastics. A term covering a number of resin-like synthetic substances which can be moulded by heat and pressure. The development of new and better plastics has been proceeding apace for some years and the products are increasingly used in costume jewellery. Some very attractive colours can be achieved, and metallic films can be applied to the surface to give the illusion of gold, silver or platinum. (Plastic can be electroplated if it is first given a coating which renders it electrically conductive.)

Plastic is in most circumstances extremely easy to identify: it is very light, it is warm to the touch, it is soft and can easily be scratched with a knife blade, and it nearly always just 'looks like plastic'. There are some ornamental stones, however, of which it can provide quite a passable imitation: these include amber, ivory and tortoiseshell. Translucent to opaque stones may also be imitated with some success as regards appearance, but plastics do not have a high enough refractive index or take a good enough polish (because of their softness) to provide a convincing imitation of a transparent stone. The main types of plastic likely to be encountered in jewellery are as follows. (A large number of plastics can be obtained by modification, and there are numerous trade names.)

Cellulosic plastics. Celluloid was the first plastic to be invented (1865); it is derived from natural cellulose and is highly inflammable. One way of identifying it is to take a small scraping of the material on a knife blade and introduce it into a flame, when it burns very readily. It is made transparent and in various colours. The refractive index is 1.495 to 1.52, the hardness about 2, and the specific gravity in the clear type is 1.36 to 1.42 but can rise to 1.80 when various fillers are incorporated, as in the case of celluloid imitations of ivory (q.v.). Amber is also imitated. Celluloid is readily sectile, and softens under amyl-acetate and acetone.

Cellulose acetate ('safety celluloid') is made from cellulose and acetic acid and is less inflammable. A peeling heated on a knife blade burns slowly with a vinegary smell. The refractive index and hardness are similar to those of celluloid, the specific gravity is usually 1.29–1.40 but can be increased with fillers. It is used in similar ways to celluloid, is sectile, and reacts similarly to amyl-acetate and acetone.

Vinyl plastics. Polystyrene, a vinyl benzene product, is a clear plastic which may be dyed in a range of colours and has been used to make moulded faceted 'stones'. It is also used for the beads in imitation pearls. It is very light (S.G. about 1.05), has refractive index 1.59 and hardness $2\frac{1}{4}$, is sectile and will dissolve in benzene, toluene, bromoform and amyl-acetate.

Acrylic plastics. These bear a resemblance to glass and can be made colourless and transparent or in any colour. They are best known under the trade name 'perspex'. Like polystyrene, this plastic has been used for moulded imitation gems

and in the beads of imitation pearls. It can also be used to imitate organic substances such as wood. It is very light (S.G. 1.18), and has a refractive index of about 1.50 and a hardness of $2\frac{1}{4}$. It is resistant to many acids and alkalis but is attacked by acetone.

Phenol plastics. The plastic known as bakelite (first produced 1909) is a phenolformaldehyde resin made in opaque colours and also in a clear transparent type which can be dyed. The clear type has a specific gravity of 1.25–1.30 but this rises with the incorporation of fillers. The refractive index is about 1.62–1.66 and the hardness $2\frac{1}{4}$. Bakelite has been used to simulate amber and to produce imitation faceted stones. It has the disadvantage of yellowing with age.

Amine or *amino plastics* are produced by the reaction of formaldehyde with urea or thio-urea, and can be made in delicate translucent colours much superior to those obtainable in the older type of bakelite. The specific gravity is about 1.50, the refractive index 1.55–1.62, and the hardness about $2\frac{1}{4}$.

Casein plastic is partly derived from the protein in milk. It is semi-transparent to opaque and is used to imitate tortoiseshell, amber and ivory. When burnt it gives off a smell of burning milk, and it may be tested with nitric acid, which stains it yellow. Specific gravity is about 1.33, refractive index 1.55 and hardness $2\frac{1}{4}$.

Nylon, derived from coal-tar and ammonia, is an extremely tough and durable plastic, is translucent to opaque, and is well suited to imitate semi-translucent stones such as agate. Its toughness makes it a favourite material for stringing imitation pearls. It is soft and very light (S.G. about 1.13), and has refractive index 1.53. It discolours slightly in sunlight and is attacked by strong acids.

Plating. See *Electroplating*, also *Gilding*.

Platinum. A recently-discovered strong white metal with a very high melting-point (1755°C) which has been used in jewellery since the nineteenth century. Platinum is a noble metal; i.e. it resists the attack of almost all substances except aqua regia (q.v.), a potent mixture of nitric and hydrochloric acid. It does not tarnish, which makes it preferable to silver as a setting for diamonds, it is quite highly reflective, though less so than gold and silver, and it has good working qualities. Its main disadvantage is its weight: it is even heavier than gold. It is also considerably more expensive.

Platinum is one of a group of metals, the other members of the group being palladium, rhodium, osmium, ruthenium and iridium. Palladium (q.v.) is used in jewellery as a substitute for platinum, rhodium (q.v.) is used for plating silver, and ruthenium and iridium are used as alloying metals for platinum and palladium. Osmium has no use in jewellery. The platinum metals appear to have been unknown until the eighteenth century, when a white metal which had sometimes been used by the Indians to make beads was discovered in Columbia by the Spaniards and named 'platina' – 'little silver'. By primitive methods the metal was unworkable in any processes requiring heat because of its high melting-point, but its properties were investigated in Europe and in 1789 a platinum chalice was made for presentation to the Pope. In the early years of the nineteenth century the six metals comprising the platinum group were isolated. A few jewellers experimented with platinum – two Paris jewellers were making mourning rings in platinum as early as 1828 – but it was not until the invention of the oxy-hydrogen blowpipe in 1847 that it really became a viable material. In 1855 the French jeweller Fontenay used platinum in some of the settings of a diamond diadem, and towards the end of the nineteenth century the metal was increasingly used in the settings of diamond jewellery. (It is highly suitable for this purpose because of its strength, and also of course its colour, which is more flattering to diamonds than the colour of gold.)

Platinum at this time was too expensive for regular use in jewellery because of its rarity: almost the only source was South America. In the 1920s, however, large quantities of platinum began to be recovered as a by-product from the silver and copper mines in Ontario, and platinum since then has been much more readily available. Another source is Rustenburg in South Africa. The refining processes are similar to those used for gold (q.v.).

Like gold and silver, platinum has to be alloyed with other metals to give it satisfactory working qualities. The metals most commonly used are palladium, iridium and copper. Unlike the other precious metals, however, platinum in Britain does not have to be hallmarked. There are therefore no legal standards for its quality, but the proportion of 950 parts platinum per 1000 is generally accepted by the trade.

Play of colour. See *Iridescence.*

Pleochroism. See *Dichroism.*

Pleonaste. Alternative name for ceylonite.

'Plexiglas'. (Trade name.) An acrylic plastic. (See *Plastics.*)

Pliers. Jewellers' pliers are usually of cast steel with wide-curved handles for

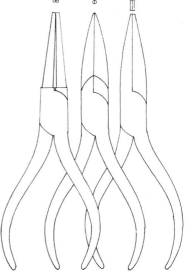

Pliers: round-nosed, snipe and flat-nosed

maximum grip. The jaws may be serrated or smooth and are made in a variety of shapes – round-nose, flat-nose, half-round, snipe (see illustration). Pliers are used for a multitude of purposes including bending and shaping wire, strip and thin sheet metal, forming ring-bezels, making chain links and holding hot objects.

In addition to the ordinary type in which the jaws pivot, there is a parallel-action type in which the jaws remain parallel when they are opened. These are made with flat, round or pointed jaws and some have a cutter at the side. (See also *Nippers*.)

Plique-à-jour. A type of cloisonné (q.v.) enamelling in which the enamels have no backing but are open to the light. (See *Enamel*.)

Point. A hundredth part of a carat (q.v.); a term used in expressing the weight of diamonds. (See also *Weights for gemstones*.)

Poison rings. Rings with a hidden compartment, usually concealed in a hinged bezel, which are believed to have contained poison. There are numerous stories of rings having been used for this purpose in the sixteenth and seventeenth centuries (Cesare Borgia, for instance, was said to carry poison concealed in his ring and drop it into the wine of his guests), but although a number of rings of this period with locket-bezels are known none of them is an authenticated poison ring; the compartment may well have been used to carry perfume or to contain a devotional relic (see *Devotional jewellery*). It has been suggested that not enough was known about poisons in the sixteenth and seventeenth centuries for a substance potent enough to be lethal to be carried in such a small compartment. This seems unlikely, however. Some vegetable poisons are exceedingly potent, and there are several well-authenticated cases of suicide by means of a poison ring in classical history. Hannibal swallowed poison from a ring rather than be taken in triumph through Rome, and the guardian of the Capitoline temple, when the gold deposited in it was seized by Crassus, broke his ring-stone

between his teeth and died immediately.

Polishing (gemstones). See *Diamond-cutting* and *Gem-cutting*.

Polishing (metals). Jewellery is polished in several stages and there are numerous variations in the tools used and the procedures adopted. The following is an outline of modern polishing procedures.

When the construction work is completed the piece is finished off with files and with whatever hand tools are appropriate, and is rubbed over with progressively finer grades of emery cloth and with wet Water-of-Ayr stone (q.v.). It is then boiled out in pickle (q.v.). The final polishing, which used to be done by hand, is now carried out in most workshops on a polishing lathe (q.v.) fitted with appropriate brushes and mops (see *Polishing mops*). A wet brass wire brush is used first to 'bring up' the metal after pickling, after which a bristle brush charged with a mixture of oil and emery powder or with tripoli (q.v.) is used to get into the undercuts and narrow spaces in the metal. This is followed by polishing with a coarse calico mop charged with tripoli, and then a soft calico mop charged with rouge (q.v.). The article may now have sufficient polish, or may require a final buffing with lambswool or a soft cloth. For polishing the inside of ring shanks a felt cone is fitted to the spindle of the polishing lathe.

Flexible-shaft drills similar to dental drills are sometimes used instead of a polishing lathe; these are fitted with small felt polishing mops.

Abrasives of the same type are used in hand polishing. Tools for hand polishing include the buff stick, ring stick, and burnisher (qq.v.). Burnishing (q.v.) is a polishing technique which works by compression instead of abrasion, and may be used for polishing small areas which other polishing tools cannot reach.

For polishing in the crevices of filigree and openwork, a string charged with tripoli is fixed at one end to the workbench, threaded through the crevice, and the piece is run up and down it.

For a list of abrasives and polishing agents, see *Abrasives*.

Polishing lathe. An electrically-driven machine (it is not in fact a lathe) with a rotating spindle to which are attached various brushes, mops, and felts for polishing jewellery. (See *Polishing* [*metals*].)

Polishing mops, brushes, etc. Interchangeable polishing heads fitted to the rotating spindle of a polishing lathe (q.v.); pieces of jewellery are held against them for polishing.

The calico mops consist of a number of separate calico discs held together at the centre. When the mop is rotating at speed these discs form a solid wheel against the rim of which the piece is held. They are obtainable in hard and soft grades and in various sizes, of which 6-inch diameter is the most commonly used. (The larger the mop, the greater the polishing action.)

The brushes are made in bristle, brass and steel and in wheel-shape, cup-shape and pencil-shape. They are used for the preliminary cleaning-up before polishing with the calico mop.

Small felt mops of various shapes are used on flexible-shaft drills for polishing. (See also *Polishing* [*metals*].)

Polka-dot agate. Translucent chalcedony with dots of red, brown or yellow.

German pomander, made about 1500. Nationalmuseum, Munich

Pomanders. Pendant scent-cases, worn in various forms from the Middle Ages to the eighteenth century. They were not only something of a necessity in a time of rudimentary hygiene, but were also thought to be a protection against the plague. The perfumes were enclosed in a metal case which was perforated to allow the scent to escape. The shape was often that of an apple or pear (the name comes from 'pomme d'ambre', meaning 'perfume apple'). In the simpler type the perfumes were mixed together into a ball and were inserted by opening the case across the middle, but more elaborate pomanders were made in which each perfume was enclosed in a separate compartment, the compartments fitting together like the segments of an orange. These were richly decorated and often jewelled. Many were at the same time pomanders and devotional jewels: a beautiful example made in about 1470, probably in Germany, opens into four segments the walls of which are engraved with the figures of saints while the central portion contains a small statuette of the Virgin. This was comparatively modest; some pomanders had as many as 16 compartments, with the name of the perfume engraved on the outside of each.

Pomanders were worn hanging from the girdle, and sometimes from a long chain round the neck. During the seventeenth century, when a preoccupation with death manifested itself in many types of jewellery (see *Memento mori jewellery*), they were sometimes in the form of skulls. They ceased to be a normal part of dress in the eighteenth century, but shortly before their disappearance they assumed very elegant forms – some were decorated with painted enamels (the British equivalent were in Battersea and Bilston enamels, qq.v.), and in France many were made in onyx or crystal with applied decoration in gold. They were often worn hanging from chatelaines (q.v.).

'Pomegranate ruby'. Indian misnomer for red spinel.

'Pompadour pearls'. Trade name for imitation pearls.

Poppy stone. Red orbicular jasper (see *Jasper*) from California.

Porcelain. A type of fine earthenware sometimes used to make imitation stones. (See *Earthenware*.)

Porcelain opal. White common opal which is more opaque than milk opal (q.v.). (See also *Opal*.)

Posy rings. So called because from the fifteenth century they were engraved with a verse or 'poesy', posy rings developed from the earlier medieval fashion for inscribed jewellery. Rings exchanged between lovers were frequently inscribed. In the fifteenth century the chivalrous mottoes borne by knights at tournaments began to appear on jewellery, and there are rings engraved with such mottoes as 'Joie sans fin' and 'For ever'. The early inscriptions were usually in Lombardic lettering or black-letter, and would be on the outside of the shank unless this was already decorated.

The inscriptions of the sixteenth century are sometimes brief to the point of terseness ('Deal truly' is a fair example), and are normally in capitals. However, by now the mottoes had come under the influence of courtly literature and the composition of elegant 'posies' was increasingly a literary pastime. Commonplace books written in the sixteenth and seventeenth centuries list many examples such as

'Povertie preventeth mee',
and
'True love hath led my heart to choose,
My heart is dead if you refuse'.

The form of most posy rings was now a plain gold or silver hoop with the inscription, usually in italics, on the inside – the message on the ring was essentially a private one.

In the early seventeenth century there was a renewed fashion for inscribed jewellery, and the inscription reflected the current literary preoccupation with clever allusions and word-play. The wedding-ring given by Thomas Lyte of Lyte's Cary to his wife was inscribed 'Lyte's love is little worth': this referred to her small stature and the fact that Worth was her maiden name. The traditional sentiments of lovers – 'Let deathe lead love to rest', etc. – were still the most popular, but chivalry had declined sadly. The blunter sentiments of the age range from:

'Love him who gave thee this ring
of gold,
'Tis he must kiss thee when th'art old.'
to

'If thee dosn't work thee shasn't eat'.
Most of the seventeenth and eighteenth century posy rings were probably used as wedding rings.

The plain inscribed posy ring lost its popularity at the end of the eighteenth century, and rings began to be worn which had decorative inscriptions in French enamelled on the outside of the shank. The shift of emphasis from a hidden and personal message to something intended to be seen marks the end of the traditional posy ring.

Potato stone. A rounded geode (q.v.) containing crystals, commonly of quartz. When removed from the rock formation these geodes often look very like potatoes.

Potch. Australian miners' term for opal which although colourful does not have a lively play of colour. (See *Opal*.)

Prase. A name applied both to crystalline (q.v.) quartz which contains fibres of actinolite, giving a leek-green colour (this stone has also been called 'mother of emerald'), and to dark green jasper (q.v.).

'Prasiolite'. Brazilian amethyst heat-treated to produce a green quartz.

Precious metals. Gold, silver, platinum, and palladium. (See also *Noble metals* and *Base metals*.)

'Precious stones'. A term conventionally reserved for diamond, emerald, ruby and sapphire. However, the value of a stone does not depend only on its species and in this sense the term is misleading. (See '*Semi-precious stones*'.)

'Precious topaz'. A term sometimes used in America to distinguish genuine topaz from citrine, which is often called topaz quartz.

Prehnite. (Hydrated calcium-aluminium silicate. S.G. 2.88–2.94; R.I. 1.61–1.64; H. 6.) An opaque oil-green or brown stone sometimes seen in cabochon form or used for carving. Some cabochons of translucent yellowish prehnite show a cat's-eye effect.

Sources of ornamental-quality material include Bourg d'Oisans in France, Cape Colony in S. Africa, Renfrew in Scotland, Prospect, near Sydney, Australia, and China.

President Vargas diamond. A superb diamond weighing 726.6 carats in the rough, found in the alluvial deposits in Minas Gerais, Brazil in 1938. It was named after the President of Brazil, Dr. Getulio Dornelles Vargas.

Pressed amber. See *Amber.*

Princess cut. An earlier name for the profile cut, q.v.

'Prismatic moonstone'. Misnomer for chalcedony.

'Prismatic quartz'. Misnomer for iolite.

Profile cut. A cut for diamond invented in 1961 by Mr. Arpad Nagy, making possible very economical use of the material. (See *Diamond-cutting* for description.)

Pseudochrysolite. Moldavite. (See *Tektite.*)

Pseudoemerald. Malachite.

Pseudomalachite. (S.G. about 3.6; R.I. 1.80; H. 4½.) An opaque green copper phosphate similar in appearance to malachite (q.v.) but slightly harder and less common. It comes from Rheinbreitbach in Germany and Nizhne-Tagilsk in Russia.

Pseudophite. (Hydrated aluminium-magnesium silicate. S.G. about 2.69; R.I. 1.57; H. 2½.) A green rock found in Burgenland, Austria, and used ornamentally. It is a type of aluminous serpentine.

Pudding stone. A mineral conglomerate often used as an ornamental stone; it consists of numerous rounded pebbles cemented together by a finer-grained mineral.

Pudding stone jade. Nephrite (see *Jade*) in the form of nodules cemented together by a darker material. (See also *Pudding stone.*)

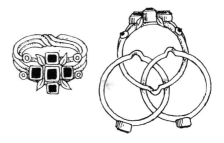

Seventeenth-century gold puzzle ring with white-enamelled scrolls, set with a central diamond between four rubies. British Museum

Pumice. A cellular volcanic rock used in powdered form as a polishing agent.

Pumicite. A material of volcanic origin and similar in composition to pumice, used as a polishing agent.

Punch. A tool for impressing a shape or pattern on an object, or for piercing or indenting it. Punches are often used in conjunction with a hammer. Many different types are used in the manufacture of jewellery: see *Carat punches, Centre punch, Chasing tools, Cutting punches, Doming punches, Letter punches, Repoussé tools.* The cameo part of a die which forces the metal into the hollow mould is also known as a punch. (See *Stamping* and *Machine-stamping.*)

Purple gold. An alloy consisting of 25 per cent aluminium, 75 per cent gold. It is very brittle.

Putty powder. A dioxide of tin, used as a polishing agent.

Puzzle rings. Rings made of a number of twisted interlocking hoops which readily come apart and which it is extremely difficult to put together again. It is not known when puzzle rings were first used, but in the seventeenth century they became popular as lovers' rings. In Turkey it was apparently the custom for a soldier going off to war to give his wife a puzzle ring; if on his return he found her trying to fit it together he knew that she had had occasion to take it off during his absence.

The hoops of puzzle rings were usually set with stones or surmounted with knobs of metal, which, when the hoops were correctly put together, formed a pattern. There might be any number of hoops from three to nine or more. In the past few years cheap puzzle rings of base metal have become popular in England as novelties.

'Pyralin'. (Trade name.) A cellulose plastic. (See *Plastics*.)

Pyrite. See *Marcasite*.

'Pyroemerald'. Misnomer for green fluorspar.

Pyrope garnet. (Magnesium-aluminium silicate. S.G. 3.7–3.8; R.I. 1.74–1.75; H. $7\frac{1}{4}$.) A transparent garnet usually of a fine blood-red colour, sometimes approaching the purplish colour of almandine (q.v.) as it approaches almandine in chemical composition. The name means 'fiery'. Some pyropes have a yellowish tinge and are much less valued. It was the latter type of pyrope garnet that was found in great quantity near Trebnitz in the old kingdom of Bohemia and extensively used in Victorian jewellery. Better quality stones have since been found associated with diamond in the South African mines, which are now the best source for pyrope. These stones are sometimes wrongly called 'Cape rubies'. Other localities are

Russia (Transbaikalia), and the U.S.A. In Arizona pebbles of pyrope are dug up and deposited on the top of earth-mounds by ants in the course of their excavations. Pyrope is usually free from flaws and a stone of good colour is therefore very attractive. The crystals are generally small, but occasionally very large stones are encountered, such as the one weighing 468 carats which used to belong to the kings of Saxony.

Pyrope may be distinguished from ruby by its single refraction and absence of dichroism, its lower specific gravity and (usually) its faint tinge of black. From the valuable red spinel, which is also singly refractive, it may be distinguished by its higher specific gravity and the fact that unlike spinel it does not fluoresce under ultra-violet light.

Rhodolite. (S.G. 3.84; R.I. 1.76) is a rose-red sub-variety of garnet, intermediate between the pyrope and almandine groups. It was first found at Cowee Creek, Macon County, N. Carolina, and similar stones have been found in Ceylon. (See also *Garnet*.)

Pyrophyllite. (Aluminium silicate. S.G. about 2.8; R.I. 1.55–1.60; H. $1\frac{1}{2}$.) A mineral of which some varieties are occasionally used as ornamental stones. The massive variety is white, grey or greenish, has a greasy lustre and resembles steatite (q.v.). 'South African wonder-stone' (q.v.) is a greyish variety used ornamentally.

Pyroxene. A group of minerals with similar physical and optical characteristics. Diopside, enstatite, spodumene (qq.v.) and jadeite (see *Jade*) are members of the group.

Q

Quahog pearl. Pearl from the quahog or hard clam (*Venus mercenaria*), found off the Atlantic coast of North America.

Quartz. (Silicon oxide. S.G. about 2.65; R.I. 1.54–1.55; H. 7.) The commonest of all minerals. In its *crystalline* form quartz provides the gemstones *amethyst, cairngorm, citrine, rose quartz, rock crystal* and *smoky quartz*, with the chatoyant varieties *quartz cat's eye* and *tiger's eye* (qq.v.). All these varieties have the specific gravity, refractive index and hardness given above.

Quartzite is quartz formed by the metamorphic process. It provides the gemstone *aventurine quartz,* and may also be dyed and used in beads or sold as an imitation of jade.

Cryptocrystalline or *microcrystalline* quartz is a combination of crystalline quartz and amorphous hydrated silica (opal). The gemstone varieties of this are *chalcedony* (giving the sub-varieties *agate, bloodstone, chrysoprase, cornelian, onyx*) and *jasper* (qq.v.). *Opal* (q.v.) may be regarded as a quartz gem on account of its chemical composition, but is usually treated as being in a class on its own because of its peculiar structure and lack of crystalline form.

Quartz occurs all over the world. Material which is not of gemstone quality has numerous industrial applications – glass, building sand, resonators and oscillators in radio transmission equipment, etc.

Quartz cat's eye. (See *Quartz, crystalline.*) A chatoyant stone sometimes very similar to chrysoberyl cat's eye (see *Cat's eye*) and often mistaken for it, although it is softer and lighter than chrysoberyl. The colours are usually honey-yellow, brown or greyish-green. The chatoyancy is caused by fine parallel fibres of asbestos which reflect the light.

The best quartz cat's eye comes from the gem gravels of Ceylon and from India. Poorer quality greenish stone is found at Fichtelgeberge in Bavaria.

Quartz glass. Fused quartz.

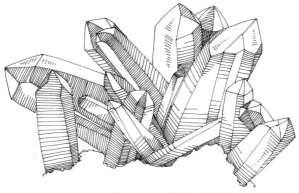

Group of quartz crystals (amethyst)

'Quartz topaz'. Misnomer for citrine.

Quartzite. See *Quartz*.

'Quebec diamond'. Misnomer for rock crystal.

Queen Elizabeth's earrings. The now traditional name for the four drop pearls suspended from the intersection of the arches of the Imperial State Crown in the British Regalia. The history of these pearls is shrouded in remarkable obscurity; it is impossible to say which, if any, of them belonged to Queen Elizabeth, or to which Queen Elizabeth they belonged.

When the crown was refurbished for the coronation of George IV (1820) the jewellers found two very badly shaped and poor-quality pearls suspended from the cross. The Jewel Office stated that they were extremely valuable and had once been pawned to the Dutch government for £50,000. The crown jewellers disregarded this information and exchanged one of the pearls for a better one for the sum of £5, selling the original to a dealer for £1. The other was subsequently replaced for the coronation of Queen Victoria. In the early part of this century a story became current that after Queen Victoria's death a paper packet had been found in the palace containing a pair of pendant pearls and marked 'Queen Elizabeth's earrings', and that Edward VII had ordered them to be placed in the crown. There is no official record of this having been done, but the pearls thereby acquired their present name. If there is any truth in the story, it is likely that the Queen Elizabeth referred to was not Elizabeth I but Elizabeth Queen of Bohemia, daughter of James I, whose jewels passed to the Hanoverian royal house and were inherited by Queen Victoria. The Stuarts were very fond of pendant pearl earrings. On the other hand, Elizabeth I, to judge from her portraits, was also much addicted to the wearing of pearls.

Queen pearl. A large American fresh-water pearl found in Notch Brook near Patterson, N.J. in 1857. It weighed 98 grains (4 pearl grains = 1 carat) and was pinkish in colour. It was bought by Tiffany and Co., who sold it to a French dealer. It was subsequently bought by the Empress Eugénie, wife of Napoleon III, who had a predilection for pearls.

Queenstownite (Darwin glass). (S.G. 2.27–2.29; R.I. 1.47–1.50.) A natural glass, thought to be from a meteoric crater, found near Queenstown in western Tasmania. The colours range from colourless through yellowish-green to black. (See also *Obsidian* and *Tektite*.)

Quenching. The cooling of heated metal in water or an acid solution. (See also *Annealing*.)

Quetzalitli. Mexican name for translucent green jade.

Quoin facet. One of the facets on a brilliant-cut diamond (see *Diamond-cutting*). The term is sometimes used for four of the bezel facets (q.v.), sometimes for four of the pavilion facets (q.v.).

R

Rainbow agate. See *Iris agate*.

Rainbow obsidian. Iridescent obsidian.

Rainbow quartz (Iris quartz). (See *Quartz, crystalline*.) Rock crystal containing numerous tiny cracks which, being filled with air, produce an iridescent effect through interference of light. The effect is artificially created in the so-called firestones (q.v.).

Raspberry spar. Rhodochrosite or pink tourmaline.

Rati. An Indian unit of weight for gemstones. In the past it has varied considerably in different districts and at different times. At present the rati equals 0.91 carat. (See *Weights for gemstones*.)

Reconstructed stones. Small crystals or pieces of crystal fused together to make larger stones, usually with the addition of some colouring oxide. The process was used mainly with rubies (see *'Geneva rubies'* for the earliest example), and the stones were apt to betray their nature by the inclusion of air-bubbles. Reconstructed gemstones are no longer made because synthetic stones of greatly superior quality can now be produced (see *Synthetic gemstones*). There is, however, a reconstructed amber; see *Amber*.

Red Cross diamond. A canary-yellow South African diamond weighing 375 carats in the rough, fashioned into a 205-carat square-cut brilliant. The stone contains a series of inclusions which when seen through the table facet appear in the form of a Maltese cross. In 1918 the London Diamond Syndicate donated the stone to the art sale in aid of the funds of the British Red Cross Society and the order of St. John of Jerusalem. It was sold by Christie's on behalf of the Red Cross for £10,000. Its present whereabouts is unknown.

Red gold. An alloy of gold with copper or copper and silver.

'Redmanol'. (Trade name.) A phenol plastic. (See *Plastics*.)

Red Sea pearl. Correct name for a pearl fished in the Red Sea, or incorrect name for a bead of coral.

Reflection. The throwing back of light from a surface into the medium from which it has come. The light is returned at an angle equal to the angle of incidence. When light strikes the surface of a transparent or translucent gemstone some of it is reflected from the surface and some penetrates the stone and is refracted (see *Refraction*) within it. Some of the refracted light may then be reflected within the stone. (See *Total internal reflection*.)

The amount and quality of the light reflected from the surface of a stone or metal is responsible for its lustre (q.v.).

Reflectometer. Alternative name for refractometer.

Refraction. The bending of light from its original path when it enters a medium of different optical density. Light is bent towards the perpendicular when it enters an optically denser medium, and away from the perpendicular when it enters an optically less dense medium. Since a gemstone is an optically denser medium than air, the angle of refraction in a stone is therefore smaller than the angle at which the light struck the stone (the angle of incidence). The extent to

Refractive index

which stones refract light varies considerably and is one of their most important properties. The refractive power of a stone can be measured in various ways and is expressed in a figure known as the *refractive index* (q.v.). Transparent stones with a high refractive index possess considerable brilliance.

According to the refractive index of the stone and the direction in which the light is travelling, light may not be refracted out of the stone but may be thrown back into it by striking the facet-surface at a certain angle. This phenomenon is called *total internal reflection* (q.v.) and is one of the principles used in refractive index measurement.

In minerals of the cubic system (see *Crystal systems*) and amorphous minerals a single incident ray of light emerges as a single ray, but in other minerals the ray is split up into two rays which travel independently through the stone and emerge separate. (See *Double refraction*.)

Refractive index. A measure of the power of a substance to refract light (see *Refraction*). Light entering a gemstone from the air is bent towards the perpendicular, making an angle with the perpendicular which is smaller than the angle at which it struck the surface of the stone (the angle of incidence). The refractive index is the ratio of the sine of the angle of incidence to the sine of the angle of refraction, the resulting figure always being greater than 1. The figure is constant for the variety of gemstone and in singly-refracting stones is independent of the angle of incidence (Snell's law).

Doubly-refracting stones have more than one refractive index and the indices are dependent on the direction of the light ray. This is further discussed under *Double refraction* (q.v.).

Where the identity of a stone is in doubt it can usually be determined by the refractive index. There are various methods of measuring this.
Measurement of refractive index.
1. Refractometer. This is a straightforward and very useful method of measurement since gemstones can usually be examined in their settings. The stone is placed table facet downwards on a piece of highly-refractive glass set in the refractometer, and by means of total internal reflection of light a shadow-edge is produced which, being projected on to a calibrated scale, enables the refractive index to be read off. The method is explained more fully under *Refractometer*. The disadvantage of the method is that stones of very high refractive index are beyond the scope of a normal instrument, but it is adequate for nearly all gemstones.

2. Immersion methods. These serve as a rough guide to the refractive index of a stone and are particularly useful for beads, very small stones and fragments of stone. A transparent stone when immersed in a liquid of similar refractive index to its own will become almost invisible. The simplest of the immersion methods therefore is to place the stone in a series of liquids of known refractive index and note the one in which the stone most completely 'disappears'. A refinement of this procedure is the *Becke method*, in which the stone immersed in liquid is studied under a microscope. The microscope is first sharply focused, and then the focus is raised or lowered. When this is done, a band of light appears to move from the stone into the liquid, or vice versa, according to which has the higher refractive index; when the focus is lowered, the line of light passes into the medium of lower refractive index, and when the focus is raised the light passes into the medium of higher refractive index. By making several trials, two liquids can be found between the refractive indices of which lies the refractive index of the stone. The *immersion contrast* method works on the same principle but does not require a microscope, and several stones can be examined at once. They are immersed in a suitable liquid in a glass dish, which is placed on a sheet of glass under an overhead light. Seen from underneath by means of a mirror, the stones show varying effects according to their refractive indices. In stones with a lower refractive index than that of the liquid, the facet edges appear as black lines and the edge of the stone is bordered with white. In stones with a higher refractive index than that of the liquid, the facet edges are white and the stone is bordered with black. The effect is marked when there is a considerable difference between the refractive indices of the stone and the liquid, and faint when the difference is small. A fairly simple test is the *shadow method*, in which the stone, immersed in liquid in a glass dish, is placed on a bright surface, and a piece of straight-edged black card is slipped under the dish so that, seen from above, the card and the gemstone overlap slightly. If the stone and the liquid have the same refractive index, the card-edge will follow the same line where it passes under the edge of the stone, but if the refractive indices differ the light rays will be deviated and the edge of the card that lies under the stone will appear to be displaced – it will advance into the stone if the liquid is of higher refractive index, and retreat out of the stone if the liquid is of lower refractive index.

Liquids used in testing. There is a range of several dozen suitable liquids. The following are some of the more useful ones: water (R.I. 1.33), chloroform (1.45), olive oil (1.47), cedarwood oil (1.51), clove oil (1.54), monobromobenzene (1.56), bromoform (1.59), acetylene tetrabromide (1.63), monobromonaphthalene (1.66), methylene iodide (1.74), methylene iodide and sulphur (1.78). The contact liquid generally used with refractometers is a mixture of methylene iodide, sulphur and 18% tetraiodoethylene: this has a refractive index of 1.81. For measuring stones of very high refractivity, phenyldi-iodoarsine (1.85) and West's solution (2.05) are used; both these liquids are dangerous.

3. *Minimum deviation.* This is the most accurate method of measuring refractive index and there is no upper limit to the refractivity of the stones that can be tested. However, the procedure requires fairly complex apparatus and involves considerable calculation. It also requires

that the stone should have well-cut facets.

The instrument used is a table spectrometer. This consists of a fixed collimator which controls the amount of incident light and renders the rays parallel, a graduated circle marked in degrees, in the centre of which the stone is set, and a telescope which can be moved on a vertical axis around the circle. Two facets of the stone are selected which together form a prism (usually the table facet and one of the back facets are used), and the angle formed by these facets (the prism angle) is measured. The stone and telescope are then rotated until the light from the collimator passes through the prism and is received by the telescope. What is seen through the telescope will be either an image of the collimator-window (if monochromatic light is used) or the spectrum (if ordinary light is used) (the image is double in doubly-refracting stones). If the stone is then again rotated, and the telescope with it, this image will move until it reaches a point beyond which it will not pass. This is the position of minimum deviation, where a ray of light enters and leaves the prism at the same angle. The position of minimum deviation for each of the two facets is read off in relation to the incident light from the collimator; theoretically the two angles should be identical but as in practice there is always a slight difference a mean is taken, and this is the angle of minimum deviation. When the prism angle (A) and the angle of minimum deviation (D) have been measured, the refractive index of the stone can be calculated by the formula

$$\text{R.I.} = \frac{\sin \frac{1}{2}(A+D)}{\sin \frac{1}{2}A}$$

Refractometer. An instrument for measuring the refractive index (q.v.) of gemstones. Various models are available, but basically the instrument consists of a series of lenses, a hemisphere or prism of dense and highly-refractive glass, and a calibrated scale of refractive indices. The principle on which the instrument functions is the total internal reflection of light (q.v.), which occurs when light travels from a medium of greater optical density to one of lesser optical density at an angle greater than the critical angle. In this case the medium of greater optical density is the glass, and the medium of lesser optical density is the gemstone, which is placed on the flat surface of the glass with its table facet downwards (a drop of contact liquid, a liquid of higher refractive index than the stone, must be placed on the glass, as otherwise a thin layer of air will prevent proper optical contact between the stone and the glass). Light (which should be monochromatic, to avoid a dispersion effect by the stone) is passed through the glass from below and strikes the surface between the glass and the gemstone. The light which is travelling at an angle less than the critical angle is refracted out through the stone; that which is travelling at an angle greater than the critical angle is totally reflected back into the glass. The observer looking through the eyepiece sees part of the field dark, where the light has been refracted out through the stone, and part light, where the light is internally reflected in the glass; at the boundary of these areas is a line, known as the shadow edge, which marks the critical angle of the glass for the stone in question. The position of this shadow edge bears a regular relation to the refractive index of the stone, and it is projected on to a scale seen (usually) through the eyepiece which gives a direct reading of the refractive index.

Singly-refractive stones show one shadow edge and have one refractive index; doubly-refractive stones have two, separated by a small interval. If a doubly-refracting stone is gently rotated on the glass the interval between the shadow edges will vary slightly; the most widely separated readings are the maximum and minimum refractive indices of the stone, and the arithmetical difference between them is the stone's birefringence, or degree of double refraction.

Measuring the refractive index of a cabochon-cut or carved stone on a refractometer is more difficult. The domed surface of the stone is placed downwards on the dense glass in a spot of contact liquid. The observer looks through the eyepiece from a distance of about 15 inches, and sees a small disc which, when the eye is moved slowly up and down, changes from being completely dark to completely light. Between these points is a stage where a line of shadow bisects the disc. This position is read off on the refractometer scale, but since the shadow-line and the scale cannot both be in focus at the same time the position of the shadow-line has to be carried mentally for a moment. Recent models of refractometer incorporate modifications which make the process slightly easier.

Regard ring. A ring set with a row of small stones, the initial letters of which spell the word 'regard'. The usual combination is ruby, emerald, garnet, amethyst, ruby, diamond. It was fashionable to give regard rings as tokens of friendship and sentiment in the later part of the nineteenth century. Most of the rings consisted of a single hoop set with the stones in a row, but in some of them each stone is set on a separate hoop and the hoops are joined under the finger. The stones form a row along the top of the finger. The effect is interesting but exceedingly unattractive.

(Jewellery of this period is discussed under *Nineteenth-century jewellery*.)

Regent diamond. See *Pitt diamond*.

Reitz diamond. See *Jubilee diamond*.

Religious jewellery. See *Devotional jewellery*.

Reliquaries. See *Devotional jewellery*.

Renaissance jewellery. (Late fifteenth century to early seventeenth century.) The rediscovery of classical art which marked the end of the Middle Ages influenced the forms of jewellery and the way in which it was worn, but the influence was indirect. Greek and Roman jewellery was not copied because it was not yet known; it was the sculptures and monuments of antiquity which had been

Sixteenth-century enamelled chain

Elaborate pendant in the Mannerist style,
with pendant emeralds and rubies and six
table-cut diamonds

Sixteenth-century gold ring with figure of a
river god, set with rubies

rediscovered, and these inspired the
painters and sculptors of the sixteenth
century, who in turn influenced the work
of the goldsmiths. The relationship
between goldsmiths' work and the major
arts was very close at this time because
many painters were first apprenticed as
goldsmiths; Botticelli, Ghirlandajo, Ghi-
berti, Pollaiulo and many others received
their first training in this way. Hans
Holbein the younger designed jewels for
Henry VIII, and Benvenuto Cellini (q.v.),
popularly regarded as the greatest Renaissance goldsmith, abandoned his craft
towards the end of his life to devote
himself to sculpture. The two most
characteristic personal ornaments of the
sixteenth century, hat-badges and pendants, show unmistakably the influence of
contemporary sculpture.

Sixteenth-century jewellery is notable
for its emphasis on superb stones. These
were table-cut or faceted in simple shapes,
and diamonds were either table-cut or left
in their natural pointed octahedral form.
As a method of faceting which exploited
the fire of the diamond had not yet been
discovered, diamonds were less highly
valued than rubies and emeralds. It was

Spanish eagle pendant in enamelled gold; the
body consists of a large baroque pearl.
Wallace Collection, London

303

normal practice to use a coloured foil at the back of a stone to improve its colour, and diamonds were usually given a black tint to increase their sparkle. Paste gems of high quality were now being made, particularly in Milan.

Greek and Roman engraved gems were the only small-scale examples of classical art the sixteenth century possessed, and they were highly prized (see *Cameos* and *Intaglios*). Contemporary gem-engraving flourished in Italy under the patronage of wealthy collectors such as the Medici, and portrait cameos became very fashionable. Another characteristic of the century is the lavish use of enamel. Enamelling was now a highly sophisticated art; the difficult technique of encrusted enamel (q.v.), which had been used for a brief period around the end of the fourteenth century, reappears on the splendid figured pendants of the later Renaissance, and the art of painted enamel had been established at Limoges by the end of the fifteenth century. Its development was made possible by the discovery of counter-enamelling, which allowed thin sheets of metal to be safely enamelled without the use of cloisons (see *Enamel*). Painted enamel was used less on jewellery than on church ornaments, but it appears on medallions, hat-badges, and often on devotional jewellery.

Hat-badges were almost universally worn by men of the wealthier classes. The custom of wearing a brooch in the hat had originated in the Middle Ages, but such brooches were usually devotional or a sign of allegiance. In the Renaissance, when men asserted their individuality, they often bore the personal device of the wearer. Others showed scenes from mythology or from the Scriptures. There are two superb examples embossed in bas-relief with John the Baptist in the wilderness, and St. John the Divine mounted on the back of the eagle, writing his gospel. Hat-badges were usually set in jewelled rims, and many were enamelled. Portrait cameos of rulers were also worn in the hat, and around 1520 portrait medallions in enamel were fashionable. The finest surviving example is a portrait of the emperor Charles V, now in Vienna. These portrait cameos and enamels were also worn as pendants. Another popular hat decoration in the sixteenth century was the *aglet* – a small jewelled brooch-like ornament which could be sewn to the clothing; these were usually worn in sets.

Pendants in the first half of the sixteenth century were of various kinds, but were mostly fairly simple in form and dominated by precious stones. Some were in the form of initials – initial jewellery was popular in northern Europe, although little has survived because of its personal nature. Pendants in the form of the Tau cross were popular and were believed to have protective powers; much sixteenth-century jewellery, indeed, had a magical element, since the belief in the miraculous properties of stones, and in astrological signs, still lingered (see *Magical jewellery*). The great jewelled *collars*, such as the collar of balas rubies shown on several portraits of Henry VIII, were probably the prerogative of monarchs. Long, heavy gold *chains*, however, were widely fashionable from the 1520s onwards. They might be plain or with decorated links; one in Stockholm is made of rectangular links decorated with fine filigree. In France and England such chains were worn chiefly by men and in England were frequently presented by the monarch as a sign of favour or gratitude; in Flanders and Germany they seem to have been worn mainly by women. They were often worn with pendants attached.

Rings were extremely popular; several were often worn on one finger. Ornamental rings were usually of a fairly heavy form, with cabochon or table-cut stones in high enamelled settings. Signet rings were often set with antique or contemporary intaglios. There were numerous rings of office and rank, and of course the many love-rings and betrothal rings which had remained more or less unchanged from the Middle Ages. The ring illustrated is very unusual, but the sculptural form is typical of the period.

Bracelets began to be worn again in the sixteenth century after several hundred years of neglect, but were not very common. In Germany they were worn over the sleeve.

Towards the middle of the sixteenth century political and artistic changes took place which influenced the nature of later Renaissance jewellery. The political change was the increasing importance of Spain, founded largely on her lucrative conquests in the New World. As a result of this, Spanish fashion, with its stiff and formal dress and high lace ruffs, was adopted almost throughout Europe. The artistic change was the development of mannerism, a style which replaced the classical simplicity of early Renaissance art with elaboration and virtuosity, and with abstract forms such as moresques, scrolls, and strapwork (qq.v.). This style dominated the minor arts from about 1560 to the beginning of the seventeenth century.

It was quickly spread by the engraved pattern-books for jewellers which had begun to circulate in the earlier part of the century. These books were produced in most of the countries of Europe and account for the international nature of Renaissance jewellery. Among the highly gifted designers of the mid-century were Virgil Solis, Jacques Androuet Ducerceau, Pierre Woeiriot and Etienne Deaune (qq.v.); later Erasmus Hornick, Hans Collaert, Corvinianus Saur and Daniel Mignot (early seventeenth century) (qq.v.) developed and refined the style. It is rarely possible to match an existing jewel with a known design, but the general influence of the designs is obvious.

This is particularly so in the case of the figured *pendants* which show later Renaissance jewellery at its most magnificent. Erasmus Hornick published many designs for pendants in the form of dragons and sea-monsters, and numerous pendants of this type exist. Hans Collaert's later designs are similar. Other existing pendants are in the forms of mermaids, lizards, insects, birds (particularly popular in Spain), ships (popular in maritime countries including England), and animals.

These pendants, which were worn fastened to the sleeve as well as on a chain round the neck, are often very large, and are exquisitely enamelled and jewelled. In many cases a large baroque pearl is used as an integral part of the design. (See illustration.) In the last quarter of the century pendants of a different type, enclosed in an architectural frame set with square-cut stones, also became popular. These frequently had mythological or Biblical subjects, and were mostly made in Germany.

The *chains* and *necklaces* on which the pendants were worn were often equally magnificent. The women of the royal houses of Europe (jewellery was increasingly becoming a feminine prerogative) wore richly jewelled carcanets (short necklaces) with matching shoulder-collars and long chains. When ruffs became too large to allow for a necklace or collar, jewelled belts following the pointed waist were worn instead. These ornaments were typically in the form of linked enamelled plaques set with large table-cut stones and pearls, enamelled on the back with the moresque designs of the period.

At the beginning of the sixteenth century women had worn a simple chaplet of pearls or precious stones in their hair. By the latter part of the century this had become a formal and elaborate diadem of pearls. Other head-ornaments were jewelled hat-pins and aigrettes. With the increasing luxury of the European courts many accessories to dress were set with jewels, including the heads and claws of sable skins, worn on a short chain.

The first watch had been made in the early years of the sixteenth century and for a time it was fashionable to wear a watch round the neck. Throughout the century watches were incorporated in other types of jewellery, not yet having found a form of their own; they appear in pendants, miniature cases, as pomanders, and set in the clasps of bracelets. A superb example in Munich, with an alarm mechanism, is set in a finger-ring, and the

305

inside of its lid opens to reveal an enamelled scene of the Crucifixion. It was made about 1580, and illustrates the contemporary delight in ingenuity and in scientific things. Other rings were fitted with miniature astronomical or mathematical instruments (see *Rings*).

A similar delight in ingenuity lies behind the fondness for symbolism which is particularly characteristic of English sixteenth-century jewellery. Many jewels were clearly intended to convey a meaning; the inventories of Elizabeth I's jewellery list, among others, a jewel in the form of a lamp containing a hart in a flame, with an opal serpent, and another enamelled with Victory standing on a rainbow, holding a garland and a pair of compasses. The example *par excellence* of this type of jewellery is the Darnley or Lennox jewel (q.v.) made for Lady Margaret Douglas, a heart-shaped locket enamelled with numerous symbolic figures alluding to the political intrigues and hopes of the house of Douglas.

By the beginning of the seventeenth century the ingenuity and extravagance of Renaissance court jewellery were all but exhausted; jewels were worn in profusion but the designs were undistinguished. The decline was arrested by a change in fashion (see *Seventeenth-century jewellery*) which created a need for jewellery of a different type, suitable for a more restrained age.

(Other illustrations of Renaissance jewellery will be found under *Baroque pearl, Canning jewel, Rings*.)

Repoussé hammer. See *Chasing hammer*.

Repoussé tools. Steel punches of square or rectangular section, and about 5" long, used for punching up metal in relief from the back (see *Repoussé work*). Many tools can be used either for repoussé or chasing (q.v.), but *bossing* and *cushion* tools are used primarily for repoussé work. These have smooth, rounded and highly-polished tips and are used to drive the metal up in bumps or ridges. *Modelling tools* with convex tips can also be used to create areas of relief. *Tracers*, shaped like blunted chisels, are used to create lines, *matting tools*, which have patterned tips, are used to give texture to the surface, and a variety of tools with specially-shaped tips are used to produce shapes such as circles with a single impression. These tools may be used on the back or the front of the metal according to whether a concave or convex impression is required. (See also *Chasing tools*.) A special hammer is used for chasing and repoussé work: see *Chasing hammer*.

Repoussé work. The modelling of sheet metal in relief from the back, using a hammer and punches. The design is transferred to the metal and lightly scratched in, and the metal is laid on a firm but yielding surface. A block of wood or sheet of lead can be used if only shallow relief is required, but for high relief the metal is laid on a bowl of pitch (q.v.). The pitch and the metal are both heated slightly before work is started. The relief is then punched up, starting with the areas which are to be in lowest relief. From time to time the metal has to be annealed (see *Annealing*) to prevent its becoming brittle.

Repoussé work is nearly always done in conjunction with chasing (q.v.) (modelling and texturing from the front), and to a great extent the tools used in the two processes are interchangeable. On the whole the tools used for repoussé work are rather more blunt and rounded, and they are held nearly upright whereas chasing tools are held at more of an angle to the work. The punch is held between the thumb and the first and middle fingers of the left hand, while the tip of the third finger rests on the metal. (For tools, see *Repoussé tools, Chasing tools* and *Chasing hammer*.)

Gold and silver, being extremely malleable, are ideal materials for repoussé work and have been worked in this way from very early times – at least since the third millennium B.C. (see also *Gold*). A variant of repoussé much used in the ancient Greek world was stamping: the metal was embossed from the back with a punch which imprinted a complete pattern on the metal. This made it possible to cover a sheet of metal with identical patterns and to produce a series of identical plaques for necklaces, etc. (See *Stamping*; also *Greek jewellery*.) Much later, magnificent repoussé work resembling bas-relief sculpture was produced by the goldsmiths of the Renaissance, notably in the elaborate hat-badges popular in the sixteenth century (see *Renaissance jewellery*). In the nineteenth century stamping became mechanized and was used extensively for the production of cheap jewellery (see *Machine-stamping*). Repoussé work is not much used in modern jewellery, which prefers untextured surfaces, but it is still an important technique in silversmithing.

The term 'repoussé' is often used to include chasing.

Résille (Resilla). A fine network, usually of small beads sewn in patterns.

'Resinoid'. (Trade name.) A phenol plastic (see *Plastics*).

Resoglanz. German trade name for a polystyrene plastic (see *Plastics*).

Retinalite. Serpentine of a honey-yellow colour.

'Rhine diamond'. Misnomer for rock crystal.

Rhinestone. A somewhat meaningless word. It seems to have first meant rock crystal. Later it was used for glass imitation stones with variegated colours. It is now sometimes used in Britain for paste which has a slightly iridescent effect, or for coloured paste; in America and Canada it usually means colourless paste. It may also still be used to mean rock crystal.

Rhodium. One of the platinum group of metals (see *Platinum*), first isolated at the beginning of the nineteenth century. It is harder, whiter and more reflective than platinum. It is now widely used for plating silver to give it a tarnish-resistant surface, and also for plating platinum and white gold. The plating is extremely thin and makes little difference to the appearance of the metal, but is very durable.

Rhodium plating. See *Rhodium*.

Rhodizite. (Potassium [caesium/rubidium] aluminium borate. S.G. 3.4; R.I. 1.69; H. 8.) A rare mineral cut mostly for collectors. It was first found in rose-red massive form in the Urals; yellowish and greenish crystals have since been found in Madagascar.

Rhodochrosite. (Manganese carbonate. S.G. 3.5–3.6; R.I. 1.6–1.8; H. 4.) A rose-pink stone with radial bands of varying shades of pink. Grey, fawn, and brown stones also occur. The banding is due to stalagmitic formation. Rhodochrosite has only been used as an ornamental stone in the past 30 years, since its discovery in quantity in a silver and copper mine in Argentina said to have been worked by the Incas. Ornamental material now also comes from various localities in North America.

'Rhodoid'. (Trade name.) A cellulose acetate plastic. (See *Plastics*.)

Rhodolite. See *Pyrope garnet*.

Rhodonite. (Manganese silicate. S.G. 3.6–3.7; R.I. 1.73–1.74; H. about 6.) A rose-red stone, varying from translucent to opaque, which is made into beads and cabochons and very rarely, in the case of almost transparent material, into faceted stones. It occurs most commonly in a massive form resembling pink marble, veined with black. Sources of gem-quality material include the Sverdlovsk district in Russia, the Broken Hill mines in Australia, Sweden, Mexico, various localities in the U.S.A., and Cornwall.

Ribbon jasper. Jasper (q.v.) with bands of colour.

'Richelieu pearls'. (Trade name.) Imitation pearls.

Ricolite. A banded serpentine.

Riffle (Riffler). A double-ended steel file gripped in the middle, having curved and usually tapered ends. It is used for filing work which an ordinary file cannot

Ring clamp

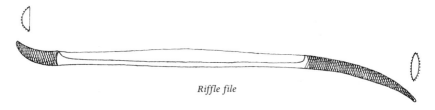

Riffle file

reach. Rifflers are made in numerous shapes and sections to suit various requirements.

Ring clamp. A roughly cylindrical tool made of two pieces of box wood, used to hold small objects, particularly rings, while they are being worked on. There are several types. In one type the two parts of the clamp are held together with a metal band and the jaws are brought together by forcing a wedge into the space at the bottom end. In another type the jaws are tightened by means of a screw at the side. In a third type the ring is held from the inside in a recess at the top of the jaws; the jaws are expanded by a screw set in the bottom of the clamp. (See illustrations.)

For other holding tools see *Vices*, also *Tweezers*.

Ring clip. A strip of hard springy metal fixed to a ring-shank to hold a loosely-fitting ring securely on the finger. One type is a plain strip, one end of which is soldered to the inside of the shank. Another type is a strip with lugs at each end; the strip is placed inside the shank and the lugs are bent over the edge of the shank to keep it in place. (See illustrations.)

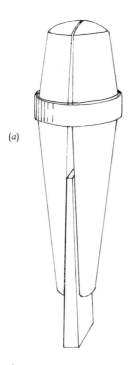

(a)

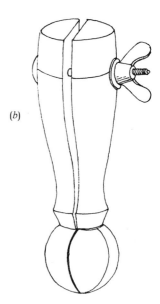

(b)

Ring clamps: (a) wedge type, (b) wing nut type

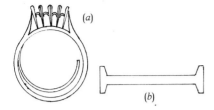

Ring clips: (a) soldered type, (b) lug type

Ring clips are made in silver and in various gold alloys.

Rings. Rings mean many things. No other article of jewellery is so charged with personal significance or has been used for so many purposes. Rings have been used in the past to confer high office, to impress the owner's mark on documents, to indicate social rank, to convey secret messages (the news of his accession to the English throne is said to have been conveyed to James I by a ring depicting a darkened lantern, indicating that the light of the Queen's life was extinguished), to invoke magical powers, to commemorate political events and personal disasters, to carry perfume, poison and religious relics, and as a sign of marriage or betrothal. They have even been used as offensive weapons (see illustration of a German pugilist's ring). They have been worn on every finger, and on every joint of every finger, as well as on the thumb, and they have also been worn over gloves, strung round the neck, threaded onto the cords of hats, sewn to garments, attached to legal documents and dedicated in shrines. Rings play an important part in all the best literature from fairy-stories to Shakespeare, and sometimes they have

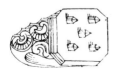

Bavarian pugilist's ring, brass. Victoria and Albert Museum

played a part in history. There are numerous stories of rings having been sent as tokens in a time of crisis. One of them concerns a ring given by Elizabeth I to the Earl of Essex with the promise that if ever he incurred her displeasure and sent her the ring the sight of it would restore him to her favour. Some years later, under sentence of death for treason, Essex gave the ring to a boy with instructions to deliver it to his cousin, Lady Scroop, who would give it to the Queen, but the boy delivered it by mistake to the Countess of Nottingham who was one of Essex's greatest enemies and who, guessing the meaning of the ring, kept it. The Queen was expecting to receive the ring and when it did not arrive concluded that Essex was too proud to make this last appeal, and therefore ordered his execution. It is said that the Queen finally learnt the truth when the Countess was dying, and, visiting her on her death-bed, exclaimed bitterly that God might forgive her, but she could not.

The decorative use of rings, which is the subject predominantly considered here, is of course very old. The simplest ring of precious material is a circle or coil of metal wire, and rings of this type were made in the ancient civilizations as soon as gold wire could be made – some time in the third millennium B.C. In ancient Egypt, although jewellery was elaborate and complex (see *Egyptian jewellery*), rings do not seem to have been very important decoratively but they were extensively used to carry signets. For about a thousand years they were made with a swivelling bezel which had the carved back of a scarab beetle on one side and the signet in the form of hieroglyphs on the other (see *Scarabs* and *Signet rings*). Apart from their practical use, these rings, in common with the rest of Egyptian jewellery, had an amuletic significance.

The use of the signet ring was continued by the Greeks but from early times Greek rings were also made purely for decoration – some which look like signet rings were in fact probably not used as such. From the fourth century

Rings

B.C. signet rings were set with an engraved gemstone in a fixed bezel, but with this exception stones were little used in Greek jewellery until Hellenistic times and the rings were mostly of gold decorated with filigree or repoussé work. There were several types including the spiral snake-ring; one of these is illustrated under *Greek jewellery* (q.v.).

In Rome rings attained an importance they had not possessed elsewhere; they became part of the social system. In the early days gold was scarce in Rome and austerity was a national virtue; as a symbol of this, early Roman rings were mostly of iron. The wearing of a gold ring was restricted to certain classes, at first to patricians who had held high office and to their male descendants. By the end of the third century B.C. the privilege had been extended to the *equites* or knights, and gold rings could also be awarded as a military honour. By the end of the Republic a certain frivolity had crept into the honours lists and gold rings were being awarded to actors, who were normally considered to be a very disreputable class of people. Under the Empire, when gold was flowing into and out of Rome at a steady rate and the old social distinctions were becoming very blurred, gold rings were bestowed with increasing freedom by the emperors until in the end any soldier and any freed slave might have one and the symbol became meaningless.

As the wealth of the Empire increased so did the wearing of rings; a contemporary satirist speaks of a man who wore six on each finger – doubtless an exaggeration, but presumably founded in fact. The Romans did not usually wear a ring on the middle finger, but they wore them on all other fingers and the thumb and sometimes on the upper joints. The rings were usually set with stones (a variety of gemstones had become available through trade and conquest in the East) or with paste (the Romans were skilled at glass-making and paste was not necessarily regarded as inferior to a real stone). They were often very elaborate and heavy. The early Empire was a period of great interest in gem-engraving when some very fine work was produced (mostly by Greek artists), and many rings were set with these stones as signets. A type of ring characteristic of the later Empire has an imperial gold coin set in the bezel; these may have been military decorations, or they may have been worn in flattery of the Emperor, whose portrait appeared on the coin. Another feature of Roman rings is the use of niello (q.v.) for decoration.

Certain types of ring are peculiar to Roman jewellery or first appeared in the Roman period. The most important of these is the betrothal ring, which was first used (as far as is known) in republican Rome and was originally of iron. Its history is described under *Betrothal rings*. The fede ring (q.v.), bearing the motif of two clasped hands, also originated in Rome; it was obviously suitable for a betrothal ring but was not exclusively used for this purpose. Key-rings (q.v.), in which a key projects from the bezel or hoop, were often worn on a chain but were sometimes made to be worn on the finger, and a few are in precious metal. A series of bronze rings have been found engraved with Roman numerals; these were previously thought to have been the numbers of Roman legions and the rings are known as legionary rings (q.v.) – they probably had nothing to do with legions but were almost certainly worn by soldiers. Another class is the poison ring; the existence of this article has been doubted, but it certainly existed in Roman times if not later (see *Poison rings*).

Roman ring set with an onyx, third century A.D. British Museum

310

Finally, rings were worn by the Romans, as by every society, as amulets. Since all manner of precious and non-precious materials were popularly credited with strange powers (see *Magical jewellery*) it is difficult to be sure now which surviving rings were worn for this purpose, but it seems fairly safe to say that rings set with or made out of materials which have no decorative value, such as nails, were amuletic. One material popularly used as an amulet in Roman times was coral.

The use of rings for decoration, as signets, as amulets and as tokens of betrothal and/or marriage continued more or less unbroken after the fall of the Empire. The use of signet rings by the early Christians is described under *Signet rings* and *Devotional jewellery*. The signet was supposed to be the only ring worn by Christians but this ruling was not strictly observed, particularly in Byzantium where amulet rings were much worn. Byzantine decorative rings are very diverse in style, reflecting the many elements in Byzantine culture. Some have peacock designs which are inspired by Oriental art, others are descendants of Roman types. Cloisonné enamel appears on some, niello is extensively used, and granulation is quite common. On the signet rings the devices are usually religious. By the seventh century the Church had begun to use the ring as a symbol of investiture: bishops were invested with a gold ring set with a gem that was not engraved (see *Ecclesiastical rings*).

The Teutonic tribes were fond of rings and also used the signet. The signet rings usually had a metal bezel engraved with a portrait, monogram or Christian emblem: it is doubtful how many of the symbols on these rings, adopted from Roman types, were understood. Some rings were set with Roman intaglios. The commonest type of barbarian gemstone ring worn on the Continent had a circular bezel set with slices of garnet. Some barbarian rings had extremely high bezels projecting nearly an inch. The Anglo-Saxons used garnet but it does not normally appear in their rings, which for the most part are very simple. An exception to this simplicity is the series of so-called 'royal rings', which are in gold decorated with designs in niello. One of these, the ring of Queen Ethelswith, is illustrated under *Anglo-Saxon jewellery*.

In the early part of the Middle Ages such decorative rings as were worn were mostly copies of antique styles. Little attempt was made to fashion the stones, which were very often left in their irregular shape and simply polished. The bezel was shaped to the stone, which was usually held by four claws attached to the outside of the bezel. The shoulders of the ring might be chased or moulded in the form of dragons' heads: a memory of more barbaric times. Stones or pastes which had been properly cabochon-cut were often set in rectangular bezels. In the thirteenth century the stirrup-shaped ring, a graceful type which had earlier been used by the Romans, became common (see illustration), and it became more usual to fashion stones as cabochons instead of leaving them practically uncut. High collet-settings fashioned to the shape of the stone were now replacing the claw-settings. Towards the end of the Middle Ages the shoulders and hoop of the ring began to be much more elaborately decorated; many English fifteenth-century rings are enamelled with floral patterns. In the late fifteenth century a new style appeared in which the bezel was in the form of a quatrefoil; this developed in the subsequent century into a striking and characteristic Renaissance style.

Stirrup-shaped ruby ring, thirteenth century.
Victoria and Albert Museum

311

Rings

Many rings worn during the Middle Ages were of a religious nature; they bore religious inscriptions, were decorated with the figures of saints, contained spaces for relics, etc. These are described in more detail under *Devotional jewellery*. This class overlaps with that of magical rings, since the inscriptions, relics and so on were in most cases believed to have some magical power. Many rings were overtly magical: they were engraved with talismanic signs or set with stones believed to have magical properties. Rings of this type are further discussed under *Magical jewellery*. In addition to these types, and to some extent overlapping with them, there were numerous other classes of rings. The commonest is probably the love/betrothal ring. As it is impossible to know at this distance in time whether a ring carrying, for instance, a lover's inscription was a pledge of betrothal or a suggestion of something less honourable, these are discussed for the sake of simplicity under *Betrothal rings*. (See also *Wedding rings*.) There were also

Thirteenth-century gold ring, probably a ring of office. Victoria and Albert Museum

rings indicating special office. Several types of ecclesiastical ring were now in use, and as a secular example a gold ring which probably belonged to a Venetian dignitary (it bears the lion of St. Mark) is illustrated. The use of a ring at coronations was well established, and rings could also be regarded as evidence of certain rights and duties including the legal tenure of land. Richard I had attached his ring to a charter relating to the exchange of land in Normandy for certain other properties. The heavy gilt-bronze ring illustrated, engraved with a ducal coronet, probably had some such significance, as perhaps did the so-called Papal rings (q.v.).

312

Heavy fifteenth-century Italian ring in bronze gilt, engraved with a shield of arms on each shoulder and a ducal coronet on each side of the bezel. British Museum

During the sixteenth century rings became much more popular and many were worn at a time, sometimes several on one finger. Sumptuary laws were passed in some countries to restrict the number of rings that might be worn by the various classes, but they seem to have had little effect. The characteristic rings of this period have a high and complicated setting in the shape of four petals – a development of the late medieval quatrefoil bezel. The settings were lavishly enamelled and the stone itself was usually table-cut. Diamonds, however, were often still worn in their pointed form, this being the shape of the natural crystal. The point was used for writing verses on window-panes – a fashionable pastime. (One of these rings is illustrated under *Diamond*.) The rich decoration on these rings was not confined to the bezel; the shoulders, the hoop and often the underside of the bezel were enamelled and chased with as much care.

Typical Renaissance ring with high setting

At the beginning of the seventeenth century the heavy magnificence of these rings gave way to lighter styles. There was a growing tendency for a number of small stones to be used instead of one large one. Stones were now being cut in more elaborate ways and were becoming more important than their enamelled settings. One common type of seventeenth-century ring, however, has no stones; it is a circlet of enamelled metal and the decoration is usually floral. (See *Seventeenth-century jewellery* for illustration.) The seventeenth-century fondness for flowers and floral patterns found logical expression in the *giardinetti* ring (q.v.) which appeared at the end of the century and was in the form of a floral spray set with small coloured stones. (See illustration.)

Giardinetti ring

During the seventeenth century the custom of distributing mourning rings (q.v.) at funerals became common in England. These rings followed a style of their own and lasted well into the nineteenth century. Another and quite different type of ring which made its appearance in the late sixteenth or early seventeenth century was what one might call a 'scientific' ring. This reflected the tremendous increase in scientific knowledge which had begun with the Renaissance and attracted the interest of almost all educated men. There were rings fitted with watch-mechanisms and with mathematical and astronomical instruments. The example illustrated is a silver-gilt ring which opens out into an astrolabe.

The giardinetti ring became extremely popular in the eighteenth century, but on the whole rings were not very im-

Folding astrolabe ring. German, seventeenth century

portant during this period. Stones were now by far the main feature in jewellery and this is reflected in the rings. In the second half of the century the marquise ring, with an oval or shuttle-shaped bezel, became fashionable. In England it seems to have been more often used for mourning than for decorative rings.

By the nineteenth century most of the old classes of ring had lost their meaning, become unrecognizable, or passed out of use. Signet rings were no longer needed, amulet rings were no longer believed in, the traditional forms of the betrothal ring had given way to gem-set engagement rings in the prevailing fashion. Compared with their predecessors, the rings of the nineteenth century show a sad poverty of imagination, coupled often with a determination to make the best of a bad stone. In the second half of the century Oscar Massin developed the illusion setting in which a small stone was set in a piece of reflective metal sheet held in claws; the effect was to increase the stone's apparent size. Another innovation was the gipsy ring, introduced in the 1870s, in which the stone was sunk deeply into the metal. Many nineteenth-

Typical eighteenth-century ring with large stone surrounded by diamonds

*Victorian pearl half-hoop ring
with small diamonds*

century rings, especially towards the end of the century, were machine-made. Conventional floral motifs, hearts, diamond clusters, stones set in half-hoops and serpent rings are characteristic of this period (see also *Nineteenth-century jewellery*).

Most of the rings of the present century have followed the same path. Machine-production has increased enormously, and mass-produced diamond-milled wedding rings, and eternity rings made from mass-produced hoops and standard-size stones, have long been a feature of every jeweller's shop except the most exclusive. In recent years, however, there has been a great increase in the wearing of rings and this has been accompanied by the emergence of new and experimental designs. Rings of bold sculptural form are now seen which are unlike any rings that have been made before. Modern designs of this type are becoming increasingly popular, and in the field of more traditional designs there is also evidence of increasing interest in rings which are hand-made and not mass-produced.

(In addition to the special classes of rings mentioned above, see also *Commemorative rings*, *Gimmel rings*, *Jewish marriage-rings*, *Posy rings*, *Puzzle rings* and *Serjeants' rings*.)

Gold ring with balls of haematite and turquoise. Friedrich Becker, 1962

Ring sizers. Tools for measuring the size of rings (inside the shank), or for taking finger-measurements to which rings are to be made. For taking finger-measurements, two main types known as finger-ring gauges are used. One is a stencil of stiff card or some other material with graduated holes marked with the sizes, the other is a series of metal rings in graduated sizes strung on a large hoop of wire.

Finger-ring gauge

For taking the size of the ring itself, a type of mandrel (q.v.) is used which is marked with graduated sizes. The ring is slipped over the tapered end and the measurement taken at the point at which it fits the diameter of the mandrel. Ring-sizing mandrels are made in a variety of materials including aluminium, plastic, and wood covered with a metal sheath. Some are made with a longitudinal groove to accommodate rings in which the stone-setting projects inwards into the area bounded by the shank.

Ring sizing machine. A machine for enlarging the size of rings, used instead of hammering the ring on a triblet (q.v.). Various types are available.

Ring stick. A round, tapering rod of wood (a type of mandrel, q.v.), covered with leather, used for polishing the insides of rings.

Ring tool. See *Chasing tools.*

Ripe pearl. A pearl with a fine orient. (See *Pearls.*)

River pearls. Freshwater pearls. (see *Pearls.*)

River sapphire. A name for pale-coloured sapphire from Montana.

Riveting. This process is used for joining jewellery parts which cannot be soldered because they must not be subjected to heat, or where one of the parts has to swivel. A hole is drilled through the parts, a rivet is passed through and the head of the rivet is rounded over, usually with a pein hammer (see *Hammers*). Rivets in silver and gold alloys are produced by refiners.

Riveting is rarely used in preference to soldering, but it was exclusively used for joining metal by the Celts (see *Celtic jewellery*).

Rivière necklace. A necklace consisting of a single row of graduated stones.

Rock crystal. (See *Quartz, crystalline.*) Transparent colourless quartz, said to take its name from the fact that when the Greeks discovered it in the mountains they thought it to be a form of perpetually-frozen ice and named it as such (*krystallos* = ice). Rock crystal is a common mineral and is now rarely used as a faceted stone because the material is hardly worth the cost of cutting. However, when perfectly clear quartz occurs in large crystals it provides an excellent medium for carving, and has been used for this purpose at least since Mycenaean times. It may also be used for carved seal-stones. Other minerals are sometimes found enclosed in a matrix of colourless quartz and the whole specimen may then be used in cabochon form as an ornamental stone. Examples of such inclusions are crystals of rutile (rutilated quartz), chrysocolla, dumortierite, tourmaline and actinolite.

Rock crystal may easily be distinguished from glass by its coldness, greater hardness and double refraction. It is occasion-ally used to simulate other colourless stones; the so-called 'Cornish diamonds', 'Alaska diamonds', etc., are rock crystal. Its lack of fire and low specific gravity and refractive index usually distinguish rock crystal from other colourless stones without difficulty.

Rock crystal has various industrial applications which make use of its piezoelectric properties (i.e. property of developing an electric charge when subjected to pressure); it is used in radio transmission, in the construction of accurate clocks, for underwater signalling, etc. Its transparency to ultra-violet light makes it suitable for certain lenses and prisms, and it is often used in cases where a material similar to glass but harder is required.

Some of the more important sources of rock crystal are Brazil, the Swiss and French Alps, Madagascar, the U.S.A., New South Wales, Japan and Upper Burma.

Rock glass. Obsidian.

'Rock ruby'. Misnomer for pyrope garnet.

Rock turquoise. Turquoise matrix with considerably more matrix than turquoise. (See *Turquoise.*)

Roebling opal. A mass of precious opal from Virgin Valley, Nevada, now in the Smithsonian Institute. It weighs 2610 carats and is said to be the largest mass of precious opal known.

Rogueite. Local name for greenish jasper from the gravels of the Rogue River, Oregon.

Rolled gold. A type of gold plating developed in the early nineteenth century. Rolled gold is made in a similar way to Sheffield plate (q.v.). Gold is fused under pressure and heat to a block of base metal and the two metals are rolled out into sheets of the required thickness. Rolled gold tube can be made from the sheet (see *Tube*). Rolled gold wire (which, strictly speaking, is not 'rolled') is made by surrounding a base metal core with seamless gold tube. The base metal used may be gilding metal (q.v.), a bronze alloy, nickel silver or silver. When silver is used, the gold surface is often engraved or diamond-milled to show the silver beneath.

The gold surface may be of various qualities (9, 10, 12 and 14-carat are the most used) and colours (yellow, red or white). The thickness of the gold layer is usually expressed in microns: a micron is one-thousandth of a millimetre and 20 microns is rolled gold of good quality. This unit of measurement is used where the thickness of the gold layer is uniform; where it is not uniform, the proportion of gold to base metal may be measured in milliemes. Rolled gold of 10 milliemes has 10 grams of fine gold to every kilogram.

A considerable quantity of rolled gold of several qualities is produced at Pforzheim in Germany, which was a major centre for the production of rolled-gold jewellery in the later nineteenth century.

For other methods of covering base metal with gold, see *Gilding*.

Rolling mill. A machine somewhat like a mangle used for rolling out sheet metal to reduce its thickness, for rolling down ingots or bars of metal preparatory to drawing them into wire, and for reducing the gauge of wire.

For rolling out sheet metal, plain-surfaced rollers of hardened steel are used. These are set at an adjustable distance; they are first set so that the metal will easily pass between them, and are then tightened. The distance between the rollers is gradually decreased until the metal is of the required gauge. After a certain amount of rolling the metal needs annealing (q.v.) or it will become brittle.

Rollers with grooves in graduated sizes are used for rolling down wire. On some mills these rollers are interchangeable with the plain-surfaced rollers; other mills accommodate both types of rollers, and some rollers are made with half their length plain and the other half grooved. Wire which is to be reduced is passed through each groove at least twice, and for further reduction a drawplate (q.v.) may be used. Round wire may be made into strip by running it through the flat rollers.

Rollers with patterned grooves are used to produce patterned wire. Various designs and widths are available.

Roman jewellery. Jewellery was not a feature of Roman life until comparatively late in Roman history. Under the Republic it was frowned on as a luxury: the wearing of gold rings was restricted to certain classes (see *Rings*), and the amount of gold that might be worn by a Roman lady was fixed in the third century B.C. at half an ounce. As the power of Rome expanded eastwards, however, the Romans absorbed some of the more luxurious ways of the conquered nations, and by 27 B.C., when the Roman Empire was inaugurated, republican austerity had been discarded and jewellery was becoming more and more widely worn. At this time there was no truly Roman jewellery because the Romans had always borrowed from the arts of other races; Roman jewellery until about 250 B.C. is virtually identical with Etruscan, and from 250 onwards it is Hellenistic, with a few Etruscan survivals. (See *Etruscan jewellery* and *Greek jewellery*.) Not until the end of the second century A.D. does Roman jewellery really assume a character of its own with new styles and techniques.

The most important of these innovations were a new type of pierced gold-work called *opus interrasile*, in which patterns were cut out of sheet-gold with a chisel, the use of niello (q.v.) on rings and brooches, and a new emphasis on colour which led to the massing of coloured stones and glass with little regard paid to their setting. In the later Roman Empire the very hard stones (emerald, sapphire, aquamarine, topaz and even uncut diamond) were increasingly used, particularly emerald (q.v.), which came from the Egyptian mines near the Red Sea. Certain new types of earring and bracelet were introduced (see below). Alongside these new forms and techniques, of course, many Hellenistic forms survived though usually with some modifications. The techniques of filigree and granulation so extensively used in Greek and Etruscan jewellery had almost died out by this time, and enamel was also very rarely used.

The important items of Roman jewellery were earrings, necklaces, bracelets and rings. In the eastern parts of the Roman empire the animal-headed or human-headed *earring* which had originated in Hellenistic Greece survived until the second century A.D., but in the west other types developed. One was a hoop threaded with small beads. Specifically Roman is the ball-earring, which appeared in the first century A.D. and consisted of a simple hemisphere of gold fitted with a long S-shaped hook for insertion into the ear.

The ball-earring was replaced in the following century by new types of pendant-earring which were again characteristically Roman and unrelated to the Greek varieties. One type consists of a mounted stone with a drop pendant. A very common type which survived into Byzantine times consisted of a mounted stone below which hung a horizontal bar

Roman necklace inlaid with sapphire, garnet and rock crystal. First century A.D. British Museum

with two or three drop pendants set with stones (see illustrations). Garnets were popular for these earrings.

Some of the *necklaces* were developments of Hellenistic types. The necklace of linked bezel-set stones was taken directly from Greek jewellery and lasted for several centuries. In an attractive example of this type the necklace is partly of linked collet-set stones and partly of chain, and has a butterfly-shaped pendant also composed of mounted collet-set stones (see illustration). Collet-set stones were also used in combination with the pierced gold-work referred to above. Necklaces of chain were worn throughout the Imperial period, with and without pendants. The oldest form of pendant was the Etruscan bulla (see *Etruscan jewellery*), which had been very commonly worn, especially by children, in the later Republic and, being an amulet, was exempted from the laws controlling the wearing of gold; it finally died out in the first century A.D. Gold coins and medallions bearing the head of the emperor were commonly worn as pendants in the second and third centuries, possibly for reasons of policy rather than for decoration. Other popular pendants were a wheel (believed to have magical properties), a crescent with knobbed ends (a Syrian form), and ornately-mounted coloured stones and glass. Towards the fourth century necklaces of chain threaded with hexagonal crystals of emerald were introduced.

Bracelets were popular and there were many types. The ball-earring has its

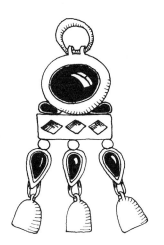

Roman pendant earring set with garnet and glass, about third century A.D. British Museum

317

Roman jewellery

counterpart in bracelets made of linked hemispheres of gold. The Hellenistic snake-bracelet continued to be worn until the end of the first century A.D.; the Roman variety was rather more solid than the Greek. Slender bracelets of twisted gold wire were also worn. An unusually splendid bracelet has been found, dating from the first century A.D., in the form of a wide openwork gold band decorated with leaves and berries, with an ornate centrepiece in the shape of a vase inlaid with squares of green glass. In general, however, bracelets were simpler than this, and the characteristic bracelet of the later Empire is a thick hoop, usually of twisted gold wire, with a large circular bezel-set stone (see illustration). In the fourth century, when pierced gold-work had become established, bracelets were also made in broad openwork gold bands.

Roman bracelet with sardonyx. Third century A.D. British Museum

The wearing of gold *rings* under the Empire was still theoretically a privilege, but it was a privilege so freely bestowed as to be almost meaningless (see *Rings*). The fashion for collecting fine and engraved gemstones which began in the first century A.D. resulted in the wearing of many more rings than before, and contemporary satirists speak of people wearing as many as six on each finger. There were naturally very many types of rings, and it is impossible to list more than a few. The Romans were the first to use rings as tokens of betrothal, but these do not seem to have been of any particular type, although rings inscribed with a man's and a woman's name are probably of this class. Seal-rings were commonly worn and the style varied with the period: thick hoops expanding at the

Roman openwork gold ring. Fourth century A.D. British Museum

bezel were popular in the early Empire, and thin hoops with bevelled shoulders in the later Empire. Sometimes a gold coin was used instead of a stone. Snake-rings survived from Hellenistic jewellery into the first century A.D., and a Roman variant of this type consists of a hoop with a snake's head at either end instead of the usual spiral form. Two late varieties are a ring consisting of a band of pierced gold (see illustration), similar to the bracelets mentioned above, and an octagonal ring, sometimes of pierced gold set with a stone, sometimes of solid metal. The latter type was worn with a devotional inscription by the early Christians. An extremely popular type from the second century onwards was the purely ornamental ring prominently set with one or more stones: amethyst and sapphires were particularly favoured. In the third and fourth centuries stones were sometimes set all round the hoop.

Of other kinds of jewellery, the *safety-pin brooch* was the most important. The Romans adopted it from the Celts and during the second century A.D. evolved their own variety, the 'crossbow' fibula with a high arched bow (see *Brooches*). It was made mostly in bronze, occasionally in precious metal, and was sometimes decorated with niello. Gold *hairpins* were sometimes worn, and one very elaborate Roman hair-ornament has been found consisting of a row of mounted stones in a border of pearls set in gold, with two pendant pearls and a sapphire suspended from a horizontal gold bar at the bottom. Contemporary statues indicate that this type of hair-ornament was not unusual.

With the founding of Constantinople as the second capital in A.D. 330 Roman power began to shift eastwards, and within a few centuries the process was complete. When the old Empire fell to the barbarians classical traditions were carried on in Constantinople, now capital of the new state of Byzantium, and in Byzantine jewellery (q.v.) the forms of late Roman jewellery survive for several centuries until they become inextricably mingled with the forms of Eastern art.

Roman pearls. Wax-filled imitation pearls. (See *Pearls*.)

Roman setting. A setting used for seal-stones; a groove is cut in the metal around the stone and the rim raised by this is pressed down over the stone. (See also *Settings*.)

Romanzovite. A dark brown variety of grossular garnet.

Rondelle. A pierced disc-shaped piece of metal or gemstone material strung between the beads in a necklace. The edge is often faceted.

Rosaline. Thulite.

Rosaries. See *Devotional jewellery*.

Rose. A rose-cut (q.v.) diamond.

Rose cut. A style of cutting for diamonds introduced during the fifteenth century and very popular during the sixteenth and seventeenth centuries, after which it was almost entirely superseded for important stones by the brilliant cut. The standard rose cut consists of a flat base with a convex crown cut with 24 triangular facets. The name is said to derive from the resemblance of a stone cut in this way to an unopened rosebud. There are several variations of the rose cut. (For fuller description and diagrams, see *Diamond-cutting*.)

Rosée. The delicate tinge of pink highly prized in pearls. (See *Pearls*.)

Rose garnet. Xalostocite (see *Grossular garnet*), or rhodonite.

'Rose kunzite'. Trade name for synthetic pink sapphire. (See *Synthetic gemstones*.)

Roselite (Rosolite). Xalostocite. (See *Grossular garnet*.)

'Rose moonstone'. Misnomer for pink scapolite.

Rose opal. Rose-coloured common opal.

Rose quartz. (See *Quartz, crystalline*). Pink quartz, varying in colour from rose-pink to almost white. The colour is liable to fade on exposure to strong sunlight. The stone is nearly always cloudy and fissured, and for that reason is more often used for carving than as a gemstone. It is sometimes cut *en cabochon* or in bead form to display the diasterism (q.v.) which is commonly present.

The best quality rose quartz comes from the valley of the Jequitinhonha in Brazil. Other sources are India, Madagascar, Japan, Russia, U.S.A., S.W. Africa and Bavaria.

Rosinca. Rhodochrosite.

Rosolite. See *Roselite*.

Rosterite. Rose-coloured beryl from Elba.

Rotten-stone. A soft, finely-textured substance largely composed of silica, used in the polishing of gemstones and metals.

Rouge. Red iron oxide, used in the final polishing of precious metals and also in the polishing of gemstones. (See also *Green rouge*.)

Roumanite. Amber (q.v.) from Rumania.

'Royalite'. Trade name for a purplish-red glass.

Royal topaz. Blue topaz.

'Rozircon'. Trade name for pink synthetic spinel. (See *Synthetic gemstones*.)

'Rubace' ('Rubasse'). Trade name for crackled quartz dyed red.

Rubasse. A spangled reddish quartz coloured by iron oxide. The material comes from Brazil and is rare. It is

319

imitated by artificially crackled and dyed quartz. (See 'Rubace'.)

Rubellite. Pink or red tourmaline.

Rubicelle. The old name for orange-red spinel.

Rub-over setting. A setting in which the stone is placed in a rim of strip metal, and the top edge is pressed over to hold it in place. A setting generally used for signet rings.

Ruby. (Aluminium oxide. S.G. 3.96–4.01; R.I. 1.76–1.77; H. 9.) The transparent red variety of corundum (q.v.), coloured by chromic oxide. The colour ranges from pale pink to deep red (the pale stones are sometimes classed as pink sapphires), the most prized colour being 'pigeon's blood', a purplish-red found most frequently in Burmese stones. Flawless ruby of a good colour is rare and extremely precious. Ruby often contains fine mineral inclusions, cavities, or wisps and swirls of colour ('treacle'). Star-stones (see *Asterism*) showing a 6-pointed star of light when cut *en cabochon*, are highly prized.

Other characteristics of ruby are its double refraction and dichroism (qq.v.) – the twin colours being purplish-red and yellowish-red – and extreme hardness. These qualities distinguish it from red spinel, garnet and red glass, all of which are used as imitations of ruby. (For distinction between natural ruby and the extensively-manufactured synthetic rubies, see *Synthetic gemstones*.)

The principal sources of ruby are Burma and Thailand, where rubies and sapphires occur together. The finest stones are found in the Mogok Stone Tract in Upper Burma, which has been mined for gemstones since prehistoric times. The history of the ruby mines is largely one of terrorism and exploitation of the native miners. The area was so unhealthy that for a time captives were sent to work in the mines, and towards the end of the eighteenth century the Stone Tract was a place of exile. Shortly afterwards the region was placed under the control of local governors who levied

taxes on the mining, forced the miners to sell their stones for less than their true value, and declared that all stones of the value of 2000 rupees and over were the property of the king. When in 1863 a governor was appointed with the responsibility of collecting a considerable sum in tax to be paid to the king, in addition to what he collected for himself, the exploitation became so severe that a rebellion took place and many miners deserted their villages. The king attempted to remedy the situation by making mining free but imposing a comparatively small tax on the buying and selling of stones, but none of the officials who were in a position to extort money was content to leave the situation as it was, and in 1885 a governor was appointed with the task of furnishing £16,000 in taxes from the mines. His attempts to levy the tax resulted in chaos; gangs of robbers moved into the mining districts, terrorized the villagers, and extracted money in return for a safe-conduct on the roads.

In 1886 Upper Burma was annexed by the British and a company (the Burma Ruby Mines Ltd.) was floated to work the mines under a concession from the British government. After some initial difficulty (the company paid a very high rental because it was supposed to have a monopoly of the rubies, which it did not because the native miners of course smuggled out stones and sold them on the open market) the mines were for a period systematically and successfully worked. However, after 1908, when the first synthetic rubies were marketed, the situation deteriorated, and the company went into liquidation in 1931. The panic occasioned by the synthesis of ruby was unfounded, for natural rubies have held their price over the years and do not suffer from the competition. This, however, is only because synthetic rubies can be reliably identified (see *Synthetic gemstones*).

The Burma mines are still worked by native miners using fairly primitive methods. Narrow shafts are sunk on to the gem-bearing alluvial deposits, known as 'byon', and the earth is loosened with a spade and hauled up to the surface in baskets. Similar methods are used for mining Siamese rubies, which occur in a coarse sand near the surface. Siamese rubies are generally darker than Burmese, often have a brownish tint, and are less highly prized. Rubies are also found in Ceylon, Australia and the U.S.A., and there are commercially unimportant deposits in various other countries.

Ruby has been highly prized from very early times. Its name in Sanskrit may be translated 'king of gems', and it was an ancient Indian belief that a man who offered rubies to the gods would be reborn an emperor or king (depending on the quality of the ruby). Its colour, suggestive of both blood and fire, inspired beliefs that ruby contained an inner heat and if placed in water would cause the water to boil, and that it conferred invulnerability to wounds and would cure haemorrhages. These superstitions attached to all red stones, and in Europe ruby was not clearly distinguished from other stones such as the red spinel until after the Middle Ages.

There are few famous true rubies, as rubies rarely occur in a size large enough to have individuality. Perhaps the best known are the 43-carat Peace ruby, found in 1919, the 167-carat Edwardes ruby crystal given to the British Museum by John Ruskin, and the 100-carat De Long star ruby in the J. Pierpont Morgan collection in the American Museum of Natural History. The two fine 'rubies' in the British Regalia, the Black Prince's ruby and the Timur ruby (qq.v.), are both red spinels.

'Ruby balas'. See *'Balas ruby'*.

Ruby glass. Bright red glass.

Ruby spinel. Ruby-coloured spinel.

Ruby tin. Red cassiterite.

Ruin agate. Agate (q.v.) with markings which resemble ruins.

Ruin marble. A greyish-green marble in which yellow iron oxide has infiltrated in angular patches which look like the outlines of ruins. Also known as Florence marble. (See also *Marble*.)

'Russian chrysolite'. Misnomer for demantoid garnet.

Rutilated quartz. Rock crystal (q.v.) which contains fine needle-like inclusions of rutile crystals (see *Rutile*). It makes an attractive stone which is usually cut *en cabochon*. It is also known as Venus' hair stone and by other similar names. (See also *Sagenitic quartz*.)

Rutile. (Titanium dioxide. S.G. about 4.2; R.I. 2.6–2.9; H. 6–6½.) Except when it occurs in the form of *rutilated quartz* (q.v.), natural rutile is not normally used as a gemstone as it is opaque and dark in colour. Synthetic rutile, however, is a commercially important material. (See *Synthetic gemstones*.)

S

Sabalite. See *Variscite*.

Safirina. Blue spinel or quartz.

'Safranite' ('Saffronite'). (Trade name.) Citrine.

Sagenitic quartz. Rock crystal with needle-like inclusions of other minerals, rutile, actinolite and black tourmaline being the commonest. When the inclusions are of rutile (q.v.) the stone is also known as rutilated quartz.

St. Edward's Sapphire. A fine sapphire, now rose-cut, set in the cross on top of the orb in the Crown of State. It is probably the oldest stone in the British Regalia; according to tradition it was originally mounted in the ring of Edward the Confessor, the last of the line of Anglo-Saxon kings.

'Salamanca topaz'. Misnomer for reddish citrine.

The Sancy diamond

Sancy diamond. A 54-carat almond-shaped Indian diamond with a long and involved history, of which there are several conflicting versions. According to one story the diamond reached Burgundy some time in the fifteenth century, and was taken from the dead body of Charles the Bold by a soldier after the battle of Nancy in 1477. By devious routes it came into the possession of the King of Portugal, who gave it to Count Nicholas Harlai de Sancy. While on a mission abroad the Count sent the diamond to Henry III of France as a token of loyalty, but his servant was attacked by robbers and, rather than surrender the stone, swallowed it. The servant was murdered and Sancy later recovered the diamond from his body. The diamond was subsequently acquired by James I of England, but Charles I pawned it and it found its way eventually into the collection of Cardinal Mazarin, and ultimately into the possession of Louis XIV.

Another version of this part of this story is that the stone was purchased by Sancy (who at the time was Ambassador to the Turkish court) in Constantinople in about 1570. On his return to France Sancy lent it to Henry III in return for a military appointment. After Henry III's assassination Sancy, now Minister of Finance, used his position to redeem the stone and, knowing the critical state of the national finances, decided to send it abroad. At this point in the story the faithful servant appears, is attacked by robbers and swallows the stone. Sancy's second attempt to get the diamond out of the country was successful: he entrusted it to his brother, who was the Ambassador to England (according to another version he was himself the Ambassador), and it was bought by Elizabeth I.

Here the stories diverge again: according to one version the stone was later pawned by Charles I to the Duke of Eperon, was subsequently bought by Cardinal Mazarin and on his death passed, with his other jewels, into the possession

322

of the French crown; according to another it was sold in 1695 by James II to Louis XIV for 625,000 francs.

All the stories agree that the diamond was among the French crown jewels and in 1792 was stolen with the other jewels from the *garde meuble*. For a time nothing was heard of it. It may or may not have been the stone later pledged by the Marquis of Iranda to pay his troops and, later still, the property of Queen Maria Louisa of Spain, but it seems fairly certain that it was the stone bought by Prince Demidoff of Russia in 1828, shown at the Paris Exhibition of 1867, and bought in 1906 by Lord Astor, in whose family it has remained. Unless, that is, one chooses to believe the story that in the late nineteenth century it passed into the possession of an Indian maharajah and has been in India ever since.

'San Diego ruby'. Misnomer for red tourmaline.

Sapphire. (Aluminium oxide. S.G. 3.96–4.01; R.I. 1.765–1.767; H. 9.) Transparent corundum (q.v.). The word 'sapphire' with no further description refers to the blue stone, which is coloured by traces of iron and titanium, but the name also covers all other tints of corundum except the red (ruby, q.v.). Thus white (colourless), yellow, brown, violet, green and pink sapphires are spoken of. Blue sapphire ranges in colour from pale cornflower to deep blue; pale stones have comparatively little value. The colour in corundum is often irregularly distributed, and some faceted stones, particularly blue sapphires from Ceylon, contain only a single patch of colour near the base, but the stone is cut in such a way as to look, from above, as though the colour is evenly distributed. Sapphire shows strong dichroism (q.v.), the colours in a blue stone being deep blue and a yellowish or greenish blue. Sapphire is less valuable than ruby because large crystals are more commonly found, but fine specimens nevertheless command very high prices. (This applies much less to sapphires of other colours than blue, which are not, on the whole, very highly regarded and are often passed off as stones of a different species. Colourless sapphire is used to simulate diamond.)

Sapphire, like ruby, has characteristic internal features, and the stones from Siam usually show a system of fine canals known as 'feathers'. Star sapphires (see *Asterism*) show a star of light, usually 6-pointed, when cut *en cabochon*. The most important source of sapphire is Battambang in Thailand, where the sapphires occur in association with ruby in a coarse sandy soil. Although many fine stones come from the Mogok Stone Tract in Burma, Burmese sapphires are commonly held to be inferior to Siamese and good Burmese stones are therefore often sold as being of Siamese origin. Mining is by native methods. Kashmir produces some magnificent cornflower-blue sapphires and rather pale blue sapphire is found in Ceylon, which yields a large number of star corundums. Dark blue and attractive yellow and green sapphires are found in Australia. Other deposits have little commercial significance.

A stone called sapphire makes several appearances in the Bible; it is one of the stones in Aaron's breastplate and one of the foundations of the New Jerusalem, and according to tradition it was on tablets of sapphire that the law given to Moses was engraved. However, as Pliny describes 'sapphire' as an opaque blue stone with spots of gold, a description which applies to lapis-lazuli but not to corundum, it seems that lapis-lazuli is the sapphire referred to in ancient writings. On the other hand the stone known in ancient times as jacinth ('hyakinthos') is almost certainly the modern sapphire. (The modern jacinth, however, is orange-coloured zircon.) Blue traditionally has a spiritual significance and symbolizes purity, and sapphire is accordingly one of the stones used in ecclesiastical rings (q.v.).

There are few blue stones capable of imitating sapphire; benitoite (q.v.) is one of them, but is rare. The recently-discovered sapphire-blue stone tanzanite (q.v.) is lighter than sapphire, has a lower refractive index and is very much softer. Blue spinel is also lighter, less highly refractive and softer, and does not show double refraction (q.v.). Most of the blue doublets (see *Doublet*) and glass imitations show a strong red colour through the Chelsea colour filter (q.v.), whereas sapphire does not. Synthetic sapphires are now manufactured on a considerable scale; for distinction between them and the natural stone, see *Synthetic gemstones*.

Sapphire glass. Sapphire-blue glass.

Sapphire quartz. Blue chalcedony or falcon's eye.

Sapphire spinel. Blue spinel.

Sapphirine. A name applied to blue chalcedony, blue spinel and blue glass.

Sard. (See *Chalcedony*). Brownish-red translucent chalcedony. The name is less used than previously as sard is merely a darker shade of cornelian (q.v.). It was used for carved seal-stones (see *Seals* and *Intaglios*) in ancient times. As used in the Bible, the name may refer to the stone we now know as sard, or to jasper – at any rate a red stone is intended. The name is usually said to be derived from Sardis, the ancient capital of Lydia, but it has also been suggested that it comes from the Persian word *sered*, meaning yellowish-red.

The sources of sard are the same as those of cornelian (q.v.).

Sardium. Sard artificially coloured brown.

Sardonyx. (See *Chalcedony*). Chalcedony with alternating straight red and white bands; the red is sard. It is used for cameos and intaglios, which are carved in such a way that the relief is of one colour and the background of the other.

Sark stones. Amethyst from Sark in the Channel Islands. It is now in fact amethyst from Brazil, sold in Sark.

Satelite. Fibrous serpentine from California, slightly chatoyant. (See *Serpentine*.)

Satin spar. A name applied to both fibrous calcite and fibrous gypsum (qq.v.); it is white or pink in colour.

Satin stone. Satin spar.

Saussurite. (S.G. 3.0–3.4; R.I. 1.70; H. $6\frac{1}{2}$.) A white to greenish-grey, tough, compact mineral with a resemblance to jade. A decomposition product of plagioclase feldspar (q.v.), it was originally found near Lake Geneva but also occurs in Corsica, various parts of Italy and Germany, at the Lizard in Cornwall, and elsewhere.

Sautoir. A long necklace, usually of pearls or chain, often with a tassel at the bottom. Sautoirs were popular towards the end of the nineteenth century.

Saws. See *Piercing saw*.

'Saxony chrysolite'. Misnomer for topaz.

'Saxony diamond'. Misnomer for colourless topaz.

'Saxony topaz'. Misnomer for citrine.

Scaife. The cast-iron lap (q.v.) on which diamonds are polished. (See *Diamond-cutting*.)

Scapolite. (Sodium-calcium-aluminium silicate. S.G. 2.6–2.7; R.I. 1.55–1.57; H. 6.) Gem-quality scapolite was first found in about 1913 in the Mogok Stone Tract in Burma. The colours are pink, violet, yellow or white. Burmese stones have a fibrous structure and give a cat's-eye effect when cut *en cabochon*. A clear yellow scapolite is found in Madagascar and the state of Espirito Santo, Brazil. These yellow stones strongly resemble beryl and chrysoberyl of similar colour, but have lower refractivity. The same test distinguishes the pink scapolite from pink beryl. Opaque massive yellow scapolite, suitable for use as cabochons, is found in Quebec and Ontario.

Scarabs. In ancient Egypt the scarab was a religious amulet, an article of jewellery, and the upper side of a seal-stone; it sometimes makes its appearance in modern jewellery as a carved ring-stone

Scarab

or lucky charm. The scarab was a formalized representation of a species of beetle revered by the Egyptians as a symbol of the sun-god. The salient characteristic of this beetle is that it rolls its food in the shape of a large ball of dung along the ground to its burrow; the Egyptians connected this with the movement of the sun across the sky and inferred that the sun was similarly propelled by its god. They also believed (mistakenly) that the young beetles emerged from this ball and that all beetles of this type were male. This obviously suggested the idea of a self-generated sun-god, and in the course of time the scarab beetle became the centre of a complex system of ideas concerning rebirth in the next world.

Egyptian scarabs are a carved representation of this beetle in glazed steatite, faience (glazed pottery), and occasionally gemstones such as amethyst, jasper, cornelian and lapis-lazuli. Very rarely they were made in precious metals, but these were more generally used for mounting the scarabs. The materials used varied according to the period, as did the style of carving. At times the shape of the beetle was merely suggested in a few lines, on others the wing-cases and head were clearly marked or the legs carved in relief, and sometimes the beetle was given a human head.

The size varied according to the use to which the scarab was put. When scarabs first appeared in the sixth dynasty (2345–2180 B.C.) they were of purely religious significance and were buried with the dead. They then began to be worn by the living, strung on necklaces

as beads. They were made with a flat base, which soon suggested itself as a surface for an engraved seal (seals [q.v.] had been in use from earlier times but had mostly been cylindrical). The scarab now became the standard form of seal in Egypt for the next thousand years. It was perforated along its length and usually worn either on a ring of gold wire strung on a chain, or mounted as a swivelling bezel in a finger-ring. In the latter case it was worn with the carved back of the beetle facing upwards, and was twisted round when the seal-surface was needed.

Large scarabs measuring several inches in length were placed over the hearts of the dead. These heart-scarabs were usually carved in green stone and mounted in gold, and they were inscribed on the base with a part of the Book of the Dead. The intention was that a man's heart should not give evidence against him when his life was weighed in the balance. Heart-scarabs in the Middle Kingdom (about 2080–1785 B.C.) commonly have a human face, and this form later developed into the scaraboid, with a negroid human head.

During this period the amuletic character of the scarab was more important than its use as a seal, and a great many were made of faience, which was not hard enough for a seal-stone. They were covered with an attractive blue or green glaze and universally worn by the poorer people in necklaces.

Towards the end of the eighteenth dynasty (1567–1320 B.C.) the solid signet-ring with an engraved bezel was invented and the use of the scarab as a seal declined. It was revived some centuries later when there was an interest in archaic styles, but its use declined again in the fifth century B.C. and thereafter it disappeared entirely.

Meanwhile, however, the scarab form had been copied by the Phoenicians and spread to Greece, where for a time it was quite widely used for intaglio stones. The back of the beetle, carved in relief, became the ancestor of the cameo. (See also *Amulets*, *Intaglios* and *Egyptian jewellery*.)

325

Scheelite. (Calcium tungstate. S.G. 5.9–6.1; R.I. 1.92–1.93; H. 4½–5.) A rather soft mineral which has sometimes been cut into gemstones. The material is rarely transparent and is usually yellowish to brownish, but some attractive orange-coloured scheelite comes from Sonora in Mexico, and California and Arizona also produce good cuttable material. Scheelite is also found in Australia and various parts of Europe. There is a synthetic scheelite. (See *Synthetic gemstones*.)

Schiller. The sheen or play of colour in a stone which is caused by the reflection of light from an intergrowth of mineral layers in the stone. It is characteristic of the moonstone. 'Schillerization' is the name given to such a mineral structure or to the process of bringing it about artificially, for instance by heating. The word is German and means iridescence or glitter.

Schiller spar. Bastite. (See *Enstatite*.)

Schmelze. Decorative glass.

Schnide. A blue glassy common opal from Queensland.

Schorl. Black tourmaline.

'Scientific brilliant'. A name given to the first synthetic colourless sapphires (see *Synthetic gemstones*); it was quickly discontinued.

'Scientific emerald'. A misnomer for beryl glass (i.e. fused beryl) or – sometimes – for a glass imitation of emerald.

'Scientific ruby/sapphire'. Misnomer for red or blue glass.

'Scientific topaz'. A name given to the first pink synthetic sapphires (see *Synthetic gemstones*), which were similar in colour to pink heat-treated topaz. The name was discontinued, but has since been sometimes applied to topaz-coloured glass.

Scissors cut. Alternative name for the cross cut, q.v.

Scorper. A steel tool with a sharp tip used for engraving metal and for various other jobs such as raising pieces of metal to grip a stone. It is the same tool as the graver (q.v.), but is more likely to be referred to as a scorper when it is used for other things than engraving.

Scorpion stone. Coral or jet.

Scotch stone. See *Water-of-Ayr stone*.

'Scotch topaz'. Misnomer for yellow or brown quartz (citrine, cairngorm or smoky quartz.)

Scottish jewellery. For this see *Brooches, Celtic jewellery, Luckenbooth brooches* and *Nineteenth-century jewellery*.

Scraper. A steel file of triangular section used for cleaning up the surface of metal, particularly the insides of ring-shanks.

Seal cut. A type of step cut (q.v.) with a low crown and a wide table. (See also *Gem-cutting*.)

Seals. A seal is an object used to impress the owner's mark on some substance such as wax or clay. For thousands of years seals played an essential part in everyday life; it is only in the past few centuries that the written signature has made them redundant. Although essentially utilitarian, they have often also been works of art, and in so far as they have been made of precious materials and worn on the person they form a class of jewellery.

The earliest seals so far discovered are of clay, are roughly the size of a postage stamp and bear geometric patterns. These were made in Western Asia some time between 6500–6000 B.C. At a later date amulet-seals came into use; these were often in the form of carved representations of animals and had the owner's personal mark engraved on the base. Their function was protective as well as utilitarian, and they were drilled with a hole to enable them to be worn on a thong round the wrist or neck. During the fourth millennium B.C. the cylinder-seal was developed in Mesopotamia; it continued to be used for several thousand years. It was engraved on a cylinder of stone drilled longitudinally down the middle and worn on a thong, and when in use it was rolled along to give a wide impression. The designs on the early cylinder-seals included wild and domestic animals, houses and everyday scenes, and religious symbols. With the development of writing these pictographs were replaced by cuneiform characters. The stones used were at first soft stones such as steatite, but during the third millenium B.C. hard stones such as cornelian, haematite and marble were engraved. The work was done with a bow drill (q.v.), using powdered quartz or, for harder stones, powdered beryl or corundum as an abrasive.

The cylinder-seal was adopted in ancient Egypt but was supplanted by the native Egyptian form of seal, the scarab. Scarab-seals were worn round the neck or set in rings. (See *Scarabs*.) In Greece too the cylinder-seal was introduced but was ultimately discarded in favour of the Egyptian scarab, which in time lost its distinctive form and was in turn replaced by the signet ring with an engraved stone set in a fixed bezel. This form of signet ring, which appeared in Greece at about the beginning of the fourth century B.C., remained in use until modern times.

With the exception of large official and state seals, which were not worn and do not come into the category of jewellery, seals until the seventeenth century were

Seventeenth-century seal

mostly in the form of signet rings. (See *Signet rings* for further information.) During the seventeenth century, however, a new form appeared: an engraved stone was set in the base of a small gold or silver fob, and this was worn on a chain or hanging from a man's chatelaine (see *Chatelaines*). These fobs took elaborate and fanciful forms (see illustration) and were an important item of men's jewellery during the seventeenth and eighteenth centuries. By the nineteenth century, however, both the seal fob and the signet ring were objects of ornament rather than of use, and in the present century the wearing of either is purely decorative. (See also *Intaglios*.)

Seal sapphire. A brown silky variety of sapphire.

Seastone. Amber.

Sectile. Capable of being cut cleanly with a knife or similar instrument. A distinguishing characteristic of most plastics (q.v.).

Seed pearls. Small round pearls weighing less than a quarter of a grain. (See *Pearls*.)

Selenite. Colourless crystallized gypsum.

Semiopal. Common opal or hydrophane. (See *Opal*.)

'Semi-precious stones'. A commonly-used term violently disapproved of by all professional bodies representing the jewellery trade and all gemmological associations. The grounds of this disapproval are that the term is both hopelessly vague and potentially misleading. It is vague in that it encompasses all gemstones other than diamond, ruby, sapphire and emerald at one end of the scale, and the common ornamental stones such as marble at the other. Within this class it gives one no hint as to the relative value of the stone, and the value of these gemstones varies enormously. It is misleading in that it gives the impression that there is some fixed relationship between the value of a 'semi-precious' stone and the value of a precious stone, and that any topaz, for instance, will always be worth less than any ruby. This is quite untrue; if one excepts the commoner stones such as agate, the quality of an individual stone is at least as important as its species, and a fine topaz is in fact more valuable than a poor-quality ruby.

It must nevertheless be admitted that the term does have some use in referring to a gemstone which has a *certain* value (i.e. is not just a pretty piece of rock) but yet is not of *great* value. The term 'gemstone', which is the alternative suggested, does not carry quite the same meaning for the public, and until it does the phrase 'semi-precious stone' will doubtless continue to be used.

'Semiturquoise'. A term occasionally used for pale turquoise or for something that looks like turquoise but is not.

Senaille. A trade term for small chips of diamond cut with a flat base and irregular triangular facets. This is a cheap version of the rose cut (see *Diamond-cutting*) and is used for the cheaper diamond jewellery.

Serjeants' rings. Rings customarily presented, from the fifteenth to the nineteenth century, to the sovereign, princes of the blood and numerous officials, by barristers called to be Serjeant-at-Law (a post now abolished). They were normally in the form of a flat gold band with a moulded rim along top and bottom, engraved on the outside with a suitable Latin motto. Mottoes on surviving examples include 'Vivat rex et lex', 'Lex regis praesidium', etc. Serjeants were usually called in batches of about fifteen, and normally they would all take the same motto for their rings.

The weight of the rings varied according to the rank of the recipient. In 1705 the Queen was presented with a ring costing £6 13s. 4d., the Lord Privy Seal and other high officials with a ring costing 18s., the Attorney-General and others with rings costing 12s., and so on down to the Clerk of the Council whose ring cost 2s. 6d. There were a great many recipients and the tradition was ex-

tremely expensive. In 1737, for instance, 1,409 rings were presented by 14 serjeants at a total cost of £773, and this did not include rings privately given by the serjeants to friends at the bar. In the nineteenth century some judges refused to accept the rings presented to them, and in 1875 the custom came to an end when the Judicature Law made it unnecessary for a barrister to be called to be Serjeant before he became a judge.

Some recipients, particularly the monarchs, must have accumulated a sizeable collection of rings. There is a story that at one time there was a drawer full of them at Windsor Castle but that they were melted down to make gold plate. According to another version, they were soldered one on top of another to make candlesticks.

Serpentine. (S.G. 2.5–2.6; R.I. about 1.56; H. about 4.) A greenish ornamental stone which can be roughly divided into 2 classes: a fairly hard, translucent variety consisting of a relatively pure hydrated magnesium silicate, and a softer, impure type which occurs in large rock masses. Most of the harder type is *bowenite* (H. about 5½), a jade-like material used in making carved ornaments and sometimes in jewellery. The serpentine rock is dark green or red with green or blackish veins and spots, and is used for ornaments such as vases. It occurs in quantity on the Lizard peninsula in Cornwall and various other localities. The 'Connemara marble' from Eire, also used ornamentally, is a cloudy green variety of serpentine in combination with other minerals (See also *Marble*.) The 'Verde Antique' used in classical times was a variety of serpentine marble quarried at Casambala, near Larissa in Thessaly.

'Serpentine jade'. Misnomer for bowenite. (See *Serpentine*.)

Serpentine cat's-eye. Satelite.

Setting edge. See *Girdle*.

Settings. The simplest way to set a stone is to encircle it with a rim of strip metal (a collet), one edge of which is soldered to the backing while the top edge is pressed slightly over to hold the stone in place. This was the style of most early settings, and being a closed setting it had the advantage of enabling the jeweller to paint or foil the back of the stone to improve its appearance. (See *Tinting* and *Foil.*) Claws attached to the outside of the setting sometimes assisted in gripping the stone; these disappeared in the thirteenth or fourteenth century. In Renaissance jewellery (q.v.) the metalwork was still more important than the stones and was lavishly enamelled; ring-stones were set, foiled, in closed settings in high decorated bezels (see *Rings*).

During the seventeenth century (see *Seventeenth-century jewellery*) stones became increasingly important and this trend reached its height in the eighteenth century when the metal was no more than an unobtrusive framework for a display of stones (see *Eighteenth-century jewellery*). Several types of setting were now in use. A characteristic eighteenth-century setting, often used for fine stones, was the cut-down setting, in which the metal was carefully worked up round the edge of the stone into a smooth wall, reinforced at intervals with narrow vertical ridges of metal. In the best eighteenth-century pieces this is done with such skill that the metal almost seems to merge into the stone. Small stones were pavé-set in groups: holes were drilled in the metal and the stones placed in these, held in position by a rim or grains of metal raised by a scorper and pressed over round the edge. The simple collet setting was still used for undistinguished stones.

The nineteenth century (see *Nineteenth-century jewellery*) saw the beginning of mass-production on a serious scale, and towards the end of the century settings were commonly stamped out by machine. This could not be done with the cut-down setting but it could be and was done with the collet setting, which became a thin curved band of metal, whereas in earlier work it had been heavy and usually straight-sided to accommodate square-cut stones. The cut-down setting, requiring patient skilled craftsmanship, gave way to two other types of setting, claw and millegrain, which are very widely used in modern jewellery. In the claw setting the stone is gripped just above the girdle by metal claws, and usually rests on a metal rim soldered inside the claws. This type of setting allows light into the stone and is used for transparent faceted stones. The ring of claws may be sawn out of strip metal, or ready-made gallery strip (q.v.) may be used. (Refiners also now produce claw settings ready made.) In the millegrain setting the stone is placed in a thin rim of metal and tiny grains of metal are pushed over from the rim to hold it in position. The grains are usually raised by drawing a serrated wheel round the rim to create a milled edge.

Several other types of setting, mostly variations on the types already described, are used in modern jewellery. The peg setting is a modification of the claw setting in which the stone is let into recesses cut into the walls of the claws. In the thread setting the stone is held in a thin line or thread of metal raised with a steel wheel and pressed over (the technique is similar to that for millegrain setting). The simple collet setting, now generally known as the rub-over setting, since the rim of the collet is rubbed over to hold the stone, is widely used for opaque stones. A variation of the rub-over setting is the cramp setting in which small triangular or square pieces are sawn out of the rim to leave projecting cramps or claws which hold the stone. The gipsy setting, developed in the late nineteenth century, in which the stone is deeply sunk into the metal, which may be engraved with a radiating pattern, is not normally used in modern jewellery, but another nineteenth-century invention, the illusion setting, in which the stone is set in a reflective metal plate and the plate is held in claws, is used for small stones in order to increase their apparent size. For seal-stones in signet rings the Roman setting (a modern version of a style used by the Romans) is often used. For this the stone is set flush with the metal. A groove

329

is chiselled out of the metal all the way round the stone; this raises a rim which is pressed over to hold the stone in place.

Setting tool. A short steel or brass rod of square or rectangular section with a flat end, set in a small handle like the handle of a graver (q.v.), used for pushing over the metal claws of a claw setting (q.v.). Some types have a wide concave tip which fits over all the claws at once and brings them together as it is pushed down. Jewellers often make their own setting tools.

Seventeenth-century jewellery. For the first quarter of the seventeenth century jewellery was much as it had been in the later sixteenth century (see *Renaissance jewellery*); dress was stiff and artificial and a profusion of jewels was worn with it. During the 1620s there was a reaction against this style; flowing garments which emphasized the natural shape of the body began to be worn, and with them a more restrained type of jewellery. The flamboyant pendants of the Renaissance were replaced by brooches, and earrings became fashionable now that there were no ruffs to get in their way.

Seventeenth-century jewellery is dominated by the increasing importance of gems at the expense of enamelled settings, and by a passion for floral designs. The latter reflected a general interest in horticulture which had originated in the Netherlands. At the turn of the century jewels began to be decorated with elongated curving leaf-like or pod-like forms; this style, which is known as 'pea-pod' or 'cosse de pois', (q.v.) continued for several decades and was used both in the shape of jewels and in the enamelled patterns on the back. It was spread by books of engravings, notably those of Gédeon Légaré and Balthasar Lemercier. The leaf-forms gradually became more naturalistic and by mid-century jewels were being decorated with delicate floral patterns that were botanically correct. Some of the most beautiful jewellery in the style is that of Gilles Légaré (q.v.), court jeweller at the time of

Louis XIV, who published a book of engravings in 1663.

The increasing emphasis on gemstones, particularly diamonds, was partly a result of advances in gem-cutting. The rose cut (q.v.) for diamonds had been invented and was increasingly popular, and diamonds were also relatively plentiful, for rich deposits had been found in India. The arts of the jeweller, the goldsmith and the enameller, which had begun to diverge in the late Middle Ages, were by now quite distinct, and the jeweller held the commanding position.

Although enamelled settings for the fronts of jewels were less and less in evidence, exquisite painted enamels were produced in the seventeenth century and the backs of jewels were enamelled with elaborate floral designs. *Miniature cases* became very fashionable about 1600 and for much of the century these were enamelled on front and back, usually in translucent champlevé-enamel, but occasionally in the difficult technique of *émail en résille sur verre* (q.v.) – enamelling on engraved glass.

Watches, hitherto incorporated in all types of jewellery (see *Renaissance jewellery*), were now developing in a class of their own and had mostly adopted a round shape, sometimes elaborated into the form of a shell, flower, etc., and their cases were similarly enamelled. Miniature cases resisted the encroachment of gems for many decades, but by the end of the century they too had gem-encrusted lids.

Jewellery had now become women's wear. Men's jewellery was almost entirely restricted to jewelled buttons, preferably diamond, and a few rings. With the revival of a classical style in dress and in the arts generally, striking individual pieces of jewellery became unfashionable and the emphasis was on a harmonious ensemble. The floral motif was joined in mid-century by the bow, which lasted as a dominant motif well into the following century.

The bow was the basis of many earrings and brooches, especially the *girandole earring*, which was popularized by the engravings of Gilles Légaré and replaced the pendant pearl earrings of the first half of the century. The girandole was a pendant earring in which three, or sometimes five, pear-shaped stones or pearls hung from a bow-shaped ornament, or sometimes from a large central stone or jewelled plaque. The large bow-shaped *brooch*, later known as a *Sévigné*, was worn below the décolletage and echoed the glitter of the earrings. Coloured stones for these earrings and brooches were not unfashionable – emeralds were particularly popular in Spain – but the preference was for rose-cut diamonds, which were generally set in silver.

Detail of a gold necklace enamelled in blue, white and black, and with a large cabochon amethyst. French, made about 1670. Victoria and Albert Museum

Necklaces in the seventeenth century very often took the form of a simple string of fine pearls. In the later part of the century, however, jewelled necklaces became more common and again were often based on the ribbon or bow motif.

Other types of jewellery were not much worn. Jewelled *aigrettes* might be worn in the hair, and a few *rings*, though not many, on the fingers. The main characteristic of seventeenth-century rings is that the whole circlet is enamelled, generally with a floral design (see illustration), and the shoulders are no longer elaborately modelled, as in Renaissance rings. The modern wedding ring, a plain band of gold, made an early appearance in this

Enamelled floral ring of the second half of the seventeenth century, German. Nationalmuseum, Munich

century, but was often worn on the thumb. Lovers' rings and betrothal rings (q.v.) had not altered much since the Middle Ages.

A preoccupation with death, never entirely absent from jewellery since the Middle Ages, became particularly marked in the seventeenth century, largely as a result of religious fervour and persecution. It took several forms, which tend to overlap: mourning jewellery worn by the bereaved, in which faceted jet and jewels in the form of Death's heads figured prominently; jewels commemorating the

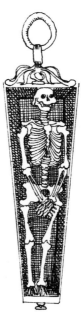

The Torre Abbey jewel. Victoria and Albert Museum

death of certain celebrated people (there was a fashion in England among Royalists for commemorative portraits of Charles I worn in rings and as slides on ribbons – see *Commemorative rings*); and *memento mori* jewellery (q.v.), which had no specific reference but simply encouraged the wearer to contemplate his or her inevitable end. Perhaps the most famous example of the third category is the Torre Abbey jewel, made in about 1600 (see illustration). This is a pendant of enamelled gold in the form of a coffin; the lid is removed to reveal a white-enamelled skeleton, beautifully made. The sides of the coffin bear the inscription 'Through the Resurrection of Christe we be all sanctified.' Pendants of similar form but with specific commemorative purpose were made after the death in 1632 of Gustavus Adolphus II of Sweden; they consist of enamelled silver coffins containing a wooden figure of the dead king.

Sévigné. A bow-shaped ornament which became the fashionable form for brooches in the mid-seventeenth century and was worn until the end of the following century. Sévignés were usually of gold or silver openwork lavishly set with diamonds. An example is illustrated under *Eighteenth-century jewellery*. They were named after Madame de Sévigné, the letter-writer.

Shah diamond. An engraved Indian diamond, with a faint yellowish tinge, weighing just under 89 carats. It is a roughly-faceted octahedron and has a groove to allow it to be worn on a thread round the neck. The diamond was found in the Golconda mines in the sixteenth century and is inscribed in Persian with the names of three of its owners. The inscriptions read: 'Nizam Shah 1000 (A.D. 1591); Jahan Shah 1051 (1641); Ali Shah 1242 (1826).'

The stone passed into the possession of the Shah of Persia but was presented to the Tsar in 1829 as compensation for the murder of the Russian ambassador to Teheran. It is now part of the Russian State Jewels.

Shank. See *Hoop*.

Shears. Tools for cutting sheet metal and wire by hand. They have short hardened-steel blades and are made in both straight and curved forms.

Sheen. The shimmering effect seen in certain gemstones, caused by the reflection of light from surfaces of differing refractive index (q.v.) within the stone. Sheen is to be distinguished from lustre (q.v.), which is the reflection of light from the stone's surface.

Sheffield plate. A type of plated silverware invented in 1743 by Thomas Bolsover as a cheaper substitute for solid silver. It was made by fusing a block of silver onto a block of copper and rolling out the resulting bimetallic block into sheet of various thicknesses, which was then decorated by stamping or rolling. (Rolled gold, q.v., is made in the same way.) Sheffield plate (it is usually called 'Old Sheffield plate' to distinguish it from modern plated wares) found a ready market among the middle classes who could not afford solid silver on their tables, and it was produced in considerable quantities in Sheffield and Birmingham for about a century. In the 1840s, however, electroplating (q.v.) was developed, and as this was a cheaper process it gradually displaced Sheffield plate, which ceased to be made in the middle of the nineteenth century. Although the decoration on Sheffield plate was mechanically produced, the work was of very high quality and surviving pieces are valuable.

Sheffield plate was not used for jewellery.

'Shell'. Name sometimes used for a hollow cabochon. (See *Gem-cutting*.)

Shell. The shell of various molluscs is used ornamentally and in jewellery; the most important commercially is the shell of the pearl-oysters *Pinctada maxima* and *Pinctada margaritifera* (mother-of-pearl). The iridescent material which covers the inside of the shell is nacre (q.v.), the substance which makes up a natural pearl.

The most important fisheries for this shell are in the northern and western coastal waters of Australia, a source discovered in the 1860s. The shells were at first recovered by skin divers, but diving suits are now worn. The divers go out in sailing luggers. When the shells are brought up they are opened with a knife and the meat of the oyster is removed and searched for pearls; the shells are then trimmed, taken ashore, sorted into grades of quality and despatched to Europe and the U.S.A.

Pearl shell from the Persian Gulf is fished by skin divers and is known as Bombay shell since it is usually marketed from India. The shell from this area is commercially much less important than the pearls. Shell is also obtained from the Red Sea (Alexandria shell), the Mergui archipelago (Burmese shell), the Philippines (Manilla shell), Singapore, Tahiti, the Gulf of Panama, and New Guinea. The value of the shell varies – the silver-white shells from New Guinea, for instance, fetch high prices, while the shell from Panama is of comparatively poor quality and is not valuable.

The pearl shell is used, among other things, for buttons, inlay, and carving. The latter is a long-established industry in Bethlehem. The black-lip pearl oyster has a dark shell which when suitably cut is sometimes chatoyant (q.v.), and pieces of this are sometimes mounted in jewellery.

A pearl-mollusc of a different species, the Abalone (q.v.) or *Haliotis*, has a brightly-coloured shell which is used ornamentally. The shell of the sea-snail (*Turbo*) is sometimes cut into small pieces which resemble pearls; these are known as Antilles pearls (q.v.) or Oil pearls. The central whorl of the nautilus shell is used to produce the *'coque de perle'* (q.v.), which resembles a blister pearl, and the septa or inner walls of the shell are used for inlay.

Shell is also carved into cameos; the Helmet shell (*Cassis madagascariensis*) from the waters of the West Indies is the most used for this purpose, and the pink shell of the Giant conch (*Strombus gigas*) is also used. (See also *Shell cameos*.)

An attractive oddity is the so-called 'Shell cat's eye', which is the 'door' of the shell of the sea-snail. (See *Operculum*.)

Shell cameos. Cameos have been cut in shell since about the beginning of the Renaissance. A variety of shells have been used, including the shell of the pearl-oyster. The Helmet shell and the shell of the Giant conch are now the two most commonly-used types. Very large and fine cameos have been cut on Helmet shells; the carving is in white relief on a brown background. In the Giant conch the colours are white and pink. The carving is done with steel tools similar to those used for carving and engraving metal, and when it is finished the cameo is polished with a soft polishing material such as rottenstone. The best shell cameos are carved in Italy.

Shell cameos became extremely popular in jewellery at the beginning of the nineteenth century; they were a cheap substitute for the hardstone cameos fashionable at the time. (See *Cameos*.) Although no longer actually fashionable they have continued to be popular ever since. As the material is easy to work and great numbers of them have been produced they have very little value, but the standard of workmanship is nevertheless often very high.

Shell cameos are now imitated in injection-moulded plastic. The difference between the two is quite apparent, and in any case the plastic imitations are usually sold in the cheapest of settings. (See also *Shell*.)

'Shell cat's eye'. See *Operculum*.

Shell marble. Lumachella.

Shoulders (of ring). The parts of a ring-shank which are next to the bezel or central ornament.

'Siam aquamarine.' Misnomer for heat-treated blue-green zircon.

'Siberian chrysolite'. Misnomer for demantoid garnet.

'Siberian ruby'. Misnomer for red tourmaline.

Siberite. Reddish-violet tourmaline.

Siderite. Blue chalcedony.

Signet rings. Seals (q.v.) to impress the owner's mark on documents and other articles were first developed in Western Asia, but the earliest use of the seal in rings was in ancient Egypt. The owner's device was engraved on the flat base of a scarab (see *Scarabs*), which was perforated lengthwise and threaded on a wire, and mounted as a swivelling bezel in a finger-ring. Stones such as jasper and cornelian were used for this purpose. (For the methods of engraving, see *Intaglios*.) In about the fifteenth century B.C. a new type of signet ring with a fixed metal bezel was introduced, and thereafter the use of the scarab as a signet declined.

The art of gem-engraving had meanwhile been developed in the Minoan civilization and reached a high level of artistry. Subsequently it seems to have been completely forgotten for many centuries, but in the Mycenaean culture which was an offshoot of the Minoan, a number of fine signet rings in gold were produced. (There is some doubt whether they were all intended to be used as signets, as in several of them the design is not reversed, as it would be for the purpose of making impressions.) They are

Mycenaean signet ring; the bezel is made of two sheets of gold with the decoration punched into the upper sheet. About fourteenth century B.C. National Museum, Athens

of two types: one is of solid gold, and the design is engraved with gem-cutting techniques; the other is made of two pieces of sheet gold with some kind of filling between them, the design being punched into the top sheet before it was attached.

After a lapse of several centuries (the 'dark age' of Greece) the forgotten art of hardstone engraving was re-introduced. At first this was used for swivelling seal-stones of the scarab type adopted from Egypt, but during the Classical period, when many extremely fine intaglios were engraved, the scarab top lost its distinctive shape and was eventually discarded. In the new form of signet ring the design was engraved on a fairly thin oval section of stone and the stone was set with the design facing upwards in a fixed ring-bezel. This type, which first appeared at the beginning of the fourth century B.C., has remained the normal form for signet rings. The stones used included garnet, amethyst and agate, and the designs covered a wide range of subjects (see *Intaglios*). Signet rings of similar form were also used in Rome from Republican times. Under the Republic the ordinary material for rings was at first iron; these were sometimes set with engraved stones or pastes. (Paste became a common material in Roman jewellery.) As the power and wealth of Rome increased, rings, including signets, began to be normally made of precious metals, and in the first century B.C. it became fashionable to make collections of engraved gems. By this time many Greek gem-engravers had migrated to Rome.

The early Christian Church rejected luxury and ornament, but the signet ring was a necessity for many of the transactions of everyday life and Christians were therefore permitted to wear one. St. Clement of Alexandria suggested a number of symbols appropriate for Christians (see *Devotional jewellery*). Most of these early Christian rings are in engraved metal, usually base metal, but engraved stones with suitable subjects (and sometimes unsuitable – the meaning of Graeco-Roman engraved gems was not always understood) were worn by the bishops of the early Church. In Byzantium gold signet rings engraved with religious subjects were commonly used. After the fall of the Roman Empire the use of the signet was continued by the barbarian peoples who had adopted it from the Romans, because in a time of widespread illiteracy it was even more important to have a recognizable mark.

This was equally true of the Middle Ages, particularly when trade began to develop. A certain number of antique intaglios were still in circulation and some of these were used as signets, but they were so rare and, in the early part of the Middle Ages, regarded with such superstitious reverence, that most of them were set in Church ornaments or reserved for the use of the king. In the thirteenth century gems began to be engraved in Western Europe after a lapse of about four centuries, but until the fourteenth century most signet rings were of engraved metal, usually gold. The design cut on the bezel was often a monogram or the owner's portrait; both these types became less common as the Middle Ages advanced. The owner's initials beneath a crown (the crown has no significance) or within a wreath became a popular device in the fourteenth century, and in the same century the merchant's mark appeared.

Fifteenth-century gold signet ring, once enamelled, the bezel engraved with a merchant's mark. British Museum

This was often a very odd-looking design with no apparent meaning, but it had the virtue of being distinctive and easily recognized by the illiterate. The merchant himself would probably be able to read, but the people he dealt with on the whole would not. Another type of design used on signets of the late Middle Ages was the rebus, which had been employed in antiquity. A rebus is the representation of a word or phrase by a set of pictures, letters, etc. which in combination give when pronounced the sound of that word or phrase. An example is given by a sixteenth-century gilt ring in the Victoria and Albert museum engraved with the picture of a vine and the letters CENT, signifying 'Vincent'.

A new element entered the devices on signet rings in the fourteenth and fifteenth centuries when heraldry was established. The signet engraved with a coat of arms was almost universally adopted by those entitled to bear arms. A type which became popular in Elizabethan England was engraved in rock crystal and the tinctures of the arms were painted in underneath the stone, so that the colours would not be worn away through use of the signet for sealing. A historically-interesting example of this type is the signet of Mary Queen of Scots in the British Museum.

The Renaissance brought a more informed interest in antique cameos and intaglios and a great revival of gem-engraving. The stones unearthed in excavations in Italy and those engraved with great skill by contemporary artists (see *Intaglios*) were often used as signets, but to an even greater extent they were collected for their value as works of art. Seals of this quality form only a small proportion of the signets actually used at this time; the merchant classes and poorer people continued to use signet rings of engraved metal with the devices that had been in use for several centuries, particularly initials and the merchant's mark. The merchant's mark, however, fell into disuse in the course of the seventeenth century, partly because literacy was increasing and partly because business methods were changing.

By the eighteenth century the need for signet rings had considerably declined. There was however another great revival of interest in engraved gems, and large

Silhouettes

numbers of intaglios were engraved during the century, often in imitation of antique gems and sometimes as forgeries (see *Intaglios*). Paste intaglios were made in large quantities by James Tassie (q.v.) among others, and an earthenware variety was produced by Wedgwood (q.v.). Although the manufacturers of these imitations stressed their suitability for use as seals, they were on the whole made and bought for collections. Nevertheless some were set as ring-stones.

Signet ring set with an onyx intaglio in antique style, made about 1800. Museum für Kunst und Gewerbe, Hamburg

German pendant with portrait silhouette, late eighteenth century. Nationalmuseum, Munich

Since the eighteenth century the signet ring has been deprived of its practical function so completely that in modern usage the name 'signet ring' often simply means a man's gold ring worn on the little finger, suggesting that it never had a practical function at all. Engraved signet rings are still worn but they are worn for ornament, and with the exception of mass-produced machine-cut intaglios, the design in modern rings is engraved in metal, not on a hard stone. Not only have labour costs risen so prohibitively that it costs much less to buy an antique intaglio stone than to have one engraved, but there are now very few craftsmen still practising this type of work.

Silhouettes. A form of decoration popular in England and Germany in the late eighteenth and early nineteenth centuries. Silhouette portraits of friends and relatives were hung on walls, and they also appeared in jewellery – in pendants, brooches, and sometimes rings. The fashion was part of the Romantic en-

thusiasm for things simple, sentimental and home-made. (Hair jewellery [q.v.] was another example.) The originator is said to have been the French finance minister Etienne de Silhouette, who in 1759 decorated his mansion with silhouette portraits to set an example to his extravagant contemporaries. Silhouettes went out of fashion when photography was invented.

Silica glass. (S.G. 2.21; R.I. 1.46; H. 6.) Natural glass containing about 98 per cent silica, occasionally cut into faceted stones. It is a yellowish-green colour and is usually rather cloudy. The stones are not particularly attractive because of their lack of fire, but they are of interest to collectors. The glass is found in the Libyan desert, in the form of large lumps weighing up to 16 lb., and its origin is unknown.

Silk. A whitish sheen seen in some corundums, due to the presence of many microscopically small canals which reflect light. (See *Corundum*.)

Sillimanite. See *Fibrolite*.

Silver. The commonest of the precious

metals, silver has working qualities almost as good as those of gold (q.v.) and the advantage of being very much cheaper. It can be rolled into sheet 0.005" thick, and a Troy ounce can be drawn into a mile of wire. It is a soft metal but has considerable tensile strength and is ideal for raising under the hammer or spinning into tableware. It has greater reflective power than gold and weighs only about half as much, which is an important consideration in the making of tableware although less important as regards jewellery.

Silver is resistant to the attack of many chemical and organic substances (hence its use by surgeons for electrodes and other articles inserted into the human body) but it is attacked by strong nitric acid and by sulphur. The latter is the cause of tarnish. Tarnish was not much of a problem until the beginning of the industrial revolution because the air in the cities was relatively pure, but when coal-gases began pouring from factory chimneys in the eighteenth century silver required constant polishing to keep it bright. When servants ceased to be readily available in this century silver suffered a marked decline in popularity, but the problem has now been to some extent solved by the invention of new cleaning agents and methods of tarnish-proofing. The most important of these is rhodium-plating (q.v.), which gives silver a tarnish-resistant surface. It is not a completely satisfactory answer, however, because the rhodium does slightly alter the appearance of the silver and of course prevents it from achieving the mellow patina so prized by collectors. This patina is the result of use; being soft, silver does not suffer by being scratched because the scratches are not sharp-edged – in time they blur and give the metal a pleasantly aged appearance.

Silver, like gold, is in fact too soft in its pure state to be a satisfactory material. It has to be alloyed with a harder metal, and the metal used is copper. In sterling silver the proportions are 925 parts per thousand silver and 75 copper. (This is British sterling; in America the minimum hall-marking quality for sterling is 921 parts per thousand.) The other legal standard for silver in Britain is Britannia, also known for some reason as Better Nine. This contains 95.84 per cent silver. It was introduced in 1697 to prevent silversmiths from melting down the coin of the realm, which was sterling, to make silver plate (see *Hallmarking* for more detailed account). The law making Britannia the compulsory standard for wrought silver was repealed in 1719, but silversmiths are still free to work in metal of this quality if they wish to do so. Before being offered for sale, silverwares must be sent to an assay office to be tested and hallmarked. (See *Assaying* and *Hallmarking*.)

The fact that silver is alloyed with copper creates another problem which has only recently been solved. Copper when heated oxidizes and blackens. When sterling silver is annealed (see *Annealing*) by the refiners and later by the jeweller and silversmith, this results in the formation of a dark stain both on and below the surface of the metal; this stain in time becomes difficult to remove without removing an excessive amount of metal. Recently, however, it has become possible for silver to be annealed at the refineries in an oxygen-free atmosphere so that the copper oxide cannot form (see *Firestain* and *Fire-free silver*).

The big refining companies produce silver of the required hallmarking standard in a variety of forms, including sheet, strip and wire of different gauges, seamless tube, findings (catches, ready-made stone-settings, etc.) and silver solders (these must also be of hallmarking standard). Special silvers for engraving, spinning, enamelling, etc., are also produced.

Unlike gold, silver is not often found naturally in usable metallic form. It occurs as sulphide in ores, and most of the silver used in the modern world is a by-product from the refining of other metals – lead, zinc, copper, tin, gold, etc. Lead is particularly important; about 45 per cent of our silver comes from lead mines. There are two methods of extracting the silver from the lead, known as the Parkes process and the Betts process. In the Parkes process, any impurities such as copper are first separated out from the ore, then the remaining mixture of lead and silver is melted, and zinc, which has an affinity for silver, is added. It combines with the silver, and by a distillation process the silver is then recovered. In the Betts process an electric current is passed through the lead and silver when they are placed as the anode in a bath containing lead fluosilicate, and this removes the lead. The silver recovered by these two processes is about 90 per cent pure; it is then further refined electrolytically until it is over 99.9 per cent pure. In some cases, particularly in the Mexican mines, silver is the principal product. These rich silver ores are crushed and dissolved in a cyanide solution, and zinc is added to precipitate the silver. The precipitate is washed in acid to remove excess zinc, and then melted in a stream of air so that the base metals oxidize; the oxides are then removed and the silver (about 98 per cent pure) is sent to the refinery to be purified electrolytically.

Mexico is now the world's leading source of silver, producing about 35 per cent of the silver mined outside Communist countries. The U.S.A. produces about 25 per cent, Central and South America 20 per cent, and Canada and Australia about 15 per cent between them. The production in Communist countries is not known, but is estimated to be about one-twentieth of that produced in the rest of the world.

History. Gold, being found in appreciable quantities in usable form, was almost certainly being worked before silver, but in areas of Europe and Asia Minor where silver occurs quite commonly in galena (an ore of lead) natural events such as forest fires would have smelted the ore and in the right conditions left a lump of more or less pure silver. According to the historian Diodorus Siculus (first century B.C.), the inhabitants of these regions eventually took to starting forest fires on purpose. Silver was being worked in Asia Minor in the fourth millennium B.C., and by

the third millennium B.C., when soldering was invented, virtually all the techniques now used on silver, excepting of course those requiring powered machinery, were in use: chasing, engraving, piercing, casting and filigree-work (qq.v.). The techniques were the same as those used for gold (see *Gold*, under 'History'), the only differences being that silver cannot be beaten quite so thin or drawn into such fine wire, and that silver leaf, unlike gold leaf, cannot be used satisfactorily to cover objects of base metal, etc. – it is too fragile.

On the whole, however, not much silver jewellery has survived from the ancient world. This may be because silver is more perishable than gold, or it may be because not much was made. Gold was the prerogative of kings and was made into ornaments which were both a symbol of power and a portable exchequer, but silver was more readily available and, because its value was universally recognized, furnished the ideal currency for ordinary trading. References to silver currency in the Old Testament and in early records are innumerable. Organized mining, probably at first open-cast but later underground, had started in Asia Minor by the fourth millennium B.C. and spread eastwards and also westwards to the Aegean. Mines in northern Greece were worked from about the eighth century B.C. onwards, and in the fifth century B.C. a rich vein was discovered at Laurium in Attica. The silver from this area was the basis of the prosperity of Athens and its chief support in the Persian wars. The deposits were worked out by about 100 B.C.

Rome took most of its silver from Spain; the Spanish mines had previously been worked by the Carthaginians. As the austerity of the Roman republic gave way to the luxury of the Roman Empire silver began to be used for tableware by the upper classes. After the fall of the Empire the Spanish deposits continued to be worked for a time, but the Moorish invasion put a stop to the mining in the eighth century. There followed a period of disruption when most of the silver in circulation was obtained by plunder, although a certain amount was mined in central Europe. As stability began to return to Europe standards were established for the silver coinage and for the silver plate manufactured for the Church, etc. The sterling standard was established in England in the thirteenth century and hallmarking was instituted in 1300 by Edward I.

In the early sixteenth century the Spaniards found extensive and very rich deposits of silver in Mexico, Bolivia, and Peru. These sources provided the bulk of the world's silver until 1800, when the colonies revolted. For more than three centuries the same traditional method was used in Mexico for treating the ore. It was crushed and mixed to a mud with water, and to the mud were added salt, the roasted sulphide ores of copper and iron, and mercury. This mixture was then trodden by mules for several days. The silver became metallic and amalgamated with the mercury. The mercury was evaporated off and the silver, still containing some impurities, was sent to a refinery for cupellation (q.v.).

The discovery of silver in Spanish America came at a time when silver was being increasingly used for elaborate Church plate and for the tableware of the nobility. Silver spoons and salt shakers had appeared in western Europe in the thirteenth century, followed shortly afterwards by silver plates, and in the sixteenth century silver tankards with lids were introduced. The nobility had elaborate centrepieces of silver, but the merchant classes also had their silver plate, and the great demand for table silver in England at the end of the seventeenth century led to the introduction of the Britannia standard (see *Hallmarking*). In 1743 Thomas Bolsover invented Sheffield plate (q.v.) – silver fused on to a block of copper and rolled out into sheet – which made silver tableware accessible to the less wealthy. Sheffield plate was superseded in the following century by electroplating (q.v.), which began to be used commercially in the 1850s and offered an even cheaper substitute for solid silver.

At the time when electroplating was developed there was a world shortage of silver, owing largely to the revolt of the Spanish American colonies. Within a few decades, however, vast silver resources were discovered in the Sierra Nevada in the United States, and the price of silver fell. The use of silver in jewellery had previously been restricted largely to peasant jewellery (q.v.) and to the cheaper jewellery worn by the middle classes. In the latter category, silver had had to compete with gold imitations such as pinchbeck (q.v.) and, later, low-carat gold alloys. When silver suddenly became readily available and cheap, however, it became a fashionable metal, and in England in the 1870s silver jewellery was the rage. In the long-term this had disastrous effects on the manufacturers of cheap jewellery (see *Birmingham*). By the 1880s the fashionable world was sick of silver jewellery and it was no longer worn. In the eighteenth century, after the invention of the brilliant cut (see *Diamond*), silver had been extensively used for setting diamonds because it had greater reflectivity than gold and did not give the stones a yellow tinge, but towards the end of the nineteenth century platinum (q.v.), which does not tarnish, began to be used for this purpose instead.

Silver was not long neglected by jewellers, however; the Art Nouveau designers made skilful use of it in combination with such stones as amethyst, and the Danish firm of Jensen (q.v.), founded at this time, has specialized in silverwork ever since. The price of silver has fluctuated considerably in this century and there are now very few countries which still have a silver coinage ('sterling' ceased to be sterling in 1920 and has contained no silver at all since 1946); the industrial use of silver in such fields as photography has on the other hand increased. Silver has now, however, become accepted as the metal for medium-priced and in particular hand-made jewellery, and it is usually set with what are popularly known as 'semi-precious' stones – agates, cornelians, amethysts, etc. It is cheap enough to be available to the ordinary person, but at the same time expensive enough to make the commercial production of silver substitutes worthwhile. One of these substitutes is, of course, silver plate, which varies considerably in quality according to the thickness of the silver coating and the techniques by which it is applied. The other white metals which are cheaper than silver – nickel silver, chromium, stainless steel, pewter (qq.v.) – bear little resemblance to silver, which even when highly polished has a certain softness of colour that no other white metal possesses.

Simetite. Sicilian amber. (See *Amber.*)

Single cut. See *Eight-cut.*

Single refraction. Refraction (q.v.) in which a ray of light is refracted into a gemstone as a single ray. This occurs only in minerals of the cubic system (see *Crystal systems*) and in glass and amorphous substances; in all other gemstones the ray is split into two on refraction. (See *Double refraction.*)

Sinhalite. (Magnesium-aluminium-iron borate. S.G. 3.47–3.50; R.I. 1.67–1.71; H. $6\frac{1}{2}$.) A transparent golden-yellow, yellowish-brown or greenish-brown stone similar in appearance to brown chrysoberyl and brown zircon. Cut specimens of the stone were thought for many years to be olivines with a high percentage of iron, but it was discovered in 1952 that they represented a new mineral species. The name 'Sinhalite' was chosen as the only known specimens originated from the Ceylon gem gravels. A deposit in Warren County, N.Y. has since been found but the stones are not of gem quality.

Sinopal. A reddish aventurine quartz.

'Sira'. (Trade name.) An abrasive made from artificially-manufactured aluminium oxide.

Skew facet. Another name for some of the cross facets (q.v.) above the girdle of a brilliant-cut stone. (See *Diamond-cutting.*)

Skiagram. An X-ray shadow photograph, used in the detection of cultured pearls. (See *Pearls.*)

Skill facet. Another name for some of the cross facets (q.v.) on a brilliant-cut stone (see *Diamond-cutting*).

Sleeper. A small gold hoop-earring worn in the perforation of the ear-lobe to keep it open.

Smalto Roggio. A rich transparent red enamel developed in the early Renaissance period; until this time all red enamel had been opaque. (See *Enamel.*)

Smaragdite. A bright green zoisite-type rock resembling jade and sometimes used to imitate it.

'Smaragdolin'. (Trade name.) A green beryl glass (see *Glass*).

'Smaryll'. A type of soudé emerald consisting of two pieces of beryl joined with a green cement. (See *Doublet.*)

Smithsonite. (Zinc carbonate. S.G. about 4.3; R.I. 1.62–1.85; H. 5.) An opaque or sometimes translucent green or bluish-green stone sometimes used in cabochon form in jewellery. Some stones have blue and green banding, and pink and yellow smithsonite is also occasionally seen. Some smithsonite has been sold under the name 'bonamite' by Goodfriend Brothers of New York, who first marketed the stone. Sources of smithsonite include Greece, S.W. Africa, Spain, Sardinia, and parts of the U.S.A.

Smoky quartz. (See *Quartz, crystalline.*) Brownish clear quartz with a smoky tinge. The colour varies from light to very dark. Sources of good-quality material include Pike's Peak, Colorado; Hinojosa in Cordoba, Spain; Japan, and Manchuria.

Snake chain. A strong flexible chain consisting of linked cups of metal, also known as Brazilian chain. (See also *Chain.*)

Snarling iron. An iron rod, sometimes Z-shaped and usually about a foot in length and $\frac{1}{2}''$ thick, used for raising bosses and bumps in relief on narrow-necked objects such as bowls in which a hammer or repoussé punch cannot be inserted. One end of the iron is held in a bench vice, and the other end, which has a rounded knob, is placed inside the object against the place where the boss is to be produced. The part of the iron near the vice is given a sharp blow and this causes the other end to rebound against the side of the object; the blows are repeated until a boss of the required size has been beaten out.

'Snowflake jade'. See 'Wyoming jade'.

Soapstone. See Steatite.

Sodalite. (Sodium-aluminium silicate with sodium chloride. S.G. about 2.28; R.I. 1.48; H. $5\frac{1}{2}$–6.) A royal blue stone which is one of the constituents of lapis-lazuli (q.v.) but is also used as an ornamental stone in its own right. It may appear very similar to lapis-lazuli, but never attains the same ultramarine blue and does not usually contain the specks of pyrites commonly seen in lapis. Being a massive mineral it is cut in cabochon or bead form or is used for inlays.

The major source of sodalite is Dungannon in Hastings County, Ontario. It also occurs at Litchfield, Maine and Salem, Massachusetts, U.S.A., in southern Norway, in the state of Rajputana, India, in Brazil, British Columbia and S.W. Africa.

Solder. A metal used in molten form to effect a join between two other metal surfaces (see Soldering). The solders used in gold and silver jewellery must by law contain the proportion of precious metal required by the hallmarking standards (see Assaying and Hallmarking). Gold solders are thus produced by refiners in 9-carat, 14-carat and 18-carat qualities, and silver solders in the sterling and Britannia standards. All these solders are available in a range of melting-points from hard (high melting-point, say 870°C for gold and 770°C for silver) to extra easy (say 645°C for gold and 680°C for silver). The middle ranges are for general-purpose soldering, but when a piece is to be soldered several times a hard solder is used for the first joint and an easy solder for the second so that the first joint will not melt again when the second is being made. Gold solders are also made in yellow, red and white gold. Platinum solders are also produced although platinum in Britain does not yet have to be hallmarked.

Soldering. The process of joining two or more pieces of metal by running molten metal (the solder) between them, so that when it solidifies a firm joint is made. In hard-soldering the solder has a melting-point not very much lower than that of the metals which are to be joined and actually penetrates them, and the resulting joint is very strong. In soft-soldering the melting-point of the solder is considerably lower and the joint is weaker; this type of soldering is not used in jewellery except in special circumstances, such as the repair of a piece which will not stand the heat of hard-soldering. The solders used in gold and silver jewellery have to contain the same proportion of precious metal as the rest of the article (see Solder) in order to meet the hallmarking requirements, which is a further reason why soft-soldering, which uses base metals, is not used in the manufacture of jewellery. Although there are as yet no legal requirements for the hallmarking of platinum, platinum jewellery is normally soldered with platinum solder. Platinum (q.v.) has a very high melting-point and an oxyacetylene flame is used.

The surfaces to be joined must be absolutely clean before the work is started, and they are usually scraped or filed to ensure this. They are then coated with flux (q.v.). The purpose of the flux is to encourage the flow of the solder and dissolve the oxide which forms on the metals as they are heated: the presence of a film of oxide would prevent a proper joint being made. The pieces to be joined are arranged in position and if necessary bound together with binding wire (q.v.), and small pieces of solder which have been dipped in flux are placed along the join. The work is gently heated (usually with a gas flame, see below) until the solder runs. Other ways of applying the solder

341

are to raise the work to soldering heat and then apply a thin strip of solder, held in pliers, to the joint, or to mix filings of solder to a thick paste with flux and apply this with a brush to the join before heating. The latter method is useful for soldering the links of chains and catches.

A gas or gas-and-air flame is generally used for soldering. Some jewellers use a hand-held blowtorch, others a swivelling gas jet fixed to the workbench. The heat of the flame may be controlled and the flame directed by means of a mouth blow-pipe (see *Blowpipe*) or a foot-bellows. The work is usually rested on a charcoal or asbestos block or on a soldering wig (q.v.). When a number of complicated pieces have to be held in position together for soldering, they are sometimes embedded in plasticine and then covered with a fine plaster-of-Paris mixture poured over them from the back; when this is set they will be held securely.

After soldering the work has to be immersed in a pickle solution (see *Pickle*) to remove the flux, which will have hardened, and any loose oxide. If the work is held together with iron binding wire this must be removed before pickling. Hard-soldering has been used in jewellery since the third millennium B.C. The metal-workers of the ancient world used a charcoal fire, controlled by a blowpipe, as the source of heat, and probably natron (a naturally-occurring carbonate of soda) or the burnt sediment of wine as a flux. Certain pieces of ancient goldwork appear too intricate to have been hard-soldered (see *Gold*), and for these the process known as colloid hard-soldering (q.v.) was probably used.

Soldering wig. A mop made of iron wire, used to support work being soldered (see *Soldering*). It allows the heat to spread underneath the work.

Soldier's stone. A name for amethyst.

Solis, Virgil (of Nuremberg). (1514–1562). One of the earliest Renaissance designers of jewellery and engraved ornament. His most characteristic work is

Soldering wig

a series of nearly 30 designs for pendants; these feature cabochon stones in high settings, and strapwork frames with caryatid figures. The backs are to be enamelled in moresque patterns. Solis also produced engraved designs for belt-harness with elaborate moresques, as well as designs for other goldsmiths' work. (See also *Moresque*.)

Solitaire. A stone of fine quality, usually a diamond, set by itself. Solitaire rings became very popular towards the end of the nineteenth century.

'Soochow jade'. Misnomer for bowenite (see *Serpentine*) or green steatite.

Soudé stones. Composite stones. (See *Doublet*.)

'South African jade'. Misnomer for massive green grossular garnet.

'South African wonderstone' (Koranna stone). A pyrophyllite (q.v.) rock from the western Transvaal, dark grey in colour, used ornamentally.

'Spanish emerald'. Misnomer for green glass.

'Spanish topaz'. Misnomer for yellowish-brown quartz, often heat-treated. (See *Heat-treatment*.)

'Sparklite'. (Trade name.) Colourless zircon, heat-treated. (See *Heat-treatment*.)

Specific gravity. The weight of a substance compared with the weight of an equal volume of water at 4°C, at which temperature water is at its most dense. (The density of a substance is its weight per unit volume. Any unit of measurement can be used, but in scientific work density is given in grams per c.c., and since one gram is the weight of one c.c. of pure water at 4°C, the terms 'density' and 'specific gravity' can be used interchangeably. The former term is usually applied to liquids and the latter to solids.)

The specific gravity of any particular species of gemstone is constant, and as the specific gravities of stones range from about 1.10 (amber) to 3.96 (corundum), the determination of the approximate specific gravity of a specimen can help considerably in identifying it. The main disadvantage of this method of identification is that the stone tested must be unmounted; this obviously limits the usefulness of the method to retail jewellers.

There are two main methods of determining specific gravity. Each is capable of modification.

1. Hydrostatic weighing. This is an accurate method of weighing stones of over 2 carats, but is rather lengthy and requires a good set of balances. The stone is first carefully weighed (the unit of weight is usually the carat). It is then placed in a wire cage suspended from one arm of the balance, and weighed when totally submerged in a beaker of distilled water. The weight of the empty cage in water must also be ascertained. This last weight is subtracted from the weight of the stone and cage in water, giving the weight of the stone alone in water. The difference between the weight of the stone in water and the weight of the stone in air is divided into the weight of the stone in air, and the resulting figure is the specific gravity of the stone.

The Jolly's Spring Balance allows the specific gravity to be calculated more quickly. It consists of a spring balance fitted with two scale pans, the lower of which is immersed in water. Readings are taken when both scale pans are empty (A), when the stone is in the top pan (its weight in air) (B), and when the stone is in the bottom pan (its weight in water)

(C). B minus A divided by B minus C is the specific gravity of the stone.

2. Heavy liquid method. This makes use of a range of liquids heavier than water, and is basically a quick and simple method. When immersed in a liquid of higher density than itself a stone will float to the surface; in a liquid of lower density it will sink, and in a liquid of the same density it will remain suspended at the level at which it is left. By immersing a stone in a series of liquids of known density, therefore, it is possible to find quite quickly the approximate specific gravity of the stone. Comparisons between stones of similar appearance can be made by immersing them together in the same liquid. The three basic liquids used are bromoform (density 2.90), methylene iodide (3.32) and clerici solution (4.15). Clerici solution is a poisonous aqueous solution of thallium salts; it is generally diluted with distilled water to a density of about 4.0. Other liquids which may be used are ethylene dibromide (2.19) and acetylene tetrabromide (2.96). Liquids of intermediate densities are obtained by diluting a heavy liquid with a lighter. Methylene iodide may be diluted with bromoform, and bromoform with toluene (0.87) or monobromonaphthalene (1.49). Very accurate results can be obtained by gradually diluting the liquid until its density exactly matches that of the stone being tested (i.e. until the stone remains suspended in it), and then ascertaining the density of the liquid.

There are various ways of measuring the density of a liquid. One is to fill a pycnometer (a bottle with a glass stopper which when completely filled holds a known weight of water) with the liquid and weigh it; the weight of the liquid (the weight of the bottle must of course be subtracted) compared with the weight of the water gives the density of the liquid. Another way is to use a Westphal balance, which incorporates a plunger that displaces a known weight of water; when the plunger is immersed in a liquid other than water the density of this liquid may be calculated by reading off the number

343

and position of the weights needed to restore the balance. A quick way of measuring density is by a hydrometer. This is a bulb-shaped instrument with a calibrated scale at the top – when immersed in a liquid it takes up a level relative to the density of the liquid, and the point on the scale which is level with the surface gives a direct reading of the density. Unfortunately hydrometers are not always available for the range of densities required. Finally, there is an accurate method based on the fact that there is a direct relationship between the density and the refractive index (q.v.) of a heavy liquid mixture. If as a heavy liquid is gradually diluted samples of it are taken at three different stages and the density determined by testing with stones of a known density, and the refractive indices of these samples are then measured by refractometer (q.v.), then on the basis of these three relationships a graph can be drawn up which will show the density of the liquid in any stage of dilution when its refractive index is measured.

Opal and turquoise should not be tested in heavy liquids because they are likely to discolour.

Spectrograph. An instrument used for the examination of bright-line and absorption spectra (qq.v.) in gemstones. A more complex instrument than the spectroscope (q.v.), it disperses light into the colours of the spectrum, but instead of the spectra being viewed directly they are photographed on to a plate inside the instrument. On being developed, this gives a picture of the spectra which can be either measured or compared directly with the known spectra of the elements more commonly encountered in gemstones. Quartz prisms and lenses are used so that lines in the ultra-violet region can be recorded.

Spectrometer. An instrument which disperses light into the colours of the spectrum and enables the wavelengths to be read off or calculated. The smaller type used in gemmological work is also known as a spectroscope (q.v.). Table spectro-

meters are used in the measurement of bright-line spectra (q.v.) in gemstones and in the measurement of refractive index (q.v.). For the observation of bright-line spectra the light is dispersed by a glass prism supplied with the instrument or by a diffraction grating, and the wavelengths are read off using a graph. In the measurement of refractive index the stone itself provides the prism. For further description of the table spectrometer see *Refractive index.*

Spectroscope. An instrument which disperses light into the colours of the spectrum and is used for examining the absorption-spectra (q.v.) of gemstones. When a stone is viewed through the instrument with a strong light behind it, dark bands are seen on the spectrum of light transmitted through the stone. These correspond to the wavelengths of light selectively absorbed by the stone and are determined by its chemical composition. The absorption spectra thus constitute an important means of identifying gemstones.

Spessartite (Spessartine). (Manganese-aluminium silicate. S.G. 4.12–4.20; R.I. 1.80; H. 7¼.) A transparent yellowish, aurora-red or brownish-red variety of garnet, in some cases similar in appearance to hessonite (grossular garnet, [q.v.]). Spessartite is rare, but crystals suitable for cutting come from Ceylon, Burma, Madagascar and U.S.A. The original source, from which the variety takes its name, was Spessart in Bavaria, but no gem-quality material appears to have come from there.

Sphalerite. See *Zinc blende.*

Sphene (Titanite). (Calcium-titanium silicate. S.G. 3.52–3.54; R.I. 1.91–2.06; H. 5½.) A transparent and strongly dichroic yellow, brown or green stone with high refraction and greater fire than diamond. These qualities make it a splendid gemstone when freshly cut, but it is not hard enough for constant wear. The name 'titanite' is generally applied to the brown or black material which is not of gem quality.

Sphene comes from the Austrian Tyrol, the St. Gotthard district of Switzerland, Ontario, California, Brazil, and Madagascar.

Spherules (Spherulites). Spherical aggregates of needle-like crystals occurring in another mineral; when the material is cut and polished they appear as circles. The best-known example is orbicular jasper.

Spinel. (Magnesium-aluminium oxide. S.G. 3.58–3.61; R.I. about 1.72; H. 8.) A transparent gemstone usually seen in various shades of red, blue and purple, the preferred colour being a deep ruby-red. Spinel and ruby (q.v.) represent two distinct but related mineral species, and in the past there has been considerable confusion between the two. The old term for a red spinel was 'balas ruby' (q.v.), and many famous 'rubies', including the Black Prince's ruby in the British Regalia, are red spinels. The confusion is still perpetuated by the use of such ambiguous terms as 'ruby spinel', and the fact that spinels and rubies frequently occur together does nothing to clarify the situation.

Spinels make very attractive gemstones, but they are inevitably compared with ruby and sapphire and suffer by the comparison – they do not possess the same richness of colour. Spinel is softer than corundum, although still hard enough to make a very durable ring-stone, and being a cubic mineral (see *Crystal systems*) and therefore singly-refractive it lacks the dichroism of corundum – an easy way of distinguishing red spinel from ruby.

Spinel is manufactured synthetically, usually as an imitation of other gemstones such as alexandrite, aquamarine, etc. (See *Synthetic gemstones*.)

Sources of spinel include the Mogok Stone Tract in Burma, the gem gravels of Ceylon, Afghanistan, Thailand, Brazil and parts of the U.S.A.

Spinel ruby. Ruby-coloured spinel.

Spodumene. (Lithium-aluminium silicate. S.G. 3.17–3.19; R.I. 1.66–1.68; H. 7.) The mineral species which includes *hiddenite* and *kunzite* (qq.v.). The term 'spodumene' is usually applied, in the jewellery trade, to transparent yellow or yellowish-green stones which differ from hiddenite (emerald-green) in that they contain no chromium. All spodumene is dichroic and is characterized by a strong cleavage which makes the stones difficult to cut. Opaque spodumene is of commercial value as the principal ore of lithium.

The sources for the yellowish spodumene are North and South America and Madagascar. It also occurs in the Mogok Stone Tract in Burma.

Staining (gemstones). See *Dyeing of stones*.

Stainless steel. An alloy which was invented in 1913 but was not widely used for some decades. The original constituents were iron, carbon and chromium, but stainless steel now contains little or no carbon and nickel is an important constituent. The chromium makes the metal rustproof (but not actually stainless – it does stain, for instance in contact with vinegar).

Stainless steel tableware has been popular since the 1950s, but more recently stainless steel has come to be used in jewellery, mostly for rings and bracelets. Compared with silver it has a harsh appearance (it is of course much harder), but its use in modern designs is quite effective. It can be electroplated with gold or silver if a plating of nickel is applied (electrolytically) first.

Stakes. Tools of hardened steel on which metal is hammered into shape. A great variety – T-stakes, round-head, oval-head, square-head, mushroom, etc. – are made for metalworkers and silversmiths, but the types used by jewellers are mostly the beck-iron and the mandrel (qq.v.).

Stamping. The process of imprinting a pattern on sheet metal by driving a punch into it. Stamping is basically a development of repoussé work (q.v.), but the punch impresses a complete pattern instead of a single mark and the process can therefore be used to produce a number of identical pieces.

Stamping first appears as a process in jewellery in Greek work of the second millennium B.C. The punches were made in two parts; on one the design was in cameo and on the other in intaglio. The design was usually driven in with the cameo punch from the back and the metal was forced into the matching intaglio mould. Most of the early punches were of bronze.

Stamping has continued to be used in jewellery, but was never a very important process until the nineteenth century, when it became mechanized and began to be used extensively for mass-production. (See *Machine-stamping*.)

Star facet. The name for the 8 small triangular facets which surround the table facet of a brilliant-cut stone. (See *Diamond-cutting*.)

'Starilian'. Trade name for strontium titanate.

'Starlite'. (Trade name.) Blue zircon.

Star malachite. Chalcedony with inclusions of malachite arranged in a star-like pattern.

Star of Africa. See *Cullinan diamond*.

Star of Egypt. A fine Brazilian diamond first heard of in Europe when it appeared on the London market in 1939. It was said to have been found some time in the middle of the nineteenth century and to have belonged to the Khedive of Egypt, at which time it was an oval stone weighing about 150 old carats (see *Carat*). The Khedive sold it in about 1880 and it was re-fashioned as an emerald-cut stone weighing about 107 metric carats.

Star of South Africa (Dudley diamond). One of the first large diamonds to be discovered in South Africa; it was found in 1869 in the Vaal River diggings and weighed $83\frac{1}{2}$ carats. It was cut into a pendeloque brilliant weighing just under 48 carats and was bought by the Countess of Dudley.

Star of the South. The largest diamond found in Brazil. It was discovered at Bagagem in Minas Gerais in 1853; it was a perfectly colourless stone weighing nearly 262 carats. It is said to have been found by a negress slave who was rewarded with her freedom and a pension. The stone was sold for £40,000 and cut as a brilliant; it was subsequently bought by the Gaekwar of Baroda.

'Starolite'. Trade name for a doublet (q.v.) using star rose quartz.

Star stones. See *Asterism*.

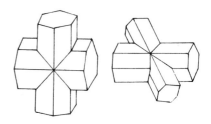

Forms of staurolite crystals

Staurolite. (Hydrated aluminium silicate. S.G. about 3.7; R.I. 1.736–1.746; H. 7–$7\frac{1}{2}$.) This stone is most often used in its natural form, owing to the cruciform shape of the twinned crystals (see illustration). In this form it is used as an amulet in some European countries. It is usually translucent or opaque, and the preferred colour is a deep reddish-brown. Transparent crystals are occasionally found and may be faceted.

Staurolite is found in Switzerland, Brittany, Scotland, Russia, Brazil, and parts of North America.

Steatite. (Hydrated magnesium silicate. S.G. 2.20–2.80; H. 1–$1\frac{1}{2}$.) Steatite is the massive variety of talc, and is also known as soapstone on account of its greasy texture. It is usually green, brown or greyish and its softness (even when containing impurities it can often be scratched by a finger-nail) makes it very suitable for carving into small ornaments. It has been carved from very early times – many of the Mesopotamian cylinder-seals and Egyptian scarabs are of this material. In spite of its softness it takes a certain polish.

In powdered form the mineral has numerous industrial uses including the manufacture of talcum powder. It occurs worldwide; there are important deposits in central Africa and India.

Steel. Iron to which has been added a proportion of carbon to increase its hardness and tensile strength. There are numerous different steels, some of them containing nickel and chromium.

Steel had a lasting vogue in jewellery in the eighteenth and early nineteenth centuries (see *Cut-steel jewellery*). Recently stainless steel (q.v.) has begun to be used in cheap modern jewellery. The most important use of steel to the modern jeweller, however, is in tools.

Steel block. A flat block of steel, machined and polished on at least one surface, used whenever a hard flat surface is required for truing-up or hammering metal. It can also be used for smoothing metal flat – a piece of emery paper is placed over the flat surface and the metal rubbed across it.

Step cut. A popular cut for coloured stones. The table facet may be oblong, hexagonal or of a variety of other shapes, and is surrounded by rectangular facets; similar rectangular facets cover the base of the stone. (See *Gem-cutting* for illustration.)

Sterling. Silver which is 92.5 per cent pure, the remaining proportion being a base metal, normally copper. (The standard is slightly lower in America – see *Silver*. The sterling standard was introduced to America by Charles Tiffany.)

Sterling was from early medieval times the normal standard of the silver coinage in England, although it was periodically debased, notably in the reign of Henry VIII. It was made the compulsory standard for wrought silver in England in 1238, and in 1300 provisions were made for hallmarking it (see *Hallmarking*). It is still one of the legal standards for silver-

ware in Britain, the other being Britannia silver (q.v.).

The word 'sterling' is derived from 'Easterling', this being the name given in the Middle Ages to the Germans (who lived towards the East) called in by King John to refine silver for the coinage. The coins made from this silver were at first called 'easterlings', but in time the first two letters were dropped, and in a statute of 1343 ordaining that 'good sterling money should be made in England' the word is used in its modern sense.

German stomacher made in the second half of the eighteenth century; diamonds and pearls set in silver. Schatzkammer der Residenz, Munich

Stomacher. A long and usually triangular bodice-ornament popular in the eighteenth century. It covered much of the front of the dress. The designs were based on floral and ribbon patterns and offered an opportunity for a lavish display of diamonds or pastes. Many stomachers, including the example illustrated, were made in detachable sections so that the size of the jewel could be varied to suit the occasion. (See also *Eighteenth-century jewellery*.)

Stone tongs. Tweezers or similar tools specially made for handling gemstones. Some of them are also suitable for some jewellers' work, such as placing snippets of solder in position. They often have blunt, rounded ends which are ribbed inside, and are made with a fairly weak spring. Some of them have a locking device which enables the stone to be gripped when the finger-pressure is removed. One type with ring ends is made specially for holding pearls, and another type has three prongs which project to grip the stone when a spring-loaded plunger is pressed. Another name for them is 'corn tongs', a term of unknown origin.

Strapwork. A kind of decoration very popular in later Renaissance jewellery, consisting of flattish metal straps or bands in folded, crossed or interlacing patterns. (See *Renaissance jewellery*.)

Stras, Georges Frederic. (1701–1773). Parisian jeweller widely believed to have invented a new lead-glass paste in the eighteenth century. He may not have invented it but he certainly sold a great quantity of it; a rival jeweller once complained that women were wearing little else.

Stras, the son of a pastor, was born near Strasbourg, was apprenticed to a Strasbourg goldsmith, and in 1724 went to Paris where he began to work in a small jewellery shop on the Quai des Orfèvres. Shortly after his arrival the shop, previously an obscure establishment run by a widow, began to attract the attention of the fashionable world. In the early 1730s Stras's paste jewellery became famous and in 1734 he was appointed jeweller to the King of France. His activities were not by any means confined to paste jewellery; he also made and sold fine diamond jewellery and dealt in jewellers' materials such as foils. In 1752 Stras left the business to his niece's husband, G. Bapst, who later became jeweller to the French court.

Stras had many imitators and competitors; by 1767 there was a corporation of paste-jewellery manufacturers in France with over 300 members. He was not the first to use a highly-refractive glass paste suitable for jewellery (experiments had been carried out for centuries and George Ravenscroft had produced a suitable paste in England in about 1675), but he was so successful that 'stras' has since become a synonym for paste. (See *Paste* for further information.)

Stras (Strass). A glass paste invented (or sold) by Georges Stras (q.v.). Also a name for any paste.

Strawberry pearl. A pink baroque freshwater pearl with a pimply surface.

Striae. Roughly parallel growth lines seen on the surface and in the internal structure of stones. The curved striae in synthetic gemstones (q.v.) serve to identify them from natural stones, in which the growth lines are straight. 'Cooling striae' are seen in glass.

Strontium titanate. A synthetic stone used as a simulant of diamond. (See *Synthetic gemstones*.)

Stuart sapphire (Charles II's sapphire). A large sapphire ($1\frac{1}{2}$ inches in length) set at the back of the Crown of State in the British Regalia. It was used at the coronation of Charles II but was taken by James II when he fled to France in 1688, and subsequently passed to his son James Edward the Old Pretender. The last direct descendant of the Stuart line bequeathed it, with other Stuart treasures, to George III, and it returned to the Crown Jewels. For Queen Victoria's coronation it was set in the front of the crown under the Black Prince's ruby (q.v.), but for the coronation of George V it was moved to the back to make room for the second Star of Africa, cut from the Cullinan diamond (q.v.).

'Styrian jade'. Misnomer for pseudophite.

Sugar stone. Pink datolite from Michigan.

Sulphuric acid. A powerful acid used, diluted, as a pickle (q.v.) to clean up metal after soldering, etc., and for various other purposes such as etching (q.v.).

Sun opal. Fire opal (see *Opal*).

Sunstone. See *Aventurine feldspar*.

Boules of synthetic spinel (left) and synthetic corundum

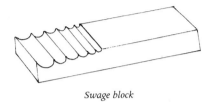

Swage block

Swage block. A tool for making wire or mouldings. It is a kind of modified draw-plate (q.v.) in which the metal is drawn through grooves in two adjustable steel dies held by a screw.

Sweetwater agate. A fluorescent moss agate (see *Agate*) from Wyoming.

Swiss cut. A simplified form of the brilliant cut, having a total of 34 facets including the culet. (See *Diamond-cutting* for description.)

'Swiss jade'. Misnomer for jasper dyed green.

'Swiss lapis' ('German lapis'). Jasper dyed blue. It often contains flakes of transparent quartz. (See also *Dyeing of stones*.)

'Symerald' (Trade name.) Pale or colourless beryl coated with a deposit of synthetic emerald. (See *Synthetic gemstones*.)

'Synthetic alexandrite'. Trade name for synthetic corundum or synthetic spinel made as an imitation of alexandrite. Alexandrite is not made synthetically. (See *Synthetic gemstones*.)

'Synthetic aquamarine'. Trade name for synthetic corundum or synthetic spinel made as an imitation of aquamarine. Aquamarine is not made synthetically, at least not on a commercial scale. (See *Synthetic gemstones*.)

Synthetic gemstones. A synthetic stone is a man-made stone which has the same crystal structure and chemical composition as the natural stone to which it corresponds. The mode of synthesis may involve some slight variation of the chemical composition, but unless this is so the stone cannot be distinguished from its natural counterpart by its refractive index or specific gravity, but only by internal features visible under a microscope which reveal its artificial mode of formation. In some cases even this distinction is difficult to make. Synthetic stones of certain varieties can now be manufactured on a large scale, which makes the cost of production relatively cheap, but even so it is not cheap enough to justify the synthesis of stones which occur commonly in nature unless there is an exceptional reason for doing so. (During the Second World War, for instance, experiments were carried out into the synthesis of quartz, which has important uses in electronics. Untwinned crystals of quartz are necessary for this purpose and such crystals occur principally in Brazil, which was not a source that could be relied on in time of war.) Synthetic stones furnish a cheap and convincing substitute for natural stones and have the additional advantage that they can be made in much larger sizes than usually occur in the natural crystals. Suitably coloured, they are often marketed as substitutes for natural stones of a different species – this is true particularly of the synthetic spinel (see below).

Experiments in the synthesis of gemstones were begun in the nineteenth century, but it was not until the beginning of this century that commercially-viable techniques became known.

Ruby and sapphire. The first experimenters to meet with much success in the synthesis of corundum were the French chemists Frémy and Feil, who in 1877 produced thin crystals of ruby and other colours of corundum by dissolving alumina (aluminium oxide, of which corundum is composed) in lead oxide at a high temperature in a crucible, and allowing the alumina to crystallize out slowly. The method was not of any use commercially. In the 1880s some rubies appeared on the market which had been made by fusing together small ruby crystals with an oxyhydrogen blowpipe (see 'Geneva rubies'), but this method was a reconstruction rather than a true synthesis. In the closing years of the nineteenth century, however, the French chemist Verneuil, who had worked with Frémy in the earlier experiments, developed a form of furnace which was capable of synthesizing large crystals of corundum and is still used with modifications for the production of synthetic stones today.

The Verneuil furnace is basically an inverted blowpipe into which oxygen and hydrogen are piped under pressure. The oxyhydrogen mixture is ignited at the orifice at the bottom of the pipe, producing an intensely hot flame. In the upper chamber of the furnace is a hopper with a sieve at the bottom; this is filled with powdered alumina and the appropriate colouring mineral (chrome oxide in the case of ruby), and a mechanical hammer administering a series of taps on a metal rod connected with the hopper causes the powder to be released at intervals into the downward stream of oxygen, which carries the powder into the flame. In the hottest part of the flame it fuses, and falls on to a ceramic 'candle' placed underneath in a fireclay chamber. There it solidifies around a core of previously-fused alumina, and as powder continues to be fed into the flame, a crystal of corundum grows upwards like a stalag-

mite, and its support is gradually lowered to keep only the tip of the crystal in the hottest part of the flame. The boule, as the crystal is called, is grown to an appreciable size – up to 200 carats for a ruby – and then allowed to cool slowly. When cool it is broken away from the candle and from the core at the bottom, and tapped lightly with a hammer to make it split longitudinally into two halves suitable for cutting. Although externally the boules resemble a lump of glass rather than a crystal they have the internal features of a crystal (i.e. their atoms are arranged in a definite and orderly structure) and it is along the plane of their crystallographic axis that they are split.

The Verneuil process is now used to produce synthetic corundum in a wide range of colours, some of which do not normally occur in corundum. There is for instance a green variety which appears purplish-red in artificial light and is marketed as a substitute for alexandrite (q.v.) (it has of course the refractive index, etc., of corundum). Some synthetic corundums have been made in America which are blue at one end and red at the other. The colours are obtained by the addition of the metallic oxides which are known to colour the natural stones. When no colouring agent is added, synthetic white sapphire, often used to simulate other colourless stones including diamond (q.v.), is produced. After their initial success with ruby the chemists had considerable difficulty with blue sapphire, the colouring of which was thought to be due to cobalt. When cobalt oxide was used in the process, however, the colour tended to concentrate in patches instead of spreading evenly, and so magnesium oxide was added as a flux. The result was a stone of even blue colour, but the blue was not the blue of sapphire and nor were the physical characteristics those of sapphire. The stones were cut and marketed under the not-inappropriate name of 'Hope sapphire'. It was subsequently realized that they had the composition (magnesium-aluminium oxide) of another gemstone altogether, and thus the synthetic spinel was born. After further investigation the tinctorial agents in sapphire were found to be titanium and iron, and Verneuil succeeded in producing a blue sapphire with traces of these minerals in 1910. The manufacture of synthetic corundum now extends even to star-stones: the star is produced by mixing a small additional percentage of titanium oxide with the powder before fusing, then heating the boule to a high temperature so that the titanium is precipitated in the form of needles of rutile (q.v.) lying in directions related to the crystal axes.

Under a microscope, most synthetic corundum made by the Verneuil process shows evidence of its artificial formation in the form of curved structure lines – in natural stones the lines of growth are straight and the slight differences in colour which are often observed also occur in straight-sided zones. Curved lines are thus diagnostic of synthetic stones, but their absence does not necessarily mean that the stone is natural, because in some synthetics the curved lines do not show even under a good microscope. Gas bubbles are also a common feature of synthetic stones and serve to identify them. If the nature of the stone is still in doubt after microscopic examination, more sophisticated laboratory tests can be applied – ultra-violet light, which is transmitted much more freely by synthetic than by natural corundum, and X-rays, under which most synthetic corundums exhibit strong phosphorescence. (See *Luminescence*.)

Synthetic rubies are now also produced by the hydrothermal method (see below, under 'Emerald'), and some of them show similar inclusions to the emeralds grown by this process. They do not show the typical curved bands of stones produced by the Verneuil method.

Spinel. The synthetic spinel, discovered by accident in an attempt to synthesize blue sapphire, began to be manufactured on a commercial scale in the 1930s. Its main use is as a simulant for stones of other species such as aqua-

marine, green tourmaline, Brazilian emerald (a pale green type of emerald), blue zircon, diamond (the colourless synthetic spinel is very brilliant), etc. Although made by the Verneuil flame-fusion process these synthetics do not generally show the curved structure lines and colour-bands seen in synthetic corundum, and rarely contain bubbles. (The red stones are an exception – see below.) There is however another way of identifying them from natural spinel. Synthetic spinels usually contain a much higher proportion of alumina than the natural stones, since equimolecular amounts of alumina and magnesium do not produce good results. The effect of this extra alumina is to give the synthetics a slightly higher specific gravity (3.63 instead of about 3.60) and refractive index (1.73 instead of 1.72) than natural spinel. These constants also of course distinguish synthetic spinels from stones of other species they may resemble. Spinel crystallizes in the cubic system (see *Crystal systems*) and is therefore singly-refractive, but the excess alumina in the synthetic stones strains the crystal lattice and causes the stone to exhibit anomalous double refraction (q.v.) when examined under a polarizing microscope: the light and dark areas occur in stripes and this effect is characteristic of synthetic spinel. The above remarks do not apply to the red synthetic spinel, which has proved more difficult to synthesize than other colours and is made with more or less equimolecular amounts of alumina and magnesium. These stones therefore do not show anomalous double refraction and have a similar specific gravity to the natural stone, but their refractive index is slightly higher (up to 1.725) owing to the use of chromium for colouring. The red synthetics generally show pronounced curved lines and colouring bands under a microscope, and numerous gas bubbles.

Two unusual types of synthetic spinel are a heat-treated colourless synthetic made as an imitation of moonstone, and an opaque blue stone made to simulate lapis-lazuli. The latter is produced by sintering coarsely-powdered synthetic spinel and cobalt oxide in a furnace; sometimes specks of gold are incorporated to simulate the specks of pyrites commonly seen in lapis-lazuli. The synthetic is a good colour, but is much heavier (S.G. 3.52) than true lapis-lazuli and when viewed through a colour filter (q.v.) shows a brilliant red.

Rutile. Natural rutile has virtually no use as a gemstone, being dark and opaque, but since 1948 synthetic rutiles have been commercially manufactured in a range of colours. The method employed is a modification of the Verneuil process and the boules produced are opaque black. On subsequent heating in a stream of oxygen they change colour – from black to deep blue, green and then yellow, and sometimes to red and orange shades. The type most commonly used in jewellery is a very pale yellow, almost colourless, stone, which has an extremely high colour dispersion (q.v.) and is used to simulate diamond. However, as its fire is six times that of diamond this alone betrays it to the experienced eye, and it is also very much softer than diamond, having a hardness of only about 6. Synthetic rutile of other colours is not often seen. The specific gravity is 4.25 and the refractive indices are 2.62 and 2.90: this marked birefringence also distinguishes it easily from diamond, which is singly-refractive. The stone is sometimes sold under the trade name 'Titania'.

Strontium titanate. This stone, which does not occur in nature, was first synthesized in America in 1955. It is produced by the flame-fusion process and, like synthetic rutile, is black until heat-treated. It then becomes colourless and is used to simulate diamond. It is a cubic mineral and therefore, like diamond, singly-refractive, but it is soft (hardness 6) and very heavy (specific gravity 5.13). The refractive index (2.41) is very close to that of diamond, and the colour-dispersion about four times that of diamond. The stones are marketed under the trade names 'Fabulite' and 'Starilian'.

Emerald. Attempts to produce synthetic emerald were made in the nineteenth century but the resulting crystals were far too small to be cut into gemstones. The first real success was achieved by Nacken, who after many years of experiment produced in the late 1920s emerald crystals weighing up to one carat. Early attempts to synthesize emerald by the Verneuil flame-fusion process had failed because after fusion emerald solidifies not as a crystal but as a glass (this beryl glass is sometimes used in jewellery: see *Glass*). (Some emerald crystals were produced by flame-fusion in America in 1964, but the chemicals which had to be used were so toxic that the method could not be commercially adopted.) Nacken therefore used a hydrothermal method, similar to that used in the quartz experiments mentioned earlier (quartz also solidifies as a glass after fusion). The basic principle of the hydrothermal process is that water is brought to a very high temperature, beyond that at which it normally boils, by heating it under pressure; at this temperature it is capable of bringing silicates, including emerald (beryllium-aluminium silicate), into solution. This mineral-rich solution can then be made to deposit its mineral content on a 'seed' crystal suspended in it, producing in time a large well-formed crystal. The process is carried out in a steel-walled container called an autoclave which can be sealed to withstand high pressure. A process similar in many respects to the hydrothermal method is to dissolve the mineral not in water but in a solid solvent with a relatively high melting point. This is called the flux-fusion or flux-melt method and is used for both emeralds and rubies.

Following Nacken's success, synthetic emeralds were produced in 1934 by the German combine Farbenindustrie. Stones were cut from the crystals and some were placed on the market under the trade name 'Igmerald'. The method of synthesis was not disclosed, but is now known to have been a flux-melt process. Since the war several firms have started manufacturing synthetic emeralds. First in the field was C. F. Chatham of San Francisco; the first one-carat crystal produced by the Chatham laboratory in 1935 was followed by much larger ones, and a crystal of good quality exhibited at the Smithsonian Institute weighed 1014 carats. Chatham emeralds are now produced on a large commercial scale, but the process – probably flux-melt – is a lengthy one; about 12 months are needed to produce crystals of the required size, as against a matter of hours for crystals produced by the flame-fusion process. During the 1960s Chatham's monopoly was broken when several other firms began producing synthetic emeralds: Zerfass of Germany, Gilson of France, and Linde Air Products of America. In 1967 green beryl coloured with vanadium was synthesized in Australia (these stones are not strictly emeralds – see *Emerald*).

Synthetic emeralds do not show the curved structure lines and gas bubbles which are prominent features of the stones produced by flame-fusion. They do however have other distinctive characteristics: they are, with the exception of the Linde emeralds, considerably lighter than natural emeralds, having a specific gravity of about 2.65, which is similar to that of quartz. The specific gravity of natural emeralds ranges from 2.68 to about 2.77. The refractive indices are also lower, about 1.560 and 1.563. The constants of the Linde emeralds are slightly lower than those of the other synthetics. Through the Chelsea colour filter (q.v.), which was invented to distinguish true emerald from its commoner simulants, all the synthetics show the red colour of emerald but it is a much stronger red than that shown by most natural emeralds. The microscope also reveals an important difference: although synthetic emeralds, being grown by a process very close to the natural mode of formation, contain inclusions similar to those seen in natural stones, they do not contain the inclusions which are particularly characteristic of natural emerald (three-phase inclusions, crystals of pyrites, etc.). The typical inclusions in synthetic emeralds are wispy, liquid-filled cavities known as 'feathers' (see *Inclusions in gemstones*).

A labour-saving synthetic emerald was produced in about 1960; the 'seed' is not a crystal but an already-faceted piece of green or colourless beryl, over which synthetic emerald is deposited in an even layer so that the stone has only to be polished. The outer layer can be seen as such when the stone is immersed in liquid. The trade name is 'Symerald'.

Diamond. Diamond poses an interesting problem: its chemical composition (pure carbon) is much simpler than that of other gemstones which have been successfully synthesized, yet it has so far proved quite impossible to synthesize it in crystals which are both transparent and large enough for use as gem material. Diamond is the form in which carbon crystallizes at very high pressures (above 15,000 times normal atmospheric pressure); at lower pressures carbon forms the soft mineral graphite. Diamond is however the less stable form of carbon: when it is heated in a vacuum to a temperature above 1750°C its atomic structure disintegrates and it re-crystallizes as graphite. Its natural occurrence is in pipes of volcanic material which have been forced up from great depths in the earth. From these facts it is evident that diamond can only be produced under enormous pressure and that its synthesis from graphite must be carried out at a very high temperature (to enable the carbon atoms to regroup). Early experimenters had difficulty in achieving these high pressures and temperatures, and particularly in achieving them simultaneously. An additional problem was how to raise the temperature of the carbon sufficiently without destroying it, since when heated in air it burns long before it approaches melting point and it will not dissolve in any ordinary solvent. It was found to dissolve to some extent, however, in molten iron.

The first important experiments were made by a Glasgow chemist, J. B. Hannay, who published his results in 1880. The principle of the experiments was that if a gas containing carbon and hydrogen was

Synthetic gemstones

heated under pressure in the presence of certain metallic elements, the hydrogen would combine with the metal and the carbon would crystallize out, possibly as diamond. The ingredients (lithium, bone oil and paraffin in the most successful experiments) were heated in welded iron tubes. Hannay made some 80 experiments, and in all but three or four cases the tubes either exploded under the pressure or otherwise allowed the gases to escape. In the few surviving tubes, however, Hannay found small hard particles which were identified at the time as being diamonds. Surprisingly, Hannay's achievement attracted little attention at the time. Recently some doubt has been cast upon it. X-ray examination in 1943 of the particles said to have been presented to the British Museum by Hannay in 1880 revealed that 11 of the 12 specimens were indeed diamonds, but because their accession to the museum's collection had not been registered until 1901, and then not by the official who had originally identified them, it was impossible to establish beyond doubt that they were actually Hannay's diamonds. There are reasons for believing it very unlikely that Hannay could have made diamonds by the method described.

The French chemist Moissan investigated the solubility of carbon in various molten metals in the 1890s and, finding that iron gave the best results, dissolved sugar carbon in molten iron and heated it to 2200°C in an electric furnace. He then chilled the mass of iron suddenly in molten lead so that a rigid crust was formed and the slow cooling of the core set up enormous internal pressure (iron expands on cooling). When cool the iron was dissolved away with acids, and tiny particles were found in it which appeared, on testing their hardness and density, to be diamonds. Moissan's particles have been lost and so cannot be tested by up-to-date techniques, but his experiments were repeated by other workers – Crookes (1919) and Hershey (1929) – who claimed to have succeeded. Other scientists, however, reproduced all the experiments

which had so far been carried out in the field and declared all of them incapable of producing diamond. Among the more unusual claims were Friedlander's claim to have produced diamonds by stirring molten olivine with a rod of graphite, and Hershey's to have produced diamonds from gum arabic and from starch in a manganese steel bath. These claims and many others like them have never been proved.

In 1955, however, the General Electric Company in America announced that they had succeeded in synthesizing diamonds by a process outlined by Dr. Percy Bridgman, the Harvard physicist. A 'carbonaceous compound' was used to supply the material and the company's success was largely due to the attainment of very high pressure and temperature simultaneously. A 1000-ton hydraulic press was used to create pressures up to 1,500,000 pounds per square inch, and a temperature of 2760°C was achieved. (Considerably higher pressures and temperatures than these can now be achieved and maintained.) The diamonds were small – the largest had a maximum length of 1.2 mm – but they were unmistakably diamonds. After further research the company began manufacturing them commercially and considerable quantities are now produced, but they are industrial-grade diamonds, too small and too dark to cut as gemstones. Many other companies announced the synthesis of industrial diamonds within a few years of the General Electric Company's success, and with the political disturbances in the Congo, which is the world's major source of natural industrial diamonds, the commercial production of synthetic diamonds was undertaken in many parts of the world. As yet, however, no crystals approaching gem quality have been made in a size suitable for cutting: the few that are of any size have been found to be multi-crystalline.

Other stones. Many types of crystals have been synthetically produced in recent years for scientific purposes, and some of these supply stones which can be used in jewellery. Among them are the garnet-type synthetics, which are not true garnets because they are not silicates, but which nevertheless have a similar structure to garnet (q.v.). The most important are the *yttrium aluminium garnets* (specific gravity 4.6, refractive index 1.83), which may be made in a whole range of colours but are mostly made colourless to imitate diamonds. Like natural garnet they are singly-refractive. Their unusual absorption-spectra and behaviour under irradiation can usually identify them in cases of doubt. Scheelite (q.v.), a mineral not often cut when it occurs naturally, has been made synthetically in colours much more attractive than those that occur in nature. The specific gravity of the natural stone is 5.9 to 6.1 and the refractive indices are 1.918 and 1.934, but this is not much help because the 'doping' (artificial colouring) of synthetic stones may alter their normal properties almost beyond recognition. Some unusual colourless synthetics may be used as diamond simulants. One is synthetic lithium niobate (hardness about 6, specific gravity 4.64, refractive indices 2.21 and 2.30) marketed in North America as a cut stone under the name 'Linobate'. The humble fluorspar (q.v.) has also been synthesized and artificially coloured; cut specimens are of interest mainly to collectors, as fluorspar is too soft to provide a durable gemstone.

'Synthetic turquoise'. Trade name for imitation turquoise. There is no synthetically-made turquoise. (See *Imitation stones*.)

'Syntholite'. Trade name for a synthetic-corundum imitation of alexandrite. (See *Synthetic gemstones*.)

T

Taaffeite. (Beryllium-manganese aluminate. S.G. 3.60–3.61; R.I. 1.72–1.73; H. 8.) A very rare pale lilac stone first identified in 1945 when Count Taaffe, a Dublin gemmologist, noticed that one of a parcel of cut stones which he had bought as spinels showed signs of double refraction (q.v.). Altogether only four of these stones have been identified, but it is possible that others are in circulation and are believed to be spinels. The source of the stones is probably Ceylon.

Tabasheer. An opal-like silica found in the joints of some types of bamboo in India, Burma and South America.

Tabby extinction. See *Anomalous double refraction*.

Table. See *Table facet*.

Table cut. One of the oldest styles of cutting stones, used in the Middle Ages and into the seventeenth century. There is a large rectangular table facet (q.v.) surrounded by a bevelled edge or a series of small facets. The cut is based on the shape of the octahedral diamond crystal and was used for both diamonds and coloured stones. The modern step cut (q.v.) may be said to be a development of it. (For further information and diagram, see *Diamond-cutting*.)

Table facet. The large central facet at the top of a cut gemstone. (See *Diamond-cutting* and *Gem-cutting*.)

Taille d'épargne. A type of champlevé enamel (q.v.) popular in the eighteenth century. A pattern was chiselled out of the ground metal and filled in with enamel so that the surfaces were flush. The colours were generally blue or black and the designs fine; it was a type of decoration much favoured for mourning rings (q.v.). (See also *Enamel*.)

Talisman. A magical charm, normally in the form of a ring or stone, on which occult or astrological characters are engraved. Some definitions restrict the talisman to charms of a strictly astrological nature, in which the engraved sign denotes the astrological influence under which the talisman was made and from which it derives its powers. A wider definition allows other signs of an occult nature (which however were often connected with astrology), and written texts such as the Hebrew phylacteries, to be classed as talismans. The distinction between talismans and amulets was at the beginning of the Christian era fairly clear: the Church condemned the former and with some exceptions permitted the latter. However, since both were worn for the same protective purposes when magical jewellery was in common use, the distinction became blurred and the two words are now used synonymously.

The theories on which the use of the astrological talisman was based originated among the Babylonians and were developed at Alexandria and later by the Arabs. Talismans began to be used in Europe in the late Middle Ages and continued until the end of the seventeenth century (see *Lapidaries* and *Magical jewellery*). A popular talisman in the Middle Ages was the abraxas stone (q.v.), which originated among the Gnostics. By the time that talismans began to be used in Europe many different strands of mysticism, magic and astrology had become interwoven in their symbolism, and it is probable that the meaning of the characters engraved on them was very rarely understood. (See also *Amulet*.)

Tallow cut. A flattened cabochon cut. (See *Gem-cutting*.)

Tang. The clamp in which the dop (q.v.) holding a diamond is held for polishing. (See *Diamond-cutting*.) The word is also used to refer to the tapered end of a tool (e.g. a file) which is inserted into a handle.

Tangiwaite. Bowenite (see *Serpentine*) from New Zealand.

Tanzanite. (Calcium-aluminium silicate. S.G. 3.35; R.I. 1.69–1.70; H. 6.) A transparent bluish-violet variety of zoisite discovered in Tanzania in 1967. The crystals occur in a variety of colours and are usually heat-treated to produce the preferred blue. (See *Heat-treatment*.)

'Tasmanian diamond'. Misnomer for rock crystal.

Tassie, James. (1735–1799). Manufacturer of moulded glass imitation cameos and intaglios (qq.v.), at a time when engraved gems were a fashionable enthusiasm but comparatively few people could afford the genuine hardstone variety. Early in the eighteenth century copies had begun to be made of the antique cameos and intaglios in European collections; the first were made by the chemist Homberg, who was commissioned to make glass replicas of the gems in the Duke of Orleans's collection. Later, reproductions of other collections were made by Baron Stosch and Rieffenstein in Rome, and Lippert in Dresden. As well as paste reproductions of the gems, impressions were taken from them in sulphur. The main purpose was educational; Lippert's casts and impressions, in particular, were widely circulated among universities and schools. Tassie's pastes were more than just the British version of this idea; his replicas were both more attractive and cheaper than any produced earlier, and were frequently mounted and worn in jewellery.

Tassie was a Scotsman from Pollock-shaws; his family are thought to have been of Italian descent. He started his career as a stonemason, but began to study modelling at the Foulis Academy in Glasgow and in 1763 went to Dublin. He worked in the laboratory of a Dr. Quinn, whose hobby was making imitation antique engraved gems. In Dublin Tassie learned to mould and take impressions in glass, and developed an easily-fusible glass composition (the recipe was never divulged) which took impressions well and could be attractively coloured.

In 1766 Tassie settled in London and began to manufacture his pastes commercially. They were an immediate success. He went to great pains to reproduce antique gems as accurately as possible in the original colours. The reproductions were taken from the many private collections of antique gems, and in time Tassie's collection included most of the gems previously reproduced by Stosch, Lippert, etc., as well as many others (he also made pastes from designs by contemporary artists). A catalogue of his collection drawn up by R. E. Raspe in 1786 lists over 15,000 subjects. He had by this time been commissioned by the Empress of Russia to make for her as complete a collection as possible of ancient and modern gems in paste reproductions and in impressions. The impressions were taken in a white enamel composition, and the pastes – both cameo and intaglio – in coloured glass. Libraries and teaching institutions bought collections of Tassie's gems, and ordinary people bought them out of interest or to wear. They were set in bracelets, necklaces, etc., and the intaglios were of course also used for their proper purpose, as seals. They were very cheap – from 1s. 6d. for a small intaglio. Cameos were considerably more expensive – from 10s. 6d. upwards – being much more difficult to make. Almost as soon as Tassie's gems had become popular the Birmingham manufacturers produced their own imitations, but these were of inferior quality and offered little serious competition. The cameos and intaglios in a porcelain composition produced by

Wedgwood, however, were very popular, but they were not really in the same class as Tassie's work and Tassie had in fact supplied Wedgwood and Bentley with many of their casts in about 1769. (See *Wedgwood.*)

Tassie was also an original artist in his own right; he modelled from life a number of portrait medallions of eminent contemporaries and cast them in paste. It is for his reproduction gems, however, that he is remembered. On his death his nephew William Tassie (1777–1860) inherited his property and continued the business at Leicester Square. He added further subjects to his uncle's collection, produced new impressions in enamel and sulphur, and made additional casts for the Imperial Russian collection. The business continued to thrive well into the nineteenth century, but by the time William Tassie died the fashion for engraved gems was waning and great collections were no longer being amassed.

Tassies. Imitation cameos and intaglios made by James Tassie (q.v.) or his nephew William.

Tawmawite. See *Epidote.*

Taxoite. A green serpentine from Pennsylvania.

Tecali. Mexican name for onyx marble.

'Tecla pearls'. Imitation pearls. (See *Pearls.*)

Tektite. (S.G. 2.34–2.39; R.I. 1.488–1.503; H. 5½.) A type of natural glass generally believed to be of extraterrestrial origin. The only variety used as a gem material is moldavite (R.I. 1.488–1.503), a transparent bottle-green, brown or greenish-brown glass first found near the river Moldau in Bohemia and in Western Moravia in 1787. It contains about 75 per cent silica and shows peculiar fissuring on the surface.

Tektites are found in various parts of the world, and in great numbers in southern Australia. Their distribution is apparently quite unrelated to the character of the earth's surface and it is therefore assumed that they are of cosmic origin, but as they are completely different in structure and chemical composition from meteorites the question remains doubtful.

Templet facet. An alternative name for the four bezel facets (q.v.) on a brilliant-cut diamond which are the first to be ground after the table. (See *Diamond-cutting.*)

Tests for gemstones. See *Identification of gemstones.*

Tests for precious metals. See *Touchstone testing* and *Assaying.*

Texas agate. See *Jasp-agate.*

Thallium glass. Flint glass containing thallium; it has a high refractive index and high colour dispersion and is sometimes used for glass imitation stones. (See also *Glass.*)

Thetis' hair stone. Sagenitic quartz (q.v.) with inclusions of black tourmaline or green actinolite.

Thomsonite. (Hydrated calcium-sodium-aluminium silicate. S.G. 2.3–2.4; R.I. about 1.52; H. 5.) A translucent stone with radial banding similar to that of agate. The colours may be white, red, yellow, brown or green. An olive-green variety which does not have the characteristic markings of thomsonite is known as *lintonite.*

Gem quality thomsonite occurs as aggregates weathered out from the lava along the shores of Lake Superior. Lintonite is found along the shores of Stockley Bay, Michigan and near Grand Marais, Minnesota.

Thread setting. A setting in which the stone is held by a thin thread of metal, raised by drawing a steel wheel over the metal around the stone. (See also *Settings.*)

Three Brothers. The name of a famous fifteenth-century jewel; the 'three brothers' were the three enormous rubies with which it was set. Charles the Bold inherited it from his father in 1467, but on his defeat at the battle of Grandson in 1476 it was taken from his tent by a

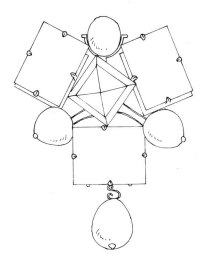

From a contemporary painting of the Three Brothers jewel in the Historisches Museum, Basle

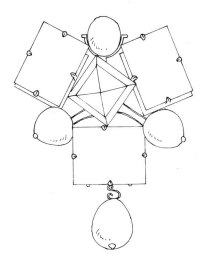

'Thunder eggs'. Nodules of agate (q.v.) found in parts of the U.S.A., which when cut across often show the agate filling to have a star-like form.

Tiaras. See *Diadems*.

Tiffany & Co. World-renowned American firm of manufacturing and retail jewellers and silversmiths. The famous store on the corner of 5th Avenue and 57th Street, New York, sells jewellery ranging in price from a silver key-ring at $5.25 to diamond rings in the $250,000 class, as well as high-class stationery, glass and china, but will not sell men's diamond rings at any price or anything made of a synthetic material.

The firm was founded in 1837 by Charles Lewis Tiffany and John B. Young as a stationery and fancy goods store. Within ten years the store was selling diamond jewellery and silverware, and in 1850 a branch was opened in Paris. In 1852 Charles Tiffany introduced the British sterling standard for silver sold by Tiffany's, and this standard was later adopted by the American Government. The firm was now known as Tiffany and Co., and in 1868 it merged with the silversmiths Edward C. Moore and Co., who had been supplying Tiffany's with silverware from the early days. In the same year a branch was opened in London. Meanwhile the firm had been awarded a gold medal for work in silver at the Paris Exhibition of 1867. In 1870, when stability and prosperity were returning after the Civil War (during which Tiffany's had been busy on badges, gold braid and swords), the firm moved to Union Square and began to be regularly patronized by American society, including President Lincoln.

The remarkable success of the company in the first few decades of its existence was largely due to the resourceful imagination of Charles Tiffany, who obviously had a keen eye for what the public wanted. In 1858, when the first Atlantic cable was laid, he purchased the unused length of cable (there were several miles of it) and made it into souvenirs

soldier. Some time later it was bought by Jacob Fugger, of the great merchant family of Augsburg. Henry VIII, a collector of fine jewels, acquired it shortly before his death. It then remained in the English treasury, but in 1623 it was broken up and the three great rubies were re-set for Charles Prince of Wales to take with him on his embassy to Spain. What became of the rubies after that is not known.

It was inevitable that the stones would be re-set sooner or later, for a fifteenth-century painting of the jewel (see illustration) shows it to be far from attractive. The three rubies are arranged roughly in a triangle, interspersed with three pearls, and with a pendant pearl below. In the centre is a large pointed diamond; this stone was particularly esteemed as it was believed to have been the first diamond cut by Ludwig van Berghem (q.v.).

Thulite. (Calcium-aluminium silicate. S.G. about 3.10; R.I. about 1.70; H. 6.) An attractive rose-pink ornamental stone, a variety of zoisite. The finest material comes from southern Norway, from the ancient name of which – Thule – the stone takes its name.

Tiffany diamond

such as paperweights, bracelets and umbrella-handles. There were so many buyers that the police had to be called in to keep order. Thirty years later he was buying the French crown jewels. Charles's son Louis Comfort Tiffany (1848–1933), a highly gifted designer with an interest in all the decorative arts, brought Art Nouveau to America (he patented a new oxidized iridescent glass as early as 1880) and on his father's death became the firm's Art Director. The store was now on 5th Avenue and 37th Street, in a building designed by Stanford White.

In 1940 Tiffany's moved again to their present seven-storey premises. Fifteen years later the present chairman, Walter Hoving, assumed control of the firm and decided that a new image was needed. Antiques, goods made of non-precious materials such as bronze and leather, and old patterns that had been kept in stock for years, were all discarded. The Paris designer Jean Schlumberger was brought over and installed in his own suite on the premises; he is now the firm's Vice-President. A new Display Director (Gene Moore) was appointed and told to make the window displays beautiful and not to try to sell anything; the windows have since displayed such things as eggs, brown paper, spaghetti, and miniature fountains playing gin (in the New York drought). Tiffany's will not sell anything which they consider to be poorly designed, in bad taste (diamond rings for men), or just plain unexciting. At the meetings of the company's editorial boards new products are discussed with two questions in mind: is it attractive, and is it exciting? The question, will it sell?, is not considered. One might imagine that a store with such a marketing policy would not survive very long, but Tiffany has increased its profits by over 900 per cent in the past 15 years.

Tiffany diamond. A canary-yellow diamond weighing 287 carats found in the Kimberley Mine in 1878. It was purchased by Tiffany and Co. (q.v.), and cut in Paris to a cushion-shaped brilliant with

The Tiffany diamond, in a setting by Jean Schlumberger of Tiffany & Co.

90 facets weighing 128.5 carats. It was exhibited unmounted at the World Fairs in Chicago 1893 and New York 1939, and is now on display at Tiffany's New York store mounted in a gold, platinum and diamond clip designed by Jean Schumberger (see illustration). It is the largest and finest canary yellow diamond in the world, and is valued at 2 million dollars.

Tiffany setting. A pronged setting for solitaire diamonds introduced by Charles L. Tiffany in 1886. (See *Tiffany and Co.*)

Tigerite. Tiger's eye.

Tiger's eye. (See *Quartz, crystalline.*) A chatoyant golden-brown stone with a silky lustre. The stone shows alternate bands of brown and gold, and the colours are reversed when the stone is seen from the opposite direction. Tiger's eye is a variety of asbestos (crocidolite) which has decomposed into quartz, and the brown colour is caused by oxidization of the iron present. When oxidization has not occurred the stone is the colour of the original crocidolite – greenish blue. The blue stones are known as *Hawk's eye* or *Falcon's eye*. The material is usually cut into cabochons, beads or flat pieces.

Most tiger's eye comes from Griqualand West in South Africa.

Timur ruby. A fine unfaceted red spinel weighing 361 carats, now in the British Crown Jewels. It is thought to be by far the largest red spinel known to exist. The stone had a long history in the East before it was brought to Europe; its traditional name is Khiraj-i-Alam, which means 'Tribute of the world'. The stone once belonged to the Tartar conqueror Timur or Tamerlane (1336–1405); it is said to have fallen into his hands when he plundered Delhi in 1398. A long inscription on the stone in Persian, but in Arabic script, records that it was once in Timur's possession: 'This is the ruby among the twenty-five thousand jewels of the King of Kings, the Sultan Sahib Qiran, which in the year 1153 (A.D. 1740) from the collection of jewels of Hindustan reached this place.' Sahib Qiran ('Lord of the auspicious conjunction') was the name by which Timur was generally known in the Moslem world. The inscription was engraved by order of Nadir Shah, who took possession of the stone in 1739, and 'this place' was Isfahan, to which Nadir Shah took it. There are five shorter inscriptions on the stone, recording the names of the Mogul rulers who owned it from the early seventeenth century onwards.

On Timur's death the stone passed to his successor, his fourth son, Mir Shah Rukh, who was in turn succeeded by his son Mirza Ulugh Bey. The latter, a famous astronomer, was murdered by his son Abdul Latif after a reign of only two years. These three names were also once inscribed on the stone but were subsequently removed, probably by the Mogul emperor Jehangir, to whom the stone was presented in 1612 by Shah Abbas Safavi; the Safavi family had taken power when the Timur dynasty declined. When Jehangir was given the stone he had his own name and that of his father, Akbar Shah, engraved on it. Jehangir's successor Jahan set the stone in his great Peacock Throne. There it remained until the Persian conqueror Nadir Shah captured Delhi in 1739 and took most of the jewels from the Peacock Throne back to Persia with him. The Koh-i-noor diamond (q.v.)

was also among the booty, and for the next century or so the two stones shared the same fate: both were taken to Afghanistan by Ahmad Abdati, to Kabul by Timur, and finally to Lahore, where they were appropriated by Ranjit Singh. When the jewels at Lahore were annexed in 1849 by the East India Company the Koh-i-noor was recognized but the Timur ruby apparently was not. It was despatched to London by ordinary transport, was shown at the Great Exhibition of 1851, and was subsequently presented by the Company to Queen Victoria, but it was not until 1912 that it was identified by means of its inscriptions. It still retains these and has not been re-cut. It is mounted in a splendid necklace with other Indian red spinels.

Tin. A white, soft, malleable metal which does not tarnish and looks rather similar to silver when polished. As a constituent of bronze (q.v.) it was much sought-after in ancient times, and the Cornish tin mines were being worked as early as 1500 B.C. The high resistance of tin to organic acids makes it a useful metal in the modern world for plating food containers and copper pans. The jeweller is likely to encounter it only in a few alloys such as Britannia metal (see *Pewter*). *Tin oxide* is used as a polishing agent. (See also *Cassiterite*.)

The melting-point of tin is 231.90°C.

Tin-cut. Term applied to cheap glass imitation stones which have been polished on a tin lap. (See *Glass*.)

Tinstone. See *Cassiterite*.

Tinting. The pavilion facets of stones are sometimes painted to improve their colour. The stones are then often, but not always, placed in a closed setting. Among the stones likely to receive this treatment are yellowish diamonds, which can be made to appear water-white by painting the rear facets with violet dye (violet is the colour complementary to yellow, and the combination of the two produces white). Usually hot water or alcohol removes the dye, but sometimes acids have to be used. The tinting of diamonds is far from a new idea; it was customary for diamonds to be tinted in the sixteenth century because a style of cutting which brought out the brilliance of the stone had not yet been discovered (see *Diamond*), and a black or indigo tint increased their sparkle. Jewellers had their own favourite and often secret recipes for tints. Cellini in his *Treatises* gives a detailed recipe involving lamp-black.

Another stone sometimes tinted is the Mexican water opal (see *Opal*), which may be painted black on the back. Any transparent stone may in fact be tinted, but the practice on the whole is not common.

See also *Foil*, and for other ways of altering the colour of stones see *Colouring of stones* (*artificial*).

'Titania' (Trade name.) A simulant of diamond consisting of synthetic rutile. (See *Synthetic gemstones* and *Diamond*.)

Titanite. See *Sphene*.

Toadstone. A stone believed to have miraculous powers, particularly against poison, and to be found in the head of a toad. It was often set in rings as an amulet in the Middle Ages and Renaissance, and was also taken in powdered form as a medicine. It was in fact the palatal tooth of the fossil fish *Lepidotus*. (See also *Magical jewellery*.)

'Tokay lux sapphire'. A brownish-black obsidian from Hungary.

Toluene (Toluol). A liquid (formula $C_6H_5.CH_3$) of low density (0.87) used as a diluent for heavy liquids and as a medium for hydrostatic weighing in the measurement of specific gravity (q.v.).

Tomb jade. Jade which has been buried, usually in a tomb. It is usually reddish or brownish although many other colours may occur. The colours are due to oxidization and may be created artificially.

'Tooth turquoise'. Misnomer for odontolite.

Topaz. (Fluo-silicate of aluminium. S.G. 3.53; R.I. 1.62–1.63; H. 8.) A transparent stone which, contrary to popular belief, is not always yellow; blue and greenish-blue stones very similar to aquamarine are quite common, pink and red are occasionally found, and most topaz crystals are colourless. The sherry-brown stones are the most prized of the natural colours, and many yellow stones are heat-treated to produce the popular rose-pink topaz (see *Heat-treatment*). Topaz takes a brilliant polish and is usually cut in the mixed-cut style (see *Gem-cutting*). The stones are often oval or drop-shaped to take advantage of the long prismatic shape of the crystals. Unfortunately topaz has a very strong cleavage parallel to the basal plane and needs to be carefully treated, as a sharp blow may cause internal flaws or break the stone completely.

The derivation of the word 'topaz' is uncertain beyond its use in Greek to describe a stone now identified as peridot. More recently the term was used to cover all yellow stones, and although it has now been officially restricted to true topaz some confusion still persists owing to the use of misleading terms like 'oriental topaz' (yellow sapphire), 'topaz quartz' (citrine), etc. At one time topaz was not very highly regarded, but fine specimens now fetch quite high prices.

The sole source of sherry-brown topaz is Ouro Preto, Brazil. Other regions of Brazil produce white and blue topaz. Fine crystals of many colours are found in various parts of Russia, and other sources include Japan, Australia, Tasmania, U.S.A., Ceylon and Saxony, which was the principal source for yellow topaz in the eighteenth century. In the British Isles topaz is found in the Cairngorms of Scotland and St. Michael's Mount, Cornwall, and also in the Mountains of Mourne, but the deposits are of no importance commercially.

Synthetic topaz is not manufactured commercially. The stone known as synthetic topaz is in fact suitably coloured synthetic corundum. Tourmaline, aquamarine, danburite and citrine (quartz) may bear a strong resemblance to topaz but are all lighter; they will float in methylene iodide whereas topaz will sink.

Topaz is the stone for November.

'Topaz cat's eye'. Misnomer for chatoyant yellow sapphire.

Topaz glass. Topaz-coloured glass.

Topazolite. An uncommon greenish-yellow to yellow variety of andradite garnet.

'Topaz quartz'. Misleading term, common in the U.S.A. but regarded in Britain as a misnomer, for citrine.

'Topaz saffronite'. American term for citrine; regarded in Britain as a misnomer.

Torre (Tor) Abbey jewel. See *Seventeenth-century jewellery*.

Tortoiseshell. (S.G. about 1.29; R.I. about 1.55; H. $2\frac{1}{2}$.) The material obtained from the carapace of the hawk's bill turtle. The best colour is translucent golden yellow mottled with brown. Blond tortoiseshell, known as 'yellow-belly', is an orangy-yellow variety without mottling which is obtained from the belly of the turtle. The material is in the form of overlapping plates (known in the trade as 'blades'), weighing up to 9 ounces each, which are separated from the bony skeleton by heat. Tortoiseshell is easily worked under heat and can be moulded to shape for objects such as cigarette cases by pressing it into the mould after it has been immersed for a time in boiling water. It is also easily joined: the thickness or surface area can be increased by placing the pieces together under pressure in boiling water (or the equivalent dry heat), and the join is perfect. Care has to be taken in exploiting these thermo-plastic properties of tortoiseshell, however, since overheating darkens the colour, and salt, which may be added to prevent a change of colour during boiling, has the disadvantage of making the material rather brittle.

Tortoiseshell has been periodically fashionable for inlays, toilet articles and some items of jewellery since Roman times. Bracelets of carved tortoiseshell were fashionable in the mid-nineteenth century and tortoiseshell combs with decorated crowns were worn at most times throughout the Victorian period. More recently there was a fashion for gold and silver tortoiseshell piqué (small pieces of gold or silver inlaid in tortoiseshell by pressing them in under heat, and then immersing the article in cold water.) Mother-of-pearl is inlaid in tortoiseshell in the same way.

This art was brought to England in the seventeenth century by Huguenot refugees and was used for snuffboxes and other small decorative objects. In the 1860s it was also fashionable for brooches, earrings and buttons. The work was done by hand and was very delicate. In 1872 however, mass-production of piqué began in Birmingham, using plain and geometrical designs, and the old craft of hand-working the material died out.

Tortoiseshell is not very popular today, but good imitations of it are made in various plastics. If it is possible to cut off a small piece of the material and burn it, the substance can be identified by its smell: tortoiseshell smells like burning hair, and the casein plastics smell like burning milk. The microscope is a better means of identification: tortoiseshell will be seen to contain numerous round, reddish particles, which are absent in the plastics and also in stained horn, another simulant of tortoiseshell.

Total internal reflection. The phenomenon which occurs when a ray of light travelling through a stone does not escape into the air but is reflected back into the stone. When the light strikes the surface of the stone from the inside it is deflected (see *Refraction*) at an angle which depends on the refracting power of the stone and on the angle at which it strikes the surface (the angle of incidence). At a certain angle of incidence, known as the critical angle, the light will be deflected in such a direction that it grazes the surface of the stone. If the angle of incidence is any greater than this the light will be thrown back into the stone, where it will be reflected (see *Reflection*) from one surface to another until it strikes the surface at an angle which enables it to escape. The higher the refractive index (q.v.) of a stone, the smaller is the critical angle. In a diamond, for example, the critical angle is 24° 21', and all light which strikes the bounding surface at an angle greater than this undergoes total internal reflection. In quartz, which has a lower refractive index, the critical angle is considerably greater and therefore much less light is internally reflected. The faceting of diamonds in the brilliant style (see *Diamond-cutting*) takes advantage of this phenomenon; the light is internally reflected from one facet to another so that the whole stone flashes with it.

Touchneedles. Thin pencils of various carat golds, used in conjunction with a touchstone (q.v.) for ascertaining the carat quality of gold. (See *Touchstone testing*.)

Touchstone. The stone on which metals are rubbed to test them. Traditionally the jeweller's touchstone is of basanite (q.v.), but most touchstones are now made of some ceramic material such as Wedgwood ware. The qualities necessary in a touchstone are that it should be black, fine-grained, and harder than the metals which are tested on it. (See *Touchstone testing*.)

Touchstone testing. This is one of the oldest methods of testing the quality of precious metals. It is not particularly useful for silver, but in experienced hands it provides a reliable test for gold, and is still used in many Continental assay offices. (In British assay offices it has been replaced by a more sophisticated technique involving refinement and precise weighing: see *Assaying*.) Touchstone testing is used by retail jewellers to identify metals which have not been hallmarked. The test achieves two things; it determines the nature of the metal, and in the case of gold it enables one to know the carat quality. The metal is first scratched in an inconspicuous place to see whether it is gold-plated, rolled gold, etc. The metal is then rubbed on a touchstone (q.v.) so as to leave a small streak on the stone, and a few drops of nitric acid are

applied to the streak. Nitric acid has no effect on pure gold, but it attacks the base metals with which gold is alloyed. If the acid dissolves the streak, the metal is a copper alloy (if the streak is yellow) or a silver, nickel or tin alloy (if the streak is white). If the streak darkens under the acid the metal is 9-carat gold, or a platinum or palladium alloy, stainless steel, or a lead or aluminium alloy.

A drop of hydrochloric acid is then placed on the streak (this, mingling with the nitric acid, produces aqua regia, q.v.). This enables one to identify the streaks which were unaffected by the nitric acid. If a white film develops when the hydrochloric acid is added, the metal is a lead alloy. If the streak dissolves quickly it is an aluminium alloy. If the streak is still unchanged the metal is platinum 950/1000 fine. If the streak dissolves very slowly, it is either stainless steel, palladium 950/1000 fine, or a white gold of above 9 carats. To distinguish between the last three, the acid on the streak is absorbed with a piece of white blotting-paper. A brown stain on the blotting-paper indicates palladium, a faint brown stain indicates a white gold containing palladium. A faint yellowish-green stain indicates that the metal is either stainless steel or a white gold containing nickel. If a new streak is made on the touchstone, the touchstone is warmed and a drop of hydrochloric acid is applied to the streak, the acid will dissolve a streak made by stainless steel but not one made by white gold containing nickel.

To ascertain the carat quality of golds, a streak is made on the touchstone with the gold to be tested, and other streaks are made with touchneedles (q.v.) of known carat quality. The behaviour of the streaks when touched with various acid solutions is then compared. This requires considerable experience. Silver is usually tested with a solution of silver nitrate (2 grams silver nitrate in 30 c.c. distilled water, plus a drop of nitric acid). This will have no effect on a streak made by sterling or Britannia silver but will create a brownish stain on silver less than 900/1000 parts fine, and the more base metal is present the darker the stain will be.

It is often more convenient to place a drop of acid on the metal itself than to make a streak on a touchstone with it. If this is done the metal must be free of grease, and the test should be made at a spot which has been lightly scraped to see whether there is base metal underneath.

Tourmaline. (Complex boro-silicate of aluminium with alkalis, magnesium or iron. S.G. 3.02–3.25; R.I. 1.62–1.64; H. 7–7½.) A transparent gemstone which may be of almost any colour according to the chemical composition. Tourmalines are often parti-coloured, showing a fairly abrupt change of colour rather than a gradation, and some have a dark or colourless centre surrounded by a coloured rim ('watermelon tourmaline'). Special names are sometimes used for particular varieties: *rubellite* is pink or red tourmaline; *achroite* is colourless; *indicolite* is blue; *siberite* is reddish-violet. Opaque black tourmaline, which occurs commonly but is seldom cut except for mourning jewellery, is called *schorl*. Some tourmaline contains fibrous inclusions and gives a cat's-eye effect when cut *en cabochon*.

Tourmaline is strongly dichroic except in the paler stones. This quality made it suitable for the production of plane-polarized light before the invention of nicol prisms (q.v.). It always shows the strongest colour when viewed along the optic axis, which means that dark stones must be cut with the table facet at right angles to the vertical axis to obtain the deepest colour. (See *Dichroism*.) An unusual property of some tourmaline is that it develops an electric charge when heated to about 100°C and can attract small objects. It also develops an electric charge when pressure is applied to it in the direction of the vertical crystal axis, and this effect (piezo-electricity) is utilized in certain depth-recording apparatus in underwater craft.

Tourmaline may be distinguished from most of the other gemstones which it

resembles by its low specific gravity (q.v.): it will float in methylene iodide whereas, for instance, garnet, zircon and corundum will sink.

The main sources of gem tourmaline are Russia, Brazil, Southern Africa, Madagascar, San Diego Co., California, Maine, and Ceylon (probably the original source). It is said that the name 'tourmaline' is derived from the Sinhalese 'turmali', the local word for yellow zircon, which came to be applied to tourmaline when in 1703 a parcel of tourmalines was mistakenly sent under this name to the stone dealers in Amsterdam. Certainly in Ceylon a definite confusion between tourmaline and zircon (q.v.), which are mined together, still prevails.

'Tourmaline synthetic'. Misnomer for synthetic spinel or corundum (see *Synthetic gemstones*) made in a colour which imitates tourmaline.

Design (1619) for a miniature case by Jean Toutin

Toutin, Jean, of Châteaudun. A seventeenth-century French enameller of distinction, whose designs for lockets, watch-cases, etc., published in about 1619, show a very delicate use of the leaf-patterns and arabesques of the period. The designs were intended to be enamelled in white on a black ground. A fashionable enamelling technique, in which the ground was covered with opaque monochrome enamel and the design, in opaque colours fusible at a lower temperature, painted on top of this, is ascribed to the Toutin family.

Trace. A type of chain with oval links of equal size. (See *Chain*.)

Tracer. See *Chasing tools* and *Repoussé tools*.

Trainite. See *Variscite*.

Transparency. The term used to describe the ability of a substance to transmit light. Gemstones are said to be transparent when an object can be clearly seen through them; semi-transparent when the object appears indistinct, translucent when light penetrates but no object can be seen through the stone, and opaque when no light penetrates the stone at all. (This assumes a reasonable thickness of the material, since light will pass through any substance if it is thin enough.) Most gemstones are transparent unless they are flawed.

'Transvaal emerald'. Misnomer for green fluorspar. (See also *'African emerald.'*)

'Transvaal jade'. Misnomer for grossular garnet.

Trap brilliant. A step-cut stone with an approximately circular girdle. (See *Gemcutting*.)

Trap cut. Alternative name for the step cut (q.v.)

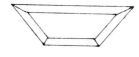

Trapeze outline

Trapeze. Name for a stone with a trapezoid outline (a truncated triangle). The facets are usually cut in the step-cut style (see *Gem-cutting*).

Trapiche emerald. A remarkable type of emerald crystal first found in Columbia in 1964. It consists of a central hexagonal prism of emerald, on the faces of which six more prisms of emerald have grown, giving a radial effect. The interstices between the prisms are filled with colourless beryl. The whole system forms a large hexagonal prism. Small emeralds are cut from the green material. These emeralds are characteristically rather cloudy and show a series of fine straight lines internally.

The name 'Trapiche' comes from the Spanish word for the radial machinery used for crushing sugar-cane.

Traversellite. Green diopside.

Travertine. Stalagmitic calcite. (See *Onyx marble*.)

Treblet. See *Triblet*.

Tree agate. Moss agate: see *Agate*.

Tremolite. (Calcium-magnesium silicate. S.G. about 2.98; R.I. 1.60–1.62; H. $5\frac{1}{2}$–6.) When in a compact mass of pale-coloured felted crystals this mineral is better known as the nephrite type of jade (q.v.). It also provides a green chatoyant stone (the material comes from Ontario, Canada) and a transparent lilac-pink variety (from St. Lawrence Co., New York). The latter is also known as hexagonite.

'Trenton diamond'. Misnomer for rock crystal.

Trezzo, Jacopo da (1514–1589). Milanese sculptor, gem-engraver and medallist. He was acknowledged to be one of the foremost gem-engravers of the Renaissance, and in 1557 distinguished himself by cutting a seal with the arms of Philip II on a diamond. His other famous gems include portraits of Philip II and his son on a yellow sapphire, and a cameo with portraits of the Emperor Charles V and his family. As well as numerous cameos, intaglios, engraved cups and vases, his work for Philip II included two reliquaries set with precious stones and part of the decoration of the Escurial. He died in Madrid. (See also *Cameos* and *Intaglios*.)

Triblet

Triangle. Name for a stone with a triangular outline; the facets are usually cut in the step-cut style (see *Gem-cutting*).

Triblet. A tapering rod of metal, of circular, oval, oblong or square section, on which rings and collets are hammered to the required shape or enlarged. It is a type of mandrel (q.v.).

Trichinopoly chain. Very compact loop-in-loop chain (see *Chain*).

Trichroism. See *Dichroism*.

Triphane. Spodumene.

Triplet. See *Doublet*.

'Tripletine'. (Trade name.) An emerald-coloured beryl triplet. (See *Doublet*.)

Triplex opal. An opal doublet with a layer of colourless quartz cemented over the top. (See *Doublet*.)

Tripoli. A finely-grained form of silica, obtained chiefly from the U.S.A., used for polishing gemstones and metals. It is available in powder form and blocks.

Troy weight. A system of weights hitherto used for precious metals and sometimes gemstones. It has now been replaced by metric weights. Troy weight was introduced into England in the fifteenth century and made statutory in 1526; its name comes from Troyes in France, where it was in use before its adoption in England. For Troy and other weights, see *Weights for precious metals*.

Tube. Metal tube can be made by the craftsman from strip metal. A strip about 3 times as wide as the required diameter of the tube is cut with one end tapered and this end is beaten concave with a hammer. The end is fed into a suitable-size hole in a drawplate (q.v.) and drawn through so that the strip curls. The process is repeated with holes of decreasing size until the edges meet.

Refiners produce a very large range of seamless tubes in various precious metals and alloys; these are made in dies. They include round, half-round, oval, square and rectangular section tube and are used for, among other things, hollow bangles and wedding rings. The latter are usually cut from round tube on diamond-cutting machines.

Tugtupite. (Sodium-aluminium-beryllium silicate; S.G. about 2.36; R.I. 1.496–1.502; H. 6.) A cyclamen-red ornamental stone discovered in Southern Greenland in 1960.

Tumbling. This is a method of grinding and polishing rough ornamental stone and gemstone material to produce baroque stones in quantity. It has recently become a popular hobby, particularly in America, since suitable stone can be picked up on any beach as well as bought from the numerous rock shops, and the equipment can be made at home by the mechanically-minded. The stones – if small enough – can be used to make necklaces, earrings, etc.

The usual equipment is a rotating barrel driven by an electric motor and mounted on a stand. The barrel may be of metal or wood and should preferably be lined with rubber (this helps to prevent the formation of hydrogen gas in a sealed barrel). Open-ended barrels tilted upwards at an angle, like cement-mixers, are often used. The barrel is filled half to three-quarters full with the rough stone, a small quantity of coarse silicon carbide grit is added (about 1 lb. to each 8 lb. of stones), together with enough water to cover the stone, and the barrel is rotated (the speed of rotation varies with the shape and size of the barrel) for about 100 hours (the duration also varies). The constant friction of the stones against each other and against the wet grit grinds them smooth and rounds the corners; it is simply a speeded-up version of the natural process that produces pebbles. When the stones are smooth they are removed and washed and the coarse grit (which should have been worn away by this time) is replaced by fine grit; the stones are tumbled in this, with water, for a further 150 hours or so. They are then cleaned again and tumbled for up to 72 hours at a slower rate of rotation in polishing powder and water. Various polishing agents may be used – tin oxide, cerium oxide, tripoli, etc. Finally the stones are tumbled for about 12 hours in a detergent solution. They are then ready.

It is of course very important that stones tumbled in the same batch should be of approximately the same hardness, since harder stones take much longer to grind and polish.

A range of barrel-polishers are made commercially, and, as already remarked, they can be made at home. A more sophisticated but more expensive alternative to the rotating barrel is the vibrating type. These grind faster than a revolving barrel and can accommodate more material in proportion to their size; there is also less wastage from broken stones because the stones are not moving about so violently.

Turkey fat. Yellow smithsonite from Arkansas.

Turkey stone. Turquoise.

Turquoise. (Hydrous copper-aluminium phosphate. S.G. 2.60–2.85; R.I. about 1.62; H. 6.) An opaque and rather porous blue-green or pale blue stone with a waxy lustre, sometimes cut with its matrix of sandstone or limonite and then known as turquoise matrix. It is cut *en cabochon* or in flat pieces for inlay work. The most valued colour for turquoise is sky-blue, which is the colour of the pure material; the green is caused by the presence of iron. Greenish stones are sometimes stained with Prussian blue to improve the tint; a spot of ammonia removes the stain and the true colour can be seen. Some turquoise, originally of good colour, fades or becomes greenish in time, and this is thought to be due to dehydration. It is said that the miners often bury the stones in moist earth before selling them to improve the colour.

Turquoise is extensively used for ornamentation, particularly inlay, in the East, where it has been highly regarded for several thousand years. It was in use during the earlier dynasties of Ancient Egypt. It is traditionally regarded in the East as a talisman for riders and as a protector of virtue; in the latter capacity is known as the 'young maiden's stone'.

Turquoise crystallizes in the triclinic system (see *Crystal systems*) but is a virtually amorphous material, occurring as nodules, incrustations and veins. The turquoise of Ancient Egypt probably came from deposits in the sandstone along the south-west coastline of the Sinai peninsula. These mines were forgotten for many centuries but are now spasmodically worked by the Bedouin. Much of the material is greenish, but some is of a good blue colour and this characteristically contains small circles of deeper blue. The blue stone has a higher density (around 2.8) than the green. The finest sky-blue turquoise comes from the district of Nishapur in Persia, which has been worked for many centuries. The turquoise is found only on the mountain peak of Ali-Mersai. It is marketed at Meshed, 15 miles away, and usually exported to Russia or India. The density of good Persian turquoise is around 2.79.

The southern part of North America produces turquoise which was used in earlier times by the Aztecs and later the Pueblo Indians for jewellery and inlay work. The old sources were New Mexico, Arizona, Nevada and California. These are still productive with the exception of the Californian deposits, which used to be worked by the Pueblo Indians using stone axes and scoops made of tortoise-shells. Turquoise is now also mined in Colorado. The only known example of distinctly crystalline turquoise was found at Lynch in Virginia in 1912. American turquoise is lighter in colour and more porous than material from the Eastern hemisphere, and its density is between 2.6 and 2.7.

Stones with a natural resemblance to turquoise are *odontolite* and *lazulite* (qq.v.), both of which are heavier than turquoise, *wardite* (q.v.), which is softer, and *variscite* (q.v.) which is softer and lighter. There are many ways of simulating turquoise: glass has been used for this purpose since antiquity. Modern glass turquoises are heavier (S.G. about 3.3) than true turquoise and usually contain small air-bubbles which betray their identity. Blue-dyed chalcedony is also used; it is much more translucent than turquoise, has a lower refractive index (1.53) and is slightly harder. The artificially pressed or plastic-bonded materials such as 'Viennese turquoise' (q.v.), which are marketed as turquoise imitations, are all lighter than true turquoise (the specific gravity is not usually above 2.4), and, if tested with a spot of hydrochloric acid, will turn the acid greenish-yellow, which true turquoise will not do. (The test should be done on an inconspicuous spot, as the polish is likely to suffer). A reconstituted turquoise is produced in Arizona from small pieces of true turquoise bonded with resin; it does not react to hydrochloric acid in the same way as the synthetic plastic-bonded material but its density (2.18–2.55) is lower than that of natural turquoise.

Turritella agate. Shell of the mollusc turritella which has been fossilized in the form of chalcedony (q.v.) and is used for ornamental purposes.

Turtle back. A name for (1) chlorastrolite, especially green with patches, (2) turquoise matrix, (3) variscite matrix. (See also *Turtle-back pearl*.)

Turtle-back pearl. A blister pearl with a fairly high dome, or a pearl with an uneven surface resembling that of a turtle's shell, or a pearl from the American clam known as the turtle-back.

Tuscany diamond. See *Florentine diamond*.

Tweezers. Special pointed tweezers are used by jewellers for placing small objects, e.g. snippets of solder, in position for soldering. Various other types of tweezers are used for particular purposes, for instance cross-locking tweezers, which are sprung and will hold small objects such as gemstones securely without pressure. (See also *Stone tongs*.)

Twinning. A phenomenon often seen in crystals, in which the crystal is composed of two individuals in reverse position to each other. There are three main types of twin crystals. In *contact* twins, the form of a normal crystal would be obtained by rotating one half of the crystal through 180° around the plane of joining. The flattened diamond crystals known as macles belong to this type. In *repeated* twinning the process has occurred several times, and as a result the crystal may appear to have a higher degree of symmetry than it in fact does. This type of twinning is not uncommon in alexandrite. *Interpenetrant* twins are twin crystals which have grown into one another; this phenomenon is common in fluorspar, and is responsible for cross-shaped and star-shaped crystals such as staurolite (q.v.), which are often used in jewellery in their natural form.

Twin stone. Staurolite.

U

Uigite. A variety of chlorastrolite from Uig, Isle of Skye.

'Ultralite' (Trade name.) Red-violet synthetic sapphire. (See *Synthetic gemstones*.)

Ultra-violet light. The use of this in gem-testing is described under *Luminescence*.

Unakite. A variegated rock used mainly by amateur lapidaries for producing tumbled and cabochon stones (see *Tumbling*). It is a granite containing quartz, feldspar, and epidote, and the colours include red, green and pink. The physical characteristics of the material – density, etc. – vary with the proportions of the different minerals included. The name of the material is taken from the Unaka range in North Carolina, where it was first found.

Uncle Sam diamond. The largest diamond ever found in North America. It weighed 40.23 carats in the rough and was found in the 'Crater of Diamonds' in Arkansas in 1924. It was fashioned into a $14\frac{1}{2}$-carat emerald-cut stone and is now owned by a firm of jewellers in New York.

Uniaxial crystals. Doubly-refracting crystals which have one optic axis (i.e. one direction in which they are singly-refracting). (See *Double refraction*.) Minerals in this class are those belonging to the tetragonal, hexagonal and trigonal systems. (See *Crystal systems*.)

Unicorn's horn. A material believed to have miraculous properties, particularly against poison, in the Middle Ages and Renaissance (see *Magical jewellery*). It was in fact the horn of the narwhal, and is described under *Ivory*.

Unionite. Pink zoisite.

Union pin. A pin in two parts: the point of the pin fits into a socket in such a way that the pin appears to be made in one piece. A fitting used in nineteenth-century jewellery.

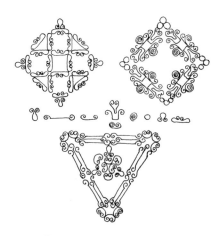

Jewellery made out of units of silver wire

Unit construction. The building-up of a form by repetition of identical units. Unit construction is not a new idea in jewellery but there appears to be a current wave of interest in it. It differs from the traditional way of making jewellery in that, instead of creating a design and then making up the necessary components out of metal sheet and wire worked to the required shape, the craftsman takes a single ready-made unit and sees what can be created out of the juxtaposition of numerous such units. The designing and the making are virtually one process, and because of the limitations of the material the technique is essentially an exploratory one.

The basic units are often very simple, such as rings of wire, which may be bought ready-made (jump rings) or made up from a length of wire. Other simple units are ready-made washers, sections cut from hollow tube (made in a variety of shapes by refiners), and blanks stamped out from metal sheet with a cutting punch (q.v.). Very attractive units can be made out of ready-made perforated metal sheet. These 'grids' are made with several different types of perforation, the commonest being circular, and by cutting into the grid at selected points with a piercing-saw the perforations can be enlarged into holes of interesting shapes. The sections containing these holes are then cut out and used as units. Sheets with rectangular perforations can be cut into strips or other geometrical shapes. The resulting units may be soldered or riveted together in various ways, and rivets themselves may also be used as units.

Unripe amber. Gedanite.

'Unripe diamond'. Misnomer for something that will never be a diamond: usually rock crystal or zircon.

Unripe pearl. A pearl of inferior quality.

'Ural (Uralian) chrysolite (emerald/olivine)'. Misnomers for demantoid garnet. (See *Andradite*.)

'Uralian sapphire'. Misnomer for blue tourmaline.

Utahlite. See *Variscite*.

'Utah turquoise'. Misnomer for variscite.

Uvarovite. An uncommon green garnet which so far has not been found in crystals large enough to have a use as gemstones. (See *Garnet*.)

V

Vabanite. Brown-red jasper from California flecked with yellow.

'Vallum diamond'. Misnomer for rock crystal.

Variolite. Dark green orthoclase feldspar with spherical markings of lighter colour.

Variscite. (Hydrous aluminium phosphate with chromium and iron. S.G. 2.4–2.6; R.I. about 1.56; H. 5.) A massive green or bluish-green ornamental stone. A variety similar in appearance to turquoise comes from Utah, and is called *Utahlite*. (It may be distinguished from turquoise by its lower hardness and specific gravity.) Utah also supplies banded material known as *sabalite* or *trainite*.

Most of the gem-quality material now comes from America, but the original source was Messbach in Voightland, previously called Variscia, from which the name is derived.

Vegetable ivory. See *Ivory*.

Venus' hair stone. Rutilated quartz.

Verdite. (Micaceous rock. S.G. about 2.9; R.I. about 1.58; H. 3.) A bright green rock, often with yellow and red spots, which makes a fine ornamental stone. It is found mainly in the Barberton district of the Transvaal.

'Vermeil' ('Vermeille'). Descriptive term applied to orange-red stones.

Verneuil process. See *Synthetic gemstones*.

Verre eglomisé. An elaborate technique for decorating glass, often used in sixteenth-century Spanish reliquaries. The under-surface of a sheet of glass or rock crystal was first covered with gold leaf.

The outline of the design was traced on this, the design was protected and the remainder of the gold leaf removed. The outline was then filled in by painting, beginning with the fine detail and shadowing. Varnish was applied over this as a protection and to add further gradations of colour, and silver leaf was sometimes added in very small quantities to provide highlights. When the painting was completed the whole sheet was backed with a reflecting metal foil.

Verre eglomisé was an ancient art, but was brought to perfection during the Renaissance. The name by which it is now known apparently originated much later, when an eighteenth-century French craftsman by the name of Glomy invented a special black and gold varnish for the backing and bequeathed his name to the entire process.

Verroterie cloisonné. An inlay of flat-surfaced paste or sliced gemstones set in cells on a metallic ground and flush with the surrounding metal. Also known as cloisonné inlay. (See *Inlay*.)

Vesuvianite. See *Idocrase*.

'Vesuvianite jade'. Misnomer for californite.

Vever, Henri (1854–1942). One of the leading French creators of Art Nouveau jewellery (q.v.), and author of a monumental and classic history of French nineteenth-century jewellery. Together with his brother Paul (1851–1915), Henri Vever inherited his father's jewellery firm in 1874. At their first exhibition in 1889 the brothers won one of the two Grands Prix, and two years later they were awarded the Croix de la Légion d'Honneur at the French exhibition in Moscow. Vever's work in the Art Nouveau style, which is second in importance only to Lalique's, differs from Lalique's in making much more use of synthetic and geometric forms. It has a stiffer and somewhat heavy quality. A superb pendant by Paul and Henri Vever is illustrated under *Art Nouveau jewellery*.

Vices. A variety of vices are used by jewellers. A general-purpose bench vice is essential for holding not only objects to be worked on (in fact other types of vice are often better for this) but also tools and equipment such as the mandrel and drawplate (qq.v.). Objects which it is not convenient to hold in a fixed vice are held in a hand vice (q.v.), and finger-rings are held in a ring-clamp (q.v.). Very slender objects can be held in a pin vice (q.v.). For engraving a special type of vice is required that will permit the object held to be rotated: see *Engraver's block*. C-clamps (q.v.) are used to hold metal down for other specific jobs such as sawing.

Victorian jewellery. See *Nineteenth-century jewellery*.

'Victron'. American trade name for polystyrene. (See *Plastics*.)

'Vienna turquoise'. An imitation of turquoise made by compressing a precipitate of aluminium phosphate coloured blue by copper oleate. (See *Turquoise*.)

'Vigorite' (Trade name.) A phenol plastic. (See *Plastics*.)

Violane (Violan). (S.G. about 3.23; R.I. 1.69; H. 6.) A translucent to opaque violet-blue variety of diopside. It is used for ornamental purposes and is sometimes made into beads. It is found at Saint Marcel, Piedmont.

Violet stone. Iolite.

'Violite' (Trade name.) Purple synthetic sapphire. (See *Synthetic gemstones*.)

Virgin metal. Metal which is taken from the ore and has not previously been used.

'Viscoloid' (Trade name.) A celluloid plastic. (See *Plastics*.)

Vitreous lustre. See *Lustre*.

'Volcanic chrysolite'. Misnomer for idocrase.

Volcanic glass. Obsidian.

Vorobievite. Pink beryl (morganite).

Vulcanite. Hard black rubber, occasionally used as a black imitation stone.

W

'Walderite'. (Trade name.) Synthetic white sapphire. (See *Synthetic gemstones*.)

Walrus ivory. See *Ivory*.

Wardite. (Hydrated aluminium phosphate. S.G. 2.81; R.I. 1.590–1.599; H. 5.) A granular bluish-green stone bearing some resemblance to turquoise. It is found at Cedar Valley, Utah.

Wart pearl. Baroque pearl.

Warty-back pearl. Pearl from the mussel *Quadrula pustulosa* (the 'warty-back clam') from the Mississippi valley.

'**Washita diamond**'. Misnomer for rock crystal.

Waste-wax casting. See *Lost-wax casting*.

'**Water chrysolite**'. Moldavite. (See *Tektite*.)

Water-gilding. A technique of gilding brass and copper by simple immersion. The ingredients are 1½ parts gold chloride and 60 parts hydrogen potassium carbonate to 200 parts water. These are boiled in a fireproof glass dish for about 2 hours until the solution turns green, when it is ready. The article is immersed in the hot solution for half a minute.

Nickel silver can be gilded in the same way if it is placed in contact with a zinc or copper wire.

Water of Ayr stone. A grey slaty stone used wet for polishing metals.

'**Water sapphire**'. Misnomer for light blue iolite from Ceylon.

Water stone. This can mean several things: hyalite opal, moonstone, or the nodules of chalcedony which sometimes contain water. It is also a Chinese name for jade.

Wax agate. Yellow or yellowish-red chalcedony with a waxy lustre.

Wax-filled pearl. A common form of imitation pearl. (See *Pearls*.)

Wax opal. Yellowish opal with a waxy lustre.

Wedding rings. The wedding ring developed from the Roman *anulus pronubis*, the ring given by the man to the girl at the betrothal ceremony (see *Betrothal rings*). The early Christians incorporated the ring-giving into the marriage ceremony and the ring thus became a symbol of marriage. The custom of placing the ring on the third finger of the left hand also dates from Roman times; this finger was chosen because the Romans believed that there was a vein in it (the *vena amoris*) which was directly connected with the heart.

Since, however, the wedding ring had developed from the betrothal ring, and since various forms of marriage and betrothal were in use in the succeeding centuries, the respective roles of the wedding ring and betrothal ring overlapped considerably and it is impossible to say of any surviving medieval ring that it was definitely a wedding ring and not a betrothal ring or simply a lover's token. The rings which could have been used as wedding rings are of many types – the fede ring (q.v.), decorated with two clasped hands, the later gimmel ring (q.v.), made of two or more hoops fitted together, rings decorated with hearts or lovers' knots or love-inscriptions (see *Betrothal rings* for fuller details of these), and, of course, ordinary decorative rings. A wedding ring mentioned in a will of 1503 is simply described as 'having a dyamond and a ruby therein'. Thomas Lyte of Lyte's Cary in the seventeenth century gave his wife a wedding ring consisting of a gold band with a punning inscription inside (see *Posy rings*). Martin Luther's wedding ring is said to have borne the figure of the crucified Christ and the Instruments of the Passion.

In post-classical times, rituals for blessing the wedding ring and placing it on the bride's finger can be traced back as far as the eleventh century. The Roman custom of placing it on the third finger of the left hand, however, had become obscured; the *vena amoris* was thought in the Middle Ages to be in the third finger of the right hand, and it was accordingly on this finger that the ring was placed. It is not clear how this confusion arose, but presumably by the sixteenth century the reference to the *vena amoris* in the writings of Aulus Gellius (second century A.D.), from whom the tradition was derived, had been rediscovered, because in the 1549 Book of Common Prayer it is decreed that the ring should be placed on the left hand. Shortly after this the Roman Catholic church followed suit. The fact that the ring was placed on the third finger of the left hand during the ceremony, however, did not mean that it was *worn* on that finger thereafter. It might be worn on any finger, and in the seventeenth and eighteenth centuries it was commonly worn on the thumb.

It is not possible to say when the plain gold wedding ring of modern times first became popular. When Queen Mary married in 1554 she decided that her ring should be a plain gold hoop, 'because maydens were so maried in old times'. Possibly this is a reference to the gold posy rings (q.v.) of the later Middle Ages. During the time of the Commonwealth in the seventeenth century some Puritans were in favour of abolishing the wedding ring as a piece of vanity; they did not succeed, but it is possible that the plain type of wedding ring first became generally accepted in this period. In the nineteenth century, when the custom of having separate rings for engagement and wedding became established in England, the plain gold wedding ring became normal. It remained (with its counterpart in platinum) the usual form for well over a century, but in recent years there has been a return, particularly in America, to gem-set wedding rings, and there is also something of a fashion for wedding and engagement rings in matching pairs. In England, where the gem-set wedding ring is still not generally accepted, variations on the plain gold band have nevertheless appeared: the hoop is faceted, or diamond-milled (these are very popular), or made in different-coloured golds.

Modern diamond-milled wedding ring

The wearing of wedding rings by men seems never to have become an established custom in England, although it has been much commoner in the past than it is now. It is now so unusual as to cause surprise; the surprise is rooted in an unspoken idea that a woman's wedding ring symbolizes that she belongs to her husband, and that it is neither necessary nor quite suitable for a man to wear a corresponding symbol. This is a fairly modern attitude, but it was foreshadowed by Dr. Johnson in the eighteenth century (when men did wear wedding rings) who, forsaking momentarily the scholarly detachment proper to a lexicographer, defined a ring as 'a circular instrument placed upon the noses of hogs and the fingers of women to restrain them and bring them into subjection.' The prejudice against men's wedding rings does not extend to other European countries or to America, and in many countries they are worn as a matter of course. In the Eastern Orthodox Church, for example, the bride and groom exchange rings and each wears the ring on the right hand. The bridegroom is given a ring of silver, and the bride a ring of gold. (See also *Jewish marriage-rings*.)

Wedgwood. In the 1770s, when the enthusiasm for antique cameos and intaglios (qq.v.) was at its height, imitation cameos and intaglios began to be manufactured by the pottery firm of Wedgwood (then Wedgwood and Bentley). The cameos were made in two materials: a white porcelain bisqué (a porcelain with a smooth wax-like surface) for collectors' cabinets, and the famous unglazed jasper ware, consisting of a white relief on a pastel-coloured or black background, which Josiah Wedgwood invented in 1774 and which was used for ornamental cameos. The intaglios were made in black porcelain bisqué; by the time Wedgwood and Bentley published their 1787 catalogue they were being made in two layers, the upper layer blue and highly polished to imitate nicolo (q.v.).

The 1787 catalogue lists 1,764 different cameos and nearly 400 intaglios. The subjects for the cameos are mostly classical – scenes from Greek and Roman mythology and Roman history, portraits of ancient philosophers, poets and rulers, etc. – but there is also a group of 'illustrious moderns' which includes Cromwell, Milton and Isaac Newton. Josiah Wedgwood was a pious man, but his catalogue reflects how completely unfashionable religious subjects had become: Jesus Christ and the Virgin Mary appear almost at the end of the list, under 'Miscellaneous', between 'a man firing a rocket, in the character of Mars' and a brace of birds, a pointer dog, an elephant, a horse and a rattlesnake. The intaglios have similar subjects, but include a number of contemporary portraits and a series of initial letters for intaglios which are to be used as seals. Many of the moulds used by Wedgwood were provided by Tassie (q.v.), who was producing a rather more ambitious series in paste.

A considerable number of Wedgwood's cameos and intaglios found their way into jewellery. The intaglios were mounted as seal-stones in rings and pendant seals, but the small cameos were to be seen in bracelets, lockets, rings, buttons, brooches and chatelaines. Many were mounted in cut steel (see *Cut-steel jewellery*), and for a period Wedgwood worked in association with Matthew Boulton (q.v.), the Birmingham manufacturer of cut steel. Others were mounted in pinchbeck and – occasionally – gold. Large cameo medallions were also made, but these were primarily intended for inlaying in cabinets and similar work. The cameos continued popular into the nineteenth century and many were exported to France.

For a short time after their first appearance Wedgwood cameos and intaglios were forged. The culprit was a man named Voyez who had been engaged by Wedgwood as a modeller; his work was excellent, but he was dismissed for drunkenness. The forgeries, which were made with the Wedgwood mark, appeared up to 1776.

Weights for gemstones. The unit of weight normally used for gemstones and pearls is the *metric carat*. (For history of this unit, see *Carat* [1]). The metric carat (here referred to as the carat) is one-fifth of a gram (0.200 g.) Parts of a carat are expressed in decimals (or should be, but it is common practice to speak of half a carat and quarter of a carat). Stones are normally only weighed to the second place of decimals, the third figure being ignored.

In the case of diamond, the decimal parts of the carat are often referred to as points. Thus a diamond weighing 0.60 carat is said to weigh 60 points, and is called a 60-pointer. Another unit of weight sometimes used for diamond (less now than in the past) is the grain; there are 4 diamond grains to the carat.

Pearls are usually weighed in carats, but the weight is expressed in grains and the value of the pearl is calculated on this basis (see *Pearls*). There are 4 pearl grains to the carat. Japanese cultured pearls are sold by the momme, which equals 18.75 carats or 75 pearl grains.

The less valuable gemstones are often sold by the ordinary metric system of weights – the milligram (1/1000th gram), the gram and the kilogram (1000 grams). These weights may be converted to carats as follows:

1 gram	= 5 carats
500 milligrams	= 2.5 carats
200 milligrams	= 1 carat
100 milligrams	= 0.5 carat
10 milligrams	= 0.05 carat, etc.

Synthetic stones and pastes are usually sold by their *size* in millimetres, instead of by weight.

Weights for precious metals. Until very recently Troy measures (see below) were used in Britain for weighing precious metals. They have now been replaced by the metric system of weights based on the gram:

1000 milligrams	= 1 gram
1000 grams	= 1 kilogram.

The Troy system is:

24 grains	= 1 pennyweight (dwt.)
20 pennyweights	= 1 oz.
12 oz.	= 1 lb.

The relationship between metric and Troy weights is as follows:

0.1 gram =	1.543235 grains Troy
1 gram =	15.432349 grains Troy
100 grams =	3.215073 oz. Troy
1 kilogram =	32.150727 oz. Troy
1 grain Troy =	0.0648 gram
1 ounce Troy =	31.1035 grams.

The Troy grain weighs the same as the Avoirdupois grain, but the pound and ounce weights in the two systems are different. 1 oz. Troy = 480 grains, and 1 lb. Troy = 5760 grains, whereas 1 oz. Avoirdupois = $437\frac{1}{2}$ grains and 1 lb. Avoirdupois = 7000 grains. The use of the Troy pound was discontinued in the nineteenth century.

History. Before the reign of Henry VIII, the basic unit for silver coins and silver plate was the Tower pound sterling, which was the equivalent of 5400 grains Troy. This was both a unit of weight and a unit of value, and in old inventories the weights of articles of plate were recorded in pounds, shillings and pence. The penny or pennyweight was one-twelfth of a shilling, and the shilling one-twentieth of a pound. There was another unit called a mark, which was two-thirds of a pound or 160 pennyweights.

During the fifteenth century another system of weight was introduced from Troyes in France, and in 1526 this system, Troy weight, was established by royal proclamation and the Tower pound was abolished. The Troy pound had 12 ounces, but the Troy ounce was originally divided into 24 parts called carats, and each carat into 4 grains. The carat ceased to be used as a general unit of weight for metals but was retained as a way of expressing the fineness of gold, for which purpose it is still used (see *Carat* [2]). The subdivisions of the Troy ounce were then fixed at 20 pennyweights and 480 grains, as given above. Since, however, the weights of gold and silver were always given in ounces, pennyweights or grains, there was little point in retaining the Troy pound, and in 1878 it was abolished as the standard unit and the Avoirdupois pound of 7000 grains was legalized in its place.

Westphal balance. See *Specific gravity*.

West's solution. A highly-refractive liquid (R.I. 2.05) used in measuring the refractive index (q.v.) of highly-refractive stones. It is a mixture of yellow phosphorus, sulphur and methylene iodide in the proportions 8:1:1, and is spontaneously inflammable.

Whistles. Jewelled pendant whistles, presumably for summoning dogs, etc., were worn by men in the sixteenth century. Surviving designs by such artists as Dürer show them to have been made in fanciful and elaborate forms well worthy of the Renaissance goldsmith's skill.

*Design for a pendant whistle by Hans
Brosamer, mid-sixteenth century*

Many were probably in chased metal, but one listed in an inventory of Henry VIII's for 1519 was set with a ruby and seven diamonds; it was attached to a finger-ring.

'White'. When applied to transparent stones, this word means 'colourless'.

'White garnet'. Misnomer for leucite. There is a translucent whitish grossular garnet.

White gold. An alloy of gold with silver, nickel, palladium or platinum. The proportion of gold depends on the other metal used: if silver or nickel, there will be less than 50 per cent gold, if platinum or palladium, 70–75 per cent gold.

White opal. A general trade term for precious opal with a light body colour, as opposed to black opal. (See *Opal*.)

Willemite. (Zinc silicate. S.G. 3.9–4.2; R.I. 1.69–1.72; H. $5\frac{1}{2}$.) A mineral chiefly important as an ore of zinc, although transparent stones are sometimes cut from it. These are yellow, greenish-yellow or orange. On the whole they do not polish well.

The mineral was named after King William I of the Netherlands. Most of the gem-quality crystals come from Franklin Furnace, New Jersey, U.S.A.

Williamsite. A translucent oil-green variety of serpentine (q.v.).

Wilsonite. Purplish-red scapolite.

Wiluite. A greenish idocrase from Siberia.

Winchellite. Alternative name for lintonite. (See *Thomsonite*.)

Wing pearl. A wing-shaped baroque pearl.

Wire. Precious-metal wire began to be used in jewellery in the third millennium B.C. The earliest method of making it was probably to roll a strip of metal between two flat stones or plates of bronze. Later the drawplate (q.v.) was introduced and is still in use for drawing wire. Rolling-mills (q.v.) are now used for producing wire in quantity. Wire in a variety of gauges is produced by refiners. (See also *Filigree*.)

Wire gauges. See *Metal gauges*.

Wisconsin pearls. Good-quality fresh-water pearls from the Mississippi valley; the name may also be used for freshwater pearls from other areas.

Wolfers, Philippe (1858–1929). Foremost designer of Art Nouveau jewellery in Belgium and member of a family firm of Belgian court jewellers and silversmiths (Wolfers Frères). His work at first made use of the conventional flowers and insects of Art Nouveau design but soon became more original and abstract. In the early years of this century he achieved an international reputation as a jeweller, but after 1905 began to concentrate on sculpture and silverwork.

Wolf's eye. A name for both moonstone and tiger's eye.

Wood agate. See *Agatized wood*.

Wood opal. See *Opalized wood*.

Worshipful Company of Goldsmiths of the City of London. One of the oldest of the great livery companies, and the first body to be established in England with powers to regulate goldsmiths' affairs and test the quality of precious metals. Assaying (q.v.) is still one of the important duties performed by the officials of the Company at its headquarters in Gold-smiths' Hall, but over the centuries the Company's role has broadened to include the stimulation of public interest in gold and silverware and a considerable amount of educational and charitable work.

Worshipful Company of Goldsmiths of the City of London

It is not known when a guild of goldsmiths was first formed in London, but there was certainly one before 1180, because in that year a number of guilds including a goldsmiths' guild were fined for being established irregularly without the King's licence. It was not uncommon at the time for goldsmiths to defraud their customers by debasing gold and silver or plating base metal, and in 1238 after numerous such frauds had come to light Henry III directed the Mayor and Aldermen of London to choose six 'discreet goldsmiths' in the city to superintend their fellows. The custom continued, and in 1300, when a statute of Edward I laid down the standards for wrought gold and silver, the superintendents were referred to as 'gardiens' of the craft whose duty it was to assay and mark with a leopard's head every vessel of silver before it left the workshop (see *Hallmarking*). The wares of provincial goldsmiths were also supposed to be sent to London to be assayed by the wardens, but needless to say in the travelling conditions of the Middle Ages this requirement was not observed.

In 1327 the guild of London goldsmiths was incorporated by royal charter under the title: 'The Wardens and Commonalty of the Mystery of Goldsmiths of the City of London.' In 1392 a charter of Richard II re-incorporated them with extended powers, and in 1462 by charter of Edward IV they were constituted a body corporate and politic and given various privileges and duties, including the right to use a common seal and the right to hold lands in perpetual succession. From time to time these privileges and duties were re-affirmed and further enlarged.

In 1423 provision had been made for a number of assay offices to be set up in the provinces (see *Assay offices*), since it was clearly unreasonable to expect provincial goldsmiths to send their wares to London. The charter of 1462, however, invested the wardens of the London guild with powers to search for and test gold and silver wares not only in London and its suburbs, but in all fairs and markets and all cities, towns, boroughs and other places throughout England. As a result the London goldsmiths claimed jurisdiction over the working of gold and silver in the provinces. They were not, however, any more eager to go and inspect the work done in the provinces than the provincial goldsmiths had been to send their wares to London, and most of the time there was little or no communication between the London goldsmiths and those of the provinces. The London goldsmiths regarded the standards of assaying in the provinces with a certain contempt, and in the light of some of the findings of the Parliamentary Commission in 1772 (see *Assay offices*) one cannot say that they were altogether wrong. Nevertheless the opposition at Goldsmiths' Hall to the setting up of new assay offices in Birmingham and Sheffield (the reason for the Parliamentary Commission) was founded in self-interest, and the new offices were set up in 1773 in spite of the Company's disapproval. Birmingham, Sheffield and London are now the only three assay offices in England.

Over the centuries the finances of the Company fluctuated (at one point they had to sell their plate to rebuild their hall – see *Goldsmiths' Hall*), but gifts, bequests, rents from lands and revenue from assaying ensured at least relative prosperity and at times considerable luxury. The fourth hall (see *Goldsmiths' Hall*), opened in 1835, was hardly on a modest scale for the time, although in recent years there has been pressure on the accommodation.

In addition to Goldsmiths' Hall, the Company have property in other parts of the City and in East Acton, where they own almshouses. They administer numerous other charitable trusts, and have for several centuries taken an active interest in assisting students, in particular sons and daughters of freemen of the Company.

The Company seeks to promote the interests of the jewellery and silversmithing trade in various ways. These include arranging exhibitions in Britain and overseas of antique and modern plate

Xaga. Obsidian (Californian Indian).

Xalostocite. See *Grossular garnet.*

Xanthite. See *Idocrase.*

X-rays. X-rays (electromagnetic waves of very short wavelength, a kind of 'invisible light') are used in gem-testing in a variety of ways. Firstly, they may be used to excite luminescence in gemstones; the characteristic glow emitted by the stone serves in many cases to identify it. This effect is described under *Luminescence.* Secondly, stones may be tested for their transparency to X-rays. The extent to which a substance is opaque to X-rays increases with the atomic weight of the element or elements composing it (this is why X-ray plates of the human body show the bone structure clearly while the flesh is almost invisible; the calcium and phosphorus in the bones are much heavier than the elements of which the flesh is composed). Thus diamond (composed of carbon, atomic weight 12.0) is almost transparent to X-rays and barely shows on an X-ray photographic plate, while a lead-glass imitation stone (atomic weight of lead 207.2) is opaque and shows as a dense black shape. Gemstones show pronounced differences in their degrees of transparency: for instance beryl is virtually transparent and corundum nearly so; quartz and topaz are translucent, spinel and hessonite semi-translucent, while tourmaline, turquoise, sphene, rutile and almandine are nearly opaque to opaque. The method is therefore very useful in distinguishing between gemstones of different species, and will also of course detect a doublet (q.v.) in which the crown and base are made of two different materials. X-rays are also used in the detection of cultured pearls; see *Pearls* for description. The third method is to take what is known as a lauegram (after Max von Laue, who first used the technique) of the stone. X-rays are of such short wavelength that they are diffracted (split up) by the internal atomic layers of the stone and are reflected by these layers. If a very narrow beam of X-rays is directed through the stone and a photographic film placed on the far side, the film will show a pattern of spots (the lauegram) which is produced by the reflection of the X-rays from the atomic layers. When the X-rays are directed through the stone parallel to one of its axes of symmetry (see *Crystal systems*) the resulting symmetrical pattern is a 'photograph' of the internal symmetry of the stone, and thus reveals the crystal system to which the stone belongs. This is of great value in identifying it. A development of this method is to scrape a sample of powder from the stone and subject it to the same process; the resulting photograph shows not a pattern of dots but a series of concentric rings, the strength of which, and distance apart, are characteristic of the stone tested. This method of course requires the photograph to be compared with corresponding diffraction photographs of all other minerals.

Some gemstones, notably kunzite, change colour under X-ray radiation. The induced colour fades after some hours in strong sunlight.

Xyloid jasper. Jasperized wood.

'Xylonite' (Trade name.) A celluloid plastic (see *Plastics*).

Xylopal. Opalized wood.

Y

Y.A.G. See *Yttrium aluminium garnet.*

Yanolite. Violet axinite.

Yellow-belly. A type of tortoiseshell (q.v.).

Yellow brass. An alloy consisting of approximately 65 per cent copper, 35 per cent zinc, with melting point of 1660°F. It is a good material for wire, chains and beads. For copper–zinc alloys. (See *Gilding metal.*)

Yellow gold. An alloy of gold with silver and copper; higher proportions of copper produce a redder gold. Yellow gold is the type of gold most often used.

Yellow pearls. Yellowish pearls from the *Margaritifera carcharium* fished off the coast of Western Australia. (See also *Pearls.*)

Yogo sapphire. Sapphire from Montana.

Yttrium aluminium garnet (Y.A.G.). A new synthetic garnet used particularly for the simulation of diamond. (See *Synthetic gemstones.*)

Yü. Chinese name for jade, also for other precious stones.

Yui Ko Iu jade. Tomb jade (q.v.) coloured green by bronze objects in the vicinity.

Z

Zeasite. Opalized wood.

Zebra crocidolite. Crocidolite in which part of the material has remained its original blue colour, the rest having been stained by iron oxide to produce a particoloured effect. (See *Tiger's eye*.)

Zebra jasper. Brown jasper with darker and lighter streaks.

Zeuxite. Green Brazilian tourmaline.

Zinc. A bluish-white metal used in the ancient world and in India, whence it was introduced into Europe by Portuguese traders. The commercial smelting of zinc in Europe began in the mid-eighteenth century. The principal use of zinc is as a corrosive-preventing agent for iron and steel, and an important by-product of the purifying of zinc is sulphuric acid. Zinc appears in jewellery as a constituent of gilding-metal (q.v.), as an alloy in silver solder (see also *Zinc chloride*), and in dust form is used in the refining of gold and silver (qq.v.). The melting point is 419.4°C.

Zinc blende (Sphalerite). (Zinc sulphide. S.G. 4.09; R.I. 2.37; H. $3\frac{1}{2}$–4.) An important ore of zinc; usually nearly black, it is occasionally found in yellowish-brown transparent crystals which can be cut as gemstones. The comparative softness and easy cleavage of the material prevent its having any importance as a gemstone.

Zinc blende resembles galena (lead sulphide) but contains no lead. To this fact it owes its name: 'blende' is derived from the German word 'blenden', meaning 'to deceive'. The name sphalerite, by which it is known in North America, has a similar meaning.

Zinc blende occurs worldwide: transparent material comes from Mexico and northern Spain.

Zinc chloride. A flux which can be used in soft-soldering (see *Soldering*). It can be made by adding small pieces of zinc to hydrochloric acid; this has to be done gradually or the acid will boil and crack the container. When sufficient zinc has been added to 'kill' the acid, so that it is no longer effervescing, the liquid is ready for use.

Zinc chloride is also used, mixed with copper sulphate, to colour copper and brass dark green. (See *Colouring of metals*.)

Zincite. (Zinc oxide. S.G. about 5.68; R.I. 2.013–2.029; H. 4–$4\frac{1}{2}$.) An orange to deep red stone usually found in massive form but occasionally in transparent crystals. A few pieces have been cut as gemstones. The gem quality material comes from the zinc mines of New Jersey, U.S.A.

Zinc spinel. See *Gahnite*.

'Zircolite'. (Trade name.) Synthetic white sapphire (see *Synthetic gemstones*).

Zircon. (Zirconium silicate. S.G. 4.67–4.70 and 3.95–4.10; R.I. 1.92–1.98 and 1.78; H. $7\frac{1}{2}$ and $6\frac{1}{2}$.) A transparent yellow, golden-brown, green, sky-blue or colourless stone. Most zircon on the market was originally reddish-brown in colour and has been heat-treated in the rough to produce more interesting colours, the most popular being blue, golden-yellow and colourless. (See *Heat-treatment*.) As zircon has an adamantine lustre and almost as much fire as diamond, a colourless zircon may on occasion be mistaken for a diamond. (For distinction between the two, see *Diamond*, under 'Identification'.)

Zircon cut

The discrepancy between the physical properties of zircons is explained by the fact that zircon occurs in two basically different forms. 'High' or 'normal' zircon, to which type most of the gemstones belong, is a completely crystallized zirconium silicate; the second type, 'low' zircon, has no crystal form and results from the breakdown of the crystal lattice, believed to be caused by the presence of a radioactive element in the zircon. There are also many stones which are at an intermediate stage of the disintegration process. Low zircon is not used in jewellery. If heated to about 1450°C it reverts to high zircon.

Zircon is simulated by glass and by synthetic blue spinel. Synthetic spinel and glass are not doubly refractive, whereas zircon shows strong double refraction (q.v.). The usual cut for zircon is a modification of the brilliant cut which is generally known as the zircon cut. (See *Gem-cutting* for description.) Fine stones may be step-cut.

The most important source of zircon is Indo-China; stones from here are cut and marketed at Bangkok. Other sources are Ceylon, the Mogok Stone Tract in Burma, Norway, France and Australia.

Zircon cut. A style of cutting used extensively for zircon, exploiting the fact that zircon has almost as much fire as diamond. It is similar to the brilliant cut (see *Diamond-cutting*) but has extra facets around the culet. (See *Gem-cutting* for illustration.)

'Zircon spinel'. Synthetic pale blue spinel. (See *Synthetic gemstones*.)

'Zirctone'. (Trade name.) Bluish-green synthetic sapphire. (See *Synthetic gemstones*.)

Zoisite. (Calcium-aluminium silicate.) A mineral producing three gemstone varieties: *tanzanite* (transparent blue-violet), *thulite* (opaque pink) and *anyolite* (rubies in a matrix of green zoisite). These are described separately.

Zonite. Local name for jasper or chert found in Arizona.

Zonochlorite. A green banded prehnite, very similar to chlorastrolite, found in the Lake Superior region.

Zylonite. A celluloid plastic. (See *Plastics*.)

BIBLIOGRAPHY

Allen, J. Romilly. 'Celtic art in pagan and Christian times.' London, 1904.

Baerwald, M., and Mahoney, J. T. 'The story of jewelry.' London and New York, 1960.

Banister, J. 'Changing fashions in memorial jewellery.' In *Antique Dealer and Collector's Guide,* vol. xxii, iv, 1967.

Bates, K. F. 'The enamelist.' Cleveland and New York, 1967.

Blakemore, K. 'The retail jeweller's guide.' London, 1969.

Boardman, J. 'Engraved gems.' London and Evanston, Illinois, 1968.

Board of Trade. 'Working party report on jewellery and silverware.' London, 1946.

Bradford, E. D. S. 'Four centuries of European jewellery.' London, 1967.

Budge, E. A. Wallis. 'Amulets and superstitions.' Oxford, 1930.

Burgess, F. W. 'Antique jewellery and trinkets.' New York, reprint of 1919 edition, 1972.

Butler's 'Lives of the Saints', revised by H. Thurston and D. Allwater. London, 1956.

Butts, A. (ed.) 'Silver. Economics, metallurgy and use.' Princeton, N.J., 1967.

Canning's handbook on electroplating, polishing, bronzing, lacquering and enamelling. Birmingham, 1953.

Castellani, A. 'Antique jewellery and its revival.' London, 1862.

Cellini, B. 'Treatises on goldsmithing and sculpture.' Trans. C. R. Ashbee. London, 1888; New York, 1966.

Cellini, B. 'Autobiography.' Trans. J. Addington Symonds. London 1949; Garden City, New York, 1966.

Clarke, J. R. 'The Alfred and Minster Lovell jewels.' Oxford, 1961.

Clifford, A. 'Cut-steel and Berlin iron jewellery.' Bath and Cranbury, New Jersey, 1971.

Copeland, L. 'Diamonds, famous, notable and unique.' New York, 1966.

Cunynghame, H. H. 'European enamels.' London, 1906.

Cunynghame, H. H. 'Art enamelling upon metals.' London, 1899.

Dalton, O. M. 'Byzantine art and archaeology.' Oxford, 1911.

Dalton, O. M. 'Catalogue of the finger-rings . . . in the British Museum.' London, 1912.

Dalton, O. M. 'Catalogue of the engraved gems of the post-classical periods in the British Museum.' London, 1915.

Davenport, C. 'Jewellery.' London, 1905.

Davis, M. L., and Pack, G. 'Mexican jewelry.' Univ. of Texas, 1963.

Dickinson, H. W. 'Matthew Boulton.' Cambridge, 1937.

Bibliography

D'Otrange, M. L. 'The exquisite art of Carlo Giuliano.' In *Apollo*, LIX, 1954.

Elkington & Co. Ltd. 'Catalogue of silver, plate, jewellery, etc.' Birmingham, 1905.

Emerson, A. R. 'Hand-made jewellery.' Leicester, 1953.

Evans, J. 'A history of jewellery, 1100–1870.' London, reprinted 1970.

Evans, J. 'English posies and posy rings.' Oxford, 1931.

Evans, J. 'Cut-steel jewellery.' In *Connoisseur*, 1917.

Evans, J. 'English jewellery from the fifth century A.D. to 1800.' London, 1921.

Evans, J. 'Magical jewels of the Middle Ages and Renaissance.' Oxford, 1922.

Evans, J., and Serjeantson, M. S. 'English medieval lapidaries.' London, 1933.

Flower, M. 'Victorian jewellery.' London, 1967.

Fontenay, E. 'Les bijoux anciens et modernes.' Paris, 1887.

Forrer, L. 'Biographical dictionary of medallists, coin-, seal- and gem-engravers, 500 B.C.–A.D. 1900.' London, 1904–30.

Fortnum, C. D. E. 'On some finger-rings of the early Christian period.' In *Archaeological Journal*, vol. XXVI, 1869.

Fox, C. 'Pattern and purpose.' Cardiff, 1958.

Frégnac, C. 'Jewellery from the Renaissance to Art Nouveau.' London, 1965.

Gems. London.

Gerlach, M. (ed.) 'Primitive and folk jewelry.' New York, 1971.

Gregorietti, G. 'Jewellery through the ages.' London and New York, 1969.

Hackenbröch, Y. 'New knowledge on jewels and designs after Etienne Delaune.' In *Connoisseur*, vol. CLXVI, 1967.

Hackenbröch, Y. 'Eramus Hornick as a jeweller.' In *Connoisseur*, vol. CLXII, 1966.

Hall, H. R. 'Catalogue of Egyptian scarabs . . . in the British Museum.' London, 1913.

Higgins, R. A. 'Greek and Roman jewellery. London, 1961; New York, 1962.

Higgins, R. A. 'Jewellery from classical lands.' London, 1965.

Holme, C. (ed.) 'Modern design in jewellery and fans.' London, 1902.

Hughes, G. 'Modern jewellery.' London, 1963; New York, 1968.

Hughes, G. 'The art of jewellery'. London and New York, 1972.

Hulme, F. E. 'The birth and development of ornament.' London and New York, 1893.

Jackson, C. J. 'English goldsmiths and their marks.' New York (reprinted), 1964.

Jackson, W. A. 'Jewellery repairing.' London, 1948.

Jessup, R. 'Anglo-Saxon jewellery.' London, 1950.

Jones, W. 'Crowns and coronations.' London, 1883.

Jones, W. 'Finger-ring lore.' London, 1898.

King, C. W. 'Talismans and amulets.' In *Archaeological Journal*, vol. XXVI, 1869.

Lapidary Journal. San Diego, California.

Lewis, M. D. S. 'Antique paste jewellery.' London, 1970.

Marryat, H., and Broadbent, U. 'The romance of Hatton Garden.' London, 1930.

Marshall, F. H. 'Catalogue of the finger-rings, Greek, Etruscan and Roman, in the British Museum.' London, 1907.

Maryon, H. 'Metalwork and enamelling.' London, 1959; New York, 1971.

McLintock, W. F. P. 'A guide to the collection of gemstones in the Geological Museum.' London, 1951.

Meyerowitz, P. 'Jewelry and sculpture through unit construction.' New York and London, 1967.

National Museum of Antiquities of Scotland. 'Brooches in Scotland.' Edinburgh, 1958.

O'Dell, A. C. 'The St. Ninian's Isle Treasure.' Aberdeen, 1960.

Oman, C. C. 'Catalogue of rings in the Victoria and Albert Museum.' London, 1930.

Oved, S. 'The book of necklaces.' London, 1953.

Pack, G. 'Jewelry and enameling.' New York, 1941.

Pack, G. 'Jewelry making by the lost-wax process.' Princeton, N.J., 1968.

Percival, M. 'Chats on old jewellery and trinkets.' London, 1912.

Raspe, R. E. 'Account of the present state and arrangement of Mr. James Tassie's collection of pastes and impressions . . .'' London, 1786.

Roche, J. C. 'The history, development and organization of the Birmingham jewellery and allied trades.' Birmingham, 1927.

Schwahn, C. 'Workshop methods for gold- and silversmiths.' Trans. W Jacobsohn. London, 1960.

Selwyn, A. 'The retail jeweller's handbook.' London, 1962.

Shipley, R. M. 'Dictionary of gems and gemology.' Los Angeles, 1951.

Smith, H. Clifford. 'Jewellery.' London, 1908.

Smith, G. F. Herbert. 'Gemstones.' London, 1958.

Snowman, A. K. 'The art of Carl Fabergé.' London, 1953.

Soapmaker, C. N. 'Erotic jewellery of East Anglia.' (unpubl. thesis).

Speight, A. 'The lock of hair.' London, 1871.

Steingräber, E. 'Antique jewellery; its history in Europe from 800 to 1900.' London, 1957.

Stone, P. 'Baroque pearls.' In *Apollo*, LXVIII, 1958.

Stopford, F. 'The romance of the jewel.' London, 1920.

Sutherland, B. B. 'The romance of seals and engraved gems.' New York and London, 1965.

Sutherland, C. H. V. 'Gold'. London, 1959.

Theophilus, trans. Hawthorne and Smith. 'On divers arts.' London and Chicago, 1963.

Theophrastus, trans. J. Hill. 'History of stones.' London, 1746.

Tolansky, S. 'The history and use of diamond.' London, 1962.

Twining, E. F. 'The history of the crown jewels of Europe.' London, 1960.

Untracht, O. 'Enameling on metal.' Philadelphia, 1957; London, 1958.

Untracht, O. 'Metal techniques for craftsmen.' New York, 1968; London, 1969.

Vever, H. 'La bijouterie française au XIXe siècle.' Paris, 1906.

Von Neuman, R. 'The design and creation of jewellery.' London and Philadelphia, 1961.

Wainwright, J. 'Discovering lapidary work.' London, 1971.

Walters, H. B. 'Catalogue of the engraved gems, Greek, Etruscan and Roman, in the British Museum.' London, 1926.

Ward, J. 'Historic ornament.' London, 1909.

Webster, R. 'The gemmologists' compendium.' London, 1967.

Webster, R. 'Gems: their sources, description and identification.' London

Bibliography

and Hamden, Connecticut, 1970.

Wedgwood, J. 'Catalogue of cameos, intaglios, medals, etc.' 1787.

Weinstein, M. 'The world of jewel stones.' New York, 1958; London, 1959.

Wilkinson, A. H. 'Ancient Egyptian jewellery.' London and New York, 1971.

Williamson, G. C. (revised). Bryan's 'Dictionary of painters and engravers.' London, 1904.

Wilson, H. 'Silverwork and jewellery.' London, 1912.

Worshipful Co. of Goldsmiths. 'Goldsmiths' Hall.' London, 1969.

Worshipful Co. of Goldsmiths. 'Hall-marks on gold and silver wares.' London, 1957.

Younghusband, G. J., and Davenport, C. J. 'The crown jewels of England.' London, 1919.